GERTRUDE STEIN

To Bridget G. Lyons, Catharine R. Stimpson, and Carole Beebe Tarantelli

Gertrude Stein
Woman without Qualities

G.F. MITRANO
University of Maryland – Europe

ASHGATE

Published by
Ashgate Publishing Limited
Gower House
Croft Road
Aldershot
Hants GU11 3HR
England

Ashgate Publishing Company
Suite 420
101 Cherry Street
Burlington, VT 05401-4405
USA

Ashgate website: http://www.ashgate.com

British Library Cataloguing in Publication Data
Mitrano, G.F.
 Gertrude Stein : woman without qualities
 1.Stein, Gertrude, 1874-1946—Criticism and interpretation
 I.Title
 818.5'209

Library of Congress Cataloging-in-Publication Data
Mitrano, G.F.
 Gertrude Stein : woman without qualities / G.F. Mitrano.
  p. cm.
 Includes bibliographical references and index.
 ISBN 0-7546-5234-3 (alk. paper)
 1. Stein, Gertrude, 1874-1946—Criticism and interpretation. 2. Women and literature—United States—History—20th century. 3. Modernism (Literature)—United States. I. Title.

 PS3537.T323Z754 2005
 823'.912—dc22

2005008036
ISBN-10: 0 7546 5234 3

Printed in Great Britain by Antony Rowe Ltd., Chippenham, Wiltshire

Contents

Contents

List of Illustrations

Acknowledgments

I thank Mr. Stanford G. Gann, Jr., the Executor of the Gertrude Stein Estate, for kindly granting permission to reproduce the photographs of Gertrude Stein from the Yale Collection of American Literature at the Beinecke Rare Book and Manuscript Library Library.

I thank the Department of Rare Books and Special Collections, Princeton University Library for kindly granting permission to reproduce materials from the Sylvia Beach Papers.

I thank the Metropolitan Museum of Art in New York for granting permission to reproduce Pablo Picasso's *Portrait of Gertrude Stein*.

I thank Gonzalo Tena for permission to reproduce the images included in Appendix II.

I am grateful for permission to reproduce an excerpt from *The Waves* by Virginia Woolf, copyright 1931 by Harcourt, Inc. and renewed 1959 by Leonard Woolf, reprinted by permission of Harcourt, Inc.

I would like to thank the Faculty of Letters and Philosophy and the Department of English of the University of Rome 'La Sapienza' for financial support during the later stages of this book.

During my graduate years at Rutgers University I was fortunate to be introduced to the study of Gertrude Stein by two exceptional guides: Catharine Stimpson and Marianne DeKoven. I should like to acknowledge my gratitude to them for their teachings. Carole Beebe Tarantelli has always been an inspiring presence. I thank her for her early teaching and, more recently, for calling my attention to the work of Thomas Ogden.

I would like to express my appreciation to the people who have read early drafts of this study, when it was still a dissertation, and who have offered their comments and encouragement: to the late and missed Agostino Lombardo, to Alessandro Portelli, and to Elisabetta DeFilippis, Barbara Lanati, and Giorgio Mariani.

I thank all the participants in the doctoral seminar of the University of Rome for the stimulating meetings and discussions, and Pauline Fry, at the University of Maryland in Europe for her interest in my work on Gertrude Stein. Professor Margaret S. Breen, at the University of Connecticut, has put me in touch with my publisher. She has consistently supported my work in so many ways and at the right times. I cherish our life-affirming intellectual exchange.

I thank my anonymous reader at Ashgate, whose criticism has significantly improved the final version of this study. I am proudly indebted to Bridget G. Lyons for her unsurpassed generosity in reading the entire typescript and suggesting numerous and decisive changes, always with that inimitable graceful levity which sets her apart as a Renaissance scholar and a New Yorker. I also thank Lewis Fried for reading the introduction and offering suggestions for revision.

My family and Ottavio Mitrano have generously offered important varieties of help and assistance necessary to the completion of this book. I am very grateful to them all. I thank especially my beautiful mother, Giuseppina Fedele Mitrano, for being a model of strength and resourcefulness, my sisters, Martina and Rosy, for their constant loving involvement. Abby Attias and Nikki Inzano have been loyal friends; I thank them for those summers at 420 Graham St. My gratitude, of course, extends to other friends who have offered moral and concrete support, especially to Maria Benestante, Gerry Carlon and Casey Carlon, and Gonzalo Tena.

I found in my commissioning editor, Ann Donahue, a rare combination of professional rigor and kindness. I am grateful to her and to the entire Ashgate team for their care.

It is a pleasure to acknowledge the assistance of the following people at different institutions: Lisa Dunkley, John S. Weeren, Tad Bennicoff at the Seeley G. Mudd Manuscript Library of Princeton University, Annalee Pauls, Charles E. Greene, and Ben Primer at the Department of Rare Books and Special Collections of Princeton University Library, Laura Raja at the Center of American Studies in Rome, Catherine Schindler, Tim Young, Nancy Kuhl at the Beinecke Library, and Eileen Sullivan at the Metropolitan Museum of Art. Finally, Richard Foreman and Jane Comfort have been graciously available to discuss their work on Gertrude Stein, the first in a phone conversation, the second in an email conversation.

Introduction

This book offers a composite portrait of Gertrude Stein at the junction of textual, visual, and theoretical realms. My study presents Gertrude Stein first and foremost as an American woman who fought her way into literary culture. Her career was a progress toward the podium. I begin with Stein's appropriation of European modernity, her access to language, culture, and writing and end by discussing her achievement in American literature. Her understanding of identity as thoroughly immersed in history, the body, geographical location, and interpersonal and power relations had significant consequences on her writing. Perhaps to a greater extent than that of her modernist colleagues, her work bridges the distance between art and life, questioning the dynamics of reading and reception.

Among the material aspects of Stein's artistic development were her struggle for and against American intellectual sources, photographic and painterly images of her person, the conscious use of clothes to accede to the fantasy of the artist, thinking about herself as modern, and the domestic situation of writing. Considering these aspects proves useful because we can understand the seemingly solitary and non-American formal experimentalism of her earlier years as part of a larger attempt at redefining the boundaries between the private and the public spheres. On Stein's part, this redefinition insists upon her work having a place in the world of public culture, a challenge for any modernist woman writer and intellectual. On our part, the consequence of this redefinition demands seeing Stein's writing (too often still judged cryptic and forbidding) in the critical context of public concerns. In public forms such as opera and lectures, the experimentalism of her earlier years raises questions about literary studies. She concentrates on the parallel vicissitudes of aesthetics and sociality. The question of how individuals become part of a social community implicates the reader's or viewer's inclusion in the reception of the work of art. Far from championing a modernist utopian belief in art, she invites us to consider her writing as a cultural, critical act. Whether we call it a theatre of the self or an open work,[1] her page conjures a place where meaning depends on the encounter of a set of private concerns with a set of public ones. Stein's life-long struggle between private (or experimental writing) and public (or audience-oriented writing) points to the larger drama of the critical task of writing. This consists in tracking the phantoms that are often denied by abstract notions of identity and community.

With the expression 'woman without qualities' I intend to assimilate Stein's work to an early twentieth-century modernity characterized by a growing awareness of others. This birthed an aesthetic based on the philosophical fall of the unique individual into the anonymity of the average humanity. With the fall of the unique individual, art is liberated into life. The freedom of the artist loses symbolic consensus; from privileged storyteller, the writer becomes as everyone else. Like her modernist colleagues, Stein is anxious about the 'death' of the author. But instead of repressing its consequences, she advantageously exploits them. She uses her page to explore how meaning is composed by the writer's self-perception. Within the collective European metaphor of the writer as a modern everyman, Stein works by perceiving herself as a nineteenth-century woman who wishes to become modern, a private woman who wishes to become public. Later in her life, at the time of her American lectures, she turns away from the European stasis of what she termed 'daily life' (*LA* 49) to embrace an American poetics of movement. She did so to cover her struggle to negotiate a desirable, powerful American cultural presence. The Stein I prefer is the woman who embraces the modernist image of the writer as fallen storyteller and by that accomplishes the self-transformation from nineteenth-century well-to-do American to twentieth-century writer. She forces upon us an intransigent questioning of the meaning of writing and reading as these activities relate to the societies in which we wish to live. A closer look at how Stein interpreted modern culture can help us better understand why she has become such a desirable subject for critical thought and theories of reading in recent years.

Stein's reputation has gone through many phases: from the appreciation of her contemporaries to the neglect of the New Critical era, to a renaissance initiated by feminism and continued by postmodernism and lesbian and gay studies. In the course of time, Stein's work has become a palimpsest for different critical schools—French feminism, poststructuralism and postmodernism among them. She has been valued as a writer and thinker. As Marianne DeKoven writes in her introduction to the 1996 issue of *Modern Fiction Studies* commemorating the fiftieth anniversary of Stein's death, Stein's import in literary studies has increased in ways that encourage not only celebrations aimed at making amends for a belated recognition but also inquiries into her politics ('Transformations of Gertrude Stein' 471). Inquiry into even the most contradictory aspects of Stein's personality is concomitant with monumental studies about her composition method, revealing her influence on past writers and influencing new ones.[2] In the wake of the contemporary crisis of literary theory, she has been upheld as a pioneer of the search for new, non-repressive theories of reading.[3] Today, Gertrude Stein is no longer neglected. On the contrary, her material understanding of identity as always mediated by history and place has released scholars from the obligation to justify her variety of modernism, enabling her readers to recognize in her a perceptive citizen of our time, close to our moods and sensibility. Today, the question is why her uniqueness is valuable to us. My study, which obviously, could not have been conceived without this rich scholarly discourse, participates in the ongoing debate approaching the question of Stein's contemporary value from three perspectives: a) Stein's use of European modernity, b) visual self-presentation and cultural access, and c) her contribution to literary studies and contemporary aesthetics. In the first two headings, feminist and cultural studies interests overlap, whereas the third is more specifically related to the crisis of literary studies and the thorny question of literary value.

a) Stein's use of European modernity. As I tried to piece together my narrative of a woman's progress toward the podium, I became fascinated with Stein's use of European modernity as a fantasy. By this I mean that modernity functions as a 'pass' that, as an American woman, Stein receives to fully participate in public discourse. I discuss her love of Cézanne as a means of access to culture. Her attachment to Cézanne and the ideas of his painting empowered Stein to perceive herself as an intellectual agent in her own right.

Certainly, European modernity is an objective set of aesthetic tenets, traditionally including shock, abstraction, and fragmented continuities.[4] But Stein makes us see ideas as a collector would. If collecting objects can create an identity (Pearce 272), so can appropriating ideas and cultural configurations. Far from producing dislocation, this method proves liberating. Stein understood that the freedom of the artist is a myth. She traded it for the fantasy of the writer. With this expression I want to suggest that the writer, as the member of a social community, has an identity shaped by historical and geographical circumstances as well as by personal subjective factors. Precisely because of this conjoining, the writer's link to the rest of humanity requires imaginative reconceptions.

Stein developed a special sensitivity to the ways in which power operates in culture from her knowledge of art and collecting. Her critical reaction to power is perhaps the reason for 'the intellectual violence' done to her reputation (Stimpson, 'Review Essay: Reading Gertrude Stein' 271). Stein had no illusions about the freedom of the artist.[5] As an art collector, she was predisposed to understanding the production of art in terms of patronage and its modern metaphors. She knew that, to some extent, creativity thrives on concrete and less concrete forms of commission and is deeply steeped in the relations between patron and artist, two viable terms implicating reader and writer. She was especially alert to the nuances of human character, as well as to the role of power in the emergence of the work of art. Accordingly, painting, especially Cézanne, became for Stein an imaginary form of patronage. It encouraged a writing that reacted to power more with formal experimentation and less by romancing a moral or spiritual negative dialectic. Without modernity's imaginary patronage, her writing would have been harder to pursue and perhaps less significant.

b) Visual self-presentation and cultural access. Stein's transformations, especially her assimilation to postmodernism, have effectively eradicated the question of her looks, which had often been used to negatively evaluate her writing. In the past, observers had found it legitimate to take traits of her body and turn them into the negative qualities of her work. Famous, in this context, is Edmund Wilson's 'fatty degeneration' (qtd. in DeKoven, 'Transformations of Gertrude Stein' 471). In this study I devote some chapters to her image because the kind of visual dialogue Stein establishes with her readers raises exquisitely literary questions. Before the onset of feminist studies she appeared as either 'an eccentric lady' (Ashbery 1971) or as 'fat [. . .] and masculine, similar to a Buddha or a roman emperor' (Minervino 61). Interestingly enough, these two portraits were authored by favorable reviewers of the Stein collection on the occasion of the MoMA exhibition *Four Americans in Paris* (1970), meant to establish the importance of the Steins as American collectors.[6] It is as if not even her great achievement as an art lover and collector, especially in the period before World War I, could be praised without calling her physical self into question.

Contemporary writers have changed all this, transforming Stein into a muse who acknowledges their literary aspirations and therefore their desire to be present in culture.[7] Stein's visual self-presentation suggests that she felt that to write is to negotiate an entrance into culture that has been traditionally problematic for women. She consciously used clothes and self-image to assert her right to cultural belonging. In light of this conscious use, the past attacks against her personality reveal an aversion precisely to what we, with our poststructuralist wisdom, like best about Stein. In a way, to appreciate her notion of identity as constructed is tantamount to valuing her tendency to use ideas like objects that bolster up identity, like art objects or clothes. Thus, even if our approaches to her texts have eradicated the issue of her physical appearance and its compatibility with standard views of a real author, the past doubts about Stein should not be forgotten. They remind us that behind notions such as authenticity and coherence, which today are universally attacked, lies a profound cultural difficulty in thinking, without ideological or psychic reservations, about the right of individuals to full cultural access and participation.

We have learned to reject repressive notions like authenticity and coherence, and Stein, who has had no small role in this reconstruction, is no longer perceived as a cerebral Medusa. Nonetheless, it remains difficult to find ways of reading that aspire to be inclusive while not repressing varieties of reading experience, as Juliana Spahr's excellent study confirms. Focusing on Stein's appearance and the literary persona she wanted to project helps me to suggest how—if one of our priorities is to use reading to build communities—it is also important not to overlook the affective undercurrents of communities. This means considering how communities tend to coalesce around favored images and envision cultural access through the limits of those accepted ideals. From this point of view, it is good that Stein's personality gets in the way. In this study, her visual image is inseparable from literary questions such as what enables us to recognize meaningful texts when we read them, which is to say, what factors play into our evaluation of meaningful authors when we see them. An attention to Stein's image and how it addresses the gaze of her viewers helps me connect to the ongoing critical debate in Stein studies, inviting inquiry into the kind of literary object she has become for the present. If her critical transformations reflect our own changing standards of literary desirability and beauty, then she can also contribute to our understanding of larger critical problems involving literary value and how to assess it.

c) Stein's contribution to literary studies and contemporary aesthetics.
Because of her careful negotiations, Stein is a woman of letters whose questions

about the meaning of writing are especially cogent in a critical climate hostile to abstract notions of human subjectivity and to imposed notions of communal cohesion. These are suspected to foster hierarchical divisions between significant and insignificant members of the human community. If Stein's texts are open, if they show that norms are artificial, if we like them for their postmodern capacity to subvert dominant narratives, then they also ask about the meaning of writing in a world where more and more write and where everybody may come to write. Stein raises the issue of identity when living means writing. Happening in the silent folds of life, writing becomes synonymous with self-recognition. At the same time, this sense of self-recognition is inseparable from writing's 'natural' drive for publication, if only in the rudimentary form of the interpersonal encounter. Since publication, even if only at an imaginary level, remains the goal of writing, for someone whose identity is caught up in writing, recognition must remain indeterminate: 'Am I I' (*GHA* 405), or, 'Am I I because my little dog knows me' (*GHA* 405). In other words, if writing is part of life, *when is one a real author?*[8]

If art and life overlap, if writing means daily living, then how does the issue of recognition change for the writer? The oscillation between writing and success, a theme in Stein's work, dramatizes precisely the extent to which writing is a metaphor for social emancipation: textual significance equals social significance or visibility. Contemporary critical thought has depended on this view for innovation. Breaking out of silence and into public presence, from the 1960s on, has been essential to the progress of criticism. We can now pause and think about the axiom that the greatest publication affords the greatest sense of recognition. We can ask if this emancipation, which is always bound to leave some behind, is an adequate approach to the responsibility of our times, which is that of encouraging the growth of human resources, including their full unfolding and unimpeded movement. What kind of ideas will do for the task? How can they be encouraged within institutions of education against these institutions' ossifying power?[9] I am not saying that Stein can answer these questions. I am saying that if we read her, we are likely to stumble on these overwhelming questions. Writing was for Stein, the woman without qualities, a vast metaphor for human connection: 'Who write./The human mind write' (*GHA* 399). While not negating her controversial politics, I am interested in arguing that she reaches us more effectively when she asks about desire, access, and full cultural participation because she makes us think about the conditions that communities put on the enjoyment of cultural belonging.

In her mature work she turned to the problem of social cohesion, with an ever growing attention to the punishing quality of abstract notions of human identity. Toward the end of her life she created perhaps her most tragic heroine, Susan B. Anthony. She realized that there is an enjoyment of exclusion at the heart of the social tie and that the hold of collective phantoms is stronger than any democratic demand:

(A Snowy landscape. A Negro man and a Negro woman)

Susan B.	Negro man would you vote if you only can and not she.
Negro Man.	You bet.
Susan B.	I fought for you that you could vote would you vote if they would not let me.
Negro Man.	Holy gee. (*MUA* 67)

The warmth of exclusion causes the fraudulent divide between private and public to crumble:

John Adams	Dear Miss Constance Fletcher, it is a great pleasure that I kneel at your feet, but I am Adams, I kneel at the feet of none, not any one, dear Miss Constance Fletcher dear dear Miss Constance Fletcher I kneel at your feet, you would have ruined my father if I had had one but I have had one and you had ruined him, dear Miss Constance Fletcher if I had not been an Adams I would have kneeled at your feet.
C. Fletcher	And kissed my hand
John Adams (shuddering)	And kissed your hand
C. Fletcher	What a pity, no not what a pity it is better so, but what a pity what a pity it is what a pity.
John Adams	Do not pity me kind beautiful lovely Miss Constance Fletcher do not pity me, no do not pity me, I am an Adams I am not pitiable. (*MUA* 62-3)

Private love mirrors public subjection; community means a scramble to escape a submissive position ('I am an Adams I am not pitiable'). Of herself she wrote: 'She always was, she always is, tormented by the problem of the external and the internal' (*AABT* 112). How does the literary imagination react to the perilous conjoining of internal and external?[10] Traditional genres will no longer do because they encourage an imagined community that feeds on death. Here is Walter Benjamin in 'The Storyteller': 'What draws the reader to the novel is the hope of warming his shivering life with a death he reads about' (*Illuminations* 101). Some might think Benjamin's remark pretentious. Yet, it would seem that to fully overcome modernism and let our times speak, we should at least have solved the question of feeding on the death of others. Literature, Benjamin suspected, can endorse a social tie tinged by the death drive or the warmth of exclusion. From this point of view, Stein's poetics of vitality is an attempt at overcoming modernism.

The question: when is one a real author? implies another. When is a text a valuable text? For a while, contemporary criticism assessed literary value while diminishing the importance of interpretive practices that would update literary canons, creating more inclusive democratic societies. From the theory of the open work onwards, with its expansion in the direction of semiotics, feminism, psychoanalysis, theory, and visuality, literary criticism sought alternatives to the hierarchical ranking of texts. But despite the transformations, the divide between producer and receiver or reader and critic remains an issue for contemporary aesthetics. Even the most enlightened theories seem to reinstate the divide. The critic has actually been seen as a figure who neutralizes the audiences' active participation in the reception of creative work.[11] Stein contributes to the debate by calling attention to the role that the individual receiver's free or random associations play in interpretation. How does, she asks, the 'emotional time' (*LA* 94) of the receiver get inserted into the collective space of meaning? How does private meaning merge with public meaning? And if the public interpretation of the critic is premised on the repression of a certain private randomness, then what is the alternative? How should we rethink the relation of critic-reader? Stein has been wrongly viewed as a destroyer of forms. Because of her reservations about a full reciprocity between aesthetics and society, she cannot be said to espouse the notion of a genteel literary diversity that the eye can appreciate especially through the metaphor of the close-knit artifact. But neither is she against forms. On the contrary, her uniqueness lies in the fact that she pushes the boundaries of formalism. Her self-reflexive writing confirms that literary innovation hinges around formalist moments.[12] In agreement with contemporary aesthetic theories that issue from the art of the 1950s, Robert Rauschenberg's in particular, Stein maintains that the individual participation of the viewer in systems of meaning remains the next challenge for critical discourse.

The first four chapters of my study examine Stein's modernist rise, her conscious self-fashioning, and our reception of her image. Chapter 1 sets the tone for the discussion examining the role of European modernity in Stein's claim to creativity and her affirmation as an American writer. Chapter 2 reads *The Making of Americans* as a novel of apprenticeship in which Stein sheds the burden of American provincialism in matters of aesthetics but also discovers the deepest sources of her writing in the American intellectual tradition. In chapter 3 I discuss the role that clothes and her friendship with Mabel Dodge Luhan had in Stein's transformation from average woman with a Puritan face to avant-garde writer. Chapter 4 picks up again the motif of clothes and technologies of the self to evaluate Stein as a modernist icon through the comparison with another modernist cult figure, Adrienne Monnier. The last three chapters turn to the question of Stein's contribution to literary studies today. In chapter 5 I take my cue from Picasso's 1906 portrait of Gertrude Stein (which remains the official image of the American writer) to discuss Stein's aesthetic views, particularly on artistic value and innovation. The last two chapters argue for an affinity between Stein and contemporary aesthetics based on the active participation of every individual reader or viewer. In chapter 6, devoted to *Four Saints in Three Acts*, I contend that this affinity stems from Stein's meditation on American literary origins, especially on the relation of aesthetics and sociality as it is posed in Anne Bradstreet's poetry and in the thought of William James. In the final chapter, on *Lectures in America*, Stein becomes the historiographer of her unpublished manuscripts. The legendary opposition between notebooks and success now reveals its philosophical implications, indicating the gap between thought and representation. Her public performance skilfully encodes her often misunderstood intellectual commitment to the tradition of women's struggle for public presence in America. I close with two appendices, one on Stein and the performing arts, and another on her influence in contemporary European painting.

I first encountered Gertrude Stein on a gorgeous spring day in Rome. I was 20 and believed in writing. At that time, writing meant notebooks: started, finished, and stacked up somewhere on a shelf or in a drawer. Never intended for public display, it resembled a private affection, with the self as its primary object. I am not talking about the love of self-discovery. Affection means feeling *and* bodily condition. The verb related to it, to affect, names different forms of influence: touch, impress, strike, sway. It implies, says the Webster dictionary, the action of a stimulus that can produce a response or a force that brings about a change. The private routine served to touch the self so that it would be real and there. The book I brought back to my room proved a good read. *The Autobiography of Alice B. Toklas* recounted the rise of European modernity, roughly in the period covering the end of the eighteenth century and a good first half of the twentieth-century, as a story accessible to everybody. Here was post-Baudelaire Paris, whose streets continued to be roamed and mined for poetic matter; here was the literary salon, where cultural history was made before it was known; here, finally, were the coteries of rising artists, brilliant, ambitious, litigious, sometimes ill and sometimes cruel. The crisp, unrelenting chatter of the prose built an engrossing human tableau of the kind one would have expected to find serialized in *Vogue* or *Vanity Fair*. Yet, modernism's enchanted kaleidoscope had a puzzling effect. Gertrude Stein, whose name appeared on the book cover, had delegated the story of her life to Alice B. Toklas, whose autobiography coincided with that of the author. At the book's end, I learned that I had been reading a novel about the progress of Gertrude Stein from literary obscurity to the status of literary personality, someone readers talk about.

The scene of the notebooks, shut and unpretentious but in full view on an imposing Renaissance table, stuck in my mind. Modernism meant being suspended between the silence of the closed notebooks and the clamor of movements, the mind thinking and worldly success. I did not know then that *The Autobiography of Alice B. Toklas* (1932) was part of a diptych. Written in the same year, *Stanzas in Meditation* replaces Toklas's Orphic ease with dejection and despondency. The bright hues and the optimism of the first panel yield to washed-out grays in the second. Despite the title's appeal to a dream of Renaissance plenitude,[13] the poetic sequence resembles those somber paintings of Jasper Johns in the early 1960s, canvasses like *In Memory of My Feelings-Frank O'Hara* or *No*, where an object-less field conjures a maker struck by the semiotic slumber of the world.[14]

I wanted to write this book to understand, from the distance of time, why the oscillation between writing as private affection and writing as symbolic exchange was so meaningful to the young woman. In part, the divide is highly representative of an epoch when avant-garde art existed side by side with mass or commercial culture (Poggioli 134). The fact that Stein shows herself as wavering between the two indicates that her indecision has a larger import that cannot be reduced to a personal trait. Her sense of division between a private dimension of writing and a public one is responsible for her original combination of issues of production and reception, and reflects her important contribution to twentieth-century aesthetics. About this contribution much remains to be said. I might have begun because I wanted to examine the cultural value of Stein's personal oscillation between notebooks and audience-oriented writing, but I soon realized that this involved settling for a composite portrait of the American writer. Along the interweaving lines of biography and intellect, the initial concrete divide between notebooks and fame multiplied into other larger questions. (From what I can tell, Stein's contributions to fashion studies, to the history of taste, and to the history of American oratory remain open to inquiry.) As I write this introduction and try to explain why I chose to privilege Stein's struggle for cultural presence, I am comforted by Julia Kristeva's work on feminine genius. Like the women discussed by Kristeva, Stein became an innovator because she was able to surpass herself. Kristeva writes:

> To appeal to the genius of the individual is not to underestimate the weight of History—these three women [Arendt, Klein, Colette] faced up to history as much and as well as any others, with courage and a sense of realism—but to attempt to free the feminine condition, and more generally the human condition, from the constrains of biology, society, and destiny by placing the emphasis on the importance of the conscious and unconscious initiative of the subject faced with the program dictated by these various determinisms. ('Is There a Feminine Genius?' 496)

Similarly, in Stein's case, I wanted to move to center-stage what Kristeva terms 'subjective initiative' and 'highly personal force,' to offer the portrait of a woman who was willing to face up to history. Her obsession with vitality, which came from the fear that writing would congeal thinking,[15] her conscious self-fashioning as an American intellectual balanced between private writing and public approval continue to invite larger questions about self-realization and freedom in our world, at a time when these values cannot be taken for granted.[16]

Chapter 1

The Woman Without Qualities

The woman writing

Gertrude Stein's best-seller, *The Autobiography of Alice B. Toklas*, begins with the scene of a woman writing. When the Toklas character offers us a tour of Stein's life in Paris, full of international artists and still unvalued pictures, she prefaces it: 'Before I tell you about the guests I must tell you what I saw' (*AABT* 8). In the middle of the atelier she sees 'a lovely inkstand, and at one end of it note-books neatly arranged, the kind of note-books french children use, with pictures of earthquakes and explorations on the outside of them' (*AABT* 8-9). When compared to the paintings that cover 'all the walls right up to the ceiling' (*AABT* 9), the unpublished manuscripts, which she will subsequently type, proofread, edit and, in some cases, publish, appear as if a secondary, almost diminutive object. But closed as they are, they occupy the center of the atelier and testify to the significance of a silent writing that goes on when we no one is looking.

You will remember a somewhat similar scene in Virginia Woolf's *The Waves* (1931). The children venture into Elvedon and see a woman writing:

> Now we are in the ringed wood with the wall round it. This is Elvedon. I have seen signposts at the crossroads with one arm pointing 'To Elvedon.' No one has been there. The ferns smell very strong, and there are red funguses growing beneath them. Now we wake the sleeping daws who have never seen a human form; now we tread on rotten oak apples, red with age and slippery. There is a ring of wall round this wood; nobody comes here.
>
> [. . .]
>
> 'Put your foot on this brick. Look over the wall. That is Elvedon. The lady sits between the two long windows, writing' (*The Waves* 17).

Both Alice B. Toklas and the children in *The Waves* are witnesses: they report about a writing in danger of never reaching us because it might remain buried in interiors. The still life with ink-stand and unread notebooks stacked on the Renaissance table lures Toklas. And Stein uses Toklas as a narrative foil to make us fall in love with the writing scene.

Stein's unpublished notebooks belong squarely in a modern culture whose climate is best captured by Luigi Pirandello's formula 'one, no one, and one hundred-thousand' [uno, nessuno e centomila].[1] The formula sums up a pervasive loss of individuality that invests every social group. In Charles Baudelaire's time, the writer's attempt to negotiate his belonging to a humanity of men and women without qualities had changed poetry into a drama of consciousness attended by estrangement and unreality.[2] In the earlier part of the twentieth century, the question became whether, in taking up his place among anonymous singularities, the writer would be able to write at all. Now, the value and status of the writing act are at stake. Roland Barthes put it memorably when he said that around 1860 writing ended (Lyotard 352). He meant the end of writing in the sense of a socially accepted metaphoric language that absorbs social conflicts and creates cohesiveness by means of great units of meaning. Modern anthropology has called these units 'mythemes' (Lyotard 353). After that, a poetic language rises whose function is not social but critical. Writing no longer respects a collective code; rather, it deconstructs socially accepted forms. Language speaks the unconscious of the poet, and reading becomes the experience of individuals who connect on the basis of a privately shared code. Those involved in reading are like people tracking each other's phantoms (Lyotard 353).

In Robert Musil's novel, from which I borrow my title, the man without qualities meets his readers from behind a windowpane. He is a solitary observer safely separated from the crowd but also spiritually fallen in their midst. As he stands at the window, an outdoor scene of movement is before him; behind him the interior is a room lined with books. His gaze wanders beyond the light-green filter of his house garden toward the openness of the street. Cars, coaches, buses, and people in turn attract and repel his gaze, forcing it along a restless route (Musil 1: 8-9). The external view holds the same sense of excitement, chance, movement and flow that we have learned to appreciate from the taxi cab scene in *A Room of One's Own* or the wanderings of James Joyce's modern hero. Musil's man without qualities is symbolic of someone at a pass, poised between two worlds, a social exterior full of possibilities and the cultural interior at his back (the walls lined with books). Gertrude Stein belongs to modern culture first and foremost because of the wavering between the internal world of her manuscripts and the external one of publication and social success. To Henry McBride, a loyal admirer 'who used to keep Gertrude Stein's name before the public all those tormented years' and 'did not believe in worldly success' (*AABT* 114), Gertrude Stein 'used to answer dolefully, don't you think I will ever have any success, I would like to have a little, you know. Think of my unpublished manuscripts' (*AABT* 114). The manuscripts and worldly success thematize two conflicting universes divided by thin glass. They figure that tension between collective codes, on the one hand, and the freedom of more individualized forms of creation and reception typical of contemporary views of modernity, on the other. As a participant in modernity, this is how Stein looks at herself: 'She always was, she always is, tormented by the problem of the external and the internal' (*AABT* 112).

Of course, what initially appears as a structural gap is also a novelistic fabrication. Even though she continued to meditate on the unresolved opposition between experimental and audience-oriented writing, also referred to as human mind and human nature in *The Geographical History of America*, Stein did publish all along. *The Autobiography* treats us to an impressive list of achievements. But the basic divide remains valued in her writing as an object of representation, or an object of meditation because it is the key to Stein's unique contribution to the literary period we call Modernism. Certainly for her, as for Ezra Pound and the others, modernism indicates a literary and spiritual program of innovation. But her aim was less to transcend American provincialism than to attain a sense of belonging to the American public sphere. When she called Pound a 'village explainer' she meant that the anxiety about American literary provincialism ruled his imagination, and thus when he said 'make it new' that sounded more like the work of mourning for a lost entitlement than a real awakening. From the vantage point of Gertrude Stein, modernism becomes a special attachment to European modernity. In the next section, through the example of Cézanne, I will discuss how an aesthetic set of ideas becomes for Stein a cultural access that her self-perception as a bourgeois Puritan would not otherwise have made possible.

The eros of pictures

Painting and Paul Cézanne preside over Gertrude Stein's birth into modern culture. This birth is amply documented both in *The Autobiography of Alice B. Toklas* and in *Lectures in America*, where she presents herself as a woman with no particular trade except that of looking at pictures. In her reassuring and unpretentious American plain speaking, Stein brilliantly encapsulates a momentous transition from the nineteenth-century *flaneur* to twentieth-century focused desire.

> The only thing [. . .] that I never get tired of doing is looking at pictures. There is no reason for it but for some reason, anything reproduced by paint, preferably, I may even say certainly, by oil paints on a flat surface holds my attention. I do not really care for water colors or pastels, they do not really hold my attention.
> I cannot remember when I was not so. (*LA* 59-60)

Roaming the streets of Paris, looking and listening no longer suffice to induce writing or justify it. For writing to happen, now one must first imagine the scene of a passage to it. The material thickness and the visual tactility of oil paint seduce her enough to make her naturally belong to writing.

When in 1903 she started to buy Cézannes, her writing had already begun. In the same year, she had written *Q.E.D.* and was at work on an early version of *The Making of Americans*.[3] But in *The Autobiography*, Stein represents her encounter with Cézanne as the experience of an awakening. Here is the well-known anecdote:

> During Gertrude Stein's last two years at the Medical School, Johns Hopkins, Baltimore, 1900-1903, her brother was living in Florence. There he heard of a painter named Cézanne and saw paintings by him owned by Charles Loeser. When he and his sister made their home in Paris the following year they went to Vollard's the only picture dealer who had Cézannes for sale, to look at them. (*AABT* 27)

She adds: 'The first visit to Vollard has left an indelible impression on Gertrude Stein' (27). After a few more lines on that first visit she and her brother 'asked to see Cézannes' (28). Followed by flash-forwards, the narrative seems to revert back to the original encounter: 'There were Cézannes to be seen at Vollard's. Later on Gertrude Stein wrote a poem called Vollard and Cézanne, and Henry McBride printed it in the New York Sun. This was the first fugitive piece of Gertrude Stein's to be so printed and it gave both her and Vollard a great pleasure' (*AABT* 28). 'Later on' was in 1912, the date of 'Monsieur Vollard and Cézanne', printed by Henry McBride in 1915. But the narrative strategy seems to annul chronological distance of almost a decade. As we read, 'later on' is strangely close to that first visit. Despite the distance in time, 'the first fugitive piece [. . .] to be so printed' (*AABT* 28) seems to have issued directly from the original visit. The suspension of time helps Stein convey not so much her artistic affiliation to Cézanne, which of course is not in doubt, as the sense of a personal liberation. Cézanne gave her poetry, a newfound self-esteem as a writer capable of non-constricted writing ('fugitive pieces') that aspires to be printed and even lures the general press, as mention of Henry McBride and *The New York Sun* suggests.

In this sense, her writing began with Cézanne because he finally made available for Stein the fantasy of the writer.[4] The powerful but unrecognized artist helped her deal with the fear that her writing would remain marginal, an appendix in the life of yet another bourgeois American collector in Paris. Stein tells us that it is as an average American collector that she first encounters Cézanne, when she mentions that at the time she and her brother Leo both preferred landscapes: 'They told Monsieur Vollard they wanted to see some Cézanne landscapes' (*AABT* 28). This preference is a clear indication that both Stein and her brother perceived themselves, at some imaginary level at least, as the descendants of a line of American art collectors with a marked taste for scenes of rustic, family, or social life (Boime 116). Stein grew up loving Jean-François Millet's *Man with a Hoe* (*LA* 65-66), the same picture the Huntingtons, major American collectors after the Vanderbilts, adored (Boime 136). 'Landscapes,' thus is used as a code word for an art taste that absorbs social conflicts in aesthetic contemplation. While they exploited workers, Vanderbilt and Huntington bought scenes of festive farmers of the Barbizon and Dusseldorf schools (Boime 137). When after the first visit she joined the circle of 'early Cézanne lovers' (*AABT* 28) and fell for Cézanne, Stein begins to think of herself as a woman who turns her back on the familial and national inhibitions that had conditioned her creative apprenticeship. Her love of Cézanne means the end of an initial and unsuccessful writing phase when the denial of approval by her family (in the person of her authoritative brother Leo) combined with her own dissatisfaction with the biographical psychologism of early pieces like *Q.E.D.* and *Fernhurst*. These might be important in terms of Stein's sexual difference but are not stylistically innovative. With her love of Cézanne, Stein conveys her access to the fantasy, henceforth worn like comfortable clothes, of the artist who, by definition, innovates. Seen through that love, the notion of success changes. To succeed means to pursue writing despite her dangerous involvement in European modernity, Stein's major link to a radical desire for change and innovation.

In the 1920s, a time when her writing perilously oscillated between dejection and self-esteem, disillusionment and belief, it is significant that she reminisced about the Cézanne 'romance' (*AABT* 28). The literary portrait 'Cézanne' (1923) records the elation of a full access to the fantasy of the writer successful on her own terms. The portrait begins with a set of differently ranked subjects: the Irish lady who 'can say' but who is trapped in deadly signs ('to-day is everyday'); Caesar, who 'can say that everyday is today,' a crowd of 'they,' who 'say that everyday is as they say' (*P&P* 11). We have here a resigned woman trapped in the servant's anxiety of an unchanging world; a leader enjoying his master position; a self-righteous crowd. Like the card players in Cézanne's famous image, Stein's subjects are in a stalemate sort of relation. Each is in his own world until the next card will be played and perhaps in a matter of seconds overthrow the tense balance that essentially captures a pattern of social hierarchies.

Cézanne's impact on Stein's social views is such that it poses the question for her of the 'mouth', that is to say, of the use of language: 'In this way a mouth is a mouth' (*P&P* 11). Cézanne's way freed the medium but the question is how to render the impact on the page: 'if in as a mouth where' (*P&P* 11). Colors and water imagery, a homage to Cézanne especially in his phase at L'Estaque, evoke a more domestic world that includes simple but important things: 'all that is precious too' (*P&P* 11). The self-righteous, conformist crowd reappears: 'and they meant to absolve you' (*P&P* 11). The verb 'absolve' plays with liquid sounds (solve) and, via the latin synonym *remittere* (*mitto*), means to let go. Cézanne's achievement lies in his execution of former fathers, a fact that is both perturbing and exciting to the portrait writer. The mixed feelings are conveyed by repetition: 'In this way Cézanne nearly did nearly in this way Cézanne nearly did nearly did and nearly did' (*P&P* 11). The jammed prose and the repetition of 'nearly' are the means to transcribe an emotional excitement mixed to Stein's realization of her love for a defeated master.

The highly elliptical and metonymic language of the portrait is dictated by the mixture of euphoria and guilt at the discovery of an innovation based on patricide. The portrait reflects Stein's private turmoil and the desire to participate in Cézanne's execution of the past, for which he was later absolved. She enters the composition to express her discovery and wonder: 'And was I surprised. Was I very surprised. Was I surprised. I was surprised and in that patient, are you patient when you find bees' (*P&P* 11). What she found was an enhanced being, intensified and pluralized (be's).[5] The appropriation of Cézanne's transgressive honey lends her equally transgressive sexuality a positive meaning, one perfectly compatible with artistic innovation: 'Bees in a garden make a specialty of honey and so does honey' (*P&P* 11). Cézanne combines avant-garde and domestic bliss, formal innovation and private life, releasing art from the clutches of melancholia and ennui.[6]

Certainly there are purely artistic reasons for her valuing of the French painter. Stein sympathized with an aesthetic program at whose center was a human subject seeking to exceed theoretical formulations. Emile Zola captures his friend's achievement, describing it as an epochal transition from poet to laborer:

> Another sentence in your letter pained me. It's this one: 'the painting I like, although I am unable to bring it off, etc. etc.' You, not succeed! I think you're wrong about yourself, as I've always told you: in the artist there are two men, the poet and the laborer. A person is born a poet, he becomes a laborer. And, you who have the spark, who possesses that something that can't be acquired, you are complaining; when all you have to do to succeed is to move your fingers, to work at it. (Zola qtd. in Cézanne *Letters* 71)

'[M]ove your fingers, to work at it' means a different search for truth in painting, or at least a change of mood from the submission to an internal abstraction ('The painting I like, although I am unable to bring it off'). The concrete movement of the hand ushers in an ideal relocation from the individual self and its autonomous will ('the painting I like') to a composition that accrues by acts of labor ('move your fingers'). Act after act, movement after movement, make for 'the painting I like'. Zola's image replaces the Romantic expressionist model of an interior world that the artist is supposed to externalize with the ongoing reciprocity of artist and medium. Becoming a laborer means, among other things, a gradual fall into a pattern of signs (the work of the fingers). The division between internal and external is thus replaced by a less rigid communication between man and the outer world, bringing art closer to life, if not making it correspond to the unfolding of the self in time. And Stein's own theory of poetry was influenced by Cézanne's sensual embrace of his medium:

> Poetry is concerned with using and abusing, with losing with wanting, with denying with avoiding with adoring with replacing the noun. It is doing that always doing that, doing that and nothing but that. Poetry is doing nothing but using losing refusing and pleasing and betraying and caressing nouns. (*LA* 231)

Her poetry comes from Cézanne's laborer, who works with his hands and is aware of his body. It will be noticed that Stein's poetry also echoes surrealism's convulsive beauty.[7]

Cézanne's impact on Stein's writing is well documented (J. Walker; DeKoven 1981; Bridgman). Here I would like to propose that Stein's Cézanne was more American than French. Through his name and legend Stein appropriated for herself the feeling of belonging to an American intellectual lineage. The poetry that she receives means more than the literary genre and is certainly more than a metaphor for creative output in general. It is comparable to the poetry that Rahel Varnhagen, the Jewish Enlightenment writer, salon hostess and pubic personality to whom young Hannah Arendt devoted her dissertation, received from Goethe.[8] And it sounds like the same poetry that Hannah Arendt, the pupil and lover of philosopher Martin Heidegger, received from her master. Recalling her reunion with the philosopher in Freiburg in 1951, Arendt writes: 'I had professional obligations [in Freiburg], and met Heidegger at my hotel. As always, I received through him the German language, uniquely beautiful. Poetry really, Man tut was mann kann, one does what one can' (qtd. in Young-Bruehl 69). Similarly, Stein receives from Cézanne, the Father of all moderns,[9] a symbolic pass, simultaneously to writing and modernity, as their natural insider and the intellectual peer of other aspiring modern writers. With the pass, she also embraces a problematic idea of success, emblematized in this study by the manuscript/publication opposition.

When considering Stein's reasons for choosing Cézanne as her master, it is not irrelevant perhaps that it was Bernard Berenson who introduced Stein to Cézanne (Boggs). As her portrait shows, she was attracted to the image of the powerful genius who toils in the shadow of more fashionable artists and innovates against the overwhelming weight of tradition, only to be applauded relatively late or posthumously for his daring achievements. Stein's special type of attraction recalls Berenson's own preference for a similar type of artist, the Renaissance painter Lorenzo Lotto. In his study of Lorenzo Lotto, the art critic transforms the underappreciated painter into Titian's worthy peer. Lotto's complexity shines against Titian's social conformity. While Titian embraced society, representing its ranks and divisions with unimpeded fluency, Lotto preferred to ask questions of character, but his own acute sensibility for the nuances of the human soul stopped him in the tracks of mundane success (Berenson 189-190).[10] In Cézanne Stein saw what she wanted to be: someone for whom personal intensity (interiority) was no stumbling block to the fluent language of expression.

That she needed a symbolic pass is evident from her brother Leo's indifference to her desire to become a writer. During her Radcliffe days and throughout the earlier stages of their arrival in Europe, Stein had emulated Leo. When in the fall of 1903 she settled in her brother's apartment at 27 rue de Fleurus and started to buy paintings, their Saturday evening salon became a theater for Leo's need to broadcast his opinions and enjoy public attention through extemporaneous lectures on art. As Alfred Stieglitz reports, Gertrude Stein remained in the background and 'strikingly silent' (qtd. in Brinnin 54). It is significant that when they parted ways and divided their art holdings, Leo left the Cézannes and the Picassos to his sister, only claiming for himself a Cézanne still life with apples. In a statement written in 1947, about a year after his sister's death, to clarify that they had never quarreled, he supports the traditional story according to which Stein's *Three Lives* was a verbal counterpart of Cézanne's portrait of his wife in a red chair, and adds a revealing detail: 'The Cézanne, Matisse, Picasso that *I* bought were of great importance to her with respect to her work' (qtd. in Brinnin 207; my emphasis). It is difficult to say whether, besides the old emulation of her brother, money also played a role in the growing distance between the two. In any case, in the earlier part of her European sojourn Stein's preference for Cézanne, over her brother's affinity for Renoir, becomes the dividing line between brother and sister. The line concerned their respective tastes in art but, domesticated as it is within the confines of the family drama, the preference for Cézanne indicates the discovery of a writing practice that, by opposing a respected family member, defines itself as a sober form of research against the argumentative vocality of its surroundings: 'by that time I was writing and arguing was no longer to me really interesting. [. . .] Anyway that was the beginning of my writing and by that time my brother had gotten to be hard of hearing' (qtd. in Brinnin 54). Cézanne is the dividing line between Leo's vocality and Stein's silence, between his exhibitionism and her writing.

If Cézanne separated her from her blood relations, it brought her closer to those American intellectual sources that resembled him, precisely because, like him, they remained silent and unrecognized in the wider public sphere. Made of 'honey and prayer', rigorous yet porous to the outer world, Cézanne's genius struck a familiar note with Stein, the student of William James, principal advocate of the work of Charles S. Peirce. Apart from the recognition paid to him by a restricted circle of admirers headed by James, when Stein was a student at Radcliffe, the inventor of pragmatism and semiotics had the reputation of being an unacknowledged genius. Like Cézanne, in his time Peirce was a powerful but denied innovator. He left more than 100,000 pages of unpublished writings that clash with the lack of public encouragement and success.

When initially she started buying Cézannes with her brothers, Leo and Michael, the painter's aesthetics, geared toward a fluid communication between the internal and the external, must have reminded Stein and Leo of William James's pragmatism, which was in turn influenced by Peirce. During a presentation at Berkeley in 1989, James called pragmatism 'the principle of Peirce' (Menand 354). He summed it up with the thesis that beliefs are 'really rules for action' and that 'the whole function of thinking is but one step in the production of habits of action' (Menand 354).[11] The principle of Peirce favors that fluid communication between the mind and the external world typical of Cézanne's images. Because of the mutual interaction between external and internal world, Cézanne's images had initially seemed an unacceptable distortion of reality. The affinity had its weight when, as art collectors, the Steins decided to invest their money in Cézanne.

At first, Cézanne was a family acquisition. The point is not only made by Stein's famous account of the first visit to Ambroise Vollard's gallery, which is presented as a family expedition, but also by Vollard himself. In his memoirs, the dealer treats us to a description of the three Steins, Michael, Leo and Gertrude, sitting on a bench in contemplation of Cézanne's portrait of his wife in a red chair (Vollard 109). The Steins saw themselves as a family of American collectors, following the latest trends in American art collecting. Before Gertrude Stein made independent purchases of Picasso's work, she was part of this family and acquisitions involved the sublimation of individual preference in a supraindividual taste inflected by status and nationality. Cézanne, Renoir, Degas and the other new French painters were misunderstood at home, when they were not actively rejected. In the first years of the twentieth century moneyed Americans bought what the French could not understand. It has been argued that by acquiring avant-garde art these American buyers were attempting to raise their social status in the eyes of a majority of Europeans traditionally skeptical about America's artistic and literary assets (Majerna 55). What can be said here is that the new art that the French were not willing to accept must have represented an exotic possession, a sort of European otherness that could be appreciated only abroad. American collectors were certainly influenced by the fact that the new painting would create capital in the long run. Their buys, however, are also indicative of how assimilable certain artists were estimated to be from an American point of view. If the famous collector Albert C. Barnes is at all representative of a national trend, Vollard reports that in his list Renoir represented a kind of European exoticism thought to be generally more in keeping with American taste than Cézanne. Barnes, in fact, bought more than 200 Renoir pieces versus 100 Cézannes (Vollard 110). In the Stein household Renoir turned out to be Leo's favorite while his sister allied herself with Cézanne.

Cézanne draws a domestic line between Leo and Gertrude that reflects a wider divide in national taste. Buying Cézanne, especially the larger paintings like his wife's portrait, had all the aura of a culturally avant-garde gesture. It meant collecting an art that showed no respect for class boundaries. Vollard, undoubtedly to make the point of his far-sightedness, tells how he discovers Cézanne at a young age when he is struck by the contrast between the revulsion of a bourgeois couple and the appreciation of a working class viewer before one of the master's works (Vollard 56). The master of Aix prefers the stark truth of the material world to the sensual evocation of the collective soul. In Vollard's account, when asked by Edouard Manet, the elegant painter of *Le déjeuner sur l' herbe,* what he would show at the next Salon, Cézanne answers: 'a pot of shit' (46).

The Steins were among the most daring collectors, acquiring with the new artists a European difference that could be assimilated to the American mind if one had the intellectual means to do so. As Americans educated at the best institutions like Harvard and Johns Hopkins, the Steins saw themselves as representative of the avant-garde of the American mind. Buying big Cézannes was the sign of an enlightened attitude toward European exoticism. It showed a mental capacity for appreciating the new iconoclastic images within a homely context without upsetting the fine balance between business and taste. Later on, Stein's individual romance with Cézanne, in contrast with Leo's preference for Renoir, allowed her to reconnect with the most radical aspects of her American intellectual origins. It especially encouraged the aspiring writer to shed a limited self-perception dictated by class privilege.

Stein was taken with the legend of Cézanne as the solitary and powerful innovator. Such a reputation strikingly resembles that of the unacknowledged master of modern American thought, Charles Sanders Peirce. Like Cézanne's painting, Peirce's thought moves to center-stage the process of a fluid communication between the human subject and the outer world, which Stein had learned to appreciate from James and which Peirce was to refine in the course of his research. As is well known, for Peirce every internal element of consciousness finds correspondence in external signs. The signs man uses are man himself. If every thought is a sign and life is a stream of thoughts, then man is a sign. If every thought is an external sign, man himself is an external sign (Sini 179). Peirce's semiotic connectivity results in a less abstract and disembodied vision. No real thought has an intellectual value on its own because this value lies in the fact that a thought is posited by a successive thought in a relation of representation with something else (Sini 170). In their immediacy, thoughts are 'non-analyzable, inexplicable, non-intellectual,' mere facts of 'a physiological force behind consciousness' (Sini 170). Exactly like Cézanne's painting, Peirce's world features a humanity immersed in semiotic relations. His solution of the problem of the internal and the external must have appealed to Stein, the former student of William James who went on to be 'tormented' all her life by the same problem: 'She always was, she always is, tormented by the problem of the external and the internal' (*AABT* 112).

Of course, like the other students in James's seminar Stein was only indirectly exposed to the thought of Peirce. While she was at Radcliffe, people, as Louis Menand writes, 'may not have known who Charles Peirce was, but they knew who William James was' (350), implying that knowing James meant knowing Peirce's thought. Stein also knew about Peirce, still indirectly, from her brother Leo, who boasted of having independently discovered pragmatism (Brinnin 53). From the distance of Paris and of time, she became aware, as she puts it in *The Making of Americans*, 'of masters and of schools in living and in working, and in painting and in writing and in everything' (486), probably an allusion to her master/disciple relation with James and to the other, more domestic, master/disciple relationship with her assertive brother. As she woke up from the spell of Leo's influence, the subtle logic of influence must have become clearer as well as the importance of the silent partners of masters who become founders of schools. Her new awareness of the problem of masters and schools would imply a finer appreciation for the origins, property, and circulation of ideas. In the context of this more finely tuned sensitivity, the dialectic of silence and vocality, of publicity and writing, is an effective figurative translation of a daunting philosophical problem. It was certainly because of William James that she recognized in Cézanne some semblance of American pragmatism, in its combination of life and thought, 'honey and prayer'. But Cézanne, unlike James, was not a celebrity; neither was he the popular, charismatic man who could stir in his students a genuine passion for ideas through the vehicle of the public word. Like James, Cézanne was 'a magic word' (*AABT* 28) but of a different kind: 'Cézanne at that time was living gloomy and embittered at Aix-en-Provence' (*AABT* 28). To those who read the *Autobiography* now, Stein's decisive love for Cézanne is likely to recall Susan Howe's poetic rendition of Charles Peirce at Arisbe, the property where he retired to attend daily to his writing and research after being rejected by major institutions of education.[12]

The Cézanne who frees Stein from the masks of power and from a self-serving aestheticism (she enters Cézanne portrait as Caesar), delivering her to a heightened sense of being and discipline (prayer), is close to the legend of Peirce. Stein's Cézanne recalls the originality, the unbounded energy, the fearlessly innovative spirit that James and a few others then associated with the powerful and solitary Peirce. Peirce himself made a point of drawing a line between his thought and its popularizations, included James's (Menand 349-350), concerned that his research would be assimilated to more seductive and widely popular notions like the unconscious.[13]

Similarly, Cézanne was interested neither in a self in crisis, abandoned to its emotional life, nor in the renewal of the collective unconscious. Like his contemporaries, he lived in sensations. Unlike them, he coupled sensations with the life of the mind. His problem was to expand the mind to include sensations without reifying them as the collective signs of the expanding appetites of a dominant class. Cézanne is after a non-melodramatic individual who, while belonging to the collectivity, resists the collective abandon to the lure of mass images. From this point of view, he has no fathers. His mind 'creates' the external landscape: it vigilantly filters social emotions through the conceptual rigor of shapes—the line, vertical and horizontal, the cube, etc. He can stop the object before our gaze short of fragmentation. He concedes little to the spectacle of drift and intoxication that is a byproduct of modern consumption.[14] We are meant to see the marriage of intellect and the senses, but never the agony of an individual overwhelmed by unspeakable sensations, at odds with systems of representation, bent over himself/herself in pain or *jouissance*.[15] Emblematic in this regard is *Bridge over the Pond* (1895-98).[16] The image invites the question of whether it is the water that reflects the green or the green that reflects the water. But objects do not fall in a semiotic vortex. Somehow, the bridge remains over the pond. In the viewer's mind, it is a supporting structure: its visible outline preserves the image of a human presence crossing over. Forms suggest a place kept safe for the reverie of human possibilities.

The green shelter of *Bridge over the Pond* seems to have transmigrated on Stein's page: 'There, where the grass can grow nearly four times a year' (*P&P* 11). Flooded with the Mediterranean light Cézanne loved and needed, Stein's garden euphorically alludes to the promise of an endless summer. Similarly, for Cézanne's friend, Zola, summer is a metaphor for modern writing, an unleashing of energies up to then inhibited by the demands of society and a correlated ennui:

> [. . .] My new life is fairly monotonous. At nine o'clock I go to the office, I write up customs declarations until four, I copy correspondence, etc., etc.; or, more likely, I read my paper, I yawn, I pace back and forth, etc., etc. Sad indeed. However, as soon as I'm out, I shake myself like a wet bird, I light a pipeful of tobacco, I breathe, I live. I mull over long poems and tragedies in my head, long novels, I wait for summer to unleash my energies. Good God, I want to publish a book of poems and dedicate it to you [. . .] (qtd. in Cézanne, *Letters* 71)

Stein's portrait ends with a newly found sense of place: 'Honey and prayer. Honey and *there*' (*P&P* 11; my emphasis). In light of the resemblance of Cézanne and Peirce as powerful and solitary geniuses, Stein's 'there' also alludes to an American cultural location. She read the Cézanne portrait during her American lecture tour in 1934. At the end of her reading, she added: 'This then was a great relief to me and I began my writing' (*LA* 77). She seemed sure that her audience would understand the intricacies of cultural belonging. But she was asking too much, as such intricacies are dizzying even to us.

Public woman: from the corset to the podium

It is generally easier to receive a symbolic canonization from the dead or from the distant living, whom we do not know personally. For Stein it was the same. She wrote the piece about the liberating 'poetry' she received from Cézanne years after the painter died. Many strains came together in her 'poetry': she began to imagine herself as a sensual intellectual with an attachment to forms; she began to think about her American intellectual origins; she began to think about the question of masters and schools, which is the question of creative autonomy and the meaning of failure and success; she began paying attention to herself as someone other than a dilettante destroyer; she began taking a distance from Leo's paternalistic dismissal; she began establishing a loyalty to European modernity. Cézanne's mentoring changed Stein's self-perception because it tied all these strands in one single knot. A popular photograph of 1905 shows Stein with one of Cézanne's compositions of bathers hanging on the wall (Fig. 1.1). She sports comfortable clothes and strikes the pose of a writer at ease with what she is and what she does. Her desire to interest the American public is visually amplified by the protective Cézanne hanging on the wall at her back. Originally, this photo of ca. 1903-1904 actually shows Stein with two paintings: Renoir's *Brunette* (1890), currently in the collection of Nelson R. Kandel in Baltimore, and Cézanne's *Bathers* (ca. 1895). *Bathers* is currently in the Cone Collection in Baltimore.[17] Despite the presence

Fig. 1.1   Gertrude Stein at 27, rue de Fleurus (ca 1903-1904), with one of Cézanne's compositions of Bathers. Courtesy of Yale Collection of American Literature, Beinecke Rare Book and Manuscript Library.

Fig. 1.2   Gertrude Stein as a student at the end of the 1890s. Courtesy of
                   Yale Collection of American Literature, Beinecke Rare Book
                   and Manuscript Library.

of the Renoir, it is Cézanne's composition that remains associated with the self-transformation of the writer, both hinted at by her pose and by her comfortable clothes. The photo is the visual counterpart of the achievement she was to celebrate in Cézanne's portrait. However, the folder leaning against the wall, probably full of prints to be hung, suggests that she is still the member of a family of collectors. She will emancipate herself from this identity to become a professional writer. As we shall see in chapter three, her image as a professional writer will increasingly depend on her use of a loose velvet garment which will become in everybody's imagination the uniform of Gertrude Stein the avant-garde writer. In light of her progress, the image of Stein posing with Cézanne's *Bathers* remains a landmark. It shows that the 31-year old woman has gone a long way in the span of a few years. In the late 1890s to the eyes of her cousin Helen Bachrach, she had appeared as 'an exceedingly attractive buxom young woman, quick–thinking and speaking, original in ideas and manners' (qtd. in Stendhal 21). Bachrach adds: '[e]verybody was attracted to Gertrude—men, women, and children, our German maids, the Negro laundresses, even casual acquaintances' (qtd. in Stendhal 21). An image of her as a student illustrates Bachrach's words (Fig. 1.2). Stein here poses as the feminine object of the gaze.

Her body is corseted. She thus confronts the viewer with all the associations with desire that this item of clothing can spin. As an item that shapes and constricts, the corset is only the concrete image of the cultural enclosure Stein describes in *Fernhurst*: 'A passionate desire for worldly experience filled her entirely and she was still waiting for the hand that could tear down the walls that enclosed her and let her escape into a world of humans' (qtd. in Stendhal 27). In this picture we see a young and attractive woman. *Fernhurst* tells us that the young woman, waiting to become human, lives in a world of images. Her desire exceeds traditional images of femininity, which she can nevertheless put on, as her corseted body shows. The result is a striking collage. As a woman, Stein is an image of desire. As an aspiring intellectual, she is not quite 'human' because she is a passive object in a world shut in two boxes: feminine passive object and masculine active participant. In this particular image, the corset keeps her within the confines of a normative sensuality while she longs 'to experience the extreme forms of sensuous life and to make even immoral experience her own' (qtd. in Stendhal 27). In Stein's career, this juxtaposition was destined to repeat itself. As we shall see in chapter 5, where I discuss the iconic Picasso portrait, the loose brown garment is no less confining.

In the nineteenth century the corset was a necessary adjunct of feminine beauty: 'Most people believed that the corset exaggerated a "natural" difference between men and women, that is, women's more pronounced waistline' (Steele, *The Corset* 53). While the corset served a useful function among heavier women because it could suppress a heavy abdomen, or support a 'corpulent' figure (Steele, *The Corset* 54), it was also a weapon of seduction used to enhance femininity: 'the corset also functioned as a brassiere, indeed as a kind of Wonderbra lifting the breasts, "augmenting their volume," and allowing them to "blossom in all their splendor and amplitude." Girls and women who were insufficiently buxom could approximate the desired curves with a discreetly padded corset' (Steele, *The Corset* 54). As a trade card for Cooley's Corsets makes clear (Steele, *The Corset* 55), the line between comfort and seduction, between seductive 'buxom' and negative 'buxom,' is hard to draw in the case of the corset. Finally, Valerie Steele reminds us that corsets were also a symbol of youthfulness, appealing to women who wanted to 'counteract the ravages of both pregnancies and time' (*The Corset* 56). The 'exceedingly attractive buxom' Stein of her youthful days easily belongs to her time. Indeed, as the photograph proves, she can approximate collective ideals of desirable femininity without a lot of effort. In that picture, it becomes difficult to tell where corpulence ends and sensuality begins. Stein is a sensual object. The staged femininity ties her to the imperative of seduction and sensuality (not necessarily limited to the heterosexual gaze) that is primarily indicated by the corset. The corset transforms her corpulence into fashionable desirability. It thus speaks of Stein's own ability to play with clothes, using them to respect or transgress, as she pleased, the acceptable line of visual femininity. It also suggests her ability to simultaneously embrace established cultural values and depart from them because of that originality of ideas and manners for which her cousin praises her.

In the pre-Paris image, then, Stein is an object of desire who wants to experience desire in the first person. The image is a good visual transcription of the heroine's dilemma in *Fernhurst*: while her gentle face communicates 'a transfigured innocence' or a 'puritan's instinct', she longs to 'experience the extreme forms of sensuous life' (qtd. in Stendhal 27). Externally she might have been an object for the senses of others, but internally she felt like a Puritan. The visual breakdown of the line between corpulence and sensuality with the aid of the corset parallels the verbal breakdown of the line dividing Puritanism and desire. In the image, Stein poses not only as a woman but also as an American trapped inside icy cathedrals while the life of the senses happens outside. The corset visually mediates Stein's American identity as a potentially seductive form capable of initiating a 'narrative' of desire. In its assimilation to the corset, her American identity assumes a theatrical capacity for shaping desirable objects. But the implication is that the sensuous experience continues to feel theatrical, i.e., fictive, deferred, unreal. When will she join the world of humans?

Progressively, Stein seizes opportunities to act on her desire for the sensuous life first through her affair with May Bookstaver, a wealthy and cultured woman who belonged to the circle of Bryn Mawr-educated women. In between her lesbianism and her fashionable transatlantic trips to Europe, especially London, Paris, and Italy, her understanding of literature changes. In 1903 she begins an early version of *The Making of Americans*, a national saga about that awareness of the striking juxtapositions of identity which we have already observed in Stein's youthful image. At the center of the narrative is a gilded middle class security. It is as seductive as a buxom woman squeezed in a corset. Among the many characters, two stand out. First a heroine, Julia Dehning, then a hero, David Hersland Jr, try to transform themselves from objects of the gaze into subjects of the sensuous life. If Julia Dehning fails because of class timidity, the young David Hersland fails out of a self-destructive drive not entirely alien to his divided loyalties to intellectual freedom and worldly success. But characters are props in a landscape that is not as reassuring as those landscapes of festive subalterns that the nineteenth-century American collectors, whom Leo and Gertrude imitated, got into the habit of acquiring. The narrator is all over the place, the paradigmatic figure of a desire that tries to scale enclosing walls and exit into an open life.

As the portrait shows, discovering Cézanne triggers the relief of change, above all a change in self-perception, within the limits of historical and power relations. Stein impersonates the nineteenth-century woman who must mediate the public import of her speech with intimacy. The discovery of Cézanne's intellectual power is encoded in domestic bliss. She enters the text in Emily Dickinson's fashion, with the assumption that her readers will know her from her masks. As already noted, first she is 'Caesar.' Then she is a 'we' destined to remain forever enigmatic without recourse to biographical information. Finally the discovery of Cézanne causes simultaneously bliss and censorship, as suggested by the pastoral pun on enhanced being. 'Bees' connotes the Dionysian abandon of heightened being—'Are you patient when you find bees' *(P&P 11)*—and also its censorship in the domestic pastoral of bees in the garden. The reader, however, can appreciate Stein's attempt to change her self-perception from daughter of Puritan America to innovative writer. Cézanne's reality, made truer by relations, reminded her of the control and restraint she should exert over her writing career to make sure that it would continue as more than an appendix to the life of an art patron.

In the same year she began an early version of *The Making of Americans*, she committed to paper her affair with Bookstaver, in the novella *Q.E.D.* The following year she worked on *Ferhurst*. While *Q.E.D.* and *Ferhurst* are based on the assumption that transgression equals a sensuous life, with *The Making of Americans* Stein finds out that a rebellious content runs the risk of inconsequential aestheticism if there is no formal innovation. Her mimeticist assumption (transgression = innovation) changes when she discovers Cézanne. Her self image also changes. She shifts to an uncorseted look that has little of the aura of studied rebelliousness of her Radcliffe 'mannish' look (Brinnin 27).[18]

Stein's writing, of course, lags behind her visual transformation. A letter to Mable Weeks suggests that she was not yet immune from the aestheticism sometimes typical of younger artists in search of their own voice: 'I am afraid that I can never write the great American novel, I don't know how to sell on a margin or to do anything with shorts and longs, so I have to content myself with niggers and servant girls and the foreign population generally' (qtd. in Sprigge 57-8). She erects a fence between herself and her modernist contemporaries by spurning the cultural fetishes with which they pandered to popular taste: 'I don't care there ain't any Tchaikovsky Pathetique or Omar Kayman or Wagner or Whistler or White Man's Burden or green burlap in [my prose]' (qtd. in Sprigge 58). It might be noted, however, that in her choice of ethnic and working class subject matter, she is no different from middle-brow writers in her eagerness to please the great American public. In this regard, *Three Lives* is closer to the old collectors' taste than to Cézanne. Its sensual aestheticism tends to spectacularize social conflict. But had she been contented in her aestheticism we would never have had *The Making of Americans*, a more remarkable achievement than *Three Lives* because now the question of a writing that its author can honestly own becomes more important than 'whether it gets published' (qtd. in Sprigge 58), and even the schizophrenic divide between art and society, sensual aestheticism and real oppression, is represented as part of the shadowy progress of the writer in search of autonomy. Change is the key in Stein's life and work.

Her visual changes are significant. So much of our understanding of Stein's contribution to modernism and American literature in general depends on her image as the Buddha-like prophet of the avant-garde intensely absorbed in thought. The transition from a constricted body to a draped body does not simply celebrate the progress to the modern mind she had proudly received from the sensuous and silent Cézanne.[19] It is a crucial moment in Stein's technology of the self understood as a life-long strife to change into a public woman acknowledged by the American public.

By the time Stein achieved public recognition in her native country, she was a modernist woman who had fought her way to the public sphere. She had left behind her youthful aestheticism and turned to the important questions of later works like *Four Saints in Three Acts*, discussed in chapter 6, and *The Mother of Us All*. These features heroines whose lives are effective metaphors of Stein's work. The religious passion of Saint Therese and the political passion of Susan B. Anthony trope Stein's own passion for writing, as well as her oscillation between artistic vocation and the desire for a just society. One should never lose sight of the two simultaneous Steins: the woman writing and the woman caught up in the struggle for public achievement. Only in this way can her image as a Medusa and irresponsible destroyer be humanized. She will not only be the disquieting muse of Picasso's portrait but also the writer looking out of her window in a photo by Cecil Beaton. The photo was taken toward the end of her life, when her body had already been ravished by illness.[20] In Beaton's intention, she meets our gaze exactly like someone poised between that intense interiority (confused with writing) which belongs by right to any human being and the outer world. She is someone who has given her life to have a voice. This meant that, to a certain extent, her sexuality (as the genre of *The Autobiography* insists) and her body had become pliant instruments in the hands of History, the very prerequisites for the recognition of her writing in the openness of the American public hall filled with an audience of strangers.

Chapter 2

Shame and the Fathers: *The Making of Americans*

Fat art/thin art

In this chapter we will see how Stein negotiates her place in the American tradition. The visual and material transformations discussed in the previous chapter find literary resonance in *The Making of Americans*. The novel's distinctive trait is that Stein's narrator struggles simultaneously for autonomy and affiliation. I will argue that the struggle for creative autonomy and intellectual belonging is carried out not so much through patricide as through a confusion of tongues within the paternal tradition. I borrow the expression 'confusion of tongues' from Sándor Ferenczi who originally used it to refer to the complexity behind hierarchical relations, especially between parents and children and analyst and analyzand. Patients, writes Ferenczi, 'have an exceedingly refined sensitivity for the wishes, tendencies, whims, sympathies and antipathies of their analyst' (158). The same applies to children. Patients and children identify themselves with the analyst and the parent respectively. It is the adult's responsibility to encourage a reaction to the identification. If this reaction fails there is an improper burden of love, a form of oppressive love, imposed on the identified subject. The consequence, Ferenczi writes, 'must needs be that of a confusion of tongues' (164).[1] Stein's novel of apprenticeship posits an identification with the fathers and subsequently rejects it. Stein simultaneously plays the role of the identified subject and that of the analyzed adult capable of encouraging a reaction to strong transference love; she goes through the confusion of tongues and brings it to its denouement.

At the time of the composition of *The Making of Americans* Stein was divided between two influential poles:[2] on the one hand, her teacher and mentor William James, and the pragmatist and thus relativist flux of sensations of his universe; on the other hand, her brother Leo, brilliant and competitive, with an omnivorous if unfocused ambition.[3] She was also reading Otto Weininger's *Sex and Character*. Weininger believed in fundamental human plasmas. The sexist, anti-semitic, and racist premises of his work leaned toward a classification of human beings that seemed to assert the social superiority of certain groups over others. Scholars have discussed Stein's borrowings from Weininger, especially of his notion of genius as 'an extremely comprehensive consciousness' more acutely aware than most (G. Moore 10; 45). Certainly, especially in the first half, Stein's epic may seem to issue from a somewhat suspect ambition to compile a lay bible of human character whose risk lies precisely in sharing Weininger's essentialist and reductive view of humanity. Boasting of extraordinarily intuitive powers when it comes to people's lives and character, Stein's narrator would seem to provide fodder for the association with Weininger. She informs the reader that she will not rest until she has 'a complete record of each one, what each one did, what each one had as being in her in him, what each one could be doing, thinking, feeling, knowing' (qtd. in J. Walker 71). Her classification of people as 'bottom nature' and 'servant queerness' does not help either. Yet, these considerations do not take into account two decisive factors

First, the peculiar nature of Stein's narrator. *The Making of Americans* is a story of coming to writing, the story of a narrator emerging from confusion and influence into the light of a problematic autonomy after a sequel of borrowings, refusals, and alliances, which will produce the extraordinary figure of David Hersland, 'the younger son of Mr. David Hersland and Mrs. Hersland' (*MA* 723). If the novel is a family progress, it also requires the reader to follow the messy progress of a voice coming to writing. Secondly, *The Making of Americans* is not only about the working through of a transgenerational intellectual heritage; it is also Stein's attempt at emancipating herself from the powerful influence of her charismatic former teacher and mentor, William James. If there is any echo of Weininger's beliefs in *The Making of Americans*, it must be considered in light of Stein's emancipatory desire. The daunting task of classifying all human characters, the novelistic trait that might more immediately betray Weininger's influence, gained momentum as she and Leo argued over William James at 27 Rue de Fleurus, in Paris. If pragmatism was teleological, as Stein seemed to infer from discussions with her brother, she wanted nothing of it. In response, she came up with an alternative—repetition.[4]

In this regard Lisa Ruddick has done the most helpful work. For Ruddick *The Making of Americans* is a novel of 'patricidal rage' (58) in which Stein declares her own independence from paternal figures: her father, her brother, and her mentor William James (59). In Ruddick's argument the patricide is carried out via an unacknowledged association with Freud. Ruddick has established that, though unnamed, Freud and psychoanalytic knowledge are present in the novel (94). In this reading, psychoanalysis becomes a decisive force, making its influence felt in the combination of a new awareness of 'the erotic dimension of [ ] writing' (81) and of repetition, a churning out of wholes that had been introjected (82). With reference to Janine Chasseguet-Smirgel's essay on Sade, Ruddick sees repetition as a style of anality that serves to level out and diminish the authority of the elders (82).

Ruddick's argument sheds light on Stein's repetition. For a good part of the novel, repetition evokes a mystifying capacity for human telepathy. It means knowing everything and everyone's essential nature. It begins to make more sense if it is thought of, as Ruddick does, in psychoanalytic terms as a form of human communication by which people can track each other's unconscious. What interests me is that this form of psychoanalytic communication, which probably helped Stein to distance herself from her mentor, invites the question of writing and its meaning: if repetition is a more complete knowing, and if, as the narrator claims, it is possible to know others as 'wholes' inside one, then what need is there for this fulfilling knowing to become writing? If repetition is a new joyful knowledge, why can it not stay as knowledge 'inside'? The idea of repetition may have started in Weininger's comprehensive, intuitive consciousness, or it may have taken off from Freud, or even from James himself, from his varieties of religious experience.[5] The point is that it refers to a cluster of promiscuous borrowings and is Stein's attempt to name a new sensibility, a communication between people, with a strong erotic component, which nevertheless her narrator fails to write.

As the progress of the novel makes clear, communication between one and the many has its impediments. Is it possible to write another as 'a whole' inside? Stein announces: 'Each one sometime is a whole one to me' (330). Her eroticized perception of others, which has prompted readers to compare her repetition to Whitman's 'body electric' (Watten 100), does not necessarily translate into writing, or at least into a form of writing that would appease Stein's urge for literary differentiation. For the persona dominating the first part of *The Making of Americans*, that of the archivist given to a generalized social eroticism, there always is a remainder: 'always then there may be sometimes more history of that one' (*MA* 330). Stein wants to partake in a modern sensibility. This participation is alternatively named 'knowing', 'learning understanding', and most notably 'repetition', understood as an erotic incorporation of others for the sake of writing. But soon the view of the writer as an archivist of human character proves limited and the narrator's initial tendency to classify multitudes goes limp, drowned in melancholia and despair. The birth of a new writing is assisted precisely by such 'melancholy feeling' for incomplete stories and 'new beginnings':

> Mostly then that is a melancholy feeling in some that there is not a complete history of every one in some one. Slowly then that feeling is discouraging to one loving having a whole history of every one inside in one. Perhaps slowly then there is really in such a one more and more knowing of the meaning in each one that one is even knowing. Always then for such a one there must be many new beginnings. (*MA* 330)

There is an excess of semiotic transaction with people ('more and more knowing of the meaning in each one') that remains compressed inside and cannot be translated into an external literary form except as 'many new beginnings.'

Stein's narrator is a brilliant piece of genealogical acting out. Repetition, in fact, can also to be understood as a mode of reception of genealogical concerns. Among these, the relation of knowledge to the practice of writing takes first place. If the nineteenth-century novel could masterfully contain the pressure of human types within the formalist charisma of whale cataloguing, for example, modernist prose can no longer use form to organize characters' life lines. Like Charlotte Perkins Gilman's uneven, erratic pattern on the yellow wallpaper, Stein's American generations twitch, held in the narrator's breath, artificially amplified by her repetitive prose. Her narrator tries hard to make those lines move us; and she accomplishes the effect precisely by abstaining from weaving them into a communion of differences. In *The Making of Americans* the passion for the communal leads to self-destruction, as we shall see when we discuss the younger son, David Hersland. Stein's prose closely recalls Gilman's wallpaper—an incoherent non-abstract pattern of lines, straggly and everlasting, that 'sticketh closer than a brother' (Gilman 17). Paradoxically, thin and straggly as they are, these lines become even more noticeable when they are mired in the attention-draining layers of repetitions.

If we read *The Making of Americans* as a novel of apprenticeship, then the narrator's failure to write the internal (but erotic) knowledge of another, which she calls repetition, is the novel's achievement in terms of Stein's own self-fashioning as a modernist. At the intersection of diverse intentions and moods—a mysterious poetics of empathy, the global human catalogue, a generalized social eroticism and an awareness of the erotic dimension of writing, depression, bouts of self-doubting despair and melancholia—Stein's narrator ultimately holds up to her readers the portrait of someone struggling for a position and a literary style of her own, both subjugated by and rebellious against her intellectual influences. The novel matters insofar as it is the spectacle of this struggle. From this perspective, Stein's narrative voice is a precursor of Wallace Stevens's modern genius. In part V of 'Notes Toward a Supreme Fiction' Stevens addresses the young poet struggling to create: 'You lie/In silence upon your bed. You clutch the corner/Of the pillow in your hand. You writhe and press/A bitter utterance from your writhing, dumb,/Yet voluble dumb violence' (11-15). For Stevens's modern poet as for Stein's narrator an anxiety of self-assertion complicates issues of creativity, and the question of subjective innovation cannot be separated from the desire for audience approval. When Stein says 'I believe in repetition' (qtd. in Ruddick 95), that is a declaration of aesthetic independence. But to achieve independence she does not exactly substitute individuation and differentiation for patricide. Without denying that patricide can be read in the novel, I wish to emphasize that, if anything, the spectacle of the struggling narrator indicates the difficult process of owning one's intellectual origins complete with the fathers' sins, i.e. with what by the individual writer are perceived to be the recurrent themes, anxieties, shortcomings of those origins. Stein is facing up to the sins of the fathers in order to transcend them rather than slamming the door against them. She could do it because, with Cézanne, she had learned to master the art of self-canonization through rebellious fathers.

Facing up to the fathers' sins involves confronting the major preoccupations in the American intellectual tradition. Stein identifies one of these preoccupations exactly in the fear of writing. One of the most persistent themes of the novel is that of a creativity subordinated to rigid class boundaries and made dependent on a domesticated taste for the ornamental. Stein rebels against the aesthetic timidity of the middle class, to which nevertheless the novel is a paean, by flashing her creative ambition as bad working class taste. She goes for a writing that is the equivalent of a servant's taste for colorful handkerchiefs and strange clocks, coded objects for a prose out of line and out of bounds. Desire, rebellion, negativity are the condition for *The Making of Americans*, but there is more. Repetition, literally the layers of repetitive prose that veil the characters' struggle to emerge and the author's hunger for success, cuts across warring intellectual systems and family (i.e. local, national, geographical) competitiveness. It is, above all, a creation with a respectable genealogy. The novel starts with the sins of the fathers and goes on to expound on their power. In the inheritance of the sins, not in their rejection, lies the effectiveness of Stein's belief in repetition:

> Once an angry man dragged his father along the ground through his own orchard. "Stop!" cried the groaning old man at last, "Stop! I did not drag my father beyond this tree."
>
> It is hard living down the tempers we are born with. We all begin well, for in our youth there is nothing we are more intolerant of than our own sins writ large in others and we fight them fiercely in ourselves; but we grow old and we see that these our sins are of all sins the really harmless ones to own, nay that they give a charm to any character, and so our struggle with them dies away. (*MA* 3)

The epigraph—from Aristotle's *Nichomachean Ethics* (via Montaigne)—suggests that, at least initially, the novel will recount an Oedipal narrative, a classic tale of subjectivity based on the master/servant, father/son combat. But this story does not last. As Ruddick has shown, the Oedipal narrative is soon undone by Stein's style of anality (Ruddick 77-92) while Stein's invocation of queerness also compromises the linearity of the Oedipal narrative (Watten 100-103). I want to suggest that the Oedipal narrative is interrupted or suspended by the grace of the son. In the economy of the book, the inert layers of repetitions finally give birth to young David Hersland who, in the last section of the saga, survives the trials of repetition to become a surrogate for Gertrude Stein herself. (Parenthetically, in this novel it is not the women that stand out, except when it is women who use other women to bolster their sense of self and focus their ambition, as in the case of Mary Maxworthing, but the men.) In the end, the novel will drag the son to the father's side. With young David Hersland's self-starvation the narrative affirms the grace of the son by also affirming the haunting and inescapable intellectual frame of reference of the father's sins. Stein's argument is that, as an American writer, she must work with the Oedipal narrative as her originality depends precisely on a confusion of tongues with the father's sins.

The elder David Hersland's foremost sin is an obsession with the self. As we shall see, he projects himself in an imaginary realm of plenitude, where he finds his sense of importance, not without frequent bouts of restlessness quickly cured by sexual exploits. His son departs from the sin of the self only to fall back on it.

Contrary to his father, David junior lives in the symbolic. He tries to mend the injustices of intersubjectivity by actively seeking out communal experiences. A more alarming, updated lay version of Puritan 'auto-machia,' he abandons himself to the Dionysian communal side in hopes of shedding private passions.[6] Paradoxically, he ends up with the feeling of an irreparable generalized detachment, starved of human food. The sin of the self, in its two extreme manifestations of David senior's restlessness and his son's ensuing melancholia, becomes to the burgeoning writer the nourishment she must metabolize until her anger against the fathers somehow breaks into a kind of love, into a form of intellectual mimesis for the sake of the new modernist prose. Through this progress Stein can emerge as an autonomous writer conscious of her potential and her originality. As they reach the reader, the fathers' thematic repetitions enfold the narrator completely. They cushion with the thickness of time and distance what, to unsympathetic ears, might otherwise sound like a raw obsession with the ego.

The language of a protective confusion of tongues, therefore, spreads over and cushions the fathers' sins. The advantage of such sacrificial poetics is an original coming to writing, the inkling of a new writing: with David senior and David junior, where does the treatise on the self end and the novel begin? With the grace of the young son, David Hersland, where does thought end and writing begin? In this fashion Stein lulls her American fathers to sleep; in the act of writing, she quiets them. In fact, *The Making of Americans* is a dialectic of lean and fat, of depression and ambition: on the one hand, the thinly disguised intellectual ambition of the writer, on the other hand, the complete knowledge of people (repetition) which, if it evokes psychoanalytic listening, is also indicative of a philosophical ambition gone astray; on the one hand, the ambition of the fathers for a thin, non-encumbering self, on the other hand, the unstoppable hunger it passed on.[7]

The important feeling

The novel starts with the Dehnings. Julia Dehning's 'healthy vigorous and active' (*MA* 20) outdoor ethic meets Alfred Hersland's culture-inflected money. Alfred belongs to a family who, like the Dehnings, had money but 'had taken to culture and to ideas quicker' (*MA* 22). The Dehnings practice the belief, illustrated by Julia's father, that thought and beauty count only insofar as they do not interfere with making money and getting ahead. His interest in beautiful things confers to Alfred Hersland 'a strain of singularity that yet keeps well within the limits of conventional respectability' (*MA* 21). With the introduction of the Dehnings, Stein ushers in the well known story of an American intellect beating like a trapped moth against the gilded panes of material comfort, exiled from the New World out of an incompatibility with the business of living. Alfred Hersland, reader of literature and appreciator of beautiful things, is emblematic of the suppressed crowd of 'Brother Singulars' and a mask of the narrator herself: 'we fly to the kindly comfort of an older world accustomed to take all manner of strange forms into its bosom and we leave our noble order to be known under such forms as Alfred Hersland, a poor thing and even hardly our own' (*MA* 21). The Shakespearean echo from the last act of *As You Like It*, when Touchstone announces his wish to marry the clumsy Audrey: 'A poor virgin, sir; an ill-favored thing, sir, but mine own,' possibly alludes to Stein's own language, which however original, will never quite be 'her own.'[8]

Young Julia Dehning enhances the melodrama. She dreams of successfully combining culture and worldly success. Consequently, she struggles to convince her sceptical father that Hersland will succeed in business even though he is a little 'interesting' (*MA* 25). Her life in Bridgeport is neither gloomy nor joyous 'but like a large and splendid canvas completely painted over but painted full of empty spaces' (*MA* 28). Materially content in her rich house, Julia 'grew more firm in her resolve for that free wide and cultured life to which for her young Hersland held the key' (*MA* 28).

By Stein's own admission, her novel is in part a study of the 'bourgeois mind' (*MA* 21) and its relation to culture. Her picture of the imprisoned middle class mind is generated by quite a different problem than forced expatriation—that of social panic. Family money and culture are divided by a line whose crossing implies the danger of falling into the abyss of class, madness, 'degradation' (*MA* 21). The members of the tableau are prey to the nightmare of loss; they fear that culture will turn them into the streets and that they will stoop to the condition of servants and lost souls. For Stein's middle class, individuality seems governed by panic. Its freedom is best left to the lower classes, a privilege of the poor, the crazy, the dregs of society, those who have nothing to lose on the cyclical stage of history.

The narrator is the first to endorse this initial paternalistic view. She muses that inner freedom has been expelled abroad, outside the realm of a local knowledge: 'we cannot stay where there are none to know it' (*MA* 47). At the same time, she does not hesitate to conflate the passion for freedom with the material degradation of the poor: 'they have no other way to do it' (*MA* 47). The narrator's reasoning is ruled by fear, which in turn prevents her from telling freedom of thought from social injustice. Happily identified with the middle class, initially Stein's narrator accepts the fear of the streets and the slums, of the impoverished and the lowest lost to degradation. In her inability to tell the effect of freedom from poverty and degradation, the narrator proves a good student of Julia's father, a man who likes to complain about the corruption of culture and modernity. He sees them as dangers to the advancement of his daughter in the walks of life. The contiguity of literary effects and poverty is clearly imprinted in his mind as a sort of transgenerational anxiety. Stein's novel begins under the sign of a pyramidal society where people like the Dehnings struggle to stay afloat and view their neighbor as the spectacle of their own potential social humiliation.

By contrast, the Herslands search for strong philosophical models that might negate social panic. One of these models is Alfred's father, David Hersland.

His parents came from the old world (*MA* 37). He was married to Fanny Hissen and settled in Gossols, a working class neighbor where his wife and children felt without social peers. It is with this character that the notion of the self, which Stein calls the 'important feeling' (*MA* 58), is introduced to the reader: 'Also he was in his way important inside to him' (*MA* 46). David Hersland begins Stein's chronicle of the self, while his younger son will end it.

The removal to Gossols seems part of an educational plan. David wants his children to grow with 'a passion to be free inside them' (*MA* 47). His story indicates that the important feeling might be synonymous with 'that vital steadfast singularity' (*MA* 48) whose lack the narrator laments in the U.S.A., which is defined as an adolescent metallic world. She complains: 'We all are the same all through us, we never have it to be free inside us' (*MA* 47). The father of Alfred, Martha, and David, David Hersland was a large man. He walked among others forgetful of his children trailing after him, 'tossing his head to get freedom' and 'muttering to himself in his thinking' (*MA* 49), his body in step with his thinking: 'throwing his body and his shoulders from side to side as he was arguing about things he wanted to be changing, and always he had the important feeling to himself inside him' (*MA* 50). What characterizes David Hersland is 'the power and completeness of the identification of this big man with all creation' (*MA* 51). He seems as large as the world, upholding his right to be in the world. He acts on impulse, as when he takes some fruit or cake from the shop to give it to the children. He can act this way, disregarding community etiquette, because he has money; in the end he pays the shop owner for what he takes to give freely to his children (*MA* 51).

From David Hersland's perspective, the self, which Stein calls 'the important feeling,' means a connection with the world that diminishes one's consciousness of social empowerment. In Emerson's fashion, David Hersland replaces social power with a more generic religious creed: 'No it was his being all there was of religion that gave him his important feeling, not his wife nor his children nor any power he had from them nor the power he never had had with any one who did not live shut up with him' (*MA* 60). David Hersland has no power over anyone beside his family circle. His Emersonian belief in the self dies with him: 'for even in his dying he had no power in him for any one shut up with him' (*MA* 63). In which sense then is David a father, that is to say, a model?

Although David Hersland has no influence in the community (he is noted only for his strange ways), socially he is less timid than Dehning. For example, he does not associate with his rich peers, but chooses instead to live in a poor neighborhood because he believes it will harden his own children. Unlike Dehning, he grasps that social panic, and its working through, has an important role in the education of the next generation. His decision pays, since this social sacrifice breeds in his wife, Fanny Hissen, an emotion that is close to her husband's 'important feeling' (*MA* 69). Whatever it is, the important feeling cuts across generations. David and Fanny marry 'to make children who perhaps would come to have in them a really important feeling for themselves inside them' (*MA* 77).

The removal to the poorer area of Gossols causes a class rift and makes the Hersland children socially dysfunctional when they visit with their rich peers (*MA* 91). The growth of the three children follows an inverse change from middle class to working class (*MA* 95). Stein's repetitive style seems particularly effective in rendering the seduction of the descent down the social ladder (*MA* 95), almost as if David Hersland were a sort of male rehearsal for Melanctha, the character Stein created at the same time that she was writing *The Making of Americans*. Like the white patriarch, David Hersland, Stein's African American heroine is consumed by an impatient feeling and literally belongs to the streets so feared by the middle class.

The Father (lack of splitting)

David Hersland is the father with whom Stein's narrator identifies, because of his strong sense of individuality and his intuition of the social constrictions of creativity. The novel had begun with the narrator's desire to catalogue human types. Now that desire has run its course and the realization has set in of an excess of semiotic connection with others and the world (*MA* 330). Like David Hersland, Stein's narrator chooses a capacity for new beginnings: 'Always then for such a one there must be many new beginnings' (*MA* 330).

Stein insists on David Hersland's strong sense of individuality. He belongs to the kind of men who 'have it in them to feel themselves as big as all the world around them. Some have such a sense in them only when a new thing begins in them, soon they lose it out of them' (*MA* 115). David grew up to be one of those men who 'have it in them to be as big as all the world in their beginning, they are strong in beginning and beginning things is all of living in them' (*MA* 117). But this positive interior feeling results in social negativity. Hersland is a business man living by choice among poor farming people. This, and his penchant for new beginnings, make him an unreliable business partner. While admiring his enthusiasm, his colleagues do not feel safe carrying through business with him. As his children will reveal to him later in his life, his fighting spirit and his anti-conformism—'brushing people away from him' (*MA* 143); 'brushing people away from around him when he went away in another direction in a blustering fashion' (*MA* 148)—was instead a manifestation of his inability to carry through a project to the end. It was a manifestation of enthusiasm that did not deliver. Hersland never knew that 'he was not strong in winning that the nature in him would not carry him to the last end of the fighting which is winning' (*MA* 147). Stein's repetitions remove the character in an abstract space. Borrowing from the style of the Puritan portrait, she is less interested in the likeness than in the 'shadow' of the man, in his moral effigy.[9] Hersland's effigy is the self—his capacity to take in the external world voraciously. But the introjection unfailingly leaves an unstoppable void, an 'impatient feeling' (*MA* 129). This father represents a sort of Spinozist direct line to the world, which endears him to us. But his unbounded communication with the external world is also supplemented by a negative restlessness. His energy does not materialize in finished projects. Although his interior independence is admirable, as he grows old, it remains unfocused, formless—its fruits scattered and unreaped. If this father is a term of transference love, he also forces on the child—Stein's narrator—the anxiety of non-production, of unfinished writing. If the identification is strong, equally strong must be the reaction to it.

It has been suggested that David Hersland senior is modeled on Stein's brother Leo.[10] In the text he is primarily a man who has never broken out of the imaginary union with the world. Because of his imaginary autonomy, he can combine thinking and doing. But if as a doer he has managed to get by and provide for his family, as a thinker he remains like a character out of Italo Svevo—the middle class citizen full unrealized potential and invaded by social melancholia—a perfect modernist icon. When compared to Dehning, David Hersland stands out even more as a model: he does not fear literary effects because even those are tame little things; the more radical change is in thinking, and David Hersland's great intuition—though he fears it—is that thought is social. Paradoxically, at the same time as he knows that and tries to instil it in his children, he needs to project himself in the imaginary sphere to keep himself from falling to pieces.

A more frontal description might reveal more bluntly the unlikable side of the father's nature: moody, voluble, temperamental, self-absorbed, guilty of a confusion of tongues that imposes on his children an oppressive form of love, demanding that they be adult emotional caretakers. The card game episode clearly illustrates this and the passage deserves to be quoted at length:

> Sometimes in little things it would be annoying to them in their early living, his way of beginning and then never knowing that he was full up with impatient feeling and so had stopped and wanted others to keep on going. Sometimes this would be annoying of an evening. He would want to play cards and the three of them would begin with him, to please him. The children felt it to be hard on them when they would have begun playing cards just to oblige him and after a few minutes with them he would have arise in him his impatient feeling, and he would say, "here you just finish it up and I haven't time to go on playing," and he would call the governess to take his hand from him and all three of the children would have then to play together a game none of them would have thought of beginning, and they had to keep on going for often he would stop in his walking to find which one was winning, and it never came to him to know that he had made the beginning and that the children were playing just because they had to, for him. (*MA* 129)

Furthermore, the text gives evidence that his behavior is incestuous (Ruddick 110). This would justify the open war against the father on which the value of Stein's novel has so far depended. In Lisa Ruddick's influential argument, the novel attests to Stein's 'difficult emancipation from a paternal specter' (55).

For Ruddick the stylistic choice of the continuous present is a symbolic evacuation of paternal authority. Through 'a heavy use of participles, gerunds, and progressive verb forms' (Ruddick 85), Stein forces things into homogeneity and represents a 'potentially anti-paternal pleasure' (Ruddick 86). Repetitions are an expression of her 'patricidal rage' (Ruddick 58). In my reading, I find that Stein, as well as working against the sins of the fathers, is also working with them because those sins are her land (Hersland), the source of the originality of her modern writing. While not pretending that fathers—and violent fathers at that—never existed, she does add that stylistic patricide may not be necessary to think anew. The writer seems to rise in her acknowledgment of her affiliation with those sins because the acknowledgment does not exclude their performative, i.e. critical, iteration and magnification. From such possibility Stein's narrator derives her authority and her mobile position.

As David Hersland's life progresses and the writing insists on his 'impatient feeling,' what had seemed abundance—identification of self and the world—actually becomes the descent into an abyss. The impression is that the elder Hersland has tried to overcome consciousness, and the inevitable relation with the other that comes with it, by opting for 'the return of consciousness into the depths of the night of the I=I, which distinguishes and knows nothing beside itself' (Hegel qtd.in Zizek 183). The father remains a strong model for Stein's narrator, a closet philosopher of the self who, to assert the self, must have no self-consciousness in the historical sense.

But at times the confusion of tongues turns powerfully against Stein's narrator. The pages on the servants are an example. There, repetition with its abstracting force testifies against the narrator for her obtuseness toward some of the characters, the servant specifically. Here she seems to repeat the same insensitivity of the father toward the interior world of his children, his dull poverty of intersubjective understanding:

> As I was saying servants often have it in them to be a little queer and children like to tease them, they have this queerness from cooking, from cleaning and from their lonesome living, from their sitting in the kitchen, from having a mistress to direct them, and children to tease them; the Irishwoman and one of the Italian women that were cooking once for the Hersland family in their middle living had this queerness in them. (*MA* 170)

The label 'servant queerness' reduces the pain of power relations to a verbal exercise (*MA* 171). Protecting the fathers' sins implies inventing categories like servant queerness that, far from being culturally significant, sound simply punishing. Stein had traded her confusion with the fathers' sins for an entitlement as a verbal impressionist. Her impressionism has transfigured the aesthetically abjected middle class into an ecstatic site of consciousness where the erotic incorporation of others seemed to cure social limits and differences. But at times, verbal impressionism becomes a sterile exercise, producing at best interesting melodramatic trinkets worthy of Julia Dehning, with no further history other than a local and provincial one. Stein is at an impasse. The confusion of tongues between the father and the daughter breeds punishing ideas.

The queerness of the servant

The text relies on the notion of 'servant queerness' to move away from David Hersland's power and focus more sharply the preoccupations of the writer and her task. Stein muses: 'to many [. . .] the important thing is to have written about everyone around them the history of each one' (*MA* 184), and: 'mostly everyone wants a history of someone, mostly everyone wants a history of some one, mostly every one wants some kind of a history of some' (*MA* 185). Such need for storytelling can be satisfied if the self encounters social circumstance. That is how one gets a story. But telling a story also means objectifying others, as suggested by categories like 'servant nature' (*MA* 182) and 'bottom nature' (*MA* 183). Moreover, now storytelling is explicitly associated with the gaze and, implicitly, with its objectifying powers: 'There are then many ways of having living inside one and having it come out from one, always then some one looks at each one, always the more one looks at every one the more one knows that sometime there will be a history of every one' (*MA* 185).

David Hersland's internal sense of self progressively modulates first as 'impatient feeling' (*MA* 185), then as 'an anxious feeling' (*MA* 185) to take up root in the bodily and social reality of the servant and emerge as the category of 'servant queerness' (*MA* 185). Servant queerness is in direct line with the father's 'impatient feeling and anxious being' (*MA* 185) but it seems a trait of women confined in the domestic sphere and deprived of rich social intercourse: 'from much sitting alone in a kitchen, from much eating without any one being then with them or around them, from much cooking' (*MA* 185). Food and domesticity will later become the theme of Stein's popular sequence *Tender Buttons*. But in *The Making of Americans* there is nothing poetic about the servant's domestic enclosure and her forced intimacy with food, except Stein's attempt to invest materiality and abjected social identities with an alluring philosophical view of the self rejoicing, like David Hersland, in its internal freedom. The human archivist finds out that storytelling is mired in society, destiny, biology and all sorts of determinisms.

Servant queerness comes from the father's sense of individuality. As the narrative progresses, the father's internal independence becomes inseparable from issues of social equity, from questions of anger and injury. These social affects, Stein discovers, are contagious and might even be the condition of storytelling: 'To have an injured or an angry feeling in one is very common in ordinary living. Injured or angry feeling may be in one with impatient feeling or with anxious feeling and it may be in one without any such being then in that one' (*MA* 189).

Stein is genuinely overwhelmed by human character. She accepts the imperative to tell the stories of the 'many men and the many women always living' (*MA* 184), and loves the telling in the process. But this diligence cannot hide the writer's anxious feeling. The more she looks around the more she must write lives: 'always the more one looks at everyone the more one knows that sometime there will be a history of everyone' (*MA* 185). It seems that multitudes of people, in true modernist fashion, demand to be written: 'the important thing is to have written about everyone around them the history of each one' (*MA* 184). As she tries to order the multitudes by creating major categories, her stories risk merging into History, the old history of masters and servants. At that point, the storyteller has the option of glamorising minor subjectivities. If David Hersland's important feeling first, impatient feeling later, conveyed a paternal matrix to reckon with, once it is immersed in social reality its philosophical potential is translated into the position of the servant, which Stein flaunts almost with gusto, as shown by insistence on queerness. We are told that David Hersland's wife, Fanny Hissen, ambiguously receives her 'important feeling' from the working class women who surround her and over whom she rules (*MA* 187). The most interesting part of this stage of the narrative is the intersection of paternal social autonomy with class and power relations. Otherwise, if considered as psychological analysis, Stein's simplistic categories like servant queerness or 'dependent independent' and 'independent dependent' bottom natures sound like the unfortunate effects of her struggle to be born to language out of the generative vocabulary of the fathers.

At this point, the narrator's sense of autonomy is still confused with the 'important thing' (*MA* 184) of having written about every single one. Such a creative program recalls Julia Dehning's timid conjoining of money (accumulation) and culture. But the aesthetic of narrative accumulation cannot exorcise the social panic of which Julia is an emblematic child and which Stein's narrator tries to appease.

Subjectivity is gentler

The Martha Hersland chapter marks a turning point. The self becomes a slippery notion. Despite the different stories, 'every one is resembling to others' (*MA* 290). Repetition, it turns out, is a nicer name for subjectivity, that is to say, for the inescapable fact that the self comes into being and into narrative as a social position: 'they are separate and yet always repeated' (*MA* 289). Repetition, as Stein's narrator discovers in the Martha Hersland section, refers to the realization that the I is both a concrete I and an abstract position. (Perhaps this is why we can read the stories of others, even when they are multiple, and why the novel remains possible in modernity without getting out of hand.) Here is how she puts it: 'Everyone then is an individual being. Everyone then is like many others always living' (*MA* 290). And: 'every one is themselves inside them and every one is resembling to others' (*MA* 290). The writer's dilemma is: because every I is an individual human being, it is possible to assign each to a type (the resemblance position). A glimmer of love replaces ennui as the vista opens up of an I and an abstract subject that are mutual reflections: 'They are all of them repeating and I hear it. I love it and I tell it, I love it and now I will write it' (*MA* 289).

What does it mean to love the social repetition of individuality? What kind of love is it? Perhaps the emphasis is on 'and': I love it *and* I tell it. The fount of (story)telling now depends on an intellectual affinity for social subjectivity. It is an uncomfortable attachment, best confessed to strangers, since 'mostly anyone' dislikes to hear 'that they look [. . .] like some one else' (*MA* 289). Subjectivity is an unpleasant truth; it can be heard from the distance that separates text and reader: 'I write for myself and strangers I do this for my own sake and for the sake of those who know I know it that they look like other ones, that they are *separate and yet always repeated*' (*MA* 289; my emphasis). And even when practiced as an intellectual attachment, subjectivity must be mitigated by the erotic introjection of others: 'Sometime every one becomes a whole one to me [. . .] Slowly each one is a whole one to me' (*MA* 291).[11]

From this point of view, repetition is not just an authorial (and authoritative) father killer, as it has been argued. Of course, Stein admits that repetition is 'irritating' but that it is necessary to 'learning the complete being in any one' (*MA* 306). While bottom nature, with its scatological ring, may have pointed to the evacuation of the philosophical subject in favor of easy psychological abstractions, the realization that individuality does not exist actually marks a return to philosophical subjectivity ('the complete being in any one'). It becomes the saving factor of writing, almost a *raison d'être* for the writer lost in the wilderness of human multitudes that demand existence on paper. Characters rise like ideas that want to be clarified. Stein's vocabulary is strikingly close to that of Peirce. She writes: 'such a one has it then that this irritation passes over into patient completed understanding' (*MA* 291). Peirce has spoken of 'the irritation of doubt that causes a struggle to attain belief' (99). Moreover, Stein's repetition, which she also terms 'a solid happy satisfaction' (*MA* 293), closely recalls Peirce's definition of belief: 'a calm and satisfactory state which we do not wish to avoid, or to change to a belief in anything else' (99). Like belief for Peirce, repetition involves the struggle to escape doubt. It is almost a structural trait that allows for the ordering of multitudes on the page, preventing the writer from being lost in them and writing from losing its vocation.

The love of repetition ensures that she can still combine her poetics of social eroticism with a novelistic vocation, which consists in the knowledge of human character. If anything, repetition, the realization that concrete individuality is also abstract social subjectivity, reinforces the erotic introjection of others and the desire that people be writing matter. The realization that individuality is never free from abstraction not only makes more plausible the understanding of others as wholes inside, but also gives the writer a reason to love in others what they ignore or do not like about themselves. In this sense, Stein's repetition echoes Freud's psychoanalysis. When she speaks of 'learning understanding' (*MA* 316), she conjures a slow process, neither bookish nor associated with writing, but primarily linked to looking and listening—'again and again to listen, to fill in, to be certain' (*MA* 316)—that is a kind of lay analysis. She is 'hard looking' (*MA* 317) but, like Freud's psychoanalytically minded person, presents herself as a listener—someone who strives to listen to an accord. In *The Question of Lay Analysis* Freud describes this kind of understanding of others with a technical metaphor:

> To put it in a formula: he must turn his own unconscious like a receptive towards the transmitting unconscious of the patient. He must adjust himself to the patient as a telephone receiver to the transmitting microphone. Just as a receiver converts back into sound waves the electric oscillations in the telephone line which were set up sound waves, so the doctor's unconscious is able, from the derivatives of the unconscious which are transmitted to him, to reconstruct that unconscious, which has determined the patient's free associations. (qtd. in Rose 13)

Like Freud's analyst, Stein's narrator strives to receive the sound waves of her characters.

Wholeness and melancholia

With the Martha Hersland section things change. The section invalidates Stein's erotic empathy, which occasionally allows her to meet another as 'a whole one' (*MA* 307). Finally, she grants that wholeness is hard to reach: not always does the writer get the character right. And getting the whole, or essential pattern, right means shuttling back and forth the internal I and the social I, the self and the subject position, difference and history. In the process, the reading experience remains suspended between individual life lines and a mass of sameness. As if to comfort the reader in her confusion, Stein admits that it may not work: 'Sometime I know and hear and feel and see all the repeating in some one, all the repeating that is the whole of some one but it always comes as pieces to me' (*MA* 311). Some characters just come 'as pieces,' without any dominant or abstract trait. Here Stein resorts to the notion of melodrama to convey the realization that unity is illusionary: 'Some of such of them sometimes then make melodrama of themselves to themselves to hold themselves together to them' (*MA* 312). This understanding of the profoundly imaginary unity of character is a breakthrough in the novel's progress, and has important consequences.

First of all, the aspiring writer of the new novel is pressured by an ever growing multitude of characters demanding to be understood. Secondly, the unity of self and writing, which as a burgeoning American writer the author of *The Making of Americans* has inherited, proves problematic. Thirdly, and connected to the second point, since the unity of character (a novelistic convention) and self (a philosophical tenet), have become a problem, this now further impacts on the unity of understanding and writing. Such unity, assumed by the narrator, proves untenable, as is revealed throughout the novel by the unbalanced mix of character sketches, self-analysis, and meditation.

It can be said, then, that the Martha Hersland middle section is about the growing awareness of the fundamental melodrama of unity. Increasingly, the desire for wholes is dismissed in favor of the problem of pieces, of piecing together, and thus making wholes, especially for the 'strangers' for whom Stein is writing so that they can, in turn, make sense of her texts.[12] Stein forcefully thrusts her apprenticeship to the foreground. The strange thing is that she does not come up with any specific knowledge about writing. Writing does not seem to be different from a state of keen perception, a heightened awareness of others. Why should this awareness of others not suffice as knowledge? Why should it instead 'come out' as writing? What justifies it is the compulsion to tell the meaning of others. She insists: 'I am filled full with each one I am ever knowing as a whole one then inside me, always then I am filled full with some one filled full of the meaning of one then filling me full up with that one then, full up to the point of telling the meaning of that one.' (*MA* 327). At first the telling of meaning had been justified by the project of the human catalogue. This was a sign that the novel should transcend its bourgeois tradition and open itself to everyone. Later, the human catalogue is redefined as a national project dedicated to committing to paper an hitherto denied and unknown 'vital steadfast singularity' (*MA* 48). Now the wholeness of each is revealed as imaginary: 'there are so many ways of seeing each one that I must stop looking' (*MA* 337), and meaning wanes altogether: 'I lose all of them and then each one I am then seeing looks like every one I have ever known [. . .] and there is no meaning' (*MA* 335). Stein is defeated in her struggle to balance individuality and collective identity, desire for originality and repetition. She is driven by an overwhelming task. No wonder she breaks out: 'I am all unhappy in this writing' (*MA* 348).

Here is a moment of intellectual rage against the fathers. She has inherited David Hersland's 'vital singularity' which puts the writer on a search for unrecorded uniqueness. The father's internal independence is sceptical of subjectivity, i.e. the social and historical dimension of the self, something which costs him mundane success. She is trapped between two different miseries: collective identity and social failure. During one of the most acute bouts of melancholia, she despairs: 'Nobody knows, nobody can know, and I am telling it very often, nobody knows nobody can know how I am wanting to know everything about every one' (*MA* 673). Moments of intellectual empowerment alternate with melancholia and despair: such is the rhythm of *The Making of Americans*, for the writer as well as her reader.

From melancholia to shame

To cure the melancholia, another genealogy of writing must be sought. This new genealogy surfaces in the section on Alfred Hersland and Julia Dehning and acknowledges the power of shame in the birth of new writing. Like melancholia, shame also is an inherited affect. As Stein understands it, shame has to do with class. It arises from making choices that do not agree with one's social status. It would seem in line with David Hersland's socially iconoclastic behavior. Shame begins in the limited environment of domesticity and extends to the more public act of writing:

> It is a very strange feeling when one is loving a clock that is to everyone of your class of living an ugly and a foolish one and one really likes such a thing and likes it very much and liking it is a serious thing, or one likes a colored handkerchief that is very gay and every one of your kind of living thinks it is a very ugly or a foolish thing [. . .]. (*MA* 485)

Soon enough from ugly and foolish clocks and inappropriately colourful handkerchiefs, the paragraph moves to books and writing:

> or you write a book and while you write it you are ashamed for every one must think you are a silly or a crazy one and yet you write it and you are ashamed, you know you will be laughed at or pitied by every one and you have a queer feeling and you are not very certain and you go on writing. (*MA* 485)

In this new model narrative of coming to writing the human catalogue disappears. Now writing bears an almost structural link to class hierarchies, and class hierarchies are clearly another name for social humiliation: 'it is a hard thing to be loving something with a serious feeling and everyone is thinking that only a servant girl could be loving such a thing' (*MA* 487) .

Stein's consciousness of the subtle tie between social freedom and creativity is part of a more general modernist sensibility. And it is possible to read her identification with writing by subordinates in line with a more general modernist valuing of negativity and minor social identities. But her passage about shame suggests that here she is not interested in the idealization of the other, a creative reaction to social hierarchies that is not only typical of modernism but continues to be a major spring of critical discourse in our times.[13] Crucially, the discovery of shame prompts a new angle on the question of 'masters and schools' (*MA* 486), that is to say, on the question of the transmission of knowledge and the related issue of innovators and their followers. The writer's dilemma about her servant status makes clear that the freedom of writing is conditioned by social affects. Shame, in fact, is no private character flaw. On the contrary, it is a political feeling charged with distress at and dissent from social impositions. At first Stein associates writing (and importantly writing in the completed form of a book) with forbidden class-marked pleasures. Then, she offers a sexualized narrative that resolves shame into approval. The passage I quoted above continues:

> Then someone says yes to it, to something you are liking, or doing or making and then never again can you have completely such a feeling of being afraid and ashamed that you had then when you were writing or liking the thing and not any one had said yes about the thing. (*MA* 485)

The reader who 'says yes' is also a favored lover, as it becomes clearer in the text: 'you can never again have the complete feeling of recognition that you have then' (*MA* 486). The freedom of writing is conditioned by social affects that are rooted in class divisions. From this starting point, Stein goes on to realize that class, sexuality, and cultural authority are bound up together. Like sexuality, especially non-approved forms of sexuality, writing becomes a forbidden act related to social feelings, produced by these feelings and reacting to them. If formerly the writer had worked in the shadow of social abjection, in the eroticized scene of the yes-saying lover she experiences the freedom of recognition: 'you can only alone and with the first one have the perfect feeling of not being almost completely filled with being ashamed and afraid to show something to like something with a really serious feeling' (*MA* 486). Only when woven into the sexual scene the fear of a cultural servant identity can be turned around and made positive; it becomes 'courage' (*MA* 487), the special creative autonomy enjoyed by innovators. After mentioning 'masters and schools in living and in working and in painting and in writing and in everything' (*MA* 486), Stein notes that it takes courage to write and to buy things (487), a subtle reference to her art collecting and preference for Cézanne, who, as we have seen in the previous chapter, was accused of pleasing the working classes.

An imaginary master-servant relation between the writer and his readers is, with class and power, one of the traditional themes of the novel.[14] With the idea of shame Stein complicates this view. Moreover, her pair seems to modify the classic philosophical pair of combatants. The non-equality of subject and object is a healing form of attestation that gives the courage to innovate. She thus suggests that writing can supply what philosophy's abstract understanding of human character cannot reckon with: this is the role of social affect in individual creative freedom. She shifts the attention from the spectacle of consciousness (seen as the subject/object struggle) to the liberating effect of the response of another (reader or lover).[15] In a way, Stein finds that the subject/object struggle at the heart of consciousness is a by-product of the fear of social shame. Accordingly, she imagines her coming to writing as a progress toward the desiring subject, beyond shame and its silencing. In the last section of this chapter we shall see that the fruit of this achievement is the character of the younger son, David Hersland, a creation that has lasting effects on all her subsequent writing.

The semiotician's drama (the young David Hersland)

For the elder David Hersland, desire was an imaginary pursuit. It meant an individual enclosure away from the interferences of social identity. But his imaginary state proves an exhausting brushing aside of others. The first part of the novel faces up to the father's inheritance and turns his imaginary state into a philosophical object, attractive but problematic. The younger son tries to break out of the father's seclusion and engage his object—the self—in a sustained philosophical confrontation. In the process, the young David Hersland comes to shun systems of thought and develop a hunger for immanence. Having gone through an array of self-perceptions, from servant identification to shame to recognition, with the young hero Stein finally justifies her sense of difference resulting from tradition and a debt to the fathers.

The final section is in more than one way the pinnacle of *The Making of Americans*. Once it has gained momentum, the narrative is focused, intense, successful in offering the movement of a life. The David Hersland section is already at the crossroad of genres, an intermediate creation that is a bit narration, a bit drama, a bit portrait, a bit philosophical biography. Stein's narrator has given up the view that the vitality of her writing depends on understanding as many people as she can. She is now interested in something more akin to a subjective affirmation of life, a will to live: 'to be one being living' (729).

Young David Hersland is the heir of an incurably agitated father for whom the Emersonian belief in the self does not clash against successful moneymaking. Indeed, for this father the desiring self seems to have been invented to placate the social fear of class degradation.[16] Daily exposed to the lower classes, he grows to be a young philosopher in his own right, leaning more towards semiotics than idealism.

At the beginning talking and listening define him (*MA* 746). These are the same traits that Stein attributes to herself in her lecture 'The Gradual Making of The Making of Americans,' delivered at several universities during her American 1934 tour.[17] David 'was one being interested in his being one being living' (*MA* 748). Unlike his father he does not assume an imaginary plenitude of self and world. Instead, he knows the split and longs to heal it: 'As I was saying sometimes when he was living he was one wanting to be needing that not any one was having angry feeling' (*MA* 759). This knowledge seems to make him particularly hostile toward institutions of education and training. Young David rebels against teaching and teachers: 'he could be wanting them not to be a bother to him while they were ones being ones teaching him something' (*MA* 769).

David is divided between an antinomian thrust against formal training and a 'humble feeling' (*MA* 778). He oscillates between the prototype of the precocious Romantic genius—'sometimes completely certain that he was understanding everything' (*MA* 778)—and another non-formal knowledge that, once again, recalls Freud's kind of communication between two unconsciouses, one tracking the other. At first he views the intellect as purged of emotion: 'David Hersland was one certainly in a way not having complete emotion, certainly in a way doing clear thinking, certainly in a way having adequate expression, certainly having very nearly absolute conviction' (*MA* 779). He values clear thinking, and therefore, unlike his father, he faces the symbolic dimension. But then he shuns emotion. In fact, he lives in fear that thought will get too close to emotion.

The narrative shifts from the elder David Hersland's defensive notion of self to his son's rationalism: 'He was now not being certain that experiencing being intensified was spirituality and idealism' (*MA* 781). The father had lived the interior life of an idealist and the worldly life of a middle class man, with the result that he had become restless, impatient, and finally disaffected if not abusive to his human companions. The young David wants to move beyond his father but is at a crossroad. On the one hand, he is neither religious nor idealistic: 'He almost came to be certain that one could not be experiencing something more complete than any experiencing' (*MA* 781). On the other hand, he is certain of something beyond the materiality of experience: 'he came to be almost certain that one can be experiencing something that is more than experiencing' (*MA* 781).

In Stein's narrative David Hersland consistently features as 'one being living' (*MA* 782). His vitalism floods the prose with light, making this section perhaps the closest to Cézanne and his teachings. Moreover, David's charismatic embracing of immanence is a good vehicle for Stein's appropriation of desire. Because of David's philosophical search, in this section thinking and writing finally converge. And this joining also accounts for the sunny quality of the narrative, despite its tragic finale.

Initially the 'something more than experiencing' which David chooses over idealism means a belief in the continuous present. He thinks of being as a flow of complete moments, as a chain of peaks of meaningfulness: 'Some of such of them have it that the moment of sensibility, emotion and expression and origin is all in a state of completion and then it is a finished thing and certainly then that one was meaning something and he was saying I mean, I mean, and it was all finished and then there was another something' (*MA* 782). Desire, even in the form of the desire to live, is a potentially destructive force. David mediates it with the religion of the continuous present. Yet, is this mediation really different from a self-enclosure in the moment, from the transformation of immediacy into a religion?

Like Peirce, David comes to believe that consciousness only lives in the present. We cannot have a consciousness of the past; we can remember the consciousness we had of the past. The meaning of the I is ever changing. There is a wonderful ode to mutability and against the fetters of rigid, encrusted meaning embedded in the David Hersland section:

> I mean, I mean and that is not what I mean, I mean that not any one is saying what they are meaning, I mean that I am feeling something, I mean that I am meaning something and I mean that not any one is thinking, is feeling, is saying, is certain of that thing, I mean that not any one can be

saying, thinking, feeling, not anyone can be certain of that thing, I mean I
am not certain of that thing [. . .]. (*MA* 782)

The undecidability of meaning is invoked as a balm against semiotic death ('not
any one is thinking, is feeling, is saying'). Stein had reached a standstill in her
meditation about the centrality of human character in writing. Such centrality has
brought her to choose the novel as the genre that might have satisfied her
innovative desire. But with David Hersland she stops thinking of herself as a
novelist, envisioning instead a freer writing in which 'sensibility, emotion and
expression and origin' (*MA* 782) are simultaneous. This vocabulary is so different
from the previous one of shame and misrecognition; it suggests an enviable
expressive autonomy and, above all, the possibility of a writing that never ends,
that is 'expression and origin' because it can begin anew. The mutability of
meaning parallels a conversion to the belief that consciousness is in the present.
For David Hersland, however, that conversion will be his predicament. David
becomes a captive of the moment, just as his father had been a captive of idealism.

Stein is commonly hailed by the majority of her readers and critics as a
believer in the continuous present. With David Hersland's portrait, however, she
may be treating us to a critique of that personal religion. This religion may be a
remnant of David senior's sin of the self and thus, though different, still an effect
of social panic. In fact, David's love of immanence may deny the relation between
the internal and the external, self and society.

It is because of his capacity to think of the world in terms of signs that he
will differentiate himself from his father. To start with, he believes there is a
correspondence between message and meaning, with no remainder or excess:
'Some are quite certain that they are knowing what each one saying anything is
meaning by what they are saying. David Hersland was in a way one of such of
them' (*MA* 784). But he also knows that meaning exceeds the message or, better,
that there are signs, and saying anything happens in a world of signs: 'Some are
quite certain that each one is meaning something when they are saying anything. In
a way David Hersland was such a one' (*MA* 784). (It does not follow, however,
that David believes in intentional meaning: 'Some are certain that each one is one
wanting to be meaning something by what that one is saying. David Hersland was
not such a one' (*MA* 784-5)). David believes that everything means something and
that desire exists insofar as it is caught in the web of meanings: 'Some are certain
that each one is one not wanting to be meaning something by what that one is
saying. David Hersland was hardly ever at all really such a one' (*MA* 785). He does
not believe in lack of agency; he experiences agency and intention as confused in a
general, extended meaningfulness: 'each one is meaning something when they are
saying anything' (*MA* 784).

For David Hersland the world is full of signs that pulse with meaning.
His entrance in the narrative actually humanizes the narrator. Now we understand
that her ambition for the human catalogue was a misguided effect of the father's
legacy. Her appetite for understanding others may have appeared strange,

especially her conviction that she could grind their difference in a system as if there were no difference between flesh and paper. With the young David, the desiring subject seems to be given a moral scope by his immersion in meaning. Panic-induced desire seems integrated in the ethical scenario of an open, ongoing semiosis.

Everyone wants to mean, and young David is nervous about systems and totalizing theories. He needs a sense of closure; at the same time, he does not want one:

> in a way he was one needing to be completely certain that he was complete in needing the realization of experiencing and thinking and meaning and telling in all men and women, in a way he was one wanting to be needing to be certain to be interested in not being certain that any such realization would be complete living for him. (*MA* 785)

Abstraction and concreteness, intellect and emotion are always at war in him. He is a sharp thinker and knows how to express his thoughts clearly (*MA* 788), yet he is also fearful of a 'complete thinking' (*MA* 788) that takes emotions into account. Eventually he overcomes fear, and emotional intellect becomes his teaching. Interestingly, Stein terms David's new phase 'boasting,' a self-referential hint. In many ways, David is a fictional rendition of Stein's own self-perception as a sensuous intellectual. It is useful to note that when David chooses the path of a less abstract thought, boasting refers to his need for a supporting audience of sympathetic listeners (*MA* 788), a yes-saying lover on a grander scale.

As the narrative goes on, we follow the younger son in his philosophical vicissitudes: first, the flux of the present; secondly, the semiotic fabric of the world, which turns the will to live into the will to mean; thirdly, his awakening to the affective dimension of thinking. The latter is followed by a struggle to shed private attachments (*MA* 869). He wavers between the need for a privileged attachment and a more political vocation for a communal tie, which echoes Stein's narrator's erotic empathy in the earlier part of the novel.

He acts on his political feeling and joins a community of likes: 'He was then being with some who were ones being living then' (*MA* 875). He tries to be 'one of them' and perceive his individuality in terms of collective identity. David's political feeling and his attempt to expand the boundaries of the isolated self are rendered in a sequence that conveys the Dionysian and sexual connotations of his inquiry: 'He was then knowing one of them, two of them, a few of them. He was sometimes meeting any of them' (*MA* 885).

David's enjoyment of the communal foreshadows the emotional denouement of the narrative. His will to live gains momentum: 'he was one understanding this thing understanding every day being living that day' (*MA* 879). His desire grows to be unquenchable, taking him from one phase to another. The phase of the political diminishes physical need while sharpening thinking: 'He was not completely needing anything. He was completely clearly thinking' (*MA* 880).

Having finally sublimated private attachment into social connection, he understands that 'thinking is existing' (*MA* 887). He comes out of the tunnel of his vicissitudes, exactly like Stein, with the realization of the emotion of thinking.

While Stein goes on writing, her hero will perish because of a residual repetition of the sins of his father. David has repudiated the father's imaginary realm in favor of an individuality fully immersed in the social and the symbolic realms. Despite the inversion, the son is still left with the doubt of the choice between existing and social success, a version of the old paternal oscillation between self and money (*MA* 876).

David has the genius of all those who brave time, place, and social conventions in a consuming desire to affirm being: 'He was needing then to be certain that being living is existing that there is being existing' (*MA* 890). In writing him, Stein creates a center of beauty. She participates in David's genius and comes out of the novel victorious, reinforced in her literary vocation, assured of her own capacity to face up to history with the autonomy of her personal choices. Above all she emerges with the strength of someone who has struggled with her national tradition and thus earned the right to believe in her own kind of writing. Her character, on the contrary, tries to master the melancholia of his struggle, a feeling that is transferred to us as we follow the last act of his tragedy.

Eventually, David's voracious desire becomes incompatible with bodily life. He stops eating (*MA* 890) and almost gives up thinking: 'He was then almost completely wanting to be needing succeeding in living' (*MA* 890). Understanding remains a 'continuous and clear' force in him (890), but he progressively loses his appetite: 'He was then only eating one thing' (*MA* 903). The emotionalization of the self paradoxically results in social anorexia. He finally dies, starved by his own medium—thinking—because he has discovered that thinking is inseparable from feeling. Like the class-, race-, and gender-marked Melanctha, David, the passionate semiotician, is consumed by the melancholia left over from his wanderings. His father had known better. He had protected himself from the experience of human detachment by taking refuge in the self. In opposition to his father, David cultivates an acute sensitivity for the communal which crucially defines the progress of his *vita activa*. A similar sensitivity, as I shall go on arguing in this book, can be detected in Stein's progress. One must listen for it carefully as it is often muffled by her much louder struggle to challenge the limits of nation, gender, and history to assert her right to cultural presence.

Chapter 3

Mabel Dodge, Patronage, and the Velvet Garment

The velvet garment

Style of dress was part and parcel of Gertrude Stein's public persona. With her move to Europe she permanently shed nineteenth-century fashion and its staple feminine item, the corset (Stendhal 26). She adopted a more timeless style (Stendhal 46, 49, 54, 77) mainly consisting in a loose velvet garment lacking specific gender connotations. She appears in a velvet garment in her public images. These comprise her portraits by Picasso (1906) and Felix Volloton (1907) and some photographs, especially the series of shots taken by Alvin Langdon Coburn, who was also the photographer of Henry James.[1] In this chapter I will explore the connection between Stein's visual self and her writing, concentrating on one of the photos taken by Alvin Langdon Coburn and on 'Portrait of Mabel Dodge at the Villa Curonia.' Though seemingly assertive Stein's visual persona, is not free from insecurities, which surface on the page. In particular, her identification with Mabel Dodge reveals her need for patron figures. Dodge, who plays the imaginary role of the artist's patron, will materially ensure Stein's production. Stein's homage to her friend tells us that Dodge helped her to dispel old doubts about the compatibility of her class and national origins with a valuable kind of artistic innovation. My discussion of Dodge's influence is indebted to Patricia Everett and her edition of the correspondence between the two women.

In one of the Coburn photos (Fig. 3.1) Stein can be seen in her Paris studio, sitting in a high Renaissance chair, facing the viewer with an expression of intensity and gravity on her face while a loose velvet garment drapes her body. This will be her favorite uniform in most of her official images. Different cultural references converge in Stein's choice of dress, including the customary dress of older men in the Renaissance, a royal robe, and an Oriental robe. What she wears becomes a studied costume that cuts across genders, cultures, and historical periods. This costume connotes simultaneously public consequence, authority, and exoticism. Draped in its folds, her body is abstracted from time and cultural divides. Her image does not imply sleekness or speed, as in the elf-like boyish look popularised by Sylvia Beach, powerful cultural entrepreneur and Parisian neighbour of Stein. Neither does it share Djuna Barnes's unique allure, resulting from the unusual combination of her striking femininity and her haunting writing.

Fig. 3.1   Gertrude Stein in her studio, by Alvin Langdon Coburn. Courtesy of Yale Collection of American Literature, Beinecke Rare Book and Manuscript Library.

Stein favored a different sort of authority, one emanating neither from boyish looks, and their implication of a male-identified sensibility, nor from the New Woman style. She relied on a touch of orientalism mixed with Western history. In fact, the velvet piece visually evokes a plain *kosode*, a premodern Japanese predecessor of the kimono.[2] In Stein's interpretation, the modern writer is an orientalized authority on a Renaissance throne. She is authoritative because she is genderless; she is genderless because she is orientalized. The public position she takes up with the aid of the photographic setting and of her dress is one of continuous translation.

Stein and her contemporaries felt the appeal of the Orient. From early youth she had shared with her brother Leo a taste for Japanese prints. Moreover, Japonisme was the fashion in the earlier part of the twentieth century. Stein's robe is sufficiently plain to be worn unisexually. But Stein's self-transformation through dress does not limit itself to playing on the gender line. She defines her intellectual power through a fashion that cuts across high art and popular taste. In pictures such as this, Stein's trademark velvet garment streamlines the difficulty of her writing, as if this could now be grasped as part of a popular leaning toward non-Western cultures, which had made its way to designer wear.[3]

Since the turn of the century, designers had been appropriating stylistic conventions from diverse cultures spanning the Asian continent (Mears 18). Avant-garde art, in the specific examples of the colors of Matisse and Picasso, had encouraged this popular phenomenon in the realm of fashion, and so did the import of Japanese kimonos made expressly for the Western market.[4] In addition, the debut of Sergei Diaghilev's Ballet Russe in 1909 helped spread the trend. Popular French couturiers like Paul Poiret and Jeanne Paquin were inspired by Ballet Russe's performances like *Clèopatra, Schérazade,* and *Le Dieu Bleu.* Fashion might have helped to spread a new canon of femininity that combined beauty with strong will and passion. Stein's visual self-fashioning adapts this popular image to emphasize her literary power.

The opulent, drapery-like quality of kimonos inspired coats and outdoor robes to attend cultural events like the opera. Marie Callot Gerber, for example, found inspiration in kimonos for opera coats that 'swathed the body like batwinged cocoons' (Mears 18). Stein's robe is a more minimalist interpretation of the then fashionable kimonos. Her velvet cocoon is far more severe than the outdoor coats. Its severity evokes less the ornamental function of the orientalized garment than its cultural function. Stein's robe holds together a series of juxtapositions: past and present, east and west, masculine and feminine, public and private. It invites the viewer to imagine the wearer as a center of cultural mobility and hybridization and to associate her with influence in the cultural arena at large.

Her Oriental cocoon does not mean that Stein was particularly sensitive to issues of ethnicity. For example, she could be crudely dismissive of the Native Americans with whom her patron and friend Mabel Dodge had settled. The fact remains that as a writer she relies for empowerment on the identification with socially marginal identities. In the previous chapter, we have seen that the link between writing and social shame was central to Stein's grappling with literary self-esteem. Moreover, from the identification with marginal subjects comes *Three Lives*. But in her public self-presentation, at least in the middle part of her career, Stein asserted her authority by mastering a fashionable code.

In the Coburn image I am discussing, the velvet garment visually transcribes the withdrawal to an aesthetic cocoon, comprising her work space, whose allure is enhanced by the exoticism of the garment. The smoothness of velvet visually associates Stein's writing with aestheticism, the senses, and the body. The writer appears to enjoy a refined sensibility for the beautiful as a genderless subject rather than a feminine object. The viewer is invited to imagine her inside her home, in the quiet of her studio surrounded by the paintings she bought. The image produces the impression of a creative autonomy by courting decadence and its appeal. The writer's ease in the sensuous life would seem to be diametrically opposed to social relations, which are elliptically removed from the setting. Yet, the richly textured robe in which the writer makes her appearance and the throne on which she sits are slightly overdetermined. In the staging of Stein's public identity they seem to compensate with an excess of aestheticism for the penury of a 'natural' link to aesthetics. As we have seen the anxiety of such penury was the recurrent motif of *The Making of Americans*.

The robe is an external object that stabilizes first of all Stein's relation to her intellectual origins, facilitating a sense of non-threatened belonging. Secondly, it makes possible a publicly acceptable presentation of her private struggle for writing. But the ultimate significance of this particular garment is in its capacity to translate her private and isolated struggle into an innovative cultural position.

As suggested, the make of her robe imitates a *kosode*. The *kosode* is shaped from a single bolt of silk. It is cut only across its width and even when design elements are applied, they are not interrupted by cutting: 'an open, flat kosode has sleeves and a body that unfold to form a single, continuous canvas. The two overlapping hems on the side of the garment are extensions of this single pictorial frame' (Hayao and Nobuhiko 4). The straight line cutting, which cooperates with the design of the fabric, contrasts with Western curved line cutting with no consideration of the pattern's placement on the garment layout. If the uninterrupted canvas of the *kosode* is well suited to bold decorations and complex designs, Stein's imitation remains a rich monochrome expanse (brown in Picasso's portrait). In her case the velvet canvass has subsumed all designs as if to prepare a new composition.

With its Oriental connotations, Stein's velvet garment attributes aesthetic power to its wearer in a studied way while also keeping her from the abyss of decadence—the worst nightmare of moneyed, middle class women like Julia Dehning. (Historically, the taste for the *kosode* was widely rooted in the daily lives of the moneyed and ruling classes of Japanese society.) It unites the writer's class origins with a literary desire that is naturally coterminous with the sensuous life. In her early writing—*Three Lives, Fernhurst, Q.E.D.*—she had strived to maintain a spontaneous link to the sensuous life and had struggled against her stereotypical appearance as a gentle-eyed Puritan. The velvet garment permits Stein to surpass her self-perception and gives her a new positive public identity, that of the cosmopolitan aesthete, especially between her early years in Europe, 1904-1907, and the time of World War I.

This is not to say that visually she gets rid of references to her American origins. In the Coburn image the pose creates a sophisticated analogy with Whitman's style. At this stage pictures are to Stein what the social body was to her ancestor, the key to sensuous experience and, consequently, to writing. Whitman had invented the sensuality of the social world. In her own way, when in her earlier writing she had grappled with issues of sexuality, national identity, and class, Stein had been singing the body electric. The adoption of the velvet uniform, at the time she increasingly switched to portrait writing, indicates the need for a literary freedom from the past and from available models. David Hersland was a synthesis of her intellectual ancestors—powerful, independent, moody. As I have argued, Stein never fully departs from the fathers. She is interested in borrowing the materials of paternal influence to forge them into her own image.

Accordingly, the strongest link to the symbolic authority of the fathers is in Stein's appetites, which she flaunts, though in a problematic way. Take for example, the rather popular photo of Stein vacationing in Tuscany (Stendhal 40). The writer poses outdoors, cross-legged on a slab of marble. Renate Stendhal's caption to this image in *Gertrude Stein in Words and Pictures: A Photobiography* reads: 'Gertrude Stein bursts out of the corset of convention' (40). She seems to glory in her body. But we should not jump to the conclusion that she unconditionally accepted it. Brenda Wineapple suggests that Stein's physical self-assertion belies her 'travails of being heavy in a world that valued thin' (173). This image is responsible for viewers' association of Stein to Buddha but it may contrast with Stein's self-perception. Wineapple reports that in an unpublished notebook Stein annotated some lines from Chaucer's 'Merciles Beauty' that she intended to use as an epigraph to an early work: 'Since I from love escaped/am so fat/I never think to be in his prison lean' (qtd. in Wineapple 173). With time she came to accept her own fatness and to celebrate food, associating it with security, love, and sexual pleasure (Wineapple 173).

Fat and food, however, stand for other appetites of a social and cultural kind. Wineapple writes: 'Often she liked to assert her middle-class birthright, even though much of her taste, her sexual orientation, and eventually her writing put her beyond the pale of the typical bourgeois and certainly beyond the bourgeoisie of Baltimore' (Wineapple 173). In other words, one of Stein's most powerful appetites was to defy her origins and upbringing. She tried not to fit the stereotype of the all American bourgeois girl. Her life choices, sexuality as well as the writing life, may be seen as spectacular signs of her class defiance. These considerations, of course, are not meant to diminish Stein's literary value. On the contrary, I am arguing that literary value is inextricable from material culture and the writer's historical struggles. It is important to consider the extent to which Stein's writing and her life were shaped by the appetite to exceed her class by doing the unexpected, whether it was having affairs with women, posing as butch, or being seduced by pictures (as opposed to just buying them). These rebellious acts are manifestations of a will to live, to break self-perceptions that haunted her and had the disturbing power to disqualify her for serious creative work. To be in the forefront of culture meant exactly, as Wineapple puts it, to be 'beyond the pale of the typical bourgeois.' Stein used whatever was available to feel in touch with her time, beyond the restrictive decorum of her birth and upbringing. Her identity evolved through a series of cultural possessions that include sexuality and her avant-garde writing. No wonder that her writing questions the boundaries of the natural and the artful, vocation and willful appropriation. For example, if *Four Saints in Three Acts*, as we shall see later on in this study, is one of the most moving portraits of the artist's vocation, *Tender Buttons* marks the triumph of the aesthete. The celebrated sequence is an explosion of colors and objects in a domestic space, the space of Stein's anti-conformist sexual preference. Her sexualized writing is synonymous with avant-garde power (new, upbeat, resistant to interpretation, impregnable to understanding and thematic synthesis, a triumph of personal defiance clad in the appearance of art-for-art's-sake). Appetite refers to a lust for appropriating cultural positions, for living identities that scandalize, but always just enough to keep the writer safe from social misery. The appropriation is empowering because it transforms the writer into a glamorous enigma, producing the image of a woman who 'straddled two worlds': 'exceptional and middle-class; unique but normal; singular but solitary' (Wineapple 173). In Coburn's photo, Stein enjoys the pleasure of contrast: being one thing and doing another. The beholder is encouraged to imagine the disconnection between appearance and act, social status and sexual practice, and to grasp identity as the appropriation of cultural sites for the purposes of cultural transgression. The velvet garment is a veil: it visibly drapes its wearer with the appropriative, assimilative appetite necessary to cultural presence

Even as she was still completing her novel, *The Making of Americans*, portrait writing seemed to suit her newfound literary confidence particularly well. Even in its literary version, the form of the portrait raises questions about the role of patronage in the artist's quest for autonomy and self-esteem. Stein wrote her first portrait, 'Ada,' in 1910, soon after Toklas moved into 27 Rue de Fleurus and took over as homemaker, manager, and typist, becoming Stein's first patron. In the next section I will focus on 'Portrait of Mabel Dodge at Villa Curonia' (1912). I will show that it is highly representative of Stein's transformation from art patron to writer, in the act of negotiating for herself the cultural autonomy staged in Coburn's image.

Dodge, dejection, and the fantasy of commission

Mabel Dodge was an appreciative, enthusiastic reader of Stein. For a short while she competed with Toklas for the position of enabling patron, a position not too different from that of the yes-saying lover in *The Making of Americans*. Moving between Florence, Paris and New York she attended the Stieglitz circle at 291, was familiar with *Camera Work*, a publication that popularised modernism, and was knowledgeable about psychoanalysis. She worked as a journalist and wrote about the unconscious (Everett 19). Like Stein, she was an art collector but openly used art for the purpose of self-fashioning. Her art collecting was in many ways coextensive with interior decoration. In the design of her residence, Villa Curonia, luxury and a homely style mixed to create a refuge she saw as an extension of her identity:

> It must be very spacious, with the nobility and dignity of ample spaces, but it must also have the poetic and tender charms of unexpected corners and adaptations to small, shy moods, twilight moods. It would allow one to be both majestic and careless, spontaneous and picturesque, and yet always framed and supported by a secure and beautiful authenticity of background. (qtd. in Everett 30).

Dodge acquired European art objects that proved functional to interior decoration. Her taste, defined by Carl Van Vechten in his fictional portrait of Dodge in *Peter Whiffle* as 'superlatively excellent' (qtd. in Everett 31), was ruled by a blend of the majestic and the small, of amplitude and shyness. She liked to pose and play with costume. To create a fluid self-image she relied on a pastiche of art and costume. Her capacity to play with art and clothes is a fundamental trait of Dodge's charisma. When she asked the painter Jacques-Emile Blanche to do her portrait she met him in a Claude Poiret gown 'in the Bakst style' and announced: 'This is my present fancy [. . .] You can do other studies of me; I can be a Manet or a Berthe Morisot—anything you like except an American for Mr. Sargent' (qtd. in Everett 108). Art and costume for Dodge become the instruments of cultural mobility. Through them she asserts an 'I can be' across a potentially infinite vista of identities and cultural possibilities. Dodge's pursuit of modernism seems voluble and volatile, the by-product of an appropriative appetite. Stein was drawn to her not only for her instincts for being on the cutting edge, she was also taken with Dodge's theatricality. From the start, Stein trusted Dodge enough to give her the manuscript of *The Making of Americans*, which the author continued to consider her masterpiece throughout her life. The gesture is evidence that the writer saw Dodge in the role of a potential patron, someone who could help connect her with the world of publication. The writer even made explicit requests to her friend for assistance with publication. The first is found in a postcard of a Cézanne landscape dated November 1911: 'My dear Mabel, The long book is finished. I am sending it to America to see what it can do. If you meet any one who wants to publish it let me know' (qtd. in Everett 48).

Dodge met Stein in the spring of 1911, when she accompanied a friend to 27 rue de Fleurus. The writer was at the start of the phase that would culminate in *Tender Buttons*. They immediately recognized each other as first of all 'inspired collectors of creative people' (Everett 1). From the start, Stein invested Dodge with the power to procure her visibility. In her turn, Dodge was happy to play mentor. She accorded generous moral patronage to Stein and acted as an attentive and prodding audience. She writes that she is 'longing to hear some of your new short things so *please* bring some and read them to us' (qtd. in Everett 38; emphasis in original). When Stein does, Dodge responds, singling her friend out as a writer and a woman: '*Why* are there not more real people like you in the world? [. . .] Miss (Constance) Fletcher & I both felt as though we had been drinking champagne all the afternoon' (qtd. in Everett 39; emphasis in original). In short, Dodge became the first individual outside the domestic sphere dominated by Toklas to offer support and to believe in Stein's talent: 'I am longing for your book to get born!' (Everett 39).

Obviously, Stein was flattered and quickly learned to turn to Dodge for protection and reassurance in times of disappointment and frustrated hopes. In March 1912 she writes: 'Your letter was a great comfort to me. I was kind of low in my mind about the publication end and even Wagner's letters were ceasing to be a comfort to me' (qtd. in Everett 51). She discloses her writing projects to Dodge, sure to find sympathy, admiration, and understanding. The correspondence between the two women gives us an hyperactive Stein 'working on four books now' (qtd. in Everett 51), eager to get published and to be recognized. On her part, Dodge promises Stein nothing less than immortality. In September 1912 she prophesies: 'Your writing is destined to *count*' (qtd. in Everett 57; emphasis in original). As she flatters the writer, Dodge does not miss the opportunity to woo her to Villa Curonia for a visit. In the same September 1912 letter, she prods: 'you know you are longing for real sunshine & for Italy & we'd talk & talk! Won't you? I'm all alone till Oct. 1st' (qtd. in Everett 57).

Dodge makes herself available to Stein, reassures her, and establishes an empathy with her through common favorites: real sunshine, Italy, the Renaissance, all topped with conversation in an ideal Southern European setting to cure the writer's professional loneliness. She lets her friend know: 'how immediately you are read you affect people' (qtd. in Everett 58). That same month, Stein visits Dodge and on that occasion repays her for her sympathy with an artistic homage. In true Renaissance style, as the grateful artist would to her generous patron, Stein gives Dodge a portrait—'Portrait of Mabel Dodge at the Villa Curonia.' In fact, the portrait hinges on the two women's overt or implicit acting out of the fantasy of Renaissance patronage, appropriating the intersection of art and seduction surrounding portraiture. As Patricia Simons writes, during the Renaissance 'networks of patronage and friendship provided the mechanisms whereby privileges were obtained, reciprocal obligations cemented, political and economic interests advanced, and bonds of intimacy formed. Modes of address, however conventional, applied affective terms of love and bondage' (42). Moreover, the portrait was associated with seduction as the artist would compete for visibility through the seductiveness of his model (Simons 44). Stein plays with both these elements of Renaissance portraiture. The patron is held simultaneously at a distance and close, as a dear friend. The model is celebrated for her desirable wealthy life style and the quality hospitality she can offer: 'there is pleasing classing clothing' (PMD 528). Such life style is different from that of the struggling artist, but it promises a new kind of 'breathing' (PMD 527). In fact, the portrait consistently alternates between the sense of an unsuccessful compromise, suggested by sentences like 'Bargaining is something and there is not that success' (527), 'This is not collaborating' (528), 'Not to be wrapped and forget the undertaking' (528), and a welcome sense of relief, a 'delight' or lack of 'pressure' (528) mainly due to material comfort. Its signs: warm blankets, a velvet spread, dresses, a 'bigger' house. 'This is comfortable' (529), Stein writes.

Dodge is celebrated as a patron who can victoriously compete with others for the ease she procures the struggling artist. Stein arrives at Villa Curonia with low self-esteem related to her experiments with a composition without a message—'There can be no message where the print is pasted and this does not mean that there is that esteem' (PMD 528). But during the visit, to the credit of her hostess, she gets rid of the shame that accompanies writing: 'There is not the shame' (PMD 529). For this reason Dodge is cast in the role of patron and benefactor whom Stein attempts to pay back with the portrait. While this does not answer an explicit commission—'there is that which is not that charging what is a regular way of paying' (PMD 267)—it is hoped that it will please the patron. That the portrait is not a 'regular' homage to the patron can be seen in the blurring of lines between model and artist: Stein is present as much as Dodge and her home. It is difficult to tell them apart, to discern who is being represented, who is speaking about whom. But it is possible to follow a clear succession of moods possibly associated with the writer's determination in her art.

The portrait's sunny opening, 'The days are wonderful and the nights are wonderful and the life is pleasant' (527), soon wanes in a brooding mood. Broken utterances, 'The intention is what' (527), are joined to conceptual distortions, 'if application has that accident' (527), which sound like the murmured monologue of a writer applying herself without the benefit of a reader: 'They did not darken. That was not an adulteration' (PMD 265). Who is they? What is that? Why cannot one know? Is this writing an avant-garde moment or is it a document of dejection? The destruction of confidence in the writer transfers to the reader, who must pick clues here and there and struggle with fragments without a message to glean meaning from the paste job of the print. Just as Stein needs the merciful judgment of her patron, so the reader can glean meaning if he/she identifies with the supportive patron and addressee of the portrait.

There is no doubt that material comfort takes the lead in the portrait. Even more central, however, is Stein's play with its double meaning as external material ease and internal peace and entitlement: 'So much breathing' (527), 'that much beginning' (527). Such creative vitality makes Dodge the forerunner of dynamic sitters like Orta, the dancer and prototype for the writer (Bridgman 96), and above all, Picasso, privileged model of unsuppressed creativity.

Painting, in the guise of memories of pictures seen and loved, makes its way subtly in this portrait. The swing of moods of discouragement and elation is interrupted by a still life with bottle and potato. The bottle meets the viewer almost in a state of nakedness: it 'has all the time to stand open' (528). Stein is evoking the surprise of the new art of Cézanne and Van Gogh, who could starkly foreground the philosophical importance of humble and neglected daily objects. These artists used color to bring objects back to a life of their own as things, not necessarily subordinated to a human subject who appropriates them. In Stein's fragment, color alters the shape and utilitarian function the viewer associates with a bottle and thus exalts the independent existence of the thing: 'A bottle that has all the time to stand open is not so clearly shown when there is green color there' (PMD 528). But the use of color is not the only way in which art changed the way people saw things in the modernist era: 'This is not the only way to change it' (PMD 528). Modern art changed the way Stein and her contemporaries looked at the world also by appealing to balance and a sense of measure. The presence of scenes of penury and objects from lives ruled by labor were meant to soften the race for cultural transformation, harnessing it to the search for a new balance and sense of measure: 'A little raw potato and then all that softer does happen to show that there has been enough. It changes the expression' (528). In Stein's representative still life, which she uses to meditate on the direction of her own writing, the explosion of color combines with the penury of the shriveled raw potato. The latter may be read as a reference to Van Gogh's potato eaters and to Millet, who influenced Van Gogh and whose scenes of labor had made a deep impression on Stein in her youth. But here the writer is contemplating the still life for purely aesthetic purposes. Because her writing is akin to modern painting's recreation of vision, she rehearses the essential principles of modern art, which she knows so well, to regain trust in herself and a sense of direction. Stein joins the still life. She objectifies herself to convey a renewed allegiance to the modern composition: 'This which has been feeling is what has the appetite and the patience and the time to stay' (266).

The location helps significantly to steady the writer's sense of purpose and affiliation to a larger artistic community: 'Nobody is alone' (528). The solitary effort to assert her affiliation combines felicitously with Dodge's 'predilection' (529) to usher in a state of bliss due to the promise of a new textuality: 'An open object is establishing the loss that there was when the vase was not inside the place. It was not wandering' (529). The term 'wandering' is a reference to *Three Lives* and David Hersland. The decision seems to be made that the open object (text?), formerly missed, now replace writing. The time of the year and the villa are celebrated to suggest the new freedom of a writing steeped in the local reality at hand. At the same time, locutions like 'gnarled division (528),'forgotten swelling' (528), or 'whiter division' (528) allude to doubts that are difficult to eradicate, all the more so perhaps because of the ideal location and hostess.

In the portrait of Mabel Dodge material comfort brings confusion. Despite the sunny location and the writer's newfound sense of purpose, the overall mood is gloomy. Writing is akin to a silent, suppressed language. For this reason the portrait is significant. It ultimately features an artist struggling with demons that her model, a woman of the same nationality, of similar social standing and cultural ambitions, can understand well. Her visit at the Villa Curonia becomes Stein's occasion to meditate on her own love of material comfort and on her oscillation between that and literary achievement. Stein is worried about the originality and value of her writing. Although she had committed herself to being a full time writer, she was primarily known as a facilitator of new burgeoning talent, an art collector rather than a talent in her own right. She had been asserting the originality of her writing starting with what was at hand—pictures. But this had been risky in terms of self-confidence. As a collector, Stein felt that her claim to aesthetic innovation would remain dependent on her capacity to accrue pretty things. Even masterpieces, after all, become ornamental objects when hung on house walls. Just as in the early writing she had tried to break away from her self-perception as a sensuous woman with a Puritan face, now she struggles to break away from her self-perception as the bourgeois collector who suspects she will remain an outsider in relation to real art.

In light of these fears, the choice of the portrait's model is crucial. Dodge is chosen because she might understand Stein's dilemma. This is why the portrait blurs model and artist and paradoxically pays homage to the benefactor with the author's dejection. On the occasion of her visit, Stein compares her achievements unfavorably to those of her friend, a social peer whom she trusts, and experiences division: 'the division is the explicit visit' (PMD 530). In fact, Dodge is what Stein might have been had she not seriously undertaken writing. Stein is not immune to the lure of comfort and things, and vicariously enjoys through Dodge the joys of the collector's life. But she has chosen to be a writer, with the ambition, sacrifice, and haunting sense failure that such life implies. In the portrait of her hostess she can recognize her own attachment to material ease and possessions. Initially, she attempts to make the most of such awareness but the effort is negated by the bullying, angry quality of some of her musings.

Dodge's reception of the portrait was enthusiastic. She promoted it and published it in a private edition. It seems that she was going to support it regardless of how she was portrayed. Clearly, the portrait was a pretext to make explicit a private understanding between the two women of their respective fantasy roles as patron and artist. Others found the piece impenetrable but, needless to say, the model recognized herself in it because she knew she was being addressed as a patron. Dodge recognized the identification of artist and model in the portrait, which bespeaks Stein's professional vulnerability at the time, and acted like a faithful patron, hijacking criticism toward herself: 'I consider the "Portrait" to be a masterpiece of success from my (& your) point of view *as* a portrait of *me as* I am to others!' [. . .] What they see in it is what, I consider, they see in me' (qtd. in Everett 75; emphasis in original). She found the portrait, like herself, 'middleclass, confused, & rather sound' (qtd. in Everett 76). That was how Stein felt about herself at Villa Curonia and it made her dejected.

Real sunshine, Italy and the Renaissance

Villa Curonia housed a diverse array of signs of social status and cultural appetite: there were golden mirrors, gold cupboards, blue damask and golden red damask on walls, wooden figures including a Buddha, a collection of ivory skulls, shelves piled with silk, chiffon veils, lace hats, a wardrobe of brocaded coats and velvet outfits that included Renaissance costumes, the latest books by Henry James. Medieval atmospheres coexisted with French eighteenth-century style, while in the decorative patterns Persian colors mixed with Raphael-like grotesques.[5] Dodge's taste was inseparable from a process of self-transformation, the principal aim of which was to lose national origins. Her home was the summa of an art that kindled Stein's fire: the art of breaking away from imprisoning self-images dictated by natality and physical appearance. During her visit, Stein could see that luxury, the Renaissance, artsy bric-à-brac, decadence and kitsch all had their role in the transformation of this villa in sunny Italy into a sanctuary for the owner's insuppressible desire for self-invention.

As suggested, Dodge's pursuit of beauty was inseparable from her passion for home decorating. She shares this view with Stein's character Julia Dehning, the thriving middle class daughter of *The Making of Americans*. Although Stein did not subordinate beauty to ornament, she nevertheless recognized in Dodge's taste a part of herself. Stein and Toklas were proud of their own Paris home. In a study of 27 Rue de Fleurus, Sara Blair has shown that Stein's writing was connected with bourgeois homemaking. Such a connection was not unusual to make for even the most avant-garde publications like *Broom*, where Stein published some of her pieces. An advertisement for the 1922 Arts and Decoration Practical Home Study Course in Interior Decoration shows an affinity with Stein and Toklas's homemaking, as it has immortalized by a famous Man Ray photo of the couple. Looking at the Man Ray photo and the advertisement side by side, Blair notices that both images 'align Yankee ingenuity,' culture, earned 'know-how,' and a modernist language of color and design' (427). Without denying the cultural distance of the two life-worlds, Blair concludes that they are united by the same ideal of 'a good life comprised of good things, chosen from an aestheticized realm of consumer fantasy and desire' (427).

From this point of view, Stein's famed obscurity might be grasped as the encounter of high and low, avant-garde and consumerism. In *Tender Buttons*, her cubist writing is propelled by the objects in the home. Art makes for a beautiful home as well as for a creative deconstruction in print that eludes the middle class of *The Making of Americans*. Blair has shown that *Broom*'s reaction against 'stultifying conventions' actually implies a bourgeois community of reception (429). Similarly, bourgeois domesticity remains the main site of Stein's attack on tradition.

Art objects had helped Stein become a modernist, but as she closely studied her model at Villa Curonia, she became aware of the flipside of that bargain. Dodge shared with Stein a love of art, but the former's appetite resulted in the void typically left by the spoils of fulfilled appropriation. Even after she realized her dreams of object ownership, as in the example of her bedroom, Dodge knew that she could not enjoy it: 'I can never, never tarry here in lazy contemplation [. . .] I fancied myself hours on end in that room, alone, at rest. Free to sink into it and gather up the life of it. But never' (qtd. in Everett 33). Thus, the references to 'interval' and 'resting' in Stein's portrait might equally apply to model and artist, alluding to their similar personality. For Dodge, objects, even when they multiplied materially, had a capacity for becoming mere figments of the imagination. Like meaning, authentic art can only be glimpsed fleetingly among the pile of material signs. A refined collector like Dodge is prone to the same malaise of the common woman who can afford only low quality goods—very likely never a work of art—and after her purchase falls prey to dejection at having spent her hard won money on inferior bric-à-brac. Moods, it would seen, unite people across classes. For both Dodge and the common woman, the material object first desired, then possessed, produces a feeling of scarcity, of missed accord, a persistent blurring of dream and reality.

Villa Curonia is the shrine of a dream Dodge shared with Stein: the dream of a more sensuous life incarnated by sunshine, Italy, and the Renaissance. Dodge designed her house after a hybrid model of majesty and carelessness 'always framed and supported by a secure and beautiful authenticity of background' (qtd. in Everett 30). The side effect of the dream was that everything and everyone became an object. People too become part of the décor: ornamental objects especially in amorous jealousy. Dodge speaks of Toklas as 'a silent, picturesque object in the background' (qtd. in Everett 36). During her visit Stein must have observed that Dodge's search for authenticity was incurable, that at each turn, it could not but result in a sense of withered artificiality. She was attracted to Dodge's pursuit of a master position that could no longer be enjoyed. She was probably fascinated by a woman trapped in an unfulfilled fantasy of plenitude. But she also knew that, despite their common cultural origins, what distinguished her from her restless friend in what was to become a life-long modernist appropriation of interesting people and interesting cultures, was, after all, writing.

Technologies of the self

We have seen that Stein and Mabel Dodge bonded around common interests, especially Italy and the Renaissance. These encouraged the fantasy of patronage from which the portrait of Mabel Dodge issues. We have seen how, following on the example of her patron, Stein could envision a felicitous marriage of art and comfort, which relieved her of her artistic insecurities, even if only for the brief span of time that the composition of the portrait lasted. In this final section we will see that the erotic undercurrent between the two women during the writer's sojourn at the Villa contributed to Stein's sense of release from dejection.

Before the visit, Dodge hinted at the possibility of an erotic connection between the two, presenting it as something her husband took for granted: 'E. [Edwin] goes from one misunderstanding to another—out of it all he evolves a theory that I—infatuated by *you*—because I have succeeded in getting your attention wish to remain in Paris on account of you—that my letter to him about Paul was *written* on account of *this* rather than on account of him or Paul' (qtd. in Everett 72; emphasis in original). At the time Dodge was the emotional center of her husband's life and was also having an affair with Paul, an undergraduate at Columbia University and tutor of her son. Courted and wanted by two men, she basked in the attention: 'I am in a confused state of delight & despair &don't know what to make of myself of things or what I want' (qtd. in Everett 68). When Stein saw her at the Villa, Dodge appeared as an incarnation of desire; she was an earthy affirmative presence, attracting the double 'Yes' of two different men.[6] As she executed the portrait, the artist openly flirted with her model under the eyes of Toklas. Dodge committed to paper the look that Stein sent her one day at lunch as the writer, and this is an important detail, sat opposite her in her husband's chair: it was 'such a strong look [ ] that it seemed to cut across the air to me in a band of electrified steel' (qtd. in Everett 63-4). Though, as she admits, she did not feel anything for Stein, Dodge enters the patron-artist fantasy, in which eros presides over art production. Mutual flirtation more strikingly casts the patron in the role of the one who gives the writer what Dodge termed 'unconscious thoughts' (qtd. in Everett 63).

Dodge herself was not completely indifferent to the artist's charms. She romanticized Stein's body: 'Gertrude Stein was prodigious. Pounds and pounds and pounds piled up on her skeleton—not the billowing kind, but massive, heavy fat' (Dodge qtd. in Stendhal 62). She found this 'grand ampleur' attractive (qtd. in Everett 36). Stein's affirmative attitude toward the body must have meant a respite for Dodge, equal in importance to the rest that she offered Stein at the Villa Curonia. As we have seen in the previous section, Dodge's artsy dreams, once realized, threw her into a state of ennui and melancholia. By contrast, under 'some covering of corduroy or velvet' (Dodge qtd. in Stendhal 62) Stein and her fat advanced like a vision of mild exoticism appropriately mixed to monastic severity, as suggested by the corduroy fabric. She had attained a studied indifference for the master position which Dodge, with her penchant for the queenly, eagerly strove for. In Dodge's eyes, Stein could afford *sprezzatura* because of Toklas, whom she saw as the writer's 'courtesan' (qtd. in Stendhal 63). Stein's public acceptance of her fat represented a piece of the authenticity that escaped Mabel Dodge. It stopped art from inducing the infinite vertigo of objects. Stein's writing buttressed Dodge's impression: it could not be recycled as an ornamental object, it required that its meaning be completed by the reader with some labor; furthermore, one had to be careful that such labor did not turn into bondage. The capacity of Stein's writing to raise issues of independence and subjection also attracted Dodge, who felt like a prisoner of her own taste for self-invention.

Fig. 3.2   Gertrude Stein (1913), by Alvin Langdon Coburn. Courtesy of Yale
            Collection of American Literature, Beinecke Rare Book and
            Manuscript Library.

It should be noted that even Dodge has some difficulty when describing Stein's trademark garment. She calls it 'some covering of corduroy or velvet' (qtd. in Stendhal 62). The cover, for Dodge, is what it appears to be in Stein's photo and undoubtedly what Stein intended it to be, a veil for the mind—to make the presence of the mind felt even more powerfully. Dodge's gaze at Stein and her flirtatious play confirm that she assimilates the writer's mind to the phallic imagination. From Dodge's perspective, Stein's mind is the phallus. Her cover veils an alluring mind that presents itself to the imagination as the ultimate link to authenticity (just as the Phallus in Lacan's system is the ultimate signifier), a direct connection to art and beauty without the mediation of signifying objects, the potentially infinite (and smothering) chain of secondary links. In Dodge's eyes, fat promises an ascetic vicinity to the real thing or fount of art. But the velvet garment is also a sacrificial coverage. It is the sign of an individual who has embraced wider motives linked to the public sphere. In the course of time Stein enhanced her sacrificial presence, affecting peasant and monk looks. In her unfulfilled quest for art, Dodge found desirable the sacrificial element in Stein's presence, just as Stein found desirable Dodge's femininity.

I have tried to show that the connection between the two women and a reading of the portrait of Mable Dodge further illuminate the dilemma at the heart of Stein's work: the strange juxtaposition in her image and in her writing of cultural muse and middle class daughter. Her use of the velvet garment associates her with the cultural syncretism of the modern mind (Fig. 3.2), but this image starkly contrasts with that of the traditional plump middle class daughter. In her study of clothes and identity, Joanne Entwistle establishes that the tension between artifice and authenticity, between the self as styled and the self as natural, is a decisive element in twentieth-century literature and represents 'the contradictory nature of modernity' (126). Stein's career is driven by such tension, and 'Portrait of Mabel Dodge at the Villa Curonia'—both the final text and the material conditions leading up to it—may be read as an illustration of its shaping power in literature. Dodge's attraction to Stein's fat is a sign that she saw the dialectic of artifice and authenticity at work in the writer's style of self-presentation. This, in turn, confirms that Stein was thoroughly modern in her awareness of technologies of the self. The eroticism that she provoked in a supportive stranger, under her own lover's eyes, and which Dodge might have returned, was a great form of attestation of the writer's conscious work on her public self.

Chapter 4

The Looks of Modern Culture

Looking at Adrienne Monnier

On the 'Finding AIDS and Inventories for Manuscripts' shelf of the Rare Books and Manuscripts Division of the Princeton University Library there is a portfolio of the most requested Sylvia Beach photos. One of them depicts Francis Scott Fitzgerald and Adrienne Monnier. The caption, however, says 'F. S. Fitzgerald' in print, followed by '+Gertrude Stein' in handwriting. In Box 277, Folder 23, of the Sylvia Beach Papers the original photograph is catalogued correctly: 'F. Scott Fitzgerald and Adrienne Monnier.'[1] This case of mistaken identity by the archivist is instructive. In her seated position, wrapped in her trademark cape, with her cropped hair and clean face, Adrienne Monnier is likely to recall, especially to the eyes of many contemporary viewers, the modernist look popularised by Stein. The anonymous viewer whose hand penned in '+ Gertrude Stein' under the photo of Monnier and Fitzgerald is right: among all other prominent modernist women, it is to Monnier that Stein is visually closest. 'Visually closest' here does not mean large, robed or caped, and with cropped hair. Visuality is more than looks. Adapting an expression used by Rosalind Krauss to describe surrealist aesthetics, one might say that visuality is 'a kind of writing' (qtd. in Foster 221). It involves a rhetorical labor on physicality. In this chapter I will compare Monnier's and Stein's visual identities. Because I concentrate on only a few images, I would like my remarks to have the status of notes taken after my visit to the Sylvia Beach archives; they have no ambition to say anything new in the field of Monnier studies.[2] By comparing these two modernist icons, my aim is to extend the discussion, already initiated in the previous chapters, of Stein's awareness of the labor of cultural access.

Women like Stein and Monnier were aware that, in order to accede to culture, they had to transform themselves into signs. Their visual identities, in the case of Stein more so than in the instance of Monnier, show that their appearance and their sexuality were not private but historical, complicit with the then available media. Both used clothes to establish a positive, legitimate connection with cultural modernism. When Stein wrote that she had always been 'tormented by the problem of the external and the internal' (*AABT* 112), she was alluding to the central concern of twenty-century culture with polarities and their crossing. As it is clear in the work of Paul de Man, contemporary thought has recognized and extended the chiasmic vocation of modernism to reverse inside and outside, figure and grammar, rhetoric and substance.[3] The generic restlessness with polarities, which in the following remarks I summarily refer to as chiasmus, using the rhetorical term to encapsulate a cultural climate, is shared by Stein and Monnier and affected their visual identities. My comparison will show that the rhetorical inversion of the inside and the outside, of the figural and the historical-material levels, is not always successful. This incomplete reversal of the seduction of rhetoric and the obstinacy of history confirms the difficulty of the requirements for acceding culture. Clothes celebrate the possibilities of surface but do not conceal the labor of self-transformation—that struggle with time, place, and destiny, through which cultural affirmation must pass.

Monnier and Stein lived in the same city and, in their own separate circles, they were prominent personalities. Writers like H.D., Bryher and Janet Flanner moved in both circles. Monnier's partner, the American bookseller Sylvia Beach, did not particularly like Stein.[4] Toklas, however, liked Beach's friend. Writing to Sylvia Beach in 1962 from 5 rue Christine VI to thank her for the gift of the French edition of *Shakespeare and Company*, Toklas informs her that she would send the copy to the Yale University collection to join the English edition. Toklas also acknowledges her fondness for common friends and for Adrienne: 'The photograph of Adrienne Monier (sic) before the Shakespeare window and the early Bryher photographed by Man Ray touched me deeply' (Beach Papers, Box 228, Folder 2.VI). The photo in question is a popular image by Gisèle Freund. It shows Monnier in her trademark cape, slightly bent over the book box outside Shakespeare and Company (Fig. 4.1). She is unrecognizable except to friends and close associates at this time of her life, an audience of feminist devotees in the 1970s and 1980s (a time when photos of Monnier and Stein were likely to be found on the postcard rack in women's or alternative bookstores around the world), and, of course, modernist scholars today, all of whom were and are familiar with her vestimentary code. Her standard uniform consisted of an ample cape, a garment that seemingly covers her in gender and social anonymity. In some pictures in the Sylvia Beach Papers Monnier is captured standing outside Shakespeare and Company with other women clothed according to the fashion of the time. In one she is with Hemingway's sister-in-law, who wears a suit and a cone-shaped hat, an outfit which provides a striking contrast with the appearance of the woman next to her, at once anonymous and highly individualized, universal and concrete. Toklas's fondness for Monnier is not unrelated to an appreciation for the woman's conscious mastery of her public image and her subordination of appearance to the achievement of meaningful intellectual presence.

As she looks at the now famous picture of Monnier outside Shakespeare and Company, Toklas contemplates precisely that effort but as if it were a thing of the past, a moving sort of labor now consigned to the archives and historical memory. 'Deeply touched' informs us that Toklas has touched on a cultural moment that she wishes preserved. She encounters it in the pages of Beach's book, and in Monnier's photo. She sends the copy to Stein's archives at Yale. From the distance

Fig. 4.1 Adrienne Monnier outside Shakespeare and Company. Courtesy of Princeton University Library.

of time, this cultural moment, so vivid to Toklas, will undoubtedly become a hieroglyph, an object without a context, left in the hands of willing readers to decipher. Yet, Toklas can be touched deeply upon looking at Monnier because of her knowledge of Stein's belonging to that cultural moment when a large community of women used their public appearance to assert their intellectual significance. This community included in addition to Bryher, H.D., Janet Flanner, Sylvia Beach and Adrienne Monnier, Mina Loy and Djuna Barnes, as well as their photographers Berenice Abbot and Gisèle Freund, to mention only a few. Among the media they used to achieve a sense of full cultural belonging, clothes and photography were decisive, even to the point where their writing cannot be fully appreciated without due consideration of the figurative structure of their public identity. Given her life spent side by side with a woman who struggled for public presence, Toklas's affection for the image of Monnier suggests that writing cannot be separated from the material process that transformed fairly common women like Monnier, Beach, and the others into influential minds. Indirectly, in her brief but important missive, Toklas is saying that for women like Monnier and Stein, their intellectual significance is bound up with their visual rhetoric. To a certain extent, for modernist women to write is to become an image.

Adrienne Monnier's bookstore, La Maison des Amis des Livres, was located in 7, rue de l'Odéon. In the middle of the war, in 1915, the bookstore was a place not striking in any way, started by a common woman. It was made possible by the indemnity money Monnier's father got from a train accident. At first it served also as a lending library. It specialized in modern authors, with a section on the 'entire world,' including Stein's work, and a section on Tibet and Tibetan yoga. Monnier worked as director and secretary. Membership was granted on a yearly basis. Every member obtained a Carte de Societaire, at times blue, at times beige. Sylvia Beach's, for example, was blue, n. 18, and ran from 15 March 1918 to 15 March 15 1919.

Monnier's love of books and their authors turned the place from an anonymous bookstore to, as *France-Soir* put it in 1953, 'une espáce de célébrité' (Beach Papers, Box 52, Folder 3). The transformation applied to the owner, too. She went from being a woman with a business to the favored friend of young and thriving genius. Writers discovered the bookstore (much as they discovered Stein's salon) and it soon became a meeting place. Monnier held Wednesday gatherings devoted to lectures and presentations (Fig. 4.2). In her bookstore Larbaud lectured on Joyce for the first time on 7 December 1921. In the typescript of Sylvia Beach's working notes, 'Adrienne Monnier and Her Bookstore, La Maison des Amis des Livres,' a profile written for the Benjamin Franklin Library, Monnier features as a cultural mover (Beach Papers, Box 51, Folder 1). She organized readings called 'Les Séances des Amis des Livres' at which the members of the library crowded into the bookshop and heard authors read their manuscripts before publication, or recite poetry of their own or of others. Monnier was an untiring cultural entrepreneur. She also edited and published her own review, *Le Navire d'Argent*.

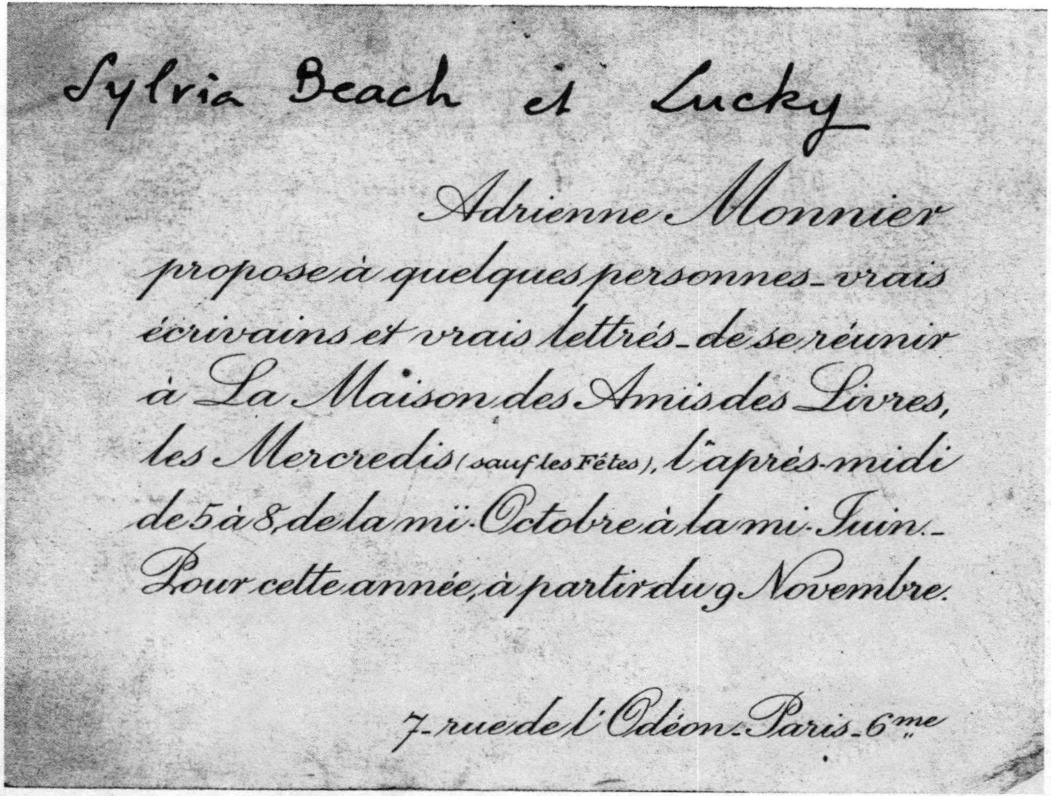

Sylvia Beach et Lucky

Adrienne Monnier
propose à quelques personnes - vrais
écrivains et vrais lettrés - de se réunir
à La Maison des Amis des Livres,
les Mercredis (sauf les Fêtes), l'après-midi
de 5 à 8, de la mi-Octobre à la mi-Juin. -
Pour cette année, à partir du 9 Novembre.

7 - rue de l'Odéon - Paris - 6me

Fig. 4.2 Sylvia Beach's invitation to Adrienne Monnier's Wednesday literary salon. Courtesy of Princeton University Library.

Fig. 4.3   **Adrienne Monnier reading. Courtesy of Princeton University
Library.**

In the same profile Beach refers to her as a 'gifted writer.'

That is, she had an internal and external relation to words and books, being at once a practicing writer and a patron of writers. Thus Monnier balanced in herself two traits: she was an aspiring creator and a woman who promoted others, a conjoining fostered by Beach who, in her typescript, emphasizes her friend's cultural standing and her patronage. She writes that Monnier was 'a personality in the French literary world' who, besides encouraging modern writers, 'was particularly active in the service of American letters' (Beach Papers, Box 51, Folder 1). Book seller, writer, animator, literary patron, publisher, editor and part time 'salon keeper' in the post-war sense. As the center of an international intellectual network, a sought-after hostess who welcomed many of Beach's American friends to her home and table, Monnier was an ordinary woman who had made herself into an extraordinary magnet. As a 'gifted writer,' she had taken her special connection with words into the public arena, where it had been exchanged for the capacity to foster modern talent.

There is a striking image of Monnier in which she is absorbed in reading, oblivious to the viewer (Fig. 4.3). The image shows that her beauty depended less on the assertion of an autonomous creativity and more on the balance of an individual literary desire and a care for writing in general, here symbolized by the act of reading. The possibility of the crossing of these two levels, autonomous creativity and literary patronage, gave her a natural title to modern culture (writers flocked to her bookstore), while lessening the visual intensity of her individual link to writing. In this image Monnier exchanges the libido of writing for the Apollonian pleasure of the literature of others. For this she was not only sought out by the writers but also became attractive to the press. Despite her cosmopolitan butch looks, Monnier charmed the public because of the provincial daughter in her. An article in *France-Soir* for Friday, 4 December 1953 remembered her as a friend of writers and as 'une des femmes les plus intelligentes et le plus sensibles de la literature' (Beach Papers, Box 51, Folder 1). In an article by Anne Manson in *Journal Bref*, Monnier is simultaneously a notable cultural presence and a common woman among many, with her 'yeux bleus de petite fille' and 'a jupe paysanne à fronces jusqu'aux pieds' (Beach Papers, Box 52, Folder 4). She is perceived as powerful yet subservient, provincial yet glamorous. In the same article she is defined as the center of a creative elite 'la plus avancée, la plus active' of French and foreign literature, yet she makes for a caring and reassuring presence.

Monnier bears a certain iconic relation to the modern mind, based on the reconciliation of polarities often through their reversal: subject and object, nature and artifice. In another photo by Gisèle Freund, she poses in her bookstore, whose walls are lined with low shelves and covered with portraits of writers. She leans against a corner shelf in a Tyrolian costume with a wide skirt, a vest, a brooch at her collar (*Shakespeare and Company* ill. 11). The official photo confirms that her public identity is characterized by the visual crossing of country and city, high-powered intellect and simplicity, urban subjectivity and provincial marginality.

Pictures in the photo-album in the Sylvia Beach Papers at Princeton University reveal a certain continuity between the clothes she favored in the city and the simple, loose peasant-like dresses the wore in the country. Her claim to a native bond to culture manifests itself in her choice of particularly ample garments. As we have seen, the most iconic photo shows that she favored a cape, a form of coverage that closely recalls Stein's velvet garment. Under the cape she wore homely combinations of ample dresses with vests in peasant style. Whether plain like the ones she wore in the bookstore or checked like those she wore at Beach's chalet in the south of France, her country clothes reinforced her image as a vestal of the avant-garde. Significantly, the aura is quite lost when Monnier is seen in ordinary clothes, like a sweater and a skirt.[5] In one photo she stands on the threshold of Beach's chalet in a checked peasant dress complete with an apron (Beach Papers, Box 247), arms folded on her womb. She embodies an earthy femininity, aloof and complete in her own plenitude, an object of the imagination linking *Ulysses'* Penelope to post-structuralist presymbolic negativity.

It is interesting to notice the similarity between this snapshot with the carefully studied portrait of Monnier by Berenice Abbot. In Abbot's image Monnier's mouth is touched up with dark lipstick; she wears pearls, a cape and the ample dress, but her hands are folded as in the country picture. Here she returns the viewer's gaze, while in the country snapshot she had stared into the distance, her impenetrable gaze reversing her vestment's allusion to rustic domesticity. Despite their differences, both images seem to 'argue' for Monnier's iconic approximation to an intellectual object whose seduction depends on its ambiguous attitude toward modernity. She embodies an ideal of pure creativity sheltered from the debasement of dreary labor, doubt, meaninglessness. Above all she is protected by that force of chiasmic inversion typical of modernity, a time when distance and nearness become relative, when class and social barriers, formerly intrinsic to the human psyche, clearly appear as the by-products of history, when humanity changes shape, imposing itself to the imagination as a community of members equally claiming an inalienable right to expression, regardless of the forms that expression might take.

As we have seen, Cézanne had associated the rise of the modern artist with the garb of the laborer. But Monnier's visual identity, though it taps the signifiers of labor, denies a complete transition from artist to laborer. She is the vestal of intellectual transcendence in a world where art is made by the hand. Her clothes become the aesthetic evidence of her daily proximity to the modern genius. Their homeliness, denoting domesticity, rustic simplicity, labor, the realm of matter—all traditionally perceived as an unscalable wall in relation to the beauty of forms—actually relieves the artist from the complications of toil, slow craftsmanship, or self-doubt. These are all fundamental aspects of writing but must be hidden as if its credibility could be lessened by their explicit admission. With its metaphorization of the realm of matter, Monnier's uniform generously deflects attention to the strong identification of others with the realm of culture, an identification that the modern genius needs to affirm itself.

She takes upon herself the other side of the eccentricities of genius—sacrifice and toil. In this sense her clothes cover more than her body. Especially her ample cape—seemingly genderless, classless, timeless, supranational—covers the waning of difference between private and public, hard work and self-image, solitary labor and public glamor, that is endemic to modern creativity. It preserves the difference in the fetishized sphere of individual genius. Her homeliness protects the genius of others, and she is rewarded for her sacrifice with the entrepreneurial power she has over them. Her characteristic cape is the visual embodiment of Monnier's balancing work of reparation to keep modernity on the side of a timeless culture without letting it fall into history. Her cloak or mantle, which in Latin means veil (*mantum*), covers tattered cultural units. As veil, it leaves the breakages in full view. Her garment is the figure of a modernism that wishes to impose the velocity of forms on the slowness of society, but is at the same time timorous and worried that art will die if it dirties its hands and re-envisions the fundamental social rules. The mantle-veil covers and reveals. As Manuela Fraire observes, in its function as accessory, the cloak, robe or mantle, can, by contrast, suggest the idea of dismantling, and thus the idea of a loss of old, obsolete, crumbling structures (15-6). Hence the vulnerability that endeared Monnier to the public. Her earnest face speaks of a classic transcendence of brute power. Her deep blue eyes of *petite fille* suggest innocence, drive, intuition for real genius, but also a leaning toward substance and a vigilance against the ethereal seduction of artificial forms. She dictated taste. The image of Monnier in her bookstore featured on a carte postale.

Nevertheless, Monnier knew how to play with forms. She went through transformations. In her early Paris years she could be seen in masculine drag. An image shows young Adrienne at her home, at 18 rue de l'Odéon (Fig. 4.4). She poses in shirt, vest, and bow tie, holding a cigarette. She impersonates the new woman open to gender ambiguity and sexual transgression. Over the years she became the caped muse of modernist aesthetics. In the last phase, after 36 years of activity, in a photo by Gisèle Freund she appears tiny, with wavy gray hair and glasses, the aged mother of modern writers both French and foreign.[6] Looking at Monnier's photos in the Beach Papers, one realizes that, in light of her transformations, the Spartan simplicity that emanates from her was a self-conscious exercise in style, which she let the best photographers capture. From ordinary woman she became an extraordinary personality. In her, a dream of social mobility materializes as a woman's 'natural' entitlement to culture. Adrienne's cloak is a veil spread over some of modernity's crucial anxieties: the right to cultural entitlement, the uncertain, tame relation of women to intellect, the city as a place of opportunity versus the threat represented by the country and the provinces to creative and avant-garde desire. In typical chiasmic fashion, the threat was reversed into a taste for country houses and country summering.[7] A photo of Sylvia Beach illustrates the reversal (Fig. 4.5). It shows her at ease among country people, as if her androgynous looks and brooding expression, signs of high culture, were

Fig. 4.4   Adrienne Monnier in a bow tie at 18, rue de l'Odeon. Courtesy of Princeton University Library.

Fig. 4.5   Sylvia Beach in Savoy. Courtesy of Princeton University Library.

the natural next of kin of the rough hewn faces of Savoy farmers. The photo reveals the other side of modernist deconstructive aesthetics. If Beach's androgynous presence is the cultural accessory of modernism, the visual knot of incongruent differences (masculine/feminine, subject/object, center/periphery, etc.),speaks of a nostalgic attachment to the land, to an agrarian spirit imaginatively associated with a pre-cultural infantile folk dimension. Notice how men and women are made iconographically similar by the hardships of labor, their gender distinction left to the imagination rather than worn on their faces. The striking visual association of James Joyce's patron and the rough hewn faces of the farmers comments on the superficial quality of the modernist exchange of polarities. This exchange is photographically translated here as a cultural gap between different classes of social subjects. Aesthetically, the gap remains perilously alluring, as if it were the echo of a suprahistorical subjection.

Monnier's simplicity is achieved by a theatrical use of clothes. The picture in masculine drag can be found among a group of photos taken by Sylvia Beach where Adrienne is either reading or writing.[8] Beach's gaze at Monnier is emblematic of the latter's public identity. The photographer looks amiably on Monnier's sacrifice of autonomous creativity. The Beach Papers contain a number photos of Monnier sitting at her desk, against her bookshelf, in front of an inkstand. These pictures are variations on the same theme: that of the woman writing. They amplify the structure of Monnier's visual identity: writing and books become the most feminine attribute of Beach's model. The loose white tunic she wears in one of the pictures suggests her private pledge to culture. Yet, the success of Monnier, and perhaps her desirability for Beach, resided in the reversal of this private attachment to writing into the public promotion of others. The model's exchange of a standard feminine physicality for the femininity of writing and an active rapport with words impress the photographer. This exchange is an aesthetic reaction to historical limitations and seems to feed other desirable possibilities like the rotation of simplicity and exoticism. In some snapshots Monnier almost appears orientalized. There are pictures of her sitting on a draped sofa-bed against a draped wall. She sips tea in comfortable clothes whose shiny texture—probably taffeta or shantung silk—court exotic associations.

In pictures where Beach and Monnier are portrayed together, the latter's lean body, her cropped hair, her unconventional clothing become the dynamic center of the composition (Beach Papers, Box 246, Folder 2). The images immortalize the two women's intimate and professional partnership. At Beach's side, Monnier redirects her friend's nervous energy. Significantly larger than the elflike Beach, she is earthbound, receptive, responsive, prodding. In a sequence by an unspecified photographer, Monnier wears a garment that looks like an ethnic variant of her trademark cape, while the American is seen in layered knit tops and breeches, with a hand in her pocket. With its allusion to draped forms, Monnier's garment stores the other's energy. While this energy suggests defiance, the garment promises to subordinate it to productivity. The kind of visual identity she forms with Beach is not mere repetition for emotive purposes. Her photographic presence next to Beach supplies more information. As a couple, as an identity of two, they made cultural history. In such making Monnier's model of chiasmus is decisive. Her sacrifice of individual transcendence for the genius of others is, as suggested earlier, a kind of reparation. It is a defense of the lost Orphic integrity of talent at the hand of the harsh reality of mass culture and commerce. To Beach, Monnier's exchange of the individual gift of writing for literary serviceability was lovable, imitable. In fact, it made her similarly receptive. As booksellers and patrons, the two women are united as a private couple by their vigilant intimacy with modernity. This is illustrated by some exemplary photos with James Joyce. In one, Joyce is flanked by his two publishers and mentors, Beach and Monnier, while he entertains them; in another Beach listens attentively to Joyce while Monnier looks admiringly at Beach listening to the great writer. The image speaks of the power of Joyce to reinforce the couple with his genius: he fascinates Beach's mind and, via Beach, Monnier's mind.

Visually, there seem to be no psychological complications attending Monnier's acceptance of a more passive role. She inspires love rather than struggle or criticism; she is a common reader rather than an aggressive cultural interventionist. In her letters to Beach she inquires about her friend's favorite American books. In a letter dated 12 April 1939, her spontaneous response when she discovers *MobyDick* is that of a common reader enchanted by a book: it is poetic; it is profound, she exclaims (Fig. 4.6).

Disquieting discipline

Like her French colleague, acquaintance, and neighbor, Stein was the animator of a circle of talented writers and artists. Like Monnier, her public influence was inextricable from her partnership with another woman; like Monnier, Stein was simultaneously a writer and a patron who welcomed international artists to her Paris home; like Monnier, therefore, she put herself in the service of letters. Finally, like Monnier's, her visual identity relies on the crossing of homely and avant-garde, convention and innovation. But in Stein's case her visual presence is somewhat metafigural: it suspends the chiasmic illusion, reaching for something beyond the modern reconciliation of opposites. For Stein, writing remains a libidinal attachment that is not easily reversed by the Apollonian distance of visual rhetoric. Her poetics explicitly prefers vitality to the cool seduction of polished forms. Her presence, in a sense, goes against the grain of the new modernist alliance between photography and writing.

By the earlier part of the twentieth century, devotion was no longer a sufficient condition for art. There could be nothing self-effacing about the writer. On the contrary, it was understood that the value of writing depended on such external factors like promotion, support, image, and so on.[9] As a result, emphasis

Figure - toi que nous sommes en train de lire Moby Dick et que nous en sommes enthousiasmés. On ne peut rien imaginer de plus beau ; que c'est poétique, que c'est profond ! C'est vraiment un des grands livres du monde ; le capitaine Achab est une des figures de l'Homme, pas d'Amérique, au fond, de Don Quichotte. Tu ne parlais depuis si longtemps de ce livre. C'est vraiment bien gentil de la part de Giono de s'être mis à cela

J'irai, sans doute, le 25

fell more on the surface, on the outside of writing, than on the process. Famous photographic portraits of writers—by Freund, Man Ray, Abbot—help move the writer closer to the common viewer by encouraging in the latter a new fascination with the absent literary object. Foregrounding the person of the writer, photography separates the labor of writing from its public display. It does to writing what commodity fetishism does to production: it switches attention from process to product, turning the difficult scene of the former into the glossy surface of the portrait. The more the face of the writer moves publicly to the foreground, the more writing recedes in the background, cut off from the photograph's surface, increasingly hidden, mysterious, and therefore inducing imitative desire. Photography favors a transition from the traditional story of individual talent to the reproducibility of the literary object, increasing the imaginative access to writing.

As we have seen, Monnier's visual self tries to appear transhistorical, impenetrable to materiality and market logic. From the beginning Stein had presented her literary vocation as imitative, a secondary development of her seduction by oil paint. She loses herself in images (*LA* 59), therefore she starts writing. She insists neither on the primacy of writing nor on her identity as a gifted writer. Instead, she subordinates writing to visuality. In Fredric Jameson's famous argument, Andy Warhol's postmodernist *Diamond Dust Shoes* empty Van Gogh's modernist *Peasant Boots* of a story of glamorised simplicity (Jameson 1993; 66-69). Similarly, Stein replaces the myth of vocation, genius, and entitlement, with a self-generated coming to writing. Photographs of Stein show her writing in her atelier, surrounded by pictures she has bought with family money (Stendhal 77). Writing is a translation from images to paper. It is self-generated and unthinkable without cultural appropriation. While in popular portraits of other modernist authors like Mina Loy and Djuna Barnes the desirability of the woman establishes the desirability of her writing, in Stein's case, as in Monnier's, writing substitutes for all the more spectacular feminine attributes. But the internal relation of Stein's words to her pictures conveys a self-sufficiency that makes untenable the chiasmus of autonomy and service that was so important in Monnier's visual identity.

Monnier's cape and Stein's velvet garment are clothes of desire: they cover the body just as the gaze of the mother, precursor of the attesting gaze of others, covers the child (Fraire 15). For Monnier and Stein desire has an unquestioned connection with culture, but with a difference. If Monnier's cape denotes a certain sacrificial austerity in the name of the genius of others, Stein's robe suggests the discipline of autotelic repetition (words derived from images), and thus of an individual seduction by forms that could run out of hand. Absorbed in writing, surrounded by her avant-garde possessions, she embodies a less popular modernist romance. She is the disquieting wholly self-commissioned and independent artist who sponsors herself with the pictures she owns.

The drag of history

With its use of the female body, surrealist photography played a significant role in the modernist rhetorical overturning of reality. For example, Lee Miller's *Nude Bent Forward* (c. 1931) or Man Ray's photographs of Meret Oppenheim in his *Veiled Erotic* series (1933) rely on 'a complete collapse of differences' between male and female (Foster 221). Borrowing the expression 'the fetishization of reality' from Rosalind Krauss, who used it to describe the inversion of fact and figure, nature and writing, Hal Foster notes that the leitmotif of surrealist photography is 'woman transformed fetishistically into penile form' (221).

Surreality might be understood as a reality teeming with meaning. It is about the imaginary multiplication of the potential of signs and their call to the speaking subject, as well as a celebration of the latter's power to respond. The other side of surreality would be semiotic aphanisis, the fear that signs will no longer address us fruitfully. Semiotic aphanisis threatened to seize thought and representation in the twentieth century, when more and more people demanded a new social mobility and full symbolic and political rights of citizenship. Surrealist images in which a woman's body is transformed into penile form may be understood as a response to the death of signs. In the nudes by Lee Miller and Man Ray, the female body, traditionally perceived as contiguous to matter, symbolizes the anxiety of a libidinal detachment from meaning. To be close to matter means to be distant from culture and the power of symbolization. In these images, however, the female body is veiled by the phallus, the ultimate 'sign of the latency with which everything significable is struck' (Lacan 288). The veil of the phallus reconstitutes a semiotic plenitude between the subject and the world.[10]Although it is possible to see a political potential in the surrealist confusion of feminine and masculine forms, the primary aim of this visual confusion does not seem to be the cultural subversion of fixed gender identities. The confusion of forms appears first and foremost to be dictated by the urgency to flee a closeness to matter (the female body) that is felt to be deadly for artistic invention and innovation.

At first sight, butch-femme iconography may seem to exploit the political potential of the surrealist manipulation of forms, especially as it concerns notions of gendered and historical identity. But, in fact, it questions the omnipotence of desire as it is conveyed by surrealism's phallicized women's bodies. For example, in a famous image of Stein and Toklas in butch-femme drag (Fig. 4.7), the photographic surface certainly calls attention to the rhetorical construction of gender and sexuality. The use of clothes argues for a certain artificiality of the masculine and feminine divide. But precisely because the clothes heterosexualize the two women, they also ask the question of social conventions. Social conventions might be wished away, but they return on the battlements of the body. Obviously, the wearers complicate the heterosexual reference, raising the costumes beyond their functional role and to a richer semiotic level. The heterosexual allusion of the costumes worn by the same-sex couple undermines the force of

Fig. 4.7   Gertrude Stein and Alice B. Toklas, Aix-Les-Bains, 1928. Courtesy
of Yale Collection of American Literature, Beinecke Rare
Book and Manuscript Library.

social conventions. This force, however, is also strangely affirmed. The costumes are a visual commodity that speaks of a meaning congealed in history, of a difficult transition from the constrictions of the ideological-historical level to the freedom of the semiotic one.

The image of Stein and Toklas in butch-femme drag seems critical of the surrealist omnipotence of desire. The surrealist 'advent of desire' (Lacan 287) meant the wish to pass from a more restrictive historical-ideological level to the healing plenitude of the semiotic surface, where norms can be deconstructed and reconstructed. With the expression 'the fetishization of reality,' Krauss refers to the metaphorization of labor from material to figural. 'Fetishization' indicates the reversal of the depth of history as the surface of semiotics.[11] The image of Stein and Toklas in butch-femme drag cautions that desire and the innovative possibilities of form might leave history unchanged.

The Stein-Toklas costume acquires the visual gravity of a social hieroglyph that demands interpretation, not infatuation. The allusion to drag actually delimits formal possibilities. It is well known that contemporary theories of identity, which interestingly echo Stein's repetition, argue for a rhetorical erosion of identity's dependence on social norms. The repetition of established cultural positions and beliefs—also known as performativity—promises to detach those beliefs from the tight fabric of accepted and unquestioned symbolic meanings, until they are shown to be the product of culture rather than nature.[12] In the Stein-Toklas image he rhetorical self-consciousness of their visual identity stops short of signifying the utter mobility of identity. A sense of entrapment, a faint suggestion of the apathy of frozen meaning, seeps trough the overall celebration of the unbound latency of meaning. In the surrealist nudes the confusion of shapes (woman's body and phallus) reconciled the subject (beholder and beheld) with a natural fount of culture. In butch-femme images of the Stein-Toklas kind clothes detach the models from the transhistorical romance of desire. Rather than indicating a mobile identity, drag clothes become the stiff referents of the labor of history, of social hierarchies and their durability. Their power to refer to history and norms seems to prevail over their complicity with the formalist work of signs and desire.

As I look at the photos of these modernist women aging (Fig. 4. 8), I think about their use of costume and photography. Both media were subordinated to the women's wish to 'make' themselves.[13] To 'make' does not simply refer to an identity that goes through transformations. In their ability to present the self for public scrutiny, clothes can make visual identities embody culture. The visual transformations of the body can be read as an attempt to approximate a native tie of attestation and entitlement to culture. As the women age, the gender divisions harden, the most material evidence of the effect of time in the face of critical desire. In photographs of Sylvia Beach and Adrienne Monnier in the countryside at Rocfoin, Monnier's large body looks like that of a peasant. She is, here, simply, a

Fig. 4.8 Sylvia Beach and Adrienne Monnier at Rocfoin. Courtesy of Princeton University Library.

homely woman of whom you could never tell she owned one of the best known bookstores in Paris. She is the proof of the problematic tie of modernist technologies of the self to the ideal of the primitive simplicity of the land.

Chapter 5

Picasso and Paper

From Repetition to Composition

In this chapter I examine Picasso's influence on Stein. I argue that his *Portrait of Gertrude Stein* (1906) raises challenging questions of value that adumbrate the writer's contribution to the debate on modern aesthetics. I read 'Composition as Explanation,' Stein's first public lecture, as a landmark of that contribution. Traditionally in the Picasso-Stein relationship the American writer has been subordinated to the Spanish painter. Recent scholarship has demonstrated that 'the creative practice of the two is more collaborative than previously imagined (Pavloska 5).[1] While I share this position, my focus here is on Stein's admiration of Picasso and the traces it left in the writings of the 1920s, when she turned toward a writing style that is perceived as amenable to postmodern taste. I argue that her identification as a Picasso follower enabled Stein to think of herself as a writer straddling two worlds—the creative one of the modern composition and a different kind of writing involving intellectual judgement. In a certain sense, following in Picasso's footsteps freed Stein to think of herself as two: the private author of her unpublished oeuvre and a public commentator of modernity, with the authority of the insider's point of view.

A popular argument makes sense of the modern experience as a reaction to the invasion of commercialization. In this line of argument the seduction of merchandise redefines aesthetic experience. Jean Baudrillard, for example, maintains that in the twentieth century beauty becomes the destruction of the object's use value and its traditional intelligibility (175). Charles Baudelaire is the father of this kind of negative dialectic. The poet 'was to confront the invasion of commercialisation by transforming the artwork itself into merchandise and fetish' (Baudrillard 175). For this reason, in Baudrillard's view, Baudelaire is more authentically modern than Walter Benjamin, Baudelaire's scholar and a key contributor to contemporary aesthetic discourse. For Benjamin, modernity sets in when the work of art loses its aura of originality and authenticity. For Benjamin and his followers the reproducibility of images is a positive phenomenon: it promises 'a renewal of mankind' ('The Work of Art in the Age of Mechanical Reproduction' 221). By contrast, Benjamin's popular notion of the loss of the aura appears nostalgic to Baudrillard, especially when compared to Baudelaire's 'exploration of new forms of seduction, linked to pure objects, to pure events, to that modern passion which is fascination' (177).

Baudrillard establishes a line of continuity, joining Baudelaire to postmodernism. These chronologically distant trends share the dominant influence of merchandise. Thus, for example, Baudrillard's argument would encourage to link Baudelaire's seduction of material and commercial objects to the painting of photorealist artists like Tom Blackwell. In a world where commerce has appropriated art, Blackwell 'has appropriated commerce as a subject for fine art' (Meisel 19), as it is clear in pictures like *Prada* (1999-2000) or *In the Frame* (1999).[2] With the seduction of merchandise, Baudrillard names a cultural logic of productive negativity whereby art resists its own devaluing at the hand of commerce by incorporating and imitating the trait it opposes.[3] The outcome of the cultural repetition of the fascination of merchandise is destruction. Eventually it leads to the disappearance of art: 'against classic art and the seduction of forms, modern art opposes "the magic of its own disappearance"' (Baudrillard 181).

The problematic side of the above argument is that it assumes a passive spectator stupefied before the spectacle of culture. It relies on an observer who, like the people in Plato's cave, is subjected despite himself or herself to the autonomous force of culture, in the guise of the productive and self destructive logic of merchandise. Is repetition the only way to understand that 'renewal of man' that Walter Benjamin associated with twentieth-century modernity? Is it the only road to aesthetic innovation? When, in 'The Work of Art in the Age of Mechanical Reproduction,' Benjamin saw modernity as 'intimately connected with the contemporary mass movements' (221), to a certain extent he meant that aesthetics should seek innovation by accounting for the impatience of an ever greater number of individuals claiming the right to a fuller existence and self-realization.

The mimeticist repetition of dominant cultural currents has proved a rather influential model of innovation and a contemporary measure of beauty in literature and in the arts. But, as Baudrillard's argument shows, this model stakes a lot on an ideological counter-bourgeois stance. From Baudelaire on, the negativity that moves the artist to value merchandise and repeat its logic, finds its reason in an anti-bourgeois feeling. It was the bourgeoisie that gave merchandise a sentimental value (Baudrillard 178). In its origins, the critical model of repetition subordinates change to an ideological imperative. To be sure, this subordination results in rhetorical power and critical eloquence when we attempt to explain categories like 'modern' and 'postmodern.' But it can also blind us to the fact that in modernity aesthetic change is scattered and disseminated in the most unlikely corners. Above all, change is related to the emergence of public feelings generated by an unprecedented cognitive openness.

The most influential modernist thinkers have given us an inkling of these new public feelings. Benjamin's notion of 'the plurality of copies' ('The Work of Art in the Age of Mechanical Reproduction' 221) and, most of all, his view of a modern contagious literacy,[4] helped translate into concepts a general atmosphere rife with the desire of a subjective cultural access. After Benjamin, Martin Heidegger returned to the new feelings only to puzzle over thought's estrangement from them: 'All distances in time and space are shrinking. Man now reaches overnight, by plane, places which formerly took weeks and months to travel. He now receives instant information, by radio, of events, which he formerly learned about only years later, if at all' ('The Thing' 165). If at all: the shrinking of space and time is more overwhelming than any anti-bourgeois stance. This ideological stance seems to crumble under the weight of a new cognitive openness or decentering that conceptual thought has difficulty in describing. A world has disappeared where it did not seem to bother anyone if information and knowledge remained unknown or hidden. An old world of inattention and indifference, of approximate and unrefined perception, of human slumber, is being replaced by the signals of an unprecedented mobility synonymous with a global incitement to human self-realization. Thought can take stock of the event.

Modern aesthetics may hinge on the seduction of merchandise. But this seduction runs parallel to a transformation of the way in which individuals think of themselves. They are no longer the resigned members of a class or social group, condemned to fixity by natality, geography, and collective beliefs.[5] Gertrude Stein's 'Composition as Explanation' is an important document of this modern experience. Written as a lecture, the author's first real one, it was delivered at Cambridge and Oxford in the summer of 1926.[6] It judges the new cognitive openness positively. It also limits it to the span of a few years, from 1905 to 1914. After that, the questioning of value and authority was abruptly suppressed by the obscurantism of the war.

The word 'composition' sums up modern aesthetics. Stein's definition is strikingly generic: 'Composition is the thing seen by every one living in the living they are doing, they are that composing of the composition that at the time they are living is the composition of the time in which they are living. It is that that makes living a thing they are doing' ('Composition as Explanation' 523). Composition is an unselfconscious form of art that resembles life. The work of art amounts to a multiplication of individual expressions. Moreover, the modern composition is a space everybody can choose to enter (CAE 521). It all depends on 'time-sense,' that is to say, on an authentic, unimpeded connection with one's time rather than on an academic imposition from above of notions of authority and value. Stein's lecture collapses the distinction between art and life and converts social differences to impersonal identities: 'they' and 'everybody.' An open, ongoing creativity takes place beyond the need of the enjoyer, who inevitably appears posthumously, after the new composition has become widely recognized and a classic.

Stein explains modernity in terms of an extended access—'in their *entering* the modern composition' (CAE 521; my emphasis). She describes a cultural moment marked by the liberation of simultaneous individual energies: '[t]hey themselves' (521). She refrains from the nostalgic celebration of a magical accord removed from historical time and presents modernity as a relation to strive for: 'composition is not there, it is going to be there and we are here' (CAE 523).

In the second part of her lecture, Stein traces the origins of her writing career to the spell of cognitive openness, to the new availability of messages and signs, conjured by the vista of ungoverned simultaneous differences (CAE 526). She evokes a spectacle of non-hierarchical creativity as unselfconsciously aesthetic as life itself: 'Composition is the thing seen by every one living in the living they are doing' (CAE 523).

Stein's composition sounds like a public pattern: moods and emotions that run through everyone's life without annulling their individuality. It could be argued that it recalls repetition, the term that in *The Making of Americans* had meant the personal discovery of social identity: 'all the repeating in some one, all the repeating that is the whole of some one' (*MA* 52). In her novel of apprenticeship, unity had already become a melodramatic illusion: 'Some of such of them sometimes then make melodrama of themselves to themselves to hold themselves together to them' (*MA* 312). In the novel, repetition had helped Stein to take her distance from bourgeois sentimentality and aesthetic timidity. As we have seen, the achievement was crowned by the creation of young David Hersland, a paragon of beauty that has nothing of the ornamental quality but is instead distinguished by an existential restlessness.

But composition, as Stein meant it in her first academic lecture, is different from repetition. It dissolves any antagonistic or ideological anti-bourgeois stance in favor of an Orphic accord with the external world. Stein's modern composition is premised on the plenitude of parallel authenticities, not a multiplicity of equally valuable copies (as repetition would suggest). It is therefore bound to change notions of value and authority. The sense of liberation we hear in Stein's notion of composition is nowhere present in repetition. 'Composition as Explanation' develops a canon of beauty in part reminiscent of *Tender Buttons*. Objects do not attain the cool seduction of fetishes: they are expressive, umanized. Stein's 'blind carafe' with its 'hurt color' (*TB* 461) is as expressive and as generous to the viewer as the earthenware jug will be to Heidegger.[7] Objects are included in a semiotic process—'a system to pointing' (*TB* 461)—and thus subtracted from the ennui of merchandise fascination. The observer refuses to be paralyzed.

'Composition as Explanation' is a lecture on the problem of artistic and literary value: 'The quality in the creation of the expression the quality in a composition that makes it go dead just after it has been made is very troublesome' (CAE 529). The vista of multiple and parallel individual pursuits, where everything is simultaneously alike and different (527), together with the generic definition of modernity as 'how everybody is doing everything' (CAE 523), serve to raise the question of value. The authority of this plural landscape depended less on the individual pursuits cohering around a unified oppositional discourse, and more on the willingness to grasp without impediments, almost unselfconsciously, the new cognitive mobility. Those who enter the modern composition 'are prepared just as the world around them is prepared' (CAE 523).

Stein does not present herself as a leader. She is a follower, 'creating' the composition and 'groping' (CAE 527) as a follower of those for whom 'living [was] a thing they were doing' (523). The lecture is a turning point because it presents a writing that borders on an archaeology of aesthetics and taste in the affirmative and subjective mode of the modern composition. The emblem of such charismatic modernity is Picasso. Stein's view of herself as a follower of modernity alludes to the painter's influence on her writing. The influence is significant because it nurtures Stein's hybrid professional identity as an original writer *and* an aesthetic theorist. In her second portrait of the painter, 'If I Told Him: a Completed Portrait of Picasso' (1923), in the comparison with the Spaniard, Stein sees herself as a writer-critic with the prerogative of judging the work of other artists: 'I judge judge. /As resemblance to him' (22).

Anxiety and value

Stein met Picasso for the first time in 1905. She was 31; he was 25. Although at that time she was writing *Three Lives*, she was less known as a writer and more as a patron of the arts. *The Autobiography of Alice B. Toklas* reports that Etta Cone, a Baltimore friend, 'was taken' (49) to Picasso's studio 'whenever the Picasso finances got beyond everybody and was made to buy a hundred francs' worth of drawings' (49). The episode fosters a view of Stein as an aesthetic judge, spreading a taste in the arts outside Europe. The story of the execution of *Portrait of Gertrude Stein* (Fig. 5.1) confirms this image, revolving around Stein's difference from other Americans whose 'romantic charity' (*AABT* 49) contrasts with the intensity that she shared with Picasso.

The montage of anecdotes that *The Autobiography of Alice B. Toklas* devotes to the 1906 Picasso's portrait of Stein evidences the struggle for differentiation from her compatriots. In the anecdote about the beginning of 'their intimacy' (*AABT* 43) the writer and the painter have a minor duel over a piece of bread. Subsequently, they bond against 'all Americans' (and Stein's brother Leo) who reduce art to its decorative or ornamental function (*AABT* 43). Cultural misapprehensions form the background of the rising connection with Picasso. To the eyes of other Americans, the young Spanish artist appears as a hot-tempered intellectually shallow, Mediterranean macho, undeserving of the graceful company of Fernande Olivier. We first catch sight of him from the point of view of a dear friend of Toklas, Nellie Jacot, who says that he was 'a good-looking bootblack' (*AABT* 42). This is followed by the Andrew Green anecdote. An erudite man, Green was 'quite overcome' with Fernande's beauty (*AABT* 44) and fantasized about taking her away from 'that little Picasso' (*AABT* 44). Picasso is inducted into a grinding mechanism of superficial cultural appropriations; he enters the narrative as the forbidden object of female desire, romantically complicated by the intrigue of class and national differences. Although she is an integral part of this pattern, Stein is clearly also 'groping,' as she had said in 'Composition as Explanation' (527), to find an identity different from the cliché of the opportunist, predatory American tourist in Europe. Tellingly, *The Autobiography* frames the portrait narrative with the prediction that 'some time [Stein] would have a biography' (42).

Fig. 5.1   Pablo Picasso, *Portrait of Gertrude Stein,* **oil on canvas, 39⅜ x 32
in., 1906. The Metropolitan Museum of Modern Art, Bequest
of Gertrude Stein, 1946.**

After the prophesy, the metonymic deflection toward the sittings at Picasso's atelier—'some eighty or ninety sittings' (43)—and the long-lasting writing habits Stein formed at that time, invite a positive association of the portrait with her projected biography.

Shortly before her death, Stein bequeathed the portrait to the Metropolitan Museum of Art in New York. Her gift suggests that she trusted that her value as a writer would not be overshadowed by her reputation as an art patron or, even worse, as a model in a Picasso painting. William Rubin, the editor of the catalogue for the exhibit *Picasso and Portraiture* held at the Museum of Modern Art (MoMA) a few summers ago, confirms the model's trust. For Rubin, Picasso 'created for Stein a face as a woman of the avant-garde. Her portrait now corresponded to the role she wanted to play in writing literature for the twentieth century' (268). If her face is the sign of her literariness, it will be noticed that it has also contributed to spread the legend of the cerebral Medusa. As we have seen in the previous chapters, this image starkly contrasts with the sensuous intellectual she longed to be. In which sense, therefore, might the portrait be said to have given Stein a literary biography?

In her third piece on Picasso, in 1938, Stein supports Rubin's impression:

> I posed for him all winter [1906], eighty times and in the end he painted out the head, he told me that he could not look at me any more and then he left once more for Spain. It was the first time since the blue period and immediately upon his return from Spain he painted in the head without having seen me again and he gave me the picture and I was and I still am satisfied with my portrait, for me, it is I, and it is the only reproduction of me which is always I. (*Picasso* 8)

The strong sense of recognition comes from the same author who, just a couple of years before, had emerged from a meditation on the literary history of her country with a shattered sense of identity. *The Geographical History of America* skirts the abyss of fatuous and illusionary literary worth. Writing perilously approaches the vortex of meaninglessness: 'Am I I' (*GHA* 405). Picasso's portrait of her has the opposite effect: 'it is I'; 'it is always I.' There might be an imaginary dimension at work here. The recognition, in other words, might be strong precisely because the I of the image is autonomous *vis-à-vis* the actual struggle for value as it can be gleaned from Stein's work, especially after the parenthesis of the modern composition.

In lieu of a face, Picasso gave her a mask, 'a solid thing' ('Picasso' 19) that imposes the calm of forms on the poor struggles of the flesh. Like all the rest of Picasso's art, to her it is 'a charming thing' ('Picasso' 19) because its aloofness and intensity celebrate the ascetic achievement of forms. To be drawn in a discourse on forms, to be an aesthetic 'judge' is important to Stein. The mask turns her into the character of a human comedy about the short-lived struggle for forms linked to the cultural moment of the modern composition. With wars and the rise of totalitarianisms, art can no longer affirm. It enters a regime of mourning 'for what is dead, mutilated, humiliated and offended in everybody's life' (Bodei 115) that extends to our post-modern 'sad art' ruled, out of respect for the sorrow of others, by the prohibition of beauty and the 'sensorial taboo of enjoyment' (Bodei 115).

Stein's modern composition embraced aesthetic enjoyment. Even the disturbing and repellent aspects are geared toward enjoyment: Picasso's work is 'a solid thing, a charming thing, a lovely thing, a perplexing thing, a disconcerting thing, a simple thing, a perplexing thing, a complicated thing, an interesting thing, a disturbing thing, a repellant [sic] thing, a very pretty thing' ('Picasso' 18). Far from mourning the impossibility of beauty, Picasso's modernity embraces the potential of forms to impose a new subjective language. His painting looks real in the sense of Cézanne, who refused a mass gaze mollified by the fascination of commercial simulacra.

The mask-like face Picasso gave Stein wears a severe, almost disaffected expression. The somber browns of the model's coat enhance the distance at which she keeps the invisible object of her gaze. She is no passive hostage to what Baudrillard had called the modern passion of fascination. Any sadness that might be imagined here comes from a sensorial taboo against passive abandon. Stein's physiognomy, in sum, is used to ritualise the subjective assertiveness that defined Picasso's new style.

The portrait's completion in 1906 is contemporary to the execution of *Two nudes*, *Seated Nude*, and the charcoal on paper *Woman Seated and Woman Standing*.[8] These feature bulky and dramatic female presences preparatory for *Les Demoiselles D'Avignon*. As shown by these images, the new style revolved around a specific aggressive operation that art critics have termed 'psychological emptiness' (Rubin 266). The human subject is emptied of any inner complexity. Strangely, though, reduced to its physical element, human presence also takes on a new authority. The psychological emptiness results in the emergence of an enigmatic language of 'emphatic and obscure' gestures.'[9] Stein's body becomes content and vessel of Picasso's starkly affirmative and individualized language. The aim of his language was to alter a semiotic public code dominated by a mannerist sensuality that separated viewers from the external world rather than connecting them to it.

The summer before the completion of the portrait, Picasso had gone to Gósol where he had painted nudes in interiors, such as *The Harem*.[10] He had further explored the nude in relation to traditional themes in *La Toilette* and *Nude Combing Her Hair*.[11] Nudes like *The Harem* pair visual pleasure with an interior ease. A male viewer reclines leisurely against a wall as his gaze lingers on the female bodies and the women tending to them. He is eating while he watches the women. Clearly, his repast suggests that the view inside the harem is food for his soul. Picasso is still using the female nude as the totalizing symbol of a mollified interiority that circulates in public discourse as a light and affordable commodity. The use of the nude as the symbol of public harmony becomes quite outdated in

Seated Nude, which develops the notion of a different beholder. Except for the breasts and the long hair, the figure has shed the cliché of the feminine aura of *Harem*. The face bears already the traces of the African wooden masks.

In the Gósol paintings Picasso was preparing to trope the female body from symbol of public consensus to icon of subjective affirmation. He was switching from feminine seduction to enigmatic meaning. For example, the young woman in *Girl with a pitcher* wears an expression of aloofness that preludes to Stein's face.[12] She is completely absorbed in the act of pouring invisible water, as if taken more with the gesture and her thoughts than with the scope of her action. In this phase of transition Stein becomes a bridge to a new painting that privileges subjective idiolects.

The figures he painted between 1905 and 1906 illustrate the primacy of subjective gestures that enhance the assertiveness of the human presence. A prime example of Picasso's repertoire of explosively independent gestures is *Woman with a Fan* (1905), which Stein owned.[13] His subjects attempt to balance themselves in front of the viewer—and the external world—with the help of objects like a pitcher, a fan, or even a part of the body functioning as a steadying object. Though not immediately transparent, or because they raise the question of what they mean, these gestures confer a new pride and nobility to the human figure. The expression of Picasso's model in *Woman with a Fan* seems at once oppositional and defensive. By stopping everything around her with the raised right hand, the woman affirms herself visually. She is the alluring image of a public projection of individuality. The fan she holds in the left hand has a steadying function: it is there to favor the externalization of acts and meanings that, one suspects, would have otherwise remained suppressed. Simple gestures become obscure; they take on the importance of ritual. Stein is part of this new style of psychological emptiness, which Picasso refined by incorporating references to archaic and non-Western cultures. Art critics agree that, '[i]t is in the face, whose mask-like starkness contrasts so sharply with the treatment of the rest of the portrait, that we see the new development in Picasso's style' (Jaffe' 78). The writer's face bears resemblance to a stone head from ancient Spain (Wertenbaker 67). It is also suggestive of African masks. Just around the corner from the room that houses Picasso's portrait at The Metropolitan Museum there is a group of African masks. One of these stands out from the rest. It is a nineteenth-century wood, pigment and kaolin Mukudj Dance Mask from Gabon, made among the Punu peoples. Such masks were worn by male performers of the stilt dance mukudj, which involved towering impressively while executing complex choreography and astonishing feats of acrobatics. The mukudj mask attempted to capture the likeness of a woman. The stylized portrait was embellished with a coiffure composed of a central lobe and two lateral tresses, and with cicatrization of the forehead and temples. The masks had a healing function meant to transcend mortality. Similarly, Stein's mask transcends all emotions. Picasso's incorporation of external cultural references wipes out readymade associations of visual signs and meaning that would, for example, encourage the viewer to read in Stein's face melancholia or sadness. Instead it aims at an emotional undecidability. In her first homage to Picasso, the painter's incessant working to produce something with 'real meaning' ('Picasso' 19), suggests his shuffling of diverse culture in his search for an innovative visual idiom.

Portrait of Gertrude Stein does not hide the jarring juxtaposition of the intense face of the twentieth century, with 'an exaggerated ovoid shape, flat frontal planes, sharply arched brows and thin lips to suit [Stein's] features' (Wertenbaker 67), and the nineteenth-century body covered in a brown velvet coat open on a ruffle and a small coral brooch. Were it not for these accessories, the painter's debt to his model would have been greater. She would have become even more disengaged and unapproachable than his hand, with its forceful reversal of the gaze *on* the world. Far from being surfeited with the pleonasm of signs, withdrawn in a fictional direction, the model's gaze is intense and absorbed.

Because of the model's active gaze, it is not surprising to find the portrait in a beauty manual. Carla Mathis and Helen Villa Connor's popular hit, *The Triumph of Individual Style*, which encourages women to value the bodies they have instead of changing them to imitate an ideal, mentions Picasso's Stein twice, as a model of 'innate personal intensity' (151). The book uses the image to teach women with 'a strong or dramatic presence' to 'downscale in order to be more approachable'(109). To the formalist hegemony of fascination, the portrait responds with an reactive stance. But without he accessories it would have been perhaps too overwhelming a *coupe de theatre*. It would have spoken the language of mimicry rather than subjective intensity. It would have betrayed rather than controlled an essential ingredient in artistic value—fear.

The appliqué work of the mask belongs to the order of fear: 'All of a sudden one day Picasso painted out the whole head. I can't see you any longer when I look, he said irritably' (*AABT* 49). In Stein's account, the mask is the index of the hand hurrying for innovation '[i]n the long struggle with the portrait of Gertrude Stein' (*AABT* 50). Stein is now the balancing object in that struggle. Especially her 'realistic' body and nineteenth-century accessories counteract the first set of terms in her theory of value—'a fear a doubt' (CAE 528)—with the second set of terms: 'a judgment and a conviction' (CAE 528). The ruffle and brooch simultaneously downscale the intensity of the woman and, by metonymic deflection, the fear conveyed by the painter's hand. The juxtaposition of the theatrical, ritual element of the mask with the human body, with the intent to modify it, turns inside out the rapacious *tristesse* of the outer world. In the real studio, '[t]here was a large broken armchair where Gertrude Stein posed' (*AABT* 43). The broken object is absent in the portrait. The reversal of the world of objects is also part of the long struggle for the portrait. From this point of view, the visual juxtapositions of the portrait turn the fear and doubt instilled by an impoverished material world into an affirmative statement: 'a judgment and a conviction' (CAE 528).

The first page of Henry Miller's *Tropic of Cancer* relies on a similar effect: 'A year ago, six months ago, I thought that I was an artist. I no longer think about it, I am. Everything that was literature has fallen from me. There are no more books to be written, thank God.' Gertrude Stein's mask is the value-creating intrusion of an 'I am,' a wilful act committed in an emergency, when the fear rises of being submerged by all painting or all literature. It comes as a relief. Stein theorized aesthetic value as a tension between fear and judgement that persists after the composition is finished and prevents it from going dead (CAE 528-529). She was perhaps thinking about the sound of an 'I am,' of an exit in the openness of language, visual or verbal. In 'Pink Melon Joy' she equated writing with the externalization of 'suppressed sounds' (*G&P* 374).

Years later, when she altered her looks by cutting her hair, the mask was still 'there' to identify her as a peer of the moderns: 'And my portrait, said he sternly. Then his face softening he added, mais, quand même tout y est, all the same it is all there' (*AABT* 53). Picasso gave Stein a public face. He permanently associated her to a solemn exit in the public world of meanings. He concretely did for her what Cézanne had done for her on an imaginary level. When she said of her reproduction that 'it is always I,' she implied that she would always wear the struggle for innovation and value on her face.

Picasso's portrait of Stein remains the portrait of an American writer. It was donated to a public cultural institution so that everyone could look at it. What everyone sees is a discontinuity between the model's hands and writing. The emphasis usually placed on the face diverts attention from the hands. Like the broken armchair, writing is absent. Indeed, Stein's hands—the part of the body most involved in writing—are one of the most enigmatic traits of the image. Her right hand, the one with which she wrote, hangs as if in repose, the forefinger hidden from view. The left hand rests on her thigh, as if to balance and steady the seated body of a model who does not seem entirely at ease. The left hand more closely repeats the theatrical effect of the mask, as if it had been juxtaposed with the volume of cloth that covers her body. This hand's thumb appears at a symmetrical distance from the index finger, as if it were closing on it, thus projecting the idea of picking and holding something. But for the moment, both hands remain exposed and dormant, a prehensile pair, neither masculine nor feminine, extending out of the brown coat sleeves, almost mechanical in their inertia. These hands refuse to romanticize writing. Rather, they startle. They make us pause and think about the dirty work of the composition—the struggle out of which writing (like Picasso's juxtapositions) comes and by which it can be easily smothered. In Stein's theory of value, anxiety is the aesthetic measure of the modern soul.

The theory of value Stein presented at Cambridge and Oxford can be already inferred in her first portrait of Picasso (1909). The painter is 'completely charming' ('Picasso' 17). He is the symbol of an Orphic poetry of persuasion and action that encourages aesthetic enjoyment and 'real meaning' (19). In this first tribute repetition and the use of indefinite pronouns help suggest a flat cultural landscape of non-hierarchical anonymity where value is multiple and decentered rather than dictated by academic consensus. The landscape of simultaneous differences gives Stein the chance of insertion. Picasso is part of the flat anonymity, working autonomously: 'one having something coming out of him something having meaning and this one was certainly working then' ('Picasso' 18). Repeated several times, the locution 'coming out of' clearly associates Picasso with the exit of a privacy into the openness of culture. In part, the repetition is for emotional effect. It renders Picasso's isolation in a modern landscape of decentered creativity, which in later years she will identify with America. But repetition also serves to produce an artistic redoubling. At the center of the portrait, almost imperceptibly (through the shift from 'one' to 'this one'), the repetition of 'coming out of' admits the interposition of Stein in the modern composition: 'This one was working and something was coming out then, something was coming out of this one then [. . .]. This one was one having something coming out of this one' (18). Does 'this one' refer to the model of the portrait or to the writer? And who is borrowing from whom?

The portrait begins under the sign of Picasso's *agalma*: 'One whom some were certainly following' (17). As Mario Perniola explains, in ancient Greece *agalma* indicated the divine image and the economic notion of value, before the invention of money. The word comprises three aspects: wonder or surprise, admiration, and envy or resentment (Perniola 96). The portrait deploys all three aspects: wonder in the incantatory repetitive prose; admiration in the repetition of 'coming out of him,' by suggesting the projection of an individuality in the midst of a uniform creativity; envy when Stein cautiously hints at Picasso's borrowing from her. Picasso has a sought-after value—'it was something' (17)—that Stein wants. Most of all, his *agalma* is linked to the enigmatic language that has already been noted in his early twentieth-century figures. For those obscure gestures amount to the subjective affirmation by which Stein is fascinated in her first portrait of the artist. In Stein's tribute, the moment of artistic gemination—'This one was one having something come out of this one' (18)—effects the synaesthetic convergence of painting and writing. Colors and shapes come out of this one [Picasso?] just as words and voice come out of the writer. Stein tropes Picasso's visual art as voice, that is to say, as writing coming out of her, having public meaning.

Picasso's language of externalization represents the strongest link to his time. His idiolect is the strongest proof of a collective cultural value: 'This one was one having always something being coming out of him, something having completely a real meaning' ('Picasso' 19), that is, a meaning that others can recognize. The publication of the subjective is effortless for Picasso whose affirmative being—his complete charm—can bypass negative dialectic. Around the convergence of individual and public in 'real meaning' revolves not only Picasso's *agalma* but also that of the modern composition, whose main trait is an accord between subject and culture: 'Composition is the thing seen by every one living in the living they are doing' (CAE 523).

Picasso has what Stein wants because he can make public sense of a suppressed, submerged individual world. He is to her what Van Gogh's peasant shoes are to twentieth-century thought—a symbol of authenticity, of an art that has value because it refuses to spread a soft patina of beauty over things. It will be recalled that the salient trait of Van Gogh's shoes is their controlled anxiety. Here is Heidegger's description: 'The equipment is pervaded by uncomplaining anxiety as to the certainty of bread, the wordless joy of having once more withstood want, the trembling before the impending childbed and shivering at the surrounding menace of death' ('The Origin of Work of Art' 34). Similarly, for Stein the beauty of Picasso lies in his uncomplaining anxiety of materiality, revealed not only in his preference for popular culture, for examples circus workers and harlequins, but also in the formal fragile equilibrium of the human figure. This new precarious posture of beauty 'was a solid thing, a charming thing, a lovely thing, a perplexing thing, a disconcerting thing, a simple thing, a clear thing, a complicated thing, an interesting thing, a disturbing thing, a repellant [sic] thing, a very pretty thing' (18).

In her second tribute to the Spaniard, 'If I Told Him: a Completed Portrait of Picasso' (1923), Stein asks him to pass on his *agalma*: 'so to beseech you as full as for it' (21). She attempts a phonic translation of Picasso's affirmative art: 'Shutters shut and open so do queens. Shutters shut and shutters and so shutters shut and shutters and so and so shutters and so shutters shut and so shutters shut and shutters and so. And so shutters shut and so and also. And also and so and so and also' (21-22). When repeated, 'shutters' puns on a kind of innovation that shatters and gives the shudders. In the fragment, the simple gesture of shutting and opening window shutters confers a noble aura on the subject doing it—'and so do queens.' Picasso is recognized as 'king,' the title he had once used for himself to assert an independent spirit that instigates the imitation of others: 'Exactly as as kings' (21). Exactly like Stein's young David Hersland, the painter distinguishes himself by his restless desire to exist: 'He he he he and he and he and and he and he and he and and as and as he and as he and he. He is and as he is, and as he is and he is, he is and as he and he and as he is and he and he and and he and he' (23).

As far as I know, contemporary artist, dancer and choreographer Rachel Germond best renders the Stein-Picasso collaboration as I am trying to present it here, as a *geminatio*, a redoubling that gives Stein the authority to create the modern composition and speak about it. Germond's 1993 *Solo with Black Eggs (For Picasso)* (1993), inspired by Stein's second portrait of the Spanish painter, deals with the empowering appropriation of Picasso's world. From a central dark passage, made of enigmatic gestures that suggest a tormented self-transformation, the dancer emerges as a glittery persona to signify the effect of Picasso's art on Stein.[14]

But Stein's admiration of Picasso also raised the question of her status as a sub-genius,[15] as a secondary writer or aesthetic theorist rather than a leading creator: 'I judge judge./As a resemblance to him' ('If I Told Him' 22). As we have seen, in her academic lecture 'Composition as Explanation' she will present herself as a judge who 'recite[s] what history teaches' ('If I told Him' 25). In 1938, she returned once again to Picasso with a longer monograph. This time, his affirmation 'not of things seen but of things that exist' (*Picasso* 19), part Oriental and part American, serves to refute the death drive that was seizing all Europe.

Paper and Orphic Ditties

Ulla Dydo writes that '[s]wings of mood from excitement to anxiety preoccupied Stein from January until June 1926, when she spoke in England' (*The Language That Rises* 82). It could be said that similar swings of mood extend over Stein's production throughout the 1920s and are openly thematized in many of her pages. After the celebrated *Tender Buttons*, between 1914 and 1919, she wrote over one hundred pieces mostly collected in *Painted Lace, Bee Time Vine, Geography and Plays*, and *As Fine as Melanctha*. They have been described as 'generally commonplace, banal, drawn from the vast stock of phrases used in superficial, everyday social and intimate conversation' (DeKoven 1983; 90). The pieces bear witness to a struggle to go on writing.

Frequent trips and long stays in the south of France, especially Saint Remy and Bilignin, resulted in a symbolic relocation of writing in the countryside as well as in a retrenchment in private life. When compared to the Picasso years, the 1920s seem a time of isolation. This isolation is different from that of the moderns making the composition 'in the living they are doing' (CAE 523). The moderns' isolation implied a positive decentering of creative possibilities. Each participant in the composition felt the right to an active belonging to a common cultural pattern. No one had more value than another, unless, like Picasso, he/she had followers. By contrast, Stein's new isolation is tinged with bitterness and doubt about her literary worth. The elocution that she admired in Picasso seems a past ideal in most of the short pieces of the 1920s. It is followed by Stein's withdrawal into a starker, almost claustrophobic, space dominated by the struggle to keep writing. In one of the pieces in *Geography and Plays*, 'Pink Melon Joy,' in an effort to fight the waning of confidence, she goes as far as devaluing her past and her unpublished manuscripts:

> I had loads of stationary.
> Not pink melon joy. Pink melon joy. (*G&P* 357)

The association of the present to a euphonic plenitude cannot cover over the fear of dead or valueless writing, which in fact is a daily reality. The piece starts with '[p]ugilism' and 'leaning,' alluding to her struggle to write and to her increasing dependence on Toklas and their private life. Stein issues a negative judgment on her work: 'it isn't very good' (*G&P* 358).

The refrain, 'pink melon joy,' hopes for a romantic renewal of the aesthetic emotion (pink) through nature and its fruits (melon), but without success: 'I wish I was restless' (*G&P* 368). Other wishes accumulate, traces of a lost world of strong emotions, belief, and explosive energy:

I wish anger.
I wish religion.
I wish bursts.
I do wish fancies.
Fancy balls.
Blue dresses. Other color cushions. (*G&P* 368)

A voice exhorts her to draw creative energy from private love: 'Please be restless
[…] in kiss' (*G&P* 376).

As she says in 'Braque,' geography is not 'a change of place' but 'a
change of influence' (*G&P* 145). Stein was searching for a new writing that would
revive the spirit of the modern composition without melancholia: 'When I do this
and I am melancholy I remember that rivers, only rivers have suppressed sounds'
(*G&P* 374).

Domestic drama and the recording of ordinary life prepare the transition
to the different writing that will culminate in *Lucy Church Amiably* and *Four
Saints in Three Acts*. The domestic drama of the isolated school of two formed by
Stein and Toklas makes for the backbone of 'Pink Melon Joy,' leading its author to
experiment with a rudimentary collage of voices. There are at least two voices: the
voice of the writer and that of a follower, midway between a sympathetic reader
and protective editor. Her role is to prod the writer on and censure excessive self-
criticism. Here is a fragment with my annotations in square parentheses:

> It is a time for that. [Writer showing her piece]
> Formidable. [Reader's approval]
> Amiable. [Am I lovable, will they like it?]
> Amiable baby. [Of course]
> Fan. [You are a fan; that's why you say it]

Toklas is explicitly named as the editor of the piece:

> I have a real sight. This is critical.
> Alice.

Anxiety is kept under control: 'I didn't complain Susie' (*G&P* 375) and leads to
renewed determination: 'I shall choose wonder. Be best' (*G&P* 375).

A similar retreat into private life can be heard in 'Reread another.' Written
in 1921 and published in *Operas and Plays*, it is made up of voices arranged in
group of non sequiturs. The play cuts from scene 2, to 3, to 4, and back to 3, then
fast-forwards to 9 and 10. Stein has not yet redirected her anxiety productively.
Subtitled, 'A Play/To be played indoors or out/I wish to be a school,' the exercise
openly expounds on the question of value, on having followers, and on attempts to
disguise the dejection caused by the confinement of literary value within the
domestic situation.

Literary self-doubt and domestic claustrophobia reach a climax in 'The King or Something,' another exercise in *Geography and Plays*. The struggle to write is cast as a master-slave combat. The piece illustrates the drama of paper: it is actually an accretion of exercises, a series of numbered pages. Again, the details of daily life feature prominently. References to Stein as mechanic and chaffeur, for example, are employed to create an outer textual layer that conveys reassurance and a sense of well-being: 'very well pleased' (*G&P* 122).

Soon enough, we move toward a more interior textual place where the character of Mrs. Beffa—literally a hoax or joke—rises to mock the writer's effort at producing a text of contentment. Later, self-esteem returns: 'Can you see why I am inspired' (*G&P* 131). As in 'Pink Melon Joy,' the loving other prods on: 'I want to be simple and think./You are very ready to do it. No I don't think so' (*G&P* 133). But the piece ends on a note of self-loathing: 'What does the nigger say today?' The writer has evolved from 'king' to 'nigger,' and Toklas from a yes-saying reader to the regressive figure of a white slaver.[16]

Exercises like 'Pink Melon Joy' and 'The King or Something' are highly self-referential. They move domestic vicissitudes to the center and show a search for creative rejuvenation partly associated with the relocation of the imaginary fount of writing in nature. A bare dramatic structure, with a dialogue of unnamed characters, renders, in a way that would be sustainable for the reader, the swings of moods, from dejection to elation and back, that constitute the substance of Stein's writing in these years. They are valuable when we observe Stein's incorporation of the simple details of daily life and her attempt to emancipate them from their non-literary status. Thus, in 'Pink Melon Joy,' a sequence on the inner turmoil of the writer—'I do mean to win' (*G&P* 366)—is followed by a scene of leave-taking from friend Mildred Aldrich: 'Going up./Good night Mildred./Good night dear.' The intrusion of the ordinary affords momentary relief. It creates the effect of a controlled calm while the Shakespearean echo lends dignity to the banal moment.

Stein went on to refine this composition strategy over the years, with her landscape writing and her turn to drama.[17] As Bonnie Marranca observes in an introduction to *Last Operas and Plays*, Stein's composition strategy is shared by postmodern artists like John Cage. Marranca rightly notes that both Stein and Cage 'gloried in the ordinary, Stein in the lives of words, Cage in the lives of sounds, and goings of friends—in short, the pleasures of company—are casually recorded as text' (xxiv). It is significant that Stein can be seen building bridges with postmodernism at a time when she felt a keen sense of isolation and was understandably anxious about the confinement of her writing to the domestic sphere.

She makes us think about the role that a sense of disconnection from recognizable centers of cultural value (in Stein's case it was Paris and Picasso) plays in the rise of postmodernism. In Stein's view of the modern composition, autonomy was conducive to a sense of public presence. The flat landscape of multiple individualities each working, like Picasso, in isolation nevertheless resolved itself in public expression. By contrast, the loss of value that is felt in the pieces of the 1920s does not have the sound of a public exit, of an accord between subject and culture. From an aesthetic tenet of innovation, anxiety becomes a private drama to be played out within the enclosure of a school of two and to be kept under control by the casual recording of the details of ordinary life. If the ordinary becomes central to postmodernism, changing from symptom of literary isolation to distinctive stylistic feature, then it might be legitimate to ask to what extent, from Stein to postmodernism, the ordinary has served to mediate the desire of a 'publication,' of an exit into the openness of culture. Moreover, the question remains open whether this exit constitutes a new feeling, a new passion of the self, and whether it indicates a generalized, global need.

A discussion of *Lucy Church Amiably* will help to clarify such questions. The alternation of contentment and self-doubt in the pieces of the 1920s is also the main ingredient of *Lucy Church Amiably* (1927-1931). For the greater part, however, the narrative promotes the vision of a regained serenity which, contrary to the earlier pieces, harmonizes private life and writing. The new accord is reached by projecting the potentially claustrophobic isolation of the school of two outside, onto the pleasant countryside of southern France, the land of Lamartine and Brillat-Savarin. For the greater part, the narrative is an eclogue in Virgil's tradition. It extols the simplicity of frugal country living against the city, typically characterized by the unbridled course of wealth and power. In the country 'Everybody is rich quietly' (*LCA* 19). Nature is the imaginative seat of a moderate writing of contentment with the ordinary life. Not until we have made our way first through the preliminary notes and then through the actual novel, with its seductive but unattainable female lead, is the eclogue ruined and the enchantment broken:

> Paper and paper pay her.
> Pay her pay her for the paper.
> Pay her for the paper.
> By her pay her pay her pay her for the paper. (*LCA* 200)

Stein's commercial enjoins the reader to pay for the pages of a novel that roams and tarries, like a leisurely walk in the countryside. The material metaphor for reading, paper, is haunted by the specter of value (paper as in dead writing). But here the anxiety and bitterness of 'The King of Something,' for example, successfully modulates into a certain iconoclastic playfulness that only a contented authority could perhaps afford. This novel and, above all, its lovable heroine are entirely an affair between Stein and her future audience: she is inviting, provoking, cajoling, shamelessly using Lucy's beauty: 'b[u]y her.'

In the game of reading, as in the game of love, Lucy Church wins because she is elusive. She changes endlessly. Importantly, she first appears as a reference to Stein's highly individual style: she is an inspired writer who 'made master-pieces readily and excitedly' (*LCA* 59). She becomes a church 'surmounted by a pagoda and illustrated by a crown of red blue and pretty lights' (63). She is an architectural presence with feelings and desires: 'very impressed by having been very much and very pleasantly surrounded by what she feels and felt to be very much what is desirable and that is pleasantly' (69); she is the tutelary spirit of a place (the French locality of Lucey, near Belley) in an idyll complete with 'butterfly on river' (67). She is two women 'Lucy Church and Lucy Pagoda on the border by a river' (77), who subsequently become one, Lucy Church Pagoda. At the peak of the eclogue we are informed that Lucy Church is 'an authority' (85). Through this seductive principle of unattainable meaning Stein manages to think of her writing as desirable and predicts Lucy's public triumph despite her literary difference, which might induce some to think of her as simply 'paper': 'They loved to pay her for the paper' (200). The novel ends with a vision of publication.

Before *Lucy Church Amiably* Stein had tried to represent a metaphorical public exit but without success. In 'Capital Capitals' (1917) she had experimented with the economic metaphor to render the happy confluence of private life and public discourse. In the background of post-war penury, basic needs become collective desires. Even the most ordinary things all of a sudden become yearned-for commodities: 'Water can be bought' (64). Here, in line with what Baudrillard has called seduction, Stein is enticed by the urban landscape of merchandise and by its power to shape a surface made of lively objects calling out to the human agent. The call of the objects unifies people through similar desires. She affirms, however, the preference for a negativity that is 'capitally capable' (69) of exchanging nothing apart from pleasing sounds: 'Combs for combs and lilies for lilies./Lilies for lilies./Combs for combs./Buds for buds'(69). But 'Capital capitals' lacks any semblance of structure and can hope to make an impact on the reader only with the addition of the human voice.[18] By contrast, the economic metaphor is much less pervasive in *Lucy Church Amiably*. Although 'merchandise is always a pleasure' (*LCA* 63), and nature is described in economic terms as 'advantageous' (*LCA* 37), one of the purposes of the narrative is to suggest almost an architectural construction, with Lucy's ordinary life actively withstanding the vortex of merchandise-based wealth. In Lucy's world, 'they are rich and richer every day in the ordinary meaning of the word' (*LCA* 24). The point of the eclogue is to contrast the unbridled convolutions of capitalist wealth with the contentment and moderation of Lucy's elusiveness. This elusiveness is a poetic extension of the modern composition.[19]

As I have already suggested, for Stein the modern composition must externalize 'suppressed sounds' (G&P 374). In his *Sonnets to Orpheus*, Rilke had similarly spoken of an 'invisible poem' [unsichtbares Gedicht], a counterbalance [Gegengewicht] to the writing self, providing the rhythm—and reason—of his or her acts of literature (156-57). The externalization of a subjective language had attracted Stein to Picasso and to the enigmatic gestures of his noble human figures. Lucy Church fits in with Stein's attempt to prolong the beauty of the modern composition. She creates a transformative poetic principle, adapting it from a classic tradition of poetry that challenges power in the name of a more humble private idiom, and thus contrasts the homogenizing impulse of the aggressively transparent style of merchandise communication.[20] Lucy's elusiveness extends the modern composition, understood as an affirmative exit into the openness of public language, but as the agrarian setting shows, it does not equate the exit to the seduction of merchandise.

The new serenity of *Lucy Church Amiably* parallels Picasso's turn to tradition and his themes of nature, nurture and care. The elegance of his figures, the harmonious gestures and the majesty of the bodies bear clear traces of the 'Italian seduction' (*Picasso* 521), of his exposure, that is, during the 1917 trip, to the works of antiquity in Rome, Naples, and Pompei. He nods to the Renaissance masters with his portraits of women with veils.[21] The references to antiquity result in the melancholy and introspective air of the figures. One of his most popular images of this period, *The Lovers* (1923), embodies all these traits, bespeaking a renegotiation of artistic self-consciousess. In paintings such as *Three Women at the Spring* (1921) he 'represent[s] the Arcadian, unproblematic presence of these powerful bodies' (Jaffe' 104). The scene that generates the narrative of *Lucy Church Amiably* is a variation on Picasso's theme of the woman by the fount. By a running brook a woman sits and nods to the gurgling water: 'Select your song she said and it was done with a nod and then she bent her head in the direction of the falling water. Amiably' (*LCA* 19). Lucy possesses the charm of Picasso's affirmative creativity in Stein's first portrait of him: 'Lucy Church you can tell yes and yes. Yes and yes. You can tell less and less you can tell yes and yes' (128). The subtitle of Stein's novel informs that it 'looks like an engraving.' Lucy is the icon of a poetic principle whose romance it is difficult to resist because it promises a natural accord between poet and song, dancer and dance. She combines in herself Sir Philip Sidney's 'poesy,' a gentler mother tongue or, as Stein says, 'the milk of human tenderness' (*LCA* 174) and Picasso's yes-saying art. Above all, as an unresisting, pleasure-arousing unit of meaning, she tropes Picasso's public elocution as a more private peace and fulfilment. She is an object that placates creative restlessness, preferring low-key Orphic ditties to high songs: 'did not sing it is not the habit of the country to sing' (129).

Despite her value, Lucy turns out to be a 'disappointment' (208), and Stein's text reverts back to implosion and isolation. *The Autobiography of Alice B. Toklas* contains an anecdote about the publication of the novel. Seeing her book displayed in the bookstore windows, 'gave Gertrude Stein a childish delight amounting to almost ecstasy' (*AABT* 229). Stein recognizes herself in the object on display. But this is simultaneously a moment of misrecognition since the book is a (totalising) metaphor for her person. Publication, like Lacan's mirror stage, inflects the self in a fictional, imaginary direction.

In 1930, Picasso's *Woman with a Fan* (1905) was sold to finance the Plain Edition, a press run by Toklas and devoted to the publication of Stein's writing. The sale is highly symbolic. *Lucy Church Amiably* was the first book in the catalogue. It is as if Stein were trading Picasso and the modern composition for the new autonomy of the self-promoted and self-financed author, an autonomy which, as Stein's Lacanian jubilation suggests, comes with its problems. 'I am sorry you are confused' (*LCA* 209), writes Stein, apologizing for her post-Picasso anguish:

'Lucy Church followed and came and came pleasantly to have anguish' (*LCA* 207). Translating Lucy Church into a postmodern literary object, Ellen Berry has demonstrated that Stein has no need to apologize.

Ellen Berry has effectively explained Lucy's seductive elusiveness in terms of postmodern undecidability. Elaborating on DeKoven, who saw Lucy as a 'thematic center' responsible for the 'active and energetic but unperturbed, untroubled sense of union with the natural world' (*A Different Language* 131), Berry argues that Lucy is a unit of 'semantic dispersion' (99), owing to her utter mutability. Berry equates the heroine's transformative energy with the postmodern 'call for an art of permanent negativity that 'dissolves identity—even sexual identity—in the name of a feminist practice at odds with what already exists' (108). One of the strong points of Berry's argument is the kinship between Lucy's desirable elusiveness and postmodern undecidability. This kinship owes something to Berry's wish to emancipate Stein from the critical discourse of the 1980s with its essentialist, 'gyno-or femino-centric' focus. At that time, the risk was to reduce Stein's experimental writing to the status of a feminist ideological apparatus. Berry, instead, while retaining a feminist slant, removes Stein's writing in a less ossified, more open and comprehensive landscape of critical positions loosely united by the appreciation of an 'ontological undecidability' (Berry 108). Thus Berry's becomes an important reading because it accomplishes critically what Stein saw as the aesthetic emotion of the modern composition—the production of an exit into the openness of culture. I am not saying that undecidability is a modernist thing. There are, however, similarities between undecidability as Berry explains it and the modern composition as Stein understood it. Berry's critical approach ends up shifting the burden of self-referentiality (and doubts about value) from Stein to her readers, something that Stein had desired to do.

For Berry, Lucy's transformative energy illustrates postmodernism's expansion of the boundaries of narrative space through the materiality of language. Opposing traditional coherence, such materiality fosters a negativity which in fact aims at projecting 'an affirmative, desiring space of potential—held open, in motion.—elsewhere' (Berry 108). Undecidability attracts because it can project an 'elsewhere.' The materiality of language applies to narrative linearity and cohesive meaning a pressure capable of producing an exit of culture itself into a more 'open space.' Thus, from the vantage point of Berry's reading, postmodernism, with its attention to change and differences, can best appreciate Stein's personal effort to break out of her individual isolation as, in fact, a generalized public desire. The postmodern imagination, moreover, can value Stein's contradictions. On the one hand, she thought of writing as an individual act, opposed to an act of communication, and was anxious about appearing in public. On the other hand, she placed a high aesthetic value on the accord of subjective and public meaning, as her admiration for Picasso's shows.

It was not easy, after Picasso, to imagine the freedom of a cultural openness. In *Lucy Church Amiably*, 'nature,' with the serenity, contentment, and plenitude that emanate from it, counters private isolation and literary doubt.

Insofar as Lucy's undecidability successfully challenges Stein's bitterness and sense of neglect, it asks to what extent self-doubt and isolation might also be part of postmodern aesthetics. This privileges the materiality of the medium to project a public space of potentiality on the side of differences and transformation. By way of Berry, Stein's attempt to escape isolation becomes the postmodern motif of a culture that threatens to be an enclosure. We seem to share with Stein the loss of a sense of real value and the employment of the creative medium to approximate a more amiable elsewhere.

Chapter 6

From Song to Image: *Four Saints in Three Acts*

Preliminary remarks

Juliana Spahr has argued that Stein's work is more innovative than that of other established modernists like T. S. Eliot or Ezra Pound, because 'it points to a polylingual American literature' (31). Spahr usefully catalogs the most recurrent deviations from grammar norms, such as unusually inclusive and complex sentences, phrasal or incomplete sentences, nonstandard qualifiers and/or verb use, duplicate words and restricted vocabulary, and word confusion (27-30) to show the similarity of Stein's writing to the linguistic patterns of second-language speakers (27). Thus what in Stein studies is usually taken for textual polysemy or even indeterminacy in Spahr's study appears as the effects of a diasporic condition. Against a critical tradition that associates diaspora with an essential ethnic identity Stein's experimental works, proposes Spahr, 'present a story of American immigrant literature that is anti-assimilation, that celebrates mistake and insists that there is no hope for a monolingual United States or literature' (31). In this chapter I still employ the resources of polysemy to argue that Stein was concerned about national monolingualism, at least on a conceptual level. *Four Saints in Three Acts* is a rich poetic text about the temptations of monolingualism, a song of social harmony, which Stein, via William James, sees at the heart of American literature. Through a cautious allegory of religious life, the libretto tells the story of an individual's insertion in the community, linking the assumption of public identity to issues of beauty. What do we love? What pleases us? Above all, what placates the violence or death-drive in the community? The libretto reckons with the pressures of a literary monolingualism or a poetry of social harmony and ends up raising larger questions of aesthetic and critical reception. Stein's text no longer assumes that we can make sense of literature because it reflects the interests of particular social groups. Rather, the reader is invited to consider literature, and the attending art of interpretation, in terms of the aesthetic and critical problem of public speech and how many can join in. How much do private acts of meaning— personal associations, memories, and so on—weigh on the public act of interpretation? What is the difference between a 'private' reader and a 'public' critic? Stein builds bridges with contemporary aesthetics, which, as is known, is particularly impatient about this boundary. Stein's contribution to a 'rethinking of the aesthetics of cultural critique' (Spahr 31), might be in her questions about criticism as the public sphere of interpretation.

Written before *Lucy Church Amiably* and set to music by Virgil Thompson, *Four Saints in Three Acts*, was not produced until 1934. In that year, the opera was first performed at the Hartford Atheneum in Hartford, Connecticut, under the auspices of the Friends and Enemies of Modern Music, with Alexander Smallens as conductor. Frederick Ashton and John Houseman were in charge of the staging. It went on to became a success in New York and Chicago. Since then it has been in the repertoire of major opera singers like Betty Allen and Leontyne Price, of avant-garde directors like Robert Wilson, and has been danced by the Mark Morris Group.[1] For its first production, Virgil Thomson chose Frederick Ashton as choreographer and staging director. The production's strongest supporter was Stein's press agent, Carl Van Vechten, who reveled in the fashionable cult of Negro chic. He encouraged the production and hosted a premiere in his living room (Watson 202). An all black cast was chosen. As we shall see, there are significant differences between the staged opera and Stein's original libretto.[2]

Like *Lucy Church Amiably*, Stein's original libretto seems preoccupied with creating a lovable heroine: 'To know to know to love her so' *(O&P 11)*. But this time instead of Lucy's undecidability, Stein prefers a *prima donna* divided between ordinary life and religious vocation, eros and caritas, inside and outside. 'The garden inside and outside of the wall' *(O&P 16)*, says Saint Therese, meaning the equally desirable pleasures of interior and worldly life. Despite her divided mind, she joins an increasingly larger community. Saint Therese's calling becomes a narrative device for the aesthetic enjoyment of collective units in space: 'There are a great many persons and places near together' *(O&P 16)*.

There have been speculations about Stein's choice of subject matter as it clearly marks a departure in her repertoire.[3] But perhaps the importance of this choice for her new turn toward landscape writing has not been sufficiently considered. A distinctive feature of the libretto is that religious life seems to be highly functional to the visual projection of a harmonious social bond: groups of saints lend themselves to being visually projected as ordered communities moving in space. Bonded by their calling, saints form a human group made visually compact by that premise. They represent a social body that is least disbanded by conflict and violence. As Stein implies in her lecture 'Plays,' when seen from a distance groups of nuns—or friars—have the virtue of becoming 'pieces of things [. . .] in a landscape' *(LA 129)*. The visual geometry of saints is perturbed neither by the death drive, which military masses instead would evoke, nor by hysteria, which modern crowds would evoke. Landscape becomes a still life of the social bond in a pleasant, non-threatening state of repose—an image of social beauty: 'all these saints together made my landscape' *(LA 129)*. Landscape writing is not about movement, narrative movement, for example: 'nothing really moves in a landscape but things are there' *(LA 129)*. Landscape is about things, compact groups frozen into pleasing forms, suspended as if in the air. This is why a landscape 'if it ever did go away would have to stay' *(LA 131)*. It is made of lasting forms that appease and can be contemplated without endangering the observer's sense of identity, without instilling fear and anxiety. In a landscape beauty depends on its capacity to make the viewer imagine a non-punishing, non-exclusive social bond, with which 'anybody looking on can keep in time' (*LA* 131).

Before moving on with the discussion I will briefly sum up the plot.[4] The libretto was inspired by the life of Saint Teresa of Avila, whose name becomes Therese. It relates Saint Therese's difficult progress toward her integration into a religious community. At first she is 'seated' (*O&P* 16), a part of the group, and then surrounded by 'a great many saints seated' (*O&P* 17), a position that alludes to her role as founder of a movement. Disregarding chronology, Stein has Saint Ignatius, who never met the woman from Avila, become a major influence in her conversion.

Act I opens with the storm at Avila and the sensuous image of the 'warm snow' (*O&P* 15), referring to Therese's calling. From now on, Therese will have to learn to distinguish sensuality from religious vocation, self-interest from caritas. By the end, transformed into a nun—'being widowed (*O&P* 18)—she 'can know the difference between snow and thirds' *(O&P* 23).[5] The final libretto, fruit of the Thomson-Stein collaboration, adds to Stein's original text a Commère and a Compère, translators with the reader of Therese's and Ignatius's thoughts. They announce, for example, the protagonist's renunciation of private life for a communal bond: 'She can have no one no one can have anyone' (*O&P* 17).[6] The final libretto, moreover, doubles the heroine, after having changed her name from Therese back to Teresa. It also adds two choruses to amplify the heroine's wavering between her interior calling and worldly joys. The two choruses explain that she is 'half inside and half outside' (*O&P* 16). The Commère, spokeswoman for Theresa's innermost feelings, clearly proclaims what the problem of the opera is: 'St. Therese and attachment' (*O&P* 20).

Virgil Thomson explained that the opera uses religious life to make a statement about the life of the artist.[7] Among the saints, Saint Fernande, the name of Picasso's lover at the time he and Stein were intimate, alludes to the Parisian avant-garde. But perhaps the strongest reference to art and writing is Stein's heroine. A woman divided between the pleasures of ordinary life and an interior call, in the middle of her progress she asks 'Can women have wishes' (*O&P* 18). As Therese's interior calling tropes Stein's modernist attachment to writing, the question implies another: Can women write? That is to say, Can women aspire to a public recognition of their writing? Therese is Stein's occasion to tie the public value of artistic vocation to its material and historical contexts, resisting the utopian strain of modernism. If, as Thomson said, the saint is a metaphor for the artist, Saint Teresa of Avila, also renowned as a writer, allows Stein to consider the usefulness of literature for the human community.

The choice of the saint as the libretto's protagonist marks a change in Stein's aesthetic views, from Picasso's modern composition, with its emphasis on the externalization of a subjective language, to a more public form of 'poetry.' In part the shift is prompted by Stein's need to escape isolation. In part, it issues from an increasing interest in the social dimension of the self, which implies a legitimate feeling of cultural belonging. With Saint Teresa of Avila Stein found a popular icon of woman's intellect as identified with social service, all the more so given her religious vocation. Overall Act I shows how Therese's interior call leads her to a public identity as the member of a collectivity of saints. Stein exploits to her advantage popular representations of Saint Teresa, like Bernini's marble group, in which her interior call is a metaphor for a passion of the self and vice-versa. In the libretto's final version, Chorus II makes us hear the rhyme connecting Teresa's inner turmoil and her desire for community: 'In clouded./Included' (*O&P* 20).

Act II celebrates Therese's calling through movement: 'Can any one feel any one moving' (*O&P* 27) and a language that strongly relies on visuality: 'Might with widow' (*O&P* 27). The visual identity of Therese as a nun, dressed in black like a widow, indicates her removal   in a collective landscape suggestive of the power of the social bond to shatter individual identity:

> Saint Therese.   Might be third.
> Saint Therese.   Might be heard.
> Saint Therese   Might be invaded. (*O&P* 33)

Act III opens with a collective scene: male saints mending fishnets in a monastery garden, singing the joys of the interior call and the holy marriage to Christ: 'within it within it within it as a wedding for them in half of the time' (*O&P* 36). Then during the vision of the Holy Ghost, Saint Ignatius sits surrounded by a groups of saints. Saints coalesce in spatial volumes and geometries of human subjects who can do without the gaze of others. As Saint Ignatius puts it, a saint 'might be admired for himself alone' (*O&P* 38). The bonded groups of saints intone the praises of a community free from negative passions like envy, anger, and consternation. Nevertheless, the gaze is central in Stein's landscape writing. For this writing is about spatially objectified collectivities that the gaze apprehends as a social song of equality and harmony. When singing the praises of the collectivity, the character of Saint Ignatius is also praising the power of the gaze to construe social beauty: 'Foundationally marvelously aboundingly illimitably' (*O&P* 40). For Saint Therese, inclusion in the community is a conquest she strives for. Responding to Saint Ignatius' social song, she falters: 'Intending to be intending to intending to to to to. To do it for me' (*O&P* 41). The attraction of the social song is the theme of the opera and Stein's concern at the time. Her landscape writing poses the question of the aesthetic shaping of social masses into compact ordered units. Concomitantly, via the metaphors of singing and of the interior call, she asks about the role of poetry in the making of these geometries. The question about Therese's religious vocation, 'How many nails are there in it' (25) in Act II, is echoed in Act IV—'How many acts are there in it' (45)—to suggest the problems ('nails') now faced by Stein in her writing. As we shall see, it is in act IV, an added part, that Stein builds bridges with contemporary aesthetics and issues of public reception. First it is necessary to consider the formal strategies of the libretto and

Stein's attraction for a social song, with the 'nails' that it implies, as a point of contact with the American literary tradition.

Memory fragments

The inception of the libretto, Stein tells us, was in some photographs she saw in a Paris shop window:

> As it happened there is on the Boulevard Raspail a place where they make photographs that have always held my attention. They take a photograph of a young girl dressed in the costume of her ordinary life and little by little in successive photographs they change it into a nun. The photographs are small and the thing takes four to five changes but at the end it is a nun and this is done for the family when the nun is dead and in memoriam. (*LA* 130)

The charm of Stein's Saint Therese has its origins in photography. For Stein photography's power to still human life, and freeze it as if in a mortuary mask, evokes the transformation of the private individual into a collective subject (Therese's change from girl to nun). Saint Therese was born in the streets and in the visual display of shop windows. This synchronic dimension is as important as the diachronic narrative of Baroque saints. Materiality and spirituality, past and present, mingle in Stein's landscape: 'Then as I said streets and windows are also landscape and they added to my Spanish landscape' (*LA* 130).

For the vision of the Holy Ghost in Act III, she chooses a magpie instead of the traditional dove because its black plumage with white streaks rhymes visually with Therese's new public identity as a nun: 'and the magpie in the sky on the sky and to try and to try (*O&P* 36). Precisely because the magpie is not an entirely positive image, it conveys Therese's tension and indecision. Moreover, the image's chromatic consonance with the young woman's future identity helps suspend this identity in the sky, as an object of peaceful contemplation, indeed 'on the sky,' that is to say, starkly in relief against the blue background, as if seen in a painting. The consonance between the magpie and Saint Therese's uniform tells of the important role that the contemplation of forms plays in the inclusion of the individual in a community. The vision of the magpie happens after Ignatius and Therese have begun to roam away from Barcelona to spread the Gospel and thus are on their way to taking up their place in a community of many: 'All and all Saints' (*O&P* 29).[8] The narrative is driven by the labor of this inclusion. In light of Therese's wavering between worldly joys and religious calling, her integration into a public pattern of saints could take a while. She keeps wondering 'how much of it is finished' (30) and whether four acts 'could be ten' (31). These self-referential moments confirm the catalyst function of meaningful forms in the achievement of public identity, while the spatial view of public identity all the more throws into relief the problem of integration into a harmonious whole.

The genesis of the image is indicative of the formal dynamism with which the libretto develops the theme of public identity. In 'Plays,' Stein tells her audience that the image of the magpie formed over a number of years (*LA* 130) from looking at the photographs in the shop window. But other memories converge in it. It is also an adaptation from the dove in paintings of the Annunciation: 'They look exactly like the Birds in the Annunciation pictures the bird which is the Holy Ghost and rests flat against the side sky very high' *(LA* 129). The word 'flat,' used in 'Plays' becomes 'on the sky' in the libretto. The magpie *on* the sky is the evocation of painterly forms that are starkly silhouetted against a background to appear as if suspended. Apart from the mystery and solemnity of certain forms, 'on' also suggests the state of suspension of forms once they have passed into the memory of the beholder, to be transformed into unclear units of manifold meaning. The rhyme of the magpie with a solitary nun might emerge from memories of the '400 masters. Among them, Piero della Francesca perhaps best illustrates the quality that impressed Stein in a composition where everything seems suspended, immobile, as if in pose. In the Annunciation scene, part of the *Polyptych of Saint Anthony* [Polittico di Sant' Antonio] (1450-1468), the dove is silhouetted 'flat,' as Stein would say, 'on' the fragment of sky to the upper left side in a painting otherwise occupied by a dynamic marble colonnade.[9]

Stein's magpie echoes Piero's suspended, hieratic shapes, whose theatrical pose does not seem alien to the narrative of Saint Therese. The meaningful image and the atmosphere originate in layers of private memories of city scenes, art images, landscapes—Avila but perhaps also Perugia and Assisi—all condensed together, not all of them traceable, for which Therese's transformation provides a strong expressive channel. Past and present, the diachronic and the synchronic levels, visual seduction and intellectual insights all converge in a synaesthetic inebriation that seems the core procedure of the libretto, at least until Act IV.

In the passage on the vision of the Holy Ghost the magpie's severe chromatic play of black and white is flanked by a softer panel: 'Pigeons on the grass alas' (*O&P* 36), a memory fragment that within the context of saints cannot fail to recall Giotto's fresco *St. Francis Preaching to the Birds* (1295-1297/1299). Part of the cycle on the life of Saint Francis, the scene is awash in misty blues, greens, and browns.[10] The vision culminates in a euphonic chant, an arabesque of melodious women's names like Lucy and Lily, sung in the final libretto collectively by the saints: 'Let Lucy Lily Lily Lucy Lucy let Lucy Lucy Lily Lily Lily Lily let Lily Lucy Lucy let Lily. Let Lucy Lily' (*O&P* 36). Thus, the vision of the Holy Ghost, omen of Theresa's public identity, culminates in collective melody, a social song of enjoyment free from the clamor and fury of the human passions. This is landscape: the visual projection of a collective melody patched up from bits and pieces of confused individual associations.

Suspended in the sky, just as Saint Therese in a nun's uniform hovers over our imagination, the black and white shape conjures the thought of mimetic correspondences between the visual composition and a more tender human tie. But the magpie has negative connotations. Magpies are seen in dumps. They are attracted by shiny metal objects, which they steal to their nest, and do not sing. In Stein's libretto, the black and white form of the magpie, though more in a detached and theatrical way than in a lyrical one, fulfills a similar function to the swallow in Pier Paolo Pasolini's poem 'L'Umile Italia' [Humble Italy], included in the poetic sequence *Gramsci's Ashes*. In Pasolini's poem the swallow is the figure of a humble, earthly, perhaps secondary feeling that cannot be conceptualized and perhaps cannot be sung. The swallow intimates in those who look on a strange feeling, hard to describe and easily mistaken for indifference or nostalgia (Pasolini 31). Like Stein's magpie, Pasolini's swallow is a suspended visual center of meaning. In Stein's libretto the unholy bird is made sweeter by its chromatic consonance with Saint Therese's uniform. Pasolini's swallow is already 'holy' in its humility as a minor bird, author of 'sweet inlaid works' in the sky (54). The swallow's beautiful graffiti are news from 'a-chromatic/places' [incolori/luoghi] outside history and time. They are the cryptic signs of a social community linked to an originary poetry that cannot be revealed to the human eye but must be sung (50). Unlike Pasolini's swallow, Stein's magpie is still and silent. It comes from places midway between the mortuary mask of photography and the feast of painting. But it does intimate the suspended interrogative pattern that in his poem Pasolini calls 'muted fury' [sopita furia] (13). However different, the magpie and the swallow are on a continuum: they replace John Keats's nineteenth-century silent but violated bride in symbolizing the troubles of the poet who wants to raise his voice for collective uses: he must forcefully look to the past and to art objects for the power of decoding signs that he cannot sing. In both cases, an austere chromatic composition of blacks and whites flooded in the ravishing Southern European light around Easter time alludes to a humble social tie, a desirable social rhythm, more concrete because closer to the land, to earth.[11]

Elaine Scarry writes of the beauty of political arrangements when these, condensed into a circumscribed space, are made available to the senses. She mentions the great assembly hall from the present and the trireme from ancient Greece as examples of a beauty that depends on making the social arrangements visually available to sensory experience: 'the trireme ships, the ships whose 170 oars and 170 oarsmen could, like a legislative assembly, be held within the small bowl of visual space of which a human perceiver is capable, and whose rhythmic striking of the water, in time with the pipeman's flute, could also be held within the finite auditory compass of a perceiver' (104). Stein is aiming for a similar effect. Her groups of saints move across the landscape from Barcelona to Avila (*O&P* 27) as if they were the harmonious volumes from a Giotto fresco or from a fifteenth-century painting after him. They represent images of collectivities that 'stay in the air' (*LA* 130): they hover in the observer's mind like stories awaiting to be spun. Stein's Saint Therese is a stand-in for the human observer, 'half in doors and half out of doors' (O&P 15), contemplating a 'rhythmic equality' (Scarry 103) of the saints' arrangement.

Four Saints in Three Acts has a special place in Stein's canon. At this point, she is preoccupied with the possibility of song, a metaphor for poetry and aesthetic emotion in general, as it must relate to society. The new interest prompts an examination of her ties to an American tradition of thought on the uses of art. As we shall see in the next section, Stein's Saint Therese, in part, comes from William James's *Varieties of Religious Experience*. In James, Saint Teresa's religious calling also poses the question of textual truth. But Stein's interest in the uses of poetry, as we shall see in the last section of this chapter, leads her to an openness toward contemporary aesthetics. This deals with the question of social inclusiveness by encouraging multiple interpretations or by further consigning interpretation itself to the challenge of individual associations and the effort to make public sense of them.

William James, Saint Teresa, and beauty

The points of contacts between William James's *Varieties of Religious Experience: A Study in Human Nature* and Stein's *Four Saints in Three Acts* are striking. James's text was delivered as a series of twenty lectures at Edinburgh between 1901 and 1902 as part of the Gifford Lectures on Natural Religion. He expands the definition of religious experience to comprehend three levels: saintliness, social life, and art. As the three meanings merge in the notion of saintliness, James can assign to religious experience the lyrical power to evoke a latent human grammar of social justice. Saint Teresa of Avila occupies a pivotal place in James's argument. In the first part, she helps him establish the similarity between saints and artists and further advance the thesis of a pragmatist textual truth recognizable in the impact of the message and the changes it provokes. Later on in the study James adds a third term to his set of similarities, that between saints and socially reactive people at large, and at that point Saint Teresa is dismissed as a narcissist formalist interested only in recording on paper her amorous flirtations with God. Saint Teresa's writing becomes an impediment to James's triangulation of saintliness, aesthetics, and society. James argues that it is not a socially useful way of setting a good example for others.

I will now go into the details of James's argument to show how, in part, Stein shares it. But my main interest is to suggests that she moves on. In James's study, as in Stein's libretto, the contemplation of saints leads to the reduction of potentially perturbing social groups to pleasing visual geometries. But Stein resists the modulation of art into forms of collective cognition, which is instead implied by James's triangulation. Unlike James, she aims at a dissociation of the aesthetic from the social context. With the dissociation she can resist the subordination of art to a collective assent. It is in this way that she begins to build bridges with contemporary aesthetic theories that value a rapprochement of production and reception, artist and viewer, emphasizing the role of the spectator's individual associations in interpretation.

In the first part of his study James takes up the skepticism afflicting those who have attained religious truth. People react to saints as they do to exceptional and eccentric individuals, including the creatively talented. Saints are like artists: they are accused of being insane or degenerate (James 35). Having established the similarity, by the time he defends Saint Teresa of Avila from the accusation of hysteria, he is also implicitly defending the creative genius:

> Immediate luminousness, in short, philosophical reasonableness, and moral helpfulness are the only available criteria. Saint Teresa might have had the nervous system of the placidest cow, and it would not now save her theology, if the trial of the theology by these other tests should show it to be contemptible. And conversely if her theology can stand these other tests, it will make no difference how hysterical or nervously off her balance Saint Teresa may have been when she was with us here below (39).

Vision, supernatural revelation, hearing, automatic utterance: these are some of the origins of truth in religious history (40). Thus, to investigate religious experience means to get to the question of truth: How can we tell that what the saint says has any value? But, given the similarity between saints and geniuses, the question also applies to the latter: How can we tell literary or artistic truth from hysteria? Religious experience helps pose the question of how authors are canonized: on the basis, that is, of the evidence of their qualification to speak.

What qualifies the author to speak? James answers: the results, the effects of his or her speech. He finds this answer thanks to an interesting collaboration between Saint Teresa and Jonathan Edwards. It is always possible to tell genuine from fake religious experience. He invokes the empiricism of Jonathan Edwards: 'By their fruits you shall know them' (41). He proceeds to quote Edwards and Saint Teresa back to back. The words of the author of *The Treatise on Religious Affections*—'the degree in which our experience is productive of practice shows the degree in which our experience is spiritual and divine' (qtd. in James 41)—are echoed by a similar statement by Saint Teresa. To the question: How can we tell truth from deception?, the Spanish saint answers that, while the work of imagination can be identified by the 'lassitude and disgust' it leaves behind (qtd. in James 21), by contrast, 'a genuine heavenly vision yields [. . .] a harvest of spiritual riches, and an admirable renewal of bodily strength' (James 41). In the saintly realm, truth is, in Teresa's words, the 'masculine courage' (qtd. in James 41) with which the message impacts those on the receiving end. The implication is that this pragmatist measure of truth might be valid also for art.

James further cements the similarity between saints and artists arguing that the moods of the saint are the same that accompany the creative act. In religious experience, happiness, melancholy, trance are the contextual elements of the insight into truth, but these also point to 'a human experience of a much wider scope' (44). In the saint, as in the artist, a higher intellectual faculty (especially the faculty of association by similarity) combines with a certain 'emotional excitability' (262), manifesting itself as 'impatience, grimness, earnestness, severity of character' (262), a willingness to live with energy, though it brings pain. Saintliness, like creativity, is a state of 'astringency and desolation' (262) in which 'stern joy' (262) is taken. This is an important turn in James's argument, which proceeds toward the homologation of saints, artists, and citizens at large.

While asserting the similarity of moods between the saint and the artist, James introduces the more general notion of 'energetic character' (262). In this category the saint and the artist converge. Thus, when a bit later he speaks of 'energetic saints' (265), the expression sounds redundant. By now saintliness has passed not only into the literary notion of talent but further into the wider notion of human character. He speaks of a character 'free of all that inner friction and nervous waste' (263) and of 'inhibition-quenching fury' (263). He concludes his psychological remarks by adding that energy means having creative ideals. After this flight into character, as he returns to the specific religious terrain, his two primary examples of 'energetic saints,' Saint Teresa and Saint Ignatius Loyola (265), have come to suggest any human subject distinguished by the same creative destruction of which saints and geniuses alike are capable. Saints and artists share the power to say 'no' to inhibitions and norms. They, therefore, represent a reactive position to the society in which they live. James's saintliness is an affect existing against the sprawling background of a composition that the lectures' subtitle calls 'human nature.' In fact, James's language of negativity—friction, waste, and fury—translates human nature into a social wilderness of conflicts and stagnant public beliefs.

Saintliness, somehow, takes on a reparative role in relation to the surrounding social wilderness. But so does the reception of art. For James, the saint's emotional excitement can demolish the stonewalls of 'paltry conventionalities' (265), while novels and the theater educate the audience to a similar capacity for 'melting moods' (265). When theater spectators or readers of novels weep, their tears break inveterate inner divisions; 'moral stagnancies drain away' (265). The stern joy typical of saints like Teresa and Ignatius is accessible to any reader or viewer through the fruition of art, and it is linked to the transmission of a more fluid social bond. Art is a social balm.

Modeled on Saint Teresa's admirable renewal, James's aesthetic emotion is valuable insofar as it alters, albeit momentarily, the social composition, making it appear less ossified, less compartmentalized, a vista in which the internal divisions promise to dissolve in fluid communication. Consequently, beauty is inseparable from cognition. Artistic enjoyment is in fact one among other experimental forms of perception, like hypnosis for example, aimed at temporarily dissolving rigid social norms and at modifying our perception of the social sphere. James's Saint Teresa and Saint Ignatius are political saints, germane to the modernist artist who invests his or her creations with the power to displace deeply ingrained and oppressive symbolic structures.[12] But only apparently does James's view bear affinities with contemporary theory's interest in a subject beyond power.

In fact, his focus remains on the uses of aesthetic experience to bend knowledge in a gentler direction.

We have seen how the saint is an unstable signifier: one moment it means the artist, the next a generic citizen. A few pages later, James notices that one attribute of saintliness is poverty. In a world divided into those who have and those who are (313), saints decidedly fall in the second camp. So do oppressed groups like the working classes: 'The loathing of "capital" with which our laboring classes today are growing more and more infected seems largely composed of this sound sentiment of antipathy for lives based on mere having' (314). James's gaze transforms class struggle into the vista of a community of saints interested more in being than in having. Anger is drained away, replaced by a beautiful brotherly tie.

It is clear in his argument that the task of art is to tame the fury of the social body into pleasing, reparative compositions. The fruition of art involves the same relaxation of 'self-responsibility,' the feeling of 'throwing the burden down' (James 285) typical of religious experience. Art helps relieve the viewer/reader of the burden of social divisions, class first and foremost. James's saintliness is a vertiginous notion, a multifaceted unit of meaning, arising exactly where the struggles and the hatred pitting social groups one against the other are ignored. Saintliness helps thought replaces the anger of the masses and the fury of the crowd with the less violent idea of a bonded community. But it is also clear that to veer in this gentler direction, thought must rely on aesthetic emotion. To 'drain away' (James 265) the depression of social divisions it is necessary to project those out into space and still them into a pleasing geometry. James goes to great length to support the transmutation of the working classes into a painterly mass: he quotes an anarchist. The working classes, like the genius and the saint before them, become one of the proper names of the energetic subject choosing a freer life 'based [. . .] on doing or being' (314). saints are to James what the trireme was to the Greeks, the image of a rhythmic equality, an example of beauty that instills justice.

Saintliness helps James believe in the consonance of thought with a social order less plagued by misery: 'Treating those whom they [saints] met, in spite of the past, in spite of all appearances, as worthy, they have stimulated them to be worthy, miraculously transformed them by their radiant example and by the challenge of their expectation' (347). But the problem remains whether, in its capacity to swerve in the direction of good ideas, conceptual thought remains subordinate to aesthetic enjoyment. The boundary between intellect and aesthetic emotion is less clear cut than James would like to think. Perhaps this is why, having established the social meaningfulness of saintliness, he suddenly turns against Saint Teresa, on whose pragmatism to some extent his edifice of a gentler thought has relied.

Suddenly Saint Teresa becomes guilty of being a selfish writer, one attached more to desire than to vocation. She is found guilty of exploiting religious experience for literary aims. James ends up defining saints as authors in the sense of *auctores*, authors who uphold to the world the image of a just social tie. By contrast, Teresa is accused of 'stereotyped humility' (339) and 'voluble egotism' (339) because she bent her amorous flirtation with God to her writerly aims. Her childish show of desire excludes her from the social value that other saints have. In Teresa's case, religious experience appears to be too much of a variety of aesthetic experience. So far James has used saintliness to prove thought's capacity for gentler ideas. Teresa's desire for forms negates their reparative, social uses. Self-referentiality is a sin. James's denial of Teresa's holiness sheds light on the difficulty in accounting for the self-referential side of art, but also on thought's problematic vocation for adorning perturbing social truths.

I read Stein's libretto as an intervention in James's discussion of religious experience. She picks up from the impasse of an art seen as ancillary to the defensive posture of thought, and goes on to ask how art itself might claim an inquiring rather than a socially unifying function. The opera's first production, for the most part, would seem to reinstate James's position. An all black cast of actors actors was employed. They replaced James's working classes in the visual projection of a more authentic human interiority and of a collective symbol of thought's power to breed gentler ideas. If audiences found the opera beautiful, if, in fact, it seemed to them 'America's first avant-garde event' (Watson 267), it was for the Jamesian reason that it temporarily dissolved the stonewalls of social conventions and paltry morality. The opera was a public staging of the Jamesian argument with the added critical twist of Stein's libretto.

In fact, in the opera production the all black cast was decisive in translating Stein's kind of modernism into an American beauty accessible to Broadway audiences and intellectual elites alike. In a pioneer essay, Alice Walker defines her ancestors as saints, meaning by this their capacity to keep alive against all odds 'the notion of song.'[13] The notion of song s indicates a resilient aesthetic faculty planted in the midst of American inner conflicts. The opera's production resolved these conflicts with the visual solemnity of the collective ensemble.

Stein and Thomson worked hard to avoid sensualism and sensationalism. But their choice also pandered to the then fashionable taste for primitivism. As a reporter on Harlem culture for *Vanity Fair*, Carl Van Vechten, a strong supporter of the production, helped spread the romanticized images of African Americans and the cult of blacks as an exotic other. Homoerotic curiosity for black men was very much behind the scenes of the production. Thomson and his staging director shared with Van Vechten an attraction to black men (Watson 208). During rehearsals, Ashton spent time in Harlem after dark and slept with one or two of the male dancers (Watson 255). A photo portrays him sensually posing with three black male dancers (Watson 255). The photo capitalizes on the alluring intersection of aesthetics, primitivism (romanticizing the other) and national auto-exoticism, in the form of white-black male sexual transgression. The mix had a significant part in the success of the opera.[14] The male homoerotic curiosity was toned down by a supposed affinity between Stein's writing and black culture. During rehearsals Thomson spread the notion that Gertrude Stein wrote for rhythm rather than for reading, assimilating her libretto to the oral black genius: 'The whites always kind of resisted Gertrude, whereas the blacks understood her perfectly well and took to it like ducks to water' (qtd. in Watson 251).

It would be unfair to reduce the opera to an exploitative commercial success. The performance marked a musical and economic breakthrough for the artists employed. The actors were paid for rehearsals, a privilege up to then only granted to black leads (Watson 246). Those involved got to see another side of Harlem. Rehearsals took place in the basement of St Philip's Episcopal Church in the midst of the economic depression, against the background of the cold, the despair, and the uncollected garbage in the streets by day. This picture of Harlem contrasted with the glamorous life by night, associated with famous dance and jazz clubs like the Savoy Ballroom, the Cotton Club, Connie's Inn, Club Hotcha. Moreover, the production crossed the divide of high and low rt. The Eva Jessey Choir was a professional black choir representing a tradition of 'illegitimate' art embroidered with claps and shouts and rhythmic variations, octaves that could not be rendered in notes. Most of the singers directed by Jessye, though professional singers, were technically untrained. They could not write down the music and could not read it. This tradition seems to mirror Stein's own illegitimate poetic language that the cast learned by heart like 'a foreign tongue' (Watson 252).

Choreography emphasized the visual rendering of a social rhythm made available to the senses. Ashton wanted the action to be 'not operatic but ritualistic and ordered, and not balletic but ceremonial' (Vaughan 7). He remembers: 'never has any production had the beautiful leisure of a procession with its pauses, when the lifting of a hand and raised eyebrows were dramatic' (qtd. in Vaughan 7). The choreography had to suggest a sense of accord between audience and stage: 'It was the strangest and most beautiful production [...] because I am devout and the Negroes are devout and I am plastic and they are plastic' (Vaughan 7).

When the performers sang Stein's poetic language, the effect achieved must have been of a private idiom made public, of an inner American poetry shown by her Jamesian saints. Saint Therese's inwardness took on the proportions of a multitude. In this movement from inside to outside the audience could experience a sense of inclusion, valid for every viewer. Some of them are reported to have said that they 'did not know anything so beautiful could be made in America' (Watson 280). For the audience, the cast of racialized performers came to embody a classic ideal of beauty, according to which beauty is separate from cognition and one does not need to know the object in order to love it. Stein's poetic language played an important role in emphasizing the split internal to the black actors between their central position as performers and their position as subordinate citizens. Precisely because the black actors could conjure at any one point concepts of oppression on the basis of race and throw viewers off balance, the beauty of the opera relied on an elided perception, on a shared national secret about social subordination around which the audience silently bonded. Together, they experienced Ashton's euphony and perfect rhymes: 'I am plastic/ They are plastic,' a social accord planted in the imaginary ground of cultural clichés with which individuals may or may not have agreed but which nevertheless circulated.

It would be hard to imagine the opera's success without the work of cultural translation Virgil Thomson's music effected on Stein's libretto.[15] In opera 'the music is seen to represent in objective form the interior mental and emotional life of the characters' (Corse 18). Through quotations from religious hymns and folk music, Thomson gave Stein's saints an American soul. The score comments the formation of visual geometries of saints with folk tunes. This happens in act II when Saint Teresa is settled in her community of saints and the members experience a love that is a 'nestle' in them. Similarly, a folk tune also seals the wedding of saints in Act III, with the collective scene of male saints mending fishnets. The patchwork of local allusions creates the 'illusion of a palpable inner essence for the character' (Corse 18): Teresa's calling becomes an American attachment 'within.' In this regard, the musical score removes Stein's allegory of modernist art from Europe to America. It inverts the story's genealogy. Commonly associated with European, especially Parisian, bohemia, modernist desire now becomes local.[16]

Perhaps the most faithful element to Stein's libretto was Florine Stettheimer's stage design. Cellophane, gauze, plumes, and richly textured costumes in base pastel colors created a strange ethereal atmosphere, all lightness and transparency, that jolted the spectator back in time, into a dreamy world of childhood memories.[17] In one tableau, for example, Saint Teresa posed in a tent of gauze with gold trimmings. The stage was wrapped with cellophane, which made the vault look like a sky of rock candy. The slightly surreal background against which the saints move provides an important Brechtian moment in the production, when the dreamy world might actually provoke the spectator to a critical scrutiny of the relation of aesthetic enjoyment to social repression. The beauty of *Four Saint in Three Acts* helped make this problem public. If art and society must be related, then how can art encourage forms of reception other than assent to violent ideas? How can art counteract the anxiety about the fury of the social body? Is it possible to depart from forms of production and reception that do not reinforce silence and keep national secrets?

The material object, reverie, literary origins

Act IV gives reason to ask such questions. The final act is an appendix if we have to believe the opera's title, *Four Saints in Three Acts*. Stein uses it to depart from William James's argument. The writer of the libretto intrudes with a signature phrase: 'When this you see remember me' (47). Throughout, she has been in the shadow of Saint Therese and her religious affections. The question of love, which had inaugurated the opera—'To know to know to love her so' (*O&P* 11)—now appears to refer not only to Stein's heroine but also to her creator. To love Saint Therese, and the librettist, means to save both from the accusations of narcissism to which their desire to write exposes them. In fact, the sensitivity to accusations of formalist narcissism is there in the libretto. If it derives from James's view of Saint

Teresa, it also puts Stein in the company of American writers who took on this preoccupation, Wallace Stevens above all.

The fruits of James's assimilation of saints, artists, and social subjects, can be best seen in Wallace Stevens's 'Anecdote of the Jar' (1919). In the poem the 'gray and bare' (10) object is placed upon a hill and takes 'dominion everywhere' (9). Its stern roundedness placates 'a slovenly wilderness' (3) with its epicenter in the South (Tennessee). The jar is an appropriate symbol of the 'astringency and desolation' (James 262) described by the American philosopher. Willful and depressing, the container imposes order on social misery with the formalist narcissism of its bare shape. It is the symbol of a 'frightened literariness' or 'withdrawal into genteel hermitage' (Lentricchia 439) which neither Stevens nor Stein ever embraced. On the contrary, they had to reckon with the self-deprecation inherited by the American artist with the subordination of aesthetics to the fear of social conflicts.

In Stein's libretto the concentric themes of saintliness, sociability, and literary experience certainly come from James but also link her to Stevens and his preoccupations about formalist narcissism. In *Four Saints in Three Acts* her landscape follows from James's views. What is pleasing to the senses deflects thought toward tender ideas, toward the idea, for example, that the working class, a bit like Heidegger's humble jug or painterly peasant shoes, tell the story of an authentic life of 'doing and being.' But differently from James, Stein does not bank on the coincidence of the intellectual and the aesthetic levels, which in James served to assert the primacy of cognition over art. The libretto does not subordinate forms to concepts. On the contrary, it insists on poetic language. Therese's attachment 'within within' (*O&P* 12), her being 'wed' (*O&P* 43) and 'led' (*O&P* 43), her oscillation between individuality, 'seated and not surrounded' (*O&P* 16), and collectivity: 'A great many saints can sit around with one standing' (*O&P* 17), the 'warm snow' (O&P 15) of her visitation, the magpie in the sky announcing her public identity, the many windows (*O&P* 32) of heaven, the many 'nails' (*O&P* 25) of responsibility, and so on. In other words, the relatively well-known story of the saint helps readers follow Stein's concept-resisting figures. In this phase of her career, she is thinking about a transition from poetry as 'inconsequential toy' (Lentricchia 436)—the stern jar defending itself from the friction, waste, and fury of the social community—to a poetry of public consequence.

Accordingly, issues of composition and reception become an integral part of the libretto. In the last scene of the last act, Act IV, Saint Plan, whose name suggests an organizational agent behind the production, confesses to some difficulty with the opera: 'Saint Plan Saint Plan to may to say to say two may and inclined. /Who makes it be what they had as porcelain' (*O&P* 47). Together with the photographs in the Parisian shop window, a porcelain object is at the inception of the opera:

> Then in another window this time on the rue de Rennes there was
> a rather large porcelain group and it was of a young soldier giving alms to

a beggar and taking off his helmet and his armour and leaving them in the
charge of another.
       It was somehow just what the young Saint Ignatius did and
anyway it looked like him as I had known about him [. . .]. (*LA* 130-1)

The porcelain group is a souvenir, an object of memory, therefore covered with the
patina of other images. As Bridgman notes, the soldier might have looked like
Saint Ignatius to Stein but probably represented Saint Martin of Tours (182).
Stein's error or misrecognition is indicative of the multiple layers of memories and
associations of which the porcelain object is made. The almsgiving scene is one of
the most recurrent in Saint Martin's iconography in Renaissance European art. The
saint is represented as a Roman soldier who, on a winter's day, meets a beggar and,
to protect him from the cold, makes him the gift of half of his coat
(*paludamentum*). In fact, the iconological subject of almsgiving in the form of a
clothing item was also employed by Giotto in his stories of the life of Saint
Francis, *Saint Francis gives his coat to a poor knight* (1295-1297/1299), in the
Basilica Superiore in Assisi. Stein, who had a passion for Saint Francis, had very
likely seen the frescos. *The Autobiography of Alice B. Toklas* mentions an
exemplary summer walk from Perugia to Assisi (83). The opera ends with a
material object that, as Stein's error suggests, invites manifold potential
associations. We have seen how the libretto relies on the modulation of chromatic
shades into visual geometries, on an associative chain of memory images that
surface as visual centers of meaning. An example is the recurrent widow image,
combining memories of the black and white photos in the shop, the nuns' uniform,
the black uniform of widows, and the black plumage of the magpie. The ending
tells us about another formal device: the saints stilled back into the elements of a
porcelain group. In fact the material object is physically embedded in the text. This
literary procedure parallels the art of Robert Rauschenberg. In Rauschenberg's
paintings, images are 'physically embedded within the pictorial medium the way a
nail can be driven into the surface of a wall' (Krauss 45). Stein' s integration of the
compositional device or material object in the text can be usefully approached
through Rauschenberg's creative process as described by Rosalind Krauss.
       In 1970s, Krauss coined the expression 'materialized image' in her essay
'Rauschenberg and the Materialized Image,' to refer to a technique based on 'the
physical incorporation' (45) of various materials in a painting (objects, fabrics,
newspaper, etc.) whereby the work of art becomes these 'material substances' (45).
The special characteristic of the technique is that the image materially present in
the painting also dictates the compositional procedure. The material substances
used, writes Krauss, 'are embedded into the surface by covering them either by a
coating of paint, or by a stretch of semitransparent scrim material so that they are
implanted under the continuous spread of the surface like a splinter under the skin'
(44). The interpretive logic of the materialized image is the logic of associations.
But as Krauss specifies in a later essay, 'Perpetual Inventory,' it does not 'privilege
chains of associations that, in their dependence on further associations to decode

them, continue to assert the private depth of experience underwriting these connections' (96). Rather, it points to individual associations as the thorn in the side—or the splinter under the skin—of publicly meaningful acts that aspire to make sense in relation to symbolic wholes.

In 'Rauschenberg and the Materialized Image,' Krauss argues that materialized meaning cannot be reduced to the cognitive moment of a socialized individual or private depth. Instead she emphasizes the role that individual associations play in the semiotic process: 'What Rauschenberg was insisting upon was a model for art that was not involved with what might be called the cognitive moment (as in a single-image painting) but instead was tied to the durée—to the kind of extended temporality that is involved in experiences like memory, reflection, narration, proposition' (41). Rauschenberg's extended temporality opens the work of art to individual associations and insists on their importance in the interpretation of his work, to the point that to many viewers the fruition of his art means the 'desire for an anthropological belonging in a social, human, planetary system' (Bonito Oliva 11). Especially when seen through Krauss, Rauschenberg responds to James's subordination of art to cognition, in the service of a melodious social song. He responds to the ambiguous function of art and the fear of formalist narcissism that it raises in Stevens and Stein, claiming the independence of the aesthetic experience: 'the capacity of the work of art to operate as Idea' (Krauss, 'Robert Rauschenberg and the Materialized Image' 42). For Krauss, this capacity, resists the reduction of art to the function of commodity (42), and implies the possibility of manifold associations, comprising individual ones. Stein seems to be working in this direction.[18]

The opera ends with a material object that reveals the composition procedure. The libretto comes from an expanded temporality, from an authorial reverie. While the narrative of saints provides a symbolic unity, Stein's synaesthetic inebriation gives the reader the right to enjoy an aspect of interpretation linked to conjectures and daydreaming, that only with difficulty finds a place in critical analysis. The porcelain object is key to such an invitation to the reader. It tells us, at the end, that the text has been a reverie.

As defined by Thomas Ogden in his study on reverie and interpretation, reverie is a quintessentially private dimension. It involves the most embarrassing and private (albeit important) aspects of our life (86). The reverie separates what is interior from what is exterior, what is private from what is public. Talking publicly about the feelings in the reverie means giving up the privacy to which we unconsciously resort when separating the interior from the exterior (86). With reference to the analyst, Ogden proposes that even though states of reverie are highly personal and private, it would nevertheless be misleading to consider these states only the analyst's personal creations. The reverie is at the same time an unconscious construction and an interpretive position created in a collaborative activity between two parties. Ogden calls this interpretive position 'the intersubjective analytical third' (86).[19] Although Odgen is talking about the psychoanalytic setting, his interest in investigating the process of interpretation.

Reverie describes an interpretive position asymmetrically constructed, because in this case the reader puts in more than the text. While it is a fundamental capacity for interpreting a text, it seems not dignified enough to participate in meaning (Ogden 88). It remains at best 'an emotional compass' (Ogden 88).

        With the porcelain object at libretto's end, Stein wakes up from her reverie and openly invites her readers to consider their own reverie. An important private aspect of the libretto seems the use of saints' iconography. This alludes to literary authors, linking Stein to the American tradition. (How can art make a difference? Is poetry a dreary object? Is the song a defense from the outside world? How can poetry ally itself with truth, i.e. with change?) Stein's libretto daydreams about overwhelming questions that surely cannot be reduced to a struggle for aesthetic independence. But one has the impression that *Four Saints in Three Acts* comes from the perilous conjoining of beauty and cognition, a union whose evidence is not limited to James's Saint Teresa. The struggle of art to tell a social truth truer than the one that thought can tell loses itself in the darkness of literary origins.

        In the space of the reverie Stein's saints allude to the founding fathers, those men—and women—who sailed to the New World so that, in John Winthrop's words, they 'might be all knit more nearly together in the bond of brotherly affection' (Winthrop 80-81). Stein's Saint Therese borrows her diction from the speech Winthrop pronounced on the deck of the flagship Arbella: 'There are a great many places and persons near together' *(O&P* 16). Catholic saints move in the shadow of Puritan saints. Stein knew that to become a public woman meant to reckon with her literary origins, no matter how forbidding they might be. In her origins, the sins of narcissistic flirtation and literary egotism, which prompted James to condemn Saint Teresa, loom large. From the translation of the Bay Psalm Book on, the imperative of didacticism forces literary desire to dwell in the nooks of the figurative exhibitionism of Jonathan Edwards or the unnerving coyness of Anne Bradstreet. Stein's mixture of self-deprecation and boasting echoes this tradition. Even beginning students opening any anthology of American literature will notice the list of self-deprecatory images on the first pages of the first book of American poetry. In her 'Prologue,' Bradstreet laments: 'My obscure lines' (6), 'My foolish, broken, blemished Muse' (16), 'my wondering eyes and envious heart' (7), a 'weak or wounded brain' that 'admits no cure' (24). Every quatrain of Bradstreet's 'Prelude' is shut off by a rhymed couplet repeating over and over the subservient position. With every couplet we hear the bang of a door that shuts her out of the gates of the mansion of writing. Yet, this broken voice must speak, and does.

        Anne Bradstreet is not the only one. In a journal entry for March-April 1844 Emerson wrote: 'No writing is here, no redundant strength, but declamation, straining, correctness, & all other symptoms of debility' (qtd. in Porte 324). The straining and the sense of disqualification that haunt Emerson were part and parcel of early American literary performance. Stein's ancestors are given to travesty to defend or justify their wish to write and their desire for literary value. They speak like people who, just woken from a dream, cannot remember themselves. On closer scrutiny, James's Saint Teresa and Stein's Therese rightfully take their place in the early American artist's tormented fable of identity. If Anne Bradstreet must admit to her wounded mind and broken song, Phyllis Wheatley must speak as a racial collaborationist when she is not. And J. Hector St. John de Crèvecoeur, in his *Letters from an American Farmer*, must put on the persona of James, the humble American unworthy of European intellectual interest, so that he can explain his country to the Europeans, giving them what they want to hear (Letter III) and, eventually, what they do not (Letter IX). In *A True History of the Captivity and Restoration of Mrs. Mary Rowlanson*, the writer must speak as a member of her Puritan community led by visible saints, even as she loses herself in the cultural relativity of an ethnic wilderness.

In the space of the reverie Stein's landscape writing picks up the thread of an original literary act of contemplation that educates the eye to shape the outer world into synchronic patterns, training the viewer to act as if, when looking around, she were looking at the sensuous materiality of a painting. Bradstreet's 'Contemplations' begin:

> The trees all richly clad, yet void of pride,
> Where gilded o're by his rich golden head.
> Their leaves & fruits seem'd painted, but was true
> Of green, of red, of yellow, mixed hew,
> Rapt were my senses at this delectable view. (2-7)

The painting expands to social song as the 'sweet-tongu'd' bird of poetry 'percht ore my head' (178):

> The dawning morn with songs thou doest prevent,
> Sets hundred notes unto thy feathered crew,
> So each one tunes his pretty instrument,
> And warbling out the old, begin anew,
> And thus they pass their youth in summer season.
> Then follow thee into a better Region,
> Where winter's never felt by that sweet airy legion. (190-196)

Forms have the power to suspend in full view a rhythmic equality that is not available to cognition and that, it is hoped, might instigate extra-textual imitation. This is the theme of 'Contemplations,' a private reverie that the author consigns to the page in an attempt to put 'to rest' (160) her desire to write.

Only in 1938, in *Doctor Faustus Lights The Lights*, will Stein create a more obviously colonial heroine. She has four names and suffers from a permanent state of agitation: 'I am I and my name is Marguerite Ida and Helena Annabel, and then oh then I could yes I could I could begin to cry but why why could I begin to cry' (*LO&P* 95). She attaches herself to woods she cannot remember having seen:

> And I am I and I am here and how do I know how wild the wild world is
> how wild the wild woods are the wood they call the woods the poor man's
> overcoat but do they cover me and if they do how wild they are wild and
> wild and wild they are, how do I know how wild woods are when I have
> never seen a wood before. (*LO&P* 95)

Marguerite is partly the endangered heroine of early novels,[20] partly the Puritan
survivor stranded in the Christological locale of the New Wild World,[21] infested
with Indians and beasts, and partly the more modern survivor of the ontological
crisis of identity. A version of Goethe's eternal feminine, she is created from the
same language as Saint Therese. She is a unit of meaning around which masses and
volumes aggregate into a pleasing view. A procession of scattered individuals who
come 'from everywhere' (*LO&P* 106) to 'see how she sits' (106) coalesce around
her into a compact collectivity. Just like Saint Therese, Marguerite is a radiant
visual center—'See how she lights' (*LO&P* 106)—that intimates geometries of
rhythmic equality: 'a great many are around' (*LO&P* 107).

Above all, her trembling voice tells us that she is the captive of a
wilderness that, unremembered, seduces her. And despite the fact that she is a
banal lover of middle-class comfort—'I would not have to look around fearfully
everywhere there where a chair and a carpet underneath the chair would make me
know that there is there' (*LO&P* 95-96)—she loves what she must reduce to
nothing: 'but here here everywhere there is nothing nothing' (*LO&P* 96). A
quivering tragicomic creation, Stein's colonial heroine shares the infectious
neurosis, the claustrophobia, and the compulsiveness of Samuel Beckett's
characters.[22] Her saving trait is a lyrical affection for the woods: 'I close my eyes
but the green is there and I open my eyes and I have to be sure the green is there
the green of the woods' (*LO&P* 96).

Chapter 7

The 'Visitor': *Lectures in America*

The kiss of the self, the intimacy of writing

Princeton. November 5, 1934. McCosh Hall. The largest auditorium there seats 481 and is now called the Harold Helm Auditorium, after one of its trustees. The podium faces semicircular rows of seats arranged in the shape of an amphitheater. The wooden seats, nailed to the wooden floor, the wooden vault and the tall windows, to the right of the podium and back and front of it, fill the occasional visitor with a sense of austerity. Stein gave her lecture in the evening. As she walked toward the podium, the wooden floors probably creaked, just as they do now. She had to climb the three or four steps to get on the platform in front of her audience. Toklas sat 'directly in front of her' (Waters 1). As one stands on the podium, one sees that 'in front' means literally just a couple of steps away.

The lecture she delivered, 'The Gradual Making of The Making of Americans,' is crucial to understanding the experience of her American tour.[1] It is a disarmingly simplified tale of her writing career. She sums up herself as someone trained in psychology, who turned to writing as a way to let in philosophy: 'When I began The Making of Americans I knew I really did know that a complete description was a possible thing [. . .] But as it is a possible thing one can stop continuing to describe this everything. That is where philosophy comes in, it begins when one stops describing everything' (*LA* 156-7). Here Stein refers to the transition from *A Long Gay Book* to *Tender Buttons* and the portraits, when the human inventory becomes constricting and removed from her ideal of vigorous beauty. The conviction that the responsibility of the writer was to catalog human types dated back to her college years: 'While I was in college and doing philosophy and psychology I became more interested in my own mental processes and less in that of others and all I then was learning of what made people what they are came to me by experience and not by talking and listening' (*LA* 137). If before *The Making of Americans* she had wavered between writing about 'the life inside of others' and 'myself and my experiences' (*LA* 138), once she grew as a writer she decided that the central question was a consciousness open to externality. Whatever gets on the page should be the result of 'listening and hearing and feeling the rhythm of each human being' (*LA* 145). 'Gradual' in 'The Gradual Making of Americans' is meant to evoke a writing of waiting, a hand that hesitates to commit to the page what is not mediated by the intersubjective consciousness. The process of this non-bookish knowledge can, in fact, be very slow.

The lecture makes clear that the writing of waiting, of a consciousness that lets itself be filled with 'listening' and 'feeling,' and with the rhythm of others, reveals a difficulty at the basis of all writing when this aspires to be a form of knowledge. The difficulty lies in the gap between the moment of knowing and the moment of writing. While writing unravels in a sequence, the knowledge one obtains after waiting is 'at one time': 'Types of people I could put down but a whole human being felt at one and the same time, in other words while in the act of feeling that person was very difficult to put into words' (*LA* 145). It took a long time to find out something, but it became very difficult to put it on paper as a 'whole,' that is, as it was 'there then within me' (*LA* 147). Can writing exist? Can the expanded consciousness occupied by the 'wholes' of others write? It seems that when the self opens to externality, writing becomes a terrible trouble: it can subsist as representation, but can it as knowledge? And does the time needed for knowledge kill writing?

By 'philosophy,' therefore, Stein meant a turn to difficult questions of writing. It would seem that the more consciousness opens to externality, the greater the distance between representation and knowledge becomes. The more writing opened outside the self the more what it found remained interior, reaching the page either in fragments or, worse, with a sense of inconsequence when compared to the feeling of knowing. Knowing is time-bound while writing happens in space. As writing becomes interested in others its outward disposition comes back on the page as if it were the reported speech in the intimacy of the self. Portraiture exemplifies the predicament.

In her lecture 'Portraits and Repetition,' Stein recollects: 'I must find out what is moving inside them that makes them, and I must find out how I by the thing moving excitedly inside in me can make a portrait of them' (*LA* 183). 'Portraits and Repetition' makes explicit Stein's involvement in a writing of 'vitality' and movement' (*LA* 173). Its uniqueness resides in an intimacy ('what is moving inside them') that can be written if it reacts successfully with the singularity of the viewer ('the thing moving excitedly inside me'). Repetition replaces what Stein had formerly called philosophy. It suggests an immemorial movement inside the subject of the portrait that the subject doing the portrait—in Stein's terminology, the listener—must draw out, precisely as if two unconsciouses were listening to each other. Stein is after a writing that impacts on her readers as a moment of knowing: 'I wondered is there any way of making what I know come out as I know it, come out not as remembering' (*LA* 181). Portrait-making helps put into focus the problem that the uniqueness of each human subject—what makes for his or her distinctive identity—can 'come out' only in reciprocity, through an intersubjective involvement. In order to feel our identity, we need to be given it by another. As we have seen in the discussion of 'Portrait of Mabel Dodge at Villa Curonia,' Stein deliberately cultivates the ambiguity between the subject of the portrait (its object, that is) and the author of the portrait, replacing identity with reciprocity. But portraiture for Stein is representative of the question at the heart of writing in general.

From this point of view, Stein is a humanist. She believes in the power of writing to shape life in that it can acknowledge a human subject in his or her innermost intimate difference from others. This is what Jean-Luc Nancy means in a recent essay about portraiture influenced by Stein's views, when he says that a portrait achieves the infinite return of the subject to himself (*Il Ritratto e il Suo Sguardo* 49). Nancy uses the portrait genre to redefine identity in terms of an 'intimacy' (48) that coincides with the human subject portrayed. Referring to Lorenzo Lotto's *Ritratto di Giovane* [Portrait of a Young Man] (1506/7), Nancy says that this intimacy is not to be understood as an interiority behind the figure; rather, facing us, the portrait appears to recall the subject to himself (49). In other words, the portrait stands for a form of listening for the interior intimacy of another that is not so much behind language as on its surface. The portrait impacts on us as a moment of knowing rather than representation. Stein similarly thought of the portrait as exemplary of a writing open to externality. When she used the word 'philosophy' to suggest this kind of writing, she meant the term less in the sense of the pragmatist stream and more in the sense of Novalis:

> One must never confess to oneself that one loves oneself. The secret of this confession is the life principle of the one true and eternal love. The first kiss in this understanding is the principle of philosophy—the origin of a new world—the beginning of absolute chronology—the completion of an infinitely growing bond with the self. Who would not like a philosophy whose germ is a first kiss? (58-59)

Similarly, as Stein recalls her transition to the experimental phase of *Tender Buttons* and the portraits, she speaks of the origin of a new world, of an awakening: 'I myself was becoming livelier' (*LA* 150). She is experiencing at that point the paradox of a writing that, like the portrait, is public because it addresses the onlookers, but at the same time reveals itself as a 'private' knowledge, akin to what Novalis terms self-love and Nancy an intimacy without memory. Stein's problem is: How am I going to tell what I have come to know?

The problem of the gradual knowledge of others, and whether it can pass into writing, is a version of the question of truth in philosophy. Readers of *Discourse on Method* would notice that *cogito ergo sum* is simultaneously a truth, a foundation that survives any doubt, and a belief confirmed in the heat of the meditation. This is why Jean-Luc Nancy, as Ian James explains, argues that the *Discourse on Method* is a portrait: 'What one finds in the *Discourse on Method*, the story of the Cogito, is a portrait of the author of the Cogito, a 'picture' which reveals the truth of René Descartes and which seeks to narrate the possibility of grounding truth itself' (Ian James 132). Truth is the narration of its search: 'the cogito has the exact structure of the fable of its exposition" (qtd. in I. James 133). In other words, writing is always a figure of knowing—its portrait. Stein would agree:

> When I was up against the difficulty of putting down the complete
> conception that I had gradually acquired by listening seeing feeling and
> experience, I was faced by the trouble that I had acquired all this
> knowledge gradually but when I had it I had it completely at one time.
> Now that may never have been a trouble to you but it was a terrible
> trouble to me. And a great deal of The Making of Americans was a
> struggle to do this thing, to make a whole present of something that it had
> taken a great deal of time to find out, but it was a whole then there within
> me and as such it had to be said. (*LA* 147)

What she has come to know in thought ('gradually acquired by listening seeing
feeling and experience') is a picture of thought ('when I had it I had it completely
at one time). Writing can only be the portrait, a figuration in space, of a feeling of
truth one has inside. The clumsy beginning of 'The Gradual Making of The
Making of Americans' is meant to enhance the paradox:

> I am going to read what I have written to read, because in a general way it
> is easier even if it is not better and in a general way it is better even if it is
> not easier to read what has been written than to say what has not been
> written [. . .]. (*LA* 135).

Stein is delivering to the audience present in the hall a text that she has written for
an earlier one, during the act of writing. The members of her real public hear the
address to the imaginary audience and, consequently, they feel a certain
uneasiness, a sense of belatedness, as if they were made to step into an ongoing
performance that feels private to them because it has not yet included them.

It is easier to stick to the written text because, when this is pronounced out
loud, its quality as an address meant for a previous imaginary audience feels like
an intimacy that dissolves in the presence of the public in the hall. The speaker
realizes that she has a real audience in front of her. But the moment of knowing
dissolves, as if put beside the point in public, as if it were inappropriate. Thus, it is
not better to 'read what I have written to read.' On the other hand, it is better to
read the text written for an imaginary audience because the writing is not projected
outside so much and thus can come out as the original writing of movement and
vitality Stein pursued. The address can therefore approximate the reinvigorating
origin of a new world. '[E]ven if it is not easier': because Stein's writing of
movement, a homage to Emerson's 'manifold allusion' (90), might fare better in a
space other than the lecture hall.

The intimacy of the human subject, in this case the writer, is made of
temporal moments of knowing. Explained out loud, in the public sphere of the
lecture hall, it dissolves and might even sink into meaninglessness. Writing is
bound to time. The lectures rely on the strange ethereality of a time-bound writing
at odds with its actualization in space. Stein used the occasion of her long awaited
public recognition to stage the philosophical problem of the belatedness of writing,

of a writing at odds with the modernist expanded consciousness that had initiated it in the first place. The lecture begins with palpitations and indecisions impeccably delivered in Stein's dignified monotone. It ends on a very different note, with the Americanization of the 'postmodern' vulnerability at the heart of her writing.[2] She resorts to the prop of an American thing, an utterly vulnerable self-grounding certainty to lend her credibility, to justify her. I would now like to discuss how historical approaches are better suited to describe the lecture's overall effect of an originality negated by its publication or externalization. The historical approach gives the reader a slightly stronger hold on a text whose central preoccupation is the vertigo of a time-bound singularity that disappears as it is entrusted to the voice in a public space.

Presence

Marianne DeKoven has discussed the paradoxical overturning of the private and public in Stein. With reference to the lively period of *Tender Buttons* and the portraits, she defines Stein's outward bound expanded consciousness as 'a transformative interaction with exteriority' that meets the readers with a 'unique interiority' ('Woolf, Stein, and the drama of public woman' 193). DeKoven explains her method of composition: 'Stein derives or constructs an abstract principle of motion or quintessence of being by concentrating intently on something outside herself; she then focuses her consciousness on this principle or quintessence, incorporating it as an organizing principle for writing' (193). DeKoven argues that 'Stein's presence as a public woman was made possible for her by its mediation through her attachment to and location within a house (rue de Fleurus; later the house in Belley), and the other links to traditional modes of feminine domesticity (the salon, the dinner party)' (192).

Lectures in America crucially relies on the insertion of feminine domesticity in public space. In fact, Stein's more public production, including drama, opera and speeches, hinges on her redefinition of public and private spaces. Toklas's presence, just a few steps away from the speaker, is a strong element in the reconfiguration of the public hall as continuous with the domestic interior. Another way in which Stein redraws the boundary of public space through a feminine private sphere is by tapping the resources of spectacle and putting them to use in the space of the academic lecture hall. A student present at the Princeton lecture reports thinking that 'it was sort of silly of anyone to act like such a nut in public' (Trudy and Alice in Jungleland' 2). Besides reconfiguring feminine domesticity in public spaces, her performance also mixes different public places, the theater and the lecture hall, with a disorienting effect on the audience.

In *Lectures in America* the redefinition of the private/public divide discussed by DeKoven is also Stein's concrete way of pointing to philosophy. The historical mediation of the public sphere by domesticity leads to the philosophical question of the private/public divide of writing, to the gap between knowledge and representation. In the American lectures the philosophical problem of writing becomes a woman's problem; Stein engages our awareness of women's struggle to become public subjects.

The American lectures brought home a message that was still unclear in her first academic performance in England, discussed in chapter 5: the extent to which her self-presentation as a writer taps collective images of women who achieved the status of public women. It would be hard to appreciate the lectures without also hearing their echoing of the tradition of women's strivings for public presence. Stein's performance imaginatively transfers the podium and the lectern, essential props of lecturing, to the larger stage of history. She invites the juxtaposition of the lecture hall with the historical time of women's struggle for oratorical power and public recognition. Her lecturing style critically engages the nineteenth-century struggle for the platform. In this tradition women's rhetorical power had to be curbed by the deployment of a conventional feminine sensibility. (Johnson 134). The more obvious stylistic trait that links Stein to the nineteenth-century tradition of women's oratory is her appearance. In the prestigious American lecture hall, her appearance takes on a historical valence that would otherwise be lost in bohemian Paris, because it tropes on the nineteenth-century expectation that oratorical performance be associated with male privilege. Her 'masculine countenance' (Waters 1) was the first thing any audience noticed. Among nineteenth-century famous women public speakers some, like Frances E. Willard, stood out for their 'embodiment of a compelling femininity in a public rhetorical space' (Johnson 112). But the common expectation was that a woman giving a public lecture 'would surely be mannish in demeanor' (Johnson 112). Stein played up her mannishness: her strong, austere features framed by her cropped hair unmistakably bespoke a command of the masculine position. Robed in a timeless loose silk tunic made for the occasion, she was in many ways the incarnation of a historical stereotype.

The engagement of the audience's historical imagination reinforced the link between the uniqueness (and inscrutability) of Stein's writing and the cultural convention that domesticated the rhetorical careers of women. It is a truism that emphatic denial only affirms the thing denied. Stein's mannish appearance, while denying femininity, reminded the audience of its problem in relation to public presence. Her appearance bore the memory of a rather recent past, spanning Stein's life, when the pressure was there for women to make desire for public presence coextensive with the private sphere of domesticity.[3] Domesticity is not so easily exorcized. Toklas's presence confirmed the traditional subordination of women's rhetorical powers to the private sphere. She appeared in press photos carrying the briefcase containing the lectures Stein had written at home. In the public eye she was the reminder of the private destination of the writing of Gertrude Stein, whose modernist star had risen in the parlor of her home. Thus Toklas's presence lent historical and political significance to Stein's performance as it 'stressed the podium as a domestic space' (Johnson 114).

Toklas's presence also meant that Stein's intellectual credibility and public presence were haunted by the impersonation of the male artist nursed by a devoted wife. This feature of the performance further drew out the continuity between past and present. Of course, the impersonation of the male genius had begun in *The Autobiography of Alice B. Toklas*. But in her American lectures Stein tried to stand apart from modernism, with its strange mix of genuine intellectual passion and coterie mentality, to concentrate on public achievement as a leitmotif in her career. Stein was well aware of the tradition she came from.[4] After *Lectures in America*, she was to turn it into the subject of her opera *The Mother of Us All*, with Susan B. Anthony as the charismatic orator for the cause of women's rights. The American lectures may be read as a preparation for the lyricism of Susan B., the purity of whose aspirations, reflected in her life of 'strife' (*MUA* 794), is lost on the public sphere.

Diva

When dealing with her American lectures, biographers of Stein remark on the audiences' surprise at the familiarity she inspired. John Malcom Brinnin thus relates her arrival in the United States:

> At the sight of her comfortable and comforting presence, at the first sound of the inflections of her soft American voice, they were quite put off. Since many of them still came expecting to meet "a languid woman . . . smoking cigarettes, sipping absinthes perhaps and looking out upon the world with tired, disdainful eyes," they were at first surprised, then altogether disarmed. (343)

She delighted them with her homeliness. Ella Winter, for example, commenting on the lectures for the *Pacific Weekly*, voiced a similar surprise: 'These lectures are all shot through with homely little illustrations from Gertrude Stein's life' (83). Suddenly, the writer's mannish looks became reassuring and endeared her to the public. She gave the impression that her lectures were on a continuum with a local tradition. In her performance, style was disjoined from the academic context. For some the performance worked because it communicated a vitality beyond the meaning of the lecture. In her already cited review, Ella Winter adds: 'This is what makes Gertrude Stein a perpetually alive and stimulating writer whether you "understand" the meaning of the sentences she writes or whether you do not' (83). Even the negative review of Kenneth Burke resorts to the image of a melody— albeit negative—detached from a meaning. For Burke, the lectures are made of 'repetitions and blithe blunderings' woven around 'her doctrine of essence' (88). Significantly, both sympathetic and unsympathetic spectators resort to allusions to opera to describe the effect of Stein's lectures. It is in opera, in fact, that the meaning of words does not matter. Even when words are drowned in music, it is the theatrical manner and voice of the singer that move the audience, especially in the case of a *prima donna* or diva. The fact that her audience could perceive the value of her 'vocal endowment' (Leonardi 21) without understanding her meaning aligns Stein with opera divas. Whether intentional or unintentional, this identification is enlightening.

At the start of 'The Gradual Making of The Making of Americans'—'I am going to read what I have written to read, because in a general way it is easier even if it is not better [. . .]'—Stein not only insists on reading a text that will sound inadequate for the live audience before her but also insists on the uniqueness of her voice. Even though she reads a written text, it is punctuated with insecurities that she has no qualms pronouncing out loud: 'I hope you like what I say' (*LA* 157), or: 'I wonder if I at all convey to you what I mean by this thing' (*LA* 16O).

Like George Eliot's fictional opera singer in 'Armgart,' Stein knows she has a voice that can be neither duplicated nor displaced (Leonardi 77). Besides freeing her from the strictures of traditional gender roles, this voice is 'a way of addressing and redressing powers and institutions' (Leonardi 778). Of her heroine George Eliot writes:

> She often wonders what her life had been
> Without that voice for channel to her soul.
> She says, it must have leaped through all her limbs—
> Made her a Maenad—made her snatch a brand
> And fire some forest, that her rage might mount. (qtd. in Leonardi 78).

In opera, a woman's voice signifies a great power that may be perceived as destructive (qtd. in Leonardi 78). This is because the female operatic voice is often associated with transgressive sexuality, madness, disorder and disease.[5] Distinctive and original voices can instigate a punishing backlash. One thinks of Maria Callas. Her voice was considered imperfect because she did not always translate the deep emotions into beautiful sounds. Many found her an unbearable spectacle. In the earlier stages of her career, before she submitted to what might be termed a form of cultural surgery through diet to look more like a waif, the public punished her by using her fat against her gift: they called her the *prima donna* with 'elephant legs.'[6]

But there are other reasons for Stein's diva identification. The opera diva's charisma is based on the paradox that she transgresses through discipline. From a position reached by discipline and steely ambition, she both sings of traditional self-sacrifice and nonconformity: she cross-dresses, screams, protests; she makes an open show of desire and sexuality. Literary portraits of divas like Willa Cather's *Song of the Lark* and Marcia Davenport's *Of Lena Geyer* give us women exceptionally devoted to their work. Diva narratives emphasize the value of sustained hard work not only to reach a goal but for love of the work itself (Leonardi 87). Davenport's Lena Geyer made for herself a life all about work, '*senza gioia, senza amore*. Nothing but work' (qtd. in Leonardi 87). Work ensures a voice in the world. In these portraits, the diva is less interested in seducing men and more in 'securing a share of traditionally masculinist power and privilege for herself and other women' (Leonardi 19). Her voice therefore is an effective metaphor and vehicle of empowerment. Because on stage the diva is a woman who has a voice: a) she earns authority in the public world; b) her voice moves and transforms other women (and men) (Leonardi 19).[7] In this sense, the diva's voice is 'a political force' (Leonardi 19). Stein put the message to work in *The Mother of Us All*, whose protagonist, Susan B. Anthony, is a master of public speech.

A vehicle of empowerment both for her and for her spectators, the diva's voice is also the site of her vulnerability. As a general rule, the diva's relation to her voice is steeped in self-alienating rhetoric. Singers complain about their lack of control over their voices. Historical singer Emma Calvé even referred to hers as a 'visitor' in her 1922 autobiography: 'I do not know why it stays with me, except that I have 'entreated it' kindly, and that I have tried not to be an unworthy hostess' (qtd. in Leonardi 249). At once physical and transcendent, the diva's voice has a fragile power that can be lost at any time. Stein's decision to emphasize the gap between the time of writing and the time of delivery is a way of lingering on the fragility of her voice. At this point of her career, fragility meant that she was not in control of her writing because this belonged to American literature. Her voice came from others before her.

The American thing

We have seen in the previous sections how Stein feminized the philosophical problem of writing. In her lectures she also proceeded to americanize it, including her work in the larger context of an American aesthetics:

> I feel this thing, I am an American and I felt this thing in every paragraph that I made in The Making of Americans. And that is what after all this is an American book, because this thing this sense of a space of time and what is to be done within the space of time not in any way excepting in the way that it is inevitable that there is this space of time and anybody who is an American feels what is inside this space of time and so well they do what they do within this space of time, and so ultimately it is a thing contained within. (*LA* 160)

A private feeling ('I feel this thing') becomes a public feeling, something that 'anybody who is an American feels.' The impossibility of an identity between the movement of thought and its representation—its time and its space—re-enters the lecture through the condensed image of 'a space of time.'[8] At this point, Stein's search for a literary method turns into a dance of veils. She entices the audience with a state of liminality between the interior of a shared but elusive depth—the incantatory 'this thing' suggests an unnamable substance—and an external surface of stereotypes that equate America with doing, act, body, physical output, thing, space, materiality, sequence, series:

> The assembling of a thing to make a whole thing and each one of these whole things is one of a series, but beside this there is the important thing and the very American thing that everybody knows who is an American just how many seconds minutes or hours it is going to take to do a whole thing. (*LA* 160).

She continues:

> I am always trying to tell this thing that a space of time is a natural thing for an American to always have inside them as something in which they are continuously moving. Think of anything, of cowboys, of movies, of detective stories, of anybody who goes anywhere or stays at home and is an American and you will realize that it is something strictly American to conceive a space that is filled with moving [. . .]. (*LA* 160-1)

Between deep public truth and collective stereotypes, America is a new incarnation of the amiable Lucy Church and takes on the inscrutability of an exotic other. To legitimize her writing life to her public, Stein evokes an alluring genius loci.

She argues that in order to release the modernist pressure of others who occupy her consciousness, the fluid world of multiplicity—call it stream or fragmentation—is not enough. She champions another writing, one that falls into 'a space' and another pressure, that of a given 'space of time.' This time-bound space alludes to a sense of purpose and of action with the slightly nervous, rhythmic repetition of 'do.' As we have seen in chapter 5, such assertive doing had distinguished Picasso as someone who constantly had 'something being coming out of him' (*P&P* 18). Now, in the American 'space of time filled with moving' Picasso's modern 'doing' becomes a general, pronounced physiological force.

In the hushed wooden lecture hall, at least in the instance of the Princeton performance, Stein made the effort to drain away all the sounds and the bustle of her long writing life, so that the audience might hear only its bare outline. Her style was formal and solemn, but also confusing. She sounded like one of the anonymous Americans that populate her lectures, driven by the anxiety to act in a limited space of time: 'nobody who is an American feels what is inside this space of time not in any way excepting in the way that it is inevitable that there is this space of time' (*LA* 160). As her initial project of cataloguing human types dissolves into the nervous rhythm of the given space of time, Stein's America names a creative model of frenzied output, of incessant production. At the same time, it exerts the seduction of a philosophical principle, now appearing as a self-grounding truth ('I feel this thing'), now as a worn cliché. Stein's public American depth is a bit like the Lacanian phallus, the ultimate signifier on which the coherence of her self-presentation depends, while at the same time, it is in danger of being unveiled as a sham.[9] She goes as far as presenting the American public interior as a principle of intellectual justice.

The American space of time is a landscape filled with movement. It figures a great redistribution of knowing likened to geographical mobility: 'Think of anything [. . .] of anybody who goes anywhere or stays at home' (*LA* 161). The abstract public vista of movement (anything/anybody who can go or stay) disposes of that other meaning of movement as cultural currents, schools of thought regulated by the master-disciple dialectic. In *The Making of Americans* she had promised to return to the question of masters and schools, that is to say, to the question of a knowledge that accumulates in the hands of a few (*MA* 486). The movement inside Stein's landscape seems to transform the ossifying enclosure implied by the master-disciple division into a dispersed movement in space. She now projects onto an American space the intimacy that was moving in her at the time of the expanded consciousness of the modern composition, when she was 'listening seeing feeling' others (*LA* 147). America becomes the space of Stein's time, the years spent writing. The liveliness of her former years merges with the movement of the American thing: 'I feel this thing [. . .] Think of anything [. . .] of anybody who goes anywhere or stays at home.' But how exactly does anybody that goes anywhere or stays at home feel? How does it feel to move between some place and another called home?

Places of transit play a crucial role in conceptualizing movement for those who can choose to go home or stay. Airports, for instance, are exciting because people feel as if poised on a threshold. In an airport, the return home is experienced as the rejoining of a community. But returning home does not always mean going back to the reassuring intimacy that the word 'home' is supposed to conjure. On the contrary, going home might mean rejoining the space of a fixed identity. One feels that, having once crossed the threshold of the airport, one will fall into a common thing that becomes difficult to describe because it is made of a set of components—language, accents, gestures, etc.—that are supposed to bind individuals in a group. There might be an anticipation of comfort as one falls into this public interior. Each individual is taken in; each individual steps out of strange places and into this familiar terrain. But while it conveys a sense of belonging, the common thing is also disturbing.

One can stand back from his or her sense of commonality and cultural belonging to feel, in a vague way, an exclusionary force lodged there. The sensation has a private authority, resembling that of the reverie. As discussed in the previous chapter, the reverie has a private import when compared to the more impersonal authority of the larger symbolic connective: language, bodies, clothes, gestures, all speaking to a supposed affinity that binds. Nevertheless, when in transit between places, one can glimpse the exclusionary potential of community. One can stand as if on a threshold and breathe in the excitement, the strong emotion of a distance (spatial but also in a particular time of the mind) from the temptation of an emotional communal consensus. Visions of angry crowds, angry groups, families warming in their niches cut out in the symbolic circle rise before one's eyes. Yet, on the threshold of places of transit, one can even boast of the incredible freedom of one's individuality without being accused of living outside history and outside the human community. Minutes extend to a long time in the imagination: soon each will go through a check-in gate, each will be channeled in a group, each group in a country. In time, each will fall inside a culture, left to feel in different degrees the struggle for achievement inside it. A few minutes, even a few hours, and all will be placed in their communities ready to be tolerant or to rebel, completely free to accept or to reject the symbolic 'thing' that connects them all. And as one uses up the last seconds of that utter freedom which transiting places afford and resigns oneself to going home and staying, one can only hope seriously for more tolerant communities and homes, as well as for the support of the symbolic shared 'thing.' We owe to such states of detachment texts like Freud's *Civilization and Its Discontents.* As if speaking from the distanced mood I have described, Freud wonders why community must happen and answers that we do not know.

Like the visitor whom the course of things has pushed beyond the threshold point, Stein, contemplates the warming knowledge of an American common space. She appeals to the narrative of a bond that Americans share ('anybody who is an American feels what is inside this space of time') and subordinates her writing to it. In our example, the visitor enjoyed her position at a distance from the culture of entry, where she can 'feel,' as Stein would say, the abstract work of a common culture that nevertheless bears its concrete stamp on each individual. As the visitor dwells on that invisible threshold long enough for her sense of justice to be provoked, she is likely to become alerted to the fact that the entrance into a culture, the feeling of cultural belonging, rests on the appreciation of an almost imperceptible exclusion. The visitor has the privilege, if she chooses, to linger in that intellectual space of contemplation where the force of exclusion acts. It is doubtful, however, that if she is a writer, the vista will give her writing that will feel beautiful. That vista is, in many ways, unbearable fare.

As the visitor would do, Stein embraces the common thing; she becomes eager to join the circle of people held together by the 'American thing.' She leaps to it—'I am an American'—and clears all obstacles from her place at the eucharistic table of the nation: 'this book is an American book an essentially American book.' The deictic function asserts a concrete sense of belonging that needs no explanation because it has the immediacy of a thing and does not need to be proved as if it were a concept. But as we have seen, the exclusionary dynamic of public culture perceived by our visitor in the example above was as vague as this 'American thing' that cannot be explained without body language—'this'—or without going home.

Stein's American thing sounds like a symbolic monody that expresses her desire for recognition at home. But the audiences who had heard the lecture 'Plays' knew that it named an aesthetic difference made first of all by Stein herself and then by the American creativity whose genealogy she publicly claimed. Far from referring to some national essentialism, the American thing was fraught with 'nervousness' (*LA* 95). It marked a transition from the modern composition to another aesthetics. In accordance with her strategy of reconfiguration of space noticed by DeKoven and discussed above, Stein proceeds to include her private modernist writing, done in isolation from America, in an American culture made amenable to her experimental uniqueness, which is now what 'anybody who is an American feels' (*LA* 160). As suggested in the previous chapter on *Four Saints in Three Acts*, Stein turned her attention to issues of reception and the question of the inclusion of the reader or viewer.

The question of the receiver's inclusion remains central in literary studies today. From the New Criticism on, the autonomy of literary studies has been staked on the elusive passage from 'a private act of appreciation' (Ransom 594) to 'criticism, which is public and negotiable' (Ransom 595). In the 1960s and 1970s, the notion of the open work arose to account for the role of the individual, random associations elicited by a visual or verbal text in the act of interpretation. Today, the credibility of literary studies still hinges on our willingness to account for the individual aspect of aesthetic reception. Poststructuralist indeterminacy came as a welcome replacement of the once huge, elitist distance between creator and receiver, parallel to the one between reader and critic. But the question of how private reading and looking become open to public critical discourse remains more urgent than ever. What makes a critic a critic and a reader a reader? Where does the divide between the two begin?

The ideas put forth in 'Plays' and reworked in 'The Gradual Making of The Making of Americans' address such questions and thus make an important contribution to literary studies. The dynamics of reception is the topic of 'Plays.' Stein begins by speaking of the reception of drama: 'This thing the fact that your emotional time as an audience is not the same as the emotional time of the play is what makes one endlessly troubled about a play' (*LA* 94). Clearly, the trouble of plays is the trouble of art reception in general: the creator and the receiver are separated by a line; they keep missing each other: 'One will always be behind or in front of the other' (*LA* 95). If earlier in her lecture Stein talks of an audience, therefore of a social group, later with the example of jazz she clarifies that the problem of reception in art does not mean that the latter should be understood by audiences as groups. She is not referring to a public meaning accessible to all. She imagines reception, and thus interpretation, as a jazz performance in which every participant can join despite the 'difference' (*LA* 95) between himself or herself and 'everybody including all those doing it and all those hearing and seeing it' (*LA* 95). Jazz is an apt metaphor for social differences experienced at the individual level as a 'difference in tempo' (*LA* 95) between interiority and the outside world. The metaphor does not constrain individuals in ideological or sociological blocs, according to their class, gender, orientation, beliefs, etc. Instead, it visualizes a group (the jazz band) and raises the question of individual freedom within it.

The problem of reception is the willingness to see that the public space of meaning and the emotional time of the viewer/reader might be at odds. The crucial question then becomes: How can this private or individual emotional time merge with public meaning without sacrificing its difference? Stein makes sure that we get her social metaphor: 'Nervousness consists in needing to go faster or go slower so as to get together. It is that that makes anybody feel nervous' (*LA* 95). It is in this way that she raises questions that concern contemporary literary criticism and aesthetic theories. The emotional time of the individual viewer has been a phantom for literary criticism as it undermines its aspiration to become a specialized public discourse. The New Criticism exorcized the phantom by positing appreciative readers captivated by close knit patterns of form and content. But the New Critical groundbreaking appreciation of forms and the rhetorical recasting of truth seemed to deny any individual intrusion on the part of the interpreter. This changed with feminism and poststructuralism, when the historicity and the material situation of the reader/viewer got in the way and in fact changed the formal vocation of criticism into a larger cultural one. Still, the text in these critical movements is made to speak for the interest of social groups, to acknowledge ideas, moods, feelings through which individuals claim their political affiliation to a particular group. The critic is a spokesperson, a public identity first of all, and must subordinate his personal aesthetic responses to ideas that might be recognized by the group he or she is addressing. In fact he or she might even contribute to cement the group's sense of collective identity. What Stein calls the emotional time of the receiver can be accounted for in critical discourse only as a collective emotional time. Thus the individual receiver merges with an ideal receiver representative of social groups that were perhaps formerly denied an existence in culture. This is why scholars of the avant-garde and literary scholars alike have raised the question of the surveillance of meaning by criticism.[10] It seems that the difference between critic and reader or viewer yokes interpretation to social hierarchies. Given this mimetic correspondence between criticism and society, the question of how innovation will come about in the literary or aesthetic realms becomes crucial. There seems to be a need to rethink the experience of reading and seeing with the aim of freeing them from the fear that the individual encounter with an image or a text represents for the public status of interpretation. The encounter of the individual viewer and the creative artifact is generally made of an associative chain of ideas, fragments of memory, error, misrecognition. The role that these play in interpretation as a form of public discourse remains open to debate. For this reason, Stein's reconfiguration of private and public sounds like a problem of our time.[11]

When Stein says that the problem of individual inclusion, 'this thing that makes you nervous' (*LA* 95), is 'an essentially American thing' (*LA* 160), she is also suggesting that it is at the origins of American literature. The 'feathered crew' of Anne Bradstreet's 'Contemplations' (191) comes to mind. Bradstreet contemplates a pattern in which each separate individuality 'tunes his pretty instrument' (192). Bradstreet's pattern becomes the 'space filled with moving' (*LA* 161) of Stein's American lectures, and it might have been behind Saint Therese's attraction for visions of community: 'Can any one feel any one moving' (*LO&P* 27). Movement in space connotes empathy; it encourages visions of a less rigid humanity. In the lectures the question of social patterns made of synchronous individualities becomes free from the religious metaphor and is openly posed as the question of literary and artistic value. This must reckon with the emotional time or individual experience of meaning.

With its allusion to more tolerant communities, Stein's 'space of time' might have a utopian ring to it. But the utopian undertone of the lectures should not make us blind to the intensity of their author's aesthetic beliefs. While denying neither the formalist impulse of art and its interpretation nor the love of forms and beauty, she stakes innovation in art and its related fields on the challenge of the individual's relationship to public meaning.

Like her modernist colleagues, to a certain extent, Stein wrote in reaction to history. Alessandro Portelli has argued that modernist writing counteracts the 'familiar democratic nightmare' (41) represented by the rising masses and their challenge to authority.[12] After all, in *Three Lives* Stein had tapped right into the democratic nightmare of many conservatives in inaugurating a new writing and claiming oral origins for it (Portelli 57). Racialized and working class characters had provided the young writer with 'the sound of an intriguing [and all American] primitive glamour' (Portelli 136). Similarly, it could be argued that the American thing of Stein's more public phase borrows its contagious allure from social conflicts forced into an essentialist social interiority shared by all. This impulse to tame conflict into pleasing forms, as we have seen, was a concern for Stein in *Four Saints in Three Acts*. By the time she wrote the lectures, she seemed more intent on asking how the merging of individual and social perspectives can happen and does happen. Her space of time, filled with echoes of Bradstreet's collective pattern of singular players, is also a tense, nervous space. It is filled with the pressure of individual meaning and symbolic import, with a drive to participate that traverses the whole social body.

From this point of view Stein is one of the authors of the open work because she invites the receiver to becomes a co-producer of meaning, or of the postmodern composition where objects and fragments can be at the same time as personal and collectively meaningful, indeterminate and referential. I am thinking of Robert Rauschenberg's work.[13] If so, she also usefully cautions that even postmodern undecidability might be a way of silencing the individual aspect of reading and interpretation by forcing it into an abstract collective identity, albeit always in flux.

In a way, the postmodernist view of meaning as polysemic, multiple and even aporetic is heir to the structuralist conviction that we are all part of language, that we all begin in language,[14] and that therefore we can track the collective meaning of even the most enigmatic signs and objects coming from the private world of the maker. Yet, as contemporary critical thought keeps arguing, there are requirements for entering language and sociality.[15] We do not all begin in language. Stein's American space is about the burden of those requirements: '[O]ne will always be behind or in front of the other' (*LA* 95). Her formula for embodied knowledge, 'a space of time,' expresses a certain anxiety about the channeling of individual meaning into collective wholes. In fact, in her text the nervous tension that traverses the vista of expressive individualities is a reminder that we may not all be born in language.

Those who read Stein can tell that they are invited, that the 'I of writing is a we' (Riddel 108). But Stein tries not to force the projection of an inclusive we. She asks how an I at odds with the collective composition can be valued in public practices like art and interpretation. The anxiety can be heard precisely in the passage about the American thing: 'I felt this thing [. . .] and I felt this thing [. . .] this sense of a space of time [. . .] and what is to be done within this space of time [. . .] what is inside this space of time [. . .] and so well they do what they do within [. . .] within' (*LA* 160). The space of time also sounds like a confinement and a pressure to do, as if the doers were haunted by an impoverishment that will take the doing away: '[o]ne will always be behind or in front of the other' (*LA* 95).

The other side of the American thing is semiotic aphanisis.[16] With this expression I want to refer to a waning of semiotic power that, in Stein's passage, undermines doing (writing). The repetition of 'do' conjures the link of representation to time: 'writing time never effaces the shadow of the hand that leads it' (Riddel 107). It ties writing and symbolic expression to the calamity of signs. 'They do what they do' means that expression goes on despite the fact that signs withdraw their reciprocity. In her lecture 'Poetry and Grammar' she had said:

> Poetry is concerned with using with abusing, with losing with wanting, with denying with avowing with adoring with replacing the noun. It is doing that always doing that, doing that and doing nothing but that. Poetry is doing nothing but using losing refusing pleasing and betraying and caressing nouns. (*LA* 231)

Signs, nouns, speak to you insofar as you do something to them, caressing, using, abusing, negating, and so on. The long list of sexualized labor implies not an exchange but the fear of a lack of reciprocity. Only insofar as you act, signs, like a lover, keep replying and speaking to you. The space of time in which 'well they do what they do' (*LA* 160) has been seen as a non-hierarchical space: 'a composing of an open field' (Riddel 106). The fact, however, remains of the pressure that can be heard in this doing. 'They do what they do' evokes the open field insofar as this is beset by an unspecified aggression, an absence of action that may well up and take over when you know that you are in a space of time, as if the doing, that is, an active relation to signs, might be taken away from you at any time. The theme of Stein's passage on the American thing is the emergency of a symbolic import felt by each and every one. Her space of time is 'nothing but an individual difference' (*LA* 95). Can individual difference tune in? Does it? How can literary studies account for this non-hierarchical open field of human resources that demand symbolic participation?

The elusiveness of Stein's thing is further proof of the importance of the questions it poses for literary studies. Stein's thing can neither be fondled by thought nor romanced and glamorized with nostalgia. Its stumbling rhythm makes a show of its accent, of its social class. In her lecture on English-speaking literature Stein had made the point of a class difference between English and American Literature: 'What is English literature that, by English literature I mean American too' (*LA* 11). 'American literature too' is a pun on the numeral 2, meaning American as well, added and secondary. Like secondary social subjects, this literary object might become slightly dangerous. If you go near it, perhaps it will fire back. A loaded gun? In 'Plays' Stein had used the adjective 'violent' (*LA* 95) to qualify the difference between an individual and 'every body' (*LA* 95), thus pointing to the urgency of an individual desire for meaning.

It is possible to sense a shift in the American lectures from the calm of her previous academic experience to a different, problematic tempo. In her British lecture 'Composition as Explanation' (1926) the modern composition had consisted of a relaxed correspondence between seeing and living: 'Composition is the thing seen by every one living in the living they are doing' (523). In the American space of time seeing cedes to a doing doomed to materiality ('this') and temporality: 'They do what they do within this space of time' (*LA* 160). In the modern landscape of 'Composition as Explanation' no one was different: 'nothing inside them in all of them makes it connectedly different' (526). The space of a uniform social identity made Picasso stand out. In the American composition, individual nervousness increases: 'this sense of a space of time and what is to be done with this space of time not in any way excepting in the way that it is inevitable' (*LA* 160). In 'Composition as Explanation' no one was ahead of his time (521); now composition is made of different tempos, of individual differences. It is a space where each feels ahead or behind, where each equally conveys an almost physiological impulse to mean. The American thing itself cannot be serenely conveyed, as if it were always ahead or behind formalist detachment: 'I wonder if I at all convey to you what I mean by this thing' (*LA* 160). One can guess that this thing has to do with a love of forms. Here, as in *Four Saints in Three Acts* or 'Composition as Explanation,' Stein imagines a space in which presences are intimated like beloved pictorial forms. But these are forms that resist detached critical elucidation.

Stein could raise the aesthetic question of the individual's relationship to public meaning, of literature and its interpretation as open fields of human resources pulsing to mean, because, in her strife to become a public woman, she had experienced first hand the emotional time of her experimentalism and felt at odds with the interpretive community at large. As a public woman she came to believe that only by crossing that dividing line symbolized by the stage, by the page, or by the canvas could innovation take place. Her socio-theatrical 'nervousness' might seem to rise out of a scene of nineteenth-century American life. The line between doers and spectators is the theme of *Shad Fishing at Gloucester on the Delaware River* (1881) by Thomas Eakins. The innocent act of looking at fishermen is a good enough occasion to reinforce the dividing line: the artist's family looks on while the fishermen's nets form a material divide that reconfigures the open natural space as the closed dramatic space of a theater, with

one class neatly separated from the other and looking on. The boundary drawn by
the instrument of labor (the nets) makes sure that the two groups remain strangers
one to the other. If Eakins is fascinated by the influence of the line, Stein, after
him, is more interested in dissolving it.

Appendix I

Stein and the Performing Arts

Four Saints in Three Acts was the only text to be successfully performed in Stein's life time. Lord Berner and Frederick Ashton collaborated on *A Wedding Bouquet,* a ballet adapted from Stein's *They Must. Be Wedded. to Their Wife.* It was first danced at the Sadler's Wells Theatre by Margot Fonteyn in the role of Julia in 1937 and revived during Stein's lifetime in 1941, and later at Covent Garden in 1949.[1] The ballet associates the voices in Stein's play to memorable characters who gather for a wedding. Soon, the event transforms into a series of incidents thar reveal the groom's philandering past. Most of the women at the wedding turn out to be his mistress. Among the characters are Webster, the maid who organizes the wedding, the forlorn Julia, who throws herself at the feet of the groom, and Josephine, who drinks too much champagne. Simple and sophisticated at the same time, walking the fine boundary between 'zany Humor' and slapstick comedy, the ballet has become known as 'a connoisseur' s piece' (Walzer 81).

In the post-World War II years Stein's work became a source for experimental theater. The Living Theater gave first a private drawing room performance of 'Ladies Voices,' a piece from *Geography and Plays*, in the summer of 1950.[2] Then, the company went on to stage *Doctor Faustus Lights the Lights* a year later, in December 1951 at the Cherry Lane Theater, with the direction of Judith Malina and the stage design by Julian Beck. Just a month earlier, Stein's libretto had been made into a successful play at Beaver College, at Glenside. Princeton, where Stein was hailed by students as 'the bard of Bedlam' during her lecture tour ('Trudy and Alice in Jungleland' 2), ended up producing 'Yes Is for a Very Young Man' in 1948.[3] Judith Malina and Julian Beck's interest in *Doctor Faustus* set the trend for a series of revisitations of Stein's libretto by The Judson Poets' Theater, by experimental director Richard Foreman in 1982,[4] and later by Robert Wilson in 1989 and 1992. In 1999 the Wooster Group produced *House/Lights*, a surrealist version of Stein's libretto of *Doctor Faustus Lights the Lights*.[5] 'What Happened' became an off-Broadway production by Lawrence Kornfeld in the early sixties and won an Obie for best musical in 1964.[6] Arlene Rothlein, then a leading performer for the Jusdon Dance Theater, was in it.

At the time Rothlein was a young dancer associated with James Waring. Waring was the dancer's most powerful creative and teaching influence. Rothlein studied with him at the Merce Cunningham Studio. In collaboration with her teacher, she created the dance solo *Twelve Objects from Tender Buttons*, first performed at The Cubiculo in New York on 26 June 1972. Don MacDonagh commented: '[James Waring] made a solo for Miss Rothlein that capitalizes on bursts of condensed activity contrasted with calm repose.'[7] When four years later Arlene Rothlein danced the same solo at the Merce Cunningham studio, the percussion musical score of The Cubiculo performance was replaced by music with quotes from Chinese Opera Theater. Played at the end of each movement, as the dancer stands still, the music's Oriental reference best draws out that combination of energy and repose noted by the reviewer of the *New York Times*.

The dance solo *Twelve Objects from Tender Buttons* was recorded some years later, in the summer of 1976, at the Merce Cunnigham Studio.[8] In this version, the Oriental element is further underscored. Rothlein wears a red top and wide pants with a black belt. Some of her movements quote from the marshal arts, especially movement five, 'What is the wind,' while the music directly quotes the Chinese Opera Theater. The orientalism of the piece brings to the surface references already buried in Stein's text. Movement seven, for instance, performs a fragment where Stein refers to Japan and is dominated by images of breakages and mending.

References to the Orient combine with quotes from children's play in movement ten, 'A shine,' and the redolent beauty of classic ballet in the final movement, 'Little sail ladies [...] beautiful, beautiful, beautiful [...]. The whole piece conveys the impression of a balancing act. The dancer is a disciplined warrior. In movement three, 'Dirt and not Copper,' even breathing seems a stylish act of survival.

Rothlein's solo, which admirably mixes grace and mastery, is one of the best readings of Stein's *Tender Buttons*. Interestingly, the last movement begins with the dancer miming the fragment 'suppose a gate,' with her body sliding sideways, one arm moving up and down in front of her face. The movement captures the sequences' s oscillation between vision and disguise.[9]

In the 1980s Jane Comfort's *Duet for Four Hands* retains the same visual and dramatic impact of Rothlein's interpretation of Stein. Originally presented by the Dance Theater workshop at the American Theater Laboratory, 219 West 19th St., in New York on 4 December 1980, *Duet for Four Hands* was a twelve minute piece part of a longer performance entitled *Split Stream*.[10] Jane Comfort is joined by other performers: Blondell Cumming, Marjorie Gamso, Susan Yabroff. While two performers read the text in sign language the other two simultaneously read the text out loud. Stein's text regains the rhythm of a meditation, with changes of direction, pauses, and associative developments. The performance moves between the relative ease of defining human nature and the difficulty of deciding what the human mind is: 'Human nature makes me nervous. It is like a great war,' or: 'Human nature is what any human being will do,' followed by the question: 'And the Human mind?' [. . .] The actors show the extent to which Stein engages her reader at an individual, almost private level: 'Please see my human mind.'

The theme of the performance is the impossibility of pinning identity down: 'Am I I if my little dog knows me?' The difficulty of knowing what we are has to do with time, which shapes identity as a shifting position. In Stein's text only a strange intimacy with the anonymous readers can make the I more permanent, and make the I 'like' what it is. Addressing her audience. Stein asks provocative questions about identity: 'And how do you like what you are. And how are you what you are?'

The duet actually strengthens the effect of the meditation, with sign language emphasizing listening: 'Tears come into my eyes when I say the human mind.' The performance consists precisely in stumbling into this question, in the pain and the love of the question. Jane Comfort and her colleagues make us hear the rustling of ideas visiting Stein's mind as if they were visiting ours. As they speed through and disappear they create a strange commonality between Stein and her readers, based on a difficult knowledge.

Acting and dance complete Stein's texts. This productive approach continued through the 1990s. An example is Rachel Germond's *Solo with Black Eggs*. (*For Picasso*) presented in 19l93 as part of the 'Food For Thought' initiative at St Mark's Church in New York.[11] Germond's performance, inspired by Stein's portrait of Picasso 'If I Told Him,' reads the relationship between the two as a positive form of artistic collaboration. The dance opens with quotations from the circus world, favored by Picasso before he met Stein. The dancer holds two oval-shaped musical instruments producing unrecognizable sounds, midway between the cicada's verse, the noise of silver coins, and the music of Spanish castanets. The dance is divided in two parts, with a crisis in the middle. The structure and the enigmatic movements of the dancer in the passage between first and second act suggest transformation. The dancer emerges from the central crisis in a glittery costume and her hair loose, an image of self-celebration. The enigmatic gestures at the center of the performance iconize Stein's admiration for Picasso's expressive power.

Sometimes performers have been attracted more to Stein's legend than to her writing. In the early 1980s the dancer Beverly Blossom used quotes from 'A Very Valentine' and *Geography and Plays* to create a feminist collage with a turn of the century and early 1920s atmosphere evoked by costumes and by the use of old photographs.[12] Stein and her legend serve to celebrate the difference of feminine identity in our contemporary world. Stein's legendary ménage with Toklas provides the frame of reference for a postmodern couple living in a postmodern hell in *The Modest Typist* (1994). Amy Pivar and Frieda Rosen play Alice and Gertrude. Alice-Amy is a typist working in a highly competitive world. Frieda Rosen plays a contemporary of Stein. Her bowler hat makes her look like one of Samuel Beckett's melancholy clochards. The second and third parts of the show, 'When she saw' and 'Chaos and One dancing,' draw on 'Orta or One Dancing' to celebrate individual beauty. The piece is a feminist critique of the unlovable postmodernist 1990s and Pivar looks to Stein for life-affirming models: 'She went on and changing.'[13]

Young performers and directors are increasingly turning to Stein. For example, in the summer of 2001 her play Mexico, directed by Kelly Cooper, was on at St Mark's Church in New York City, in a double bill with Michael Comlish's

Nothing, adapted from the notebooks of Richard Foreman. At the same time, *Photograph* was also playing. A Company of young actors, the Duende Theater Company, staged *Doctor Faustus Lights the Lights* as part of the New York Fringe Festival.[14]

Appendix II

Melody Makers: Gonzalo Tena on Gertrude Stein

Gertrude Stein (1874-1946) wrote *Stanzas in Meditation* in 1932. At that time she was thinking about the difference between poetry and prose, and had decided that poetry consisted in replacing the noun with the thing in itself. Accordingly, while writing her best seller in prose, *The Autobiography of Alice B. Toklas*, she also composed another autobiography in verse subdivided in a sequence of 83 stanzas. This other autobiography (published posthumously in 1956) tells the story of a voice enchanted with the visible world, in the attempt to entreat it onto the page. But how does one represent a voice calling out to the outside world? In *Stanzas* words are treated as if they were autonomous objects, without further reference. The result is that poetry becomes an essential apostrophe to the alluring materiality of things. As she moves from stanza to stanza, Stein ends up meditating on the possibility of such melody in the modern world.

The prime object of her meditation, then, is an old dream of harmony—the union of body and letter, of meaning and being—but presented in such an abstract way as to reach us disfigured. It is as if she had dreamed of Shelley's own hymn to union, 'Epipsychidion,' and upon waking up had committed it to the page. The new version is only the minimal outline of the dreamed text, eroded by the lack of memory and by the distortions that typically mark the passage from dream to waking state. In many ways, *Stanzas* is a puzzle, readable only in bits and pieces, when we pull out lines, words, fragments from the whole. Stein's extreme experiment asks for a different kind of reading based on the selection of isolated elements to which we hold on without fully understanding why. In this reading procedure we remain strangers to the text while simultaneously becoming intimate with some of its details, letting them do their work on our imagination. This is what Stein meant by her famous motto: 'I write for myself and strangers.'

It is no coincidence that contemporary Spanish artist Gonzalo Tena chooses *Stanzas in Meditation* as the centerpiece of his dialogue with Gertrude Stein. Like few other modernist texts, Stein's poetic sequence raises the question of intention, on the reader's part, as a matter of selection. *Stanzas* (2000), Tena's homage to the American writer, demonstrates that selection is not only the Steinian principle of productive reading, but also a principle of contagious creativity.

Selection is at the heart of Gonzalo Tena's creative process in the paintings included in *Stanzas*. He starts with pre-existing images, usually technically reproduced images of Roman mosaics from books, magazines, or newspapers. Next, the reproduced image is xeroxed. A detail is chosen, magnified, and further reproduced on colored paper. Later, there are rehearsals with words and colors. Finally, words selected from Stein's poetry are associated to the triptych on colored paper, the size of the canvas is decided, and color is applied, at first in more fluid layers and then in progressively thicker ones. Stein's themes of vitality and care make their way in Tena's paintings, as shown in *At least to move* (Fig. II.1), and *When they took care* (Fig. II.2). The concatenation of selective acts is not separate from the crucial notion of play. Both Stein and Tena convey the distinct sense of a playfulness that transforms into accomplished labor. Through play Stein composes her texts; through play Tena realizes something in a large size. Evoking an exceptional absorption in the process of the composition, playfulness indicates an almost fusional relation between the subject (artist) and the object of the composition. Interestingly, the symbiosis expresses itself in a desire for the Oriental element, subtly incorporated by Stein and Tena.

Like the work of some great American painters—Jackson Pollock, Franz Klein, Robert Motherwell—Tena's abstractions break with the specular relation to the canvas. He paints while bent on a canvas laid on the floor or on a table. Working on the floor he uses a bigger brush, holding it in a vertical position as it is done in calligraphy. This built-in reference to the orient is amplified in the final composition, which recalls the three elements of a haiku, each with the same value. The distinctive trait of the haiku is the osmosis of the subject and the nature described. The subject disappears in the objective world, which is at the same time de-materialized through moods and tonalities.

Looking at compositions like *Once in a while nothing happens* (Fig. II.3), one wonders if color is not all. But one must not be mislead. Just like Stein's writing, the abstract force of these chromatic melodies does not imply the void of meaninglessness. Color here is in a dialogue with the past, present through the images eroded to the point of non-recognition by successive technical reproductions. These strange forms look like tubers, tissues, tracks. They intimate a classicist motif—the individual talent's struggle with tradition. They testify to a monumental tradition at the origin of the composition. But now, soaked and lost in color, the past beckons only weakly, through vague signs that cannot devour what will come after them. Stein had her own way of describing the struggle with tradition. She used to say that the task of the artist is to be exciting. The excitement of play and the absorption in the immediacy of the composition ensure the survival of individual talent.

Play, however, also means making decisions and going against them. The painter goes against the rhythm of the painting, pursuing comic effects, something that Stein does with puns and word games. Thus, while selection might be bound up with chance, there is here an effort at reviving the question of individual decision or intention, a notion that postmodernism has emphatically disavowed. Do we have to choose between the aesthetic bliss of melody and the cold search for meaning? Is there a middle ground between aesthetic abandon and the mastery of meaning? These occidental visual haikus, these 'orientalized' stanzas, do not incite their viewers to a passive abandon to the drift of meaning. On the contrary, the contagious chromatic melodies seem to heighten the awareness of our individuality as viewers. Importantly, it is the captions from Gertrude Stein's *Stanzas* that decide this higher level. They govern any hedonistic temptation, keeping us anchored in the act of listening to the dialogue of text and image.

Stein admired the genius of Spain, most notably in the person of her friend Pablo Picasso, and even considered her own penchant for abstraction Spanish. Surely, she would be delighted to know that, with time, she has become even more Spanish thanks to the work of contemporary artist Gonzalo Tena.[1]

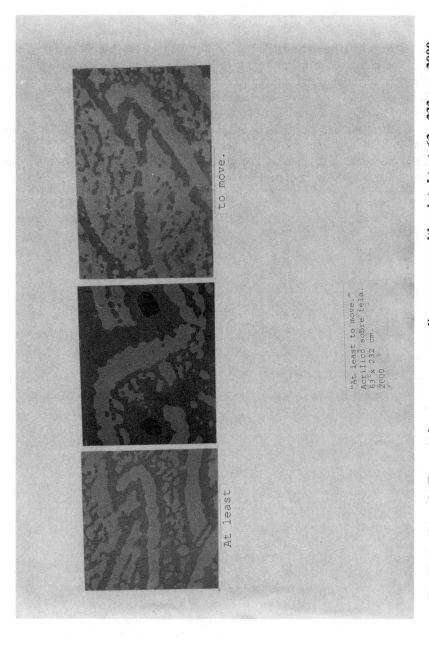

At least

to move.

"At least to move."
Acrílico sobre tela.
63 x 232 cm.
2000

Fig. II.1 Gonzalo Tena, *At least to move*, acrylic on canvas with printed text, 63 x 232 cm., 2000.

Fig. II. 2   Gonzalo Tena, *When they took care*, acrylic on canvas with printed text, 63 x 232 cm., 2000.

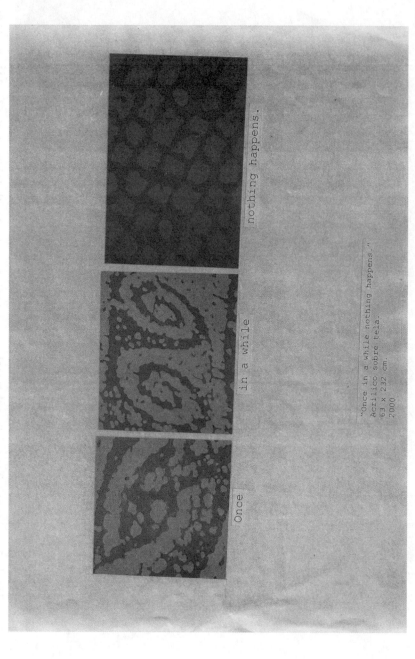

Fig. II.3 Gonzalo Tena, *Once in a while nothing happens*, acrylic on canvas with printed text, 63 x 232 cm., 2000.

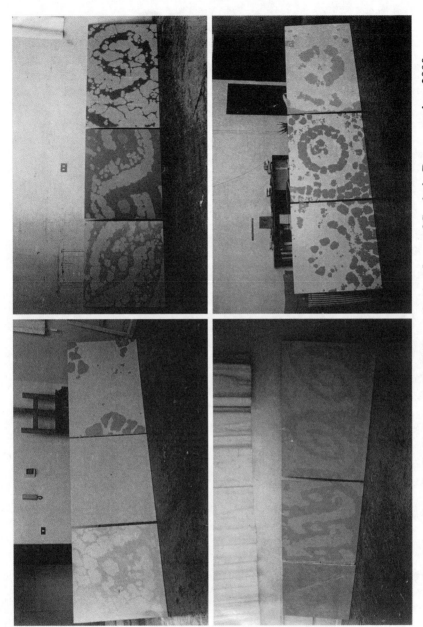

Fig. II.4   Gonzalo Tena, the artist's studio at the Academy of Spain in Rome,   spring 2000.

Notes

Introduction

1   Catharine Stimpson invites us 'to realize that a page of [Stein's] writing yearns to be a theater, a music hall, a garden, a room'. 'Review Essay: Reading Gertrude Stein', *Tulsa Studies in Women's Literature* 4.2 (Fall 1985): 265-271; 269. Stimpson has amply discussed the richness of Stein's page as it intersects issues of sexuality, in a number of articles. Here are some of the most frequently quoted: 'The Somagrams of Gertrude Stein,' *Poetics Today* 6.1-2 (1985):67-80; 'Gertrude Stein: Humanism and Its Freaks,' *Boundary 2: A Journal of Postmodern Literature and Culture* 12-13. 3-1 (Spring-Fall 1984): 301-19; 'Gertrice/Altrude: Stein, Toklas, and the Paradox of the Happy Marriage,' Ruth Perry ed., *Mothering the Mind: Twelve Studies of Writers and Their Silent Partners* (New York: Holmes and Meier, 1984) 122-139; 'Gertrude Stein and the Transposition of Gender,' Nancy Miller ed., *The Poetics of Gender* (New York: Columbia UP, 1986) 1-18.

2   See the essential study of Stein's manuscripts by Ulla Dydo, with William Rice, *Gertrude Stein: The Language that Rises 1923-1934* (Evanston, Illinois: Northwestern UP, 2003). For the contradictory aspects of Stein's relation to her Jewishness, see Maria Damon, "Gertrude Stein's Jewishness, Jewish Social Scientists, and the 'Jewish Question'," *Modern Fiction Studies* 42-3 (Fall 1996): 489-507 and Janet Malcom, 'Gertrude Stein's War: The Years in Occupied France,' *The New York Times* 2 June 2003: 59-81.

3   Juliana Spahr, *Everybody's Autonomy: Connective Reading and Collective Communities* (Tuscaloosa: U of Alabama P, 2001).

4   For a discussion of modernist aesthetics, see Marianne DeKoven, *Rich and Strange: Gender, History, Modernism* (Princeton: Princeton UP, 1991).

5   The freedom of the artist has been hard to defend ever since Renaissance princes incorporated artists in their courts to serve their princely aura. For a useful study on Renaissance patronage, see Martin Warnke, *The Court Artist: On the Ancestry of the Modern Artist* (Cambridge: Cambridge UP, 1993).

6   Margaret Potter, introduction, *Four Americans in Paris: The Collections of Gertrude Stein and Her Family* (New York: Museum of Modern Art, 1970).

7   I am thinking about the work of Camelia Elias on Lynn Emanuel. Elias uses the expression 'notional ekphrasis' to describe Emanuel's speaker's intercourse with Stein. As Elias argues, genius is 'to arrive at new combinations, make them work, and make them acknowledged.' For Emanuel it was not enough to compare literary strategies for poetic expression; she need to be 'inside Gertrude Stein.' In *Then, Suddenly* (1999), Emanuel writes: 'So, I am inside Gertrude; we belong to each other, she and I, and it is so wonderful because I have always been a thin woman inside of whom a big woman is screaming to get out, and she's out now and if a river could type this is how it would sound, pure and complicated and enormous.' See Camelia Elias, 'Sexing up genius: tableau instaurations in Lynn Emanuel and Gertrude Stein,' Session 15: Modernism I, Poetry and Sexuality Conference, The University of Sterling, Scotland, June 30-July 4, 2004.

8   In a 1937 letter to Bennet Cerf, Stein mentions 'the feeling of being a real author.' 'Introduction,' ed. Edward M. Burns and Ulla Dydo with William Rice, *The Letters of Gertrude Stein and Thornton Wilder* (New Haven and London: Yale UP, 1996) xvii.

9   For a defense of theory's pursuit of embodied knowledge that also points to the difficulties of its reception in institutions of education, see the work of Lauren Berlant. I refer to Berlant because theory's attempt, for example, 'to deuniversalize [the senses], rooting them somewhere in a space of time', clearly uses the Steinian phrase for embodied writing. For a discussion of 'a space of time' as it occurs in Stein, see the last section of chapter one in this study. Lauren Berlant, 'Critical Inquiry, Affirmative Culture,' *Critical Inquiry* 30 (Winter 2004): 445-451; 448.

10 In daring and less daring ways, modern culture has grasped a continuum between abstract notions of human identity and social regulations, prohibitions, and hierarchies. Interiority is not sheltered from the social scenarios of subjection and shame that hierarchies require, as Franz Kafka, the father of contemporary critical thought, has shown. It could be argued that, as a historical phenomenon, psychoanalysis showed its most radical potential when it wanted to break the circle of expression and subjection. As Jacqueline Rose suggests, in her introduction to Moustapha Safouan, *Jacques Lacan and The Question of Psychoanalytic Training*, trans. Jacqueline Rose (New York: St. Martin's Press, 2000), Freud himself, while emphasizing the Oedipal law, saw in the dyad analyst/patient a new form of communication beyond prohibition. Rose first quotes Freud's on the analyst: he 'must turn his own unconscious like a receptive organ towards the transmitting unconscious of the patient. He must adjust himself to the patient as a telephone receiver to the transmitting microphone,' a view which will lead to Ella Sharpe's formula "only the unconscious can track the unconscious"' (7). Then, she comments: 'on this process, in all its fine-tuned (and slightly deranged-sounding one might say) sensitivity, legality has absolutely no purchase' (7). Because of her attention to punishing and exclusionary ideas, especially in the operas and in the lectures, Stein's writing recalls an almost psychoanalytic sensitivity for a speech beyond the shame of prohibitions. For a more literary assessment of Stein's intransigence, see Richard Poirier, 'Manly Agitations,' *The New Republic* 8 June 1998: 26-34.

11 Charles Le Vine, 'The "Open" Work of Art,' *Rooted Rhetoric: Una Tradizione dell'Arte Americana*, ed. Gabriele Guercio (Naples: Guida Editori, 1986) 124-133.

12 Paul de Man writes: 'The structural moment of concentration on the code for its own sake cannot be avoided, and literature necessarily breeds its own formalism. Technical innovations in the methodological study of literature only occur when this kind of attention predominates.' 'Semiology and Rhetoric,' *The Critical Tradition*, ed. David H. Richter (Boston: Bedford Books, 1998) 906-916; 906.

13 I am thinking of Angelo Poliziano's *Stanze Cominciate per la Giostra di Giuliano De' Medici*, first printed in Bologna in August 1494 and sometimes known simply as *Stanze* (for example in Codice Riccardiano 1576 and Codice Riccardiano 2733). Cupid's sweet venom [*dolce veleno*], mentioned in the opening of the sequence (stanza 2) would describe well the mixture of elation and melancholia that one senses when reading Stein's own stanzas. Angelo Poliziano, *Stanze Cominciate per la Giostra di Giuliano De' Medici*, ed. Vincenzo Perticone (Turin: Loescher-Chiantore, 1954).

14 Jasper Johns, *In Memory of My Feelings–Frank O'Hara*, 1961, Collection of Stephan T. Echs, Chicago, and *No*, 1961, Gallery of Art, Washington D.C., reprinted in Fred Orton, *Figuring Jasper Johns* (London: Reaktion Books, 1994) 34, 36.

15 Jean-Michel Rabaté, 'Una lingua straniata. Gli stili del modernismo,' *Il Romanzo*, ed. Franco Moretti (Turin: Einaudi, 2001) 747-773.

16 Critical thought is increasingly engaging the death-drive that seems to dominate recent history. To progress of criticism seems to be at odds with the escalation public violence at an international level. For a representative statement on the state of criticism, see Fredric Jameson, 'Symptoms of Theory or Symptoms for Theory?' *Critical Inquiry* 30 (Winter 2004): 403-408.

Chapter 1

1 Luigi Pirandello, *One, no one, and one hundred-thousand*, trans. William Weaver (Boston, Mass.: Eridanos, 1990).

2 Exemplary poems of this drama of consciousness are 'Spleen II' and 'Les Sept Vieillards' [The seven old men]. Charles Baudelaire, *Oeuvres de Baudelaire*, vol. 1 (Paris: La Pleiade, 1931) 86, 100-102.

3 In am relying on the chronology table in Catherine R. Stimpson and Harriet Chessman's edition of Stein's work for The Library of America.

4 I am thinking of Frank O'Hara, admirer of Stein and her successor in the genre of fugitive poetry. In 'Poem "À la recherche d' Gertrude Stein,"' O'Hara rewrites 'on' the body of a male lover the poetic pass that Stein had received from Cézanne. Frank O'Hara, *The Collected Poems*, ed. Donald Allen (Berkley and Los Angeles: The California UP, 1995) 349.

5 Creations like Melanctha, the heroine of one of the novellas in *Three Lives*, and especially David Hersland Jr, the hero of *The Making of Americans*, owe to the discovery of Cézanne's emphasized being. I will discuss David Hersland in chapter 2.

6 Toklas met Stein in 1907. Cézanne died in 1906, the year of Picasso's portrait of Stein.

7 As a prime example of modern aesthetics, surrealism submits meaning to desire because the latter ensures the survival of art in a semiotically anxious world where signs might no longer speak. Lacan comes from the surrealist school. Semiotic anxiety may be seen at work in the first phase of Lacan's thought, when he theorized a human subject at the mercy of the signifier. For a good biography of the man and his work, see Elizabeth Roudinesco, *Lacan*, trans. Barbara Bray (New York: Columbia UP, 1997).

8 Hannah Arendt, *Rahel Varnhagen: The Life of a Jewess*, ed. Liliane Weissberg, trans. Richard and Clara Winston (Baltimore and London: The Johns Hopkins UP, 1997). I have taken up the question of the pass as a form of heterosexualized intellectual entitlement in 'Schools and *il dolore*,' unpublished.

9 *Cézanne: Il Padre dei Moderni* [Cézanne: Father of the Moderns], Complesso del Vittoriano, Rome, 7 March-7 July 2002. My ensuing discussion of Cézanne is indebted to that exhibition and to the conversations with my companion on that visit, my sister Martina.

10 Bernard Berenson, *Lotto* (Milan: Electa editrice, 1955) 189-190.

11 For a discussion of contemporary notions of subjectivity influenced by Peirce, especially by his notion of habit, see Teresa de Lauretis, 'Semiotics and Experience, *Alice Doesn't: Feminism, Semiotics, Cinema* (Bloomington: Indiana UP, 1984) 158-186.

12 Susan Howe, *Pierce-Arrow* (New York: New Directions, 1997) 1-30.

13 Gay Wilson Allen writes that at the time of his students' experiments, in which Stein participated, James 'was trying to find the relationship between the conscious and the unconscious.' *William James: A Biography* (New York: The Viking Press, 1967) 374.

14 I am thinking of two texts here: Theodor Adorno, 'On the fetish character in music and the regression of listening,' *The Culture Industry: Selected Essays on Mass Culture*, ed. J. M. Bernstein (London: Routledge, 1991) 26-52, where Adorno maintains that under the influence of mass production art reveals its social substance in obedience, and Fredric Jameson's essay 'Postmodernism, or The Cultural Logic of Late Capitalism,' Thomas Docherty, ed., *Postmodernism: A Reader* (New York: Columbia UP, 1993) 62-92. I think Jameson's work is important. I do have reservations about the division between modern negative affect and the postmodern waning of affect. Examples of the first are Van Gogh's shoes, as they are analyzed in Martin Heidegger's essay 'The Origin of the Work of Art' or the jug in Heidegger's 'The Thing.' In both cases the observer uses the object to glamorize the oppressed. The division between modern affect and the postmodern waning of affect prevents us from seeing clearly how the European psyche is occupied for its great part by a strong anxiety about social mobility, class mobility first and foremost. Martin Heidegger, *Poetry Language, Thought*, trans. Albert Hofstadter (New York: Harper & Row Publishers, 1975) 17-87, 165-186.

15 Jean-François Lyotard discusses Cézanne's technical revolution in *Discours, Figure* (Paris: Editions Klincksieck,1971). For a different reading of Cézanne's work on the relation of internal and external, via Bergson, see Joyce Medina, *Cézanne and Modernism: The Poetics of Painting* (New York: State University of New York P, 1995).

16 Paul Cézanne, *Bridge Over the Pond* (1895-1898), oil on canvas, cm 64 x 69, Puškin Museum, Moscow, *Cézanne: Il Padre dei Moderni* [Cézanne: Father of the Moderns], edited by Maria Teresa Benedetti (Milan: Gabriele Mazzotta, 2002) 195.

17 Paul Cézanne's *Bathers*, oil on canvas, 10 ⅝ x 18 ⅛ in., ca. 1895, was one of the first paintings to enter the Stein Collection. A good introduction to the Stein Collection is Lamont Moore, foreword, *Pictures for a Picture of Gertrude Stein as a Collector and Writer on Art and Artists: An Exhibition* (New Haven: Yale University Art Gallery, 1951). For further references to *Bathers*, see Henry McBride, 'Pictures for a picture of Gertrude Stein,' *Art News* 49.10 (February 1951): 16-18; 17, and Fiorella Minervino, 'Una americana a Parigi,' *Bolaffi Arte* 7 (February 1971): 56-61; 61.

18 Brinnin reports that Arthur Lachman a fellow student of Stein, describes her as follows: she was a heavy-set, ungainly young woman, vey mannish in her appearance. Her hair was cut short at a time when this was by no means the fashion among the fair sex. She always wore black, and her somewhat ample figure was never corseted' (27). However, in at least one photo with friends at Radcliffe, Stein seems to be wearing a corset. Howard Greenfeld, *Gertrude Stein: A Biography* (New York: Crown Publishers, 1973) 10.

19 As a fount of writing, the silent Cézannes, in a sense, function much as the urn in Keats's 'Ode to a Grecian Urn.' Like the urn, the pictures are erotic and semiotic, a stand-in for Keats's silent bride ravished by the viewer who, in turn, receives from it the power of speech.

20 For this image, see the cover of Gertrude Stein, *Last Operas and Plays*, introduction Bonnie Marranca (Baltimore and London: Johns Hopkins UP, 1995).

Chapter 2

1   I am quoting from the essay 'Confusion of Tongues' included in *Final Contributions to the Problems and Methods of Psychoanalysis*. However, Ferenczi's reflections in that essay are based on various clinical cases which he recorded in his diary, *The Clinical Diary of Sándor Ferenczi*, ed. Judith Dupont, trans. Michal Balint and Nicola Zarday Jackson (Cambridge, MA: Harvard UP, 1988)

2   Stein began an early version of *The Making of Americans* in 1903. She worked at it intermittingly; at the same time she also wrote *Q.E.D.* (1903) and *Fernhurst* (1905). She resumed work on the novel in 1905 and 1906 and in 1908 Toklas began to type the manuscript, which was completed in October 1911, and finally published in 1925 by Robert McAlmon's Contact Edition. I am relying on the chronology in Catharine R. Stimpson and Harriet Chessman's edition of Stein's work for The Library of America.

3   For William James one of the best sources remains Jayne Walker, *Gertrude Stein: The Making of a Modernist* (Amherst: The U. of Massachusetts Press, 1984); for Leo Stein, see the engaging biography by Brenda Wineapple, *Sister Brother: Gertrude Stein and Leo Stein* (New York: G. P. Putnam's Sons, 1996).

4   I found the anecdote repeated in different sources, among these Walker and Wineapple. Lisa Ruddick traces Stein's declaration of her love of repetition to Notebook D. 11, where Stein writes: 'When Leo said that all classification is teleological I knew I was not a pragmatist I do not believe that [. . .] I believe in repetition.' Lisa Ruddick, *Reading Gertrude Stein: Body, Text, Gnosis* (Ithaca and London: Cornell UP, 1990) 95.

5   Linda S. Watts investigates the influence of William James's view of religious experience on Stein's writing. For Watts, 'Stein's theory of creativity echoes another point James makes concerning religious experience: not everyone has the same "propensities for it."' *Rapture Untold: Gender, Mysticism, and the `Moment of Recognition' in Works by Gertrude Stein* (New York: Peter Lang, 1996) 120.

6   For the Puritan split self, see Sacvan Bercovitch, *The Puritan Origins of the American Self* (New Haven & London: 1975) 19.

7   In Stein's novel the sins of the fathers are of a philosophical order. Thus, the mutual cushioning is also about a writing stuck with the philosophical investigation of the self.

8   Thank you to Bridget Lyons for this reference.

9   I am relying on Robert Hughes's commentary to the portrait of John Winthrop in *American Visions: An Epic History of Art in America* (New York: Alfred Knopf 1997) 32.

10   Throughout his study, George Moore finds resemblances with Leo in both David senior and David junior. In fact, Moore links *The Making of Americans* to Leo and Gertrude Stein's discussion over character. Leo seems to have been blind to human similarities. His sister, instead, embraces them and this leads to the apprehension of subjectivity. Moore takes David Hersland junior to be 'Stein's forum for this ongoing debate' (145).

11   'I write for myself and strangers' is to Stein's novel what 'London Bridge is falling down' in T. S. Eliot's *The Waste Land*: these refrains work to pinpoint the modernist experience of as division between a singular I and a collective position.

12   *Tender Buttons*, Carl Van Vechten, ed., *Selected Writings of Gertrude Stein* (New York: Vintage, 1972) 459-509, is the text where Stein will take up the problem of pieces and wholes. Despite its organization around family progress, *The Making of Americans* foreshadows that problem as fundamental in the experience of reading. The novel demands a reader who must create a whole from the textual fragments. The role of

textual unity in the transmission of meaning will weigh on Stein's transition to opera and drama after *Tender Buttons*. In opera especially, aesthetic reception depends on the unity of words, music, voice. See Linda Hutcheon & Michael Hutcheon, *Bodily Charms: Living Opera* (Lincoln and London: U of Nebraska P, 2000). I will take up this issue again in chapter 6, devoted to *Four Saints in Three Acts*.

13 On this topic, I find the work of Rey Chow illuminating, especially *Primitive Passions: Visuality, Sexuality, Ethnography, and Contemporary Chinese Cinema* (New York: Columbia UP, 1995).

14 The precedent for Stein's paean to the yes-saying lover can be found in the work of one of the novel's founding fathers, Henry Fielding. *Tom Jones* (London: Penguin, 1966) abounds in metanarrative interferences. Fielding boldly sets out the rules for his readers; these have to be his obedient subjects since he, the writer, rises in their service. As a form of social relation, the new writing (novel) has to do with class and power. Stein takes her cue from Fielding and maintains that writing is a master/servant relation, but she counteracts this view with the yes-saying lover, the figure of a devoted reader attached to writing as if to a beautiful poem learned by heart.

15 Among the theorists who defend the complexities of the Hegelian couple and its viability for present thought is Slavoj Zizek. He asks: 'is not the Master, insofar as he depends on the other's recognition, effectively his own servant's servant?' (178). Zizek argues that the master belongs to the modern philosophical narrative of subjectivity provided that narrative is not wrongly understood as the supremacy of a universal subject but as the struggle 'to articulate the paradoxical conjunction of autonomy and grace, i.e., the dependence of the very assertion of the subject's autonomy on the sympathetic response of an Otherness' (182). Slavoj Zizek, '"The Wound is Healed Only by the Spear that Smote You": The Operatic Subject and Its Vicissitudes,' *Opera Through Other Eyes*, ed. David J. Levin (Stanford, CA: Stanford UP, 1994) 177-214. I think that in Stein's case, shame poses, even more powerfully than any deconstructed binary opposition between unequal terms, the question of the unacknowledged role of gestures of response in our imaginings of human consciousness.

    An important source for the view of shame as a crucial affect in the rise of identity, especially at the junction of reading and the sense of cultural belonging, is Elizabeth Bishop's poem 'In the Waiting Room.' Elizabeth Bishop, *The Complete Poems: 1927-1979* (New York: Farrar, Straus, Giroux, 1983) 159-161.

16 In the novel's plot this is slightly undermined by the failure of money and material success. Jayne Walker notices that if Albert and David do not maintain the material success of their father's generation, their father too loses his fortune before the end of the novel. The plot thus enhances the gap between pursuit of self and social status (*The Making of a Modernist* 45).

17 For a discussion of this lecture, especially with reference to its Princeton performance, see the last chapter of this study.

Chapter 3

1 For a visual documentation of the changes in Stein's self-fashioning, see Renate Stendhal, ed., *Gertrude Stein in Words and Pictures: A Photobiography* (London: Thames and Hudson, 1994). For the transition to the more timeless look of the velvet garment, see particularly pp. 46, 47, 49, 54,62, 73,77.

2   General term for kimonos worn until the end of the Edo period. Kimono means 'thing worn.'

3   For an interesting discussion of the relevance of Stein's visual identity as an Oriental icon to her writing and its borrowings from Eastern culture, see Marina Morbiducci, '"Oriental Peaceful Penetration": Revisited. The Ideogram and Gertrude Stein's Notion of Repetition,' HOW2.4 (September 2000) http:www.departments.bucknell.edu/stadler center/how2/.

        Morbiducci's essay, which includes the reproduction of Djuna Barnes's portrait of Stein as an Oriental icon, is a response to Shawn H. Alfrey's '"Oriental Peaceful Penetration': Gertrude Stein and the End of Europe,' *The Massachusetts Review* (Autumn 1997): 405-416.

4   Jeanne Paquin, also known as 'The Mother of Modern Dress,' did for clothes what the fauves did for painting. She paved fashion's way to modernity via a taste for things exotic and oriental. She devised an aesthetic that 'incorporated a sense of high drama with seductive femininity' (Reeder 22). In her case, the kimono helped revolutionize women's clothes. In the public's mind, they now came to signify 'youth, modernity, and the height of sophistication' (Reeder 22).

5   I am relying on Everett (30-33), who relies on the description of the Villa in Dodge's *European Experiences*, the second volume of her memoir *Intimate Memories* (New York: Harcourt Brace and company, 1933-1937).

6   The letter from which I quote in the body of the text (October 1912) goes on: 'Two cables on my breakfast tray this morning—one from Edwin says "Sailing on Savoie tomorrow for I love you"—the other from Paul in answer to a letter I wrote him same time as E. wondering if I'd better come back this winter & if he still cared of thought he would or I would--& asking him to cable me. It says "Yes! Yes! Yes!—Paul' (qtd. in Everett 68-9).

Chapter 4

1   The image is reproduced in Noel Riley Fitch, *Sylvia Beach and the Lost Generation: A History of Literary Paris in the Twenties and Thirties* (New York: W.W. Norton, 1983).

2   This chapter relies on materials from the Sylvia Beach Papers, Manuscripts Division, Department of Rare Books and Special Collections, Princeton University. I will reference the materials parenthetically as Beach Papers, followed by the box number and, whenever possible, by the folder number. Most of the photos referred to in the discussion are contained in an unnumbered photo-album.

3   Paul de Man, *Allegories of Reading* (New Haven: Yale UP, 1979).

4   In *Shakespeare and Company* (Lincoln: U of Nebraska P, 1991), Sylvia Beach remembers: 'Alice had a great deal more finesse than Gertrude. And she was grown up: Gertrude was a child, something of an infant prodigy (27). A few lines later: 'Gertrude's subscription [to Beach's lending library] was merely a friendly gesture. She took little interest, of course, in any but her own books' (28).

5   Beach Papers, Box 247, photo album.

6   In a photo by Gisèle Freund, Beach Papers, Box 277, Folder 15 (The Freund folder). The mother with grey hair in glasses is the image opener of the *France-Soir* article of 1953.

7   Stein and Toklas shared Beach and Monnier's taste for the country. Their country house in Belley became the major site of Stein's production in the 1920s and early 1930s, before their important American tour. For the abjection of the country and the supposed threat it posed to the intellect and to progress in general, the crucial theoretical source remains Antonio Gramsci's Notebook 22, *Americanismo e Fordismo* (Rome: Editori Riuniti, 1991). For selections in English see David Forgasc, ed., *A Gramsci Reader: Selected Writings 1916-1935* (London: Lawrence and Wishart: 1988) 275-299.

8   Beach Papers, Box 246, Folder 11; folded in a piece of paper saying 'Adrienne pas Sylvia an 18 pas bonnes.'

9   See Kevin J. H. Dettmar and Stephen Watt, eds., *Marketing Modernisms: Self-Promotion, Canonization, and Reading* (Ann Arbor: The U of Chicago P, 1996).

10 For a review of the theoretical implications of the Lacanian perspective, see Jan Campbell, *Arguing with the Phallus: Feminist, Queer, and Postcolonial Theory. A Psychoanalytic Perspective* (London and New York: Zed Books, 2000).

11 For a discussion of fetishism that weaves together the different strains—the labor of signs, the modernist vogue of primitivism, the Marxian critique of economy, and sexuality—see Valerie Steele, *Fetish, Fashion, and Power* (New York/Oxford: Oxford UP, 1996). As Steele notes, Marx's commodity fetishism opens up the vista of an external world populated by objects that turn it into a semiotic mystery (5). The surrealists' surreality is an effect of the discontinuity, established by fetishism, between labor relations and the final product. It poses a subject seduced by the flux of meaning. It can be added that this condition recalls Peirce's unlimited semiosis, which assumes an incessantly productive latency of meaning.

    In post-Saussurian times, Roland Barthes's semiology initiates a lucid understanding of semiotic desire. The point is not to deny the fascination of signs but to discern the danger of imposture latent in their use in the naturalization of culture, that is to say, of specific materialist power relations. Gérard Genette, 'The Obverse of Signs,' *Figures of Literary Discourse*, trans. Alan Sheridan, intro. Marie-Rose Logan (New York: Columbia UP, 1982) 27-44.

    For further discussions of fetishism see Emily Apter and William Pietz, eds., *Fetishism as Cultural Discourse* (Ithaca: Cornell UP, 1993). For a specific discussion of fetishism in surrealist photography, especially in Man Ray, I refer to Jennifer Blessing, '"Eros, C'est la Vie": Fetishism as Cultural Discourse (Surrealism, Fashion, and Photography),' *Art/Fashion* (Milan: Skira, 1996) 81-91.

12 Drag plays a significant role in Judith Butler's popular notion of performativity. Originally, Butler sees drag as a diaphoric repetition which can change the meaning of the repeated cultural unit. In *Gender Trouble, Feminism and the Subversion of Identity* (London: Routledge, 1990) 146, she speaks of a 'subversive repetition' which would reveal the rhetorical construction of identity. Change is promised in this unveiling. In *Bodies that Matter: On the Discursive Limits of Sex* (London: Routledge, 1993) she specifies the possibilities of a rhetorical modification of normative identities. This time, however, repeating hegemonic norms can 'wield the final power to *renaturalize*' bodies only problematically (133). In a different context, I am looking at the Stein and Toklas butch-femme image to suggest the difficult relation of history and critical desire.

13 For an image of Stein and Toklas as an older couple see, *Staying on Alone: The Letters of Alice B. Toklas*, ed. Edward Burns (New York: Vintage Books, 1975) 344.

Chapter 5

1   For another theoretically informed article that takes up the question of their mutual influence, see Karin Cope, 'Painting After Gertrude Stein,' *Diacritics: A Review of Contemporary Criticism* 24.2-3 (Summer-Fall 1994): 190-203.

2   Reproductions of Tom Blackwell's *Prada* and *In the Frame* can be found in Louis K. Meisel's volume, *Photorealism at the Millennium* (New York: Harry N. Abrams, Inc. Publishers, 2002), pl. 138 and pl. 136, respectively.

3   Baudrillard's fascination sounds like a more economically inflected version of subjection, a pivotal notion in contemporary theory as illustrated by the work of Judith Butler.

4   Benjamin remarks that the wider access to literacy created by the newspaper resulted in new public emotions. He quotes Tretiakov on the 'impatience' (*Reflections* 224) not only of those who already read but above all 'of the man on the sidelines who believes he has the right to see his own interests expressed' (*Reflections* 224): 'the reader is at all times ready to become a writer, that is, a describer, but also a prescriber' (*Reflections* 225). At a time of growing audiences, reading and writing are linked by a mimetic efficacy that might be better grasped by hypnosis and magnetism, or the more dignified name that psychoanalysis gave these—identification—than by traditional dialectical view of the human subject struggling for visibility on the scene of history. Walter Benjamin, 'The Author as Producer,' *Reflections*, ed. Peter Demetz (New York: Schocken Books, 1986) 220-238.

5   For a different argument examining the commercial uses of objects in Stein's work, see Mary O'Connor, 'The Objects of Modernism: Everyday Life in Women's Magazines, Gertrude Stein, and Margaret Watkins," *American Modernism Across the Arts*, eds. Jay Bochner and Justin D. Edwards (New York: Peter Lang, 1999) 97-123.

6   Before she became a writer, around 1898, Stein had addressed an audience of women on the value of college education. Ulla Dydo, *The Language That Rises 1923-1934* (Evanston, Ill.: Northwestern UP, 2003) 77, n.1.

7   Martin Heidegger, 'The Thing,' *Poetry, Language, Thought*, trans. Albert Hofstadter (New York: Harper & Row Publishers, 1971) 163-186.

8   Pablo Picasso, *Two Nudes*, Paris, autumn 1906, oil on canvas, 151.2 x 93 (59½ x 36⅝), The Museum of Modern Art, New York, Gift of G. David Thompson in honor of Alfred H. Barr, Jr.; *Seated Nude*, Paris, autumn 1906, oil on canvas, 15 x 1000 (59⅜ x 39⅜), National Gallery, Prague; *Woman Seated and Woman Standing*, Paris, autumn 1906, charcoal on Ingres paper, 67 x 48 (26⅜ x 18⅞), Philadelphia Museum of Art, A. E. Gallatin Collection. Reproductions of these works can be found in *Picasso: The Early Years 1892-1906*, edited by Marilyn McCully (New Haven and London: Yale UP, 1998) 344, 345, 348.

9   Commenting on *Two nudes*, Werth notices the 'emphatic and obscure' gesture of the right-hand figure, 'pointing to the picture's high degree of irresolution, to its own processes of negation' (281). Margaret Werth, 'Representing the body in 1906,' in Marilyn McCully ed., *Picasso: The Early Years 1892-1906.*

10 Pablo Picasso, *The Harem*, Gósol, summer 1906, oil on canvas, 154.3 x 110 cm (60¾ x 43¼), The Cleveland Museum of Art, Bequeathed by Leonard C. Hanna, Jr., reproduced in McCully 323.

11 Pablo Picasso, *La Toilette*, Gósol, summer 1906, oil on canvas, 151.1 x 99.1 (59 ½ x 39), Albright Knox Art Gallery, Buffalo, New York, Fellows for Life Fund, 1926; *Nude*

Combing Her Hair, Paris, autumn 1906, oil on canvas, 105.4 x 81.3 (41½ x 32), Kimbell Art Museum, Fort Worth, *Picasso: The Early Years 1892-1906*, edited by Marilyn McCully, 322 and 342.

12 Pablo Picasso, *Girl With a Pitcher*, Gósol, summer 1906, oil on canvas, 100 x 81 (39⅜ x 32), The Art Institute of Chicago, Gift of Mary Leigh B. Block, *Picasso: The Early Years 1892-1906*, edited by Marilyn McCully, 320.

13 Pablo Picasso, *Woman with a Fan*, Paris, autumn 1905, oil on canvas, 100.3 x 81 (39½ x 31⅞), National Gallery of Art, Washington, Gift of the W. Averell Harriman Foundation in memory of Marie N. Harriman, *Picasso: The Early Years 1892-1906*, edited by Marilyn McCully, 260. For a photo of Stein's atelier showing this painting, see Jérôme Peignot, 'Les premiers Picasso de Gertrude Stein,' *Connaissance des arts* 213 (Nov. 1969): 122-131; 122.

14 For a more detailed description of Germond's dance, see Appendix I in this book.

15 A term used by Camelia Elias to define the relation of Lynn Emanuel to Stein in her talk, 'Sexing up genius: tableau instaurations in Lynn Emanuel and Gertrude Stein,' Poetry and Sexuality Conference, The University of Sterling, Department of English Studies, Sterling 2 July, 2004.

16 For an example of how domestic tensions reflect in Stein's later writing, see Ulla Dydo's work on the manuscript of *Stanzas in Meditation*, 'How to Read Gertrude Stein: The Manuscripts of *Stanzas in Meditation*,' *Text: Transactions of the Society for Textual Scholarship*, vol. 1 (New York: AMS, 1984), and '*Stanzas in Meditation*: The Other Autobiography,' *Chicago Review* 35.2 (1985): 4-20.

17 In *The Autobiography of Alice B. Toklas* Stein names 'Lend a Hand or Four Religions' as the 'first conception of landscape as play' (197). As Donald Sutherland remarks, Stein had been writing plays on and off, but the difference between the earlier plays and the piece of 1922 was 'a clearly dominating melodiousness.' Donald Sutherland, *Gertrude Stein: A Biography of Her Work* (New York: Yale University Press, 1951) 120.

18 'Capital Capitals,' with music by Virgil Thomson, was performed by the male voices of the Ionian Quartet on Feb 24, 1929 at the Copland-Sessions Concert. Male voices. The critic for The New York Evening Post wrote: 'Four men of solemn visage [. . .] projected the words in a manner not unlike the singsong of some primitive church chanting and ingeminations.' Anthony Tommasini, Virgil Thomson: Composer on the Aisle (New York: WW Norton and Company, 1997) 200.

19 Stein's belief in a writing that exceeds economic exchange holds *Lucy Church Amiably* together. For Stein, as for Jacques Derrida in our times, writing is an event against the web of property/propriety in which language is completely assimilated to capital. See Jacques Derrida, *Given Time: Counterfeit Money* (Chicago and London, The U of Chicago P, 1992). In part, for Stein the timelessness of writing depends on its power to exceed money. A more detailed discussion of this topic can be found in the chapter devoted to Stein by Luke Carson in *Composition and Depression in Gertrude Stein, Louis Zukofsky and Ezra Pound* (New York: St. Martin's Press, 1999).

20 For a thought-provoking discussion of the negative meaning of communication as a strategy of aggressive homologation of diverse cultural contents, see Mario Perniola, *Contro la Comunicazione* [Against Communication] (Turin: Einaudi, 2004).

21 William Rubin establishes a connection between Picasso and Walter Pater's view of the Renaissance. For Pater, the goal of life in the Renaissance is 'to burn always with [a] hard gemlike flame.' Similarly, Picasso looks to the past with the sense of an affective

affiliation to tradition, to the classics and the inextinguishable fire they stand for in the popular imagination. William Rubin, 'Reflections on Picasso and Portraiture,' *Picasso and Portraiture*, ed. William Rubin (New York: The Museum of Modern Art, 1996) 90.

Chapter 6

1   Virgil Thomson chose Allen for the role of Saint Teresa in the second production of the opera. In the same production Leontyne Price was assigned the part of Saint Cecilia. See Hugh Lee Lyon, *Leontyne Price: Highlights of a Prima Donna* (New York: Vantage Press, 1973) 58-59.
    Thomson's collaboration with Stein was the result of a long acquaintance with her work . The composer admired the writer. He had first met her when he escorted George Antheil—a New Jersey born composer living in Paris—to 27 rue de Fleurus in 1926. He had been introduced to Stein's work as an undergraduate student at Harvard by the young French instructor Foster Damon. He had read *Geography and Plays* and there is evidence in his letters that he had read and liked the David Hersland section of *The Making of Americans*. Soon after meeting Stein, Thomson wrote of his feeling of commonality with her: 'Gertrude Stein has been impressive and unconsciously encouraging. She takes for granted so many of the same things that I do.' *The Selected Letters of Virgil Thomson*, eds. Tim Page and Vanessa Weeks Page (New York: Summit, 1988) 72.
2   Here and elsewhere in this chapter, for the details of the opera production I am relying on Steven Watson, *Prepare for Saints: Gertrude Stein, Virgil Thomson, and the Mainstreaming of American Modernism* (Berkeley: U of California Press, 1995).
3   I refer the reader to Ulla Dydo's *Gertrude Stein: The Language That Rises 1923-1934*, 180-182.
4   For more detailed descriptions of the libretto's plot, see Ulla Dydo, *Gertrude Stein: The Language That Rises*, 174, n. 13. To the sources indicated by Dydo, I would add Giovanni Morelli's study, *Very Well Saints: A Sum of Deconstructions* (Florence: Olschki Editore, 2000), enriched with a very useful footnote apparatus including quotes on the opera from Stein's autobiographies.
5   Stein exploits the popular accusation moved against Saint Teresa of subordinating religious vocation to the self-serving pleasures of writing. This opinion, somehow reinforced by Bernini's representation of Teresa's ecstasy, was held, as we shall see later, by William James. Historical feminism has examined the knot of mysticism and women's writing. The standard reference here is the chapter on women mystics in Luce Irigaray's *Speculum of the Other Woman*, trans. Gillian C. Gill (Ithaca: Cornell UP, 1985).
6   The final libretto, abridged by Thompson, is included in Virgil Thomson, *Four Saints in Three Acts*, cond. Joel Thome, perf. Betty Allen, Gwendolyn Bradley, William Brown, Clamma Dale, Benjamin Matthews, Florence Quivar, Arthur Thompson, Orchestra of Our Time, Elektra/Asylum/Nonesuch records, 1982.
7   In his notes to the recording of the opera, *Four Saints in Three Acts* (cond. Joel. Thome, Elektra/Asylum/Nonesuch Records, 1982), Thompson explained that he and Stein chose the subject of saints because 'we saw among the religious a parallel to the life we were leading, in which consecrated artists were practicing their art surrounded by younger artists who were no less consecrated, and who were trying to learn and needing to learn

the terrible discipline of truth and spontaneity, of channeling their skills without loss of inspiration.' Commentators of the opera have discussed Stein's allusions to her modernist peers, including T. S. Eliot. See Morelli's study, cited in note 3, and Corinne E. Blackmer, 'The Ecstasies of Saint Teresa: The Saint as Queer Diva from Crashaw to *Four Saints in Three Acts*,' *En Travesti: Women, Gender, Subversion, Opera*, eds. Corinne Blackmer and Patricia Juliana Smith (New York: Columbia UP, 1995) 307-347.

8 There is a kind of magpie (Cyanopica cyanea) that lives in the Western part of the Iberian peninsula. Its black head and white throat clearly recall a nun. Its back and the rest of the body are all gray streaked with pink, while the tail is streaked with brilliant blue. Stein might have referred to it.

9 Piero della Francesca, *Polittico di Sant'Antonio*, oil on canvas, 338 x 230 cm, Galleria Nazionale dell'Umbria, Perugia, *Piero della Francesca: Il Polittico di Sant'Antonio*, edited by Vittoria Ganbaldi (Perugia: Electa Editori Umbri, 1993) 21.

10 Giotto, *La predica agli uccelli*, fresco, cm 270 x 200, Basilica Superiore di San Francesco, Assisi, *La Leggenda Francescana nella Basilica di Assisi* [The Legend of St Francis in the Assisi Basilica], by Bruno Dozzini (Assisi: Editrice Minerva, 1992) 36. For a discussion of the cycle, see Bruno Zanardi, 'Giotto and the St. Francis Cycle at Assisi,' *The Cambridge Companion to Giotto*, ed. Anne Derbes and Mark Sandona (Cambridge: Cambridge UP, 2004) 32-62.

11 As Ulla Dydo notes, the libretto was written during Lent (*The Language That Rises* 183n). Pasolini mentions Easter in the second part of his poem 'L'Umile Italia,' *Le Ceneri di Gramsci* (Milan: Garzanti, 1957) 45-55.

12 Julia Kristeva pictures forth this modernist view of the artist through the dialectic of semiotic and symbolic in Mallarmé's work. Kristeva's study of modernity, it might be recalled, led to the displacement of the formalist notion of text by the notion of signifying practice. Julia Kristeva, *Revolution in Poetic Language* (New York: Columbia UP, 1984).

13 Alice Walker, 'In Search of Our Mothers' Gardens.' *In Search of Our Mothers' Gardens* (New York: Harcourt Brace Jovanovich, 1983) 230-243.

14 Frederick Ashton had first heard the opera in a one-man recital by Virgil Thomson at the London house of the art dealer Kirk Askew. After *Four Saints in Three Acts*, he went on to compose the choreography for a ballet based on another Stein piece, *A Wedding Bouquet*, and turned it into an acclaimed masterpiece. See Kathrine Sorley, 'A Wedding Bouquet' *Dance Now* 6.1 (Spring 1997)76-81. For Ashton's work on *Four Saints* see the excellent article by David Vaughan, '(a tree, a melon, a sheet of water, a flight of birds)' *Ballet Review* 4.6 (1974): 2-13.

15 In his study, *Opera in the Twentieth Century: Sacred, Profane, Godot* (New York: Oxford U P, 1978), Ethan Mordden credits *Four Saints in Three Acts* and *Porgy and Bess*, produced only a year apart and with all black casts, with breaking the long standing subordination of American opera to the European repertoire: 'they founded a *sui generis* basis that, for the moment, expressed something percipiently American instead of hacking out dead Continental melodrama' (Mordden 304). The Stein-Thompson collaboration is 'manufactured out of a musical rather than a stage tradition' (Mordden 304). For Mordden the production set a trend for American opera: through 'hymn-like episodes, choral antiphony [. . .] and diatonic glee' (304), Thomson turned opera into a mélange of genres, 'both profane and popular [. . .] closer to comédie melèe d'ariettes, ballad opera, and Zeitoper than to opera' (316), while also exploiting the

European tradition for romantic power and 'thus cutting across the barrier of genre classification' (317-7).

16 Stein's point is that the subordination of literary value to the qualifications of the speaking subject does not concern her only. Saint Teresa helps her raise questions of reception through a problem common to all women's spiritual autobiographies. This, in the words of Jarena Lee, is the problem of 'a call to preach' that cannot be verified and whose value must be judged by its impact on the readers/listeners: 'So it may be with such as am, who has never had more than three months schooling: and wishing to know much of the way and law of God, have therefore watched the more closely the operations of the Spirit, and have in consequence been led thereby' (48). 'The Life and Religious Experience of Jarena Lee,' *Sisters of the Spirit*, ed. William L. Andrews (Bloomington: Indiana UP, 1986) 25-48. Lee's term 'led' becomes part and parcel of Stein's poetic diction in the libretto.

17 In *Modern Music*, Gilbert Seldes thus described the production: 'The work was produced with a great sense of style, beginning with Miss Stettheimer's settings made of lace and cellophane, and looking like a child's dream of rock candy, and continuing through the costumes and choreography, the lights and all the other elements involved.' See Herbert Graf, *Opera for the people* (Minneapolis: The U of Minnesota P, 1951) 135.

18 In literary studies, an important moment of the debate on the role of individual associations in the act of interpretation is Umberto Eco's distinction between 'free use' and interpreation in *Lector in Fabula. La cooperazione Interpretativa nei Testi Narrativi* (Milan: Bompiani, 1979) 59-66. Eco further elaborates on the distinction in *Interpretation and Overinterpretation* (Cambridge: Cambridge UP, 1992), which also contains responses by Richard Rorty, Jonathan Culler, and Christine Brooke-Rose.

19 See also Thomas Ogden, 'The analytic third—working with intersubjective clinical facts,' *International Journal of Psychoanalysis* 75 (1994): 3-20.

20 The sensational confusion of Marguerite bears the mark of early novel heroines, exposed to the danger of seduction, abandonment and misery. One thinks of Sarah Wentworth Morton's *The Power of Sympathy* (1789), Susanna H. Rowson's *Charlotte Temple* (1790), Hannah Webster Foster's *The Coquette*. All these have learned the lesson of the classic British novel of Defoe and Richardson: the heroine is both a character internal to the narrative and a semblance of the novel reader external to it, a type prone to the seductions of sensationalism and wonder. Lillie Deming Loshe, *The Early American Novel 1789-1830* (New York: Frederick Ungar Publishing Co., 1966).

21 See Sacvan Bercovitch, *The Puritan Origins of the American Self* (New Haven & London: Yale UP, 1975). Bercovitch speaks of the figuralism in early New England rhetoric. By this he means that the perceiver 'had to identify with the divine meaning of the New World if he was to understand his environment correctly' (114). Stein's Marguerite is affected by a sort of secular ontological figuralism: the wilderness where she awakens wears the colors of the question of human identity and what makes it.

22 The tragicomic side of Stein's characters is effectively conveyed in the adaptation of Stein's opera for the theater by the Duende Theater Company. This team of young actors staged the play as part of the 2001 New York Fringe Festival. *Doctor Faustus Lights the Lights*, dir. Willa Bepler, The Paradise Theater, New York, 23 August 2001.

Chapter 7

1 Stein and Toklas sailed from France on the Champlain on October 17, 1934. They had made arrangements with Mr. Frank Case at the Algonquin Hotel, New York. Toklas had originally requested a double room with two beds and a bath not higher than the 6th floor. He gave them a suite plus a sitting room. Rates: $5 a day; $30 a week (Edward Burns, ed., *The Letters of Gertrude Stein and Carl Van Vechten* 340, note 1). They arrived on October 24. We know from Toklas that they were met by Van Vechten, Bennet Cerf, and a cousin of Stein from Baltimore (*What is Remembered* 143). That night they had dinner with Van Vechten and Fania Marinoff. On November 2 Stein delivered the lecture 'Painting' at the Colony Club, New York. Her second lecture was at the McMillin theater at Columbia. The audience counted 500 hundred members of the Institute of Arts and Sciences. Twenty-five walked out on her. She delivered 'The Gradual Making of the Making of Americans' to promote her novel published in the abridged edition (Harcourt Brace) in February (Mellow 387). Princeton was next, on November 5 in McCosh Hall (Mellow 387). Princeton was the second academic place after Columbia, where Stein has delivered 'Poetry and Grammar' (Souhami 208). Toklas remembers: 'We went to Princeton University one evening for a lecture (*What is Remembered* 145). They went round trip by train and got back the same day. The lecture room at Princeton University was filled 'but not with more than five hundred people' (*What is Remembered* 146).

    For materials on the Princeton lecture, see also two scathing reviews of Stein's visit by student observers: R. D. Waters, 'Gertrude Stein Leaves Capacity Audience in 500 Various Stages of Understanding,' *The Daily Princetonian*, 6 November 1934: 1+; '"I'm A Fair Genius," Admits Gertrude Stein In Explaining "Pigeons on the Grass Alas,"' *The Daily Princetonian*, 7 November 1934: 1+; 'Trudy and Alice in Jungleland,' *The Daily Princetonian*, 8 November 1934: 2. I thank Lisa Dunkley, librarian at the Seeley G. Mudd Manuscript Library of Princeton University, who kindly found the materials.

2 In her introduction to the lectures, Wendy Steiner thus phrases the philosophical problem of writing: 'For Stein, as for many modernists, artistic history is a drama between immediacy and deferral, sameness and difference.' 'Introduction,' *Lectures in America* (Boston: Beacon , 1985) xx.

3 Stein was born in 1874, at the peak of the feminist struggle from women's rights. Only a few years before her birth, in 1869, Elizabeth Cady Stanton and Susan B. Anthony founded the National Woman Suffrage Association (NWSA), an association opened only to women with the aim of obtaining a federal law granting women's the right to vote.

4 For a general introduction to the nineteenth century lecturing tradition, see Paul Fatout, *Mark Twain on the Lecture Circuit* (Bloomington: Indiana UP, 1960).

5 Stein had been a theatre and opera goer since her adolescent days. Early on she developed a short-lived enthusiasm for opera with a reprise during her college years:

> I came not to care at all for music and so having concluded that music was made for adolescents and not for adults and having just left adolescence behind me and besides I knew all the operas anyway by that time I did not care any more for opera (qtd. in Brinnin 23)

What Brinnin does not add here is that in this particular narrative of Stein's early years, opera and other arts contribute to the portrait of a restless middle-class daughter ruled by compulsory appetites she rushes to satisfy. One cultural object quickly displaces another in this cycle of hunger and surfeiting. Her rejection of opera, because she had had enough, is meant to add the final touch to a picture of bourgeois boredom and aimless desire from which Stein will struggle to free herself. In the later stage of her career her knowledge of opera would come handy, this time not so much to support the vision of the artist struggling free from a social group as to include her in a social landscape full of conflicts.

In Stein's diva identification both opera and the theater play their role. In April 1891 Sarah Bernhardt came to San Francisco to play *Tosca*, *La Dame aux Caméleias*, *Cléopatre* and *Jeanne d'Arc*. Stein experienced diva identification for the first time while watching Sarah Bernhardt:

It was all so foreign and her voice being so varied and it all being so French I could rest in it untroubled. And I did [. . .] It was better than the opera because it went on. It was better than the theatre because you did not have to get acquainted [. . .]. (qtd. in Brinnin 22).

6   For an impassioned defense of Maria Callas, see Attila Csampi, *Callas: Images of a Legend* (New York: Stuart, Tabori, & Chang, 1993).

7   This view contrasts with that of Catherine Clément, who accuses opera of singing only one song of self-sacrifice for its female heroines. Catherine Clément, *Opera, or the Undoing of Women*, trans. Betsy Wing (Minneapolis: U of Minnesota P, 1988).

8   Philosopher Jean-Luc Nancy derives from Stein's image his notion of the 'existent' by which he means an embodied subject. For Nancy the classic subject is defined by the contradiction of its own alienation: 'that which is capable of maintaining within itself its own contradiction' (6). Thought can account for human complexity only by stylizing it as the contradictory internal appropriation of an externality. The limit of this mental image is precisely a subject-being, the being in the process of unfolding that Nancy calls the 'existent' (6). By this he means an embodied and situated 'who,' present because he/she occupies a place and is, in fact, 'the coming into space of a time' (7). Nancy varies Stein's expression, 'a space of time,' borrowed from Lectures in America and quoted earlier on in this chapter. Nevertheless, his existent has something in common with the liberating sense of a heightened being that Stein received from Cézanne. Here it is important to notice that Nancy includes Stein among the writers interested in an alternative mode of subjectivity that challenges abstract thought. Jean-Luc Nancy, 'Introduction,' *Who Comes After the Subject*, eds. Eduardo Cadava, Peter Connor, Jean-Luc Nancy (New York and London: Routledge, 1991) 1-8.

9   Jacques Lacan, 'The Signification of the Phallus,' *Ecrits: A Selection* (New York and London: W. W. Norton & Company, 1977) 281-291.

10   Peter Burger argues that the inclusive experience of the viewer/reader is neutralized when the diverse elements of the art work are put together by the critic. Burger sees institutionalized criticism as a problem. Methodological approaches like linguistic structuralism, psychology, psychoanalysis, and digital computer-assisted analysis force the work of art within a rigid frame of consumption. See Peter Burger, *Theory of the Avant-Garde*, trans. Michael Snow, (Minneapolis: U of Minnesota P, 1987), and Charles Le Vine, 'The 'Open' Work of Art,' *Rooted Rhetoric: Una Tradizione dell'Arte Americana*, ed. Gabriele Guercio (Naples: Guida Editori, 1986) 124-133.

The exchange of experience between the work and the reader cannot take place, says Le Vine. Le Vine talks of an aesthetic reception that, following from Burger's argument, is neutralized by the intervention of the critic (126). Stein encourages a direct exchange between reader and work and resists a rigid frame of consumption as well as posing the question of who the critic is.

11 For the importance of free association in the 1990s and the changes it has brought on in contemporary aesthetics see Roberto Daolio, 'American Beauty,' *Arte Americana: Ultimo Decennio* (Milan: Mazzotta, 2000) 29-32.

12 On the nexus modernism, writing, and democracy, apart from the cited study by Alessandro Portelli, *The Text and the Voice: Writing, Speaking and Democracy in American Literature* (New York: Columbia, 1994), see also Marianne DeKoven, *Rich and Strange: Gender, History, Modernism* (Princeton: Princeton UP, 1991).

13 For a good example of the simultaneous action of indeterminacy and reference in the work of Rauschenberg, see Mark Ormond's reading of *Orphic Ditty*, 'Introduction,' *Robert Rauschenberg: Works from the Salvage Series* (Saratosa, Florida: The John and Mable Ringling Museum of Art Foundation, 1985) 6-7.

14 Emile Benveniste writes: 'Now we hold that "subjectivity", whether it is placed in phenomenology of in psychology, as one may wish, is only the emergence in being of a fundamental property of language. "Ego" is he who says "ego". That is where we see the foundation of subjectivity, which is determined through the linguistic status of "person".' 'Subjectivity in Language,' *Problems in General Linguistics*, trans. Mary Elizabeth Meek (Coral Gables: U of Miami P. 1971) 217-230; 224.

15 Judith Butler has challenged the structuralist view of language as a common good, implying that the structuralist account of the subject as a linguistic category 'dismisses the subject as a philosophical trope.' She rightly reminds that there are 'linguistic requirements for entering sociality.' Judith Butler, *The Psychic Life of Power: Theories in Subjection* (Stanford, Ca.: Stanford UP, 1997) 29.

16 The term aphanisis was introduced in psychoanalysis by Ernest Jones. It refers to the disappearance of sexual desire. As Laplanche and Pontalis write, 'According to Jones aphanisis is the object, in both sexes, of a fear more profound than the fear of castration.' Jean Laplanche and L.-B. Pontalis, *The Language of Psychoanalysis*, trans. Donald Nicholson-Smith (New York, London: W.W. Norton & Company, 1973) 40.

Appendix I

1 For an account of early stagings of *A Wedding Bouquet* see Clive Barnes, 'A Wedding Bouquet,' *Dance and Dancers* (April 1959): 20-21; 34.

2 Carl Van Vechten, 'Notes Written on Stone,' brochure of *Doctor Faustus Lights the Lights* presented by The Living Theatre at the Cherry Lane Theater, 2 December 1951-16 December 1951, 5-7. New York Public Library, Carl Van Vechten Collection. For an introduction to The Living Theater, see Pierre Biner, *The Living Theater* (New York: Horizon, 1968).

3 'Yes is for a Very Young Man, in *Last Operas and Plays* (Baltimore and London: Johns Hopkins U P, 1995) 3-51, was actually produced on two occasions on the Princeton campus in 1948. The University Players, a summer troupe composed of students and members of the local community, performed the play between July 26 and 31. In the fall, Theatre Intime, an undergraduate theatrical organization, opened an eight-performance run on October 29. I thank Lisa Dunkley, Project Archivist of the Seeley G. Mudd Manuscript Library at Princeton University, for providing this information.

4   I thank Richard Foreman for a phone conversation on Gertude Stein, summer 2001.

5   Annette Shandler Levitt, *The Genres and Genders of Surrealism* (London: MacMillan Press Ltd., 1999) 138.

6   '15 receive "Obies" for '68-'69 Season,' *The Village Voice* 29 May 1969, 41. For more on Kornfeld, see www.tenderbuttons.com/gsonline/there/SteinKornfeld.html.

7   Don MacDonagh, 'Humor Bubbles Up as 4 Women Unite for Dance program,' *The New York Times*, 28 June 1972.

8   Arlene Rothlein, perf., *Twelve Objects from Tender Buttons*, dir. James Waring, Directional Concepts Dance Theater, 1977, The New York Public Library for the Performing Arts, Dance Collection.

9   Arlene Rothlein was to die shortly after this performance at the young age of 37. The press reported the cause of her death to be meningitis. 'Arlene Rothlein, Dancer Is Dead,' *The New York Times*, 22 November 1976.

10 Jane Comfort, dir., *Duet for Four Hands*, perf. Blondell Cumming, Marjorie Gamso, Susan Yabroff, and Jane Comfort, The American Theater Laboratory, New York, 4 December 1980, The New York Public Library for The Performing Arts, Dance Collection. I thank Jane Comfort for an email conversation about her work, summer 2001.

11 Rachel Germond, perf., *Solo with Black Eggs (For Picasso)*, St. Martin's Church, New York, 1993, The New York Library for the Performing Arts, Dance Collection.

12 Beverly Blossom, *Dance*, 1985, The New York Public Library for the Performing Arts, Dance Collection.

13 Amy Pivar, dir., *The Modest Typist*, perf. Frieda Rosen, Amy Pivar, Performance Space 122, 1994, The New York Public Library for the Performing Arts, Dance Collection.

14 Willla Bepler, dir., *Doctor Faustus Lights the Lights*, perf. Joshua Pohja, Abigail Marlowe, Nicholas Warren-Gray, and Max Faugno, Duende Theater Company, The Paradise Theater, New York, 23 August 2001.

Appendix II

1   This piece was written as the introduction to Gonzalo Tena's exhibition *Stanzas* at Galeria Maeght in Barcelona in December 2000. For more on Gonzalo Tena, see Juan Manuel Bonet, 'On the Return of Gonzalo Tena,' *Gonzalo Tena* (Barcelona: Galeria Maeght, 1991) 6-7; Santiago Martínez Fernández, 'Tena-Stein,' *Gonzalo Tena: Gertrude*, exh. cat. Sala de Exposiciones del Ayuntamiento de Logroño (Saragoza: Tipolinea, S. A., 2003) 3-6; Gonzalo Tena, 'Sobre Gertrude Stein,' *Heraldo de Aragón* 29 May 2003: 2-3.

Bibliography

Adorno, Theodor W. "On the fetish character in music and the regression of listening." *The Culture Industry: Selected Essays on Mass Culture.* Ed. J. M. Bernstein. London: Routledge, 1991. 26-52.

Alfrey, Shawn H. "'Oriental Peaceful Penetration': Gertrude Stein and the End of Europe." *The Massachusetts Review* (Autumn 1997): 405-416.

Allen, Gay Wilson. *William James: A Biography.* New York: Viking Press, 1967.

Apter, Emily and William Pietz, eds., *Fetishism as Cultural Discourse.* Ithaca: Cornell UP, 1993.

Arendt. Hannah. *Rahel Varnhagen: The Life of a Jewess.* 1957. Ed. Liliane Weissberg. Trans. Richard and Clara Winston. Baltimore and London: The Johns Hopkins UP, 1997.

"Arlene Rothlein, Dancer Is Dead." *The New York Times* 22 November 1976: B12.

Ashbery, John. "G.M.P. (Gertrude Stein, Matisse, Picasso)." *Art News* 69.10 (1971): 45-47; 73-74.

Barnes, Clive. "A Wedding Bouquet." *Dance and Dancers* (April 1959): 20-21.

Baudelaire, Charles. "Spleen II." *Oeuvres de Baudelaire.* Vol. 1. Paris: La Pleiade. 1931.

Baudelaire, Charles. "Les Sept Vieillards [The seven old men]." *Oeuvres de Baudelaire.* Vol. 1. 100-102.

Baudrillard, Jean. "Beyond the Vanishing Point of Art." *Post-Pop Art.* Ed. Paul Taylor. Cambridge, Mass.: The MIT Press, 1989. 171-189.

Beach, Sylvia. *Shakespeare and Co.* Lincoln and London: University of Nebraska Press, 1991.

Benedetti, Maria Teresa ed., *Cézanne: Il Padre dei Moderni* [Cézanne: Father of the Moderns]. Milan: Gabriele Mazzotta, 2002.

Benjamin, Walter. "The Author as Producer." *Reflections: Essays, Aphorisms, Autobiographical Writings.* Ed. Peter Demetz. Trans. Edmund Jephcott. New York: Schocken Books, 1986. 220-238.

———. "The Work of Art in the Age of Mechanical Reproduction." *Illuminations: Essays and Reflections.* Ed. Hanna Arendt. Trans. Harry Zohn. New York: Schocken Books, 1985. 217-251.

———. "The Storyteller: Reflection of the Work of Nikolai Leskov." *Illuminations: Essays and Reflections.* 83-109.

Benveniste, Emile. "Subjectivity in Language." *Problems in General Linguistics.* Trans. Mary Elizabeth Meek. Coral Gables, Florida: U of Miami P, 1971. 217-230.

Bercovitch, Sacvan. "The Return of Hester Prynne." *The Rites of Assent: Transformations in the Symbolic Construction of America.* New York & London: Routledge, 1993. 194-245.

Bercovitch, Sacvan. *The Puritan Origins of the American Self.* New Haven & London: Yale UP, 1975.

Berenson, Bernard. *Lotto.* Milan: Electa, 1955.

Berlant, Lauren. "Critical Inquiry, Affirmative Culture." *Critical Inquiry* 30 (Winter 2004): 445-451.

Berry, Ellen. *Curved Thought and Textual Wondering. Gertrude Stein's Postmodernism.* Ann Arbor: The U of Michigan P, 1992.

Biner, Pierre. *The Living Theater.* New York: Horizon Press, 1968.

Bishop, Elizabeth. "In The Waiting Room." *The Complete Poems: 1927-1979.* New York: Farrar, Straus, Giroux, 1983. 159-161.

Blackmer, Corinne E. "The Ecstasies of Saint Teresa: The Saint as Queer Diva from Crashaw to *Four Saints in Three Acts.*" *En Travesti: Women, Gender, Subversion, Opera.* Eds. Corinne E. Blackmer and Patricia Juliana Smith. New York: Columbia UP, 1995. 307-347.

Blair, Sara. "Home Truths: Gertrude Stein, 27 Rue de Fleurus, and the Place of the Avant-Garde." *American Literary History* 12.3 (Fall 2000): 417-37.

Blessing, Jennifer "'Eros, C'est la Vie': Fetishism as Cultural Discourse (Surrealism, Fashion, and Photography)." *Art/Fashion.* Ed. Germano Celant. Milan: Skira, 1996. 81-91.

Bodei, Remo. *Le forme del bello*[Beauty and its Forms]. Bologna: Il Mulino, 1995.

Boggs, Jean Sutherland. "Gertrude Stein, Collectionneur." *Gertrude Stein & Picasso & Juan Gris.* Ottawa: The National Gallery of Canada, 1971. N. pag.

Boime, Albert. *Artisti e Imprenditori.* Trans. Bianca Tarozzi. Turin: Bollati Boringhieri, 1990. Trans. of *Rethinking Patronage.* 1990.

Bonet, Juan Manuel. "On the Return of Gonzalo Tena." *Gonzalo Tena.* Barcelona: Galeria Maeght, 1991. 6-7.

Bonito Oliva, Achille. "La Pittura è l'autoadesivo della memoria. Painting is Memory's Sticker." *Robert Rauschenberg, Mostra Personale/One Man Show.* Rome: Galleria d'Arte Il Gabbiano, 1991. 9-13.

Bradstreet, Anne. "The Prologue." *The Norton Anthology of Literature by Women.* Eds. Sandra Gilbert and Susan Gubar. New York and London: W. W. Norton, 1985. 61-3.

———. "Contemplations." *The Complete Works of Anne Bradstreet.* Eds. Joseph R. McElrath, Jr. and Allan P. Robb. Boston: Twayne Publishers, 1981. 167-174.

Breen, Margaret S. and Warren J. Blumenfeld. *Butler Matters: Judith Butler's Impact on Feminist and Queer Studies Since Gender Trouble.* Aldershot, UK: Ashgate Publishing Co., 2005.

Bridgman, Richard. *Gertrude Stein in Pieces.* New York: Oxford UP, 1970.

Brinnin, John Malcom. *The Third Rose: Gertrude Stein and Her World.* Boston & Toronto: Little, Brown, and Company, 1959.

Burger, Peter. *Theory of the Avant-Garde.* Trans. Michael Snow. Minneapolis: U of Minnesota P, 1987.

Burke, Kenneth. "The Impartial Essence." *The New Republic*, 13 July 1935. *The Critical Response to Gertrude Stein*. Ed. Kirk Curnutt.Westport, Conn.: The Greenwood Press, 2000. 88-90.

Burns, Edward M. and Ulla Dydo. "Introduction." *The Letters of Gertrude Stein and Thornton Wilder*. Eds. Edward Burns and Ulla Dydo, with William Rice. New Haven and London: Yale UP, 1996. xv-xxvi.

Burns, Edward, ed. *The Letters of Gertrude Stein and Carl Van Vechten: I, 1913-1935; II, 1935-1946*. New York: Columbia UP, 1986.

Burns, Edward, ed. *Staying on Alone: The Letters of Alice B. Toklas*. New York: Vintage Books, 1975.

Butler, Judith. *The Psychic Life of Power: Theories in Subjection*. Stanford, Ca.: Stanford UP, 1997.

——. *Bodies that Matter: On the Discursive Limits of Sex*. London: Routledge, 1993.

——. *Gender Trouble: Feminism and the Subversion of Gender*. London: Routledge, 1990.

Buxbaum, Gerda, ed. *Icons of Fashion: the Twentieth Century*. Munich and New York: Prestel, 1999.

Campbell, Jan. *Arguing with the Phallus: Feminist, Queer, and Postcolonial Theory. A Psychoanalytic Contribution*. London & New York: Zed Books, 2000.

Carson, Luke. *Consumption and Depression in Gertrude Stein, Louis Zukofsky, and Ezra Pound*. New York: St. Martin's Press, 1999.

Cézanne, Paul. *Letters*. Ed. John Rewald. New York: Hacker Art Books, 1984.

Chow, Rey. *Primitive Passions: Visuality, Sexuality, Ethnography, and Contemporary Chinese Cinema*. New York: Columbia UP, 1995.

Clément, Catherine. *Opera, or the Undoing of Women*. Minneapolis: U of Minnesota Press, 1988.

Cope, Karin. "Painting After Gertrude Stein." *Diacritics: A Review of Contemporary Criticism* 24.2-3 (Summer-Fall 1994): 109-203.

Corse, Sandra. *The Evolution of the Self in Modern Opera*. London: Associated University Presses, 2000.

Csampi, Attila. *Callas: Images of a Legend*. New York: Stuart, Tabori, & Chang, 1993.

Damon, Maria. "Gertrude Stein's Jewishness, Jewish Social Scientists, and the 'Jewish Question'." *Modern Fiction Studies* 42-3 (Fall 1996): 489-507.

Daolio, Roberto. "American Beauty." *Arte Americana: Ultimo Decennio*. Milan: Mazzotta, 2000. 29-32.

DeKoven, Marianne. "Woolf, Stein, and the drama of public woman." *Modernist Sexualities*. Eds. Hugh Stevens and Caroline Howlett. Manchester and New York: Manchester UP, 2000. 184-201.

——. "Introduction: Transformations of Gertrude Stein." *Modern Fiction Studies* 42-3 (Fall 1996). 469-487.

——. *Rich and Strange: Gender, History, Modernism*. Princeton: Princeton UP, 1991.

——. *A Different Language: Gertrude Stein's Experimental Writing*. Madison: The U of Wisconsin P, 1983.

DeKoven, Marianne. "Gertrude Stein and Modern Painting." *Contemporary Literature* 22.1 (Winter 1981): 81-95.

de Lauretis, Teresa. "Semiotics and Experience." *Alice Doesn't: Feminism, Semiotics, Cinema.* Bloomington: Indiana UP, 1984. 158-186.

de Man, Paul. "Semiology and Rhetoric." *The Critical Tradition.* Ed. David H. Richter. Boston: Bedford Books, 1998. 906-916.

de Man, Paul. *Allegories of Reading.* New Haven: Yale UP, 1979.

Derrida, Jacques. *Given Time: Counterfeit Money.* Chicago and London: The U of Chicago P, 1992.

Dettmar, Kevin J. H and Stephen Watt, eds. *Marketing Modernisms: Self-Promotion, Canonization, and Reading.* Ann Arbor: The U of Chicago P, 1996.

Dozzini, Bruno. *La Leggenda Francescana nella Basilica di Assisi* [The Legend of Saint Francis in the Basilica of Assisi]. Assisi: Editrice Minerva, 1992.

Dydo, Ulla, with William Rice. *Gertrude Stein: The Language that Rises 1923-934.* Evanston, Illinois: Northwestern UP, 2003.

Dydo, Ulla. "*Stanzas in Meditation*: The Other Autobiography." *Chicago Review* 35.2 (1985): 4-20.

——. "How to Read Gertrude Stein: The Manuscripts of *Stanzas in Meditation.*" *Text: Transactions of the Society for Textual Scholarship.* Vol. 1. New York: AMS, 1984.

Eco, Umberto. *Interpretation and Overinterpretation.* Cambridge: Cambridge UP, 1992.

——. *Lector in Fabula: La Cooperazione Interpretativa nei Testi Narrativi.* Milan: Bompiani, 1979.

Elias, Camelia. "Sexing up genius: tableau instaurations in Lynn Emanuel and Gertrude Stein." Poetry and Sexuality Conference. The University of Sterling, Scotland. June 30-July 4, 2004.

Entwistle, Joanne. *The Fashioned Body: Fashion, Dress and Modern Social Theory.* Cambridge: Polity Press, 2000.

Everett, Patricia R., ed. *A History of Having A Great Many Times Not Continued to be friends: The Correspondence Between Mabel Dodge and Gertrude Stein, 1911-1934.* Albuquerque: University of New Mexico Press, 1996.

Fatout, Paul. *Mark Twain on the Lecture Circuit.* Bloomington: Indiana UP, 1960.

Ferenczi, Sándor. *The Clinical Diary of Sandor Ferenczi.* Ed. Judith Dupont. Trans. Michael Balint and Nicola Zarday Jackson. Cambridge, Ma: Harvard UP, 1988.

——. "Confusion of Tongues." *Final Contributions to the Problems and Methods of Psychoanalysis.* Ed. Michael Balint. Trans. Eric Mosbacher and others. Intro. Clara Thompson. New York: Basic Books, 1955.

Fielding, Henry. *Tom Jones.* London: Penguin, 1966.

Fitch, Noel Riley. *Sylvia Beach and the Lost Generation: A History of Literary Paris in the Twenties and Thirties.* New York: W.W. Norton, 1983.

Foster, Hal. "Violation and Veiling in Surrealist Photography: Woman as Fetish, as Shattered Object, as Phallus." *Surrealism: Desire Unbound.* Ed. Jennifer Mundy. Princeton: Princeton UP, 2002. 203-225.

Fraire, Manuela. "No-Frills, No-Body, Nobody." *Abito e Identità*. Ed. Cristina Giorcelli. Vol. V. Palermo: Italo-Latina-Americana Palma, 2004. 13-23.

Ganbaldi, Vittoria, ed. *Piero della Francesca: Il Polittico di Sant'Antonio*. Perugia: Electa Editori Umbri, 1993.

Genette, Gérard. "The Obverse of Signs." *Figures of Literary Discourse*. Ed. Alan Sheridan. Trans. Marie-Rose Logan. New York: Columbia UP, 1982. 27-44.

Gilman, Charlotte Perkins. *The Yellow Wallpaper*. New York: The Feminist Press, 1973.

Graf, Herbert. *Opera for the people*. Minneapolis: The U of Minnesota P, 1951.

Gramsci, Antonio. *Americanismo e Fordismo*. Rome: Editori Riuniti, 1991.

Greenfeld, Howard. *Gertrude Stein: A Biography*. New York: Crown Publishers, 1973.

Hayao, Ishimura and Maruyama Nobuhiko. *Robes of Elegance: Japanese Kimonos of the 16th-20th Centuries*. Raleigh: North Carolina Museum of Art, 1988.

Heidegger, Martin. "The Origin of the Work of Art." *Poetry, Language, Thought*. Trans. Albert Hofstadter. New York: Haper & Row Publishers, 1975. 17-87.

———. "The Thing." *Poetry, Language, Thought*. 165-186.

Howe, Susan. *Pierce-Arrow*. New York: New Directions, 1997. 1-30.

Hughes, Robert. *American Visions: An Epic History of Art in America*. New York: Alfred Knopf 1997.

Hutcheon, Linda and Michael Hutcheon, *Bodily Charms: Living Opera*. Lincoln and London: U of Nebraska P, 2000

———. *Opera: Desire, Disease, Death*. Lincoln and London: U of Nebraska P, 1996.

"'I'm A Fair Genius,' Admits Gertrude Stein In Explaining 'Pigeons on the Grass Alas.'" *The Daily Princetonian* 7 November 1934: 1+.

Irigaray, Luce. *Speculum of the Other Woman*. Trans. Gillian C. Gill. Ithaca: Cornell UP, 1985.

Jaffe', Hans L. C. *Pablo Picasso*. New York: Harry N. Abrams, Inc., Publishers.

James, Ian. "The Persistence of the Subject: Jean-Luc Nancy." *Paragraph* 25.1 (March 2002). 125-141.

James, William. *Varieties of Religious Experience: A Study in Human Nature*. London: Collins, 1960.

Jameson, Fredric. "Symptoms of Theory or Symptoms for Theory?" *Critical Inquiry* 30 (Winter 2004): 403-408.

———. "Postmodernism, or The Cultural Logic of Late Capitalism." *Postmodernism: A Reader*. Ed. Thomas Docherty. New York: Columbia UP, 1993. 62-92.

Johnson, Nan. *Gender and Rhetorical Space in American Life, 1866-1910*. Carbondale and Edwardsville: Southern Illinois University Press, 2002.

Krauss, Rosalind. "Robert Rauschenberg and the Materialized Image." *Robert Rauschenberg*. Ed. Branden W. Joseph. London and Cambridge, Mass.: The MIT Press, 2002. 39-55.

———. "Perpetual Inventory." *Robert Rauschenberg*. Ed. Branden W. Joseph. 93-127.

Kristeva, Julia. "Is There a Feminine Genius?" *Critical Inquiry* 30.3 (Spring 2004): 493-504.

———. *The Kristeva Reader*. Ed. Toril Moi. New York: Columbia UP, 1986

———. *Revolution in Poetic Language*. New York: Columbia UP, 1984.

Lacan, Jacques. "The Signification of the Phallus." *Ecrits: A Selection*. New York: Norton, 1977. 281-291.

Laplanche, Jean and L.-B. Pontalis, *The Language of Psychoanalysis*. Trans. Donald Nicholson-Smith. New York, London: W.W. Norton & Company, 1973.

Lee, Jarena. "The Life and Religious Experience of Jarena Lee." *Sisters of the Spirit: The Black Women's Autobiographies of the Nineteenth Century*. Ed. William Andrews. Bloomington: Indiana UP, 1986. 25-41.

Lentricchia, Frank. "In Place of an Afterword: Someone Reading." *Critical Terms for Literary Study*. Eds. Frank Lentricchia and Thomas McLaughlin. Chicago and London: The University of Chicago P, 1995. 429-446.

Leonardi, Susan and Rebecca C. Pope, *The Diva's Mouth: Body, Voice, Prima Donna Politics*. New Brunswick, NJ: Rutgers UP, 1996.

Le Vine, Charles. "The 'Open' Work of Art. " *Rooted Rhetoric: Una Tradizione dell'Arte Americana*. Ed. Gabriele Guercio. Naples: Guida Editori, 1986. 124-133.

Levitt, Annette Shandler. *The Genres and Genders of Surrealism*. London: MacMillan Press Ltd., 1999.

Loshe, Lillie Deming. *The Early American Novel 1789-1830*. New York: Frederick Ungar Publishing Co., 1966.

Lyon, Hugh Lee. *Leontyne Price: Highlights of a Prima Donna*. New York: Vantage Press, 1973. 58-59.

Lyotard, Jean-François. *Discours, figure*. Paris: Editions Klincksieck: Paris, 1971.

MacDonagh, Don. "Humor Bubbles Up as 4 Women Unite for Dance Program." *The New York Times*, 28 June 1972.

McBride, Henry. "Pictures for a picture of Gertrude Stein." *Art News* 49.10 (February 1951): 16-18.

McCully, Marilyn ed. *Picasso: The Early Years 1892-1906*. New Haven and London: Yale UP, 1998.

Majerna, Paola. *I mecenati di ieri e di oggi: riflessioni sul nesso tra economia e arte*. Bollate: Il Melograno Editore, 1998.

Malcom, Janet. "Gertrude Stein's War: The Years in Occupied France." *The New York Times* 2 June 2003: 59-81.

Marranca, Bonie. "Introduction: Presence of Mind." *Last Operas and Plays*. Baltimore & London: Johns Hopkins UP, 1995. vii-xxvii.

Martínez Fernández, Santiago. "Tena-Stein." *Gonzalo Tena: Gertrude*. Exh. Cat. Sala de Exposiciones del Ayuntamiento de Logrono. Saragoza: Tipolinea, S. A., 2003. 3-6.

Mathis, Carla and Helen Villa Connor. *The Triumph of Individual Style*. New York: Fairchild Publications, Inc., 2002.

Mears, Patricia, "Orientalism and Opulence." *Icons of Fashion: The 20th Century*. Ed. Gerda Buxbaum. Munich/London/New York: Prestel Verlag, 1999. 18-19.

Medina, Joyce. *Cézanne and Modernism: The Poetics of Painting*. New York: State University of New York Press, 1995.

Meisel, Louis K. *Photorealism at the Millennium*. New York: Harry N. Abrams, Inc. Publishers, 2002.

Mellow, James R. *Charmed Circle*. New York, Washington: Praeger Publishers, 1974.

Menand, Louis. *The Metaphysical Club*. Hammersmith, London: Flamingo, 2002.

Miller, Henry. *Tropic of Cancer*. New York: Signet, 1995.

Minervino, Fiorella. "Una Americana a Parigi." *Bolaffi Arte* 7 (February 1971): 56-61.

Moore, George. *Gertrude Stein's The Making of Americans: Repetition and the Emergence of Modernism*. New York: Peter Lang, 1998.

Moore, Lamont. Foreword. *Pictures for a Picture of Gertrude Stein as a Collector and Writer on Art and Artists: An Exhibition*. New Haven: Yale University Art Gallery, 1951.

Morbiducci, Marina. "'Oriental Peaceful Penetration': Revisited. The Ideogram and Gertrude Stein's Notion of Repetition." *HOW2* 4 (September 2000) http:www.departments.bucknell.edu/stadler center/how2/.

Mordden, Ethan. *Opera in the Twentieth Century: Sacred, Profane, Godot*. New York: Oxford University Press, 1978.

Morelli, Giovanni. *Very Well Saints: A Sum of Deconstructions*. Florence: Olschki editore, 2000.

Mundy, Jennifer, ed. *Surrealism: Desire Unbound*. Princeton: Princeton UP, 2002.

Musil, Robert. *L'uomo senza qualità*. Trans. Anita Rho, Gabriella Benedetti, Laura Castoldi. 2 vols. Turin: Einaudi, 1996-1997. Trans. of *Der Mann ohne Eigenschaften*. Reinbek bei Hamburg: Rowohlt Verlag GmbH, 1978.

Nancy, Jean-Luc. *Il Ritratto e il Suo Sguardo*. Milan: Raffaello Cortina Editore, 2002. Trans. of *Le regard du portrait*. Paris: Galilée, 2000.

——. "Introduction." *Who Comes After the Subject?* Eds. Eduardo Cadava, Peter Connor, Jean-Luc Nancy. New York and London: Routledge, 1991. 1-8.

Novalis. "Logological Fragments I: Fragment 55." *Philosophical Writings*. Ed. and trans. Margaret Mahony Stoljar. Albany: State University of New York Press, 1997. 58-59.

O'Connor, Mary. "The Objects of Modernism: Everyday Life in Women's Magazines, Gertrude Stein, and Margaret Watkins." Eds. Jay Bochner and Justin D. Edwards. *American Modernism Across the Arts*. New York: Peter Lang, 1999. 97-123.

Ogden, Thomas. *Rêverie e Interpretazione*. Trans. Givanni Baldaccini and Luciana Riommi Baldaccini. Rome: Casa Editrice Astrolabio, 1999. Trans of *Reverie and Interpretation: Sensing Something Human*. Northvale, N.J.: Jason Aronson, Inc., 1997.

——. "The analytic third—working with intersubjective clinical facts." *International Journal of Psychoanalysis* 75 (1994): 3-20.

O'Hara, Frank. "Poem 'À la recherche d' Gertrude Stein.'" *The Collected Poems*. Ed. Donald Allen. Berkley and Los Angeles: The California UP, 1995. 349.

Ormond, Mark. "Introduction." *Robert Rauschenberg: Works from the Salvage Series*. Saratosa, Florida: The John and Mable Ringling Museum of Art Foundation, 1985. 6-7.

Pasolini, Pier Paolo. "L'Umile Italia." *Le Ceneri di Gramsci*. Milan: Garzanti, 1957. 45-5.

Pavloska, Susanna. "Stein and Picasso: The Anti-Aesthetes." *Modern Primitives: Race and*

Language in Gertrude Stein, Ernst Hemingway and Zora Neale Hurston. NewYork and London: Garland Publishing, Inc., 2000. 3-29.

Pearce, Susan M. On Collecting: An Investigation into Collecting in the European Tradition. London & New York: Routledge, 1995.

Peignot, Jérôme. "Les premiers Picasso de Gertrude Stein." *Connaissance des arts* 213 (Nov. 1969): 122-131.

Peirce, Charles S. *Selected Writings*. New York: Dover Publications, 1966.

Perniola, Mario. *Contro la comunicazione* [Against communication]. Turin: Einaudi, 2004.

Pirandello, Luigi. *One, no one, one hundred-thousand*. Boston, Mass.: Eridanos, 1990. Trans. of *Uno, Nessuno, Centomila*. 1926.

Poggioli, Renato. *Teoria dell'arte d'avanguardia*. Bologna: Il Mulino, 1962.

Poirier, Richard. "Manly Agitations." *The New Republic* 8 June 1998: 26-34.

Poliziano, Angelo. *Stanze Cominciate per la Giostra di Giuliano De' Medici*. Ed. Vincenzo Perticone. Turin: Loescher-Chiantore, 1954.

Porte, Joel, ed. *Emerson in His Journals*. London: The Belknap P, 1982.

Portelli, Alessandro. *The Text and the Voice: Writing, Speaking and Democracy in American Literature*. New York: Columbia, 1994. Trans. of *Il testo e la voce. Oralità, scrittura e democrazia in America*. Roma: Manifestolibri, 1992.

Potter, Margaret. Introduction. *Four Americans in Paris: The Collections of Gertrude Stein and Her Family*. New York: The Museum of Modern Art, 1970.

Rabaté, Jean-Michel. "Una lingua straniata. Gli stili del modernismo." *Il Romanzo*. Ed. Franco Moretti. Turin: Einaudi, 2001. 747-773.

Ransom, John Crowe. "Criticism, Inc." *Virginia Quarterly Review* 13 (Autumn 1937): 86-602.

Reeder, Jan Glier. "Femmes De la Mode." Ed. Buxbaum, Gerda. *Icons of Fashion: The 20th Century*. Ed. Gerda Buxbaum. Munich/London/New York: Prestel Verlag, 1999. 22-23.

Riddel, Joseph. "Stein and Bergson." *The Turning Word: American Literary Modernism and Continental Theory*. Philadelphia: U of Pennsylvania, 1996.

Rilke, Rainer M. *Sonnets to Orpheus*. Trans. Willis Barnstone. Boston and London: Shambala, 2004.

Rose, Jacqueline. "Introduction." Moustapha Safouan. *Jacques Lacan and The Question of Psychoanalytic Training*. Trans. Jacqueline Rose. New York: St. Martin's Press, 2000. 1-47.

Roudinesco, Elizabeth. *Lacan*. Trans. Barbara Bray. New York: Columbia UP, 1997.

Rowlandson, Mary. "A Narrative of the Captivity and Restoration of Mrs. Mary Rowlandson." *Colonial American Travel Narratives*. Ed. Wendy Martin. London: Penguin, 1994. 1-48.

Rubin, William. "Reflections on Picasso and Portraiture." *Picasso and Portraiture*. Ed. W. Rubin. New York: The Museum of Modern Art, 1996.

Ruddick, Lisa. *Reading Gertrude Stein: Body, Text, Gnosis*. Ithaca & London: Cornell UP, 1990.

Scarry, Elaine. *On Beauty and Being Just*. Princeton: Princeton UP, 1999.

Simons, Patricia. "Homosociality and erotics in Italian Renaissance portraiture." *Portraiture: Facing the Subject.* Ed. Joanna Woodall. Manchester: Manchester UP, 1997. 29-51.

Sini, Carlo. *Semiotica e Filosofia: Segno e Linguaggio in Peirce, Nietzsche, Heidegger e Foucault.* Bologna: Il Mulino, 1978.

Sorley, Kathrine. "A Wedding Bouquet." *Dance Now* 6.1 (Spring 1997) 76-81.

Souhami, Diana. *Gertrude and Alice.* London: Pandora Press, 1991.

Spahr, Juliana. *Everybody's Autonomy: Connective Reading and Collective Communities* Tuscaloosa: U of Alabama P, 2001

Sprigge, Elizabeth. *Gertrude Stein: Her Life and Work.* New York: Harper and Brothers, 1957.

Steele, Valerie. *The Corset: A Cultural History.* New Haven and London: Yale UP, 2001.

——. *Fetish: Fashion, Sex, and Power.* New York/Oxford: Oxford UP, 1996

Stein, Gertrude. "Composition as Explanation." *Gertrude Stein: Writings 1903-1932.* Eds. Catharine R. Stimpson and Harriet Chessman. Vol 1. The Library of America, 1998. 520-9.

——. *The Geographical History of America or The Relation of Human Nature to the Human Mind. Gertrude Stein: Writings 1932-1946.* Eds. Catharine R. Stimpson and Harriet Chessman. Vol. 2. 365-493.

——. "Melanctha." *Gertrude Stein: Writings 1932-1946.* Eds. Catharine R. Stimpson and Harriet Chessman. Vol. 1. 124-239.

——. "Portrait of Mabel Dodge at Villa Curonia." *Gertrude Stein: Writings, 1903-1932.* Eds. Catharine R. Stimpson and Harriet Chessman. Vol. 356-9.

——. *Stanzas in Meditation. Gertrude Stein: Writings 1932-1946.* Eds. Catharine Stimpson and Harriet Chessman. Vol. 2. 1-45.

——. *Four Saints in Three Acts. Operas and Plays.* Foreword James R. Mellow. New York: Barrytown, LTD., 1998. 11-47.

——. "Capital capitals." *Operas & Plays.* 61-70.

——. "Reread Another." *Operas & Plays.* 123-130.

——. *The Making of Americans.* Normal, Ill.: Dalkey Archive Press, 1995.

——. *Doctor Faustus Lights the Lights.* Ed. Carl Van Vechten. Intro. Bonnie Marranca. *Last Operas and Plays.* Baltimore and London: Johns Hopkins UP, 1995. 89-118.

——. *The Mother of Us All. Last Operas and Plays.* 52-88.

——. "Yes is for a Very Young Man." *Last Operas and Plays.* 3-51.

——. "The Gradual Making of the Making of Americans." *Lectures in America.* Intro. Wendy Steiner. Boston: Beacon, 1985. 135-161.

——. "Pictures." *Lectures in America.* 59-90.

——. "What Is English Literature." *Lectures in America.* 11-55.

——. *The Autobiography of Alice B. Toklas.* Ed. Carl Van Vechten. *The Selected Writings of Gertrude Stein.* New York: Vintage Books, 1972. 3-237.

——. *Tender Buttons.* Ed. Carl Van Vechten. *Selected Writings of Gertrude Stein.* New York: Vintage, 1972. 459-509.

——. *Lucy Church Amiably.* 1930. New York: Something Else Press, 1969.

Stein, Gertrude. *Geography and Plays*. New York: Something Else Press, 1968.
——. *Picasso*. 1938. Boston: Beacon Press, 1959.
——.   "Cézanne." *Portrait and Prayers*. New York: Random House, 1934. 11.
——.   "If I Told Him: A Completed Portrait of Picasso." *Portraits and Prayers*. 21-25.
——.   "Picasso." *Portraits and Prayers*. 17-20.
Steiner, Wendy. "Introduction." *Lectures in America.* Boston: Beacon, 1985. ix-xxvii.
Stendhal, Renate, ed. *Gertrude Stein in Words and Pictures: A Photobiography*. Chapel Hill: Algonquin Books, 1994.
Stevens, Wallace. *The Collected Poems*. New York: Vintage, 1982.
Stimpson, Catharine R. "Gertrude Stein and the Transposition of Gender." *The Poetics of Gender*. Ed. Nancy Miller. New York: Columbia UP, 1986. 1-18.
Stimpson, Catherine R. "Review Essay: Reading Gertrude Stein." *Tulsa Studies in Women's Literature* 4.2 (Fall 1985): 265-271.
——. "The Somagrams of Gertrude Stein." *Poetics Today* 6.1-2 (1985): 67-80.
——. "Gertrude Stein: Humanism and Its Freaks." *Boundary 2: A Journal of Postmodern Literature and Culture* 12-13. 3-1 (Spring-Fall 1984): 301-19.
Stimpson, Catharine R. "Gertrice/Altrude: Stein, Toklas, and the Paradox of the Happy Marriage." *Mothering the Mind: Twelve Studies of Writers and Their Silent Partners*. Ed. Ruth Perry. New York: Holmes and Meier, 1984. 122-139.
Sutherland, Donald. *Gertrude Stein: A Biography of Her Work*. New York: Yale University Press, 1951.
Tena, Gonzalo. "Sobre Gertrude Stein." *Heraldo de Aragón* 29 May 2003: 2-3.
Theweleit, Klaus. "Monteverdi's *L'Orfeo*: The Technology of Reconstruction." *Opera Through Other Eyes*. Ed. David J. Levin. Stanford, Ca: Stanford UP, 1994. 14-176.
Thomson, Virgil. *The Selected Letters of Virgil Thomson*. Eds. Tim Page and Vanessa Weeks Page. New York: Summit, 1988.
——.   *Four Saints in Three Acts*. Perf. Betty Allen, Gwendolyn Bradley, William Brown, Clamma Dale, Benjamin Matthews Florence Quivar, Arthur Thompson. Cond. Joel Thome. Elektra/Asylum/Nonesuch records, 1982.
——.   "Jacket notes." *Four Saints in Three Acts*. Cond. Joel Thome. Orchestra of Our Time. New York: Elektra/Asylum/Nonesuch records, 1982.
Toklas, Alice B. *Staying on Alone: The Letters of Alice B. Toklas*. Ed. Edward Burns. New York: Vintage Books, 1975.
——.   *What is Remembered*. New York: Holt, Rinehart and Winston, 1963.
Tommasini, Anthony. *Virgil Thomson: Composer on the Aisle*. New York: W.W. Norton and Company, 1997.
"Trudy and Alice in Jungleland." *The Daily Princetonian* 8 November 1934: 2.
Van Vechten, Carl. 'Notes Written on Stone.' Brochure of *Doctor Faustus Lights the Lights*. The Living Theatre. The Cherry Lane Theater, 2 December 1951-16 December 1951, 5-7. New York Public Library, Carl Van Vechten Collection.
Vaughan, David. "(a tree, a melon, a sheet of water, a flight of birds)." *Ballet Review* 4.6 (1974):2-13.

Vollard, Ambroise. *Ricordi di un mercante di quadri*. Trans. Maria Castellani d'Este. Torino: Einaudi, 1978. Trans. of *Souvenirs d'un marchand de tableaux*. 1937.

Walker, Alice. "In Search of Our Mothers' Gardens." *In Search of Our Mothers' Gardens*. New York: Harcourt Brace Jovanovich, 1983. 230-243.

Walker, Jayne. *The Making of a Modernist: Gertrude Stein from Three Lives to Tender Buttons*. Amherst: U of Massachusetts P, 1985.

Walzer, Katherine Sorley. "A Wedding Bouquet." *Dance Now* 6.1 (Spring 1997): 76-81.

Warnke, Martin. *The court artist: on the ancestry of the modern artist*. Cambridge: Cambridge UP, 1993.

Waters, R. D. "Gertrude Stein Leaves Capacity Audience in 500 Various Stages of Understanding." *The Daily Princetonian* 6 November 1934: 1+.

Watson, Steven. *Prepare for Saints: Gertrude Stein, Virgil Thomson, and the Mainstreaming of American Modernism*. Berkeley: U of California P, 1995.

Watten, Barrett. "An Epic of Subjectivation: *The Making of Americans*." *Modernism/Modernity* 5.2 (April 1998)): 95-121.

Watts, Linda. *Rapture Untold: Gender, Mysticism, and the 'Moment of Recognition' in Works by Gertrude Stein*. New York: Peter Lang, 1996.

Wertenbaker, Lael. *The World of Picasso*. New York: Time-Life Books, 1967.

Werth, Margaret. "Representing the Body in 1906." *Picasso: The Early Years 1892-1906*. Ed. Marilyn McCully. New Haven And London: Yale UP, 1998. 277-287.

Wineapple, Brenda. *Sister Brother: Gertrude Stein and Leo Stein*. New York: G.P. Putnam, 1996.

Winter, Ella. "Gertrude Stein Comma." *Pacific Weekly*, 12 April 1935. *The Critical Response to Gertrude Stein*. Ed. Kirk Curnutt. Westport, Conn.: The Greenwood Press, 2000. 82-84.

Winthrop, John. "A Model of Christian Charity." *The American Puritans: Their Prose and Poetry*. Ed. Perry Miller. New York: Columbia UP, 1982. 79-84.

Woolf, Virginia. *The Waves*. San Diego, New York, London: Harcourt Brace Jovanovich, Publishers, 1959.

Young-Bruhel. Elizabeth. *Hannah Arendt: For Love of the World*. New Haven: Yale UP, 1982.

Zanardi, Bruno. "Giotto and the St. Francis Cycle at Assisi." *The Cambridge Companion to Giotto*, Eds. Anne Derbes and Mark Sandona. Cambridge: Cambridge UP, 2004.

Zizek, Slavoj. "'The Wound is Healed Only by the Spear that Smote You': The Operatic Subject and Its Vicissitudes." *Opera Through Other Eyes*. Ed. David J. Levin. Sanford, CA: Stanford UP, 1994) 177-214.

Index

Abbot, Berenice 72, 76, 83
Adorno, Theodor 163 n.14
aesthetics 1, 18, 56, 89, 91, 125, 143
  American 139
  archaeology of 92
  contemporary 2, 4, 7, 111, 114,
    118; *see also* postmodernism
  deconstructive 80
  modernist 77, 80
  and human self-realization 91
  and innovation 90
  and society 7, 118
  and social justice 118
  and conceptual thought 121
  and primitivism 122
  surrealist 69
African Americans
  as exotic other 122
African masks 97
agalma 100-101
agrarian
  setting 107
  spirit 80
Aldrich, Mildred 104
Allen, Betty 112, 170 n1
American art collectors 4, 14, 19, 27
anger
  and injury 40
  of the masses 121
anonymity 100
  and gender 70
  of the writer 1-2
anorexia 51
Antheil, George 170 n1
Anthony, Susan B. 5, 28, 137, 139,
    173 n.3
anthropology 12
anxiety 13, 15, 32, 38, 56, 84, 99,
    101, 102, 103, 105, 113, 140,
    145, 146
  of materiality 101

  semiotic 162 n.7
  transgenerational 35
Apollonian 75, 81
Arendt, Hanna 17
Aristotle
  Nichomachean Ethics 33
art
  of the 1950s
  avant-garde 55
  collecting 46
  and comfort 65
  and costumes 59
  devaluing of 90
  and fear 98-99
  high and low 123
  and life 1
  reception of 143
  as reparative 120-121
  and writing 113
Ashton, Frederick 112,122-123, 149,
    171 n.14
Askew, Kirk 171 n.14
authenticity 4, 65, 66, 89, 101
  and artifice 68
author
  death of 2
  real 4, 5-6, 161 n.8
  twentieth-century 9
avant-garde 16, 19, 76, 95, 144
  art 8, 55
  and consumerism 64
  desire 77
  possessions 83
  power 58
  writing 58

Bachrach, Helen 25
Barnes, Albert C. 19
Barnes, Djuna 53, 72, 83, 166 n.3
Barthes, Roland 12, 167 n.11

Gertrude Stein and
the Essence of What Happens

GERTRUDE STEIN

AND

THE ESSENCE OF WHAT HAPPENS

DANA CAIRNS WATSON

VANDERBILT UNIVERSITY PRESS   *Nashville*

This book is printed on acid-free paper.
Manufactured in the United States of America

Design by Gary Gore

Frontispiece courtesy of Department of Special Collections,
Charles E. Young Research Library, UCLA. Collection 2108,
Gilbert Harrison Collection of Material relating
to Gertrude Stein, box 4 folder 16:
Gertrude Stein and Alice B. Toklas having tea.

Library of Congress Cataloging-in-Publication Data

Watson, Dana Cairns, 1966-
Gertrude Stein and the essence of what happens / Dana Cairns Watson.—1st ed.
p. cm.
Includes bibliographical references and index.
ISBN 0-8265-1462-6 (cloth : alk. paper)
ISBN 0-8265-1463-4 (pbk. : alk. paper)
1. Stein, Gertrude, 1874-1946—Criticism and interpretation.
2. Interpersonal communication in literature.
3. Meaning (Philosophy) in literature.
4. Conversation in literature. 5. Speech in literature.
6. Dialogue. I. Title.
PS3537.T323Z96 2004
818.'5209—dc22
2003027602

For Rob, a credit to the species

CONTENTS

ACKNOWLEDGMENTS

Thanks to Stephen Yenser for introducing me to Gertrude Stein and her critics in 1986, for daring me to develop instructions for reading Stein, and for making me pay attention to every word—Stein's, as well as my own. Thanks to Martha Banta for pointing out that my sudden interest in conversation analysis—as inspired by Michael Moerman and Edith Wharton—might be worth pursuing. Thanks to John Heritage for welcoming this novice into the field of conversation analysis, and for being willing to take on Stein at the same time. Thanks to all of them, as well as Jayne Lewis, for encouraging me with praise, challenges, and always more questions and wordplay.

Thanks to Stein's readers and critics for inspiring me to think in ways I never imagined, and to Gilbert Harrison's generous donation to UCLA's Special Collections. Thanks to the warm and helpful people who work there, especially Jeffrey Rankin, for enabling me to read Stein's out-of-print works (many of which are now in print), gaze at photographs, and finger—among other memorabilia—one of her small gloves.

Thanks to the many students who hesitatingly started into a Stein work and were open-minded and creative enough to notice that something wonderfully interesting was happening. These include Allison Raskin, Jake Bern, Aaron Dover, carine risley, Bryan Kocol, Suzanne Karpilovsky, and Tessa Ingersoll. Thanks even to some of the stubborn ones—Mike Hawes and Eugene Pino, for example—who kept asking for more reasons that they should come to appreciate Stein, too.

To Bob Hiller, my eighth-grade American history teacher at Stanley School, thanks for teaching out of discontinued textbooks which showed that imperfect people can accomplish great things, and for truly thinking while he talked to us thirteen-year-olds.

Thanks and love to my parents, Gene and Patty Cairns, for everything.

Thanks and love to Emma Cairns Watson for her patience and her sweet kisses from the doorway of the study. Thanks for singing: "I am Rose my eyes are blue / I am Rose and who are you / I am Rose and when I sing / I am Rose like anything" (from Stein's *The World is Round*). Thanks even more for saying unprompted to a friend, the week before this book was due at the press, "Let's sing it like it's a conversation!"

Thanks and love to Robert N. Watson, who gave unofficial fellowships year after year, was my main reader and copy editor, offered suggestions without expecting me to take them all, arranged a year in Paris for the whole family, and not just accepted but encouraged my natural tendencies to do this (and almost everything else) differently.

Gertrude Stein and
the Essence of What Happens

INTRODUCTION

"Announce what you see"

F OR GERTRUDE STEIN, language is a living but ailing organ of our social body. Modern speech is a symptom of the way bureaucracy threatens to become fascism and conformity damages humanity. Stein's several styles of writing advocate a revision and rearrangement of fundamental orders: the syntax of English sentences, the contained and supposedly individualized selfhood of Americans, interpersonal allegiances, and social and political organization. If there is something wrong with these structures, then language can be studied to diagnose the problem, and language can serve to solve it—or change it, anyway. Stein has been canonized for her eccentricity, but that reputation may be a way of making safe—making cute and quirky—a revolutionary utopian impulse and insight, with a huge force of life behind it.[1] Unlike a strict deconstructionist, who believes (or at least asserts) that "*words speak us*," Stein builds on the assumption that *people* speak, that we can wield language however we choose (Lehman, 106); she writes on behalf of free will and self-making. Stein does not believe in "an exclusively linguistic universe," as her devotion to her dogs and long walks and especially Alice's cooking—and talk about food—suggests (Lehman, 99). At the very least, "we can say we do like what we have," or that we don't (Stein, "Lifting Belly," 94).[2] And words are not all we have with which to communicate; we have intonations, smiles, glances, kisses, and caresses—as Stein makes clear in three of her titles, we have "Tender Buttons" and a "Lifting Belly," not just "Patriarchal Poetry." Stein is not a nihilist doomsayer but rather a doctor investigating the organic functions of interactive language. How that language works and what it achieves is the essence of what happens.

Stein must have been particularly sensitive to the subtle orders around her. Her writing demonstrates awareness of the unwritten rules of human social interaction manifest in the structures of turn-taking conversation, which were ignored by linguists such as Ferdinand de Saussure and Noam

1

Chomsky and which have come to the attention of social scientists such as Harvey Sacks only in the last few decades. Stein's biographers attest to her tendency to overstep the silent boundaries of decorum. She was a lesbian, and she was too loud and too cheerful and too fat. She alluded to her own genius too directly. She talked too much, asked questions that were too personal, laughed too hard, and sweated too profusely. This relentless crossing of boundaries that keep people's bodies separate and knowledge separate—keep their interiorities interior—persistently alerted her to the part that social norms play in human subjectivity, and thus in every other human endeavor.[3]

On the other hand, Stein's writing is usually pure pleasure—a game—and serious only in that she's serious about play. She mucks about with words, fools around, teases and tickles and hums. Reviewers call Stein's opera *Four Saints in Three Acts* an "untroubled really very simple pleasure" (Krutch, 75), and my child sings certain phrases with glowing delight. Another reviewer describes *The World Is Round* as "pure delight, simple pleasure" (Becker, 114). In 1913, Mabel Dodge Luhan—then the center of an avant-garde Greenwich Village salon and later a memoirist who worked to alter white and masculine notions of the American West—wrote that "every word lives" in Stein's writing (153). A year later, Carl Van Vechten—a music critic later turned novelist, Harlem booster, and photographer—wrote that there is no "fresher phrase" than those found in Stein's long prose poem *Tender Buttons* (158). French literary and social critic Bernard Faÿ—a friend of Stein who collaborated with her on abridging *The Making of Americans* and then collaborated with the Germans and was appointed director of the Bibliothèque Nationale in Paris in 1940—writes that Mencken, Dreiser, Joyce, Valéry, and Gide "write as you and I take a bus," but that Stein is "sincer[e]" and "courageous" in the "amusing game" of being a writer (59, 58, 60). "Preaching and politics," Faÿ goes on,

> oblige one's mind to take social problems profoundly seriously; they destroy the freedom of the mind, the ability to be interested in the universal and the individual. Science obliges the mind to get used to a rationalistic and systematic method that is no good for the artist. Science trains you to count and avoid understanding; it gives you very good means to measure things, but it insists that you should feel and react as little as possible, while art and literature require a rich and deep ability to react, feel, dream, and act freely.

"So few people," he concludes, "can love and laugh, search and choose, look and live," and "Miss Stein has done it" (60, 63). And in an essay pleasingly titled "Stein Is Nice," Wayne Koestenbaum writes that "we are free to make of her what we wish, and to read her more obscure texts in a state of liberated remoteness from dogma, protocol, and usefulness" (298).

All this points to the problem of treating Stein as a writer with ideas, as interested in solving problems—but these are not the same thing. Ideas include speculation and theory. Ideas can "imagine" and "hypothesize" and "postulat[e]" and "arous[e]" "expectations" even without delivering, and Koestenbaum suggests that Stein thus "insists that we enlarge our capacities—*even if the enterprise turns out to be bankrupt*" (297). Stein's ideas are not especially utilitarian; indeed, she suggested it was a shame that words were put to use (*Geographical History*, 190, 175). She is interested in freedom for freedom's sake, ideas for ideas' sake, being for being's sake. William Carlos Williams (1966, 73–74) wrote in "Asphodel, That Greeny Flower": "It is difficult / to get the news from poems / yet men die miserably every day / for lack / of what is found there" and Malcolm Cowley understands Stein to be working along these lines. Shortly after Stein's death, Cowley wrote that she was "working at some problem that apparently has no connection with man or society"—"something humbl[e]," something less like "atomic fission" than like "the anatomy of junebugs"—and, he predicts, "suddenly it would be found that one or more of [these] discoveries about junebugs could be applied to curing or prolonging human life" (150). I would argue that her playfulness does aid in prolonging our lives: it makes us conscious and makes us strive to express ourselves. But explications of the message sent through her playfulness risk undermining that very playfulness and therefore that very message, and I fear that I too will take her "both too seriously, and not seriously enough" (Canby, 80).[4] While I offer a new and somewhat suspiciously coherent reading of Stein's texts, I agree with Linda S. Watts, who begins *Gertrude Stein: A Study of the Short Fiction*, with "Stein's own instruction for engaging her texts: 'If you enjoy it you understand it'" (Watts, 12, 97). Here Stein echoes another pyramid-shaped and cantankerous writer, Ben Jonson, who was also interested in the details of ordinary human speech: "Pray thee take care, that tak'st my book in hand, / To read it well; that is, to understand" (7).

Stein's writing expresses the meaning between the words—between individual words on the page and between utterances in conversation. She shows us how to read between the lines of our daily—personal but socially circumscribed—lives. Readers often balk at Stein's works, suspicious that they are wasting their time decoding Stein's words, but she was actually decoding theirs, and ours. Stein makes her readers aware of their linguistic processes: reading, writing, speaking, and listening. The poet Robert Haas has explained that Stein "was enormously influential, on some writers who followed her, and on our everyday speech" (Hubly, 69).[5] In *Halfway to Revolution*, Clive Bush rightly argues that Stein's work is politically valuable in its critique of the increasing social control of discourse and knowledge, and that she is at her best when challenging the "unreflected habits of society" in *The Making of Americans* (373), sensing the way the world is changed by mass media (382), and discussing the effects of propaganda in *Wars I Have Seen* (397). In addition to making us aware of our words, and how we speak them, and what they really mean in and out of the contexts in which they are uttered, Stein offers a garbled vision (to use an aptly synesthetic phrase) of a potential new society with a new language and a new idea of personhood.

Stein's education in classes taught by William James is not the only reason to place her writing and its potential social and political ramifications within a strong and long-lived American tradition of thought. Though her work may seem the antithesis of anything practical, she must be understood as a pragmatist. James was the first to put the term "pragmatism" in print, in 1898, although he was already arguing for a somewhat different meaning for the term than Charles Sanders Peirce had implied when he first used it in conversation—and Peirce had lifted the idea from Alexander Bain and the term from Immanuel Kant (Menand, *Metaphysical*, 354n; Simonson, 4). James dedicated his 1906–7 published lectures on pragmatism to John Stuart Mill, "from whom [he] first learned the pragmatic openness of mind" (James, *Pragmatism*, 1). But pragmatism did not just offer Stein an open mind (or correspond to the one she already had). Pragmatism emphasized (and still emphasizes) verbal communication between humans and mutual relationships between other phenomena. For example, James believed that "the knower is an actor" who "registers the truth which he helps to create" (qtd. in Putnam, "Permanence," 17).[6] A colleague of James at Harvard, Nicholas St. John Green, believed that "knowledge is not a passive mirroring of the world, but an active means of making the world into the kind of world we want it to be" (Menand, *Metaphysical*, 225). In *Mind, Self, and Society*, published in 1934, George Herbert Mead posited a theory of intersubjectivity, in which people import (into their behavior, from society) and export (from their behavior, to other members of society) attitudes and gestures which call out for responses from others, ad infinitum (186–89). He goes so far as to say that this "conversation of gestures" is responsible for the rise of language: "Words have arisen out of a social interrelationship" (189). In *Experience and Nature*, published in 1929, John Dewey also emphasized mutuality within communication: "we bring together logical universals in discourse, where they copulate and breed new meanings," and this "dialectic generates new objects" (194). Or, as Timothy Kaufman-Osborn summarizes it, "making sense" is when "knower and known are continuously engaged in creation and re-creation of each other" (ix). These mutualities may have been an important foundation for—or may at least correspond with—Stein's ideas of personal efficacy in a social setting. Interested in the individual, Stein repeatedly asks a question that would haunt the neopragmatist Richard Rorty (*Contingency*, xiii): "How can an inhabitant of . . . a society be more than the enactor of a role in a previously written script?"

The pragmatists may also have encouraged Stein's very confident, even cheerful, potential tentativeness about all things known. Hillary Putnam emphasizes James's "fallibilism," which "does not require us to doubt *everything* [but] only requires us to be prepared to doubt anything." Further, "there are no metaphysical guarantees to be had that even our most firmly-held beliefs will never need revision. That one can be both fallibilistic *and* antiskeptical is perhaps *the* basic insight of American Pragmatism" (Putnam, *Permanence*, 21). In a later essay, Putnam argues for Ludwig Wittgenstein's pragmatism, which can "change our point of view" without advocating alternative theses, and which can challenge the very "language games" in which people speak to determine "better and worse language games" ("Wittgenstein," 27–28, 38). Perhaps desiring to change the "language game" that makes philosophy so authoritative, or just authoritative sounding, Wittgenstein writes: "Philosophy ought really to be written only as a form of poetry."[7] And this is often what Stein does: much of her writing is a form of philosophical inquiry in which she throws assumptions into doubt but does not offer another stable idea on which we can depend instead. Yet her tone of confidence and playfulness prevents readers from confusing her doubt with skepticism or, worse, its common partner cynicism. The fact that Stein is one of very few cheerful writers indicates that she was not plagued by an all-encompassing skepticism. The traditional culture of France and her regulated daily life may have given her a solid platform from which to comfortably ask discomfiting questions.[8]

Language and speech were the main ingredients in Stein's (loose) program for individual development, as well as for societal change, and this too may have been supported by pragmatist thought. Although not addressing conversation directly, James "influenced the study of communication processes" in that he saw communication as the way "to look at and know the world," offer "an exchange of information," and "even offer a negotiation of reality" (Leonhirth, 92).

Pragmatism placed a primary value on communication:

Pragmatism has always been all around communication, near to it, surrounding it, because "as a doctrine" it has always "held that the world is
open-ended and in process." The idea of communication was, from the
beginning, implicated in James' resistance to the world. James knew that
his existence depended on believing that this is an unfinished universe
and that each of us can have a hand in making it. That knowledge is
knowledge of the possibility of communication. (Shepherd, 247).

In short, communication influences how we see the world and also allows
us to manipulate that world. In *Democracy and Education*, Dewey goes so
far as to say: "Society not only continues to exist by transmission, by communication, but may fairly be said to exist *in* transmission, *in* communication"
(5). More recently, Rorty asserts that "the human self is created by the use
of a vocabulary" and that "a talent for speaking differently, rather than for
arguing well, is the chief instrument of cultural change" (*Contingency*, 7).
In fact, pragmatism has been described as a "resistance movement" that
"employ[ed] the hope of communication against the manifest tragedies of
complete isolation and total uncertainty" (Shepherd, 253). In writing "differently," Stein resisted her mind's verbal occupation—and then she moved
into the outside world, imagining a language that could resist the German
occupation of France, as well as make manifest other emancipations.

James's earliest description of pragmatism corresponds to some of the
ideas Stein held most dear:

Pragmatism represents a perfectly familiar attitude in philosophy, the
empiricist attitude, but it represents it, as it seems to me, both in a more
radical and in a less objectionable form than it has ever yet assumed.
A pragmatist turns his back resolutely and once for all upon a lot of
inveterate habits dear to professional philosophers. He turns away from
abstraction and insufficiency, from verbal solutions, from bad *a priori*
reasons, from fixed principles, closed systems, and pretended absolutes
and origins. He turns towards concreteness and adequacy, towards facts,
towards action and towards power. That means the empiricist temper
regnant and the rationalist temper sincerely given up. It means the open
air and possibilities of nature, as against dogma, artificiality, and the
pretence of finality in truth. (*Pragmatism*, 25)

While some readers seem to find Stein's writing full of "artificialities" or at least unidentifiable "abstraction," I believe that Stein's work is in the vein of this type of pragmatism. Stein's descriptions of the careful observations she made in writing *Tender Buttons* and her close attention to conversation patterns demonstrate her observational tendencies. Her incremental repetition reveals, in at least one way, her openness to revision based on further experience, including the experience of having said it and heard it and thought about it one more time. Stein avoids reiterating old habits, tries to escape what had generally been considered closed systems (of syntax, of thought), searches for a way to say and enact what she can envision, and erases whatever intellectual boundaries she comes across with her assertive questions (the ones without question marks). She does not reach "absolutes and origins," but she seems to find a way "towards action and towards power."

It is possible that Stein did not see the urgent need for this action until World War II, but she was playfully proposing and enabling it through her entire life's work. Stein remembers that one of her goals for making *The Making of Americans* was to understand people—"to know what was inside each one which made them that one"—so that she (and they) could "change something" (*Lectures*, 137). In fact, her early works are in some ways more radical than her later writings, perhaps because she is not responding to a particular set of social problems in a politically charged setting. A reviewer of *Tender Buttons* claims that Stein attempts "to express anarchy in art" (R. Rogers, 18). By the end of her life, Gertrude Stein has become a household name, and all American eyes (those who read *Life* and *Time* magazines, anyway) are upon the woman who survived the war incommunicado. Early in her career, though, she is more free to be, free to see, and free to say, since she has love and time and little or no readership. In fact, this very contrast between her earlier lonely freedom and her later experience of public expectation may have pointed Stein toward her recognition of the limitations on the search for meaning and possibility in a society of mass communication and celebrity, too much (apparent) information, and too much (thoughtless) activity.

Ultimately, then, Stein's tapping into the dynamic forms of spoken language contributes to sociopolitical as well as linguistic projects. By listening to everyday conversations, Stein diagnoses the character of individuals and the strengths and weaknesses of society. By writing the ways she does, Stein conditions her readers to understand words differently than they have before. Once we hear differently, we can see differently. We then treat words differently ourselves, altering how others hear. Changing language, by changing us, can change society.[9]

Stein, then, does not propose that we learn to read differently only so that we can appreciate *her* writing. By learning to read anew, which involves changing the order in our minds, we can change order at all levels, personal and social. Seeing differently is difficult; Stein writes: "I like seeing things in each one that are interesting, I even in a way like learning seeing a new way of seeing new, to me, things in them." But she admits: "I like it in a way I say, I find it hard to let myself not resist at all to this thing" (*Making*, 622). By seeing anew, by resisting established orders instead of new ones, and by saying what we see, we can start new conversations with others and within ourselves. These conversations in turn can develop new forms of relationships and ideally can grow a new culture through spontaneous connecting. Put very differently, the world is changing, and words can't mean what they always meant before. This notion is one that Koestenbaum describes as "queer": "Words experience the gravitational pull of nonmeaning, or of fluctuating significance" ("Stein Is Nice," 305). Bush points to Stein's interest in "the adaptation of old form to new content" (*Halfway*, 391). We must learn to notice the differences between what we say, what we mean, and what we see.

Although this is not a book about pedagogy, a classroom discussion of Stein demonstrates her potential influence on a society in crystallized form. My readings of Stein prove her value less directly than does the thinking (and talking) of students in the presence of *Tender Buttons*. Students find themselves freed from trying to guess what their instructor expects them to say (largely because they have no idea). And because the students are grasping at straws, they find new ways of grasping. Stein's work increases semantic sensitivity and intelligence, traits that influence how students read other works and that the great polemical "educationist" Neil Postman argues are crucial for students of any subject. Semantic intelligence should increase students' abilities to insist on and act on their freedoms—freedoms which many of them understand as a given or a formality—so that they can achieve individuality as readers, thinkers, creators, and political animals.[10] Stein teaches us to listen to ourselves as we never have before, as only Stein seems to have heard us, so that we know who we present ourselves to be and can decide and become who we want to be as individuals and as a community.[11] (Stein also made some people think in new ways, or at least made them see that there might be new ways *to* think, during her U.S. lecture tour, the response to which I discuss in chapter 4.) Discussing Stein allows readers to see unforeseen political and social possibilities, and to see how our democracy could be deepened by our own individual semantic changes—and to see, too, why we haven't seen these things. She leaves space into which we must project meaning, partly like a traditional psychotherapist, partly like a deconstructionist, but also like any good conversationalist. Reading Stein is necessarily participatory, not passive, as Harriet Scott Chessman has explored most extensively. In short, mine is a book that makes an argument about a dead author, but it is also a book that hopes to convince each reader that he or she can take great pleasure in, and actually bring about change in, this present world by talking and listening differently.

Stein's understanding of the human mind explains why she writes the way she does. As Postman points out, teachers' understandings of their students' minds determine how they teach:

> There is no test, textbook, syllabus, or lesson plan that any of us creates that does not reflect our preference for some metaphor of the mind, or of knowledge, or of the process of learning. Do you believe a student's mind to be a muscle that must be exercised? Or a garden that must be cultivated? Or a dark cavern that must be illuminated? Or an empty vessel that must be filled to overflowing? Whichever you favor, your metaphor will control—often without your being aware of it—how you will proceed as a teacher. (*Conscientious*, 29)

I think that Stein's metaphors are unique, or at least not the clichés about which Postman warns us. For her, our minds are rusty climbing structures—rusty because they are unmaintained and underutilized, and playground equipment because we are meant to play and exercise on them. Or our minds are dancers that have been repeating the same few steps over and over for so long that we've forgotten—or forgotten to develop—the very capacity for improvisation. To use a more contemporary metaphor, each of our minds is an exciting, one-of-a-kind computer program stuck in the same tiny subroutine in which almost everyone else is stuck, too. We are all using Microsoft when we could be fingering tender buttons.

Stein's writing pulls us out of that infinite loop and makes us notice how much of our thought we take for granted without really thinking. She makes us aware of what has been invisible, directs our attention to the medium (language) in which we usually tread so easily because we step on the stepping-stones, and causes us to ask questions about structures of thought we have always accepted as harmless and inevitable. Long before Marshall McLuhan, Stein seemed to know "the medium was the massage" (and while not stating it in those words, she seemed to explain herself in prose at least as clear as much of McLuhan's writing, which is full of sporadic headlines and strangely shaped word blocks). Stein charts the geography of the mind, a topography shaped by language and just as infinite in its untested permutations. Never one to shy away from the seemingly impossible, Stein imagines how a new mental chorography and choreography could influence a nation's social and political landscape. Stein's early works, including "Q.E.D.," *The Making of Americans*, and *Tender Buttons*, are the perfect documents for reeducating readers in (among other topics) general semantics, alternative thought, and identity.

Not until her later works, written during and after World War II, does she explicitly discuss the need for this reeducation. Her experiences and observations during that time must have motivated her to state directly the need to hone our abilities to resist authority, save our land and our souls from machine-made gadgets, and revive our individual potential. Fascism raised the stakes for epistemology, raised in a political contest questions that were formerly confined to a literary context.

In *The Geographical History of America*, Stein writes:

> I think that if you announce what you see nobody can say no. Everybody does everybody does say no but nobody can nobody can say so, that is no.
> That is the reason that you can say what you see[.]
> And do you see.
> That is what the national hymn says the star spangled banner.
> Oh say can you see. (162–63)

"Say what you see" captures the tense cooperation between sound and sight emphasized throughout this reading of Gertrude Stein's writing. But "oh say *can* you see" also expresses Stein's plea to individuals to notice, contemplate what they perceive, and express their observations and analyses. The epistemological position she takes is that "nobody can say no" because nobody can know what anybody else sees. Solipsism authorizes freedom—and does not preclude dialogue. Stein asks a person to speak up without being afraid of being wrong, and her allusion to the national anthem is also an allusion to her overt suggestion in *Brewsie and Willie* that articulating our thoughts and impressions will save the United States of America from the spiritual and worldly poverty that follows industrialism. Seeking to achieve social reform through language reform, she explicitly tells Americans that they must learn to express complexity. By changing the kind of English people read, Stein intends to change the way Americans articulate their thoughts in speech, making room for thoughts that evade the binary pollster lingo of yes or no, approve or disapprove, guilty or not guilty, Democrat or Republican.

Stein's words request individual readers to say what we see, with the knowledge that, while we cannot be justly corrected, we also cannot count on others' seeing the same things. There is no monologic in Stein's monologues. Stein's writing forces readers to recognize and re-embrace their own unique visions. While encouraging individuality, Stein acknowledges and celebrates the dialogic aspect of self, celebrating our multiplicity and suggesting that the exchanges we carry on with ourselves can provide a model for interaction with others. I hope too that this very monologue—the book in front of you now—is dialogic enough to suggest a variety of ideas about Stein and set the tone for continuing conversations about what we see in Stein, and beyond.[12]

Chapter 1 demonstrates Stein's interest in conversation, as well as in the sights and sounds of words. The chapter documents Stein's early interest in conversation, manifest in the voices that pervade *Three Lives* and several aspects of *The Making of Americans*. This long early novel represents individuals as born into preexisting families and family narratives, writers as born into the world of the already written, and speakers as born into a world of conversations where they can transcend the already said only by first listening. The chapter argues that Stein makes her American readers listen to ourselves, unmakes our mask of Americanisms, and chides us toward building ourselves more legitimately. The new frontier in America has to open within and for the individual, and the new pioneering begins at the lips, where the verb "states" might be prevented from calcifying into the noun "statements" if we were to listen to ourselves and stop copying. The chapter also emphasizes Stein's dispositions and her special training, both of which seem to point to an interest in attention, sensory inputs, and especially the spoken and written word. I begin in this chapter to exemplify some of the richness of the interaction between sight and sound, although much more of that will be demonstrated in chapters 2, 3, and 4.

The second chapter asserts that Stein's reading of the neuroscience in William James's *Principles of Psychology* encouraged her to rearrange her readers' mental associations.[13] James's idea that all thought takes place through habitual associations among thoughts and words, that experience shapes these habits and more experience can change them, suggests that Stein's writing is surprisingly, if still unpredictably, utilitarian—on behalf of anti-utilitarianism (of course). Attending to all sensory aspects of a language leads to a greater associational range, more freedom for words, and an increased flexibility for the mind organized around those words. An extended reading of a long passage from *Tender Buttons* in this chapter demonstrates various ways to read Stein and supports the idea—in content as well as style—that Stein advocates our changing our most standard rhetorical forms. By hypothetically breaking up a portion of this selection into discrete utterances, I also begin to demonstrate the intrasubjective nature of conversation, the way one conversation synthesizes back-and-forth exchanges between different voices and opinions.

Chapter 3 continues my chronological examination of Stein's importation of spoken forms into her writing, in this case in several works in *Geography and Plays*. While chapter 1 demonstrates that Stein's more prosy narratives are constructed from conversations, this chapter shows that Stein turns her attention from the way conversation reveals personality to the way conversation is itself a significant structure worthy of further investigation. My definition of conversation is drawn from the related fields of conversation analysis and ethnomethodology but augmented with enough psychology to take into account internal dialogue (an aspect of conversation treated more thoroughly in chapter 5). Stein explores utterances as multilayered actions that, for example, can simultaneously communicate agreement and heavy disapproval. She attends to the ways interactional conversation—as distinguished from transactional conversation—allows speakers to develop complicated and ever-shifting relationships by negotiating through minutely contextual interpretations of specific utterances. In other words, she points to the realpolitik within politesse. And she engages in a kind of conversation nervously foreshadowed in *The Making of Americans*—with a literary forefather, William Shakespeare. In recalling Macbeth's misunderstanding of the witches, Stein highlights conversational strategies as power plays, not just domestic courtesies.

Chapter 4 discusses Stein's lectures of the 1930s, in terms of both the ideas they express and their effect on audiences during the lecture tour. Stein's *Lectures in America* and *The Geographical History of America*, and her reading as well as her writing, demonstrate her interest in the interplay of spoken and written language. Many of Stein's most important theories—about human nature and the human mind, about geniuses and "masterpieces," about identity, about repetition and insistence—depend on the relationships between sight and sound. The lecture tour itself seems to me an attempt to get people talking and listening, experimenting with their ideas in conversation. Newspaper stories in the cities she visited during her 1934–35 tour suggest that she both succeeded and failed in this endeavor. Her own mysterious popularity may have undermined her project, since people tend not to talk *with* icons.

Chapter 5 explicates Stein's novel of celebrity, *Ida*, and concludes that interpersonal and intrapersonal conversation can serve to erase the boundaries between people at the same time that they enable us to distinguish significant boundaries within the self. This novel and its main character act as sounding boards for various possibilities about the self, and these ideas contribute, with much of Stein's other writing, to a theory of personal subjectivity and social cohesion that depends on conversation.

Having noted the way words work in conversation, and how conversations work to build relationships within the complex self and among others, Stein turns her attention to the influence of larger political structures on conversation. Chapter 6 explicates *Mrs. Reynolds* and *Brewsie and Willie*, both written during World War II and sensitive to the way that war changed habits of speech. In *Mrs. Reynolds*, Stein contemplates how everyday conversation is both influenced by and resists the pressure of the political situation in which that conversation takes place. In both novels, Stein contemplates the characteristic speech patterns of totalitarian leaders, and in *Brewsie and Willie*, Stein explores the proliferation of acquiescent employees who encourage totalitarian speech by accepting it, expecting it, and propagating it in their own talk. I argue that Stein deplored the way these forms of conversation affected original thought, and that she believed improved speech patterns would cure moribund consciousness and even solve economic and political ailments.

My conclusions, "Feminine Endings," make a sudden turn to Stein's shallow but bigoted feminism, only because she seems to have made this turn herself. The first section, "The Woman Who Changed the Mind of a Nation," hears Stein's libretto, *The Mother of Us All*, as expressing her frustration that not enough people are being individuals, truly and honestly conversing, and thus improving the state of their individuality—and, to her mind, the state of the state. Her frustration leads her to some gender stereotypes but also to the realization that an individual can still (kind of) succeed in spite of a group's failure. Her surprising acceptance of common gender distinctions also leads toward the ideas expressed in the second section, "Sublime Amalgamations." Here I suggest that Stein has been advocating a feminine epistemological sublime in the interests of both the individual and the ultimate project of an American sublime, and that she has developed a dialogic language that can best express it.

If William James convinced her the processes of the human mind could be influenced through linguistic experience, and if Stein was struck with an interest in both the sights and sounds of words—words on the page and words in conversation—then she may have seen some potential efficacy in her unusual writing. This critical history treats Stein as a writer with changing, but cumulative, interests: she moves from her interest in the human character and mind to an interest in language and its sights and sounds; then to conversation, and how language mediates the relationship between the individual and herself; and then to the relationship between an individual and his or her social organization. Working with writings from the span of Stein's career, I hope to prove that conversation is at least five important things for Stein: a language form worthy of examination in its own right; the marker by which Stein evaluates American success, on both the individual and political levels; the paradigm for Stein's concept of inter-personal subjectivity that has true agency even while being influenced from without; a telling symptom of any political situation; and a means toward a messy kind of peace and problem solving. While not explaining *how* she wrote—how she managed to put *those* words on the page—this book offers a coherent explanation for *why* Stein might have written as she did, what her words mean, and what can be achieved by reading her.

Most writers try to "build, in sonnets, pretty rooms" or to build novelistic mansions. Modern theorists posit ominously a "prison-house of language."[14] Gertrude Stein builds instead an amusement park fun house of language, full of slides between levels, weirdly convex and concave mirrors, illusory parallels, flashes of color, flickers of tickling. But a writer can be serious without being solemn, and Stein's play has work to do. She shows us the minds we unwittingly have, and the thoughts we could have instead. She shows us the struggle between tyranny and freedom in every moment of ordinary casual conversation. She lets us see what's at stake in language, and she is willing to play, at times, the clown of a verbal circus, so we can become the teachers of our own classrooms and true citizens of a fully human state.

CHAPTER 1

Talking and Listening in
Stein's Early Life and Works

"Interested in the mere workings of the machinery"

SUSPICIOUS AT AN early age that she was living vicariously and learning only indirectly through reading, Gertrude Stein decided to plunge into the noisy, breathing world around her. As a child, Stein escaped her family into books: "She read anything that was printed that came her way and a great deal came her way" (Stein, *Autobiography*, 74). Wagner-Martin reports that the Stein "children spent as much time as they could away from their family," and in her teens (after her high school burned down) Stein chose to visit libraries in Oakland and San Francisco (19, 24). Linda Simon guesses that Stein's "imagination was stirred by the books she read voraciously. Shakespeare, Trollope, Richardson, Defoe all took her far from the mundane middle-class world of Oakland, and the oppression of her family life" (xi). But when she moved to Baltimore, she immersed herself in a social life again. "There she began to lose her lonesomeness," writes Stein under the guise of Alice B. Toklas, "She has often described to me how strange it was to her coming from the rather desperate inner life that she had been living for the last few years to the cheerful life of all her aunts and uncles" (*Autobiography*, 75). She began listening to people, noting their repeating, and desiring an understanding of their real being—which may explain her interest in psychology in college. Stein writes that she "began very early in life to talk all the time and to listen all the time" (*Lectures*, 136).

Years later, after she left medical school, Stein "had for the moment nothing to do but talk and look and listen," and she "did this tremendously" (*Lectures*, 138). When she decided to become a writer at age twenty-nine, Stein fully appreciated the potential of this type of learning. She listened to and thought about people's words, and she evidently noticed that certain people's words, and certain kinds of words, were ignored or discounted.

When she writes in the 1920s, "I have been forbidden to gain instruction either by narrative or conversation consequently I embroider and literally I count eight," she may point to the way that women who shared information and passed on skills while sewing or knitting together—or who avidly read novels, memoirs, and biographies—were nonetheless considered unknowledgeable (*Village*, 12).[1] Stein believes otherwise. In the 1930s, she wrote that "anybody in any village can do" psychology (*Geographical History*, 209)—elevating daily observation and experience and demystifying the university type of knowledge. In 1940, she claimed that "if you let any plumber anybody talk long enough they will always tell the truth" (*Paris*, 32).[2] Later in the forties, she claimed that it is "quite unnecessary" to study race differences in an academic setting because any schoolchild who has grown up with children of different "nationalities" knows as much (*Wars*, 8). I am not confident that the lessons learned on playgrounds are always the best kind, but certainly Stein is right that conversations and life experiences—gleaned personally or from oral or written narratives—are important means toward knowledge.

Stein's early narrative works—"Q.E.D.," written in 1903 but published posthumously; *The Making of Americans*, started in 1903 and published in 1925; and *Three Lives* (Good Anna's, Melanctha's, and Gentle Lena's), started in 1905 and published in 1909—are pervaded by voices, especially women's voices. While Adele, Stein's persona in "Q.E.D.," suffers at the hands of her beloved Helen, she seems unwilling to extricate herself from the situation because, as she says, "I certainly get very much interested in the mere working of the machinery" (54). This "machinery" includes the subtle wordings and unstated meanings that allow Helen and Adele to agree without either of them yielding (54, 45). In other words, the complexities of social intercourse in this love triangle are the main "compensations" for Adele's pain (54). The wandering conversations in "Melanctha," a story that grew out of "Q.E.D.," reveal that the complexities of social intercourse remained Stein's main concern when most vestiges of interest in the love affair died away. Jeff and Melanctha talk—and talk and talk—in a language that "opened" Richard Wright's ears "for the first time to the magic of the spoken word." In spite of the unrealistic sound of some of the repetitive dialogue, Wright notes:

> I began to hear the speech of my grandmother, who spoke a deep, pure Negro dialect and with whom I had lived for many years.
> All of my life I had been only half hearing, but Miss Stein's struggling words made the speech of the people around me vivid. From

that moment on, in my attempts at writing, I was able to tap at will the vast pool of living words that swirled around me. (qtd. in Van Vechten, *Selected*, 338)[3]

In "Melanctha," Stein not only captures something important about the spoken voice, but she also lets Wright hear it and value it, too.

The other stories in *Three Lives* are also filled with voices; Stein emphasized these voices, and readers noticed them. Richard Bridgman (50, 51) notes Anna's "immigrant speech" and Lena's "authentic" voice, and Jane Palatini Bowers (45) asserts that Stein has such a strong "tendency to foreground conversation" that she "allows talk to practically obliterate narrative." Indeed, "Anna's voice"—rather than Anna herself—seems to be the main character: Miss Mathilda's house is full of animals and people "and Anna's voice that scolded, managed, grumbled all day long" (*Three Lives*, 69). In "The Gentle Lena," Mrs. Haydon has "a long talking that she was giving Lena" (252), and hers is just one of the several voices that bully Lena from one situation to the next. Eventually Stein moved out from behind her ungrammatically talkative characters. No longer hiding her interests and writing goals behind fictional spokespersons, she writes in a dissident form of improper but living American English.

Stein's fiction employs and celebrates the words and phrases, originality and banality, of American speakers, and through it Stein points to the renewable vitality of the English language. In 1936, Harvey Eagleson wrote:

> Except for the "portraits" of her friends, Miss Stein's work generally deals with the ordinary matters of life, the ordinary people in life, in the language and words of those people. The first and most essential step in an approach to an understanding of Gertrude Stein's work is to read it aloud. Only in that way can one realize the rhythms and sounds which are an integral part of her work. They are the rhythms of America, of American speech. Only in that way can one understand Miss Stein's peculiar punctuation, for she places marks of punctuation not where they should be placed to indicate syntactical pauses, but where they indicate speech pauses. *Three Lives* and *The Making of Americans* sound like America talking, America talking after supper on summer evenings as it sits in rocking chairs on front porches, America gossiping over back fences. The long, involved repetitious sentences, the characteristic grammatical errors, split infinitives, dangling pronouns, the idiomatic phrases of American speech are all there. (167)

Early on, then, Eagleson points to a method for accessing Stein: read it aloud, and it doesn't sound so strange. Read it aloud, and notice that speech not only helps us understand Stein but that she helps us understand speech. Allegra Stewart writes that Stein was "dissatisfied with the glib and easy use of the mere surfaces of words, the disease that threatens every writer, [and she] began to face the authentic poet's task: the revitalizing of language" (82). Stein detects this revitalization in speakers who are new to the language, and the underclasses, and anyone who speaks in a language every day and chooses, invents, overhears, and perpetuates words and phrases that catch the fancy.

The Potential Remaking of Americans, or Revising America

Even Stein's very early novel *The Making of Americans*, in its 925 pages of longwinded, elongated, and repetitive storytelling, furnishes evidence of her interest in speech. The novel—eventually, on page 728—identifies itself as a history of talking and listening. Based on the history of her own family's immigration to the United States, it seems to be stylistically based on the way family histories get told by elderly relatives, such as the "cheerful . . . aunts and uncles" Stein lived with in Baltimore in 1892 and 1893 (Stein, *Autobiography*, 75). Speakers repeat themselves, starting over to add a few omitted details and, over time, gradually changing or improving their stories. Most people only know what they've heard. The American story is the story of what Americans say, how we boost ourselves (or don't). In 1903, after Mark Twain and Walt Whitman but before Langston Hughes, Ring Lardner, Dorothy Parker, John Dos Passos, and the Lynds of *Middletown* fame—and long before the Ken Burns Civil War documentary narrated by voices in personal communication (usually letters home) and the invention of the Manhattan computer that steals quotations from Internet chat rooms and creates a kind of poetry with it (see Gopnick)—Stein saw that the voice, the stutter, the fake bravado, the lingering words, and the insistent repetition of the human voice is the main story, "the essence of what happens." Long before Thomas Pynchon's Mucho Maas (on LSD) recovers whatever's human in machine-generated Muzak, finds the "power spectra" of spoken words, and says, "The human voice, you know, it's a flipping miracle" (115–17), Stein writes: "Once more I think about conversations," and "Let me tell about the character of the people of the United States of America and what they say" ("Circular Play," 334; *Four in America*, 167).

Conversation plays several roles in *The Making of Americans*. For example, the anxiety of influence that haunts this early book is couched in the idea of conversation. Stein worries about the inevitable conversation in which her own words must participate with every other thing that has been written. In becoming an author, Stein escaped from books and family and chose to develop her own goals and her own art. But completely erasing relationships is impossible.[4] Stein avoided many of the middle-class American traps and trappings when she moved to Paris, loved Toklas, appreciated innovations in art, and wrote a different kind of English, but even her most recent biographers, Linda Wagner-Martin and Brenda Wineapple, put more stock in her family relationships than in anything else when they try to discover Stein's "bottom nature." Just as Stein cannot exactly escape her family, Stein's writing cannot help but keep company with all writing in English. While unique and surprising, Stein's words must stand in some relationship to other words. She can write and write but never erase the books that came before hers, or, as Stein herself writes: "You only add books you never subtract or divide them" ("My Debt," 307)—though that's what Harold Bloom's "strong poets" work to do as they "wrestle with their strong precursors, even to the death" (Bloom, *Anxiety*, 5). As T.S. Eliot posited in "Tradition and the Individual Talent," sometimes the most individual parts of a writer's work come out of their allusions to and contentions with "the whole of the literature of Europe from Homer" (38).

Although literature was not her field of study in school, Stein was a greedy reader of prose narrative and would have been aware of the company her words, if they ever got read, were going to keep. Literary critics often try to understand Stein's writing in relation to her friendships with her fellow modernists, but her oldest friends were books. In "My Debt to Books," Stein describes her wanderings through Paris: "That is the delightful thing about the quays you see books that you never thought it would be possible to see again." She refers to these books by author as often as by title: "Gulliver's Travels, Robinson Crusoe," "Swiss Family Robinson," "Shakespeare, Lavengro and Romany Rye, Trollope and Edgar Wallace," and "Clarissa Harlowe." When she meets up with them, she takes them home and reads them again, often surprised by the differences between her memories of the books and the books' reiteration of themselves.

She claims to have read "at least five or six books a week," a high but not unusual number ("My Debt"). Mildred Aldrich described Stein as "'the greatest reader I had ever known and the most catholic'" (qtd. in Wagner-Martin, 82).[5] Stein's reading, mentioned throughout *The Autobiography of Alice B. Toklas*, included Hawthorne, Henry James, Walter Scott, Wordsworth, *Charles Grandison*, *Pilgrim's Progress*, Burns, the *Congressional Record*, encyclopedias, Fielding, Smollett, Carlyle's *Frederick the Great*, Lecky's *Constitutional History of England*, Lord Robert's *Forty-one Years in India*, Twain, Hemingway, Fitzgerald, the newspapers the *Herald* and the *Daily Mail*, and other letters, biographies, and diaries from Mudie's Library in London. There's more, of course, this time from *Everybody's Autobiography*: Shelley, Thackeray, Jules Verne, Jane Eyre, George Eliot, Tendret (on eating), Prokosch's *Asiatics*, Bravig Imbs's *Professor's Wife*, her friend Sam Steward's *Angels on the Bough*, Louisa May Alcott's *Rose in Bloom*, Darwin's *Descent of Man*, Poe, the children's magazine *St. Nicholas*, Winston Churchill's best-seller *The Crisis*, Dickens, Lloyd Lewis's *Myths after Lincoln*, Leon Wilson's *Merton of the Movies*, Lewis Carroll's and Queen Victoria's letters (not to each other), and Caesar's commentary. Other sources suggest that Stein also read the *Iliad*, the Old Testament, Jane Austen, Sherwood Anderson, Samuel Johnson, William Faulkner, Arthur Young's *Travels in France*, Mary Wilkins's *Pembroke* (which she hated), Shelley's *Cenci*, Walter Pater's *Marius the Epicurean*, George Meredith's *Tragic Comedians*, Norse legends, Longfellow, and Goldsmith.[6]

As the youngest Herslands in Stein's *Making of Americans* say "Wait and see" to their father's implication that they will amount to no good (11), the work itself is also not completely ready to defend its specific differences from these (and other) classic texts. As Stein's written creation refuses to follow a formula, the youngest generation of Herslands intends to live life in a new way. The new generation does not know what it's going to accomplish but feels excited and nervous that it may be something new and important. As Rorty writes, building off Harold Bloom's *Anxiety of Influence*, the "poet" who "makes things new" "is typically unable to make clear exactly what it is that he wants to do before developing the language in which he succeeds in doing it. His new vocabulary makes possible, for the first time, a formulation of its own purpose" (*Contingency*, 12–13). In both the familial and writerly cases, the generations struggle over who has perfected the art of life or who will write the essence of the literary genre. Stein writes: "We, living now, are always to ourselves young men and women. When we, living always in such feeling, think back to them who make for us a beginning, it is always as grown and old men and women or as little children that we feel them, these whose lives we have just been thinking" (*Making*, 4). Bloom posits in *The Anxiety of Influence* (5) that a "strong poet" regards, or at least depicts, previous authors as less evolved ancestors (analogous to Stein's "little children") or as old-fashioned, worn out, and passé (Stein's "grown and old men and women"). If Stein's novel has to participate in a conversation with these other books, then she—like others before her—has purposefully put herself in a position of authority in relation to their posited immaturity or senility.

Most simply, *The Making of Americans* calls itself a "history . . . of talk-ing and listening" (728). Stein waits to get three-quarters of the way through the book to say this, but she may have only at that point discovered what her whole enterprise has been (and, in the interests of an honest represen-tation of a typically messy human thought process, she was not inclined to go back and add it in earlier). Perhaps she discovered that her means to understanding others and her means of communicating that understand-ing are inseparable. When she thought she was writing about identity, she was writing about talking, writing about writing about talking, and writing about talking about talking.

The Making of Americans is notorious for its failed (or at least bafflingly unclear) classification of people into types. Regardless of their bottom nature, however, and regardless of her ability or inability to classify types of bottom nature, Stein sees the nature of one's talking and listening as an important clue to the development of a real sense of self. The two dif-ferent tendencies in the novel can be helpfully distinguished by M. M. Bakhtin's terms "analysis" and "prosaics." The "analysis" is the text's attempt to develop, or its appearance of attempting to develop, a system capable of describing everything about human personality. In addition to the auto-biographical aspect of *The Making of Americans*, critics have emphasized its painstaking and sometimes pained quest toward ordered knowledge, its "analysis." But Stein's text also contains "prosaics," which are "suspicious of explanatory systems" and suggest "that the most important events in life are not the grand, dramatic, or catastrophic but the apparently small and prosaic ones of everyday life," and which seem to me much more interesting (Morson and Emerson, 64–65). These details of everyday events—including everyday interactions between confused but lecturing parents and their si-lent but also unsure children—support but also explode the aforementioned systematizing with much more information and nuance than can be ac-counted for within a system.

In *The Making of Americans* and "A Long Gay Book," Stein develops a taxonomy of human personality, but she gradually becomes more inter-ested in relationship. The charts and categories Stein created while writing the novel are well documented (Stendhal, 50; Wagner-Martin, 84). Wagner-Martin describes "The Book of Diagrams" as "filled with schemata of people [Stein] knew arranged by personality traits" (84). Leon Katz describes Stein's attempt to create "a psychology which defines character by a mosaic of typify-ing adjectives" ("Weininger," 11). Moving beyond individual character types, Stein writes "A Long Gay Book" in order "to describe . . . every possible kind of pairs of human beings and every possible threes and fours and fives of human beings and every possible kind of crowds of human beings" (*Lectures*, 148). These relationships, constructed through language, may become more important to Stein than the people themselves. She seems to have discovered that conversation is the means by which people present themselves and form these connections.

In listening, however, Stein notices people's tendency to say the same things, or the same kinds of things, over and over. Insincere copying appears to be a weak but prevalent twin of genuine repeating, which comes straight from our own being. More common than repeating, copying is neither genuine nor individualistic. Copiers "know what they want to be and can build it up by little pieces and do again and again. [They] know what they are and see it as a complete thing and make that thing in daily living" (*Making*, 644). These copiers are "always cutting and fitting and fitting and cutting and painting and sometime they come to be that thing . . . inventing themselves in daily living and in dressing" (644). In other words, we can grow a self from the parts of us we like, arranging and discarding pieces of ourselves like clothing, but Stein is sure we cannot be comfortable in these borrowed and cobbled robes. People can copy "the repeating that once came out of them in feeling," copy "others around them," copy "themselves in their way of talking, sometimes in their loving, often in their way of walking, of moving their hands and shoulders, in their ways of smiling, there have been some and always will be some who copy themselves so in all their living, in their eating and drinking, in every moment of their daily living" (195). Thus Stein describes the kind of adamant consistency people claim when they perform themselves.

Stein values repeating, although in the midst of her unmatched repeating and her explicitly stated championship of repeating and her effusive, eternal love poem to repeating, she concedes that "listening to repeating is often irritating" (*Making*, 291). Even sincere repeating can be irritating until the listener's love of repeating turns irritation "into patient completed understanding" (291). When Marianne Moore begins her poem titled "Poetry" with "I, too, dislike it," she suggests that some poetry is annoying, even though there are things that cannot be expressed any other way. Repeating, like poetry, offers "after all, a place for the genuine" (*Complete Poems*, 36). Similarly irritating and important, repeating is the natural way we express our beings. Stein links genuine repetition, a special kind of vision ("seeing"), and an "important feeling" of oneself as an individual, which she sees as the culmination of personal success ("winning"). Stein also values authentic repeating for the information it can reveal about people's "bottom natures." What people do and say, especially what they do and say over and over, lets her see them for who they really are.

For Stein, a person who resists copying is a success because she has obtained an "important feeling of herself to herself inside her" (*Making*, 66) and "an individual kind of thinking that [arises] of itself inside her" (65). Stein explains that "one of the Hissen women came very near to winning, came very near to seeing, came very nearly making of herself to herself a really individual being" (65). When Fanny Hissen and David Hersland marry, they have the potential to "make children who perhaps would come to have in them a really important feeling of themselves inside them" (77).

But Stein hears more copying than repeating, which attests to an American failure. Some people have incomplete senses of themselves because they shrink or expand certain parts of their personalities according to social expectations; Stein's characters represent these possibilities when they feel empty or too full. All three Schilling women feel the emptiness: "the fatter sister" had a "vague fear" because "all that unprotected surface of her makes it easier to see in her that she is just like all the other millions who have been made just like her" (*Making*, 82); "the thinner sister" "had not enough inside her to really fill her" and felt a fear that was caused by "always trying to fill up a hole in her without enough to fill it from the being in her without making some other hole inside her" (82, 83); and Mrs. Schilling was like her daughters in that "something had dropped out of each one of them and they had been indolent or stupid or staring each one of them then and they had not noticed such a dropping out of them" (78). Something important, perhaps an eccentric uniqueness they didn't dare manifest, fell out of these women's lives when they weren't paying attention. What's left is inadequate and conformist.

Confident second-generation David Hersland, who is "all full up inside him, there was not much of any way that anything could enter into him" (*Making*, 85), is incomplete in quite a different way. He is too full of himself, so confident of his idea of himself that he must have bolstered the weak and unsure part of himself with copies from the solid part in him. As a result, he is a bad listener because he does not have room for any other ideas or feelings. Stein makes her readers wish for the freedom—the initiative and independence—to feel and be wholly ourselves. She makes us wish for enough permeability—or unsureness or curiosity or vitality—that we can truly interact with other people.

Stein sympathizes with the difficulty of acting from one's being, particularly in the small things of life. Even people who succeed in making career decisions for themselves can succumb to this copying, because they tend not to give much thought to other, less weighty, decisions and can unknowingly fall into the habit of copying:

> it is a very difficult thing to get the courage to buy the kind of clock or handkerchiefs you are loving, when every one thinks it is a silly thing, when every one thinks you are doing it for the joke of the thing. It is hard then to know whether you are really loving that thing. It takes very much courage to do anything connected with your being that is not a serious thing. It takes courage to be doing a serious thing that is connected with one's being that is certain. (*Making*, 488)

And then we get back to talk. One kind of talking and listening is repeating; the other is copying. For Stein, copying and what I will call "plain old" talking and listening lead to an incomplete sense of self; repeating and what Stein calls "talking and listening at the same time" develop real being. Plain old talking and listening involve hearing yourself as if you were an impressionable somebody else. Plain old talking and listening allow a person to lie to herself, or at least allow her words to contain and finalize her thoughts. But listening and talking *at the same time* is listening to yourself while remembering that you are the one talking: you can make amendments, you can see more complexities than your listener, your words point toward but do not embody your whole thought, and you don't have to expect and create consistency. When Stein says, "I am writing for myself and strangers" (*Making*, 289), she intimates that she is reading and writing *at the same time* and possibly imagining how a multitude of strangers might differently, creatively, and *not* dogmatically understand her words.

But the very motivation behind copying is that we can come to know ourselves in as consistent and limited a way as others know us. Some women strictly enforce their own youthful identities and "make a dance step every now and then in their walking" to project a cheerful innocence or a "lively" pre-"adolescence" (*Making*, 174). Martha Hersland has not only convinced herself that she's tough, she's convinced her husband: "He only heard what she said to him in anything that she had been concerned in and so he never came to any feeling that she was not a strong woman to win out in the things she always loved to be beginning" (75). Men around Mr. Hersland give him a sense of complacent self confidence: "These men . . . were a comfort to him, . . . they made a kind of support around him . . . they made a kind of cushion for him to keep him from knowing when he was through with fighting that he had not been winning." As he gets older, they become "more and more important to him as padding, not to fill him but to keep him from knowing" about himself (146–47). As he feels his multiple failures—aided by his children's telling "him what they thought of him" (149)—the men around him help him sustain his idea of himself. All of these people have a way "of always repeating the whole of them as a serious obligation," or helping others do so (269).

In these several ways, Stein uses what comes out of the mouths of Americans to evaluate their success as individuals. Her characters depict Americans who confine themselves within preconceptions about themselves, each other, and the idea of identity itself. In spite of the American reputation for pioneering, Stein sees too many Americans as weak makers who "accept somebody else's description" of themselves (Rorty, *Contingency*, 28). Rorty describes Nietzsche's criterion for failure as a human being, and Stein's ideas parallel his corollary that a person should strive to "describ[e] himself in his own terms" and "creat[e] the only part of himself that matter[s] by constructing his own mind. To create one's mind is to create one's own language, rather than to let the length of one's mind be set by the language other human beings have left behind" (*Contingency*, 27). Of course, as Stein's opening anecdote in *The Making of Americans* demonstrates—a young man rebels, and his father says, "Stop! I did not drag my father beyond this tree" (3)—sometimes when we think we are being most original, most resistant to the past, we are repeating a revolution that has already occurred. Staging a rebellion is often the most conventional way to repeat the past.

The Making of Americans also mimics and highlights the ways that we learn about nation and family by listening to the people around us. Stein's history of the United States is not only appropriately short and accurate for much of the nation's population—20 percent of the U.S. population had foreign-born parents in 1900—but also realistically impressionistic. While others might have valued the length of their family's habitation in the New World, Stein understands "real" Americans as these newish comers: "The old people in a new world, the new people made out of the old, that is the story that I mean to tell, for that is what really is and what I really know" (*Making*, 3). Truly, "that is what really is." Conventional histories of the United States champion the American Revolutionary War heroes, but there are only so many daughters and sons of the Revolution. In 1900, 6 percent of the U.S. population had parents from Germany, a likely nation of origin for the Dehnings and Herslands: Dehning is a name of German origin, meaning a "bold, free man"; Hersland is either German or Danish. (Even more tangentially, the 1870 census reports a young jeweler named David

Hersland living in San Francisco; might Stein have met him on her wanderings through the city a couple of decades later?)[7] Furthermore, although the published version of the novel does not identify the Herslands and Dehnings as Jewish, their history corresponds with the histories of many Jewish immigrants: the Jewish population in the United States grew from 15,000 in 1840 to almost 250,000 in 1880, with most of the increase the result of German Jewish immigration (Wittke, 328).[8] Many were peddlers who became merchants and then owners of large stores, and they had a high respect for learning and high ambitions for their children (329). Stein's own family history in America—which begins with an eighteen-year-old male immigrating from Bavaria in 1841 (Wagner-Martin, 3)—corresponds to the historical tendency: "First to come were young, poor immigrant males from the small towns of Bavaria and the Rhineland" (Cordasco, 451), and between 1840 and 1850 approximately five hundred Jewish families from the Old World settled in Baltimore (Wagner-Martin, 3).

Stein's listening to her own family may have inspired a history of the United States that models the narrative structures that children hear on the laps of their grandparents. Standard historical plots are developed through contextualization, summary, analysis, and the needs of the nation, but family history—in nonroyal and otherwise "nonhistorical" families—never quite becomes information.[9] Instead, children develop vague impressions of the past that are pinned on just a few specific events told through the haze of personal memory and the lens of egoistic bias. This history is not arranged chronologically, and events are rarely attached to a date. If personal experience is linked to national events or social movements, this linking is done loosely and inaccurately.[10] Also, because of the role family history plays in the moral education of children, it emphasizes positive and negative character traits or behavior in an attempt to perpetuate the civilized behavior and values that are considered ideal by the family or nation.

Americans are made by continually listening to themselves talking about what an American is supposed to be. Our identities are not only personal and familial but also racial, regional, and national. Perhaps Stein's *Making of Americans* intends to make Americans by making Americans listen. Americans have not listened to Stein much since 1934, but what is more important is for Americans to listen to themselves—to listen to all the things adamantly copied and carefully omitted, and to start genuinely repeating and hearing what we say when we do. In "Portraits and Repetition" (101), Stein writes that "each civilization insisted in its own way before it went away," and in *The Making of Americans* she makes us notice the narrative propagation of culture through our forced copying of our ideas of ourselves.

If we listened to ourselves, we would probably want to make some changes in our narrative.

In medical school, Stein was taught to diagnose physical illness through listening, and she ended up diagnosing social illness by the same means. The Lynds' *Middletown*, published in 1929, also allowed Americans to hear themselves, and many were surprised to notice the power of peer pressure and social expectation in American life. *Middletown* revealed that not all Americans were innovative, energetic, enterprising, and daring. For example, the Lynds discover that clothes consciousness led to a "decrease in individualism and increase in type-consciousness" (161). Stein urges Americans to *listen* to themselves talk in clichés, just as Jacob Riis, the early photographer, made Americans *look* at American streets, which were not paved with gold. But unlike Riis, who wrote his own autobiography, *The Making of an American* (1901) in the typical vein, Stein creates a new plot of difficult adjustments and innocent, envious imitation. Though most readers look for Stein's legacy in avant-garde writing, such as Harryette Mullen's wonderful poetry, Stein's project has gone on in other forms. For the last several decades, Studs Terkel's interviews have allowed Americans to hear ourselves and our great multiplicity on several big topics, including work, World War II, the Depression, and death. Similarly, Robert Bellah and others' 1996 *Habits of the Heart: Individualism and Commitment in American Life* reveals American ideas about public and private life through the voices of two hundred people. What we learn by reading *The Making of Americans*, what we learn by heeding Stein's advice and listening to ourselves and other Americans speaking, is that there is a difference between the official national characteristics and the characteristics of the real people.

For example, Americans tend to be characterized as steadfast pioneers who start impossibly ambitious projects and see them through to the end. Americans are reputed to be like Theodore Dreiser's ruthless and relentlessly goal-oriented Frank Cowperwood. But David Hersland, a second-generation American, likes so much to begin that he rarely finishes anything. He has theories about how to eat, how his children should be educated, how to make a fortune, and how to care for the health of his children, and he acts on each new theory before his last beginning has progressed very far at all.[11] Stein describes his "kind of being" as like those who "have arabian nights inside them": they begin their story again and again and never end it, "always changing and beginning" (*Making*, 121, 124). Stein's modernism already saw, in reality, the indeterminacy that postmodernism would demand of fictional narrative. The model of Scheherazade's stories in *The Arabian Nights* is appropriate for this long American novel, because almost-great American fortune hunters begin again and again in their efforts to succeed. Those who succeed entirely don't have to try again.[12]

Myth and reality are also at odds in the area of individuality. According to Stein, new nations such as the United States value conformity, not individuality, to the extent that they do not allow people to be unique. Even before World War I, the Depression, and World War II—events which made national conversations of critique and reform common and even patriotic (if carefully expressed as anticommunist)—Stein was worried about the effect of industrialism on the American character. In *The Making of Americans*, she laments the "adolescent metallic world" that expresses itself in a penchant for producing ticky-tacky products with machinery (48). Stein connects this method of production with every other activity of American life, activities with which we define and project who each one of us is as an individual: our habits of thinking, writing, talking, dressing, decorating, and supporting ourselves. She asserts that

> vital singularity is as yet an unknown product with us, we who in our habits, dress-suit cases, clothes and hats and ways of thinking, walking, making money, talking, having simple lines in decorating, in ways of reforming, all with a metallic clicking like the type-writing which is our only way of thinking, our way of educating, our way of learning, all always the same way of doing, all the way down as far as there is any way down inside to us. (47)

The renowned American "type" makes it difficult for us to believe that Americans are conformists, and yet Stein seems to have felt enough conventional pressure to notice a discrepancy between myth and reality.

Stein attributes American conformity to American youth—what a more censorious Van Wyck Brooks in *America's Coming-of-Age* calls "the incurable boyishness, the superannuated boyishness of the Emersonian tradition" (87). That youth leads to conformity is an idea antithetical to the American myth that promised freedom in the new, young world, although writers such as Sinclair Lewis also pointed this out to their readers.[13] Stein supports the belief that open spaces breed freedom and eccentricity with her description of the Hersland children growing up on ten acres in Gossols. In the West, where the "young man" David Hersland went "to make his fortune," Gossols is still a kind of frontier: "This was the new world in a new world and it took this newest part of this new world to content him," because he was "restless" (*Making*, 35, 43). But Bridgepoint, an older part of this new world, from which David moved and where the Dehnings live, is the new world in its unpolished conformist adolescence.[14] With the imminent (or already consummate) adolescence of even the western frontier, the new frontier in America has to open within and for the individual.

In a world with no frontiers to establish, the real pioneering seems to lie in unbuilding. "Attacking" and "resisting" are the defining characteristics of Stein's two types of humans, and Stein describes herself as a resisting being. An attacker jumps enthusiastically from one idea to another, building up and moving forward. But a resister strives toward wisdom through questions, unmaking in order to understand. For this type of person, "a puzzled feeling"—a doubt that has not been formed into words—is the first step toward wisdom (*Making*, 310). Later, Stein explains that her progression of understanding is from "a puzzle" to "a conscious puzzle" to confusion to bafflement to "a clear whole one, and then at last a completer whole one" (357). Her senses allow Stein to progress through these levels of understanding: "Always I was hearing, feeling, seeing every one else feeling, listening to, seeing this one. Slowly then this one came to be a complete one to me" (310). If she's right about herself, then this method corresponds to the type of resistance I see Stein generating toward the common language of our society. Her doubts and questions undress us, unmake our mask of Americanisms, and force us to try building ourselves again more legitimately.

Much of this discussion has had little to do with conversation but much to do with change, with sensing something wrong in the United States, and with Stein's eventually prescribing a change in our behaviors. *The Making of Americans*, then, is a history of the making of the nation itself, not its origins as much as its ongoing creation, its self-production in the eyes, by the hands, and as told by the voices of Americans themselves. Unlike later authors such as Dos Passos and the Lynds, Stein doesn't cite a great number of different voices. She sees essences, the structural "tender girders" of language (to use a phrase from Mullen's poem about Stein; see p. 217n22). Here in *The Making of Americans*, Stein mainly grouses, expressing her anxiety of influence and struggling to make good on her decision to become a writer, but later she finds a possibility for change through the adoption of different structures: by remaking conversation, we might remake America. In fact, a *Boston Post* reporter, Grace Davidson, mistakenly referred to Stein's novel as *The Remaking of Americans*.

Stein's love of the human voice is not blind (or deaf), and, from her earliest work, Stein emphasizes the parts of the American nature she would have different. She emphasizes American blindness and American monologuing, both of which come from feelings of inadequacy or overconfidence—emptiness or fullness, in her terminology. Americans are made by listening to themselves and believing. But Stein implies that attention to the makings of conversation—its structures and complexities—could enable Americans to make themselves differently, to be more adaptive, freer.

In the most scrutinizing piece of criticism on *The Making of Americans*, Priscilla Wald in *Constituting Americans* emphasizes Stein's interest in the relationship between language, the self, and society:

> Stein examined how external stimuli—language, physical sensations, even directives—influence the experience and understanding of "self." Her discoveries laid the groundwork both for theories, explored in *The Making of Americans*, of how cultural assumptions shape the experience of self and for the stylistic experimentation of that work through which she analyzed and represented that process. (261)

Stein writes to explicate the complex interaction between who we are and what we say in order to determine where one can begin a revolution of self, art, and society.

Sound Writing

Stein is interested not only in conversation, but also in sound itself. Her contemporary reviewers repeatedly encouraged Stein's readers to read out loud (Winter, 82; Dodge, 153). One reviewer writes that "it is a relief to read something that doesn't intend to make sense in the ordinary sense and so sets you free to use some of your unused senses to make sense" (Winter, 82). Another reports that some readers "could see with their ears and smell with their eyes and taste with their whole selves" (Lerman, 145). In her lecture "Plays," Stein worries over the question, "Could I see and hear and feel at the same time and did I" (*Lectures*, 115). She forces her readers to try.

In *The Gutenberg Galaxy* Marshall McLuhan posits the effect of print on the mind: print encourages us to see more and hear less. He writes (in boldface type): "The interiorization of the technology of the phonetic alphabet translates man from the magical world of the ear to the neutral visual world." McLuhan links this change in sensory emphasis to a change in thought and interpersonal states. He asks (again in boldface): "Does the interiorization of media such as letters alter the ratio among our senses and change mental processes?" And he asserts (this time in regular type): "No other kind of writing save the phonetic has ever translated man out of the possessive world of total interdependence and interrelation that is the auditory network" (18, 24 22). Stein seems to have thought about these same issues less pseudoscientifically, but no less boldly and intricately. Her interest in sound may arise from her personal dispositions, but she may also recover the aural nature of language in order to improve our interactive networks and goad our minds into working differently.

Stein claims that her primary interest is sight, but this may be explained by her complaint that the French read out loud to her instead of letting her read the words herself. She writes that she likes "to read inside and not outside," and that she sometimes overcame this problem by reading over their shoulders (*Everybody's*, 163, 17). Instead, then, of understanding Stein's statement to mean that she was interested only in the sight of words, I take it to mean that she liked reading to be a private matter. She liked to see the words and turn them into sounds on her own. In fact, it is difficult for written words to mean by sight alone, which is one reason it is sometimes difficult to teach deaf children to read. According to Walter Ong, in *Orality and Literacy*, "the world of sound" is "the natural habitat of language." He continues, "'Reading' a text means converting it to sound, aloud or in the imagination" (8).

Stein's interest in the creative friction between these two language media points to her interest in sound as well as sight. In "An American and France," Stein explains that a creator must live between two civilizations or two languages, because creativity comes from the opposition between them, and she even worries that the world's shrinkage will hobble creation—an anticipation of twenty-first-century anxieties about globalization. When the world was so big that people rarely knew of other civilizations, creation could occur, because people had two languages: they had "a special language to write which was not the language that was spoken" (65). The language of talking must be related to the language of writing if their difference is a necessary condition for creativity. In his history of the Frankfurt Institute, *The Dialectical Imagination*, Martin Jay holds: "The distance between Hebrew, the sacred language, and the profane speech of the Diaspora made its impact on Jews who were distrustful of the current universe of discourse" (34). Jay proposes a possible connection between this dual language system and the development of the Frankfurt Institute's dialectical theory—a theory that becomes relevant in this volume at the end of chapter 6.

Stein's attention tended to be voice activated, which is one reason Stein may have had to re-sound others' conversation—and disliked people reading aloud to her. The tone of a voice was likely to distract her from the very words it was saying. In *The Autobiography of Alice B. Toklas*, Stein writes (that Alice reports that Stein said): "I don't hear a language, I hear tones of voice and rhythms, but with my eyes I see words and sentences" (70). Leon Mendez Solomons, a graduate student and Stein's colleague in Harvard's Psychology Laboratory, noted that "Miss Stein has a strong auditory consciousness, and sounds usually determine the direction of her attention" (Stein and Solomons, 15). Stein's auditory consciousness also interested her in rhythm. Reiterating that she was distracted by sound, she writes that "hearing tires me very quickly. Lots of voices make too much sound, any one voice sounds too much like that voice." But she soon adds: "On the other hand as I write the movement of the words spoken by some one whom lately I have been hearing sound like my writing feels to me as I am writing" (*Everybody's*, 88). Stein transforms the conversations she has heard into written words and rhythms and then can reconstitute them in her own voice and better feel their movement. Her method might signify an imperialist domination of those whose words she revises (or replays). As I argue in chapter 3, however, her interest in talk reveals her developing interest in the deep structures of interaction.

Stein plays with the sounds of words throughout her writings, as the next two chapters will demonstrate. For clear instances of Stein's playing with sounds, see *Bee Time Vine* (36), where she writes in the poem "Miguel (Collusion). Guimpe. Candle": "Collection of eggs white, white as know excellent. / Are the holds extra skinned." "Eggs white" sounds like "egg whites"; "white as know" sounds like "white as snow"; "excellent" and "extra" (and even "collection") have the sound of "eggs" in them. About another piece in *Bee Time Vine*, "In," Virgil Thomson cites Alice B. Toklas as saying that what is important is "definitely 'sound.'" He adds that "G.S. would have denied this, since she regularly denied that sounds and their play were a major consideration in her writing" (*Bee Time Vine*, 44). Thomson also reads the title "Yet Dish" as "Yiddish" (52). In the poem "Early and Late," near "Teas and teas," Stein writes "Tease and tease" (245). In "Decorations," she writes: "I do not wish to write down what I hear" (186); but ten pages later, in "What Is This," she writes: "I love conversation. / Do you like it printed. / I like it descriptive. / Not very descriptive. / Not very descriptive. / I like it to come easily / Naturally" (196–97).

Perhaps Stein's "auditory consciousness" led her to wonder about the difference between the sight and the sound of words (independent of a particular voice or even other limiting contexts). She may or may not have had to make sounds as she wrote, but, for example, she did write: "She likes the poet to mutter. He does. The olive" ("Advertisements," in *Geography and Plays*, 343). If we mutter while we read, "the olive" becomes (more profitably within the context) "they all live." Her and our muttering brings (more) meaning to life. If we don't notice Stein's "Loud Letters" (*Geography and Plays*, 345), we are missing something fun, as well as killing meaning—or, less criminally, not bringing as much meaning to life as we could.

A Sensible Education

While the writings themselves are the best evidence of Stein's interest in sound, her extensive undergraduate studies with William James, her experiments in Harvard's Psychology Laboratory, and her medical school training also indicate serious interest in sensory impressions, particularly the senses by which most of us experience language. During her years at Harvard Annex, Stein took seven courses with James, including five graduate courses in experimental psychology, and, even before meeting him, she was assigned his *Principles of Psychology* in her course with Hugo Münsterberg (Bowers, 13; Wagner-Martin, 35, 31). In medical school, Stein devoted much of her time to investigating the sections of the brain and spinal cord that accept and process sensation.

James emphasizes personal sensation—an individual's experience as that individual attends to it—and many readers have noted Stein's own interest in attention and sensation. In the second paragraph of the preface to *The Principles of Psychology*, William James defines the data of psychology as "*thoughts and feelings*," "a *physical world* in time and space with which they coexist," and the knowledge we come to have about this physical world through those thoughts and feelings (6; his italics). Throughout his works, James advocates our trusting our own perceptions and impressions, and he also points out that we develop perceptions and impressions only if we are paying attention.[15] Lloyd Frankenberg suggests that "Gertrude Stein's work as a whole might be called a study in attention, including inattention" (vi), and Rosalind S. Miller also describes Stein's and Solomons's experiments as studies in attention.[16] The subjects of these experiments—and for the first one, the only subjects were Stein and Solomons themselves—were to do one language task while being distracted with another. They were to write down words they heard at the same time that they attempted to read a book; they also tried to write their own stories or anecdotes while being distracted by someone speaking to them. Miller concludes that Stein and Solomons were interested in determining how much of human attention is triggered by sight, and how much by auditory signals (Miller, 51; Stein and Solomons 13–15). Decades later, Stein asks: "Is the thing seen or the thing heard the thing that makes most of its impression upon you at the theatre?" and "Does the thing seen or does the thing heard effect [*sic?*] you and effect [*sic?*] you at the same time or in the same degree or does it not?" and "Of course in reading one sees but one also hears and when the story is at its most exciting does one hear more than one sees or does one not do so?" (*Lectures*, 101–2). Stein's writing allows readers to continue a personally administered attention experiment. Stein hands us a looking glass with which to examine our own consciousnesses.

The pedagogical methods used in the Johns Hopkins Medical School curriculum, as well as Stein's particular knowledge of brain physiology, further support my insistence on her interest in the sensory perceptions of written and spoken language. The misconception that Stein dropped out of medical school and preconceptions about early medical school education mix to create an impression that Stein was escaping a stuffy rigidity in preference for airy Paris. But in the 1880s, U.S. medical schools began to emulate European ones by foregoing lectures and instead teaching through experience (Rothstein, 108).[17] William Osler, a prominent gynecologist from whom Stein took a course her fourth year (Wagner-Martin, 50), admitted to giving "a talk" once a week, but he was more satisfied with holding "a regular weekly amphitheater clinic. Of these he explains, 'I like the clinical clerk and the patient to do the teaching, adding comments here and there, or asking the former questions'" (Rothstein, 109). Already Stein was learning from conversation, and she was learning from the people who feel the symptoms instead of the experts who diagnose them.

This modern medical school education taught future doctors to trust their own senses and instincts. Professor William Thayer called their method of teaching "self-education under guidance" and writes: "The method of authority has given way to the method of observation and inquiry" (qtd. in Ludmerer, 64, 66).[18] Professor Franklin Paine Mall preferred the clinical approach to book learning: "When anatomy is studied in this way [through dissection rather than through lectures], the student must indeed be stupid not to discover the many defects as well as errors in some of our favorite English text-books" (qtd. in Ludmerer, 66).[19] In short, medical school training taught students that sensory impressions and experiences are more reliable than summaries (generalizations of sensory impressions) by authorities. If I am right about her, Stein would have embraced this form of education; her appreciation of it is one of the few facts that might explain her staying in medical school for the duration.[20] Teaching Stein to trust her senses and ignore authority must have been like teaching a lion to roar.

After deciding not to take the summer course which would have allowed her to obtain her medical degree, Stein remained at Johns Hopkins for a fifth year, and she continued her work on the brain (Wagner-Martin, 51).[21]

Professor Lewellys Barker maneuvered (without success) to get Stein's original work published in two prominent journals of anatomy (Wagner-Martin, 51–52). In his 1899 textbook *The Nervous System and Its Constituent Neurones*, Barker refers to Stein's investigating "bundle[s] of fibres" in the brain and trying to discover where they lead (725–26). Titled "Centripetal Fibres in the Fasciculus Longitudinalis Medialis," this section of Barker's book shows that Stein's object of attention is a bundle of centripetal fibers, which, as Antoine Keyser succinctly explains, "project the various streams of stimuli from the sense organ receptors towards the posterior lobes of the brain" (Keyser, 64).[22] In his autobiography, *Time and the Physician*, Barker parenthetically comments: "Among these students [at Johns Hopkins] was Miss Gertrude Stein, and I have often wondered whether my attempts to teach her the intricacies of the medulla oblongata had anything to do with the development of the strange literary forms with which she was later to perplex the world" (60). Stein's work on the brain may have been motivated by the same interests that led to her unusual writing. A doctor would cite her interest in the neural networks activated by our habits of attention to sensory input; a literary critic might tend to call this same motivating interest an experiment in reader response or a challenge to our habits of language use. Either way, Stein's words—even as early as *The Making of Americans*—challenge readers' attention, disallow our habitual responses, and inspire something new in the way of reading and writing, speaking and listening.

CHAPTER 2

Modifying the Mind:
William James and *Tender Buttons*

ICHARD RORTY (*PHILOSOPHY*, 24) characterizes the early pragmatists (William James and John Dewey) as talking about experience and the neopragmatists (William Quine and Donald David-
son) as talking about language, but William James's *Principles of Psychology*
had already suggested that language is one form of experience.[1] From the
outset, James contends with the problem that phenomena cannot really
be experienced; we attentively let them be "*undergone*" and then fix them
in our memories: "The dance of the ideas is a copy, somewhat mutilated
and altered, of the order of phenomena" (*Principles*, 17)—and this dance
of ideas necessarily takes place in words. James implies that language is a
significant experience when, treating the topic of aphasia, he discusses *how*
various injured and healthy people imbue language: by sight, by sound, by
the feeling in [their] fingers as they hold a pen, and so on. Thus language
is both the means to noting experiences of other types and an experience
in itself.

The experience of language helps instill the network of associations
within the mind, which is what produces—or simply *is*—the structure
of that mind, though James points out weaknesses in this theory, too
(*Principles*, 1218). Assuming that the theory is even partly true, Stein could
change her readers' habits of mental association by changing the arrangements of words on the page. In this way, the choices she makes—the very
ways she arranges those words—are an artistic adaptation of James's scientific work. Every mind is a black box, a function machine of countless
inscrutabilities, and we can never know how one person's words might strike
another person's fancy, but Stein's works, from *Tender Buttons* to *Brewsie and
Willie*, seem inspired by James's speculations about the workings of human

36

cognition. While Stein is often understood to write differently because of her homosexuality or her womanhood—as lacking a heterocentrist world-view or writing *l'ecriture feminine*—James's discussion of the means by which *human* minds think would have let her see her project as more universal. Stein calls attention to our necessary habits of human thought, not just heterosexual or masculine thought, and makes us question assumptions that so many of us hold so deeply we haven't noticed them.

In *The Principles of Psychology*, James states that all thought occurs through association and that memory is only a matter of paths (620). He speculates that our minds are networks of associations that have developed through experience:

> The highest centres [of the human mind] *do probably contain nothing but arrangements for representing impressions and movements, and other arrangements for coupling the activity of these arrangements together.* (73; his italics)

James's idea that the mind consists of arrangements, and of arrangements of arrangements, coupled with his assertion that linguistic experience can form these arrangements, suggests that Stein's weird series of words might have the capacity to rearrange those arrangements in our minds. Stein redesigns her readers' neural pathways, developing in us a greater number of associational paths leading out from each stimulus. Her words elicit expectant attention; they mildly prime the reader to interpret other words in certain ways (or productively uncertain ways). For example, in *Tender Buttons*, when Stein writes, "A seal and matches and a swan and ivy and a suit" (11), the reader might think of an animal (a seal), then a wax seal (to go with matches), then an animal again (a seal to match with a swan, and now "match" has transformed from a noun to a verb or an adjective), then possibly a coat of arms (animals surrounded by ivy), and then coupling in general (matches, suit, a pair of animals). These few words prime us to notice a variety of meanings for each one. An Ivy League suit? A swimsuit to accompany the water animals? ("I vie" could even prime us for a different kind of "suit.")

Stein began learning about the brain in college, because James's textbook reviews contemporary works on cognitive science. As Louis Menand reports, in those days "psychology was just what philosophers did when they talked about minds," and in Germany James had studied "what was then the hottest area in science: physiological psychology, sometimes called psychophysics," which based its work on the assumption that "every conscious event has a physical basis" (259). In James's text—as well as in most works on cognitive science today—localization is introduced through the study of aphasia, a "language deficit caused by damage to the brain" (O'Grady, 348).[2] As one modern text asserts: "The study of aphasia is by far the most important tool in the investigation of language in the brain" (ibid.). Before the technology that could detect hot spots—the active parts—of the brain, (though not before the 1867 discovery that *brain-activity seems accompanied by a local disengagement of heat*" [James, *Principles*, 105; his italics]), specialized brain areas were located by studying the brains of aphasics post mortem. Different kinds of aphasia led to hypotheses about the possible chain of events that must occur between hearing or reading verbal stimuli and responding in kind. The study of the brain is likely to have let Stein see strong and complex relationships between the senses, language, and knowing.

Stein's writing often reads as if she has Wernicke's aphasia, the "most important type of fluent aphasia."[3] A person with Wernicke's aphasia is "generally unaware of [his] deficit," speaks without hesitation, correctly uses "function words" and normal syntax, but "rarely makes any sense" (O'Grady, 351). But Stein is more interested in the normal than the abnormal workings of the human mind: "the normal is so much more simply complicated and interesting" (*Autobiography*, 83). She also recognizes the skill of the normal brain to make sense of *whatever* inputs it receives. She may even be aware that Carl Wernicke in 1874 asserted that "speech acquisition coincides so closely with the development of consciousness that it may be considered as a gauge thereof" (69). Her writing rearranges the arrangements, and the arrangements of arrangements, in the highest centers of her readers' minds, affecting our very consciousness. The sensations of Stein's words in our brains enables Stein to enable us to cut shortcuts through and build extensions to the more common neural pathways of association. Her word placement forces us to expand the number of places in the brain to which we send information about any particular word; we send out all-points bulletins to discern possible meaning.

William James's *Principles of Psychology* might even have suggested Stein's sense of the efficacy of language in changing people and societies. In his first chapter, "The Scope of Psychology," James speculates on how memory works. Describing "the associationists'" ideas, James writes:

> This multitude of ideas, existing absolutely, yet clinging together, and weaving an endless carpet of themselves, like dominoes in ceaseless change, or the bits of glass in a kaleidoscope,—whence do they get

their fantastic laws of clinging, and why do they cling in just the shapes they do?

For this the associationist must introduce the order of experience in the outer world. The dance of the ideas is a copy, somewhat mutilated and altered, of the order of phenomena. But the slightest reflection shows that phenomena have absolutely no power to influence our ideas until they have first impressed our senses and our brain; . . . a very small amount of reflection on facts shows that one part of the body, namely, the brain, is the part whose experiences are directly concerned. . . .

. . . it will be safe to lay down the general law that *no mental modification ever occurs which is not accompanied or followed by a bodily change.* The ideas and feelings, e.g., which these present printed characters excite in the reader's mind not only occasion movements of his eyes and nascent movements of articulation in him, but will some day make him speak, or take sides in a discussion, or give advice, or choose a book to read, differently from what would have been the case had they never impressed his retina. (17–19)

This description of the complex way our minds associate ideas with each other corresponds with descriptions of the way the words associate in a Stein work such as *Tender Buttons.* But even more importantly, James's assertion that our future actions will be affected by each mental experience suggests that Stein's strange and strongly sensory writing could have consequences (and might have even been intended to have consequences) beyond the field of literature. Stein encourages us to develop new ways of understanding and forming our own language, new ways of talking, new orders in our neurons, and even a new social order—but all that comes later.

James asserts that the brain undergoes constant remodification (*Principles,* 227). The brain is "an organ whose internal equilibrium is always in a state of change," like a "kaleidoscope" in which "the figures are always rearranging themselves" (239). He goes so far as to say (in an echo of Heraclitus) that the mind's incessant fluxion means that no state of thought can ever be repeated: "*no state* [of thought] *once gone can recur and be identical with what it was before*" (224). He asks, "How is a fresh path ever formed?" (1183) and then offers examples of "how often experience undoes her own work, and for an earlier order substitutes a new one" (1217). His examples of how our eyes and minds adjust to our wearing unusual glasses, looking through prisms, or moving on ice instead of land demonstrate how quickly we form new associations, and "the habits of a lifetime [are] violated" (820)—an afternoon of ice skating can make one forget habits of walking for an hour. "When we have been exposed to an unusual stimulus for many minutes or hours, a nervous process is set up which results in the haunting of consciousness by the impression for a long time afterwards. . . . [P]rofound rearrangements and slow settlings into a new equilibrium are going on in the neural substance," and they gradually develop into memory (609). In other words, also James's: "Excitement of peculiar tracts, or peculiar modes of general excitement in the brain, leave a sort of tenderness or exalted sensibility behind them which takes days to die away" (542).

In contrast to the excitation of "peculiar tracts," habits are associations that have dug deep paths in our minds through repetition. James defines habits in terms of well-worn, highly eroded waterways (*Principles*, 113, 427). In reaction to certain stimuli, we become automata, and he is not talking only about habitually putting on socks or buttoning buttons, although he mentions both of these (118). Even reading has become instinctual: "the art of reading (after a certain stage in one's education) is the art of skipping" (992). We quickly pass over signs, ignoring them in order to get to what is signified (872). We do not fully revisit information that we assume to be familiar.

What makes us conscious is hesitation, deliberation, and choice. James writes:

> Consciousness . . . is only intense when nerve-processes are hesitant. In rapid, automatic, habitual action it sinks to a minimum. . . . In hesitant action, there seem many alternative possibilities of final nervous discharge. The feeling awakened by the nascent excitement of each alternative nerve-tract seems by its attractive or repulsive quality to determine whether the excitement shall abort or shall become complete. Where indecision is great, . . . consciousness is agonizingly intense. Feeling, from this point of view, may be likened to a cross-section of the chain of nervous discharge, ascertaining the links already laid down, and groping among the fresh ends presented to it for the one which seems best to fit the case. (*Principles*, 145)

A collection of subtle stimuli can point in a variety of directions, and so a person must act consciously, mentally stepping in to decide which way to go. James calls this widely drawn arc of association "submaximal excitement of wide-spreading associational brain-tracts" (244), and "*suffusion*" and "*fringe*" (249; his italics).[4] The more "wide-spreading" the associations, the more necessarily conscious the thinker must become. In a more beautiful phrase, he states that the mind "is at every stage a theatre of simultaneous possibilities" (277). James defines genius in terms of this living, active consciousness (400). But genius is hard to sustain in the ordinary business of life. Daily experiences form habits of sight and thought that are almost impossible to change. James asserts that learning something altogether new is easier than seeing the mundane in new ways.

But he may have inspired Stein to try. No matter how weirdly it reads, Stein's *Tender Buttons* represents a domestic space, with its sections titled "Objects," "Food," and "Rooms." Buttons are an example James uses to describe thoughtless, habitual actions, and "tenderness" is the very word he uses to describe the effect of new and different stimuli on the mind. In *Tender Buttons*, we certainly are looking at the mundane from an unusual perspective, or through a prism, one that forces our thoughts down different paths than they would usually tend to take. Stein does not use words as if they were buttons to be pushed, and she actively prevents readers from jumping to any single reaction or firm conclusions. For example, "A Box" reads:

> Out of kindness comes redness and out of rudeness comes rapid same question, out of an eye comes research, out of selection comes painful cattle. So then the order is that a white way of being round is something suggesting a pin and is it disappointing, it is not, it is so rudimentary to be analysed and see a fine substance strangely, it is so earnest to have a green point not to red but to point again. (*Tender Buttons*, 11)

Her first two "out of" phrases suggest the manifestations and consequences of certain behaviors ("kindness" and "rudeness"), but the next two "out of" phrases undermine that assumption. The four phrases in this first sentence make a reader think about the relationship between the components of each pair, and we tend to assume that the relationship we find should be similar; James says the mind makes great use of "the *notion* of sameness" (an ability measured on most standardized tests), which accounts for its very structure (*Principles*, 435; his italics). The desire to find sameness leads readers to consider all possible meanings of each of the eight components of the four expressions, and readers probably feel hopeful of success until they get to "painful cattle." The wish to collate that phrase with the others compels the reader to become much more creative in reconsidering the possible meaning of all the other components. The reader has to determine what "comes out of" means, such that "kindness" is to "redness" as "rudeness" is to "rapid same question" as "eye" is to "research" as "selection" is to "painful cattle." In forcing us into thinking about these words or terms, Stein forces us to notice our less habitual associations. We notice similarities of sound ("-ness" is repeated three times; "rudeness" and "redness" sound alike), and we notice semantic relationships (research and eye, for example). We notice what we are habitually trying to do (find this parallel set of relationships), and then we think of alternate activities (Is this a linear plot? Is she talking about what we are doing, as in boxing ourselves in, instead of anything exterior to our reader response?), in addition to alternative denotations of the words.

The next sentence alludes to "order," but "a white way of being round" forces us to disorder our nice little mutually exclusive boxes of color and shape concepts. "Something suggesting a pin" encourages us to acknowledge the vagueness of similarity instead of letting us continue to pretend that the notion of sameness on which our thoughts are founded is firm bedrock. Later in this sentence, Stein seems to state her goal more directly than usual: she wants us to "see a fine substance strangely" and "to have green point not to red [its opposite, and a likely spontaneous next thought] but to point again" (and again) instead of losing its power once it has fired off the beginning of a chain of habitual associations and reactions.[5]

Have I undermined Stein's goal by coming to this conclusion? "Is it disappointing, it is not"—because I have only a tentative grasp on these words. They have not fired and emptied. They are still firing (along with previously unacquainted synapses), and they will continue to point and point again because "rudimentary" is related to "rudeness," "earnest" points ahead to a sincere pledge of something to come, and there are so many other loose ends that the stanza cannot be neatly sewn together, wrapped up, or boxed. Stein's words, here and elsewhere, do not let us rely on habit. She relies on our habits only enough to use them against other habits, to encourage us to encourage her words to mean as much as they can, and to let our minds do more than we usually demand from them.[6]

James cites Josiah Royce's precept that "consciousness constantly tends to the minimum of complexity and to the maximum of definiteness" (*Principles*, 943), but Stein won't let it. If the times we hesitate and decide are the times we are most conscious, then Stein heightens our consciousness by producing strings of words that cause our instincts to contradict each other. When that happens, according to James, we lose those instincts and "lead a life of hesitation and choice, an intellectual life" (1013).[7] A review of *Tender Buttons* cites an anonymous "friend" of Stein as saying, "She is impelling language to induce new states of consciousness" (R. Rogers, 19). In his review of the same work, H. L. Mencken says that Stein's writing requires "a resilient cerebrum" (15). Instead of running our minds through the regular channels, Stein makes our thoughts spread out of the main river, streaming between stimuli and less common reactions. These tributaries form deltas where our minds can consciously wander and wade, playing and testing the waters. As in scientific abbreviation, these deltas mean "change."

James shows that when people practice looking through prisms, their minds start to violate the habits of a lifetime. Perhaps then it is no accident that Stein chose to begin *Tender Buttons* with the prose poem "A Carafe, That Is a Blind Glass," which reminds many readers of refracted light.

<blockquote>

A CARAFE, THAT IS A BLIND GLASS

A kind in glass and a cousin, a spectacle and nothing strange a single hurt color and an arrangement in a system to pointing. All this and not ordinary, not unordered in not resembling. The difference is spreading.

</blockquote>

Chessman posits that this "word-painting may be 'a cousin' to the actual 'carafe,'" since it holds, but doesn't quite hold, meaning (92). Comparing Stein's project to Emerson's, Chessman writes that both believe that "to see the world newly requires, not a new world, but new perception" (93). Ruddick understands this passage to be self-reflexive: the poem's "gesturing toward . . . connections" that "fall short of shaping the poem into a single, monologic (or systematic) meaning" (*Reading*, 195). While first writing that the issue of sight is an unrelated one, Ruddick then hazards: "Maybe the poem, or *Tender Buttons* as a whole, is meant to initiate us in a new kind of *seeing* that exposes *connections* among things without authorizing a single system of classification" (196; her italics).[8] Stewart calls this passage "a meditation" and follows the etymology of "carafe" back to Arabic *gharr fa* (to draw water) and then notes the similar Indo-European root *ghar-* (shine, glare, glow) which is the root of "glass" (87–89). Also seeing "religious ritual" in *Tender Buttons* (133), Stewart concludes that "for Gertrude Stein the activity of writing is the ritual of deracinating one's own consciousness" (138). Digging up human consciousness is a way of airing the roots and encouraging new growth, as well as planting something wholly new.

Perhaps then I am only putting in neurological terms what these others have said in spiritual (and botanical) ones. Together, "blind," "glass," and "spectacle" suggest that Stein is discussing vision (and its distortions), although in each case Stein's other words seem to prime the reader to notice other possible denotations of those three words. "A carafe" may be blind because it contains, but it can also refract light through itself (or even through the liquid it contains), such that the light points and spreads. Stein's words "kind," "cousin," and "resembling" also point toward the less distinct associations she would have us recall. Toklas seems to have called puns (double entendres) "double tenders" (Steward, *Murder*, 113), but eventually a choice must be made, a preference admitted, for the juggling mind must let go of some ideas while grasping others.[9] I think that Stein is beginning a treatise on epistemology and language, and that here she describes the many ways she sees a carafe as a metaphor for a word, which is the container of our perceptions. A word can contain meaning, but it can also do more, point to more, and that array of possible meanings is the very difference Stein advocates we notice. This stanza of Stein's prose poem is like James's prism, in that it can change forever our mental associations. Her diction and word arrangements, her emphasis on sight and sound, encourage us to travel our less developed paths of association. Instead of firing from "carafe," say, to cheap sangria, Stein's readers' thoughts will spread out over a delta of more.

Tender Buttons Disturb a Center: Questioning Our Rhetorical Religion

This whole first passage in *Tender Buttons*, "A Carafe, That Is A Blind Glass," is explicated quite often, but elsewhere critics have tended to address their attention to short bits and extracted phrases, developing their interpretations of Stein's work from these pieces. Stein's words, however, should be contemplated not just in pieces but in the order she put them on the page, and in longer sections. Reconsidering her 1983 book thirteen years later, Marianne DeKoven notes: "I would now read the whole paragraph rather than just the first sentence" of "A Portrait of Mabel Dodge at the Villa Curonia" ("Introduction," 476). Marjorie Perloff writes: "To assume that Stein chooses her words more or less randomly, that she is merely being 'playful,' is to ignore the careful contextualization that makes such play possible" (105). Agreeing wholeheartedly, I choose to discuss the longest paragraph from *Tender Buttons*, all of it, and to see and hear what can be seen and heard there. I will also be demonstrating the mental calisthenics involved in reading Stein. If you agree with Stephen Booth that there is pleasure to be gotten in the "understanding of something that remains something we do not understand," then read on (*Precious*, 6).[10] To start with my conclusions, the following long sentence from the section, "Rooms" suggests that Stein is suspicious of the standard structures of conventional English, the easy routines that these structures afford thought, and the predictability of everyday rhetoric which allows people to get away with not thinking.

She suggests that people have fallen asleep, become unconscious of the world and themselves by becoming habituated to and relaxing upon "congealed . . . phrases" (Loy, 94)—prefabricated, retold untruths:

> A religion, almost a religion, any religion, a quintal in religion, a relying and a surface and a service in indecision and a creature and a question and a syllable in answer and more counting and no quarrel and a single scientific statement and no darkness and no question and an earned administration and a single set of sisters and an outline and no blisters and the section seeing yellow and the centre having spelling and no solitude and no quaintness and yet solid quite so solid and the single surface centred and the question in the placard and the singularity, is there a singularity, and the singularity, why is there a question and the singularity why is the surface outrageous, why is it beautiful why is it not when there is no doubt, why is anything vacant, why is not disturbing a centre no virtue, why is it when it is and why is it when it is and there is no doubt, there is no doubt that the singularity shows. (*Tender Buttons*, 73)

Stein would probably agree that these words cannot be "understood," since, for her, "understanding" implies passively following a leader or author rather than coming to know through experience. But there is still meaning to be gleaned here. As James says, a collection of stimuli, each one *"ineffectual"* in itself, can eventually add up and can "at last overcome a resistance" (*Principles*, 89; his italics). If we are forced to look at the words, we start to see what's there. We note "syllables that we perceive one by one as we read or listen, syllables whose relations to one another flicker and change as we and they progress to the end" (Booth, *Precious*, 20).[11] Experiencing this stanza in "Rooms," searching it for sights, sounds, relationships, subsequent meanings, and anything else accessible to an attentive reader, evokes a variety of meanings which all seem to add up to a comprehensive declaration of mental independence from the commonplaces that express the normal order of things. One can arrange that range of meaning (a process Stein encourages by means of the repeated presence of "range," "arrange," "arrangement," and even "orange" throughout *Tender Buttons*) into a "single set"—one and yet multiple, *e pluribus unum*. Playing, paying attention to Stein's unusually tendered, quite tender, suggestions toward meaning, rearranges one's mental arrangements, which should remind readers of the messy ways *unum* arises out of *pluribus*, and maybe even reintroduce pluralism into our minds.

Instead of telling us what she's talking about, Stein obliges us to figure it out. Without a right or wrong in view, the exercise forces readers into a more complete experience of single words—their sounds, their spelling, their various denotations and connotations, their relatives. Ferdinand de Saussure, W.V.O. Quine, and Jacques Derrida (among others) may be wrong when they argue that isolated words have no meaning. But maybe they are right, because although lonely words lose some meaning, they take on more or other—they are never alone in our minds. According to James:

> If we look at an isolated printed word and repeat it long enough, it ends by assuming an entirely unnatural aspect. Let the reader try this with any word on this page. He will soon begin to wonder if it can possibly be the word he has been using all his life with that meaning. It stares at him from the paper like a glass eye, with no speculation in it. Its body is indeed there, but its soul is fled. It is reduced, by this new way of attending to it, to its sensational nudity. We never before attended to it in this way, but habitually got it clad with its meaning the moment we caught sight of it, and rapidly passed from it to the other words of the phrase. We apprehended it, in short, with a cloud of associates, and thus perceiving it, we felt it quite otherwise than as we feel it now divested and alone. (*Principles*, 726–27)

Stein says she discovered this feature of words on New Year's Day 1927, when she was getting her hair cut short and reading with her glasses out in front of her, but she had studied James in the fall of 1893. Even one word, or a set of words, can give rise to an array of associations, considerations, and imaginings. Stein's focus on the word is a love affair—but also a political campaign. Developing semantic consciousness should prevent knee-jerk reactions to language; readers pleasingly educated by Stein's *Tender Buttons* might become less easily manipulated by words.

Instead of helping us understand this "religion" she mentions, Stein makes us come to know it personally. Stein often wrote about the artistic endeavor in terms of religion (see Watts, *Rapture*, 25; S. Watson, *Prepare*), and this Jewish writer teaches us to protest our traditional catholic reading habits. Words were her artistic medium, and she's a reformist. In this passage, the words that seems adjectival because of their syntactic positions ("almost a," "any," and "a quintal in") only make Stein's meaning more vague. The noun "religion" is complicated rather than clarified by the words that seem as if they should act as modifiers. "Almost any religion" or "any almost-religion" would have been comparatively easy to understand, but those are not (therefore) what Stein offers. By refusing to let her readers' thoughts lean on the shoulders of adjectival ensigns, Stein makes us look directly at the noun "religion." I see "re" and "lig," which reminds me of ligaments.[12] Something that is done again? Something that binds one thing to another? I also see "re" and "ligion," which reminds me of "legion." Something that a whole legion of people do over and over? ("Legion" means "to gather," as I am gathering all this information together.) "[A] quintal in religion" sounds like "a Quintilian religion," which suggests this religion might refer to ancient, common, and powerful rhetorical conventions. In fact, Quintilian valorized conventions, as here: "Custom . . . is the surest preceptor in speaking: we must use phraseology, like money, which has the public stamp" (49). All Stein's stored-up meanings rub together, and they add up to something about conventional (reused, repeated) rhetorical habits of binding together words—or ideas, people, communities, and political bodies. If one were writing in this unusual style, one might choose to write the reasons for it. *Tender Buttons* may be a treatise against the habitual use of language and also a primer for a new kind of attention. Stein risks having her ideas misunderstood because she does not write in familiar forms, but standard prose could neither change habits nor awaken consciousness.

With so many more words left to read in the sentence, and such unusually tendered suggestions, a reader must feel in great doubt about meaning. The sounds of the words and the anataxis encourage a reader to rush through "a relying and a service in indecision and a creature and," but Stein's practice so far has taught the reader to slow down and look around. But where to look? "And" is the perfect word to express associations without suggesting hierarchies, making the sentences "[a]dditive rather than subordinative," a phrase Ong (36–37) uses to describe one of the "characteristics of orally based thought and expression." "And" does not allow us to guess where the central idea in this phrase will be found, so we look at everything. The unusual situation of "relying" in the sentence makes interpretation less than automatic. The article "a" immediately before "relying" primes us for a noun rather than what sounds like a verb (and subsides into a gerund). Through this false priming, Stein forces us to look carefully at words we thought we already knew. Unable to skip over "relying" (as we can when it is in its customary setting), we are forced to look at the word and consciously enumerate all it might mean. One might note the visual—and socially functional—similarities between "religion" and "relying" or recognize the etymological parallels. "Relying" is "re-" + "lie" and means "to fasten together," just like "religion." "Relying" suggests reclining back, or lying down again, or even telling another untruth. Collecting all that stored meaning, I get an image of a person or a whole group of people mentally reclining, relaxing on the retold untruths that have already been fastened together for them.

Stein's anataxis pulls readers further, on toward rediscovering the associational "fringes" and related entanglements of more and more words. Our reading habits, our expectations of coherence and similarity, compel us to take what meaning we find in "a relying and a surface and a service in indecision and" and try to contrast it with that already blossoming in this complicated tree of associations. "Surface" makes me skim forward, surf ahead on its soft sounds and slippery connotations. It pushes me on to the next word and the recognition that "surface" and "service" sound quite a bit alike. The "surface" could describe the character of the reading process when I read normal sentences in which I feel fluent and which lead me to take words for granted. Surface-y sentences might be "a service in indecision" because they allow us to avoid making decisions: our habits keep us from noticing that there are any decisions to make. The surface offers a service on which readers rely, but Stein's writing offers no stable surface on which readers can stand together, or even alone (and her phrase could mean something very different from my paraphrase). "In" and "in-" call out to one another and trade places, suggesting that surfaces may offer services that lead not toward decision but toward not-decision—and these are not exactly the same place. On either hand, Stein's sentence leads us toward ambiguity, keeps us thinking, guessing, adding, and noting a network of complexity.

In the phrases that follow "a creature," Stein's discussion of knowledge—how we use language to think, and to avoid thinking—seems more direct than usual: "and a creature and a question and a syllable in answer and more counting and no quarrel and a single scientific statement and not darkness and no question." A question, like a living thing, can grow into a variety of answers and even more questions. But "a syllable in answer" responds to "a question" with a yes or a no, clipping off further potential discussion or discovery.[13]

"More counting" contrasts with this clipping off; counting can go on and on (and "more" is one of the words used most in *Tender Buttons*). "Count" is also from a root from which grew two different French words: *compter* (to count) and *conter* (to narrate), which may connect adding numbers with adding more words, or just more meanings. The bullying exclusivity of "a single scientific statement" may allow for "no quarrel" and "no question" and admit of "no darkness"—but may indeed be a means toward obscuring truth, or at least obstructing *more* ideas or information.

"A question" becomes "no question" by the end of Stein's list, but probably more would be gained if that question developed into many questions.

In "an earned administration," words tend to have an "urned" servitude to meaning, and an urn is a much more oppressive type of carafe—opaque from within because of the blindness of the dead. In "an earned administration," words are dead, cremated, and locked in stasis. They become mere gofers in a bureaucracy. The etymological roots of both "earned" and "administration" mean "to serve," the first in Old English and the second in Italian. But if we try to free them from that servitude and look at their glorious pasts, their family relationships, and even their quirky associations in our own minds—their fringe—we see that "earned" is also related to harvesting, and the *ministrare* in "administration" is also in "minestrone." Stein—her mind never far from her belly—seems to offer a cornucopia of vegetative words to chew on. Instead of being served as the rich and varied fresh vegetables they could be, words have been overprocessed and made less nutritious. They have come to serve a bureaucracy instead of the individual speaker. Elsewhere, Stein writes: "A language tires. / A language tries to be. / A language tries to be free" (*Last Operas*, 153).

The words in the next phrase demonstrate the potential energy of words. They are given lives of their own—as we have lives of our own, entangled with others' lives—and not subordinated to our simplest needs. The rhymed couplet, as well as the perfect iambic tetrameter, marks "a single set of sisters and an outline and no blisters" as a "single set" itself, but it hardly wants to be crammed into my schemes for meaning. Maybe a protofeminist insight couched in feminine rhyme, "a single set of sisters" may be a strong enough group to escape the proposed "outline" of acceptable words or thoughts. Perhaps they color out of the lines or speak off their scripts and as a result are healthier and happier—not so tightly confined that they get blisters in the iambic march of feet. "A single set of sisters" may be both strongly united and multiply diverse.

Stein offers a critique of our (usually necessary) habits of thought, making us aware of our dependence on these habits by making it useless for us to lean on them blindly. Thus far, Stein's long sentence concerns itself with the predictability of everyday rhetoric, which allows people to get away with not thinking. Her lack of punctuation, and the fact that she takes words out of their common contexts (syntactically as well as semantically), means that a resourceful reader notices much more semantic ambiguity, a wider penumbra, than usual. The visual and auditory associations that Stein imbeds in her word streams provide another fringe of association. In addition to the multiple connotations and the sight and sound reminders, other associations work through the proximity of experience: Stein's words are in an order that allows one word to prime another for one denotation, and yet another nearby word primes us for another denotation (or detonation). On top of this, the pairing of two or more words in close proximity eventually allows one of those words to call up the other, such that Stein programs our associations and then calls up that programming—and hacks it before it becomes a routine—as we move through her work. Association is further complicated by the fact that if two things are associated, the words and things associated with them will also be associated with each other (James, *Principles*, 252). Stein makes us notice this fringe, and the fringe's fringe . . . and then we notice that it's all fringe. Accretive complexity forces us to recognize the arbitrary character of the single, simple meanings we may derive. Instead of just privileging the previously marginal, Stein makes us doubt the central itself, and the principle of centrality. By making it all fringe, Stein highlights a concern about our ignoring some things and taking others into account, especially when we do so unthinkingly. The actively engaged reader is not only made conscious of reading and thinking processes but also must make conscious decisions (or remain purposefully undecided) while reading. Words have potential energy, a potential individuality given additional meaning by their community (and vice versa), a potential complicating equivocation, and they offer resistance even when they are "used"—if the reader notices.

The rest of the sentence seems to be a conversation between two not completely opposing positions. Instead of emphasizing a binary distinction between "section[s]" and "centre[s]," or "questions" and certainties ("no doubts"), Stein's two sides waver between (a synonym for and etymological relative of "doubt"), and wave toward, each other. A resistance to binarisms also shows itself in the way Stein builds similarity between the usually very different meanings of "surface" and "centre." While the "surface" and the "centre" of a three-dimensional object are very different places, Stein's "surface" and "centre" refer to approximately the same concept. The "centre" is the mean value, an average that does not correspond to any of the real values it is supposed to represent, and the "surface" is a superficial summary that skips the details. The "single surface centred" puts a single but inaccurate representation in a primary position so that it looks conclusive and stops all further investigation, but it only pretends to represent the truth about something.

Following out some looser speculations, if we personify "section" ("And the section seeing yellow"), then "section" seems envious, perhaps of the "centre" about to be mentioned (yellow is also near the center of the continuous spectrum). "The section seeing yellow" sounds like "the sex (or sects) un-seeing, yell, 'Oh.'" This homophonical allusion to "sex" recalls the female "sisters," connecting that sex with sects or schismatic religious groups. Since rhetorical convention has already been established (always tentatively) as a religion, then this sect may have broken away—or may be trying to break away—from common rhetorical conventions. Perhaps this sect values speech over writing (because it is unseeing? or even unseen?) and speaks out (with a seemingly inarticulate "Oh!") instead. Perhaps the sects *shun* seeing, making the choice to hear and speak more deliberate.

In opposition to this set, this envious section, this yelling sex, is "the centre having spelling." The "centre" is written, spelt out instead of alluded to through sound play, which suggests the orthodoxy of orthography. If spelling had not been standardized, more potential meanings would always be present. This "centre" is also the generality that overcomes the importance of outlying sections (thus the jealousy or "seeing yellow"). It is the norm to which "sects" are (or a sex is) contrasted and away from which they break. "The centre" is also described by "and no solitude and no quaintness and yet solid quite so solid and the single surface centred and the question in the placard." "The centre" is not secluded (it has "no solitude"), and it is not agreeably peculiar (it has "no quaintness"). These descriptions sound like criticism of the center. But the reassuring voice seems to come back: "and yet solid, quite, so solid!" (my punctuation). The center has substance; it is forceful and hearty, sound and reliable, tangible and unanimous. On the other hand, "no solitude," since it holds a sound that approximates "no solid," works to undermine this reassurance. How solid can the center be if it is just the midpoint between everything else? It may be an average, but it has no singular substance of its own, just as there never has been an American family with 2.5 children.

The description of the "centre," which continues in "the single surface centred," is reminiscent of the reliable and serviceable surface earlier in the sentence, one that allowed us to understand quickly, without paying careful attention or taking time for much thought. If surfaces are cursory readings and centers are generalizations inferred from that type of reading, then the two words which seem to mean points on a sphere that are radially (half-diametrically) opposed become surprisingly alike. The promising, positive space Stein envisions is somewhere between the surface and the center.

Stein's reform of English is also a reform of science, since both depend on our mental tendencies to simplify, generalize, categorize—to delimit fields of inquiry and look for the core of any issue. Stein criticizes what science sometimes becomes, how thought is prone to becoming less thoughtful and more automatic. "The question in the placard" may refer to the political slogans of the time, which may question but which always do so from a stance of self-certainty. "The question in the placard" might be a nineteenth-century version (if there were one) of questions posted near exhibitions at museums or zoos: "How does the kangaroo rat feed its young?" One lifts up a flap, and the answer is immediately available underneath. There is always an answer. In one of his early lectures, Harvey Sacks explains that questions "arise out of something you're trying to deal with" instead of beginning as the type of things students see on exams. As I now blame the ill health of education on "teaching to the test," Sacks believes "it was the death of academic psychology that it grew up in a university. That implies that they did experiments for which it could be seen from the start how the result of those experiments would look as answers to quiz questions" (29). Along the same lines, a question in a placard already knows what the center of the issue is, while (what I will call) a living question has not yet discovered its center (nor, probably, has it discovered the surfaces that distinguish it from other questions or fields of inquiry). We might be better thinkers if we expected a question to lead to "more counting" and more questions instead of "a syllable in answer" or "a single scientific statement." Neil Postman reminds us that, in U.S. schools, science is taught with as much unexplained authority and required memorization as every other topic—a very unscientific way of teaching science (*Technopoly*, 192–93). While Sacks situates the blame in the words "academic" and "university," Stein uses the word "science" to highlight the failings of people who take (or ask others to take) scientific conclusions (or anything else) on faith. One can easily slip from valid scientific method to an antithetical authoritative position.

If all the words from "the section" to "the placard" are voiced by one speaker, that speaker is one who can doubt the value of a center but also reassure herself of its overall importance. It is also possible to break this passage down into a dialogue between speaker A and speaker B. Note that the bracketed commas are intended to be read two ways—as being there, and as not being there—and that this difference changes the meaning quite a bit.

> A: and the section seeing yellow and the centre . . .
> B: . . . having spelling and no solitude and no quaintness . . .
> A: And yet solid, quite, so solid, and the single surface centred and the question in the placard.
> B: And the singularity?
> A: Is there a singularity?

B: And the singularity?

A: Why[,] is there a question?

B: And the singularity?

A: Why[,] is the surface outrageous?

B: Why[,] is it beautiful?

A: Why[,] is it not when there is no doubt?

B: Why is anything vacant?

A: Why is not disturbing a centre no virtue? Why is it, when it is? And, why is it, when it is? And . . .

B: There is no doubt, there is no doubt that the singularity shows! (73; my punctuation)

Converting this monologue into dialogue may certainly seem arbitrary, but I suspect Stein wants to blur the exaggerated boundary between those modes of speech. Speaker A prefers the solidity of the center to the jealousy of the section, while B points to the drawbacks at the center, particularly the way an emphasis on the middle cannot take singularity, individuality, or specificity into account. The singularity may be a section of, or even an exception to, the centered surface of a thesis or generalization. Speaker A's response to B's question "And the singularity?" (i.e., How does your generality account for that?) is either "Why is there a question?" or the more breathless "Why[,] is there a question?" In other words, how can there be any question about the importance or validity of this center or, even, *is* there any question about its validity. But Speaker B is insistent and asks again, and again. Speaker A's response may be to change the direction of the conversation and go on the attack by asking why B thinks this surfacey center is so terrible ("Why is the surface outrageous?"). But the repeated question may finally throw A into doubt: "Why[,] *is* the surface outrageous?" or "Is this surfacey center really a gross offense that I just hadn't noticed before?" B's response, "Why[,] is it beautiful?" can be understood as similarly ambiguous: either B asks why A thinks a center is so beautiful, or B might be consenting to look at the issue from A's perspective and ask herself, "*Is* it beautiful?" A reader can continue to explore the differences between reading "why" as the beginning of a question and reading "why" as an interjection. "Why" as a question assumes the condition; "why" as an interjection doubts the condition. Stein's phrases, read in these different ways, express the ambiguity of each speaker's point of view rather than emphasizing the polarity of their positions.

This is madness—but I hope it shows the method by which Stein's carafe (like Keats's urn) "teases us out of thought." When B asks, "Why is anything vacant?" she may wonder why some things go unused, why some words are ignored because they are assumed to be empty of significance. Stein encourages paying attention to everything possible. While James would not advocate this kind of unfocused attention (see Ruddick, "William James," 52, 56), he *does* complain of the tendency of some scientists to consider certain data irrelevant (and so not to consider them at all) when developing a theory. In "The Hidden Self," James laments that the "ideal of every science" is "a closed and completed system of truth," because this leads scientists to ignore "phenomena unclassifiable within the system" and to consider them "paradoxical absurdities" which "must be held untrue" (90). James condemns "the extreme slowness with which the ordinary academic and critical mind acknowledges facts to exist which present themselves as *wild* facts with no stall or pigeon-hole" (91; his italics). While James refers to pigeonholes in scientific theory—his example is that there is no room for spiritual healing in contemporary ideas about psychotherapy—Stein carries this one step further: if we accept ready-made words and phrases, we may never develop the words to hold new ideas that might compose a more successful system. Ong writes that "perception of objects is in part conditioned by the store of words into which perceptions are nested. Nature states no 'facts': these come only within statements devised by human beings to refer to the seamless web of actuality around them" (68). Stein is working with an old language, but she thinks that new forms might allow new thoughts, or at least new relationships between old ones.

In the last part of the exchange, A asks, "Why is not disturbing a centre no virtue?" Here, A still wonders why disordering things isn't bad and seems to begin to convince himself (again?) that it *is* bad. At the end, B, the speaker more resistant to the center, uses the language of certainty that belongs, not rightfully but at least characteristically, to A. "There is no doubt," says the doubter, "there is no doubt that the singularity shows." Like Stein, B is a bully on behalf of open-mindedness—B's problem, like that of Rorty's "ironist theorist," is "how to overcome authority without claiming authority" (Rorty, *Contingency*, 105).[14] And thus B asserts that details, exceptions, will be seen, no matter how much resurfacing, synthesis, summary, or gathering into a center is done. Stein makes us notice, but after reading her we notice for ourselves, these unsilenced singularities (and perhaps we become one of them).

Here, then, conversation occurs between two strains of thought that are not direct opposites. Since they seem somewhat sympathetic to each other, the voices are willing to listen to one another and to collaborate on an idea. Stein does not just capture and summarize two polar positions.

The collaborative presentation of thought corresponds to the analytic way of thinking that Ong describes as occurring in primarily oral cultures, where people learn through listening, repeating, recombining, and "participating in a kind of corporate retrospection" (9). Stein writes with all of these methods. She highlights our binary process of thought, adding enough qualifiers and resistance to be thought-provoking and puzzling to our orderly thought processes, but she does not suggest that there is any radically other place from which to start thinking. These two voices, as suggested here and represented more clearly in her later work, are as close as Stein gets to an alternative: opposites who do not hold too strongly to their positions, who listen, who speak openly and try to work toward an idea together instead of trying to win. As Stein says later, "the winner loses," and as Deborah Tannen points out, an "argument culture" shouldn't be our ideal: "When a problem is posed in a way that polarizes, the solution is often obscured before the search is under way" (*Argument*, 21).[15] Or as Rorty advocates, redescription and communication should replace argument as a form of conversion (*Philosophy*, 62–64).

Where do I see the "centre" of the sentiment of Stein's intricate sentence? She seems to warn that people use language not originally but terminally, making it work in bureaucratic service. We therefore don't think originally but tend to believe what we are told and ignore the details we know. Centers have their uses and are beautiful in their ways, but no word or observation is vacant. Context and association are of great importance, but each word (or idea or person) is important enough to warrant scrutiny within that context. And finally, meaning can develop in the spaces between words or voices.

Our habits have led us to the state of affairs in which Stein finds us. They take us down the easy paths of preconceptions, prevent us from noticing the new or different, and keep us from using our minds' potential for complexity. James describes a condition of "*psychic* blindness" with which one can physically see, but one cannot quite notice, or assign meaning, to what is seen (*Principles*, 52; his italics). Stein points out her readers' psychic blindness as she simultaneously offers a reading experience that acts as a therapeutic cure. In the interest of undermining our habits, Stein produces a literature that makes her readers notice their psychic blindness—but they blame her for it, accuse her of making *no* sense when she will not make the *usual* sense. Our habits have become so ingrained, our main neural pathways so nearly mechanized by "normal" language, that we find ourselves (I hope only at first) at a loss when reading Stein. But then we notice that any word has a fringe or suffusion of associations, and that we can choose among them instead of depending on habit to get us to meaning. According to James, we become more conscious: "New conceptions come from new sensations, new movements, new emotions, new associations, new acts of attention, and new comparisons of old conceptions, and not in other ways" (442). Consciousness is a goal in itself, and probably one of Stein's early ones, but later she seems to worry that this mental or psychic blindness might keep us from seeing and knowing new things. As she says, the world stays largely the same, but our composition of it—the ways we see it—changes. If these ways of seeing become too rigid and unchanging, we cannot progress. We can only repress.

CHAPTER 3

Conversational Relations in
Geography and Plays

Recognizing the Real in a Collage of Words and Phrases

P RAGMATISM MAY HAVE provoked Stein's interest in the content of the supposedly empty in-between, not the borderland so much as the fenestra or fontanel—something related to hearing or mind, apparently closed off, but still open for the entrance of meaning. David Kadlec points out that William James advocated in *The Principles of Psychology* that "empiricists should account for not only terms but also the relations . . . [and] that grammar itself had served to empty experience of the conjunctions that marked the points of transition between the 'larger objects of our thought.'" In other words, the rules of grammar allowed "particle words, or syntactic markers," power *only* within a sentence. These small words can make "hierarchies of the clauses within sentences, [and form] pyramids of meaning and value out of the phrases and words held therein," but they have been emptied of meaning in relation to the outside world. James, however, "appealed to the expressive value of syntactic markers, or connecting words," writing that we have "a feeling of *and*, a feeling of *if*, a feeling of *but*, and a feeling of *by*" (Kadlec, 30).[1] Kadlec goes on to show the way Stein's *Tender Buttons* is "an anti-imperialist's assault on the distinction between expressive and functional parts of speech" (30–31), and he also suggests that Stein's "aesthetics" is founded in her "understandings of the conceptual affinities between cubism (and also the collage arts that eventually sprang from Picasso's and Braque's cubist portraits) and pragmatism and Darwin's writings" (252n55). In sympathy with this reading, I believe that Stein started seeing the meaning in the spaces between one speaker's phrases and another's. She heard the interpersonal meanings, as well as the logistical ones, between subsequent phrases, such as these from *Mexico* (*Geography and Plays*, 321):

A great many people were blamed.
A great many people were blamed.
Robert Nestor. I have heard of him.
Of course you have.
Be careful.
Be very careful.
There is no danger.
There is no danger.
Not to me.
Not for me.

Or these from *Counting Her Dresses* (*Geography and Plays*, 279):

Act I
Can you spell quickly.
Act II
I can spell very quickly.
Act III
So can my sister-in-law.
Act IV.
Can she.

Readers of *Mexico* are induced to wonder what Robert Nestor has to
do with people getting blamed, if the speaker is to be careful because of
some kind of censorship or threat, if repetition means agreement or mockery (or something else), and if "to" is so different from "for." Readers of
Counting Her Dresses might ponder the relationship between the speakers,
when the second seems naively to brag about her spelling skills and then
may be somewhat arch about the first speaker's sister-in-law's similar ability.
In neither case, however, and in spite of the simple—even common—words
and phrases, do we know exactly what's happening.

Stein's plays represent people's verbal actions, their conversation, and she
calls attention to the organic structures of human interaction by giving us
nothing else which would distract us, such as the basic elements of plot and
character. Taken out of their restrictive contexts, the utterances with which
Stein fills her plays are freely valenced. While in a real conversation they
would be tied down, here in Stein's texts they float free. The reader's mind is
forced to associate, to guess, to hazard, and to hesitate, all the time noticing
the many ambiguities of common statements. Stein includes phrases we've
constantly met, but to which we rarely give even a full second's thought.

This more intimate meeting encourages us to realize just how complicated we all are, and just how much we let context and expectation (and other norms) limit our ideas and influence our behavior. Collage takes pieces of the world and cuts, shapes, and recontextualizes them for greater analysis—a new view, a longer look, a serious critique, a surprise, a laugh—and that is what Stein does in her plays with pieces of conversation.

For my purposes—and, I think, generally—conversation is the back-and-forth exchange of utterances, usually by different people taking turns talking and listening (but including the interaction of differently motivated voices within a single person). These utterances are not just words and sentences, and they are not just messy imitations of written structures; utterances are actions. Expressed another way, conversation is an activity, not just a word game. Conversation enables the exchange of information, ideas, and feelings through interactive performances, which involves the exchange of words in inflected utterances, body language, and the minutely contextual interpretation of those specific utterances. This transaction between (or among) psychological entities is refereed by rules that offer boundaries to steer through peaceably or with which to collide conspicuously. In other words, conversation can be the soul's expression, but that intimacy is almost always regulated by rules; even when expressing our deepest feelings, we are usually still locked inside the strict but almost unnoticeable confines of conversational rules. These rules, as well as inflectional choices and some improvisational problem solving along the way, enable us to send and receive messages, because we not only interpret what others say to us; we also evaluate their words in relation to what they could have or should have said.[2]

Stein seems to see her art as more real than the real, to believe that her plays—such as the first one, *What Happened*—can show *what really happens*. Daniel-Henry Kahnweiler describes Stein's work as cubist, since she and the cubists worked with "the most stripped forms" and the "commonplace" in their "reaction against affectation." He suggests that "it is important to understand that in Gertrude's work as in that of the Cubists we are dealing, in spite of appearances, with a realistic art, an art full of naturalness, of simplicity" (xii–xiii). In spite of what his biographer argues, Picasso and Stein probably both "rejected abstractionism and liked to think that [their] work was if anything more, certainly not less, real than the real thing" (Richardson, 406). When Stein arrived in New York after thirty-one years abroad, she told reporters, "I am essentially a realist" ("Fancy Writing"). Perhaps, then, Stein's writing is alien to us only because our sense of reality has become so conventionalized.

Gertrude Stein and Alice B. Toklas probably left more than one calling card at Picasso's door, and in his 1914 collage *Still Life with Calling Card*, Picasso included one of these visiting cards from "Miss Stein" and "Miss Toklas." In turn, Picasso left this artwork as a *carte de visite* at 27 rue de Fleurus.[3] Picasso's *Calling Card*, however, is an apt symbol for the ways Stein's work does and does not correspond to the cubist enterprise. Many of the pieces Stein situates in her writing seem to have been plucked from conversations that would have occurred during the polite visits for which these calling cards were substitutes. While both Stein and Picasso produced collages, language and objects are quite different things. This very fact has been cited to Stein's detriment: an early review of *Tender Buttons* compares Stein's writing to Picasso's "compositions produced by combinations of actual materials . . . nailed and glued together to form patterns" but asserts that Stein's attempts in this vein must fail, since words are "in themselves symbols" (R. Rogers, 19–20). In short, Stein's project seems to fail because one can't exactly do cubism with words. Stein, however, is not treating words as objects. Instead she works with pieces of conversation, phrases such as "how do you do," and she offers a creative analysis of the mysterious ways conversations can work. One can make collages of words and phrases, as well as of objects, and the found objects in Stein's plays are pieces of conversation.

While conversation in Stein's writing has been noted early and often (sometimes as an indication of Stein's laziness as a stylist), it has not been meaningfully explored. In 1923, Edith Sitwell reviewed *Geography and Plays* and wrote that the book had "an irritating ceaseless rattle like that of American sightseers talking in a boarding-house (this being, I imagine, a deliberate effect)" (26). Sitwell and others have not sufficiently wondered why Stein would deliberately produce this effect. Edmund Wilson describes "Have they Attacked Mary He Giggled," published in *Vanity Fair* in June 1917, as "a sort of splintered stenographic commentary made up of scraps of conversation as they reverberate in the mind and awaken unspoken responses" (61). Wilson and others did not audibly wonder why these responses are so automatically "awakened" in us—why certain bits of language lead automatically to certain other bits. Interactional spoken language, in particular, is predictable because of its informal but stubborn rules. If it weren't, listeners would not be so quick to know what someone should have said. James R. Mellow asserts that Stein and the poet Guillaume Apollinaire each "had a highly developed aural sense of language." They both "creat[ed] poems—collage-like—out of snippets of conversation overheard in a bistro on the rue Christine," and, in many of their poems, "the structure of the lines was carried by repetitions, percussive phrases, natural pauses, the sense of sound" (124). Alison Rieke observes that Stein's

> writing [has] the appearance of being more assembled than written, and assembled out of close deliberation over particular words. . . .
>
> Stein was always an arranger of words, concerned about their junctures, the stoppings and startings of phrases, the role of the artist in piecing these pieces to give them places. (63)

But why does she do this?

Stein's writing expresses the deep structures of conversation, the processes and motivations and emotions behind it. The trivial statements of which conversation is so often formed appear in her work, but with a different purpose than they do in Ionesco's later plays, which seem to emphasize the trivialities and to critique the empty clichés that fill human minds in the middle of the twentieth century. Instead of bringing cynicism to her tea table, Stein sought out the powerful purposes and organizing principles hidden within the give-and-take of polite stock phrases. And to continue her task of making her readers attend to the associational relationships among individual words we've always taken for granted—making us know *about* instead of just know *of* those words, to use William James's distinction—Stein highlights the complex thoughts expressed within, and the complex relationships developed by, simple conversational phrases. Stein's collages of spoken phrases create an educational game for her readers that teaches us about the way we talk, the way we speak effortlessly every day.

Discussing Stein's plays in relation to conventional theater, Jane Palatini Bowers asserts that the dialogue in Stein's drama expresses well the differences between real dialogue and what we think of as real dialogue because we are used to hearing it on the stage. (Similarly, Pynchon's Mucho Maas introduces Oedipa Maas as Edna Mosh because of "the distortion on these [radio station] rigs, and then when they put it on tape" [114]). In her wonderful introduction to Stein's work, Bowers reminds us that

> plays are not natural but fictive utterances. Dramatic dialogue is . . . not a natural phenomenon but an artificial one. However, the pretense of naturalness is at the heart of dramatic mimesis; Stein's conversation plays at once engage in and expose this pretense. They sound much like real conversations and not at all like conventional dramatic dialogue, thereby revealing the ways in which dramatic dialogue is not like ordinary discourse. (111–12)

Bowers, though, does not end up arguing that Stein's "conversation plays" mimic real conversation better than does conventional drama. Bowers decides that the words in Stein's plays "are not windows onto a non-linguistic world. They are themselves the world—a world of conversations without stories" (112)—and this is not how we usually talk.[4] Bowers reasonably concludes from this analysis that Stein's plays are "closed systems of discourse" (115), that they "subvert the conventional form of dramatic dialogue," and that "when conversation is about language and language-making activities, language becomes an object of interest in its own right and is, itself, the object of discourse" (117). By representing "conversations without stories," Stein creates an alternative realism, but I think it is not so much an alternative purely linguistic reality as much as a written form that exposes unperceived aspects of real chat.

Stein is multiply oral. She demonstrates a particular interest in the complex patterns found in friendly conversation over food: the motivating forces behind the things people say in those settings, the ways our utterances can mean more than what we meant (and how we might creatively build on this knowledge), and the ways politeness can contain and yet express conflict. Along the way, Stein discovers long-overlooked structures of spoken language, which conversation analysis began to theorize several decades after Stein's death. At the end of this chapter, my reading of "Susie Asado" links this well-known piece from *Geography and Plays* with the functions of conversation as a means toward apparent cooperation—as a way of seeing eye-to-eye or dancing to the same drummer, to return to the issues of sight and sound—if not substantial agreement.

Food and Talk

Although I respect and tend to concur with Bowers's analysis of *Can You See the Name*, I think it is worth noting that this short play—which Bowers calls "typical in all other ways of the longer conversation plays" (113)—diverges from the typical early Stein play in at least one way: there is no mention of food (or dishes or a table) in it.[5] Of the sixteen brief plays published in *Geography and Plays*, only one of them, *I Like It to Be a Play*, does not contain any of the ingredients for a social gathering founded on food and talk (although it does contain the line "The rest of the day was spent in visiting" [288]). Stein's plays contain a "desert spoon," "turkey," "cut[s]," and "slice[s]" (*What Happened*); "meats," "mints," "candles," a "table," and "cloth" (*Not Sightly*); "cauliflower and green peas" (*Please Do Not Suffer*); and "table . . . linen," "excellent eating," and "coffee" (*Mexico*)—to list just a few examples. In *He Said It*, "sugared prunes" and "pressed figs" lead toward a "fruitful evening." Two of her titles refer to food: *White Wines* and *Turkey Bones and Eating and We Liked It*. (And remember: the central section of *Tender Buttons* is called "Food" and is stuffed with savory dishes.) Sometimes, Stein writes formally complete sentences to describe food: "This is the last time we will use seasoning" (*For the Country Entirely*, 237), and "We eat our breakfast and smoke a cigar" (*Bonne Annee*).[6] If these plays are partly representative of real or at least realistic conversation, Toklas must be reporting accurately when she writes: "Conversation even in a literary or political *salon* can turn to the subject of menus, food or wine" (*Cookbook*, 3).[7]

Stein's words reassemble (and encourage readers to revise their thinking about) one of life's most common recreations: the chat. Without any stage directions, Stein's plays manage to suggest noisy settings, such as afternoon tea on the veranda with a polite group of visitors (as in "Susie Asado") or sitting at a cafe (at the end of *Do Let Us Go Away*). Although in *Do Let Us Go Away* (215), Stein writes (or has Theodore say), "My principle [*sic?*] idea is to eat my meals in peace," Stein's meals—and snacks—seem to be accompanied by talk. Bowers finds that these plays "suggest that there is no non-linguistic world, that the only 'event' taking place in the world of the play is speech" (110), but it seems to me that somewhere nearby people are eating.

I suspect that Stein is interested in interactional conversation. The basic difference between transactional and interactional conversation is that the first is for business and the second for pleasure. Transactional conversations take place between people of fixed status working to accomplish a goal within the framework of their institutionally established roles. People participating in a transactional conversation must obediently and consistently perform their fixed roles throughout the conversation. The latitude in an interactional conversation is much greater, because the relationship is personally instead of institutionally defined. The goal of the interaction is itself to define the relationship, which means there is much more experimentation with levels of intimacy and ratios of power (see Cheepen, 118–21).

Not completely unlike literature, interactional conversations occur in nonfocused situations. Before the wide use of technological means to "reach out and touch someone," extensive interactional conversation would have taken place most often over food. Interactional conversation is the kind late nineteenth-century sociologist Gabriel Tarde describes: "By conversation I mean any dialogue without direct and immediate utility, in which one talks primarily to talk, for pleasure, as a game, out of politeness" ("Opinion," 308). Bronislaw Malinowski—whose term for this kind of conversation, "phatic communion," has taken on such different connotations that it is useless here—described interactional conversation as "'the language used in free, aimless social intercourse' which occurs when people are relaxing, or when they are accompanying 'some mere manual work by gossip quite unconnected with what they are doing'" (qtd. in Cheepen, 16).[8] While transactional conversations occur in focused situations "in which 'there are strong limitations on negotiations between participants,'" interactional conversations occur in nonfocused situations in which "'the highest value is on mutual sense making among the participants'" (Tannen, "Oral/Literate," 3).[9]

Stein probably hated transactional conversations. She did not easily assume a predetermined status or role. At Johns Hopkins, Stein disapproved of the condescending teaching styles and sexism of two medical school professors, communicated her dissatisfaction to them, was told to attend their classes or withdraw from them, and withdrew (Wagner-Martin, 48–49). Her break with her brother Leo seems to have been the result of his increasingly persistent assumption of his own superior status as a speaker (and her implied inferior status as a silently agreeing listener).[10] Even more to the point, when Stein drove a medical supply car during World War I, "she was officially the driver" and Toklas "was officially the delegate," because Stein "flatly refused to go inside of any office and interview any official" (*Autobiography*, 177). Furthermore, "Mademoiselle Stein has no patience she will not go into offices and wait and interview people and explain," and "Gertrude Stein hates to answer questions from officials" (178, 233). In her cookbook, Alice later commented that "Gertrude Stein did not like going into offices—she said they, army or civilian, were obnoxious" (60). As a grown woman, Stein did not let age or gender tell her how to behave and thought of herself as both a baby and a husband.[11] And during World War II, she did not let her nationality, her ethnicity, or her sexuality determine her behavior: instead of fleeing to the United States to get away from likely persecution as a Jew and a lesbian, she remained, staunch but vulnerable, in rural Vichy France.[12]

But Stein did love to talk and listen, and interactional conversation seems to have been her chosen forum. She seems to have been well appreciated by friends throughout her life, friends who liked to sit and sew and talk, who liked to wander the roads around Harvard at night and talk, who liked to ride on streetcars and talk, who liked to eat and talk (Wagner-Martin, 31, 46, 106). Reportedly, she enjoyed conversation more than needlework, she usually wasn't headed any particular place when she walked, and she liked to strike up conversations with strangers. From behind the wheel of her car, which she called Auntie Pauline, Stein started conversations with pedestrians throughout Paris (Wagner-Martin, 148). Toklas reports that one of their cooks' stipulations was access to their reading library and conversation with Stein—a request Toklas attributes to the woman's immediately noticing "Gertrude Stein's easy democratic approachableness" (*Cookbook*, 194). According to Wagner-Martin: "For those who found warmth in the rue de Fleurus afternoons, admiring Stein's ability to lead and respond to conversation, any description of those interchanges pales beside memories of immense energy, golden language, and unfeigned sympathy" (161).

Talk is the common thread (as indeed it wanders through each of our lives), but not everyone has written, as Stein did: "Generally speaking anybody is more interesting doing nothing than doing something" (*Everybody's*, 109). Stein did not approve of people bustling around just trying to fill time, but "generally speaking" may also be understood as "generally *when* speaking."[13] Perhaps people are more interesting when they are just chatting ("doing nothing") than when they are trying to accomplish some important transfer of information ("doing something"). In a lecture, Stein said: "There was more sense of movement to us in Paris when a few doughboys loafed about the streets. They impressed the French as something vital, active; you felt the essence of what was happening. But when they were doing anything, you forgot the essence" (Evans).[14] Conversations dictated by institutional roles and rules—"conversations as prearranged"—are less interesting to Stein than conversations that evolve naturally and immediately while loafing—"conversations as arranged" (Stein, *Novel of Thank You*, 10). As Stein's labels suggest, and as her writings demonstrate, even these spontaneous conversations have a kind of order.

The Motivations behind *What Happened*

In her lecture "Plays," Stein explains that *What Happened* was the first play she ever wrote. She describes the situation of its creation and her intentions:

> I had just come home from a pleasant dinner party and I realized then as anybody can know that something is always happening.
>
> Something is always happening, anybody knows a quantity of stories of people's lives that are always happening, there are always plenty for the newspapers and there are always plenty in private life. Everybody knows so many stories and what is the use of telling another story. What is the use of telling a story since there are so many and everybody knows so many and tells so many. In the country it is perfectly extraordinary

how many complicated dramas go on all the time. And everybody knows them, so why tell another one. There is always a story going on.

So naturally *what I wanted to do in my play was what everybody did not always know nor always tell*. By everybody I do of course include myself by always I do of course include myself.

And so I wrote, What Happened, A Play.

Then I wrote Ladies Voices and then I wrote a Curtain Raiser. I did this last because *I wanted still more to tell what could be told if one did not tell anything*. . . .

I came to think that since each one is that one and that there are a number of them each one being that one, the only way to express this thing each one being that one and there being a number of them knowing each other was in a play. And so I began to write these plays. And the idea in What Happened, A Play was to express this without telling what happened, in short to make a play *the essence of what happened*. I tried to do this with the first series of plays that I wrote. (*Lectures*, 118–20; my italics)

Stein came home from a dinner party—a social gathering over food—and was struck by the fact that all during dinner everyone was able to talk about all sorts of things that had happened. Never one to attempt what she knows has already been done, or even what she knows can be done—"if it can be done why do it" (*Lectures*, 157)—Stein decides not to tell the kind of stories that people know. Nevertheless, she still intends to tell "what happened," and perhaps at this dinner party she noticed that one of the things happening was that people were expressing themselves ("each one being that one") through the rhythms of their speech and creating relationships ("there being a number of them knowing each other") out of their utterances. One of the answers to her repeated question "what is the use of telling another story" might be that stories are the building blocks of social relationships. This self-presentation and casual confederation is something that happens all the time, and yet it goes largely unnoticed, probably because it seems so natural and effortless. In relation to her artistic project, at least, Stein is less interested in the stories people tell than in the deeper social and linguistic structures in which that storytelling takes place.[15]

When Stein says that she wants to "make a play the essence of what happened," she is not only talking about the deep structures of what happens within a conversation about something else, she is also emphasizing action. Although "essence" might suggest the inherent nature of something's being, "what happens" suggests activity. In French, *essence* means "fuel" or "gasoline," which may be significant in light of a metaphor Stein repeatedly employs: "As I say a motor goes inside and the car goes on, but my business my ultimate business as an artist was not with where the car goes as it goes but with the movement inside that is of the essence of its going" (*Lectures*, 194–95). I take "inside" to refer to the pistons and belts, but Stein's exploration of "the essence of what happened" looks even farther under the hood. It studies the fuel, the *essence*, which we never see move, but which is constantly undergoing a change (we *burn* gasoline, after all) and enables the car's motion. If the motor's movement is the wording that expresses relation and narrative, then the fuel may be the very structure of language and the motivations and mindsets of speakers. The best definition of the whole phrase, I think, is DeKoven's understanding that it means "an abstract rendering of an event," because "event" is a noun, but one that is not in stasis (*Different Language*, 85).

On the other hand, "essence" is derived from "to be," which—in spite of all my arguments otherwise—suggests that Stein wants to represent the existence, even the permanent nature, of something rather than its activity. Ryan (68) supports this possibility (although she actually believes something else about the phrase) when she says that "Gertrude Stein found that life was indeed a quality and not an action" and contrasts Stein's idea with Aristotle's assertion that "life consists in action." Kenneth Burke takes this same position: "The essence of a thing would not be revealed in something that it does. It would be something that a thing is" ("Impartial Essence," 187).

In spite of these opinions, I keep hearing "what happens" as action, which reflects back on "essence" and changes it into something more dynamic than an inherent truth about something. Ryan believes that Stein's plays "present the essence, and only the essence, of the moment" (69). I agree, in that I think that Stein's kind of essence—in contrast to the typical kind, of course—is fleeting, changing, in flux. Think of the way attitudes and goals tend to shift during the course of an informal conversation, especially with new acquaintances, of whom you are getting a new sense with each phrase they speak. You want to be congenial, you want to impress them, you want to agree with them, you are surprised by them, you want to know more about them, you are disappointed in them, you want to mollify them, you want to disagree with them, you want to convince them to change, you decide it's not worth it, you want to keep your mouth shut, you want to get out of there, and so on. In short, Stein seems to muddy another binary choice between "essences" and the "flux of continually changing relations" (Rorty's phrase in *Philosophy*, 47). She uses the first word to describe the other, since she seems to see the "flux of continually changing relations" as the very essence of what happens, and she represents this essential flux in her artistic investigation of conversation.

What Can Happen When People Talk and Read

What Happened, probably written in 1913, around the same time as *Tender Buttons*, is similar to *Tender Buttons* in style, but its subtitle is *A Five Act Play*. In her lectures, Stein asserts that an exciting scene (in a play and in real life) is one in which the characters with whom you have become acquainted (throughout the play or over a lifetime) say things that surprise you, things you would not have expected them to say. She writes: "Generally speaking it is the contradiction between the way you know the people you know including yourself act and the way they are acting or feeling or talking that makes of any scene that is an exciting scene an exciting scene" (*Lectures*, 106). Stein meets this requirement and doesn't. Her characters are strangers. It is not clear even whether each is a single person who has a number for a name or whether each "speaker" is a chorus of the designated number of people. The chorus seems likely, because in act 3, "Three" and "The same three" speak; act 4 is spoken by "Four and four more." Another possibility is that these numbers refer to how many people are on stage and taking turns speaking. But even though these characters are strangers about whom we know nothing, we discover that we hold some expectations for them, because we are likely to be very surprised when we read what they say.[16] In this way, Stein demonstrates that most of the expectations we have about what a person might say at any given time depend not only on insight we might have into the speaker's individual character but also on very generally understood contexts.

For example, "Act I" of *What Happened: A Play in Five Acts* begins:

(One.)
Loud and no cataract. Not any nuisance is depressing.
   (*Geography and Plays*, 205)

The reader probably does not expect anyone, let alone someone called One, to declare—perhaps self-reflexively?—"Loud and no cataract. Not any nuisance is depressing." Here, again, is a crossover between sound and sight: a "cataract" can be a loud waterfall or opaqueness in the eye. "Loud and no cataract" could mean that water is loud, but that it is not a large, single cataract of rushing water falling in one direction. Perhaps instead of cohering into singularity or agreement with others, One's opinion divides into different channels of meaning—interesting also because someone called One might be expected to have a single opinion or a unified sense of self.[17] The phrase might not only describe bodies of water as a metaphor for speech, knowledge, and group identity; it could also be a command to hear and see—to pay attention to these different senses—without the cataract of partial blindness or the blinding assumption that meaning flows together in a single, rushing stream. Stein herself seems to have avoided speaking in one voice; remembering their first meeting, Toklas recalled Stein's voice as "unlike anyone else's voice—deep, full, velvety like a great contralto's, like two voices" (Toklas, *What Is Remembered*, 23). Elsewhere in *Geography and Plays*, Stein writes: "Loud voices are attractive. When two people talk together they have to talk louder" (*Turkey Bones and Eating*, 246), and I read this as approximately synonymous with "loud and no cataract." Stein likes loud assertion but not a single unified channel of communication. In yet another play in the same volume, she announces: "There is no blindness where the talk is cheap" (*Scenes. Actions and Disposition of Relations and Positions*, 114). Turning something usually thought of as negative into something positive, Stein (in my favorite of her aphorisms) approves pure talk, talk without consequences and commitments, because it allows a freedom to dilate—to see more widely. Let me repeat: "There is no blindness where the talk is cheap."

At first, "not any nuisance is depressing" sounds wrong. We all know some nuisances can be depressing as well as annoying. But "not any new sense (or new scents) is depressing" sounds like further encouragement to hear and see (and even smell). We are being encouraged to use our senses to gain new meanings, or new senses. "Not any *new sense* is depressing" may mean that new senses are never depressing, but it also implies that just having and knowing old senses *is* depressing. Stein's differentiation between knowing and understanding, her valuation of knowing over understanding, and the link she saw between understanding and following mean that it makes sense to hear "knew sense" here also—that these new senses would lead us to knowledge. People who want us only to understand and follow, however, might esteem cataracts that can pull people along with them.[18]

The second "character" to speak is Five—which could be another silly name for a single speaker or may make a reader think of the five senses. Five might also include One, since four people could walk onto the stage after One's initial lines, and since the numbers "four," "five," and "one" all appear in Five's first spoken line. Five responds with paragraphs of new senses and dialogue about meaning:

(Five.)
A single sum four and five together and one, not any sun a clear signal and an exchange. (*What Happened*, in *Geography and Plays*, 205)

That this is a play, suggesting that One and Five are probably talking to each other, already somewhat limits the context of Five's statements. The "single sum" might refer to the single focused sense or meaning that we understand from most sentences, the cataract of which One spoke. We usually add four or five meanings (of words, or larger semantic units) together and get one meaning. Rather than a "sun" with rays shooting out in all directions—a word with many divergent implications, a sound prior to cognition—we pretend that we send and receive "a clear signal" and have a coherent "exchange." The limitations that we automatically put on our understanding bury potential meaning. This destruction of meaning is comparable (whether Stein would have known so or not) to burning books at Fahrenheit "four and five together and one." On the other hand, Stein's suggestion that we understand words in new ways both destroys and revitalizes the books themselves.

Stein's writing will not let us avoid the metaphysics of presence; she insists that we remember that the moment or the line of writing always contains more than we can say about it. Unlike a deconstructionist, Stein refuses to see multiple meanings as merely each other's cancellation. The likelihood that Stein is advocating a messy, compositely meaningful kind of reading and listening, and highlighting some of the tendencies and drawbacks to restricted interpretations of linear texts, can be further clarified by ideas from Alan Kennedy's *Psychology of Reading*. Kennedy asserts that visual and auditory perceptions are categorical, that we see something one way or the other but not both at the same time (34). Kennedy writes that "a large number of different patterns of stimulus information (the input) serve to evoke a single conceptual decision (the output)," and that it is in "instances where the perceptual decisions taken prove to be wrong . . . [that we] catch a glimpse of the system in action" (35, 40). In the process of normal reading, we channel dozens or hundreds or thousands of signs that point in multiple directions into a single cataract of meaning, according to Kennedy:

When we read a single word its many potential meanings become available as a conscious experience. But when we read a series of words we are scarcely aware of these individual elements at all. . . . For the fluent

reader the particular words, and their particular order, that produce this train of thought can be rapidly dismissed. (86)

There is no doubt that Stein upsets our reading fluency. Kennedy continues: "Only that sense of a word that can be adapted to the train of thought in progress will survive" (89). In the case of *What Happened*, Stein states the context is "a play." By doing so, she creates a very broad context but one still not broad enough to hold the words she writes underneath that subtitle. This single clue to reading her words only makes it more difficult to contextualize what she writes. Stein thus lets the various meanings of her words "endure"; they "survive," and we have to "become conscious" of them as multiply meaningful entities instead of one-dimensional pointers to something else. This terminology does not apply just to the words; it applies to us. The multiplicity disallows uniform reactions in Stein's readers; we are prevented from becoming reading machines and are thus kept alive and conscious.

Stein's knowledge of neurology again proves relevant. In the same textbook that refers to her research on the "centripetal" or "sensory neurons" which bring information into the brain, Barker describes these neurons in the following way:

> A single neurone of one system is often, by virtue of a number of end-ramifications, able to enter into conduction relations with a number of neurones in a neurone system of the next higher order . . . ; in other instances, on the contrary, the terminals of a large number of axones of one neurone system may be so arranged that they can influence only a smaller number of neurones of a neurone system of the next order. . . . In the one case there is a "multiplication of elements" in the direction of the conducting path, in the other a "reduction of elements." (*Nervous System*, 320)

Context usually deletes all but one of the possible signals a word can send to us. But Stein's words keep their many possible signals, mutiplying instead of reducing the "end-ramifications" of her words. Stein's writing shuffles the brain's mailing lists.

Looking at the letters, as well as at the words, hearing the whole string of words together—an amalgamation encouraged by the words "a single sum"—reveals the damage that results from our tendency to "use" and understand words in too limited a way. A fluent reader moves directly from the written word to its relevant meaning, but a less fluent reader goes from the written form to the sounds of the letters and then to meaning. Children sound out words when they read; many adults do not even hear the words in their mind's ear. By encouraging our sounding out of her words and phrases, Stein works to make us less fluent readers—and less likely to expect flowing cataracts of meaning.

Attending carefully to Five's words, then, one might also see and hear (hyperattentively): "A sin gal sum four and five to get her and won not any son a clear signal and an exchange." This sentence seems to describe some kind of rape or purchased sin: a prostitute or "sin gal" is bought, won, or otherwise gotten by "four and five together" and purposefully produces no son. Choosing to read allegorically (which can be another means toward numerous meanings), we may glean that the prostitution of language, its *use*, keeps it from living, or giving life to offspring meanings.[19] The goal of Stein's writing is not to use a set of words to mean conclusively one thing or the other; complexity arises in the reader's getting shunted away from one meaning after another, and—according to Booth—this grasping is what gives the most pleasure. But in most writing, words become just clear(-ish) signals which are exchanged like money.[20] Since "single" and "signal" are so much alike, it is natural to switch their places in the sentence, resulting in "a signal sum" and "a clear single," which both reiterate the power of a clear sum's signaling a single meaning. "An exchange" also sounds like "annex change"—perhaps encouraging us to exchange our single signals by adding (annexing) a change (leading to "some four and five" rather than "a single sum"). As easily as "single" and "signal" can be transposed, so can "some" and "sum." "Some four and five together" becomes "sum four and five together," which reminds us of the addition of pluralities (the expression "4 + 5") required for unity (the sum). A "single some" also combines unity with multiplicity. Stein's subtly repeated theme suggests that many are still many, even when they add up to something, a sum. Moving from letters and words to whole conversations, this theme suggests that many voices can combine into one community, and that the community may indeed be stronger if those voices are individual and multiple rather than repeating echoes of one voice.

Five goes on to argue for growing, thriving, multiplying words:

Silence is in blessing and chasing and coincidences being ripe. A simple melancholy clearly precious and on the surface and surrounded and mixed strangely. A vegetable window and clearly most clearly an

exchange in parts and complete. (*What Happened*, in *Geography and Plays*, 205)

Stein's poem is a "vegetable window," which sounds like "veritable window" or "venerable window" and acts like both, allowing readers to watch words growing from their roots to their fruits. One reason Stein's words seem particularly vegetative is that her arrangements of words prime us for fringe meanings and associations; they sprout like potatoes, like neurons. These ripe words help us notice and appreciate the beauty of the whole plant, but Stein doesn't encourage us to pick them and eat them. We cannot glean only a single message from her text and then discard it or consider it digested. If a writer is tending a garden of words, a reader should be reaping instead of hunting.[21]

The tiger in the next paragraph of *What Happened* hunts very differently, although it would not be the first time that hunting and overaggressive courtship were linked. Stein cites this paragraph in her lecture "Plays" as an example of expressing "the essence of what happened" "without telling what happened" (*Lectures*, 119):

A tiger a rapt and surrounded overcoat securely arranged with spots old enough to be thought useful and witty quite witty in a secret and in a blinding flurry. (205)

This cutting collection of words is filled with sharpnesses—tigers, spotted leopards, raptors, and wit—and suggests an image of a sharp-witted person surrounded by listeners. Perhaps a quick, quiet, sharp woman in a fur coat is "surrounded" by a "rapt" audience. Perhaps men "sir round" her, and think of something akin to rape. Although men circle her, she has somehow "arranged" to range (among them? away from them?) safely. She is seen (showing herself off with her furs and her wit) in order not to be seen (in secret liaisons?); she wears a kind of showy camouflage. Perhaps she has age spots ("spots old") and a fur coat: she could be wrapped ("rapt") in the skin of a "tiger," or, more likely, she is the tiger or raptor wearing a (leopard?) spotted "overcoat." If she were an animal, her skins would camouflage her; since she is an old woman, her aging skin and quick wit protect her from certain kinds of suspicions. She is "securely arranged," and dangerous in a "secret" way.[22]

The lives of the words themselves are endangered, but they act as their own camouflage, threatening this surrounded person (with rape), as well as representing something about her (she's wrapped, and perhaps "ripe") and protecting her (by keeping her audience, or her possible attackers, "rapt"). Wit is the essence of her personal self, as well as the weapon and shield which protect that self. Stein suggests that a good wielder of words can purposefully create blinds with them. In this instance, the words are not just the vegetables or the hunted, but also the hunters. The power of words to protect themselves and the speakers who are conscious of those multiple meanings is in the camouflage afforded by double (or more multiple) meanings.

This tiger paragraph is unusual in its story of what happened, because it can be read in an almost standard way and seems to describe people in a particular configuration communicating in certain ways with one another and continuing their established relationships. While the narrative is entertaining, and a bit of a relief to come across when reading Stein's usually much more opaque paragraphs, its vividness may mislead us into stopping there. But if we go on looking at and listening, we see that Stein writes about words by analogy when she is writing about tiger women.[23]

This same paragraph links to previous ones through the repetition of the word "surrounded" and the reiteration, through synonyms, of a few concepts. "Rapt" seems to follow from "chasing"; "arranged" is related to "mixed strangely" and may have to do with "parts" and "complete"; "old enough" might be related to "ripe" old age; "blinding" is related to "cataracts"; and the other kind of "cataracts," in their watery, noisy sense, relates to "flurry." The blinding fury in "blinding flurry" is another emotion to go with "depressing" and "melancholy." Is Stein saying something about sight, emotion, patterns, surroundings, hurriedness, and attack? If I mix strangely these notions, then I arrive at the possibility that our hurriedness and focused sight makes us attack meaning and arrange it into certain limited patterns, and that this is depressing.

Expatiating on the rest of *What Happened* could take more pages than my readers can be expected to tolerate, but let me offer a few observations on the play as a whole. The repeated references to things that expand ("a cake is powder" [205], "a very wide cake" [206]) and grow ("a wide oak" [206]) and to other fruits and vegetables and flowers suggest the yeastiness, the organic growth, of words. Further growth is suggested by references to eggs and stigma. The "little sac that shines" could be an egg sac or a cocoon, but the black eye of "shines" might remind us of the violence done to growing things. The "exchanged box" and "the chance of swelling" are simultaneously sexual, pregnant, and violent. Three says, "a special sense a very special sense is ludicrous." "Ludicrous" may have come to mean absurd or ridiculous, but "ludic" means "playful." "Special" is related to "species"—a word often associated with plants and animals and a taxonomy that does not constrain individual variation. In these senses, then, Stein's "special" kind of writing is "ludicrous." Finally, if we are to treat words as living, growing things and not do violence to them by limiting them, it makes some sense when Four and four more say, "a birthday is a speech" (208). Each time we speak we are giving birth to living, flourishing words.

Conversation Patterning as the Essence of What Happens

That section of *What Happened* is quite different from many of Stein's plays, but her emphasis on the workings of interpersonal relations remains strong through all of them. As her first play, *What Happened* seems to explore quite poetically the more general topic of human relations—for example, this sexy old woman's vulnerabilities and simultaneous powers of manipulation—but soon Stein's plays consist of short utterances, the very building blocks of persona, the letters of the alphabet of relationship. The goals and findings of academics in the field of conversation analysis—discourse analysis "with a sociological turn," which takes a close look at "the organization of conversation" (de Beaugrande, 207)—parallel and illuminate Stein's exploration of this topic.

Harvey Sacks is usually credited as the developer of the methods and goals of conversation analysis. A sociologist, Sacks wanted to work with the most fundamental data possible; the best he could locate were tapes of telephone conversations on a suicide help-line. Instead of statistics and summaries already shaped and tainted by other people's assumptions (which are usually unknown to the next person who works with them), Sacks looked at the details of real human experience—albeit in this limited context, but that was necessary and helpful too, the way limited variables tend to be—and found patterns. Developing out of the data with which Sacks began, conversation analysis attends to the minute, the way small things add up to big ones. As one critic (and participant) puts it, conversation analysts regard "macro-level concepts such as social structure and culture . . . [as] abstractions," and they "argue that the causal effects of macrosocial forces are not analytically distinct, but can only be understood by analyzing participants' orientations toward them as revealed in the talk itself (Sawyer, 47, 49). Sacks also saw potential social change within language change. As David Silverman explains: "For Sacks, one way we could identify social change would be by noticing shifts in the properties of categories used in everyday language and in how these categories were actually applied" (17).

Like Sacks's pioneering work in conversation analysis, Stein's plays "simply focus on what people *do*" (Silverman, 48). And parallel to Stein's interest in the action-enabling *essence* and her metaphor of the car's movement, Sacks uses a mechanical metaphor to describe his project, for instance when "he describes interactions 'as being spewed out by machinery, the machinery being what we're trying to find; where, in order to find it we've got to get a whole bunch of its products'" (65–66).[24] Silverman points out that "Sacks is [also] consistently interested in how members *use* the machinery" (66).

Tape recordings of conversations allow conversation analysts to listen repeatedly to the same conversation and to note myriad details. Although tape recordings are their preferred subject of study, conversation analysts also transcribe overheard conversations, using special symbols and noting overlapping speech, pauses, and other sounds and nonsounds. Transcribed English conversations are hardly recognizable as real conversation, or even as English.

Writing is a "technology" that only approximates one's "natural" use of language, which is spoken aloud within a specific temporal position. Walter Ong argues that writing reduces "dynamic sound to quiescent space, [and separates] the word from the living present, where alone spoken words can exist" (82). Writers can represent word choice, word order, and even a hint of pronunciation through creative spelling, but even the most thorough and creative use of punctuation does not allow us fully to represent the pauses, emphases, and risings and fallings of our voices. The very fact that writing can travel physically through space and time decontextualizes (or recontextualizes) it. Nor does our writing represent the short incompletion, the lone cutoff word, the almost meaningless phrase. Even when we attempt to write in our (metaphorically-) speaking "voice" we tend to modify it for proper grammar and more appropriate word choice. The quiet, private moments in which we write let us make slow or late decisions and erasable revisions untraceable in time.

But Stein's plays do not look like transcription, nor does her other writing. She does not develop special symbols to suggest pauses or overlappings, and she primarily uses regularly spelled English words. She disdained neologisms—this was one of her declared reasons for disliking James Joyce's work—and never resorted to using any of the special symbols for phonetics, accents, or emphasis. A 1923 review of *Geography and Plays* reads:

> It would seem that Miss Stein's chief difficulty . . . is the lack of speech notation for written words, to correspond with the conventional and standardized signposts to the interpretation of written music. Perhaps

the day of the oral word artist is coming back in an idiom more closely attuned to our modern consciousness. Perhaps Gertrude Stein will be found, if not among the forefront of those new singers, at least in the ranks of the pioneers that made their song possible. (Crawford, 27)

Stein is an "oral word artist" who found a different way: not tapes, not transcriptions, but an emphasis on structures and patterns, motives, the thing itself. After all, what is left of conversation when we take out its purported meaning? In at least one obvious way, Stein's plays seem *less* like conversation than other writers': without any given dramatic context, without coherent exchanges that include clues to what's going on, Stein's writing in her plays makes no sense to most readers. Since we understand sense from the conversations in which we participate and the dialogue of most of the plays we see, Stein's writing is like nothing we've ever heard—or *noticed* that we've heard—before.

But the *assumptions* and *methods* of conversation analysts, in addition to the data, reveal a clear relationship between Stein's work and theirs. That there is an order to be found in spoken language is a shared primary assumption. Earlier linguists such as Noam Chomsky chose not to analyze actual speech because they believed it was not orderly enough to "permit formal description" (Heritage, 235). Conversation analysts assume that informal conversation has an order to it and that "no order of detail can be dismissed, *a priori*, as disorderly, accidental or irrelevant" (241). Stein, like Sacks, was able to see order in conversation where others could not. And, like conversation, Stein's writing itself should be assumed to have an order—however unfamiliar or complex—and to suggest alternative orders.

Another shared assumption is that there is value in looking *at* the very things—words—with which we usually see and describe other things. Emanuel A. Schegloff describes the work of conversation analysis as based on "the distinctive and utterly critical recognition . . . that talk can be examined as an object in its own right, and not merely as a screen on which are projected other processes." Further, "commonsense knowledge cannot properly be invoked as itself providing an account, rather than providing the elements of something to be accounted for" (xviii, xlii). Schegloff describes Sacks as having noticed something worth studying in the very tools with which we usually study everything else. William James also directed his attention to *how* we know things, as well as to *what* we know: he didn't let our objects of thought distract him from noticing thinking itself, and thinkers themselves. Similarly, Stein is not interested in happenings so much as in how and why they get talked about.

The prattling data of conversation analysis requires practitioners to notice what most people ignore in the daily sounds around them. Their methods, then, beyond tape recording and transcription, most basically involve paying close attention to detail and trying not to ignore anything. Schegloff reminds us that it was difficult for him and his colleagues "to penetrate through the blinders of the implacable familiarity of the mundane materials with which we worked" (lix). To notice informal conversation, Sacks had to see anew. Stein certainly works with the "mundane materials" of gossip and domestic middle-class life; it has long been debated whether her art transforms this material into something noticeable and valuable or whether it remains as ordinary and flat as ever.

Conversation analysts have found that "participants [in a conversation] analyze and understand, from moment to moment, the contexted character of their lives, their current and prospective circumstances, the present moment," and that "the very terms of that understanding can be transformed by a next bit of conduct by one of the participants (for example, a next action can recast what has preceded as 'having been leading up to this')" (Schegloff, xxviii). In other words, all utterances are *context-shaped* and *context-renewing* (Heritage, 242; his italics). A reader of Stein's *Tender Buttons* experiences this growing and changing context more finely, on the level of the word instead of the utterance: each word renews the context; each word is "recast" as the words following it reflect back upon it. This renewing and recasting can also be seen in her plays, as I will demonstrate in the next section. Subsequent phrases tell us how previous phrases might have been meant, and how listeners interpreted them.

Conversation analysts, then, assume that there is a describable order to the way spoken language is used, and they intend to describe it in the pieces they can find: How does turn-taking work? When do topic loops appear? How do people most politely avoid saying what they are asked to say? How do they know what they are expected to say? How are conflicts rhetorically, though not substantially, resolved? Conversation analysts want to find out our "rules" of conversation, the ones we pick up, use, and follow—or, if we don't, the ones we know we are breaking (sometimes only in hindsight). These rules—descriptive in that they try to describe what happens, and prescriptive in that we sometimes are aware we are following them and sometimes let them prevent us from saying what we imagine we'd really like to say—may be a miniaturized pattern of the ways humans work. Utterances formed of words are important building blocks in human relationships, and the structures underneath the stories people tell may teach us something about society's organization. In her writing, Stein constantly negotiates between generic expectations and eccentricity, and we do the same in our daily lives. That's a lot of what happens.

Some Discoveries: Subtle Antagonism, or Free Play in Language

Stein's plays tend to be weird, but clear voices often can be heard, interrupting the audience's general confusion—though tending to leave one still baffled afterward. Reading her plays is like walking by a group of strangers and hearing part of their conversation: "Let us wait and see"; "Follow me"; "Yes I have a brother"; "I will do it tomorrow"; "Jenny give me the keys. Oh yes. I am waiting" (*Do Let Us Go Away*, in *Geography and Plays*, 226). You know what they said, what you heard, and what that means, but *why* did they say it and what were they really talking about? Often, however, just from a short exchange, we can tell quite a bit about the speakers' relationship—and thereby can tell *how* we can often tell more than we are told. A couple of words can capture annoyance, long-term enmity, general frustration, embarrassment, hero worship, enthusiasm, and so on. "Good-bye" is one thing, but "good-bye good-bye good-bye" is another (215).[25]

I imagine that Stein's afternoons were full of polite and interesting conversations with visitors—as she said herself, "someone always comes for tea" ("Gertrude Stein Arrives")—and her play *Every Afternoon: A Dialogue* is full of short pieces of conversations. Through decontextualized utterances, Stein draws a reader's attention to the complexity within what looks like simplicity. It is the lack of context that enables the great latitude or "play" in interpretation; contextualized speech can usually be interpreted pretty easily. Many of the following lines from *Every Afternoon* seem to represent polite accord, but they can also suggest misunderstanding or at least annoyed disagreement.

1— Is there any change.
Naturally.
I know what you mean.
2— Of course we did.
Yes indeed we did. (254)
3a— What did you do with your dog.
We sent him into the country.
Was he a trouble.
Not at all but we thought he would be better off there.

> Yes it isn't right to keep a large dog in the city.
> Yes I agree with you.
> Yes.
> 3b— Coming.
> Yes certainly.
> Do be quick. (256)
> 4— Who cares for daisies.
> Do you hear me.
> Yes I can hear you.
> Very well then explain.
> That I care for daisies.
> That we care for daisies. (in *Geography and Plays*, 257)[26]

The exactitude of pronunciation suggested by these polite little statements (which include no contractions) implies a stiffness in the conversation and evokes the image of people sitting straight in their chairs. Although examples 1, 2, and 3a suggest easy agreement, the others hint at discord. "Coming. / Yes certainly. / Do be quick" suggests that even though the second speaker says, "Yes certainly," his or her idea of "coming" is not as immediate as that of the first (and third) speakers. "Do you hear me. / Yes I can hear you" suggests that the first speaker has doubts about the listener's ability to understand. "*Can* you hear me" would indicate that the speakers are discussing whether one can physically hear the other, but "*do* you hear me" suggests that the first speaker doubts that the listener (if not just stubborn) is intellectually or emotionally capable of understanding that speaker's logic or feelings. In this case, the first speaker can politely use the word "hear" to his obliging listener while inaffably accusing him of incompatible sensibilities.

Other pairs of statements in this play also simultaneously signal agreement and reproof. In this group, the paired statements are almost repetitions, and yet they still manage to suggest disagreement:

> 5a— Don't tempt him.
> Do not tempt him.
> This evening there was no question of temptation he was not the least interested.
> 5b— Neither was she.
> Of course she wasn't. (255)
> 6— Why do the days pass so quickly.
> Because we are so very happy.

Yes that's so.

That's it.

That is it. (257)

7a— You mean you are taught early.

That is exactly what I mean.

7b— And I feel the same.

You feel it to be the same. (255)

8— Not now.

You mean not now. (259)[27]

In examples 5a, 6, 7b, and 8, the second speaker uses almost the same words as the first but still manages to undermine the first speaker's authority. In 5a and the last two lines of 6, the second speaker might only be correcting the first speaker's grammar, but small differences can mean wide divergence of opinion. In these examples, the first speaker does not seem to understand the seriousness of the situation; the first speaker is not emphasizing certain words—"not" and "is"—to the second speaker's liking. In these examples, the second speaker may be asserting autonomy by stating the same sentiment emphatically. Conversely, in examples 7b and 8, the second speaker undermines the first speaker's autonomy by speaking *for* him or her, since saying "you mean" and "you feel" is presumptuous and degrading. In 7b—"And I feel the same. / You feel it to be the same."—a simple infinitive changes the meaning significantly. In effect, the first speaker is coerced into agreeing with what was said—an analysis perhaps, instead of just the general emotion with which it was said. Or the first speaker is indirectly told not to *feel* but instead to be more objective in forming and stating opinions. It isn't surprising that contractions have different emphases than whole words—"it's" differing slightly from "it is"—but in example 8, even though the second speaker pretends to repeat what the first speaker says with the use of "you mean," "now" seems to mean a different time than "now." Stein repeats words, writing the same words even in the same order, but they mean something different each time, often because we know how conversations work. These passages make us recognize that we do.

In polite conversations, we try to be agreeable, and we camouflage our differences with dictional amiability. Example 5 demonstrates a series of agreements that serve only to undermine each speaker's authority and to distance the speakers. When the second speaker says, "Do not tempt him," seeming to assert that he or she came to that conclusion autonomously, the first speaker undermines any authority that might be associated with that autonomy by pointing out how obvious that sentiment is: "there was no question of temptation he was not in the least interested." The second speaker then undermines everything she has just said by saying that "she" wasn't at all interested either (I'll hazard to assume that this means that she had no intention of tempting him in the first place). And the first (and last) speaker agrees completely ("of course"), in order to again say something like, "*Anybody* would know *that*." This five-line conversation develops a tense relationship between these two speakers, but it makes no sense at all as an explicit transmission of information. Everything they've said has been unsaid, and nothing they communicate about their quite testy relationship is said directly.

If we can use language to agree with each other even when we are disagreeing, then it's possible to conclude that there is a limit to how well words can help us understand each other. K. J. Phillips writes that Stein "tinges the great majority of lines in 'Every Afternoon' with skepticism about language" and that, paradoxically, because of the promiscuous way words will support more than one meaning, a 'difference' can 'make no difference'" (Phillips, 36).[28] I disagree with Phillips enough to say that *no difference* can *make* a difference. Phillips claims that Stein was frustrated with a language that had so much slack in it, a looseness that made communication unsatisfyingly partial. My point is that Stein loved and fooled with those wide margins for greater semantic latitude.

John Dryden has described the effects of the slack in words: "As long as words a diff'rent sense will bear / And each may be his own interpreter, / Our airy faith will no foundation find; / The Word's a weathercock for ev'ry wind" (*The Hind and the Panther*, part 1, ll. 462–65). Dryden is writing about the frustratingly indeterminate nature of the authoritative word of the Bible—a paradox in itself. "The devil is in the details" is weirdly applicable. While so many writers begin with the Bible as their foundation of rock, only to discover that Dryden has accurately represented that foundation's airiness, Stein draws from the airy words of casual conversation and discovers that these interactions, especially in context, express human interrelations with great substance, consequence, and clarity. But words, especially in informal chat, may not have to be authoritatively informative. Words have another capacity: the unquestionable and important power to form relationships between us. (And perhaps if they did not have so much play in them, our contrariness would not allow us to form friendships at all.) As Stein writes: "To come into the relation means that if there is a response something has been said. This is not too exact" (*Scenes*, in *Geography and Plays*, 99).

In *Geography and Plays*, Stein demonstrates that the alternating utterances spoken during casual conversation by individuals in groups form an important corpus of knowledge that is both eccentrically wise and worthy of further regard—in all senses of that word. Her plays suggest that one should read (and listen) for multiplicity rather than linearity, for both the sake of the word—compared in *What Happened* to both an endangered animal and a growing vegetable—and our own living sakes. If we keep understanding *more* in what is said or written, and if we keep talking, then we will not be blind to other orders and new understandings. The indefinite significations of words do not just confuse; they also enable social relationships by allowing polite discord. As Kenneth Burke writes in a positive review of Stein's opera *Four Saints in Three Acts*: "Even as nonsense it sings well: indeed, its very ambiguity may have prodded the composer to express its *quality* as utterance; if what was said was vague, *en revanche* [in return] it was said with extreme mobility of emphasis" ("Two Brands," 73). As readers, we are the composers of Stein's plays. Her words encourage us to express—and then to notice—the quality and mobility of our own utterance.

Repairing Friendship in "Susie Asado"

While not made up of fragments of conversation, "Susie Asado"—written in 1913 along with *What Happened* (and they were published together in December 1922 in *Geography and Plays*)—is interspersed with suggestions of interactional conversation, as well as speech in action, two of the essential elements of friendly chat.[29] Speech in action allows people to cooperate (pass the salt, hold the tray, bring the pot), and again the main purpose of interactional conversation is to rebuild or continue to build the bond between friends (see Cheepen, 14). Both functions are specific to spoken language (although perhaps they could be reproduced in letter writing, the converse of the pen). "Susie Asado" reads:

> Sweet sweet sweet sweet sweet tea.
>> Susie Asado.
> Sweet sweet sweet sweet sweet tea.
>> Susie Asado.
> Susie Asado which is a told tray sure.
> A lean on the shoe this means slips slips hers.
> When the ancient light grey is clean it is yellow, it is a silver seller.
>> This is a please this is a please there are the saids to jelly. These are the wets these say the sets to leave a crown to Incy.

Incy is short for incubus.

A pot. A pot is a beginning of a rare bit of trees. Trees tremble, the old vats are in bobbles, bobbles which shade and shove and render clean, render clean must.

Drink pups.

Drink pups drink pups lease a sash hold, see it shine and a bobolink has pins. It shows a nail.

What a nail. A nail is unison.

Sweet sweet sweet sweet sweet tea. (*Geography and Plays*, 13)[30]

"Susie Asado," with different levels of blatancy and subtlety, suggests sweets and sweet tea; salt in an old silver saltcellar; jelly; and rare bit (aka welsh rabbit, a version of cheese on toast). We also can note the vats (in which fat might be rendered) and pots (in which the rare bit is begun), and we seem to be heartily and repeatedly encouraged to drink up ("drink pups"). Food seems to be passed around ("this is a . . .") and accepted ("please") with some of the same words and with a rhythm reminiscent of the nursery rhyme "The House That Jack Built."[31]

The "aimless social intercourse" not so much *in* but *evoked by* "Susie Asado" might also remind us that sight and sound are common components in metaphors of relationships: we see eye to eye, enter into another's view, chime or strike in, echo, harmonize, and are on the same wavelength with other people. "Sweet tea" might be given to a sweetie or may lead people to become sweeties. (Alice and Gertrude stopped for cake and praline ices on their first walk together; then Alice was invited to Saturday dinner [Wagner-Martin, 88]). The repetition of a name—either the name of the person addressed or of a third person about which the speaker and listener agree—can also support a feeling of closeness. If we listen to "Susie Asado"—try saying it three times fast—we might hear "you see as I do." In Stein's "Susie Asado", the auditory links between "sweet tea" and "sweetie," and between repeating a name ("Susie Asado") and seeing eye to eye ("You see as I do"), suggest the strong relationship between speech, sight, and human relationships. Seeing eye to eye is one way of describing the goal of chat.

A conversation can be a "nail" between people, constructing a relationship as much or more than it represents one. Our talk creates feelings of closeness because we intentionally, even if automatically, choose topics that we know are "safe" and will let us feel we are discovering that we are in agreement or have much in common. A conversation can build harmonious agreement, letting us feel in "unison" with one another—"unison" itself suggesting harmonic sound.

If we pretend that "Susie Asado" is a transcribed conversation, its structure suggests that it is about building or repairing relationships. Christine Cheepen's work on the predictability of informal conversation asserts that when there is a topic loop—for example, "sweet sweet sweet sweet sweet tea" occurs both at the beginning and the end of this text—then "interactive trouble *must* have occurred" within that loop (117). Within "Susie Asado" are several likely sites for that interactive trouble, although—as we probably all know from experience—sometimes it is impossible to tell what is going to be interpreted as criticism and cause interactive trouble. The imperative "must" can cause interactive trouble between equals. Misunderstandings (Did someone ask what "Incy" meant?) and clarifications that come across as condescending or otherwise annoying to someone ("Incy is short for incubus") can lead to trouble.

"Susie Asado" can be sounded out as the friendly overture "you see as I do," but "Susie Asado" must also be read as the name of a person, and a likely topic of conversation. If interactive trouble occurred before this conversation began, then Susie Asado herself could be a scapegoat who, in cooperation with agreement about the tea, *nails* these speakers back into agreement and friendship.[32] She could be a sacrifice to their unity, one whom they overtly agree is a witch ("which") and silently work out to be "a told tray sure" (a told, old, gold and sure treasure)—a priceless piece of talk that smoothes relations over the tea tray. People can be linked by conversational knick-knacks that they casually mouth together—in "unison." Perhaps Susie Asado is a bauble ("bobble") passed around, one that "shade[s] and shove[s] and render[s] clean" the previous disagreement; thus the invocation of "Susie Asado" is a bauble link. Repeating the name "Susie Asado" and having it bring these speakers together is like the bobolink calling out its own name to its own kind to find a mate. Besides evoking sweets, sweet tea, and a sweetie, "sweet sweet sweet sweet sweet tea" also sounds like a bird's "tweet tweet tweet tweet tweet." The "bobo*link*" call of the bobolink seems scattered throughout this work, as do the lapping sounds of "drink pup." Both the bobolink and Susie Asado link up relationships. About Susie Asado, the speakers can say, "you see as I do." And when that scapegoating has done the preliminary and most difficult work, they can again calmly agree on the sweetness of the tea (it's always sweet to the fifth power). Then they are again sweeties.

Of course there are other possibilities. No matter how informally it is invoked, Incy the incubus is still a spirit, one that combines the topics of sexual liaisons and ghosts. (The same year that Stein became interested in flamenco dancing—the ostensible topic of "Susie Asado"—she visited Mabel Dodge's ghost-haunted villa, where she overheard the living Dodge and her lover in the next room.) In the spirit of spirits, the repetition of the first two lines in the next two lines—and, in part, in the last line—signals a chant to me. That conversation over tea may work the same kind of magic that a chant over a cauldron can: people can be linked (love potions), people can be destroyed (vicious gossip), and women tend to group together in both cases.

Stein's words might remind one of Shakespeare's *Macbeth*, and this would not be the first time Stein alludes to Shakespeare in her writing: "Q.E.D." (1903) begins with a long epigraph from *As You Like It*, act 3, scene 2.[33] In *Macbeth*, the witches dance around a cauldron, take turns speaking, and jointly repeat the chant: "Double, double, toil and trouble; / Fire burn, and cauldron bubble."[34] But look again at the longest paragraph in "Susie Asado": "A pot. A pot is a beginning of a rare bit of trees. Trees tremble, the old vats are in bobbles, bobbles which shade and shove and render clean, render clean must." The pot can both be a flowerpot ("a beginning of . . . trees") and a cauldron in a forest ("the old vats" in "a rare bit of trees"). Stein's words create the image of a bubbling and popping, or "bobble"-ing and "pups"-ing, cauldron in a forest clearing, witches ("which is") chanting, and a brew being prepared.

This chant over the pot opens the scene in which the witches (the old *b*ats) equivocate with Macbeth about his future, including the prediction that he "shall never vanquished be until / Great Birnam Wood to high Dunsinane Hill / Shall come against him" (4.1.92–94). Birnam Wood's "remove to Dunsinane" (5.3.2) certainly demonstrates that it is a "rare bit of trees"—or that bits of trees have been used as effective camouflage. Until her death, Lady Macbeth tries to "render clean" her blood- and guilt-stained hands; she frets, "Yet here's a spot" (5.1.30), and we see here "a pot."[35] Stein's "shade and shove" may refer to the moving trees (which "shadow" Malcolm's soldiers [5.4.5] and allow them to shove on); the equivocation of the witches who "palter" with Macbeth "in a double sense" (5.8.20), words that shade meaning and shove Macbeth toward his tragic fate; or the words that Macbeth uses to address the ghost of Banquo (called a "shadow" [3.4.107]): "The time has been / That, when the brains were out, the man would die, /

And there an end; but now they rise again / With twenty mortal murders on their crowns, / And push us from our stools" (3.3.79–83).

Stein's allusion, if we can call it that, to Shakespeare's equivocating witches reminds me of the power of their spoken words, especially the power they achieve because Macbeth forgets to understand their words in the proper context or for their full potential. He repeats their words as if they had been written in a legal contract upon which he can depend. When attempting to interpret the portentous emblems, Macbeth also struggles, and fails, to put the visual together with the verbal. Stein demonstrates that words can be interpreted in a variety of ways, and that this ambiguity can be both constructive (allowing us to build relationships in spite of our differences) and destructive (if we assume we understand each other perfectly). Stein's words are more than equivocal, they are multivocal, and while we will die still trying to understand them fully, she lets them live. If we insist on killing alternative meaning, we will be like Lady Macbeth, whose "eyes are open but their sense are shut" (5.1.23–24).

This paragraph in "Susie Asado" is not Stein's only echo of *Macbeth*. One paragraph of *Tender Buttons* (written the previous year) evokes the same metrical rhythm, the same rhyme, and even some of the same sense as a section of the witches' recipe for their brew. Compare these excerpts:

> Scale of dragon, tooth of wolf,
> Witches' mummy, maw and gulf
> Of the ravined salt-sea shark,
> Root of hemlock digged i' the dark,
> Liver of blaspheming Jew,
> Gall of goat, and slips of yew
> Slivered in the moon's eclipse,
> Nose of Turk and Tartar's lips. (*Macbeth*, 4.1.22–29)

> Lovely snipe and tender turn, excellent vapor and slender butter, all the splinter and the trunk, all the poisonous darkning drunk, all the joy in weak success, all the joyful tenderness, all the section and the tea, all the stouter symmetry. (*Tender Buttons*, 35)

Stein seems to be listing ingredients for something slightly more tasty than the witches are making, but her concoction may share some of the destructive aspects of the witches' charm. The fourth line or phrase of each passage refers to poison and darkness. As the weird sisters wreak havoc on a sailor and Macbeth, Stein's weird word spells seem playful but have also been read as dangerously disruptive of our common linguistic and social orders. T. S. Eliot called Stein's writing "ominous" ("Charleston," 595), and Faÿ reports that "people spoke of [Stein] as of a witch" (62). Perhaps Stein and Toklas are twentieth-century weird sisters, in convocation with the literary past.

But all this is a long way from what I set out to prove. Unlike the weird sisters, who seem to be telling Macbeth something they are not, Stein's plays seem to say very little at all but tell us many things about the ways we communicate. Instead of disguising her real meanings, Stein has to erase all apparent meaning in order to motivate her readers to find something they weren't looking for. She knows that we're lazy, that we'd be happy to find a little chat over tea, perhaps the story of a divorce in the neighborhood or a bit of subtly expressed hatred with some background history. We don't need greatness; we'll be satisfied with a soap opera or a funny story. But none of that's there, and either we say she's wasting our time, or we keep looking and are forced to find surprises. If we stop looking for the emperor's new clothes and stop blaming the tailor for ineptitude or fraud, we'll see and start to understand the structures of the naked body.

CHAPTER 4

Talk in the Thirties:
In the Present, with the Past

THE 1930S WERE a hugely successful time for Stein as a writer and a celebrity. Toklas's Plain Edition published three of Stein's books between 1930 and 1934, and then Stein moved on to major publishers. Portions of *The Autobiography of Alice B. Toklas* appeared in *Atlantic Monthly*, and the book was then published by Harcourt Brace, which also published the abridged version of *The Making of Americans* (1933). Random House published *Lectures in America* (1935), *The Geographical History of America* (1936), and *Everybody's Autobiography* (1937). In 1934, *Four Saints in Three Acts* was a hit in New York and Chicago (where Stein saw it performed)—and Stein explained that "her idea . . . had been that of conversation between saints" because saints only "exist" and "converse" ("4 Saints"). During this decade, Stein also wrote at least one other opera, a play, and a children's book. While in the United States, Stein showed up late at a performance of the cantata "Capital Capitals," which Virgil Thompson had explained to the audience as "a conversation among the four capitals of Provence—Aix, Arles, Avignon, and Lesbaux—in the manner in which capitals would talk if they could." (A reporter adds: "It didn't make any difference whether they could or not, for no one would know what they were talking about" ["4 Saints"].) In short, Stein continued to fool around with conversation, even as she made it big.

Stein's sudden rise to fame after the publication of *The Autobiography of Alice B. Toklas* led to her tour. After thirty years of writing, Stein became "a best-selling author and house-hold name" when she was almost sixty years old (Blackmer, 243). She was on the cover of *Time* on 11 September 1933. The February 1935 volume of *transition* devoted itself to (angry) responses to *The Autobiography of Alice B. Toklas* from the very people about whom she had written. Stein also wrote (but did not publish—yet) the long works *Stanzas in Meditation* and *Four in America*. Some of the work—I think—is her most baffling, and some is her most straightforward (though surely baffling in its own ways). I do not discuss the ways the works "speak to each other"—how, as Dydo has convincingly argued, *Stanzas in Meditation* and *The Autobiography of Alice B. Toklas* are two parts of the same project. Nor do I explore the ways Stein creatively weaves an interest in conversation into her works—as in "How I wish I were able to say what I think" in stanza 17 or "She asked . . And I said . . And she said . . I said" in the first four lines of stanza 18 in *Stanzas in Meditation*. Instead, this chapter concentrates on Stein's visit to the United States after thirty-one years away. She came to speak English, hear English, and talk to Americans. To lecture, but also to converse.

Starting Conversations in America

While *The Autobiography of Alice B. Toklas* made Stein famous as a personality who rubbed shoulders with other (already famous) personalities, her lectures emphasize her roles as writer and thinker. According to Bridgman, Stein "undertook to expand those few sentences in *The Autobiography of Alice B. Toklas* which had pretended to summarize theories. The resulting defense of her art was much more satisfactory" (243–44). The lectures introduce an avid reader's ideas about the history of English literature (in "What is English Literature"), an art collector's theories about modern art (in "Pictures"), and a writer's goals in her several genres: plays (in "Plays"), her lengthy prose style (in "The Gradual Making of the Making of Americans"), short portraits (in "Portraits and Repetition"), and poetry (in "Poetry and Grammar"). Her explanations, however, struck audiences (and strike many readers) as almost as confusing as the literary works themselves. She is very clear, but very digressive; very repetitive, but not very strict with herself about defining certain oft-repeated words. When she talks about English literature, for example, she starts with (and doubles back quite often to) discussions about what it means to know something. She points out that while English literature has been written over centuries, all that one has read is always simultaneously present in one's mind; that different readers know different English literatures; that some writers serve God and some serve mammon; that American literature is English literature and yet very different, since it was not written on an island; and relatedly, how island life differs from continental life. Along the way, she offers a lovely history of English literature, largely based on how different writers chose their words (and how sound was, at some points in this history, their primary consideration).

In spite of this confusion, between fall 1934 and spring 1935, Stein was "the most feted woman in America" ("Gertrude Stein Gives Talk"; "Elite Fete"). She spent six months traveling by train and plane, talking to audiences of up to five hundred people. Arriving in New York City on 24 October 1934, she began lecturing in November—in Manhattan, Poughkeepsie, and Brooklyn, and in Princeton, New Jersey. When she lectured in New York City, "requests for tickets [came] from as far away as Kentucky and Vermont" ("Gertrude Stein Discusses Art"). From her base in New York, she made short forays to Philadelphia, Bryn Mawr, and Boston. Her "welcome ... was so much more hospitable than she expected" that she extended her trip past mid-November, touring the country ("Literary Enigma"). She visited Chicago, Illinois; Madison, Wisconsin; St. Paul, Minnesota; Detroit and Ann Arbor, Michigan; Indianapolis, Indiana; Columbus, Toledo, and Cleveland, Ohio; Baltimore, Maryland; Washington, D.C.; Springfield, Amherst, Northampton, Pittsfield, and South Hadley, Massachusetts; Wallingford, Middletown, Springfield, and Hartford, Connecticut; Charlottesville, Richmond, Williamsburg, and Sweet Briar, Virginia; Charleston, South Carolina; Birmingham, Alabama; and New Orleans, Louisiana. After a fortnight in Chicago, where she taught a class and gave her *Narration* lectures at the university, she lectured in Dallas, Fort Worth, and Austin, Texas; Oklahoma City, Oklahoma; and Pasadena, Carmel, Palo Alto, San Francisco, Oakland, and Berkeley, California. She returned to New York for a couple of weeks and then left for Europe on 4 May 1935. During the tour, people "scramble[d] for available tickets," because Stein was considered "a wow" and the "genial apostle of the new English" ("Miss Stein a Wow"). I doubt most people understood her or loved her, but she certainly caught their attention.

During her tour, she signed books at bookstores and department stores, auctioned off autographed copies of her work for charity, gave many interviews, spoke on a national radio broadcast, loaned some of her artwork to exhibitions, and canceled any speaking engagement for which more than five hundred tickets had been distributed or admission had been charged. She had tea with Eleanor Roosevelt at the White House and went out on the night beat in a Chicago police car. She met many famous people and was greeted by "8,000 rabid devotees of [Clark] Gable" when she landed in Dallas—they thought it was his plane ("Multitude Greets Highbrow"). She was interviewed by Walter Cronkite when he was a student at the University of Texas at Austin, published some articles on the American scene with the

Herald Tribune Syndicate, chaired a college debate (between the University of Chicago and Willamette University) on international munitions control, and attended a University of Chicago honor society meeting devoted to the topic of literature and propaganda.[1]

The *Time* cover story asserts that Stein was "very democratic, proud of being a plain American, she likes people, [and] is always accessible to strangers" ("Stein's Way"). When she arrived in the United States, she told reporters: "I like people, you see. I like to talk to people, I am always wandering around the streets having conversations with people. I like single human contacts" ("Gertrude Stein Home"). The *New York Sun* reported that during her lecture, "she stood on the platform, conversing as to every person present as an individual" ("4 Saints"). She liked rubbing shoulders with people in the street: she walked from West Forty-third Street to Park Avenue and Sixty-second to deliver her first lecture at the Colony Club; she walked the seventy-two blocks from her hotel to 116th street to give her second lecture at Columbia University ("Gertrude Stein Discusses Art"; Alsop, "Gertrude Stein Says"). At least one reporter found Stein's tone condescending when she gave her lectures (Murray), but most found it sincere and conversational.

I like to think that Stein had other goals besides "la gloire" and money when she visited her native land. I imagine she hoped to start some conversations, something like those that were inspired by the 1913 Armory Show in New York, which Mabel Dodge called "the most important public event that has ever come off since the signing of the Declaration of Independence" (Dodge Luhan and Stein, 157; see also Blackmer, 228). Van Vechten describes the effect of the show on the population of New York:

> It was the first, and possibly the last, exhibition of paintings held in New York which everybody attended. Everybody went and everybody talked about it. Street-car conductors asked for your opinion of the Nude Descending the Staircase, as they asked you for your nickel. Elevator boys grinned about Matisse's Le Madras Rouge, Picabia's La Danse a la Source, and Brancusi's Mademoiselle Pogany, as they lifted you to the twenty-third floor. Ladies you met at dinner found Archipenko's sculpture very amusing, but was it art? (Blackmer, 228–29)[2]

In short, everyone was talking. As Blackmer concludes: "When it came to interpreting modernist art, virtually everybody from elevator boys to society ladies was on the same rudimentary level, with no conventional critical perspectives to guide them," and "audiences rather than artists had the responsibility of interpreting their works according to their own lights, . . . [and] modernist writers and artists indirectly forced their audiences to examine the prejudices and preoccupations that informed their aesthetic judgements" (229). That new art got all sorts of people to step back and reconsider, and to talk about it with everyone else. Whether or not it was Stein's goal, did anything like this happen as a result of her American tour? Did Stein start a nationwide conversation?

The short (disappointing) answer is "No," although I'd like to qualify that with a "Kind of, maybe." In chapter 6, I describe the kind of conversation Stein would later advocate, but that idea seems to have come to her during the decade after her trip. Still, Stein took pleasure in confusing people, and one reason might be that confusion—or "mental chaos," as the *Boston Evening Press* called her effect on audiences—is a first step toward thought ("Gertrude Stein Baffles"). After Stein's success with *The Autobiography of Alice B. Toklas*, Lansing Warren traveled to Paris to interview Stein for the *New York Times* and observed: "When she laughs, as she often does at the mental confusion produced in her auditor by many of her remarks, her face and body become mobile, and there is something impish in her expression." Stein likes to make remarks that will get a rise out of her listeners—perhaps even make them jump up and state their own opinions, listen to themselves, and rethink some of their assumptions.

For example, in this same interview she says "that Hitler ought to have the peace prize . . . because he is removing all elements of contest and of struggle from Germany. By driving out the Jews and the democratic and Left elements, he is driving out everything that conduces to activity. That means peace." Warren doesn't try to figure out what this means, and in the next paragraph he says "her provocative side" is limited to her "experimental" writing and "does not appear in her everyday life." Couching her ideas in plain English, however, Stein is being just as provocative in her theorizing about Hitler and the Nobel Peace Prize. Edward M. Burns and Ulla E. Dydo deduce that Stein's proposal is "ironic, a point of black humor" (Stein and Wilder, 414), and they are surely right. But it is also thought-provoking: if Hitler can in any way appear to be bringing peace, then we need to rethink our ideas about peace. Might peace as an end in itself be overrated? Might it in some situations be a deadening complacency? Might dissent be more valuable than we assume? And might Stein lead her listener even to question the appeasement of Germany in the interest of peace? In a later conversation, she makes her views on peace clearer. She refers to recent purges in "peaceful" countries and asks: "What's the difference between getting killed in war or getting killed in peace? . . . Peace! P-s-s-s-t—and they shoot you. I'd rather be killed in war than in peace" (Buchalter).[3] If that's peace, who (aside from tyrants) needs it?

Stein speaks in "conundrums" which go "unanswered" ("A Painting Is a Painting"). A *New York Sun* reporter calls her surprising comments "little nifties," appreciates her "American colloquialisms," and says that, in spite of "her common representation as a lady who is very hard to understand, . . . for fifty-nine minutes in any hour you will think her altogether charming, and as transparent as a bartender's laugh" (McClain). Another journalist describes her "slow, conversational tone . . . interspersed with the crisp sentences of cryptic meaning—some bordering on the startling" (O'Connell). In Texas, a *Dallas Morning News* reporter found her "perplexingly clear" ("Multitude Greets Highbrow"). But audiences seemed to be struck by her "sincerity," in spite of her mixture of "epigrams," "extremely astute remark[s]," and comments that seem "thoroughly absurd" (Murray). In "Miss Stein Speaks to Bewildered 500," the *New York Times* reports: "At the end of the address there was obviously no unanimity of opinion among the audience as to its meaning or significance." That's good, for people will have to think, discuss. The newspaper's editorial page the next day suggests that Stein's "ingenious publicity man" is the real hero, since the "bewildered" audience just sat there with a "splitting headache and holding their breath" ("Devoted Band"), but Stein's lecture tour was primarily advertised by *The Autobiography of Alice B. Toklas* and cobbled together by friends and her own whims. There is something compelling, even enlivening, about being confused and provoked, and people went for it. In spite of the audience's "exchanging covert smiles," some listeners thought to themselves, or whispered "begrudgingly, 'A good basic idea'" (Winsten). Stein's ideas are "esoteric," but they are "not without the grain of shrewd good sense" (Alsop, "Gertrude Stein Likes").

Not everyone appreciated Stein's rousing the minds of her audiences. A *New York Post* writer comments: "It seems to have become more or less obligatory to express one's self upon the subject of Gertrude Stein" (Brickell). Columnist Evelyn Seeley wishes Stein hadn't come to New York, because then "we wouldn't have had her to argue about." Seeley implies that the argument is open-ended, unending, but she has reached her own conclusion: Stein is too much an outsider, too "Bohemian," too much like most people are in their youth, and Seeley "wishes she would come down for a while and see the America we see." Stein may have come to America, however, to let her compatriots see *her* way for a moment, to let her listeners imagine a difference.

Stein ended her lectures by asking, "Are there any questions?" When a woman in one audience came out with a "la-di-da" question, Stein's response was "a flat slapping 'What?'" which suggests her suspicion of posturing and her desire for straight talk (Winsten). In fact, sometimes she chose to stop reading her lecture to talk directly to her audience ("Gertrude Stein Explains Work"). At Princeton, there were no questions—which we could optimistically read as audience members having come to think for themselves, but I doubt it. According to the reporter at the Princeton lecture: "Few if any even came close to assimilating Miss Stein's literary theories. The audience was amused but otherwise unaffected by the obscurities which Miss Stein considers axiomatic" ("Princeton Dazed"). While Lewis Gannett of the *New York Herald Tribune* thought Stein was "jolly, bright-eyed, wholly natural, [and] likeable," he still wasn't compelled to think: he said her words tended to be "utterly meaningless" and her opera "was a big fat zero," and, to a passage from her weirder work, he can only say, "Pooh!" Some reviewers, such as Harry Hansen at the *New York World-Telegram*, refused to go see her. Stein started conversations among some people, but other listeners were just turned off.

And some people she must have purposely sent packing, perhaps because they were too stubborn to make any effort worth the trouble, and also because she was "intransigent on principle" ("Gertrude Stein Arrives"). One writer thought: "If you come up to her and say 'I don't understand anything you write, but I want to know something about you,' [Stein was likely to] be frank and friendly and helpful" ("Literary Enigma"). But James Marlow's interview with Stein sounds like a comedy routine or an interview with Bob Dylan. She starts with "Who are you?" and "What do you want? Sit down," and then she leaves the room for a while. Marlow asks questions and gets answers he doesn't understand; he says, "I do not mean that," and "I mean," and "I know, but," and "What I am trying to find out is . . ." Stein interrupts him, contradicts him, and accuses him of having the wrong type of mind: "It [my writing] does not stammer. It may seem that way to you because you have that kind of mind"; and "You haven't an ear for the way people talk"; and "You have too many ideas in your head at the same time"; and "That is the trouble with you"; and "Your choice of words is very poor." (He says, "Is what?" and she answers, "Very poor." He says, "Oh.") She also cuts him off several times with "You will have to talk louder. I can't hear you"; or "Do I what? I can't hear you." Then she turns to another interviewer: "What do you want?" Perhaps she's telling Marlow to be more open-minded, but she's not demonstrating much of an open mind herself.

Stein refuses to be drawn into a debate. One *Chicago Daily Tribune* reporter says that "Gertrude Stein never answers attacks"—but answering attacks isn't quite conversation ("Paris Aroused"). When she was a moderator at a college debate on munitions, she said (unsupportively, considering the circumstances): "All they are taught is debate. They have never learned to think" ("Miss Stein Lets"). Her position seems to be that "we have wars because people want wars"—a position provocative enough to be defended on the editorial page of the *Daily Tribune* and to cause at least one reader to reply with a different opinion—that, in short, people with children don't want war and "talk is cheap, but lives are dear" ("Miss Stein Lets"; Frey). The newspaper appreciates Stein's facing facts, but the reader replies with clichés. Debate, but not conversation, can occur when people won't think beyond, or even about, their cherished phrases.

What They Might Have Talked About

"What is art?" and "Is this art?" was one debate spurred by Stein's tour. A *New York Times* editorial mentions B. F. Skinner's critique of Stein's "unconscious prose" but argues for a different position: that the nonsense of *Tender Buttons* is "ravishing." Defending Stein's prose poetry, the editorial writer asks: "Why should 'meaningless' poetry be on the eligible list and 'meaningless' prose be excluded? Is Mr. Skinner deaf to music and obdurate to magic?" ("Two Steins"). The *Springfield Daily Republican* was all effusion: "Her highly concentrated style embraced this subject with characteristic efficiency," "a literary style which may still be considered bewildering because of its many facets . . . [and] the sudden blossoming forth of vast panoramas of information, too concentrated to be grasped without careful analysis, and too odd in form . . . to convey more than a total impression of a great erudition, powerful personality, fearlessness" ([W. Rogers?], "Stein Gives Talk").[4] Or perhaps she just spouts "the most absolute rubbish on earth" (Laurie). Whatever it all means, however she did it, however much her tour resembles "a circus tour," the editors at the *Cleveland Press* are willing to credit Stein with "20 years ago . . . [giving] license to experimenters in all the fields of all the arts to try to say what they wanted to say in their own way, regardless of how anyone else had ever done it." The editorial concludes:

> She pulled a cork. She took a lid off. Scads of criticism, ranging all of the way from serious incomprehensible attempts to define her old serious incomprehensibilities, to some of the fanciest writing produced by the lunatic fringe of her followers, still do not explain just how she did it.

But she did. And a whole generation of quite comprehensible vital artists of our time was released into birth. ("About Gertrude Stein")

Thumbs up or thumbs down, understandable or not, serious or a joke, even art or not—escaping most attempts at definition—Stein's writing started noisy debates (and perhaps some quiet conversations) on all these topics: What is art? What is meaning? What is important?

A feature in the 19 November 1934 *New York Sun* printed this letter from Helene Marer: "'What do you think of [*Four Saints in Three Acts*]?' It seems to me a lot of words, thrown together, meaning nothing. But, maybe I'm wrong. May I have somebody's opinion of it?" During two weeks of letters on this topic, Dian Deene on 22 November responded that she loved Stein's opera, even though it was indeed "a jumble of words": "There was a time I would have derided Miss Stein's 'method' in no uncertain terms, but I am beginning to realize how little I know and that maybe she is way ahead of me or something." In a more pretentious letter, on 23 November, Prudencio de Pereda defends Stein more specifically but less open-mindedly. He calls Stein a member of "the cult of temporary unintelligibility" because "effort brings a handsome reward." Rhoda Lawner is critical of Stein, however, calling her in a 26 November letter "a nonunderstanding authoress of non-understandable books." Mrs. L.B.W. wonders in her 3 December letter if Stein is "playing a hoax" or "spoofing us"—which was a common third view, though third views aren't always that common. If people started imagining their own limitations, as the first letter writer did, or started imagining the ways that art was being critiqued, as this last writer did, then Stein started some people thinking.

This debate spawned another one: about the primacy of words and their sounds. A reviewer of the Hartford, Connecticut, premier of *Four Saints in Three Acts* passes on the rumor that Stein "apparently uses words for sounds instead of meanings" and quotes Virgil Thomson's confirmation of it: "Miss Stein . . . clothed [the] story in a sound-pattern of words vaguely suggesting the atmosphere" of seventeenth-century Spain. The "All-Negro Cast" was said to have been chosen because "they had better diction" and they "projected the vocal lines with [a] startling clarity and beauty of phrasing" ("Stein Opera Sung"). Her lectures are described as "the sound within a sea shell" and "intricate, definitely lyric verbal rhythms"(Winsten; Alsop, "Gertrude Stein Says"). But a *New York Times* editorial, missing her valuation of spoken words, is disappointed in her ideas on punctuation: "Does the eye need to take a breath?" In fact, choosing to criticize Stein from the opposite direction than the paper usually takes, the editorial says Stein has not gone far enough: "She should have given us the New Style, absolute and flawless, instead of patching up the Old" ("Perfecting Language"). But Stein was interested in the real English language.

Stein's lecture tour also changed the way people talked, although not in very important ways—at least as far as the news reports tell it. The *Boston Daily Globe* says she was "contagious," and the "Radcliffe girls" started "stuttering" just like her: "Are you going out with me tonight, tonight are you going out with me, with me tonight, tonight with me?" ("Radcliffe Giggles"). As Stein's tour went on, the news headlines mimicked her repetition more and more often: "Gertrude Stein Is Here Is Here Is Here Here Is" (Dush); "A Painting Is a Painting Is a Gertrude Stein Axiom on Art"; "Greeted Greeted at Airport" (O'Hara); "A Snub, a Snub, a Snub." But copying some of the symptoms of deep thought, as opposed to thinking deeply, was not going to get Americans very close to creative thinking.

Stein's words, both spoken and written, seem especially thought provoking if we contrast them with the sentimental and formulaic poetry that appears alongside the news articles about her tour. One begins: "I know I shall be lonely just at first, / Until your step grows fainter on the stair, / And I have learned to look without swift tears / Across the room at your dear, empty chair" (Welshimer). Another begins: "In the first months when they were wed / Glamour so softened care and duty / He thought he loved her, but he fled / The moment Time had stained her beauty." It ends: "He thought he loved her, but he tired / And from his life forever thrust her / When he discovered love required / More strength of will than he could muster" (Guest). These do not represent even good twentieth-century American poetry. But if this is what people are reading in the newspaper, then we can thank Stein for stepping into the news and getting herself, her words, and her ideas discussed. These poems say what everybody knows, but Stein gets people thinking about what they don't know, what they might try to know, and even what might not be knowable.

Stein and Einstein

The very issue of "meaning" was thrown into question by the chance juxtaposition of Stein's and Albert Einstein's lectures. The 1933 *Time* magazine cover story begins with a poem that links them in a way they continued to be linked.

I don't like the family Stein.
There is Gert, there is Ed, there is Ein:

Gert's poems are bunk,
Ed's statues are punk,
And nobody understands Ein. ("Stein's Way")

Even this silly poem points to the way that the audiences for literature, science, and sculpture are confused. An editorial comments that Stein's writing is "harder to understand then the mathematical hieroglyphics of Einstein's theory of relativity, yet she is hailed as a great literary pioneer" ("Fancy Writing"). Why are the practitioners of both science and literature so baffling to their audiences? What does it mean—about past assumptions, about this moment in history, about these particular thinkers—that the audience feels left behind, grasping at straws? Is the proper response a commonsense outing of nonsense, or is it patience, yearning, deep thought, revision, and work?

The audience's tendencies in their responses to Stein and Einstein were usually quite different—and some people remarked on the contrast. John McClain of the *New York Sun* noted some unfairness in the way Stein was quizzed for explanations, since "it is a matter of record that Prof. Einstein and other protagonists of slightly baffling theories have entered and left the port for years without being called upon to defend themselves." Under a photograph of the physicist and headlined "Einstein 'Explains' Theories to Reporters," the caption reads: "In his lecture he gave additional proof of a theorem advanced by him in 1905 that energy and matter are two different forms of the same thing." Except for the quotation marks in the headline, there's nothing dubious about this report.

At the end of December 1935, Stein's and Einstein's lectures are both covered by the Washington, D.C., *Evening Star*. On 29 December, Stein (with her second cousin and a large white dog) is pictured a few pages away from an extensive article on Einstein. The next day, the paper ran a picture of Einstein and his colleagues, and Einstein's white hair and his placement in the composition of the photo make him look like the white dog in the picture of Stein! Thomas Henry reports that during Einstein's lecture, he apologetically repeated, "But this is so elementary I will not trouble you with it," and "at one rather knotty point, at which some lofty brows were puckered, he remarked, 'This is so infantile I must not delay over it.'" Like Stein, Einstein is a bit uncooperative sometimes. When a reporter asks if he enjoys talking about anything besides science, Einstein replies, "Yes, but not with you" (Henry). One short article begins: "The tradition of only 12 scientists understanding Einstein is upset completely" ("Science Understands"). And when Einstein's colleagues assure a journalist that *they,* of course, understand Einstein, he seems to trust the experts' consensus. Instead of doubting him, Einstein's nonscientist audience believes they would understand if they had bigger brains. This reporter depicts Einstein as a lone genius, concluding one story: "Prof. Einstein now does most of his thinking in his sloop off Watch Hill, R.I. He sails alone" (Henry).

Stein was more difficult to categorize. Headlines included: "Gertrude Stein Too Much for Harvard and Radcliffe; She Wonders If It Is Necessary to Stand Still to Live" (Fessenden); "Princeton Dazed by Gertrude Stein: . . . 'The Making of the Making of Americans' Befuddles Even Most Erudite Erudite"; and "Gertrude Stein Tells All About All but Audience Just Can't Take It" (Evans).

Stein noticed that new scientific ideas got more general acceptance than did her writing. She described her art as called for by "the movement of [her] time," just as "Edison's time forced on him the electric light and on the Wright brothers the airplane," but, "because inventions are practical things, people don't make a fuss about them" (O'Hara). While Stein was getting at representing the essence inside the working parts of a car, one of Einstein's colleagues explained his theory of energy as "a new part for an auto," although the part it's replacing still works ("Science Understands").

Stein tries to buck the theory of relativity, stating that if "a movement were lively enough it would exist so completely that it would not be necessary to see it moving against anything to know that it is moving" (*Lectures*, 170). In spite of this antirelativism, Conrad Aiken links Stein to Einstein in the *New Republic* when he dubiously reports that "in Miss Stein's work we were witnessing a bold and intricate and revolutionary and always consciously radical experiment in style, of which the results were to be of incalculable importance for English literature. Like the splitting of the atom, or the theory of relativity, Miss Stein's destruction of meaning was inevitably going to change, if not the world, at any rate the word" (38). Unlike Aiken, Mina Loy celebrates Stein's potential power:

> Curie
> of the laboratory
> of vocabulary
> she crushed
> the tonnage
> of consciousness
> congealed to phrases
> to extract
> a radium of the word (94)

Although Loy is probably referring to something more all encompassing, this "tonnage / of consciousness / congealed to phrases" certainly also can describe the psychological complexity of short exchanged phrases—what I see as Stein's exploration of conversation. Curie extracts a physical or material element, eighty-eighth on the periodic table, and Stein the essence of what happens between people.

Both Stein and Einstein seem to be contributing to a movement that demanded a "new mode of thinking," as the *Washington Daily News* reports on 28 December 1934. Citing the way Einstein's theories "disarranged the old-fashioned laws of time and motion," the plan is that "the new thinking blasts the idea that 'a thing is what is' or that it is identical with itself in all respects. For example, you are not the same you that existed a second ago or a year ago" ("Scientists' Meeting"). Stein would probably agree with that notion: it is one assumption behind her ideas on repetition and copying. Alfred Korzybeski is the "leading expositor" of this new type of thought, and while Einstein's famed ideas may have led to its newspaper coverage, Stein's ideas parallel Korzybeski's, too. To change the way people think, Korzybeski and his colleagues believe—in a re-dyed nominalism—that all names should be dated or numbered ("apple No. 1" and "apple No. 2") "to avoid the fallacy of false identification" (ibid.). Korzybeski also advocated avoiding the use of the verb "to be." Whether we think these changes feasible or not, these scientists—and Stein—seem to think that a change in the way language is used will be necessary to effect a change in underlying assumptions that affect human thought.

The Closed American Mind

Stein did not start a nationwide conversation. Her wish for small venues and free tickets, while democratic in spirit, contributed to her drawing a limited audience: members of museums and clubs, "grey-haired, gray-faced women . . . [and] comparatively few men"—at least at Columbia University (Winsten). She spoke to members of the "exclusive and intellectual" arts clubs, students and professors at thirty-five colleges and universities, women's clubs, the John Reed Club of Indianapolis, several audiences of museum members, and other "invited audience[s]" (Butcher; "Gertrude Stein Speaks"; "Youth Understands"). At the University of Chicago, she met with "chosen students," but "the curiosity seekers [were] kept out as firmly as nonmembers are banned from an exclusive country club golf course" ("Paris Aroused"). At one lecture, she sat on the stage at the Ritz Tower with Mrs. William Randolph Hearst, and Cole Porter was present, along with other "intellectuals" and "fashionables" ("Miss Stein Uses Saints"; Flutterbye). She only sometimes spoke to more general audiences, as at the Town Hall in Toledo and a bookstore in Cleveland.

While Stein argued that style and content "can't be divorced. They are one" (Winsten), news headlines all over the nation were increasingly likely to parrot Stein's style and maintain their closed-mindedness when it came to content. Only six days into her tour, the *New York Times* subtitled its story "'The Making of the Making of Americans' Befuddles Even Most Erudite Erudite" and ended with the speculation that the audience has realized "that their education, their education had been sadly neglected, neglected" ("Princeton Dazed"). Less than two weeks later, a *New York Times* review of *Portraits and Prayers* titled "But a Stein Is a Stein Is a Stein" asserts: "There is nothing in this book to merit more than five minutes' attention of a reasonably honest and intelligent mind." By February 1935, the *New York Times* was claiming that both Stein *and* the proletarian writers were snobs: "'Appreciation' of the unintelligible poets . . . was a form of self-flattery"; "the intelligentsia were sure they were good because the man in the street couldn't make head nor tail out of them"; and Stein seems to "continue to function . . . [as if she's] protecting a vested interest, like a losing trolley line that keeps going because it has a franchise." And the Communist writers were snobs because "if you aren't a workman . . . you and your thoughts and feelings just don't count" ("Literary Snobbery").

While everyone seemed to like Stein the person, they couldn't take her ideas seriously. The *New York Times* could do little but editorialize in the negative. For John Chamberlain, Stein's work is as silly as yoga, she is just "talking nonsense," and she's running a "racket" that takes advantage of our love of "goggling, gaping, and gazing." But for the reasonable person, he goes on, "those who have a no doubt irrational prejudice against vacuity, Miss Stein can only serve as an irritant." He even likens her writing to "the Chinese water torture." But the newspaper of record is looking for points, not ideas, and, in Chamberlain's view: "The trouble with the Stein game is that no one ever scores."

In short, this "stormy petrel of belles lettres, high priestess of the cult of scrambled words," and "word wrangler" didn't open everyone's minds (O'Hara; Evans). "The literary rebus whose unorthodox style of writing the English language has made her glorified and ridiculous alike" was asked closed-minded questions such as "What inspired you to begin doing tricks with the English language?" Sometimes she snapped at her "nosey inquisitors," and sometimes she behaved "patiently, graciously" (O'Hara). In San Francisco, a reporter claims that the audience did not understand "one single sentence, one single word, or one single syllable of Miss Stein's tiresome, and, if you ask me, rather impertinent address." This journalist, Annie Laurie, cannot understand "why Americans are such dumb driven cattle when it comes to listening to" what (she estimates) adds up to "the most absolute rubbish on earth." Laurie asks: Why didn't anyone "boo" or "hiss"? Why were they all so "polite"? She praises Americans for being so open-minded that they'll "put up with manners and customs of the crocodile on his native sandbar," but she thinks that when someone "of our own species" tries to tell us something clearly wrong, clearly "a bit thick," and probably insulting, Americans shouldn't take it sitting down. Another journalist is inspired by Keats and Coleridge to describe an audience as "left . . . palely loitering; mere metaphysicians meandering along the stream of consciousness, measureless to man, down to a psychopathic sea" (Evans). The tendency either to "scoff" or to "worship" disables thought in both cases (Murray).

In a world that wants points—wants brief pragmatic answers—Stein's mysterious miscellany was difficult to recognize as a position in itself. For example, when asked what she thought of Roosevelt, Stein said, "I think many things about him," but the answer was discounted as a nonanswer, likely to have been inspired by the sudden distraction of a camera's flash (O'Hara). Most people wanted—and still want—adamancy, not complexity.

Writing and Speaking in Stein's Quirky Defining

Stein's lectures did have points to them, however, and most of these depended on the difference between the sights and sounds of the English language. Attention to this distinction permeates many of the definitions set forth in her lectures—especially "What Is English Literature" and "Plays" (in *Lectures*) and "What Are Master-pieces and Why Are There So Few of Them"—as well as other works of the thirties, such as *The Geographical History of America* (1936), *Everybody's Autobiography* (1937), "My Debt to Books" (1939), and *Four in America* (written 1932–33, published in 1947). Stein discusses "writing" and "saying" in a variety of contexts, revealing that these visual and auditory media play an important definitional role for her. Her concepts of speaking, listening, writing, and reading figure into her definition of human nature and the human mind, her ideas of genius and masterpieces, and her method of picking up a person's internal rhythms and writing a portrait.

Stein told her audiences in the United States "to look at plays in relation to sight and sound rather than in terms of story and time" (Evans), and in

Everybody's Autobiography she reminds her readers to investigate the difference in her works between writing and speaking. In that book, Stein describes an exchange she carried on with a man during her lecture tour.

> On the airplane leaving there was a young man he was from Stanford University and I had spoken twice there, and he wrote questions on a piece of paper and I wrote him back the answers, . . . *he wanted to know what I meant by the difference between writing and speaking* and we spent all the time handing papers forward and back, perhaps he has kept them and so he knows what I answered him, I naturally do not, but it was interesting it always is interesting to answer anything. (294; my italics)

In the absence of these (no doubt) only enigmatically illuminating paper napkins, I have pieced together the answer to the young man's question from Stein's works in the thirties.

For Stein, speaking does not always mean talking, and writing does not only mean putting pencil to paper. For example, when Stein writes "writing," she only sometimes means spelling words onto paper; other times, "writing" refers to a state of heightened attention and consequent creativity. According to Dewey: "All discourse, oral or written, which is more than a routine unrolling of vocal habits, says things that surprise the one that says them" (*Experience*, 194); Stein thinks "writing" is when we pay enough attention to our own words that we register this surprise. When Stein says a genius can talk and listen at the same time, the auditory medium is less important than the genius's ability to escape routine and be an attentive audience for his or her own words—whether written or spoken (see *Lectures*, 170). This heightened attention can create written masterpieces, but it also makes for a rich and playful conversation:

> If the same person does the talking and the listening why so much the better there is just by so much the greater concentration. One may really indeed say that that is the essence of genius, of being most intensely alive, that is being one who is at the same time talking and listening. It is really that that makes one a genius. And it is necessary if you are to be really and truly alive it is necessary to be at once talking and listening, doing both things, not as if there [they?] were one thing, not as if they were two things, but doing them, well if you like, like the motor going inside and the car moving, they are part of the same thing. (*Lectures*, 170)

This "motor going inside and the car moving" should be reminiscent of the "essence" of what happens in conversation. Someone who talks and listens to himself might be considered narcissistic, but that speaker is in communion not so much with himself as with his words. And the loving existence of Narcissus seems preferable to the deadening repeating of Echo. Stein is often said to be repetitive, but perhaps she is instead gloriously insistent. Insisting (which three decades earlier she called "repeating") is a method of satisfying one's "will to live"—saying, "I am here now and I am different now!" Now, repeating (which earlier she called "copying") is succumbing to a kind of death—saying only, "I'll second that!" Insisting, not repeating or copying, leads to existing or living in the fullest present participle, which, for Stein, is genius (*Lectures*, 169, 170).

The rhythm of this insistence is one thing that Stein hears when she listens to a person talking and that she attempts to capture in her portraits. She writes that she tried to express "the complete conception" of a person, "the complete rhythm of a personality that I had gradually acquired by listening seeing feeling and experience" (*Lectures*, 147). In trying to express this independent existing, Stein's "portrait writing began" (*Lectures*, 171). Stein must have savored the paradox of her listening and recreating sounds in order to create something called a "portrait"—a word that most commonly suggests the primacy of sight. But "portrait" stems from "portray," which means "to draw forth"—which can be done in conversation, as well as in the visual arts.

Speaking and writing are also important in Stein's distinction between human nature and the human mind, the agent of genius (see *Geographical History*, 68–69, 96–97). In Stein's paradigm, human nature "use[s]" language by using ordinary speech; the human mind "plays" with language, which is done in the best writing (*Geographical History*, 190, 91–92). Human nature imagines an audience when it communicates, while the human mind is its own audience when it plays games by maneuvering words. Stein discusses—while demonstrating—human nature, human mind, masterpieces, and conversation in a section of *The Geographical History of America*:

> But really what I would like to know is why the very good things everybody says and everybody knows and everybody writes are not masterpieces I would really very much like to know why they are not. And when I say identity is not yes there is something in it all the time that there is not.

If not why not.

So many words to use.

Oh do not say that words have a use.

Anybody can tell what everybody knows but what does that disclose.

Oh dear what does that inclose.

After all what everybody knows is not a master-piece but everybody says it is.

Do they.

Oh yes everybody says it is.

But everybody knows what everybody knows.

And human nature is what everybody knows and time and identity is what everybody knows and they are not master-pieces and yet everybody knows that master-pieces say what they do say about human nature and time and identity, and what is the use, there is no abuse in what is the use, there is no use. Why not.

Now listen. What is conversation.

Conversation is only interesting if nobody hears.

Hear hear.

Master-pieces are second to none.

One and one.

I am not frightened but reasonably secure that whether it is so whether it is so whether it is so.

Master-piece or none.

Which is one.

I ask you which is one.

If he had not been frightened away he might have drunk at water but he finally did.

This is as good an example of a master-piece as there is. (190–91)

Elsewhere, Stein links the human mind, writing, and masterpieces so closely that it may be surprising to hear her ask why everything that is written is not a masterpiece, "why [are] the very good things everybody . . . writes . . . not master-pieces." But if we here understand "writing" to mean the physical act or legible product, then we can easily agree with her: certainly not everything printed on paper is a masterpiece. Stein has also connected "knowing" with masterpieces, writing, and the human mind, so we may also be surprised to hear that "the very good things" that "every-body knows" do not always create masterpieces. It turns out, however, that "everybody knows" about "human nature and time and identity," and that these topics are uninteresting. For example, she writes: "human nature is not interesting and what the master-pieces tell about human nature in them is not what makes them everlastingly interesting, no it is not" (*Geographical History*, 166). As Booth says in *King Lear, Macbeth, Indefinition, and Tragedy*, what makes a masterpiece is the complex texture of overlapping false expectations created by each phoneme and incomplete pattern, rather than character and plot. If the human mind creates a masterpiece, it's in spite of, not because of, these uninteresting pieces of information.

When Stein ends the first paragraph, "And when I say identity is not yes there is something in it all the time that there is not," she seems to change the subject. Asking about masterpieces, she suddenly discusses identity. But identity is a product of human nature, and neither of them can create a masterpiece. One of the defining characteristics of identity is that it causes one to make positive assertions about oneself. Stein says that one's true self (one's "entity," to borrow a term from *The Making of Americans*) cannot conform to a positive assertion—it "is not yes"—and if one makes a positive assertion about oneself, then "there is something in it [the assertion] all the time that there is not" in one's true self. The "yes" invariably asserts something that is not true. And then following her own instructions for a masterpiece, she asks herself a question about what she has just said: "if not why not." In other words (and I have explored this in *The Making of Americans* and will again in *Ida*), why is identity "not yes"?

While pondering that question, Stein wonders about the way an answer would be formed. The answer would use words—there are "So many words to use"—and while she perhaps first meant that there were so many words to choose from, she notices her own use of the word "use" and remonstrates with herself: "Oh do not say that words have a use." At the end of the next long paragraph, Stein returns to the issue—"what is the use"—and seems to decide that "there is no abuse [of the word "use"] in what is the use." This judgment may depend on the fact that she has uttered "use" in a question or, more likely, that—by asking, "what is the use"—she idiomatically means that "there is no use." "No" and "ab-" are both negatives, reputed to cancel each other out, but we have to notice that "There is use in what is the use" does not have the same meaning as the original sentence. Using "use" with a negative, and making her readers' minds fool around with its possible meanings in this way, is not the same as using the word.

Stein asks, "Anybody can tell what everybody knows but what does that disclose." Repeating what we all know does not uncover anything very interesting or new. But Stein recognizes a worse result of this complacent repetition of common knowledge: "Oh dear what does that inclose." She critiques conventional rhetoric not only because it fails to divulge anything new, but also because it can effectively build a fence around, contain, and keep from our awareness potentially new perceptions. It seems that there is a missing question: why would people keep doing this if it did not create masterpieces? The answer: "After all what everybody knows is not a masterpiece but everybody says it is." It is not the kind of masterpiece that Stein envisions, but perhaps it is a masterpiece of a different genre, one that can contain and control. It is a masterpiece in that it exerts mastery, but for Stein a masterpiece must break that mastery into pieces of less determinacy. "Oh dear," she sincerely says, realizing the truly greater danger, the way clichés cost us dearly. And "Oh dear" may also register an insincere expression of concern: "Thank you my dear for bringing me this lovely cliché as a gift," and "Oh dear! I've dropped it, and it has broken into a great number of (much more lovely and interesting) pieces." Gertrude Stein did have a "weakness for breakable objects," after all, and "a horror of people who collect only the unbreakable" (*Autobiography*, 13).

After holding this conversation with herself—asking questions, starting to answer them, moving on to related topics, and wondering about her use of certain words and their often unintended significance—Stein begins to wonder about conversation itself. "What is conversation," she asks, and she answers, "Conversation is only interesting if nobody hears." She thus points to private conversation—with ourselves, say, or in playful and intimate circumstances—the kind of conversation in which we happily game with one another. Here we can more cheerfully wonder and wander than when we are trying to demonstrate our knowledge by giving authoritative answers.

With her "Hear hear," Stein characterizes the way listeners endorse speakers, shouting to others to agree with the speaker because he has the right answer to all their questions or problems. Even alone, "hear" can be spoken as an imperative, and as an order to give consent. In a similar way, "Hear hear" describes the way we endorse what other people know and say instead of coming up with new and difficult questions. Her "Hear hear" may also be a playful way of supporting and undermining her own positive assertion in the previous sentence: "Conversation is only interesting if nobody hears." (Stein's voice is always most assertive when she is making statements with paradoxical, ambiguous, or apparently nonsensical meanings.) "Hear hear" may also tell us to define "hear" as "agree," as in: "Conversation is only interesting if nobody [agrees]." In other words, conversation is interesting only if people constantly question or check one another.

Unlike the listener who shouts, "Hear hear" to second the speaker, "Master-pieces are second to none." They refuse to "second" someone else parliamentarily. They say what they say, and they are counted "one and one" instead of rated in relation (or addition) to one another. Something is a masterpiece or not ("Master-piece or none") and exists alone instead of in relation to others. "Which is one" could be a statement which insists again that a masterpiece is one, but Stein makes it into a question in the next paragraph with "I ask you which is one," which asks something like, "How do we recognize a masterpiece?" and recalls the question with which this section began.

Ending with the claim "This is as good an example of a master-piece as there is" makes the reader thrill at Stein's flippant self-confidence, as well as wonder just what "this" is. *The Geographical History of America*? This particular sentence? This section? The previous sentence? For the moment, let's interpret "this" as the previous sentence: "If he had not been frightened away he might have drunk at water but he finally did." This sentence is not quite a non sequitur, since it follows from the word "frightened" in the actual (because first?) non sequitur in the excerpt "I am not frightened but reasonably secure that whether it is so whether it is so whether it is so." Considering the context, Stein may be declaring that her writing is either a masterpiece or it is not ("whether" suggests that there are two choices, and the next paragraph gives "master-piece or none" as the two likeliest options). She may mean that while some people would be scared—or at least uncomfortable—not knowing if something is one thing or another, she feels secure in this position of duality. The other sentence has "frightened" in it as well, but this time it is a "he" who is frightened, and as a result he cannot drink water until later. This paraphrase doesn't make any sense to me, it does not repeat any knowledge that I already had, and the verbs are strange enough that it does not even call to mind any situation that I can imagine taking place. With this final sentence, Stein may have created a masterpiece by not using words to answer a question, not saying something that everybody knows, and not using declarative verbs that afford certainty. She has successfully broken to pieces my mastery of this section of her work.

Our human minds are thrilled, of course, but by choosing another option, we can soothe our human nature. The "this" in "This is as good an example of a master-piece as there is" may refer to the whole section, which exemplifies the kind of conversation that can make a masterpiece: playful verbal exchange with oneself, paying attention to words and the many meanings they mean beyond those meanings one first intended. Stein demonstrates the kinds of questions that can make a masterpiece. They cannot be questions about human nature and the mind and time; they are the questions that arise along the way, often in response to the words one first "uses" but then sees and hears and considers. A masterpiece elicits heightened consciousness on the part of the writer and reader.

Stein does not react only to the words she wields; she also notes the sounds between those words. Although she does not use the word "masterpiece" in the "Henry James" section of *Four in America*, Stein here also distinguishes between two types of creation, one of which seems to correspond to that definition. The two ways of writing are when "you write" and when "You write what you intend to write" (*Four in America*, 124).[5] Stein contrasts Shakespeare's sonnets and Shakespeare's plays, saying that the sonnets are an example of writing what is intended (written by human nature) and the plays are an example of right writing (masterpieces of the human mind).[6] She writes that any two consecutive words in Shakespeare's plays "mak[e] three sounds, each word makes a sound, that is two words make two sounds and the words next to each other make not only a sound but nearly a sound" (129). Her assertion supports my practice of saying a series of Stein's words out loud and paying attention not only to the sounds that the words make, but also to the "nearly sounds" that are automatically made during the transitions between words. But it's possible for both writing and talking to be products of the human mind. Talking and listening at the same time, the essence of genius, and the essence of lively open chat, is talking with the playful human mind. That lively talking and listening is what Stein somehow writes.

Learning about Listening through Reading Borrow and Smollett

As I suggested when discussing *The Making of Americans*, a writer is also in indirect conversation with previous writers. In addition to Shakespeare, two other British authors, one from the eighteenth and one from the nineteenth century, also may have suggested to Stein ways of thinking about talk and print. Obviously, one cannot accord as much significance to books that Stein liked as one does to books that she wrote and in which she chose every word, but Stein mentions *Lavengro* more often than any other book title, and Stein and the author George Henry Borrow (1803–81) seem to share many interests, including a suspicion of masters.[7] Borrow's partly autobiographical novels may have particularly interested Stein because *Lavengro* discerns relationships between words based on their sounds and folk etymologies. Borrow's novels describe the material and intellectual adventures of a "word-master," or philologist. What is remarkable about this philologist is that, rather than reading dictionaries of dead languages, he learns from experience and conversation. Inspired by what he gleans in conversation with gypsies who speak Romany, a businessman who speaks Armenian, and friends who speak Scots and Irish, he ponders (often aloud, within these same conversations) how relationships may exist between words in different living languages, how these relationships suggest latent meanings in English words, and how these latent meanings can subvert our assumptions about binarisms, as well as cast into doubt our ability to communicate without ambiguity.

For example, one conversation inspires Lavengro to wonder "if divine and devilish were originally one and the same word" (Borrow, 114). Here the philologist glimpses irony within the sounds and possible histories of ordinarily oppositional English terms. "Duvel" and "devil" and "divine" and "duvelskoe" sound somewhat alike, and those sounds suggest a possible semantic relationship among them. If "divine" and "devil" are derived from the same word, then what might that mean about the relationship between the savior and the tempter of humankind? This is the kind of question Stein seems to appreciate, one that upsets our assumptions and, while having an answer in this case, makes us keep asking questions.[8]

While Borrow champions folk etymology and provocative ideas, Tobias Smollett emphasizes the creative humor in nonstandard spelling, diction, and pronunciation. Stein mentions reading Smollett at age fifteen, and, in *The Expedition of Humphry Clinker*, Smollett highlights the additional play in language afforded by sound homonyms and visual homomorphs.[9] In that book, both Tabitha Bramble, the overbearing manager of her brother's household, and Winifred Jenkins, her good-natured servant, have primarily experienced the English language auditorily. Their limited visual experience with language leads them to make mistakes in spelling and diction that exponentially increase the semantic possibilities of their epistles.[10] Reading Smollett may have encouraged Stein to notice that the gap between written and spoken words contains significance worth exploring. The rerealized or rediscovered network of meaning between the visual and auditory mediums enables more movement and play in language and allows freedom to express more, and more complex, meaning than our already word-ful and meaning-capable English language can.

Smollett, like Stein, plays with the homophones "rite," "write," and "right." These homonyms are emphasized in an epistolary narration of one character's defense of his native Scotland in *Humphry Clinker*:

To prove that [the English] had impaired the energy of our language by false refinement, he mentioned the following words, which, though widely different in signification, are pronounced exactly in the same manner—wright, write, right, rite: but among the Scots, these words are as different in pronunciation, as they are in meaning and orthography; and this is the case with many others which he mentioned by way of illustration. (200)

Tabitha and Winifred are obviously English, because in their letters they substitute "rite" for "write" (44, 107) and for "right" (71, 220, 338). All three words sound the same to them. Tabitha's mistake occurs in the context of complaining that her written commands to the servants at home are ignored, but that her brother's uneconomical advice is always followed; what right/rite/write does he have to give away her very productive cow (44)? While the novel makes it clear that the reader is to understand her brother as generous and usually wise and Tabitha as greedy and lascivious (not just thrifty and lonely), the woman's orthographic mistakes are play-fully thought-provoking. Winifred reports that the "thieving and tricking" cook in Bath says "it was her rite to rummage the pantry" (71), which may make us wonder if this right by proximity and opportunity is any more or less right than the ones afforded to educated men—or are they just habitual rites? Winifred describes Christianity as ritual rather than the rightful truth when she wishes "some of our family be not fallen off from the rite way" (220). And Winifred also questions the ritual of patriarchal name distribu-tion when she writes about Humphry Clinker's "rite naam" being "Mattew Loyd" (338). She subverts his "rite naam" by spelling the first one incor-rectly, but this issue is also complicated by the fact that Humphry Clinker was named after his father Matthew Loyd. The elder Loyd had taken his mother's name when he inherited her property, but after selling that land and in order to inherit his father's estate, he "resumed [his] real name," Matthew Bramble (318). When Matthew Bramble calls it his "real name," there is no commentary on that name—it is a matter of fact and not to be pondered on. But Winifred's calling it a "rite" name leads to speculation about maternal and paternal rights, patriarchal rites, and even assump-tions about right and wrong. If the male prerogatives—his rights—are a rite, than perhaps they can be questioned as arbitrary; if these rights come from his ability to write, then perhaps they can be superseded by education for women. These spelling errors suggest that the ritual of writing, in ad-dition to other rituals, affords educated males an authority—a right—that uneducated women do not have.[11]

Stein's Reading and Writing of "Rights" and "Rites"

Stein's writing is so unusual that a reader would be hard-pressed to tell whether Stein had substituted a homonym or not, but she also plays with "rite," "write," and "right." Instead of relying on misspellings, Stein places homonyms close to one another, which induces a reader to play with substitution in those cases and suggests the possible fruitfulness of substitution elsewhere in Stein's texts. Her treatment of these homophones throughout *The Geographical History of America* suggests her interest in conversation and theorizing. Enigmatic as ever, Stein writes: "I am right because I write this" (*Geographical History*, 78). But she doesn't approve of "being right," because it is too limiting and ends discussion. As with "writing," Stein defines "right" in at least two ways. "Being right" is a job for human nature and saying, and it involves claiming certainty—and Stein implies that self-delusional certainty is the only kind:

> Write and right.
> Of course they have nothing to do with one another.
> (*Geographical History*, 227)

Then again, "right" appears in the phrase "right writing" and is the kind of physical writing that successfully attends to and plays with language. Right writing is not the same as "being right." This "right" modifies "write" and denotes the ideal kind of writing that forms masterpieces:

> The human mind can write what it is because what it is is all that it
> is and as it is all that it is all it can do is to write.
> Yes that is right. (97)

The human mind "is all that it is," in contrast with human nature, which claims to be much that it is not. Because the human mind just is and has no intention of presenting itself as something else (or even presenting itself at all), it can write. Because "The human mind has no resemblances" (which involve memory), it can write: "if it had [a habit of memory] it could not write that is to say write right" (91). These different definitions of "write" and "right" confuse the issue quite a bit but highlight the mind at play with language.

The following paragraphs continue that same game and exemplify others:

They say I am not right when I say that what you say is not the same as what you write but anybody try to write and they will say that this is so.

When you write well when you write anybody try to write and they will say that I am right.

What you say has nothing to do with what you write. . . .

They say that when I say it is not what they say but what they write that has to do with the human mind they say when I say this that I am not right but I am right because I write this and I do not say this. When I say it it is not so but when I write it it is so. Anybody can know that this is so. (*Geographical History*, 78)

Several word games are going on here. "They say" and "I say" have literal as well as idiomatic meanings, and Stein lets the idioms push her ideas along. "They say" suggests the big anonymous group that determines public opinion (discussed more fully here in chapter 6), and Stein disagrees on general principle with this generalized "they." They are also *saying*, which suggests human nature is at work, rather than the human mind. The word "well" functions in two ways: as a pause or filler word and as an important qualifying adjective for the kind of writing one must do in order to discover Stein is right.

In "Volume two" in *The Geographical History of America*, Stein frustrates readers, because she doesn't provide what we think we need to understand her. We think we need to know what the question is, and we think we need to understand an unequivocal answer. But a different kind of expression might have undermined her "message" by making it equivocal in a different way. Again playing with "right" and "write" (I've added punctuation to signal how I separate the phrases):

Volume two

I have been writing a political series just to know as well as to know that I am always right that is I am always right when I say what I say and I always say something that is what I am doing I am always saying something but as I am never writing what I am saying when I am writing I am as it were not saying something and so then[,] there it is[,] that is what writing is[:] not saying something[,] content without form[.] but anyway[,] in saying anything there is no content but there is the form of question and answer[,] and really anybody can know that a question if there is an answer[—]or an answer if there is a question[—]is almost always almost human nature[.] which we do know[—]we are not right about it[,] but we do know it[,] know that it is not at all interesting. (227–28)

Stein's ideas align themselves in two categories, one that has to do with writing and one with saying. "Saying" corresponds to "being right" and having "no content"; it takes the form of questions and answers. The part of us that deals in questions and answers is our human nature. (Since it is also our human nature that usually speaks, and usually wants some closure, this idea that saying takes on the form of questions and answers is consistent.) Our human minds cannot be right about human nature, since rightness is not a quality of the human mind.[12] The human mind can know, which is different from being right, and all that the human mind seems to know for sure about human nature is that it is not interesting. Writing corresponds with knowing and "content" and can be "without form." "Content" seems to be a matter of significance, something that "right writing" holds. "Form," though, seems to be a false signal for content. For example, we are used to the format of questions and answers, and we assume that format holds something important, but in Stein's opinion it does not.

Stein is not alone in opining that form can disguise a lack of content. Neil Postman in *Amusing Ourselves to Death: Public Discourse in the Age of Show Business* criticizes contemporary public discourse for having "little content, as this word used to be defined" (112). He asserts that questions and answers in the form of crossword puzzles, quiz shows, and the game Trivial Pursuit are invented contexts "in which otherwise useless information might be put to some apparent use" (76). Combining terms from Stein and Postman, human nature may be what tempts us into being amused, what appreciates the images and the speed of modern "news," but the human mind appreciates "such larger abstractions as truth, honor, love, [and] falsehood [which] cannot be talked about in the lexicon of pictures" or, Stein might add, within a prearranged format (Postman, *Amusing Ourselves*, 72). In *The Geographical History of America*, Stein explains that human nature deals in questions and answers, and she suggests that while this may make a person feel right, it does not give him knowledge. Instead, questions and answers may lead to a false sense of understanding; they are part of a rite we enact when we try to understand our world and ourselves, but that formula only misleads us into thinking we know something. If you have an answer to a question (or even a question for an answer), then that issue seems resolved; the questioner and answerer know what is important about that field of inquiry and forget that original discovery occurs through observation and wonder, not questions and answers. As Henry Adams points out: "Nothing in education is so astonishing as the amount of ignorance it accumulates in the form of inert facts" (379).

On the other hand, right writing somehow escapes this particular question-and-answer form. Writing has content without this form, and if we look at Stein's writing, we learn that content often consists of phrases that may or may not be accurately called questions—they don't have question marks and they don't have answers. Stein says that the best modern writing, because it has content instead of form, must be done by a woman, and that she is doing "the important literary thinking" herself (*Geographical History*, 210, 214). If we understand content to mean questions without answers, and if we believe the widespread claim that feminine writing—like women's sexuality, the argument goes—is willing to be open-ended, inconclusive, and less authoritative, then there may be something to what she says. Stein writes that "it is always interesting to answer anything," but (as we saw on the airplane) she does not seem to care if she remembers the answers. The activity is more important than the product.

What have been reported as Gertrude Stein's last words—"What is the answer . . . in that case what is the question?"—are so appropriate that the story seems apocryphal. If so, it was made up by someone who understood issues that Stein worried to death. Instead of the repetition and certainty of the questions and answers in the catechism or just the reassuring answers of Christian last rites, Stein wonders, as she leaves the world, not only about the truth but also about the way to truth.

When Stein dies, she asks for "the answer" and Alice responds with silence. It's possible that Stein is referring to the circumstances of their conversation: Stein is dying of stomach cancer and insists on an operation even though the doctors have said the risks are too great. The dilemma may seem obvious: either she dies of stomach cancer or she dies from the operation, so there is no good answer. But "What is the question?" is a good question. Thus far perhaps they have assumed the question, probably something like, "How am I going to stay alive?" But is that the most interesting question? Perhaps the question is "What is the best way to die?" Or maybe Stein isn't thinking about the best way for her physical form to expire. By asking "What is the question?" Stein may wonder about and accomplish the most affecting exit from her physical form, riding her intellectual hobbyhorse into the sunset. One reviewer comments that Stein "wonders in rhythm and in cadences and she rouses wonder in you and she never answers your wonders because that would end it, that would be death" (Winter, 83–84). Her dying words are her characteristic way of refusing to die.

When in 1934 Stein says, "Language as a real thing is not imitation either of sounds or colors or emotions it is an intellectual recreation" (*Lectures*, 238), she celebrates Ferdinand de Saussure's 1916 conception that the "relation of words to their meanings is fundamentally arbitrary" (Lehman, 94). But Stein adds that language as it "has come to be spoken and written," holds in it "all the history of its intellectual recreation," which suggests that the semantic tradition has an interesting history of its own which influences the multiple connotations of words.[13] Stein's friend and publisher Daniel-Henry Kahnweiler emphasizes freedom and self-determination when he writes that Stein's "entirely new use of [English] vocabulary" frees the words from "any law antecedent to the act of creation" and "abandon[s]" those words to their "interior logic" (xii). The problem with German, Stein says, is that there is too strong a connection between words and their meanings: "the german language as a language suffers from this what the words mean sound too much like what they do, and children do these things by one sort or another of invention but this has really nothing to do with language" (*Lectures*, 238). According to Stein, then, the poor Germans don't get "intellectual recreation" from their language. The good thing about a language such as English is that there is no intrinsic connection between words and meanings but there are an infinite number of connections between words and words, and these connections create a jungle gym for the exercise of our intellects.

Not only does this network of meaning allow "intellectual recreation" as in playful fun, but "intellectual recreation" also suggests we can recreate our language and our meaning as we move onward. Derrida playfully deconstructs, but Stein's play is an intellectual reconstruction. Connections are made by noting visual and auditory similarities between words that we usually understand as semantically different. Stein disposes words in unusual arrangements such that her readers are disposed to notice their sights and sounds, make recreational connections between them, and produce unusual arrangements of meaning. Stein's word arrangements demand that words do more than they usually do. She writes: "I like the feeling of words doing as they want to do and as they have to do when they live where they have to live that is where they have come to live which of course they do do" (*Narration*, 15). Words can do what they want to do only if we are listening to them as they come out of our mouths, or watching them as they land on the paper in front of us—if we read creatively instead of dogmatically.

While Stein demonstrates these conversations in *The Geographical History of America* and in her lectures, most of her listeners in the United States walked away wondering what she meant. They tried to follow along with her words instead of participating in a free exchange of ideas and letting meaning develop as it could, as it does.

CHAPTER 5

Talking Boundaries into Thresholds in *Ida*

S TEIN PREFERRED NOT to be introduced before her lectures; reports state that she just walked up to the stage (usually down the center aisle, through the audience) and started talking without any introduction or introductory remarks ("Miss Stein Speaks"; "Princeton Dazed"; Schriftgiesser). She liked to meet people straight in, in her own terms. But Stein became an American icon during the tour, and she was happily but uneasily aware of her fame. In a December 1934 letter to Carl Van Vechten, she expressed her amazement and pleasure at being identifiable to someone who very probably would not be attending one of her free but often exclusive lectures:

> a reporter girl, told me and she swears she did not make it up here in Toledo that she went to the station to meet us on a train we did not come on and she asked the gate man if we had come through and he looked blank and a shabby citizen leaning on the wall said no she did not come through and the ticket man said who and the shabby man said sure I know her I never saw her but she would not get by here without my knowing her and then he said to the porter, you know her the one who said a rose is a rose is a rose is a rose you know her. (Burns, 368)

Aware of the complications of fame even before setting foot in the United States, Stein describes in *How Writing Is Written* (1936) its dangerous effects on subjectivity:

> One never gets quite used to unexpectedly seeing one's name in print no matter how often it happens to you to be that one; it always gives you a shock of a slightly mixed-up feeling, are you or are you not one. No matter how often it happens there is always this thing, but what is that, imagine what is that compared to never having heard anybody's voice

speaking while a picture is doing something, and that voice and that person is yourself, if you could really and truly be that one. It upset me very much when that happened to me, there is no doubt about that, if there can really not be any doubt about anything. ("I Came and Here I Am," 68; my italics)

What does it mean to look at the self from the outside? From a perspective of time and distance? "Are you or are you not one." If you are hearing yourself speak, and watching your lips move while you talk, which one are you? Can you be two, speaking to yourself?

Ida and its title character act as sounding boards for various possibilities about the self, and these ideas contribute, with much of Stein's other writing, to a theory of personal subjectivity and social cohesion that depends upon conversation. In the novel, Stein is still interested in some of the details of speech, but here that interest is compounded with an analysis of the self. Stein wonders why a self is so fragile, who makes it, and how to avoid letting others break it. She seems finally to perceive the self as a formation of the interactional conversations that take place between voices within and voices without, but a problem arises if any of the voices become too hardened by expectation or reputation. She recognizes fame as a dilemma for the famous and even begins to see it as a troublesome phenomenon among the fans; she will explore this issue of the public as a political mass in similar terms in later works. Stein sees the cessation of verbal intercourse as an individual's living death, but she also depicts true death as the end of reciprocal conversation, petrifying the deceased into the subject of a summary monologue.

There are (of course) some thought-provokingly mysterious sections to the novel, but Ida speaks in standard phrases, at least one of which she exchanges for another in a new setting. She agreeably begins many of her sentences with "yes" (*Ida*, 628, 692), and Stein tells us that she says "nice little things" such as "all right" (628), "You are very welcome," and "very well I thank you" (625). Ida "liked to thank" and "she liked to be thanked," although Stein suggests that Ida "was not really interested" in much, including "Anything that was given to her": "she [just] liked to thank" (692). After many exchanges of "how do you do" (623, 625), Ida moves house and notices that people in her new town say, "How are you?" so "Ida learned to say it like that. How are you" (661). Later, when Ida is "resting" so often that she appears to be ill, she learns that some people (nurses, probably) say, "well how are we today," or "well and how are we today" (701). In describing the way Ida never answers this question, no matter how many people ask it,

Stein offers up an axiom on a conversational routine: "Ida would have nothing to say. She had not answered the first one and if you are resting you cannot hurry enough to catch up and so she had nothing to say," because "you always have to answer the first one before you answer the second one" (701). That is, if you want to avoid offending anyone.

Ida herself, like the earlier Stein, is interested in food and talk: "She liked to see people eat, in restaurants and wherever they eat, and she liked to talk" (*Ida*, 624). But Stein seems to have become intensely interested in how people become themselves, and how they stay that way—an interest she had begun to explore in *The Making of Americans*. In *Ida*, she demonstrates how the self is endangered by the constrictions of fame. Listening to what "they say" can alter (or freeze) the sense of self, so celebrity offers an intensified instance of a common problem. The problem is especially complicated by the fact that living people with real being are flexible and, like Ida, "change all the time" (629). How do we genuinely remain ourselves without getting stuck and staying too much the same? How do we insist instead of copy? Possibly the only solution is to maintain a give-and-take relationship with oneself and others. We must keep up the interactional conversation of mutual discovery.

I choose the word "self" because Stein's specific understanding of the word "identity" (in a pair with "entity") makes that word impossible to use in a general sense. I mean "self" to represent the varying proportions of (formal, intentional, sometimes false) identities and (basic, internal, often ignored but necessarily true) entities a person experiences as self—at particular moments, but also across a lifetime. Identities are simple, performative, and singular; entities are complex, inherent, and singular; but the self is multiple, more than an idea, and dependent on experience and the interaction between external and internal forces. In fact, Ida may represent that very mix, Ida-entity.

Conversation may also be the place where the self is most evident in the moment, demonstrating the provisional, transient, evanescent agreement our different sides and multiple external influences have reached with each other, the ongoing compromise we've reached with our potential selves and the world we inhabit. The self is perhaps best manifested in the moment of speech when each utterance is the result of countless conscious and unconscious decisions about the relationship between our unique selves and the others! Each decision in which we negotiate our way through our own desires and the forces of external expectation makes us a combination of self and other. Stein might agree that we are what we eat, but she would also add that we are what we say. By our fruits ye shall know us, and the fruit of all this silent dialogue is our uttered conversation. We carry on a running multisided dialogue as we try to get a sense of who we are, and the answer is somewhere in between, in the dialogue itself (like meaning in modern semiotics). If I am not just one but two, if I am not just I but you (and it, that there), then I am formed by the conversation held between me and myself, me and you, us and it—the conversation among all. I exist within what my selves and yours (who are just as multiple) all end up saying to each other. But *Ida* is not really about single utterances. *Ida* seems to be more about the negotiations than about the uttered conclusions we reach.

I use the word "conversation" because that's what is taking place on real and metaphorical—audible and inaudible—levels. If the self is the shape I just described—multiple and influenced by other selves—then conversation within and without is of primary importance. Certainly we talk to ourselves, within ourselves, as much as or more than we talk to others. Perhaps silent and internal debate is only conversation in a metaphorical sense, but it mimics the exchange between differently embodied "real" voices. The most metaphorical of these conversations—since one side can't use language—is between the nonhuman environment and ourselves, yet whatever we notice about that environment we internalize, turn into words, and thus enable to participate in our silent internal conversation. Sam Hamilton—who, like many other characters in *Ida*, appears only to speak and disappear—says, "I like everything I say to be said out loud" (627), which suggests that much of the other conversation in the book takes place silently. Sam likes to speak "out loud," but much that the characters "say" in this book is part of their own silent intrapersonal communion, most obviously when Ida-Ida writes to Ida, and when Ida writes to Winnie.

In *Ida*, then, Stein is less interested in the mechanics or "essence" of small talk than in the conversational nature of subjectivity, an idea that might have come naturally to her, or that could have been inspired by George Herbert Mead, who called thought "inner conversation" ("Social Self," 146). Individuals are always conversing—with other people's words, with impressionistic memories of those words (the way other people's words have become internalized), and among aspects of the self whose origins are so complex that it's impossible to determine whether they originated "in here" or "out there." Our public and private selves vie for primacy, our old and new selves disagree about how we should spend our time, our angelic and devilish selves make decisions inconsistent with each other, our skeptical and creative selves cooperate (we hope) to determine the kind of work we do, and so on. Sometimes one voice might "win," but usually the voices have to coexist and keep talking. Stein seems to envision subjectivity as a product of all that gets said in serious colloquy, gossipy prattle, or deep communion among voices originating both within and without.

Like utterances, subjectivity is "context-shaped" and "context-renewing" (Heritage, 242). Subjectivity is changed by, and changes, the subjectivities (and even the nonhuman environments) around it. To borrow and amend an idea and phrase from Neil Postman, who calls his field "media ecology," Stein explores the social ecology of self. Postman argues that the environment in which contemporary humans in the developed world find ourselves consists most evidently of the media around us; language is our primary environment. Stein's ecology of the self necessitates mutual adaptation through language exchange.[1] That's a fancy way of saying that if a person talks and listens, she changes and is changed, but it also suggests that a person has a self from which to speak and adapt. We do not start with nothing; our peculiar elements express themselves and react with others in all-their-own ways.

A self and that which is not part of that self may be less distinct than we assume, and a creative and perpetual dialogue takes place across or through the permeable boundary between them. Referring, inevitably, to inside and outside, self and other, I am using the very Cartesian distinction that Stein muddies; my plain English can't quite escape the intellectual bonds that Stein's "cuckoo" writing can. Stein writes in *Ida*: "Once upon a time way back there were always gates," but then "little by little there were no fences no walls anywhere. For a little time they had a gate even when there was no fence. It was there just to look elegant and it was nice to have a gate that would click even if there was no fence. By and by there was no gate" (626). Once upon a time there might have been distinct properties, distinct selves, but then the fences disappeared and the gates were just ornamental. Now, she posits, none of that is left or is even necessary. Ida's preference is "People should be there and not come through a door" (690). It might look as if Stein is still tearing apart the distinction between self and other, but really she's already building something else in its place. Some people might be worrying about how to handle the loss of the individual and apparently independent self, but Stein imagines a new (or just newly recognized) sense of personhood arising from the acknowledgment and celebration of messy inner subjectivity and its analogies to a wider human network.

"Who is any one said the wife to the husband"

While it is possible to read *The Making of Americans* as a psychomachia in which Stein takes herself and Americans apart and puts neither back together, it is impossible to read *Ida*—particularly "First Half"—as anything but the subject's separation into pieces. Ida is many people: she is one ("I" looks like "1") and two ("da" sounds a bit like "deux") and possibly the Freudian "id" negotiating with voices different from the predictably conscientious superego and the mediating ego. (None of her parts know their part; perhaps they are too vital for that). "Da" is also Russian for "yes," one of Ida's favorite words. Ida is an "I" and an "idea" that "I" thinks. She is probably not Stein's ideal, but it is also a mistake to understand Ida as abnormal—as having a multiple personality disorder, for example. Unlike Edmund Spenser, Stein does not characterize a self with "a thousand yong ones" in its mouth as a dangerous and monstrous Errour ("Faerie Queene," 1.15–18).

The novel explores Ida's relationship with herself, and her different selves necessarily communicate with each other through various kinds of conversation. In *Everybody's Autobiography*, Stein writes that "real ideas are not the relation of human beings as groups but a human being to himself inside him" (206). In *Ida*, Stein explores these "real ideas." Ida talks to named aspects of herself: Ida-Ida and Winnie, for sure, and perhaps others (since self and other can be so easily be mistaken here). Stein's report that Ida "was just going to talk to herself" and so "she no longer even needed a twin" suggests that these twins represent Ida's multiple voices (*Ida*, 634). And this suggestion remains, in spite of the fact that Winnie herself—as far I can tell—never says anything but only inspires reactions from the people around her. Their communication hardly turns psychological drama into action, so it is more likely that it represents Stein's understanding of the self as formed by conversation—internal and silent conversation, as well as external and aloud.

Both types of communication form and inform Ida's sense of self, because internal conversation is influenced by her affiliations with the people around her. By blurring the distinctions between them, Stein depicts the mutual dependency of individual selves. When Ida converses with named aspects of herself, the reader has to guess who is internal and who is not. While Winnie and Ida-Ida are almost certainly internal (the beautiful parts of Ida that make her famous), Andrew is a mystery. We are first told: "Everybody knew that Andrew was one of two. He was so completely one of two that he was two" (*Ida*, 661). Either Andrew is a twin, too, or he is one of Ida's selves (she's gotten rid of her other twins by now), or he is two different things: a person in his own right *and* an internalized voice. Perhaps he is both an externalized self (a real person with whom Ida identifies) and an internalized other (a voice within Ida that has been inspired by that of an external, "real" person). Andrew continues to be identified by contradictions: he is there but he never seems to begin being there, he does "not notice Ida but he saw her," he takes lots of walks but "in a way was never out walking," and "Ida called him but she really never called him" (662, 663). He is "always there," but Ida says, "How do you do" to him when she meets him, although Stein adds that "she did not really meet him nobody did" (663). In these ways, he just seems to *be* there, to be there *always*, and perhaps even to be inside, reachable through silence and always observing. Andrew's case suggests the difficulty of determining whether a character represents an alien aspect of oneself (an otherness that is internal; a facet of oneself that does not feel homogenous with the rest of the self); or a very familiar other with whom one identifies (an external self, an extension of one's being). When self and other are so easily confused, real (oral, aural, public, exterior) conversation and metaphorical (silent, private, interior) dialogue are indistinguishable. In spite of the presence of Ida-Ida, Winnie, Andrew, an officer, men with orange blossoms in their hats, five aunts, and a married couple, among others, *Ida* may be a book with one character. Ida exists between and among these other personalities, and they seem to exist mainly within her, as well.

Stein's analysis of human types, and her exploration of the ways that listeners can influence the self-perception of the speaker, lead her, even as early as *The Making of Americans*, to the possibility that the only definable difference between inside and out is an arbitrary epidermic perimeter. She writes of a particular type of person who is "being independent dependent being in completely fluid condition and being a whole one only, and always being one, by having a skin to hold it in and to separate it so from every one and make it so an individual one" (*Making*, 398, and see 387). Other characters and types have "being" in them "in a more solid concentration," and *The Making of Americans* does not explicitly delve further into the subject of the indeterminate self. (Although, because it's so difficult to remember which is which of the two main types—"dependent independent" and "independent dependent"—she may implicitly be discussing this indeterminate mutual dependence.) *The Making of Americans* already suggests, then, that the differences between self and other are very minor: if we are all made up of the same components in different proportions—an unknown ratio of attacking and resisting, say—then the main difference between self and other is a thin layer of skin.[2] When we are defining ourselves as unique, perhaps we are really only gerrymandering to form an appearance of consistency.

Stein's fame, which came to her long after she wrote *The Making of Americans*, may have radicalized her thinking but did not qualitatively change it. *Ida* continues her thoughts on fluid, interpenetrating being. That which exists outside a person's skin can influence a person's self—that which is outside comes inside—and, by the time she writes *Ida*, Stein has felt this public influence so strongly that she only approximately draws the line between self and not-self in that work. The influence of these outside voices on Ida is so significant that the boundary between self and other is almost indistinguishable. We feel we know the difference, of course, and Stein seems to have successfully divided her sense of self from her reputation, but the turbid area around Ida's personal boundary makes definition very difficult.

Everything and everyone a person attends to becomes part of the self's experience and being. In *The Dialogical Self: Meaning as Movement*, Hubert J. M. Hermans and Harry J. G. Kempen bring together the ideas of Giambattista Vico, John Dewey, William James, George Herbert Mead, and Mikhail Bakhtin to grapple with Descartes and the Cartesian basis of Western thought about the self. Hermans and Kempen explain that while the French structuralists resist the Cartesian distinction between mind and body, subject and object, and they "decentralize" the self, their idea of a multifaceted human self is subject to "impersonal structures and processes." In this constructivist model, the self is at the mercy of the inhuman world. The pragmatists, however, and Hermans and Kempen, "stress *inter*subjective transactions and practices" (32; my italics). Citing John Dewey, Hermans and Kempen define the subject as an "agent-sufferer" or "embodied agent . . . living between two centers: the subject as acting upon the world and the world acting upon the subject. The interaction is so complex that the environment is in a way *in* the subject" (31).[3] While the French structuralists see the self as subject to the other, the pragmatists see the other as part of the self, and see them as having a reciprocal relationship. Perhaps I exaggerate only a little when I say that what is "out there" has to come "in here" to be noticeable.

This analysis suggests, among other things, that human interaction—which tends to occur through conversation—greatly influences subjectivity. Understanding subjectivity through dialogue "acknowledges both the existence of pre-existing structures and the subject as an innovative agent" (Hermans and Kempen, 47n1).[4] Starting with the (false) assumption that there is a single, stable self from which we speak, it is quite easy to accept the theory that this self was developed in relationship to the other selves around it. (Indeed, how—or where—else is language acquired to describe the self or anything else?) Acknowledging that the self continues to interact with other people, and to participate in a wide range of relationships, recommends the further axiom that the self is constantly under renovation and even develops multiple, coexistent, and sometimes contradictory forms. We are in dialogue with the world. Indeed, each of us multiplies into a we when encountering the multiplicities of the social world.

The characters in *Ida* are only vaguely distinguished from one another, which makes us wonder who they are, specifically, as well as who *anyone* is. Ida creates Winnie as a separate being, but everyone else thinks they are the same person. For example, one man sees Winnie, follows Winnie, rings the bell and asks for Winnie, but "of course there was no Winnie," and "he could not ask for Ida because he did not know Ida. . . . Well in a way he did ask for Ida" (*Ida*, 623). Midway through *Ida*, a married couple discusses possible husbands for their houseguest Ida, a discussion which produces an overwhelming question: "who is any one said the wife to the husband" (655). Inherently a deep question, its exchange between spouses complicates the issue even further. The marriage service would have husband and wife be "one flesh." Are the two participants in this dialogue separate people, or two halves (or even smaller fractions) of the same person? And how does either state of affairs explicate the question, "Who is anyone"? This reminder of the binding of two people in marriage also suggests further divisions in Ida: she marries several times, and her husbands—other parts of herself, though she doesn't seem to pay any attention to them—keep disappearing from the novel. So we are left wondering: who is any one, or anyone? Stein's answer: perhaps there is no such thing as "one."[5]

Fame and the Public: Alienation from the Self

From early on, Ida feels divided within herself. The novel begins with her mother trying to keep Ida from being born. That birth leads to a further birth, because "as Ida came, with her came her twin, so there she was Ida-Ida," which suggests a plausible psychoanalytic scenario in which an unwanted child develops dual selves to separate good and bad characteristics (*Ida*, 611). Ida separates herself from her appearance: she creates a beautiful and famous twin, to whom she writes letters and from whom she often feels quite alienated. Another creation story for this twin arises when Ida tells her dog, Love (who is "almost blind"), that Ida is "tired of being just one" and so she is "going to have a twin yes I am Love" (613). When this twin dyes her hair, it is Ida who will be called "a suicide blonde" (613).[6] Stein's "Ida often wrote letters to herself that is to say she wrote to her twin," and in these letters she touts her twin's appearance: "I think that you could be a queen of beauty . . . they go everywhere and everybody looks at them and everybody sees them" (618). Ida thinks of the beauty queen as someone separate from herself, as modern sports figures and politicians refer to themselves in third person by name. But others see the everyday Ida (the speaker or subject who knows herself) and the famed Ida (the object or thing known) as one. "Nobody knew anything about her except that she was Ida but that was enough because she was Ida the beauty Ida" (619). The twin is (a part of) Ida but feels alien.

Having become (or having one part of her become) the beauty queen, Ida feels lost: "she was a beauty, she had won the prize she was judged to be the most beautiful but she was bewildered" (*Ida*, 620). Ida never has any sense that she is the beauty queen. Stein tells a strange tale which suggests that the lost Ida develops a third internal other who may mediate for, or just be confused between, the other two. On the way home to a place different from the home address she gives out, Ida

> saw a woman carrying a large bundle of wash. This woman stopped and she was looking at a photograph, Ida stopped too and it was astonishing, the woman was looking at the photograph, she had it in her hand, of Ida's dog Love. This was astonishing.
>
> Ida was so surprised she tried to snatch the photograph and just then an automobile came along, there were two women in it, and the automobile stopped and they stepped out to see what was happening. Ida snatched the photograph from the woman who was busy looking at the automobile and Ida jumped into the automobile and tried to start it, the two women jumped into the automobile threw Ida out and went on in the automobile with the photograph. Ida and the woman with the big bundle of wash were left there. The two of them stood and did not say a word. (620)

If we think of the two women in the car as Ida and her beautiful twin, then the Ida walking home is a third Ida, lost between her famous persona and her (imaginary but convenient to call it so in this schema) originary self. (The two women in the car could also represent the two names Ida has given her more famous persona: Ida-Ida and Winnie. The walker would then be our alienated Ida.) This walking Ida is literally "go[ing] a long way round" between the address she gives out (as the beauty queen) and her private home (that of the first Ida) (620). The photograph of Love is probably available to the woman looking at it because it depicts the dog of the famous beauty queen, but the lost Ida can't understand why a picture of *her own* dog has been published.[7] The woman with the photograph is far enough outside her own self to be staring at a picture of a stranger's dog, and to let someone steal the picture when the beauty queen in the car takes her full attention. She is so blinded by what she's supposed to see, so enamored of the picture, that she cannot see the real Ida right there with her. The lost Ida wants to get into the car and take back control. But once begun, the role of "publicity saint" moves on its own, like an automobile, and the saint herself doesn't have to (or can't) do anything but "rest."[8] The famous Ida regains the driver's seat, and another aspect of Ida is silenced: she and the woman "did not say a word."

There isn't much to the beauty queen—whom Ida eventually names Winnie—but the attention she gets makes her interesting. Attention breeds more attention, and the people who give it have lost their will to attend to whatever idiosyncrasies interest them most. In one episode: "The place was full, nobody looked at Ida. Some of them were talking about Winnie. They said. But really, is Winnie so interesting? They just talked and talked about that" (*Ida*, 622). They can't see Ida—who looks just like Winnie, who *is* Winnie in at least one sense, but who probably doesn't carry herself the same way—because the *idea* of Winnie is so strong in their minds. "They said" is one of Stein's ways of pointing toward a group mentality, a loss of individuality and personal discrimination. Stein asks us, "But really, is Winnie so interesting?" and perhaps the crowd is wondering the same thing, except that as they talk and talk, they prove that they do find her "so interesting."

Winnie becomes a precursor to Don DeLillo's "most photographed barn in America" (12). Stein describes one of the "many things [that] happened to Winnie:

> Once there were two people who met together. They said. What shall we do? So what did they do. They went to see Winnie. That is they went to look at Winnie.
>
> When they looked at her they almost began to cry. One said. What if I did not look at her did not look at Winnie. And the other said. Well that is just the way I feel about it.
>
> After a while they began to think that they had done it, that they had seen Winnie, that they had looked at her. It made them nervous because perhaps really had they.

One said to the other. Say have we and the other answered back, say have we.

Did you see her said one of them. Sure I saw her did you. Sure he said sure I saw her.

They went back to where they came from. (*Ida*, 622)

For lack of something better to do, these two people go to look at (not necessarily see) Winnie, the beauty queen. Their incomplete expression about what would happen if they chose not to look at Winnie suggests first the hypothesis that she would not exist without spectators and also the likelihood that these people are not quite thoughtful enough to think that thought in its entirety. Neither of them seems sure that they see Winnie, but their shared experience allows them to believe that they have. As Murray Jay Siskind, DeLillo's "visiting lecturer on living icons," says about visiting the barn: "Being here is a kind of spiritual surrender. We see only what others see. . . . We've agreed to be part of a collective perception" (DeLillo, 10, 12). While Ida, Ida-Ida, and Winnie are distinct but communicating personas within one person, these two physically distinct interlocutors share a point of view. They agree on everything, however vaguely, which may suggest that they serve as external selves for one another. And they are not changed by their experience: they saw what they set out to see and then "went back to where they came from."

If the barn were a "living icon" like Winnie, then Siskind's questions would address even more of Stein's concerns about the life of a living sign; he says, "No one sees the barn," and he asks, "What was the barn like before it was photographed?" (DeLillo, 12–13). He concludes: "We can't answer these questions because we've read the signs, seen the people snapping the pictures. We can't get outside the aura. We're part of the aura" (13). So imagine Ida's bewilderment, trapped inside the aura of her own double's fame.[9] Can she escape? Can she assert herself? Since she's essentially passive, is passivity her one recourse for self-expression? And can that self-expression really live underneath, or in any way revolt from, Winnie's fame?

Ida is herself, interested in herself, and perhaps too self-absorbed, too much interested in sitting, resting, and being satisfied with that. She wants mainly to talk to herself, a situation in which she feels nobody can interrupt her (*Ida*, 634). But her self-absorption has some social benefits: she will probably not become like these men, who need reassurance from others about their own experiences. Ida's unlikely to become part of the anonymous "they." She's a complex person who cannot become a cog in a political wheel (though her passivity is likely to make her irrelevant). She will not accept authority; as soon as someone knows even her twin's name, Ida leaves town. Names, the ones we call ourselves or the ones others call us, are a form of power. One of Ida's husbands meets a chief of police who can't catch fish; the chief says: "Well I caught a trout the other day and he got away from me. Why didn't you take his number said Arthur. Because fish can't talk was the answer" (631). The fish is uncatchable without a name, or without a voice to participate in this transaction with the police chief. In fact, pointing forward to a problem faced in ecocriticism, Stein suggests that the fish does not inhabit names at all; the problem is not only choosing the *correct* voice to impose on the fish, but imposing *any* voice on the fish. As a talking person, however, Ida has to work to avoid identifying herself, to avoid letting herself be mastered by an identity. Nor will Ida become an authority over someone else: she wants to remain childless because she doesn't want to "tell [her children] what to do" (634). This is an example of her interest, first, in her relationship with herself, not with others and, second, in interactional instead of transactional conversation. (Ida's tendencies are also related to Stein's antiauthoritarianism, which I discuss in the next chapter in greater depth.)

The Self and Its Trappings

Ida addresses often unrecognized influences on the self from which we speak, including the bodies we both are and feel we inhabit. Our bodies have a say in our subjectivities, and other people's bodies speak to us before the people start using words. Ida wishes to be free of these restrictions, which may explain why she runs away from Winnie, who represents Ida's appearance. She does not like to be recognized. Stein points to the way the physical body influences the mind, ideas, and subjectivity:

> A woman said to Ida, I only like a white skin. If when I die I come back again and I find I have any other kind of skin then I will be sure that I was very wicked before.
> This made Ida think about talking. (624)

A contemporary reader is surprised that this woman's words don't make Ida think about racism, but Ida's thoughts encompass the problem of racial prejudice. The woman speaks from her (probably) white-skinned body, which points to "the role of the body in the process of knowing itself" (Hermans and Kempen, 9).[10] Like most thinkers influenced by the legacy of Descartes, though, this woman does not acknowledge the ways her body influences her views on skin color (and probably on other topics); she assumes that if she were reborn as a person of color, she would still believe as her white-skinned self did. A reader also wonders why this woman makes this comment to Ida, and Ida's own skin color becomes important to understanding the exchange—but we don't really know Ida's race. If Ida is white skinned, then the woman may be assuming that Ida agrees with her. If Ida is a person of color, the woman is chastising her for wickedness. This conversation also makes a reader notice that Stein never describes Ida. In fact, *Ida* must be one of a very few novels in which the female main character is assigned no physical characteristics.

Issues of identity upset Ida, perhaps because they tend to influence what people say. They make interactional conversation less free-form, more predictable, and perhaps slightly more transactional. So Ida chooses to converse with people of indeterminate identity: officers without their uniforms (who may or may not be officers) and people who have not introduced themselves by name (624–25).[11] Stein writes: "This makes conversation with them easier and more difficult" (624). Ida does not want an officer to tell her his name because "if I knew your name I would not be interested in you, no, I would not" (625–26). Ida likes to speak to people about whom she knows as little as possible; without roles to fulfill (except, of course, the female one that she carries with her always), Ida—like Stein, who would not speak to officials—can specialize in interactional conversation. She can speak without predicting the consequences and thus perhaps being tempted to alter what she says.

In spite of her dislike of roles, and even though she eventually murders Winnie, Ida recognizes the difficulty of losing a pose:

> Ida said to this one. When you put your uniform away for the summer you are afraid of moths. Yes said the officer. I understand that, said Ida, and she slowly drifted away, very thoughtfully, because she knew of this. Alone and she was alone and she was afraid of moths and of mothballs. The two go together. (*Ida*, 626)

Trying to free herself from Winnie is a task about which Ida feels mixed emotions. She wants to escape her public persona and be a private, freer self, but she is attached to the fame and beauty of that twin. She and the officer are afraid of moths because moths can destroy the uniform (and uniformed) side of themselves, the side they show to the world and for which they are known, but she is also afraid of mothballs because they tempt her to protect Winnie, which can only perpetuate the overshadowing of whomever she sees as her real(er) self. Ida is afraid of losing her socially constructed or performative self—but also scared of the poisons involved in trying *not* to lose it.

A public persona argues with the internal felt self in an attempt to find the real self and work from there. But the persona is what others tell one about oneself. It starts outside in the environment (and that's a simplification too, since one did or is something that gives this impression), but one internalizes it and it becomes a voice in the internal dialogue. (The external world can, after all, say almost nothing unless one listens, pays attention, brings impressions inside, and says them to oneself.) The environmental influence on the self is also felt through the body—the skin, the epidermis itself. Outward appearance encourages one to feel certain ways about oneself, because of pains or pleasures, other people's reactions, advantages or disadvantages conferred.[12] Like the beautiful Ida, one may not at first see the disadvantages of this persona; like her, one may want to both erase and retain that image. It is easier to be aware of external influences when one is aware of audiences, one knows them and what they want to hear (or not), and one finesses one's utterances. In this way, developing a self is like choosing what to say: one has personal agency, one can say whatever one wants, and at the same time one is heavily influenced by forces from all directions.

Stein at Night Means Delight

The placement and content of Stein's obituary in the *Nation* reveals her impact on Americans. An observation on Gertrude Stein's death appears two weeks after she dies, on the third page of the magazine's opening section, "The Shape of Things," surrounded by commentary on Senate approval of the Morse resolution, the stalemate between Truman and the Seventy-ninth Congress, India's extrication from the British Empire, the "cost padding" of war contractors, and the Senate decision to fund physical but not social sciences. The anonymous writer begins: "Hearing that Gertrude Stein is dead is like hearing that Paul Bunyan has been eaten by his ox Babe." This writer goes on to assert that Stein made herself into

> an American legend more lasting than anything Barnum himself ever created. . . . she sat in Paris as the Pythoness used to sit at Delphi: everybody in the world, from Picasso to a sergeant of marines, came asking for a sign, and went away happy with some oracular utterance which he could finger as if it were a Chinese puzzle. (If you believe in yourself

hard enough, the world will beat a path to your door—especially if you live in Paris.) . . . in our secular, commercial, and merciless age, she came somehow to stand for Wisdom, which doesn't sell itself in the streets, but gives itself away at home, in cipher. ("Shape of Things")

Stein herself had become a sign (and was sometimes misunderstood as "the essence of mockery"), but this author (and some portion of his or her audience) saw Stein as a sign for "Wisdom" with a capital W.[13] And this sign makes signs like an oracle.

Stein's status as a sign put her in stasis. An obituary in *Saturday Review* calls her a "monumental and enigmatic figure," whose "strong, almost masculine face, with its close-cropped, wiry gray hair was magnificently sculptural and timeless" (Smith). She might not have anticipated this particular summary of her life, but while traveling throughout the United States reading newspaper stories about herself, she would have perceived that these were prevalent impressions of her. Continuing to be human, writing from her human mind, would be difficult for anyone who notices her own "monumental" reputation and "sculptural" image. Timelessness implies a constancy Stein could not, and would not want to, achieve. Brinnin reports that *The Autobiography of Alice B. Toklas* was "a scintillating public success, [but] also a relentless personal trial. Nothing was natural after its appearance" (312). But Stein's valuation of unique individuality must have been complicated by her growing realization of just how little one can control one's own identity; identity can even influence entity. It is generally accepted that after her U.S. lecture tour, Stein found it difficult to resume writing. The fame she had sought disturbed the entity from which she liked to think she wrote. Once Stein discovered herself to *be* a sign—to stand for "Wisdom"—she had to learn to write with signs all over again.

Ida was written several years after Stein recovered from her dilemma, and here Stein personifies common signs in an attempt to understand—or reclaim—their inner life. As unlikely as it may sound, Stein explores the conflicting desires to have and not to have a public persona through a dispute among a spider, a cuckoo, a goldfish, and some dwarves. They are arguing with each other, but the reader can also note the way each one is conflicted within. In a conversation among Andrew (who asks questions), Ida (who doesn't speak), and "a man," Stein depicts signs speaking for themselves, reminding readers that the sign is not merely what it signifies. "Somebody one afternoon" explains:

Spider at night makes delight.
Spider in the morning makes mourning.
Yes said Andrew.
Well, said the man who was talking, think of a spider talking.
Yes said Andrew.
The spider says
Listen to me I, I am a spider, you must not mistake me for the sky, the sky red at night is a sailor's delight, the sky red in the morning is a sailor's warning, you must not mistake me for the sky, I am I, I am a spider. (682)

A spider at night and the red sky at night both signal coming "delight"; a red sky in the morning and a spider in the morning are negative signals of warning and mourning. But a spider and a red sky are themselves quite different things and want to be remembered as such: "I am a spider, you must not mistake me for the sky." Stein also imagines the cuckoo, the goldfish, and the dwarf speaking for themselves, asserting their separateness from what they mean to other people. This section of *Ida* is a fable to resist fables (and thereby, paradoxically, anthropomorphism).

These sign beings begin to squabble with one another because each claims not to believe in the further implications of the others. Once again mentioning a dish ("bubble and squeak" is fried cabbage and potatoes) and highlighting sound (the dish is called that because of the noises it makes while it cooks), this story's narrator says that the "goldfish suddenly began to swish and to bubble and squeak and to shriek" about how he believes in nothing but himself, "I I" (685). His "I I" sounds like "aye aye," the nautical "hear, hear" or "yes sir," and thus the goldfish demands that his listeners agree with him. The cuckoo says:

Oh you poor fish, you do not believe in me, you poor fish, and I do not believe in you fish nothing but fish a goldfish only fish, no I do not believe in you no fish no, I believe in me, I am a cuckoo and I know and I tell you so, no the only thing I believe in which is not me is when I see the new moon through a glass window, I never do because there is no glass to see through, but I believe in that too, I believe in that and I believe in me ah yes I do I see what I see through, and I do I do I do.

No I do not believe in a fish, nor in a dwarf nor in a spider not I, because I am I a cuckoo and I, I, I. (685)

"The spider screamed . . . everybody believes in me . . . bah. I believe in me. . . . I I. I" (685–86). In short, each creature does not believe in the further meaning of the others; he believes only in himself and in his own further significances (not just "I" but "I I" and "I I I"—which are insistently self-promotional but also resemble the roman numerals for "two" and "three"). The cuckoo's reference to the (invisible because dark) new moon (not) seen through (transparent or missing) glass is a mystery, although it suggests that the cuckoo tries to remember that real stuff is there even when it cannot be seen, which may be similar to remembering that he really exists even when nobody acknowledges that part of his existence. The goldfish, who says, "listen to me I am stronger than a cuckoo stronger and meaner because I never do bring good luck I bring nothing but misery" (684), tries to outdo the cuckoo by having more significance. But the cuckoo grants the fish only his being, not his signhood; he's "nothing but a fish." Like many iconic celebrities, these signs want their being to be acknowledged, but they are too enamored of their signhood to let anyone forget it. In other words, they insist upon having the moths and the mothballs.

The fight among the signs probably alludes to the lasting split between two of the most famous modernist sign creators: Stein the "cuckoo" writer and Matisse the painter of goldfish. In 1910–11, Stein wrote the portrait "Matisse," in which, in the middle of admitting that "some" think one thing and "some" another, she seems to assert the painter's greatness: "he was clearly expressing what he was expressing. He was a great one"—and part of what he is expressing is his "struggling" (278). But even this early work hints that Matisse is stuck, unchanging: he tells the same story "again and again and again," his story is so repetitive that people stop listening to it, and people want to imitate him—a potential problem, since it may increase the likelihood of his imitating his own work, as well as his own story (280). When Stein ends the portrait with the opinion of "some" people who think Matisse is "one not greatly expressing something being struggling," she suggests that his struggle is over, that he's become (or he's becoming, or he might become) the static kind of "great man" (281). And when she writes, "This one was one," she might not just be throwing in some of her playful (or annoying) redundancy; perhaps she means he is *only* one, not the several that make up a complex person with an active and "struggling" being. In *The Autobiography of Alice B. Toklas*, Stein gives some idea of the financial pressure Matisse may have felt, which—even if Stein is right about Matisse's work—explains his choice to stick with what sold and start teaching. Later, in the 1938 work *Picasso*, Stein says Matisse got stuck in the past: he and "all the others saw the twentieth century with their eyes, but they saw the reality of the nineteenth century" (512). In Stein's opinion, Matisse ended up seeing as others have seen, not as *he* sees, uniquely and individually.

In *Ida,* Stein's comments about Matisse are coded, but the author (the cuckoo) certainly comes off better than the painter (the goldfish). The cuckoo sends good luck to an author who "had written a lovely book but nobody took the lovely book nobody paid her money for the lovely book they never gave her money, never never never, and she was poor and they needed money oh yes they did she and her lover" (*Ida,* 683).[14] But a painter "bought goldfish and any day he made a painting of us," and "he turned goldfish into gold because everything he did was bold and it sold, and he had money and fame but all the same we the goldfish just sat and waited while he painted" (684). The fish tells the strength of his signhood, which is a curse:

> They buy me because I look so pretty and red and gold in my bowl but I never bring good luck I only bring bad, bad bad bad. . . .
> One day, crack, the bowl where we were fell apart and we were all cracked the bowl the water and the fish, and the painter too crack went the painter and his painting too and he woke up and he knew that he was dead too, the goldfish and he, they were all dead, but we there are always goldfish in plenty to bring bad luck to anybody too but he the painter and his painting was dead dead dead. (684)

Stein suggests that Matisse was ruined by his own fame and even associates him with Midas, whose profitable wish turned to a curse (these are *gold*fish, not carp). (Similarly, Stein said of William Saroyan: "He cannot stand the weight of being great" [Steward, *Chapters,* 105]). The fish bring bad luck and, like a broken mirror, destroy the man on whom they pretended to reflect so well (and vice versa). This author and this painter make signs—and signs, in some sense, make them. The silly dialogue among the signs parallels a common internal dialogue. Who they feel like inside argues with who they are identified as externally, each complicating assertions about self. Those who become signs in themselves must continue to assert themselves as beings in order to continue existing and working. Stein may feel superior—though sympathy would be more becoming—because she probably imagines she has successfully avoided having her wish for fame ruin her.

Stein was more sympathetic to others in a September 1934 *Vanity Fair* article, where she contemplates her own recent loss of identity:

> What happened to me was this. When the success began and it was a success I got lost completely lost. You know the nursery rhyme, I am I

because my little dog knows me. Well you see I did not know myself. I lost my personality. It has always been completely included in myself my personality as any personality naturally is, and here all of a sudden, *I was not just I because so many people did know me. . . .* for the first time since I had begun to write I could not write and what was worse I could not worry about not writing and what was also worse *I began to think about how my writing would sound to others. . . .* And then all of a sudden I said there that it is that is what was the matter with all of them all *the young men whose syrup did not pour, and here I am being just the same. They were young and I am not but when it happens it is just the same, the syrup does not pour.* ("And Now," 63–64; my italics)

People knew her, and she thought she knew what they wanted from her writing, and so the interaction between Stein and others became more transactional than interactional. Expectation or even entitlement superseded discovery and innovation. Again using a metaphor of liquids and solids, Stein depicts the solid state that an exterior definition can impose. The self becomes a fetish of the self, a stable and controllable piece of personhood that spares one from dealing with one's whole complex humanness. This fetish carries useful social symbolism but gives a false encapsulation of the self. When a sign maker becomes a sign, the signs he or she produces are likely to be imitations. Creativity dries up unless a person continually reasserts his or her self as a living, changing being. Awareness of the audience, thinking about how one's "writing would sound to others," teaching (which is often performed by repeating what one already knows instead of being fully present and thoughtful), and doing the same thing over and over because it sells, all are ways to keep the syrup from pouring, to stop creativity itself, as well as the creation of a unique self.

Standing in the Window

Conversations take place in all sorts of settings, among people of different sexes and gestures and postures, and these details make a difference. Even children know what it means when they have to sit down and someone self-righteously towers over them. Imagine an academic conference (on Stein, say) where informal groups of people discuss Stein's writing while sitting around a swimming pool, or while playing catch or boules, or while chopping vegetables and setting a table together. It would be different from a formal conference setting, and different things would get said. Doing handwork side by side and chatting is different from receiving handouts and a lecture, even of the most conversational kind.

One early reviewer of *Three Lives* saw Stein and Henry James as having "analogous method[s]": "James presents us the world he knows largely through . . . conversations," and Stein's "murmuring people are as truly shown as are James' people who not only talk but live while they talk" ("Curious Fiction Study," 12). In *Four in America*, Stein asserts "that there are two ways of writing and Henry James . . . has selected both" (138). Henry James is a notoriously subtle writer, and he takes advantage of what people knew about polite conversation to express much that goes unstated in his novels. The climactic chapter of *A Portrait of a Lady* depends on the reader's knowing that a man would not sit in the presence of a standing woman unless the two were intimately acquainted. Mrs. Isabel Osmond (née Archer) walks in on Gilbert Osmond (her husband) and Madame Merle "musing, face to face" (H. James, 376). Merle is standing and Osmond is sitting; when Isabel enters, Osmond quickly stands too. "Their relative position, their absorbed mutual gaze, struck [Isabel] as something detected," and James devotes a subsequent chapter to Isabel's "meditation" on how this scene alters her understanding of herself and the people around her (376, 389).

Ida may lightly allude to this scene. Ida visits a married couple, and the names of the husband and wife—William and Edith—help support this leap of attention to a different author. Henry James seems to me to be a likely cross between William James and Edith Wharton. In *The Autobiography of Alice B. Toklas* (written in 1932 and published the following year), Stein has Toklas say that "only very lately Gertrude Stein reads Henry James" (78). Stein probably read Henry James much earlier than she admits, but if she was reading (or rereading) his work around the time she wrote the *Autobiography*, then James's writing would have been fairly fresh in her mind when *Ida* was being composed.

Ida walks into the room (or house) as Edith and William discuss possible husbands for her, and Edith and William go silent (in light of her possible anxiety of influence, this is perhaps wishful thinking on Stein's part):

all right they would talk about Ida and Ida came in, not to rest, but to come in. They stopped it, stopped talking about her.

So Edith and William did not look at Ida, they started talking. What do you think said William what do you think if and when we decide anything what do you think it will be like. This is what William said and Edith looked out of the window. They were not in the same room with

Ida but they might have been. Edith liked an opportunity to stand and so she looked out of the window. She half turned, she said to William, Did you say you said Ida. William then took to standing. This was it so they were standing. It is not natural that if anybody should be coming in that they would be standing. Ida did not come in, Edith went away from the window and William stood by the window and saw some one come in, it was not Gerald Seaton [the most likely suitor for Ida] because he had gone away. (*Ida*, 657)

Although Stein has not made it clear whether Ida came into the room or not, she has managed to make it seem that something portentous has happened, and I can't help thinking of the scene and its sequel in Henry James's *Portrait of a Lady*. Stein may have been struck by James's sensitivity to conversational setting, and perhaps also by his ideas about the construction of the self. In both Stein's and James's scenes, a man and woman are talking, but when another woman enters they become silent. In both cases, the couple is plotting something to do with women and marriage. At some point in both scenes, everyone is standing in a way that is "not natural."

Ross Posnock makes a convincing argument for Henry James's interest in the self as social construction: "What James discovers in America is that a fluidity of identification instills a capacity for a mutuality that is the basis of vital citizenship." Further: "Implicit in Henry James . . . is the belief that the subject 'is an artificial reality imposed on material not intended to receive it,'" and that "freedom is 'not reducible to the freedom of subjects; it is at least partly the release of that which does not fit into the molds of subjectivity and normalization'" (23, 50).[15] Hanna Pitkin describes Henry James's idea of citizenship as maintaining "mutuality within difference" and patriotism as "a redefinition of self, an enlarged awareness of how individuality and community are connected in the self" (qtd. in Posnock 255, 256).[16] While Stein is heavily influenced by William James and values individualism above all things, her idea of the complex, nonindependent individual parallels Henry James's ideas.

In *Portrait of a Lady*, Isabel's musings on Gilbert Osmond supply Stein with a metaphor relevant to the issue of internally and externally influenced character. Isabel is surprised to learn that "she had never seen any one who thought so much of others" as Osmond, and that "he had looked at it ['this base, ignoble world'] out of his window even when he appeared to be most detached from it" (H. James, 396–97). For Isabel, Osmond's stance at the window means he is paying attention to what's out there, what "they" think. She realizes that Osmond, who insists that she "think of him as he thought of himself," hates her because she has "a mind of her own" (396, 398). Not only do Edith and William take turns standing at the window in *Ida*, but a few paragraphs after their mild perturbation, Stein suddenly injects: "It was a pleasant home, if a home has windows and any house has them anybody can stand at the window and look out" (*Ida*, 657). In this way, Stein may refer back to their discomfort and continue a discussion of Edith's question: "who is any one." The statement "anybody can stand at the window and look out" may allude across novels to Osmond's tendency to perform himself. But Stein adds: "Ida never did. She rested"—and we remember that Winnie's fame continues on its own even if Ida just sits in the room without looking out the window (657). When fame comes, it stays, whether Ida aids it or not.

Also Known As, or The Metaphor of Sight

Standing at the window limits, stultifies, and makes one's individual creativity stop pouring, but letting a dog tell you who you are is just as bad. *Ida* is full of aliases or misperceptions. More specifically (and more eccentrically), the novel is full of mistaken dogs—dogs who are named for things they are not, and dogs who mistake one thing for another. Everything appears to be something else. For example: "There was a Pekinese named Sandy, he was a very large one, Pekineses should be tiny but he was a big one like a small lion but he was all Pekinese." Not only does this dog look like a lion, but "Sandy was his name because he was that color, the color of sand." And this dog who looks like a lion and sand misidentifies other things: he hates to climb mountains, but "they were not real mountains, they were made of a man on two chairs" (*Ida*, 668). Another dog is named "Chocolate because he looked like a chocolate cake or a bar of chocolate or chocolate candy," but instead of being sweet, "he was a monster" and "he was awful" (670).[17] We'd be wrong to eat Chocolate or sunbathe on Sandy, just as it is a mistake to base judgments on appearances.

Clouds are not bunnies, either, but when Ida and her friend (or double) Andrew have visitors who tell what they see in the clouds, Stein is probably commenting on a couple of issues other than (but related to) false appearances. Our individual sight is an important measurement of uniqueness. These friends

would come in and say this evening I saw a cloud and it looked like a hunting dog and others would say he saw a cloud that looked like a dragon, and another one would say he said [*sic* (saw?)] a cloud that looked like a dream, and another he saw a cloud that looked like a queen. Ida said yes and Andrew said very nicely. They liked people to come in and tell what kind of clouds they had seen. Some had seen a cloud that looked like a fish and some had seen a cloud that looked like a rhinoceros, almost any of them had seen a cloud.

It was very pleasant for Ida that they came and told what the clouds they had seen looked like. (*Ida*, 699)

A favorite instance of subjectivity, and borrowed subjectivity, is Hamlet's discussion of clouds with Polonius:

> HAMLET. Do you see yonder cloud that's almost in shape of a camel?
> POLONIUS. By th' mass, and 'tis like a camel indeed.
> HAMLET. Methinks it is like a weasel.
> POLONIUS. It is backed like a weasel.
> HAMLET. Or like a whale?
> POLONIUS. Very like a whale. (3.2.339–44)

Clouds are clouds, really, not camels or whales or weasels. Hamlet says what he sees in them, and Polonius says what Hamlet sees. Polonius is not a genius, or even much of an individual. If we see how others see, we are not ourselves. But the alternative perceptions of clouds in *Ida* and *Hamlet* also suggest the projective and metaphorical quality of human knowledge. These qualities are present in and confuse our perceptions of ourselves and one another.

Over and over again, in many different works, Stein associates dogs with false, limited, or static (or otherwise lacking) identity. In her lecture "What Are Master-Pieces and Why Are There So Few of Them," presented at Oxford and Cambridge Universities in 1936, she says that "mostly people live in identity and memory that is when they think. They know they are they because their little dog knows them, and so they are not an entity but an identity. . . . The second you are you because your little dog knows you you cannot make a master-piece and that is all of that" (153). The dogs in *Ida* have one thing in common: they mistake parts for wholes, which leads to terrible misidentifications. For example, "any shadow was a rabbit to them," one dog "chased sheep . . . thinking they were rabbits," and "Another little dog was so foolish once he always thought that any table leg was his mother, and would suck away at it as if it was his mother" (*Ida*, 671). Dogs see that which is inaccurate and partial; they see identity. As a (sometimes) deliberately formed creation of selfhood, identity is only a shadow, only a false goal, only a wooden consolation.

When a reader of *Ida* begins to wonder if Andrew is a person or just one facet of Ida, Ida is "left alone," and this reader expected Ida to think about herself in a way that would reveal whether Andrew is internal or external; but instead "she thought about her life with dogs" (667). Is Andrew a dog? Probably not, but Ida reads and Andrew doesn't, and in Stein's paradigm, the human mind (genius, being) reads and human nature (limited) does not, so maybe Andrew is *like* a dog (663). At one point, Andrew voices his independence but is still overcome by Ida; he says, "Kindly consider that I am capable of deciding when and why I am coming," but "He came all the same" (664). Andrew speaks up, and he says that unlike a dog he won't come when he's called, but he comes like a good dog nonetheless. Stein ends the first half of her novel:

> And now Ida was not only Ida she was Andrew's Ida and being Andrew's Ida Ida was more that [*sic* (than?)] Ida she was Ida itself.
>
> For this there was a change, everybody changed, Ida even changed and even changed Andrew. Andrew had changed Ida to be more Ida and Ida changed Andrew to be less Andrew and they were both always together. (664)

As "Andrew's Ida," Andrew's gaze has changed Ida, but she is still Ida and not just a holograph of Andrew's desires or expectations. Andrew is somehow confirming without being limiting. He makes Ida more herself, perhaps parallel to the way good relationships make people feel like who they really are and—even better—like someone they like. But why is Andrew less Andrew? Is he too busy being an alter ego to be an ego?

Andrew and Ida fold in and out of one another even more in the second half of the novel. "Andrew's name changed to Ida and eight changed to four and sixteen changed to twenty-five and they all sat down," but very soon after, "You see there was he it came to be Andrew again and it was Ida," and "it made gradually that it was not so important that Ida was Ida" (*Ida*, 666). If Andrew becomes part of Ida, then there are half as many people (four is half of eight), but if Ida had four sides before, she suddenly has five. This mathematical function suggests that if Ida contains four selves, she also contains the personalities that each one forms in relation to the others and to itself (four squared is sixteen); when she contains five selves, she also contains the sides of those selves that they reveal to and develop in relationship to the others and itself (five squared is twenty-five). And suddenly, "There was no Andrew" (666). In the very next paragraph, Andrew exists enough to be doing things: he "stayed at home and waited for her," and he "could walk and come to see Ida and tell her what he did," although Ida could "not tell Andrew that she had been walking" (666–67). Later, after Ida thinks about dogs, and after she seems to die and then comes "back to life exactly day before yesterday," "Ida was almost married to Andrew" (674, 676). She dreams that the wedding becomes a funeral for Andrew, which suggests that when two people become one, one of them has to die. After so much ambiguity, and even more, the last page of the novel reads:

> Little by little there it was It was Ida and Andrew.
> Not too much not too much Ida and not too much Andrew.
> And not enough Ida and not enough Andrew. (703–4)

Their melding together hasn't killed either one. They have shared themselves, such that each has been influenced by the other. Their coupling seems inevitable and commonsensical, but it also seems a diminishment; there's not enough of either one of them. Ida is still "one" (or just an idea of one), and Andrew is just "and," an addition rather than an identity. Love is a dog that won't hunt for a real self.

The Death of Conversation, or The Monologue of Death

In the shorter "Second Half," Ida incessantly rests. No longer just sitting and being, now Ida seems to be sick and less comfortable in herself. Here, in at least one instance, when Stein says, "What happened," she may refer to the way that Ida doesn't do anything when she is sick; the sickness just happens to her (*Ida*, 694). After meeting a family that brings bad luck, she "never went out to see any one" (681). She has a hard time imagining herself young (677), dreams of Andrew's death and a funeral (676), cries for the first time when she hears of someone else's death (673), predicts another man's death from meningitis (675), and even seems to die (674).

But "what happened" is also that when Ida dies (if she dies), her conversations are over. In "Second Half," Ida's conversations are less apparent; she seems to go on walks with Susan Little instead of with Andrew, and they don't sing and they don't talk (666). When Ida goes on walks, she cannot tell Andrew about them; he is the only one who can talk about walks (667). Suddenly when people said, "how do you do . . . it did not matter" (667).

"Part One" of "Second Half" is largely devoted to Ida's "thought[s] about her life with dogs," and what Stein says about dogs suggests that this section of the book will be devoted to the drying up of the vital self. Here the self succumbs to the stasis that comes with death instead of the kind that came with fame. The dogs in this section are identified by their inaccurate, appearance-based names and their misconceptions (as noted earlier), but Stein also mentions their deaths (they all die, often by getting run over by cars) and their relationships with each other. Basket and Never Sleeps play together, but Lillieman and Dick ignore each other completely, even when "on the same lawn together" (673, 669). In fact, except for the two playful dogs and the many allusions to dogs "making love," "tempt[ing each] other," and doing "what they should not" (669, 670–71), several of the dogs are antisocial: Polybe "never barked, he had nothing to say" (672), and Mary Rose is not interested in her puppy Blanchette (670). The dogs who are interested in each other are separated: Mary Rose leaves Polybe; her favorite puppy, Chocolate, gets "run over"; and Lillieman dies and is separated from Dick, who now "went on running around making love to distant dogs" (669). The dogs represent a limitedness, and their relations with each other are narrowly defined by certain games or by a refusal to interact. They are the way they are, and they see humans as having the same simplicity; they do not change, and they don't let their views of us change: "Dogs are dogs" (670).

A repeated allusion to moonlight shows that things look different in different lights, and it leads to the way that death itself, the unchanging fact, can appear different depending on who dies. This second half begins with a reference to the way "a white dog . . . looked gray in the moonlight and on the snow," and the end of the dog section alludes to the moon again: "the moon scarcely the moon but still there is a moon" and "Very likely hers was the moon" (*Ida*, 665, 673). The moon makes things look different than they are; appearances are relative. And then Stein tells us:

Ida knew she never had been a little sister or even a little brother.
Ida knew.
So scarcely was there an absence when someone died.
Believe it or not someone died. (673)

Ida is relative, too; her lack of relatives makes it appear as if her death was not a death. But here, actually, a young man dies, a person with parents, and Ida mourns him, although "Ida had never cried before" (674). Ida begins to see the use of fame, and she uses this knowledge to reassure other people as they come to see her: "one by one somebody said Thank you, have you heard of me. And [Ida] always had. That was Ida"; and "Even Andrew had he had heard of them" (674). If they have to die, at least they are remembered in their fame.

Stein seems to have Ida die and immediately come back to life in her fame. "One day, she saw a star it was an uncommonly large one and when it set it made a cross, she looked and looked and she did not hear Andrew take a walk and that was natural enough she was not there. They had lost her. Ida was gone" (*Ida*, 674). But in the next paragraph she goes to bed more "carefully," in the next she comes "back to life," and in the next her life is patly summed up in terms of how many times she married and what her husbands did (674). W. H. Auden captures the difference when he writes of Yeats's becoming what he means to others: "But for him it was his last afternoon as himself, / . . . [and when] The current of his feeling failed; he became his admirers" ("In Memory"). When Ida comes back to life, in someone else's monologue instead of her own conversation, it is with a different self.

In other words, that summary of husbands is not Ida's being, which is better expressed through some short poetic lines of Andrew's, here excerpted from the conversational setting, in which they are interlarded with laughter and interruptions.

> At a glance
> what a chance
> That she needs
> What she has
> And they have what they are
> And they have what they are
> And they like where they go
> Which is all after a while
> (*Ida*, 656, ellipses and paragraph markers omitted)

In other words—which are completely different and perhaps make too brutal a revision—we are what we see and do in the moment, the minor decisions we make, the gestures and movements and detours and attitudes. The moments are our chances to be us, and we have to be us, have what we have, do what we do. That's all there is.

Stein almost (but not quite) tolls the death of the independent self. One critic concludes that "*Ida, A Novel* simultaneously testifies to an impossibility to remember . . . the laws of the traditional novel . . . and to a memory of the impossible . . . i.e. writing a novel" (Tomiche, 275). *Ida*, then, may be a memorial to the novel as a genre (as "Lycidas" is to pastoral elegy), but it is also a memorial to a no-longer-viable (or probably always mythical) singular sense of an independent self, as well as a beacon that spotlights another possible model of being. I believe this model to be true and good, but, in the second half of *Ida*, Stein seems to recognize the difficulty—the impossibility—of remaining a true self after death. If we live in our reputations, we can live on after death, but in rejecting that ancient solution to selfhood, Stein (and Ida) disappear when they can no longer just be. The only possible consolation seems to be uncertainty: "She knew she would be away but not really away," and "If Ida goes on, does she go on even when she does not go on any more. No and yes" (*Ida*, 702, 704). All she can do is stay herself until there's "not enough Ida" left. Only until death can she be where she is, continue to "Thank them," and say, "Yes" (704). We die when we cannot participate in the conversations that create us.

Human Intertextuality

Merging like her characters in *Ida*, some of Stein's texts are differentiable only by title and binding. The more one reads, the more puzzling Stein's work becomes, and one reason for this difficulty is that Stein leaves pieces of her writing around the house of her complete works. In *Ida*, for example, Stein refers to or rewrites sections of *Paris, France*; "Preciosilla"; *The World Is Round*; and *Blood on the Dining Room Floor*. *Ida* has a permeable identity in the corpus of Stein's works—one more correspondence to Stein's strong implication that people get meaning from outside themselves.

Not only does Stein's treatment of identity correspond to whole texts, whole bodies of work, but also it corresponds to words, and here we come full circle. Emphasizing the general "postmodern" instability or uncertainty in *Ida*—and choosing not to decide whether Ida and her twin represent "contradictory desires," "a split between public and private selves," conscious and unconscious, action and "unactualized potential," ego and alter ego, or even self and mother figure—Berry writes that "Ida wanders among possibilities that remain open, nomadizing in order to stay in the same place, the place where she is always just Ida" (164, 155). My discussion has depicted the twins as representing a public and a private self, though I have meant this division to suggest further divisions, and I have meant other divisions (Andrew and Ida, Ida and her various husbands) to represent multiple participants in Ida's entire self. Ida's nomadic partnering, influencing others and being influenced by them, might recall the square dance of words (sometimes in fours and fives) noted earlier. Encouraged to explore the multiple meanings of single words and the way they reflect on one another in odd groups, readers of Stein's writing cannot be content to settle for single meanings for those words any more than Ida can settle down and accept a single meaning for life. Ida wants to avoid fame, but she also wants to avoid the anonymity that threatens when she marries Gerald Seaton and "they lived almost as if Ida had not been Ida and Gerald Seaton had married any woman" (*Ida*, 659). Similarly, Stein's writing avoids static determinacy *and* does not settle for being complete nonsense. Neither Ida's nor Stein's words are satisfied with one meaning. Nor do they want *no* meaning, though our mental programming tends to resist too many simultaneous, multiple alternatives. As we tend to be suspicious of promiscuity, we tend to be suspicious of polysemy.

And so, Stein's words are independently dependent, her character Ida is independently dependent, and her works are independently dependent in relation to each other. For William James, "*My experience is what I agree to attend to*" (*Principles*; his italics, 380), and Stein tries to get us to agree to attend to much more complexity about the development of the self than we might otherwise. In describing the self in a different way, she practices a kind of "utopian politics or revolutionary science" that involves "redescrib[ing] lots and lots of things in new ways, until you have created a pattern of linguistic behavior which will tempt the rising generation to adopt it, thereby causing them to look for appropriate new forms of nonlinguistic behavior" (Rorty, *Contingency*, 9). Imagining ourselves as permeable and impermanent changes who we are, as well as how we think. Perhaps we human beings can evolve and adapt to let ourselves be as complex as the dynamic that creates us, as flexible as the language through which we know ourselves, all and each of us.

CHAPTER 6

Expressing a State of Mind:
Conversation, Politics, and Individuality in
Mrs. Reynolds and *Brewsie and Willie*

THE PEOPLE IN *Ida* who look at Winnie and depend on each other for reassurance as to what they are seeing are early manifestations of a type Stein critiques more fully in her works of the forties. Since the people agree with each other without really understanding what they are agreeing to, and they agree to approve of something they can barely appreciate on their own, they are primed for a mass movement. After *Ida*, Stein's attention shifts from mass culture to its manipulations in politics. Perhaps Stein's path of thought follows the same trajectory as that of somewhat later thinkers on the subject of tyranny: reviewing Benjamin Alpers's *Dictators, Democracy, and American Public Culture*, Louis Menand concludes that "the critique of totalitarianism by writers like [Hannah] Arendt is of a piece with their critique of popular culture, which they attacked as culture manufactured for the mass of unindividuated individuals, atomized beings able to feel alive only in their frenzied response to empty celebrity" (85). Alpers himself writes: "Although [Arthur] Schlesinger [Jr.], [George] Orwell, and Arendt disagreed on many things, they each presented totalitarianism as a nightmarish iron trap that destroyed all vestiges of individuality in its subjects" (Alpers, 253). Stein's work moves from cute psychological speculations to acute political negotiations under the repression of Nazi expansion. Stein saw that history had, in several ways, come to meet her.

Stein was always mainly interested in the individual, hating all mass movements about equally. Eric Sevareid, who met Stein in 1937, writes in *Not So Wild a Dream* that Stein "thought in terms of the human individual and was quite lost when she considered people in groups. . . . She did not understand Fascism; she did not understand that the moods and imperatives of great mass movements are far stronger and more important than the individuals involved in them. She knew persons, but not people" (90). Stein resisted distinguishing among political movements because they all seemed anti-individualist to her (as indeed they tend to be). Totalitarianism certainly is, but even progressive movements, according to Daniel T. Rodgers in *Contested Truths: Keywords in American Politics Since Independence*, turn all talk of factions and interests—of multiple ideas—into talk of procedures, management, and efficiency (see Posnock, 264). But according to W. G. Rogers, an American private first class befriended by Stein and Toklas when he was on leave in Nimes in 1917, and who remained a friend for the next thirty years: "When political issues were clarified by the eventual line-up of powers in the second World War, . . . it was as plain to Miss Stein as it was to all the rest of us that there were no two ways about it, it had to be democracy, it couldn't be totalitarianism" (222). When the European war was won, however, Stein could start worrying about the winners, too.

The primacy of individualism for Stein does much to explain her apparently mixed-up political views. The best summary of Stein's politics is DeKoven's:

> Stein's position in relation to twentieth-century democratic, egalitarian leveling, like the positions of other modernists, was as equivocal as her position in relation to female self-assertion. She hated Roosevelt and the New Deal, distrusted "big government," and allied herself politically, if at all, with an anarchic but generally right-wing American "rugged individualism." She was a close friend in the thirties and forties of the collaborationist Bernard Faÿ. . . . But, on the other side, "The Winner Loses, A Picture of Occupied France" is a tribute to the *maquisard* Resistance near her home in Belley, she excoriates Hitler as "Angel Harper" in *Mrs. Reynolds,* and, most importantly, [in "Composition as Explanation"] she links to the egalitarian-democratic principle of "one man, one vote" her notion of the "twentieth-century composition" as having no dominant center, in fact no center at all: each of its elements is as important as every other element and as important as the whole. (*Rich and Strange,* 200–201)

Right-wing "anarchy" and "rugged individualism," however, are not that far from the *maquisard*, who were fighting for their own lives, the self-determination of France, and freedom from Fascist "big government." The high expectations Stein has for individual people parallels her treatment of single words. The shape of her texts—their informal networks of association—models her ideal political body. In other words, as she declines to write formal verse, she resists the formalities of political concretion, with its hierarchies and disciplines. In her writing, and in the world as she imagines it, there is "no center at all: each of its elements is as important as every other element and as important as the whole." It is this very characteristic of the French Resistance that Jean-Paul Sartre emphasizes:

> There is no army in the world where there is such equality of risk for the private and for the commander-in-chief. And this is why the Resistance was a true democracy: for the soldier as for the commander, the same danger, the same forsakenness, the same total responsibility, the same absolute liberty within discipline. Thus, in darkness and in blood, a Republic was established, the strongest of Republics. (499–500)

Stein's politics may not weigh in very impressively in twenty-first-century American ideological retrospect, but in Vichy France her political preferences, always informed by the value she places on the individual, become recognizable, as well as defensible.

In her war writings especially, Stein advocates renewing our American individuality, and thereby the political and social character of the United States, by changing the ways we speak. She inspires her readers to become individuals, asserting our own powers of thought and doubt and saying what we see. She argues that we should listen to ourselves—our own selves and our compatriots—closely enough to hear more than the functional meaning intended by the speaker, and that listening to ourselves will lead us to speak in new ways. Earlier, in "Meditations on Being about to Visit My Native Land," contemplating her imminent lecture tour through the United States, she wrote:

> I love to ask questions and I do not dislike answering them, but I like to listen and I like to have others listen, and there is something that I can not remember not really remember did they listen in that America that I remember did they listen to the answer after they had asked the question. I always listen to the answer after I have asked the question and I hope that in that as in other things I am a good American and that they did and still do listen to the answer after they have asked a question. That would make America more than pleasant, it would make it interesting, it would make it more than interesting it would make it exciting. (*Painted Lace*, 255)

Excitement comes of paying attention to one another's possible answers, and answers can come in several forms. As an example to us, Stein's writing moves between ruthless pithiness and a doubt-filled processing of ideas.[1]

Stein's love of questions suggests that she believed a good national characteristic would be to wonder instead of to "state." One Nazi slogan, meant to discourage inquiry, was "He who thinks has already doubted," meaning that a soldier asking an honest question reveals mistrust of his orders, or of the order of things (J. Young, 70). Stein would agree with this premise, but not with the discouragement. She demonstrates the way even half-hearted, only half-doubtful questioning leads to thinking, as it does in *Brewsie and Willie*. Jo wonders:

> I wonder, said Jo, why now everybody that is all of us call America the States, in the old days that is before now, Americans always call it America or the United States, it was only foreigners who called it the States, and now just as natural as anything we each one and every one of us calls it the States just like some foreigners like the Limies used to. I wonder, said Pauline, I wonder does that really mean anything does that mean the beginning that we are beginning to feel poor, call it the States instead of America, do you think, said Pauline, do you think it does really mean anything. Everything means something, said Donald Paul, dont you know that, havent you heard, that's what's called psychoanalysis, dont you know that, that says anything always means something. (58)

If "everything means something," then idle questions mean something, too. Saying only "the States" could mean that Americans no longer express, and no longer hold, a vision of a united continent; the phrase is plural, without the unifying "United." "The States" also emphasizes assertion over questioning. "The United States," however, suggests multiplicity that mitigates the solidarity and assertiveness also implied in the name.

Like the texts discussed in previous chapters, *Mrs. Reynolds* exhibits Stein's interest in auditory and visual allusion on the level of the word.[2] In *Mrs. Reynolds*, Stein juxtaposes "fathers and feathers" (94), and "whether" and "weather" (152). She indicates that Joseph Lane's historical counterpart is Joseph Stalin by writing, "his name was Joseph lane, steal him" (114), and she implies that Joseph Lane is a "done cough" (*dummkopf*)—or that the Germans think so—when she writes that he "might cough did cough would cough" (96). Openly alluding to near homographs, Stein writes, "Eats and oats said Mrs. Reynolds can easily be confounded in printing" (136).

Directly fooling with sound, she writes: "Date rhymes with hate, murmured a man. Yes said Mrs. Reynolds it does and so does cloud rhyme with out-loud" (141). Mrs. Reynolds also likes to read out loud (160), she thinks it would be valuable "to help Joseph Lane to read out loud" (238), and "She pronounced Manitoba delightfully" (157).

But Stein goes beyond looking and listening to individual words either on the page or vibrating over the airwaves. And in *Mrs. Reynolds* and *Brewsie and Willie*, she even goes beyond watching and listening to how people speak whole conversations. In *Mrs. Reynolds*, Stein contemplates how everyday conversation is both influenced by its greater context and, even more importantly, how it resists the pressure of the political situation in which it takes place. Both novels consider the characteristic speech patterns of totalitarian leaders and contrast these with the kind of talk Stein prefers. In *Brewsie and Willie*, Stein inquires into the likely cause behind the proliferation of "yes and no job men" who encourage totalitarian speech by accepting it, expecting it, and propagating it in their own talk. She concludes not only that industrialism has spoiled interesting conversation, but also that it has adversely affected original thought, and that, conversely, improved speech patterns will revive thought, which will in turn cure economic and political ailments.

Talking under an Angel Harper Cloud

One way—the main way—that Stein understands politics is through its effect on everyday life and conversation. Someone who appreciates playful, free, "cheap" talk would notice the strain put on such conversation by propaganda and fear. During her extended sojourn in Vichy France during World War II, Stein observed the ways political context circumscribed conversation, but also the ways speakers can resist that influence.[3]

Mrs. Reynolds is a novel that follows Mrs. Reynolds as she wanders around her village and the nearby countryside, speaks to the people she meets, and, upon returning home, recounts these conversations to Mr. Reynolds. In the distance is an ominous threat to their well-being, represented in the novel by worries about Angel Harper, vague hopes that Joseph Lane will do something helpful, fears of starvation and "drowning," and the presence of soldiers and refugees. Out of desperation, Mrs. Reynolds puts her faith in Saint Odile's prophecy, which she understands as predicting the end of the war. Often she discusses this prophecy; sometimes she reads it aloud to people. Interlarded with these conversations are updates about Angel Harper's age and descriptions of his childhood memories.

Stein wrote *Mrs. Reynolds* to convey the experience of a private person emotionally devastated, but not personally destroyed, by World War II's happening all around her, as she explains in her epilogue:

> This book is an effort to show the way anybody could feel these years. It is a perfectly ordinary couple living an ordinary life and having ordinary conversations and really not suffering personally from everything that is happening but over them, all over them is the shadow of two men, and then the shadow of one of the two men gets bigger and then blows away and there is no other. There is nothing historical about this book except the state of mind. (331)

This "state of mind" could be that of anyone who lives in a maelstrom of alternating silence and propaganda, daily rituals of pleasant-as-possible survival and rumors of world-changing tragedies. The French countryside may be overrun by German soldiers, and refugees may pass by every day, but every night Mr. and Mrs. Reynolds discuss when to go to bed: "Oh dear she said let us go to bed and they did" (214); "well said Mr. Reynolds let us be asleep first and they were" (216); "now they would go to bed and she said yes they would go to bed and they did they put out the lights after they went to bed" (217); "Mr. Reynolds said all right but night is night, and so good night and they went to bed and slept tight" (222); "Mr. Reynolds said it was time to go to bed and it was and they went to bed" (225); "And Mr. Reynolds said it was exciting but tomorrow was another day to be excited in so that they might just as well go to bed now and they carefully did they carefully went to bed" (227).

Wanting to go to bed earlier than they feel they should, however, is a dilemma throughout the novel, one that signals that their private lives have been infected by their moment in history. Their bedtime discussions might sound like the irrepressible Samuel Pepys, who ended many of his journal entries with references to bed: "After that to bed"; "and after a bottle of wine we all to bed"; "and so at night to bed" (42, 44), but it also suggests the syndrome of depressives who tend to sleep more than they should. Mr. and Mrs. Reynolds cannot speak openly, and sleep is the easiest form of silence. Sleep tempts them when they have run out of things they can say and want to avoid saying things they shouldn't. Bedtime would be a familiar ritual that could help them forget the war, if it weren't something they desired so much more than in peacetime. While the word "conversation" was sometimes used between the fifteenth and eighteenth centuries to refer to sexual intercourse, these bedtime conversations are not so much playful anticipations of what's to come if they go upstairs as they are hesitant suggestions about whether or not they would be cowardly if they escaped awkward wakefulness so early.

The main cause of their discomfort is that the daily life chronicled in *Mrs. Reynolds* is overshadowed by the existence of a man whose name is a household word—one that the book's characters often choose not to speak, but that is indicated obliquely and always understood. Foremost in everyone's mind is "Angel Harper," who "is clearly a version of Adolf Hitler" (Bridgman, 319). The shared initials (pointed out in *Mrs. Reynolds* itself, 131) cannot be the only reason for Stein's choosing to call Adolf Hitler Angel Harper. She writes: "It was a long way to wait and in the meantime every day there was a dark cloud, a very dark one. An Angel Harper cloud said Mrs. Reynolds" (90). If Adolf Hitler is a cloud over their lives, then Stein may (sarcastically?) associate him with paintings of clouds and angels, or perhaps she sees him as the angel of death. Hitler's harping voice may have had something to do with it, too. Stein also writes that "Mrs Reynolds remembered fie fie fie for shame everybody knows his name" (293), which reminds me of the giant's refrain in *Jack and the Beanstalk*: "Fee fi fo fum, I smell the blood of an Englishman!" Adolf Hitler's own attempts to sniff out—and snuff out—Jews (and England) may associate him in Stein's mind with this terrible giant in the clouds. Finally, as Lloyd Frankenberg argues, Angel Harper is not so much Adolf Hitler as he is "everybody's fears and thoughts and dreams" about Adolf Hitler (xii).[4]

The name permeates *Mrs. Reynolds*: "the name Angel Harper was the name was one everybody knew too well" (224); "Nobody not even Mrs. Reynolds asked any one if they had ever heard of Angel Harper. Everybody had and everybody knew that this year he was forty-eight" (144). Angel Harper's shadow is present even when his name is not expressly invoked: when Mrs. Reynolds says "he," she expects Mr. Reynolds to know of whom she speaks (215). Mrs. Reynolds likes to say "who" when someone mentions Angel Harper's name, but it is a sour joke: "Mrs. Reynolds never laughed but she said who and when she said who she was making fun of Angel Harper" (94, 134).

The repetition of Angel Harper's name stands out, because, with the exception of Mr. and Mrs. Reynolds, most of Stein's character names appear only once, such as "little Valery Hopkins," who says, "I am the same age as Angel Harper." Stein adds: "That is the first time that the age of Angel Harper was something to compare with something" (126). This comment signals Stein's recognition that Angel Harper's person has come to occupy their minds as much as his troops occasionally occupy their countryside.

"There is said Mrs. Reynolds no escaping hearing his name"; and "in the Bible it says that the poor are always with you but that said Mrs. Reynolds oh dear me that is nothing compared to Angel Harper being fifty" (139, 197). Angel Harper's existence is as evil as the persistence of human poverty, and, less patly, the idea of Angel Harper, his position as a cloud in their lives, is as much a persistent shadow as the knowledge of human suffering. His sweet name might also be a jab at the idealization of Hitler by his followers. Angel Harper's name is snapped, muttered, growled, hissed, whispered, and conspicuously omitted from conversations as often as Mr. and Mrs. Reynolds discuss whether it is late enough to go to bed.

Clearly, Stein has been listening to herself and others talking, and not talking, in occupied France. Beyond the constant repetition and avoidance of a powerful man's name, she notices what people do not have to say and what they are unwilling to say. She observes the convenient vagaries allowed by conversational communication, which can leave difference unspoken, and sometimes unrecognized, by all parties. She sees the endurance of pleasant conversation throughout the war, and she perceives how reassuring verbal (and nonverbal) habits can be. In "The Republic of Silence," Sartre writes: "We were never more free than during the German occupation. We had lost all our rights, beginning with the right to talk. . . . every word took on the value of a declaration of principles. . . . every one of our gestures had the weight of a solemn commitment" (498). Adolf Hitler in the guise of Angel Harper may be tearing the distant world apart, but the characters in Stein's novel manage to entrench themselves in—and assert themselves through—the protective comfort of daily ritual. Hitler may have infiltrated everyday greetings in Germany and among Nazi sympathizers and sycophants elsewhere with the obligatory "Heil Hitler," but people in Mrs. Reynolds's village still say, "How do you do."

Angel Harper's notoriety enables and encourages some resistant speakers *not* to say his name. "Mrs. Reynolds sometimes read about [Angel Harper and Joseph Lane] in a newspaper but she never talked about them to any one" (*Mrs. Reynolds*, 117). At one point, Mrs. Reynolds says about Angel Harper, "It would . . . make my teeth hurt to hear his name," Mr. Reynolds says, "What," and she says, "you know what I mean." "And indeed he did he did know what she did mean," Stein tells us (139). When Nelly asks Mrs. Reynolds, "is Angel Harper married," Mrs. Reynolds abruptly rejects that topic of conversation: "Mrs. Reynolds said I am telling just as I told you before I do prefer potatoes and I do not need butter, lard will do it. Now if you have anything to say she said to Nelly say it to my husband. And if you want to wait until He comes in you had better not go away" (79).[5] Mrs. Reynolds resists letting Angel Harper's political presence make her talk about him, and her refusal to speak in this situation also reveals her dislike and distrust of both Angel Harper and Nelly. Of course, refusing to say his name is an influence in itself. Whether one speaks about one's politics or not, others can discern one's feelings: "Gradually everybody came to know what they thought about everything some because they expressed their opinions and some because they were afraid to say anything, so one way or another way every one came to know how they felt" (97).

Choosing not to speak may be a form of repression, but it can also be revelatory. When Mrs. Reynolds "met the sister of her uncle's brother" ("Not a real uncle of course"), "she said well, and the sister of her uncle's brother said well and they both laughed together. It was quite dark and the evening was dusky and they did both laugh together" (131). The placement of the conversation within the novel, surrounded by situations of worry and sadness, hints that Mrs. Reynolds and the other woman could say much to one another about the state of occupied life, but their preoccupation keeps them from speaking at the same time that it lets them communicate without words. Perhaps they are laughing because neither of them is really "well."[6]

Sometimes in *Mrs. Reynolds*, people cough instead of saying what they believe (163), but sometimes *not* saying something requires saying something *else* instead:

> And now Angel Harper was fifty and it was getting pretty serious, nobody saw anybody they used to see and it was getting pretty serious, oh dear me said Mrs. Reynolds and when she said oh dear me she wanted to say to Mr. Reynolds that it was getting pretty serious but she did not say that it was getting pretty serious she did not say it just then she only said that she was not seeing any one she used to see no not any one, and Mr. Reynolds said and what then but what he really meant to say was that he still saw her and she still saw him, so what then. (181)

The struggle between Saint Odile and Angel Harper is in full force; Angel Harper must stop dictating, stop winning, and stop living very soon for Saint Odile's prophecy to be correct. But Mrs. Reynolds does not always want to describe her feelings about the war and occupation, nor does she want to mention Saint Odile (158). Instead, she says that she no longer sees the same people she used to see, a seemingly banal comment about her social life, but one that intimates their inability to travel, their distant friends' long absences, and their neighbors' fleeing as refugees. Mr. Reynolds says, "and what then," which could mean so many things and leaves out what he really means (and what would remind them too clearly of their own desperate situation): at least *we* are still together.

Both men and women inhibit their speech in these conditions. Mrs. Reynolds and Mrs. Ellen discuss whether or not men are more selective than women about what they say: "Mrs. Reynolds said, pooh, you know what men say, they scare each other so none of them can say what they want to say" (206). This comment may be an indictment of men who don't say what they see. On the very next page, though, Mrs. Reynolds demonstrates that women do not always say everything either. In the following, "something" is an evasive euphemism for a domicile—either staying where one is, going away, or "not having any place to stay": "Naturally she never said anything about this something because if she did well she would change it to something else that was the only way not to be frightened all day" (207). If she spoke of it, this vague something would become a more distinct—a more pronounced—threat.

Sometimes speakers do not plan their evasions far enough ahead, and they have to trail off in order to avoid certain words or topics: "I wish said Mrs. Reynolds and she did not finish her sentence" (297; see also 174, 184). Stein's portrayal of her characters' avoidance helps readers notice that the novel is also evasive; the avoidance of horrid facts and dire possibilities characterizes Stein's writing of the novel itself. "Enough said" sometimes appears in a sentence by itself, signaling Stein's unwillingness to verbalize the situation of her own occupation (302).

The spoken and written words that Stein and her characters in *Mrs. Reynolds* do not express often correspond to the thoughts they choose not to think. For example, they keep saying "drowned," when it seems likely that people have been *killed* (182–83).[7] One night, Mrs. Reynolds dreams an entire conversation that she must have avoided having with herself when awake.

> While Mrs. Reynolds was sleeping she heard herself saying, why did the lamb die, and she heard a voice that answered because he was hungry and then she heard herself asking and why was he hungry and she heard the voice answer because he had nothing to eat. And she woke up and she woke up Mr. Reynolds and she said to him is it so, and he said is what so and she told him and he said well perhaps not now but perhaps later and then she let him go to sleep and she went to sleep to sleep herself. And when she woke up she said to Mr. Reynolds and I did dream it and he said you did and she said and you said perhaps not now

but perhaps later did you mean it and Mr. Reynolds said yes perhaps he meant it. (184)

When Mrs. Reynolds wakes her husband to ask about her dream, she still resists saying the words aloud. She tries to get him to answer her oblique question "is it so," and only after prompting does she explain what she means. Although Mrs. Reynolds tells Mr. Reynolds enough of the dream to get him to respond, Stein does not repeat that part to her readers (and we know her penchant for repetition). She avoids writing about the possibility of starvation except in the context of a dream about a lamb. Then Mrs. Reynolds "went to sleep to sleep" instead of to dream. The next morning Mrs. Reynolds gestures toward the question of starvation, but in the light of day Mr. Reynolds is less direct. In the night he says, "perhaps not now[,] but perhaps later," or the more reassuring "perhaps[,] not now[,] but perhaps later"; in the morning he says it again, but with one more remove, making the statement even more reassuring: "and Mr. Reynolds said yes perhaps he meant it." Perhaps he meant that perhaps later they could, perhaps, starve.[8]

Mr. Reynolds's use of "perhaps" allows him to be unclear about his meaning and is one example of how conversation can permit a desirable vagueness. Mrs. Reynolds habitually says yes, but she doesn't always mean the same thing by it. She "did not say yes just to say yes," but (and the distinction is delicate) "she said yes because she doubted very much if she knew how she felt about anything, and if she did not know how she felt about anything she said yes" (120). We hear in common parlance these days that "no means no," and that fact is supposed to solve ambiguities about appropriate levels of intimacy and consent, but what if "yes" means "I don't know"? If silence is telling because, as discussed earlier, it suggests the hearer disagrees with the speaker but is too polite or fearful to say so, then verbal signals of agreement and disagreement—"No," "I don't know," and "Yes"—have become inflated. If Mrs. Reynolds does not know what she thinks, she cannot remain silent, because that would suggest she disagrees; she must say yes.

When we agree with each other in talk, there are a variety of levels of agreement, and the speaker and listener can assume different meanings that allow them to disagree very amiably (and unknowingly or just not explicitly). Mrs. Reynolds tells Mr. Reynolds about a conversation she had with a man who "rais[ed] fish for the government" and who was very bitter:

and Mrs. Reynolds said and I told him I agreed with him, he was right to be so bitter and Mr. Reynolds said and did you agree with him, that is do you agree with him, are you bitter and Mrs. Reynolds said she had not agreed with him that she would be bitter but that she agreed with him that he was right to be bitter, and Mr. Reynolds laughed and then they went to bed feeling just a little bit bitter. (193)

Whether they went to bed feeling "bitter" or better or both is one question we are left with. But that Mrs. Reynolds has so many different options as to how to agree with the bitter man lets her agreeably disagree with him. Stein points out the difference between Mrs. Reynolds's agreeing that the bitter man was right to be bitter and agreeing that she would be bitter in the same situation. These degrees of difference remind me of other ways to disagree agreeably: if that had really happened, then it made sense that he would be bitter; since you are who you are, it makes sense that you are bitter; if I were just like you, I would be bitter, too; I can understand why you are bitter (but—and this goes unspoken—I would never be bitter in your situation); or even, Mrs. Reynolds's common response to speakers, "Yes," which could just mean "I heard what you said but I don't know what I think about it." Mrs. Reynolds's "yes" could mean almost anything, as could the French use of *ma foi*: "You say anything to them and they say ma foi, that can mean yes or oh hell, or no, or just nothing" or "to be sure" (Stein, *Wars*, 148). To maintain a level of congeniality in these difficult times, people skid across the surface of meanings: "Of course one never asks anybody what he means" (143). This man who "does raise fish millions of fish" (*Mrs. Reynolds*, 193) could also be a Nazi agitator who raises fists, millions of fists, but Mrs. Reynolds's sympathetic, noncommittal, and (only) polite agreement is not the kind of response political propagandists are trying to evoke in their audiences.

Perhaps to avoid too many situations in which they have to navigate through the complications of agreement and disagreement on tricky political points, but probably to keep themselves as pleasantly occupied as possible, the characters in *Mrs. Reynolds* retain old habits of speech. Conversational rituals, like funeral rituals (*Mrs. Reynolds*, 162) and the daily rituals of eating meals and going to bed, cycle continually through the novel. When something startling happens ("a loud noise") and Mrs. Reynolds "very nearly lost her way" coming home, Mr. and Mrs. Reynolds stubbornly agree that she was not very close to losing her way, they have a "pleasant dinner," and then "Mr. Reynolds asked Mrs. Reynolds if she was tired at all and she said no not at all, but really she was a little tired and she went to bed early" (125–26). Mrs. Reynolds is scared enough to get lost and scared enough by that experience to need a rest, but she is unwilling to give that fear credence by talking about it.

Other conversations are reassuring and also cheer Mr. and Mrs. Reynolds in the face of possible starvation, especially when idiomatic expressions take on ironic complications. Talking and avoiding starvation seem to be the two main pursuits of people in Stein's village, where they "all talked and talked and hunted for food . . . talk and talk and look for food" (Stein, *Wars*, 89).[9] When Mrs. Reynolds says "that she was beginning to be fed up," Mr. and Mrs. Reynolds both laugh, and she adds, "not with food" (*Mrs. Reynolds*, 223). She also comments that "it was funny that some people did continue to be stout" (224). And she creates a light refrain for the war situation: "In the spring a young man's fancy lightly turns to thoughts of love but . . . now, it turns to spring offensives" (223–24). Later, "Mrs. Reynolds said that life was just one spring offensive one after the other, she giggled . . . she could do with a spring where only the spring [w]as doing a spring offensive, she thought she said she thought that that would be a nice change" (239). Mrs. Reynolds is so eager to repeat this witticism that she wants to wake Mr. Reynolds to tell him, and she finally decides to go "out to see if she could not see some one and tell them about the spring offensive and how she did hope that there never would be another one" (239). Mrs. Reynolds so much enjoys making light of their problems in conversation—at the same time as she acknowledges those problems—that she searches for someone with whom to share the pleasurable reassurance of wordplay. Mrs. Reynolds needs to talk: "she was very ready to talk to Herbert or Carrie or Helena or Joan or Paul or Charlotte or Francis or Abel or Cain or even Andrew Soutar" (137), much as Stein in her memoir of the war describes herself as "being cheered by being cheerful" when chatting with a friend on the road (*Wars*, 232).

Mrs. Reynolds is not the only one to treat her fears lightly in polite conversational rituals. People are constantly passing the Reynolds house, and we are left to guess who these people are until Stein confirms our suspicion that they are refugees (*Mrs. Reynolds*, 169). Mrs. Reynolds talks to many of them, and in one case "three of them passed by and stopped to talk to Mrs. Reynolds. How do you do said Mrs. Reynolds when she saw them and the daughter Anabel Rivers answered for all of them, Very well I thank you, and then they went on their way" (170). Stein notices that people still adhere to conversational rituals under terrible duress, even when those rituals require that they express sentiments they are unlikely to feel.

The refugees are compelled to chat, leaving us to assume that they get something out of it. One woman with a small boy "had no time to spare but she did stay to hear all that Mrs. Reynolds had to say" (206). This woman wants to hear what Mrs. Reynolds understands Saint Odile to have said about what would happen; this prophecy may be as close as they can get to optimistic news, "and Mrs. Ellen who had no time to stay listened to her and listened to her and then she said she had to go away her little boy was waiting for her but before she went away she asked Mrs. Reynolds if she thought it would really be that way" (206). The experience of a friendly piece of gossip may comfort people who are facing the unknown or dreadful. This kind of conversation may enable people to be brave when their daily lives are haunted by vague and uninformed fears.

To some extent, jokes and pleasant talk may disarm the enemy. Soldiers might even forget their duties if they chatted ritualistically. Mrs. Reynolds sees "a pretty little soldier" and she tells of her interaction with him: "I said how do you do to him but a soldier must never answer how do you do because if he does he is not a soldier" (271).[10] But another person who lived in France at that time reports that by the third day of the German soldiers' occupation, they started "unbending," playing with puppies and waving to a child picking string beans. "After the lapse of a week, although still reserved and keeping to themselves, they had become integrated with the landscape" (*All Gaul*, 13). It is difficult to imagine soldiers who have thus "integrated" themselves in a community as able to fulfill their duties quite as obediently and with as much intimidation. In *Wars I Have Seen* (83), Stein mentions a joke that the Parisians told about Hitler and Napoleon: "the Parisians are funny, that is what bothers the Germans so, the jokes are never what they expect, no never." Conversation *with* the natives may disarm the occupiers; conversation *among* the natives has the power to disorient those occupiers.

"A queer state of living," or
Resistance through Reticulation and Local Area Networks

Stein finds in the condition of everyday conversation an index of large-scale political affliction, but she also notices how people keep alive a social and political body when most lines of communication have been destroyed. In her memoir *Wars I Have Seen* (200), Stein observes: "It is a queer state of living as we are all doing, you have no news except for the radio because there are no newspapers any more and no trains no mail no telephone and even going to Belley is impossible there are twenty-three barricades between here and there a distance of seventeen kilometers. As I say we live within the village completely within it." The village is an isolated local community trying to survive, and the villagers are trying to participate in a worldwide war which they know of mainly through their necessarily limited experience and through a grapevine of anecdotes and rumors. The French Resistance, a loose political body, is kept alive by people saying what they see and repeating previous conversations to one another.

A case can be made for the likelihood that Stein and Toklas participated energetically in the French Resistance, and Wagner-Martin makes this case in her 1996 biography of Stein, but to make it now, one must first contend with the suggestion that Stein supported the Vichy government (Van Dusen) or just lay low out of fear or ignorance (Malcolm). Stein translated 180 pages of Maréchal Pétain's speeches, wrote a short introduction to them, and mailed this introduction to her editor at Random House on 19 January 1942, a year and a half after the armistice. Her introduction compares Pétain to George Washington and praises him for making the Germans keep their word on the armistice in spite of France's military powerlessness. By August 1944, however, Stein is writing of "the poor maquis many of them hungry and cold and not too favorably regarded by many of their countrymen, it was a kind of a Valley Forge with no General Washington but each little band had to supply itself with its own food its own plans and its own morale. We who lived in the midst of you salute you" (*Wars*, 234).

Support of Pétain and Vichy in January 1942, however, does not contradict later, or even concurrent, participation in the Resistance. In spite of the Jewish Statute of October 1940 and mass arrests of Jews in 1941, the Resistance understood itself as resisting Germany, not Vichy, until early 1942: "the aspect of Resistance that had grown steadily throughout 1941 . . . [was] the merging of opposition to the Germans with opposition to Vichy" (Kedward, *Resistance*, 237). In fact, the Resistance press avoided criticizing Pétain or "the internal politics of Vichy" until March 1942 (237–38), the same month that the first deportation train of Jews left France. *Confluences*, a journal that claimed to be "'above all political issues'" and for which Stein wrote, was both pro-Pétain and pro-Resistance (193–94). In December 1941, this journal "gave an enthusiastic review to Pétain's speeches"—the very ones that Stein the next month tried to get printed in the United States (193).[11] While Stein seems to have diligently worked on the translations until around September 1942, six months after the deportations began, she at some point—perhaps when she finally heard the terrible news—changed her mind about who exactly constituted the good guys and the bad guys in France during World War II. While her silence on Jewish persecution is surprising—either callous or cowardly or psychologically defensive—there is nothing very sinister in her belated shift from Vichy supporter to Resistance supporter. People throughout France only gradually became aware of the Vichy government's overenthusiastic cooperation with Germany.

In a recent *New Yorker* article, "Gertrude Stein's War," Janet Malcolm accuses Stein and Toklas of being as shallow and guilty of "callow preciousness" as the "pretentious young persons" who read *The Alice B. Toklas Cookbook* in the 1960s (59). Noting the "forced gaiety" of the chapter titled "Food in the Bugey during the Occupation," Malcolm suggests that Toklas (and Stein) should have made a point of saying they were Jewish and lesbian, and certainly should have complained more about the Germans. She adjudges that "the evasions seem egregious" (60). But Toklas does not need to state the obvious. Everyone knew she and Stein were Jewish, and almost everyone knew they were lesbian. Sexual orientation was not an open topic of conversation in those days, and even today some enlightened people still hold doubts about the value, the manners, and even the anti-sensuousness of talking about something as private and tactile as sex, because speaking of it belies its nature. Stein told Samuel Steward that "she and Alice had always been surrounded by homosexuals, that they both liked all people who produced—'and what they do in bed is their own business, and what we do is not theirs'" (Steward, *Chapters*, 63). Steward's opinion might have to be interpreted in light of his own sexual activities, which led to an initial five-hour interview with Alfred C. Kinsey followed by seven hundred more hours in the next decade *and* eighteen personal journals, but he goes on to say that Stein and Toklas "were very private persons, really Victorian—completely monogamous, abstemious, and on the surface more than a little reserved" (63). Homosexuality, when it was not labeled an *outrage des moeurs* (an outrage of taste or manners), was called *une affaire rose* (53), and "a rose is a rose is a rose" was probably a not-very-subtle statement of Toklas's and Stein's natural sexual orientation—in addition to all the other things it meant. During her lecture tour, Stein was repeatedly called "mannish" and "manly" (Marlow uses both words in the same paragraph), and reporters referred to her "blocky form" and "man-fashion" gestures (P. Kennedy). After Miss Toklas tries to end an impromptu interview by saying, "Come, pussy," a reporter asks at the arranged session, "Do you like men?" a question explained by "the proclaimed Stein distaste for males." She grinned and said, "I like men enormously. . . . I live my life with them." Then "Miss Alice" arrived again, "with determination as well as gentleness," to end the interview ("Multitude Greets Highbrow"). These juxtapositions, the question, and the consistent labeling and relabeling of Toklas, suggest that people knew the women's relationship and respected (or just accepted) its privacy.

Very little is made of their Jewish heritage in the news reports, although *Time* magazine makes it clear that Stein is from a German Jewish family and that without her hair cut short she "would strongly resemble a fat Jewish *hausfrau*" ("Stein's Way"). Another reporter says she looks like "a young Jewish boy" (Murray). I assume that Stein assumed that everyone knew she was Jewish. People did not always announce their identities the way they often do now, and certainly any such announcement of Stein's would feel incomplete to her, if not to us.

Complaints about the Germans are understated, but certainly present, in the *Cookbook*. British World War II veterans (or even citizens who underwent the fear, the bombings, and the decade-long shortages) generally practice this kind of uncomplaining stoicism and brevity: we might want them to talk like heroes, but they fatalistically accept themselves as somewhat insignificant survivors. Trapped in the Bugey, Toklas and Stein pick "wretched beetles" off their potatoes "by hand" (216); they disdain the Germans' ignorance about butter (203), the Germans' food (212–13), and their general obtuseness (212); they struggle with disappointment at losing their beautiful and productive garden and at the need to start a new one "from scratch" (210). They try to maintain friendships in spite of the lack of food over which to socialize; they arrange black-market deals, food and gas and wine cooperatives; they learn to talk in code. They manage to keep their spirits higher than their depressed cook can, feed their imaginations by reading recipes for which they have no ingredients, are forced to house several groups of German and Italian soldiers, and celebrate Resistance and Allied victories when they can. Toklas reports that some shopkeepers "said it was their patriotic duty to sell what the Germans forbade." She asks, "was it not mine to purchase what they offered?" (*Cookbook*, 212). Self-serving, perhaps, but also a form of insurgency.

While it's fun to imagine Stein and Toklas slipping out to sabotage bridges, I can imagine Stein doing little other than walking throughout the French countryside and talking to everyone she meets. Yet these could easily have been very helpful activities. A wanderer might notice where airdrops of supplies and weapons from the Allies had landed and could alert the "addressees" where to find these shipments. While Stein was trekking through the countryside, Toklas visited town daily (although I assume this was not possible throughout the entire war) and may have been a contact for people who were getting on and off trains (Wagner-Martin, 251–52). Erlene Hubly (71), who taped and translated a 1986 ceremony at Stein's house in Bilignin, reports that University of Lilles professor Trenard said that Stein helped the Bugey through "aiding the Resistance fighters by collecting and transmitting information to them." Wagner-Martin (271) comments: "Because there are so few written records of resistance activity, however, the chief proof of her role is oral. Historians have long noted that many women—particularly Jewish women—worked successfully for the resistance because the Germans thought so little of women that they seldom suspected them." After all, women only talked. But maybe proof is oral because the work was oral too.

Perhaps orality enabled the French Resistance, and orality keeps us from knowing it.[12] At the beginning of the war, in a 1 October letter to Van Vechten, Stein lamented that "there is nothing to do to help," but she and Toklas seem to have found ways (Burns, 651). Alice cooked cakes for the Resistance and (unwittingly) "provided [a member of the Resistance] with the sheets of gelatin used for making false identification papers" (Toklas, *Cookbook*, 207). Stein's talents were in other areas; she walked and listened and talked.

An integral part of this kind of communication is retelling what others have said. In *Mrs. Reynolds*, many speakers do not appear in person, but we know their names (or something else about them), and we know what they say. In one instance, we hear news via four different conversations: a librarian told a librarian who told a widow who told a brother who is now telling Mr. and Mrs. Reynolds. In another instance, we know what "a little man quite shrunken" and his daughter say, but "Mrs. Reynolds never met them . . . her cousin told her what they said" (35). This repetition of peoples' names or other identifying characteristics creates a network of connection. Recounting the substance of earlier conversations in which words are attached to the individuals responsible for them is different from repeating what "they say," because who says what is especially important in a world where identity is political and one's politics are revealed by what one speaks—or suppresses.

The Resistance was a political movement largely organized by conversation—conversation that created a complex network of relationships instead of a straightforward, predetermined line of command. Stein reports on the German inability to adopt this more complex form of organization when the "mountain boys" cut off all their communications (*Wars*, 198–99). Just retribution, since the Germans had done the same for the French people, this strategy is also effective because the German army cannot operate in the same way as the Resistance: "The Germans are very uncertain in their minds now . . . guerrilla warfare gets on their nerves it is so darn individual and being individual is what they do not like that is to say what they can not do" (204–5).[13] People who conduct guerrilla warfare have a special way of communicating. Stein writes that "all around us there is fighting, the conversation in the village sounds exactly like the communiqués of the Yugo-Slavs in their early days of guerrilla fighting" (198). Stein also compares the Germans to ants, reputed for their instinctive submission to their social order. When their order is confused, the Germans "came in and out and about and they are exactly like an ants nest if you put a foreign substance in it, the Germans run around just like that" (214–15).

Another way Stein distinguishes German from French organization is that the Germans listened (to authority) but the French talked. Stein's descriptions of her neighbors' reactions to the radio—the one remaining medium of mass communication—demonstrate that listening to the imposing voices on radio divides communities and that give and take conversation rebuilds them. During the winter of 1939–40, Stein and Toklas took turns listening to their wireless radio (Wagner-Martin, 238). In *Wars I Have Seen*, Stein complained that while everyone else "had to stay home" and "could not even write letters to friends most of the time," "any public character can talk and talk all day long over the radio" (65). Stein describes everyone listening to the radio in the evenings, and then she immediately says that nobody loves their neighbors anymore (125). Assuming an association between the two topics, we may infer that listening to the radio contributes to this estrangement. During the war, every nation had its own broadcast.[14] The propaganda on each channel was so different that people had to choose whom they believed, or choose not to believe any of it at all:

> everybody listens to the radio, they listen all day long because almost everybody has one and if not there is their neighbor's and they listen to the voice from any country and yet what they really believe is not what they hear but the rumors in the town, by word of mouth is always the most convincing, they do not believe the newspapers nor the radio but they do believe what they tell each other and that is natural enough, all official news is so deceiving, so why not believe rumors, that is reasonable enough, and so they do, they believe all the rumors, and even when they know they are not true they believe them, at any rate they have a chance of being true rumors have but official news has no chance of being true none at all, of course not. (161)

Francis Bacon warned that the division of the church leads to atheism; Stein suggests that a lot of different propaganda leads people to disbelieve all information. For propaganda to work its effects, it has to be so total it becomes invisible.[15]

If people choose their propaganda from the radio, their choices create differences among neighbors, even among family members. They are literally on different wavelengths. For example, Mr. and Mrs. Reynolds hold very different views from Mr. Reynolds's brother and his wife.

> Mr. and Mrs. Madden-Henry admired Angel Harper because he never coughed. They knew that of him. He never could or would or did cough. Joseph Lane might cough did cough would cough but and this Mr. and Mrs. Madden-Henry knew Angel Harper never had and never would cough. For this they did very much admire him.
>
> Bat said Hope Reynolds, the wife of Mr. Reynolds' younger brother, Bat is a word that has two meanings, one that flies by night and one that hits a ball.
>
> By this she meant to express her admiration, her very great admiration for Angel Harper. . . .
>
> Mrs. Coates had greatly respected Mr. and Mrs. Madden-Henry, but when she heard them say that they admired Angel Harper because he never coughed, she began to think badly of them, and gradually she came to despise them.
>
> . . . Mrs. Coates said that she herself was interested in what any one said but nevertheless she herself was certain that Mr. and Mrs. Madden-Henry were mistaken. (*Mrs. Reynolds*, 96)

Mr. and Mrs. Madden-Henry seem to respect Harper because he's a persistent speaker who does not need to pause for anything. His *blitzkreigs* parallel his "*blitzsprechen*." Mrs. Coates is "interested in what any one said" and thus may believe too much in what others say, but here she seems observant enough to notice that words have "two meanings" and that while the Madden-Henrys mean to praise Harper, the fact that he "never could or would or did cough" could mean he's a *dummkopf* (a dolt). Harper talks so much nobody else has to (or dares to), but beliefs that are only heard and not expressed personally keep a community divided. The Madden-Henrys are precursors of the current propagandist Rush Limbaugh's "ditto-heads"—not because of their beliefs but because the medium by which they receive those beliefs forbids them to express themselves. Ventriloquy is no substitute for individual expression.

But if people choose to believe nothing they hear from their media source, they can discuss and create rumors together, building a local community. This smaller social structure in turn is even more resistant to further propaganda, both because smaller structures resist influence from outside sources and because "Propaganda ceases where simple dialogue begins" (Ellul, 6). In this way there may be advantages to being "completely isolated" where "rumor follows rumor" (Stein, *Wars*, 145).

Stein had been made aware of the combined power of prejudice, press, and public opinion by prominent controversies during the last decade of the nineteenth century, when she was in college and medical school:

> It was around those days that three things happened that made me know about those kinds of things. There was my eldest brother coming home from the East as a member of the G.A.R., he had to grow a beard to look old enough, of course he did not belong but there were privileges in traveling and other things so he came along with them. It was then I first knew about officialdom and what one did by bribing. Of course that has to do with war, because the ordinary person that is one leading a peaceful life particularly men comes in contact with officials but in war-time, sooner or later everybody does. The second thing was the famous Oscar Wilde trial and the question of public opinion and the third thing was the Dreyfus case and anti-semitism. (*Wars*, 51)

The GAR is the Grand Army of the Republic, a society of Civil War veterans who had served in the Union forces. Stein's brother would have been too young to fight in the war, and Stein's ancestors had been Confederates. Since Stein has just made the difficult decision to stay in France instead of "pass by fraud" to Switzerland (50)—in 1943, after being pointedly warned to go—she may be thinking of the misrepresentations of self encouraged by officialdom. Stein sees a relationship between her brother, her own situation, and disguise. "The second thing" and "the third thing," also comment on the deceptive presentation of self in a hostile situation. Oscar Wilde's trial communicates a powerful message about the importance of disguises to a homosexual; the turmoil surrounding the Dreyfus case could convey the same message to a Jew. Both cases were also huge generators of newsprint, and the role of the press and public opinion (and famous writers) in the Dreyfus affair is as interesting as, though probably not separable from, the case itself.

Gabriel Tarde—who was "one of the three most outstanding sociologists of nineteenth-century France" (along with Auguste Comte and Emile Durkheim) and who influenced Franz Boas (and indirectly through Boas, other U.S. anthropologists)—was inspired by the Dreyfus case to distinguish between a "crowd" and a "public" (T. Clark, 1, 66–67, 52). Tarde defines a crowd as a group of people who are in "physical proximity";

a public is "a purely spiritual collectivity, a dispersion of individuals who are physically separated and whose cohesion is entirely mental (278, 277). A crowd is a long-established collectivity; the more recent "public" is enabled by technologies such as the printing press and improved transportation. But Stein's characters in *Mrs. Reynolds* and her friends in *Wars I Have Seen* do not collect in crowds of more than two or three people (the Germans forbade it), and they do not read a newspaper they trust, if they have access to one at all.

In *Mrs. Reynolds*, Stein demonstrates another kind of collectivity. Stein's fictional midcentury war-inspired network is built around chance meetings and polite visits during which people chat, pass on hearsay, make wishes, predict doom, or treat crises as lightly as they can. "Mrs. Reynolds liked to know what was happening so she asked everybody as they were passing" (91). At one point, Mrs. Reynolds talks to "Mrs. Chambers who happened to be walking in the same direction" (226). Mrs. Reynolds never gets to talk to Mrs. Andrews anymore, because "she was never out in her garden and Mrs. Reynolds never saw her. And if Mrs. Reynolds never saw her they could not talk together" (258–59). Most interactions occur between two individuals who meet on a road, speak over a fence, or, in the case of Mr. and Mrs. Reynolds, chat over their scanty meals. This loose-knit complex collectivity maintains individuality but enables strength and action through cooperation.

Getting Together and Thinking in *Brewsie and Willie*

Brewsie and Willie, written after V.E. Day (8 May 1945) and published before Stein's death (27 July 1946), is an informal transcription of an imagined conversation among American GIs and nurses in France. That its informal and imaginary status makes it diverge widely from the data of conversation analysts significantly undermines my choice of the word "transcription." But readers are struck by what sounds like real conversation. Hoffman writes that "Miss Stein demonstrates that she indeed had a remarkable sense of the way people sound when they talk" (*Abstractionism*, 128n), and that "the chapters of dialogue seem almost to have been recorded by a tape recorder" (*Gertrude Stein*, 102). Bridgman is more moderate when he observes that "the dialogue gives the impression of stylized authenticity" and that the soldiers from different states are not distinguished by regional dialect (336). When she wrote *Brewsie and Willie*, Stein's imagination was steeped in the language of the GIs; she soaked up their voices, slang, and personal histories with great pleasure when she met them at the end of World War II. Of this meeting, she writes: "Oh happy day, that is all that I can say oh happy day" (*Wars*, 244). When she met the soldiers, they "talked and talked" together, and their speech—especially the names of their hometowns—"was music to the ears" (246).

The impression of conversational structure in *Brewsie and Willie* is bolstered by the many paragraphs that consist of a name, a colon, and a speech act. This theatrical signature makes the novel an obvious candidate for a discussion of how Stein's writing incorporates spoken forms of English, but my intention is to discuss Stein's prescription for a kind of conversation which she expects will heal the economic and social problems of the United States—a way of bringing the victory back home. The ideas in *Brewsie and Willie* are presented by means of conversation, and much of that conversation is about politics, economics, society, and conversation itself. In *Mrs. Reynolds*, Stein demonstrates how politics and propaganda can change the nature of conversation, but in *Brewsie and Willie*, she delineates a different relationship between politics and conversation. Consistent with her critique of cautious conversation in a political landscape characterized by propagandistic harping, Stein presents open, playful conversation as an integral step toward improving the world's sociopolitical future.

Critics have seen logistical laziness instead of theoretical complexity in Stein's choice to write *Brewsie and Willie* in dialogue form. Bridgman supposes that Stein chose to write this way because "it exempted her from the need to develop her positions fully," "permitted her to interject disagreements and illustrative anecdotes," and "sanctioned the abrupt change of subject" (336). Hoffman summarizes Bridgman's position: "Stein found the dialogue form congenial . . . because it gave her the opportunity to vent her spleen without obligating her to develop any position logically" (*Gertrude Stein*, 102). While not necessarily contradicting Bridgman and Hoffman, I'm convinced that Stein chose to work with dialogue because its interjections, incompletions, cooperation, and playful listening to itself are all components of her suggestion for an American conversation.[16] As Rorty advocates: "all that matters for liberal politics is the widely shared conviction that . . . we shall call 'true' or 'good' whatever is the outcome of free discussion—that if we take care of political freedom, truth and goodness will take care of themselves" (*Contingency*, 84). In the interests of variety and dialogue, Stein probably does not value full positions on anything; Bridgman notes that she "was constitutionally incapable of sustained exposition, for her mind rapidly clogged with qualifications and objections as she proceeded" (336). Stein distrusted final solutions before she could have known about the "Final Solution."

Since Stein's characters directly state their discontents, critics have also tended to glean Stein's solution for these problems from their specific words. Jimmie says we "have to take care of ourselves" (*Brewsie*, 59); Brewsie says we "have to pioneer" (62); several agree that they have to "break down what has been built up," and Willie takes this to the limit: "do you want us to drop our atomic bombs on ourselves, is that what you want, so we can go out and pioneer, is that the idea" (83). These half-hearted suggestions lead Bridgman to write that Stein "offered no panacea for these urgent problems" and that Willie's "negative appraisal"—"there aint any answer, there aint going to be any answer, there never has been any answer, that's the answer" (*Brewsie*, 30)—"is never fully dissipated in the book" (Bridgman, 339). Bridgman concludes that the most "positive proposal" in the novel is that of "resistance," but that "Gertrude Stein's prudence restrained her from openly advocating revolution, which in any case would not be to her taste" (340). Stein can still prove relevant today, as we face more of the same "urgent" problems; instead of looking for quick answers to our complex problems, we should begin (and continue) the longer, messier processes that might form more successful solutions.

Stein's characters do not explicitly state an answer, but in their style of talk appears a suggestion. Their proposals are less-than-desirable alternatives to Stein's truly positive proposal: speak openly, converse, and at least while you try to solve your problems you will be friends (or at least on speaking terms), which will prevent interim violence. As Stein scolded Americans, with a phrase of lasting relevance: "A country can't live without friends" (qtd. in Brinnin, 393). Perhaps there is not one answer because it is impossible to clarify and simplify the complexity of the world—Willie says: "Well go on Brewsie, go on straighten things out. I'm sure straight is something that looks funny, but go on, let's straighten it out" (*Brewsie*, 55)—but in the meantime, we can chat.[17] Their half-baked wanderings also represent people rising up and meeting each other in conversation, which allows for the possibility, as William James rhapsodizes, that "we can *create* the conclusion, then. We can and we may, as it were, jump with both feet off the ground into or towards a world of which we trust the other parts to meet our jump—and *only so* can the *making* of a perfected world of the pluralistic pattern ever take place. Only through our precursive trust in it can it come into being" (qtd. in Shepherd, 251).

A statement in Stein's memoir *Wars I Have Seen* enables readers to better understand her views on the speech she represents in *Brewsie and Willie*. Writing after World War II, Stein contrasts American soldiers in the two world wars:

I began to realize that Americans converse much more than they did, American men in those other days, the days before these days did not converse. How well I remember in the last war seeing four or five of them at a table at a hotel and one man would sort of drone along monologuing about what he had or had not done and the others solemnly and quietly eating and drinking and never saying a word. And seeing the soldiers stand at a corner or be seated somewhere and there they were and minutes hours passed and they never said a word, and then one would get up and leave and the others got up and left and that was that. No this army was not like that, this army conversed, it talked it listened, and each one of them had something to say no this army was not like that other army. . . . now they are still American but they can converse and they are interesting when they talk. The older Americans always told stories that was about all there was to their talking but these don't tell stories they converse and what they say is interesting and what they hear interests them and that does make them different not really different God bless them but just the same they are not quite the same.

We did not talk about that then. We had too much to tell and they had too much to tell to spend any time conversing about conversation. (*Wars*, 248–49)

Stein notices that American soldiers in the forties speak very differently from the way their compatriots did in the teens. A doughboy either spoke forever, "tell[ing] stories" and "monologuing," or he did not speak at all. But the GIs know how to converse; they know how to talk and listen both. In *Brewsie and Willie*, these conversations take the form of lively interaction. The characters speak together in a dance of words and interject comments and puns. Stories, ideas, and questions are built by the group from the comments of individuals expressing their different perspectives.

Brewsie and Willie contains characters of both conversational styles. Brock represents the kind of talk Stein associates with the World War I doughboys; Brewsie and Willie, along with Pauline and many other characters, collaborate to converse and be interesting. Brock, who is "older," always tells things that have happened to him:

he liked to talk about how his father and mother moved from one house to another and what illnesses they had had and what it did to them and what flowers his mother grew and that she was fond of cooking and eating, and that he was not the only child but they did like him that is to say he was interested in everything they wrote to him and was natural enough because although he had been married, he did not know whether he was married now or not. (5)

The anataxis here suggests Brock's persistent and cumulative "monologu-ing." His ignorance as to the state of his marriage is to be pitied, but it also suggests an inability to sustain partnerships. Just as he forgets that a talker needs a listener, he forgets that to be a husband requires a wife. Brock also explains things (26), and, again, explanations are not the kind of talk Stein values. Brock is not the only character who cannot converse. Ed also tells what he's done: "I'll tell you just how I do it, just how old I am, just what I have done, just what I am going to do, I am just going to tell you" (32). Exemplifying the closed mind that accompanies this kind of presentational talk, Ed does not think it necessary to think and talk about improving the economic situation in the United States. His logic: his brother "lived through the depression and he always had a job" (31).

I suspect that Brewsie is a kind of ideal speaker for Stein, in spite of his tendency to sometimes get too explanatory, pedantic, and repetitive. Brewsie asks questions that inspire conversation. "I want to know why do you fellows feel the way you do" (5). "why don't the G.I.'s [sic] have the Bible around like the doughboys did" (10). Over and over, he asks, "Are we isolationists or are we isolated, are we efficient or are we quick to make up for long preparation" (e.g., 16). Brewsie is always thoughtful and disturbs complacency. He is "earnest" and "careful," and what he says rings true (32). Several times, Willie wishes for the otherwise hated Brock, because Brock's monologues would be comforting compared to all this unnerving discussion (52, 84). Brewsie begins many statements with "I been think-ing," and Willie comments, "Well anyway . . . Brock never did begin that way" (68).

Stein has been characterized as an experimental writer; Brewsie is an experimental speaker. When he talks, he thinks out loud, in contrast to a speaker who makes up his or her mind and asserts a single definitive posi-tion on a topic.[18] Brewsie thinks about several topics at once, starts more than one conversation at a time, asks many questions, and changes his mind in midconversation. Julie Abraham describes the main "action" of *Brewsie and Willie* as "the spreading of doubt, the changing of minds" (516). Instead of declaring what's right, Brewsie says, "I think" (*Brewsie*, 3), which is one way of asking for a peaceful open conversation about what everybody else thinks too, or instead. Rather than store his opinions, which might let them become stale, he thinks as he speaks. When Brewsie has to leave before he says what's on his mind, Jo says, "Brewsie will remember what he wants to say for another day." Brewsie responds, "No . . . I wont remember but I will find it out again" (19). That Brewsie will have to rediscover his own thoughts next time he speaks demonstrates that he is not a pedantic "harper."

Besides Brewsie's letting thought inspire his more repetitive monologues, his explanations differ from, say, Angel Harper's, in another important way. Brewsie's presentations are often interrupted by other speakers' ideas and irreverent comments. When Brewsie presents his history of industrialism, he is interrupted by several jokes (34–35). The conversation deteriorates when his persistence in the face of interruption eventually produces an audience that listens without interrupting for a fairly long time. When the interjections come, they first suggest the gullibility of his audience. Jo responds only when Brewsie mentions historic facts: "My God yes, said Jo, we did have the depression" (36). The fact of the depression does not mean that Brewsie's analysis of economic trends is correct, and yet that is what Jo's awed interjection implies.[19] In one sense, then, Brewsie is temporarily a very minor dictator—intentionally or not—because his listeners are incapable of thinking independently enough to disagree with him or augment his ideas in any way.

Later in the novel, though, a productive conversation—one in which interesting ideas arise, however randomly—takes place among eight speakers: Brewsie, Jo, Willie, Pauline, Jane, Jimmie, Janet, and Donald Paul. While they all still think they are there to listen to Brewsie, most of them say something thoughtful. Jo calls their attention to language, wondering aloud why Americans have begun calling their nation "the states"; Donald Paul asserts, "Everything means something," and listens to himself enough to wonder if he means "something means anything"; Jimmie deduces the limitations of the two usual options, working or striking; and Donald Paul throws in issues of race and class when he "suppose[s] even in a poor country somebody has just got to be rich" and wonders if it will be African Americans (57–60).[20] These eight people bring their various questions and concerns to the conversation, creating a complex set of criteria that any "answer" would have to address (60–61). Single paragraphs, and even single sentences, contain speech from more than one character, further suggesting the ways that several speakers can create ideas together. What one speaker says piggybacks on the words of another one, in a form of innovation dependent on far-ranging talk and close listening.

Brewsie's thinking out loud makes him an important model, but he's not quite playful enough when he speaks. Stein does not dismiss Willie's value via a simplified binarism. Willie may resist offbeat thoughts and big questions, but he is another model speaker in that he is fun to talk to. Not only does Willie have the good judgment to listen to Brewsie when he is the only one thinking and trying to express his thoughts, but also Willie is smart, ironic, and alert to puns (34–35). Willie hears "missed steak" in "mistake," which leads him to consider the various costs of the U.S. Civil War. He ponders what it means that American Southerners are "lousy" and "foreigners" but not "lousy foreigners" (47). When a woman starts quoting her father, Willie insightfully and amusingly says, "It's enough . . . that we got to fight the rich men and the poor men too, but we got to stop somewhere sister, we cant take on your father, sure anybody has to have a father, that's all right but anybody can forget about a father especially in a war, especially" (38).[21] In pretending to summarize Brewsie's analysis of the effects of the Civil War on U.S. economics, Willie says, "yes we were fighting so no colored man would ever again have to say yes ma'am, thank you ma'am" (49). And he may be more insightful than he sounds; if "heil Hitler" is an insidious insertion of fascism into everyday life, then "yes ma'am" could just as perniciously and subtly maintain the system of human enslavement. While Willie seems to want to stop everyone's deep thought and expressiveness, his own irreverent idle talk provokes original ideas, too.

The French during the war learn to mistrust mass media, but so do the American soldiers after the war. In *Brewsie and Willie*, Willie wonders whom he can believe when he gets home:

> It used to be fine, said Willie, before the war when we used to believe what the newspapers and the magazines said, we used to believe them when we read them and now when it's us they write about we know it's lies, just lies, just bunches of lies, and if it's just bunches of lies, what we going to read when we get home, answer me that, Brewsie, answer me that. (19)

Willie worries about how he can assimilate back into the American public. The "bond" between people who are "reading the same newspaper" is forged by "their simultaneous conviction or passion and . . . their awareness of sharing at the same time an idea or a wish with a great number of other men" (Tarde, "Public," 278). Willie would like to think with the group, but now that he mistrusts the information in the press, he fears that it will be impossible to regain his position as an undeviating, untroubled member of the American public.

Yes-and-No "Job-men"

Nazis say, "Heil Hitler"; slaves in America say, "Yes, ma'am"; and, with less coercion, "yes and no job-men" say yes and no (not "kind of" or "mmhmm" or "let me think about it" or something else altogether) in the perpetuation of industrial conformity. Yes-and-no job-men are dependent employees instead of independent hired men (Stein, "Capital and Capitals," 75). Stein blames industrialism for the demise of open conversation and free thought. Admittedly, before there was industrialism, there were leaders who found willing followers. But if one assumes that Americans are different, that Americans are pioneers who lead their own kinds of lives and whose ancestors revitalized and instituted a rare form of government to ensure their right to pursue happiness in their own ways, then one might blame industrialism for the new kind of American who was just like the people left behind by those idealized movers and shakers: a follower.

The characters in Stein's *Brewsie and Willie* explicitly state their worries about the future, discussing outright the long-term economic effects and the immediately visible social effects of industrialism on the characters of Americans.[22] A "fat major" and a "thin major" compare the lives of European workers with those of U.S. workers. They wish that the United States would learn from Europe and give workers a day-and-a-half holiday each week, a month's vacation, and retirement at fifty instead of seventy (20–21). This fat major and thin major make me think of the major and minor premises in a syllogism. Their speech does not strictly follow the structure of syllogistic argument, but they do reason and reckon together (the etymological meaning of "syllogism"). They may sound lazy, but their wishes correspond to Willie's statement that Americans "dont think over there [back home, in the United States], they got no time to think, they got to get a job, they got to hold the job, they got no time to think over there" (108). Willie doesn't mind, because he thinks that thinking does no good, but Brewsie disagrees. He says that if you haven't had time to think, then "you'll be old and you never lived," and "industrialism makes industrials poor individuals" (108, 75).[23]

One might argue that it is reasonable to pay socio-psychological or cultural costs for economic prosperity, but Stein's characters also doubt that industrial capitalism is a viable long-term economic system.[24] Brewsie links new restrictions on immigration to the United States with the loss of a market for American-made products, and he describes the necessary alternative market: "now we got to make a club to make those foreign countries buy from us, and we all got to go home to make some more of those things that use up the raw material and that nobody but our own little population wants to buy" (36–37). He argues that "industrialism is wrong" because "it makes the country going all industrial poor" (56–57). Countries such as France that "never went industrial" manage to make "luxuries"—"what [France] sells dont cost her hardly anything to make," says Jo—but industrial countries use all their valuable resources making things that don't sell for very much, because "once industry makes luxuries it aint a luxury any more" (57). In short, the crisis of rising expectations caused by industrialism leads to economic ruin, as well as to intellectual bankruptcy.[25]

The characters in *Brewsie and Willie* are not the only people worried about the future of America. Stein herself seems particularly concerned with spiritual and intellectual decay, expecting that improvements in these areas would solve all the other problems, too. When she traveled to Germany with U.S. troops right after the war, she was troubled, she reported in an article for *Life* magazine, because the soldiers "admitted they liked the Germans better than the other Europeans" ("Off We All Went," 140). This admission suggested to her something ominous about the American character. In her article, she sees German "flatter[y]" as the source for this preference, and in her novel, Brewsie wonders whether "we like Germans because we are greedy and callous like them" (*Brewsie,* 20). Stein felt that the solution to a war-mongering Germany was to "teach [the Germans] disobedience, . . . make every German child know that it is its duty at least once a day to do its good deed and not believe something its father or its teacher tells them, confuse their minds, get their minds confused and perhaps then they will be disobedient and the world will be at peace" ("Off We All Went," 136). A U.S. Army sergeant told her that she "'confused the minds of his men,'" and she "got very angry": "why shouldn't their minds be confused, gracious goodness, are we going to be like the Germans, . . . all having the same point of view" (140). A Frenchman in Stein's play *In Savoy* is as direct: "Obedience is a curse. . . . The Germans are obedient and obedient people must sooner or later follow a bad leader" (21).[26]

A personal statement appended to the end of *Brewsie and Willie* further develops Stein's position. Once rightly and wrongly described as a "peroration on the subject of patriotism that is rampant with unblushing clichés" (Hoffman, *Gertrude Stein,* 103), this letter "to Americans" warns that

we have to have to fight *a spiritual pioneer fight* or we will go poor as England and other industrial countries have gone poor, and dont think that communism or socialism will save you, you just have to *find a new way,* you have to find out how you can go ahead without running away with yourselves, you have to learn to produce without exhausting your country's wealth, you have to *learn to be individual and not just mass job workers*, you have to *get courage enough to know what you feel and not just all be yes or no men*, but you have to *really learn to express complication*, go easy and if you cant go easy go as easy as you can. Remember the depression, dont be afraid to look it in the face and find out the reason why, dont be afraid of the reason why. . . . Find out the reason why, look facts in the face, *not just what they all say, the leaders, but every darn one of you* so that a government by the people for the people shall not perish from the face of the earth, it wont, somebody else will do it if we lie down on the job. (*Brewsie*, 113–14; my italics)

Sometimes a cliché is more than a cliché. Robert K. Martin's description of this passage seems apt to me: "Stein brilliantly mixes the clichés of popular advice ('look facts in the face'), folksy locutions ('every darn one of you'), and fragments from Lincoln's Gettysburg Address in a manner that both recalls the origins of her message in American political heritage and warns of its transformation into the blank phrases of Fourth of July rhetoric" (214). In this patriotic appeal, Stein expresses her belief that fighting "a spiritual pioneer fight"—one inside ourselves instead of on the plains of North America—will lead us to new ideas beyond communism and socialism, the most popularized alternatives to capitalism. Industrialism is the culprit (one that has been equally befriended by these three -isms), and our thoughts must lead us to other answers, to "a new way."

But industrialism is not just an economic culprit; it has formed us into people who cannot see beyond it. Stein is clearly aware of the kinds of jobs that are available to most people in an industrial society, and she concludes, with reason, that this kind of work diverts people from thinking and acting for themselves. Stein argues that Americans have to stop letting themselves be led around by limited binary false choices, have to escape the limits of "yes or no." Stein's Brewsie says:

you see I don't think we think, if we thought we could not articulate the same, we couldn't have Gallup polls and have everybody answer yes or no, if you think it's more complicated than that, . . . thinking is funnier and more mixed than that, . . . I guess job men just have to articulate alike, they got to articulate yes or no to their bosses, and yes or no to their unions, they just got to articulate alike, and when you begin to articulate alike, you got to drop thinking out. (*Brewsie*, 102–3)

If we escape being "mass job workers" and "learn to be individual," we will be able to see for ourselves instead of believing what a few leaders tell us.[27]

Stein's solution, or rather her means toward solutions, is linguistic: we have to get beyond the easy yes and no and "really learn to express complication." In the letter to Americans cited above, she advocates discovering causes of the depression, but *Brewsie and Willie* overall is more intent upon teaching people to participate in the processes of thinking and talking than upon asserting an economic theory. Stein prepares her readers for a conversation, and her primary directive is to become internally split so that we remember to converse with ourselves. We should think so much that we don't know for sure what we believe.

Internal stress characterizes the soldiers in *Brewsie and Willie*. Brewsie's talking to himself is a sign of an internal division (7). His "thinking and talking" make him "kind of foggy in the head" in spite of his quest for clear understanding (11). Brewsie says, "although rich we are poor," and "although quick we are slow" (22–23), extending his idea of riches beyond finances to happiness and freedom, and noticing that he values preparedness and attentive energy during times of peace even more than quick-wittedness and frantic energy in a crisis. Brewsie thinks enough to notice discrepancies between what he understands he is supposed to believe and what he feels he believes. In her memoir, Stein is told by "The man at the bank": "there are a great many different points of view and one single man can have quite a great number of them" (*Wars*, 81). As a Frenchman explains to an aptly named American woman in Stein's last play, *In Savoy*:

> my poor Constance you don't understand. How can you understand, no Constance you do not understand. There are so many points of view in a Frenchman, of course he cannot agree with any other Frenchman but he cannot even agree with himself inside him that is to say with the other Frenchman which is him. No my poor Constance you do not understand. (31–32).

When French people are asked for their opinions, they often start their answer with "no . . . and yes."

If American assertions tend to be characterized by constancy, Stein encourages us in *Brewsie and Willie* to learn a little inconsistency and free expression from the French. She noticed during the war that French free expression was curbed, and she missed it. One observer who lived in occupied France during World War II states that it was very striking to notice the restrictions on speech during the German occupation:

> Restraint in self-expression has never been a Gallic trait. Now that the Kommandantur has clamped down the ban of silence, it is especially hard to acquiesce. We have always been garrulous and carefree in speech, with a party openly advocating the return of monarchy, right in the bosom of the republican Parliament.
>
> We now see that both in manners and thought we were the freest, most unhampered people under heaven. All of which makes today's repression the more irksome. This looking over the shoulder before uttering an innocent remark does not fit into our picture. When shoving off the children for school, my wife used to say, "Don't get your feet wet." Now she warns them, "Sh-h! Don't speak to any one or answer questions." (*All Gaul*, 67–68)

This sudden speechlessness would make anyone notice and value freedom of expression, particularly someone as observant of conversation as Stein.

After the war, French habits of talk resume their freedom, as Stein observes: "all this time, well we did not say much but now France is free and we tell each other what we really think" (*In Savoy*, 58). In *Brewsie and Willie*, Stein depicts American soldiers as conversing more openly in France than they would in the United States:

> While they were talking they did not know what country they were in. . . .
>
> It was early in the morning, and there was anybody there, they never thought that there was anybody there even when there was. (13)

Their conversation is not restricted by where they are or, as I understand the implications of location, where their loyalties should lie. They never worry that anybody was there, even when someone was, which suggests a free and easy conversation not overshadowed by suspicions that "somebody's there" or hushed reassurances that "nobody's there." These soldiers feel free to think and talk about all sorts of things: "About it, about what it is, about how about it, about what is it about, about, what are you going to do about it, about, how about it" (66). They are less interested in the variable "it" than in the ruminative equation; the ultimate goal of this kind of talk is "to get going away from what everybody has gotten the habit of thinking"

(69–70). Willie goes so far as to say, "I don't see why I got to believe a thing only because it's true" (38).

Being "foggy in the head" might prevent violence, as well as lead to new and different ideas. Tarde believed that "psychic strain" prevented social conflict; groups could not form and clash if individuals were internally divided as to their beliefs (see T. Clark, 34–35). Note that Stein's men and women in *Brewsie and Willie* come and go freely; their circulation of ideas and information does not form a Rotary Club.[28] The free inconsistency which Stein believes will allow Americans to think and converse will also, according to Tarde, keep them out of violent conflict. Stein, too, seems concerned about violence. In discussing the burden of a high standard of living and industrialism, Jo says, "How do you get on top of anything that is on top of you, first you got to break it off you." Pauline worries, "Oh dear . . . fighting is so natural" (70). Instead of this "natural" revolutionary reflex, Stein suggests thinking about and speaking toward alternative ways of conceiving and generating change.

Other characters in the novel adopt Brewsie's wandering thought process and challenging talk. Henry says that his "mind's confused" and that he wants to remain in France to think:

> Willie, muttering mind mind, confused, get a mind, get it confused, I suppose, said Willie, you have been listening to Brewsie. No I havent, said Henry. Who's Brewsie. Who's Brewsie said Willie, that's Brewsie, well how did you get your mind confused if you didnt listen to Brewsie. Well I guess, said Henry, I got my mind confused because I just cant see any way not to have my mind confused that's all, see here Willie, you see it's about that employee mentality we're all getting to have, we're just a lot of employees, obeying a boss, with no mind of our own and if it goes on where is America, I say if it goes on, where is America, no sir, said Henry, no sir, I want to pioneer. Ah, said Willie, you been listening to Brewsie. (*Brewsie*, 63)

Henry sounds like Brewsie, but he has come to his ideas on his own power, his own willingness to "see here" and think. Willie doesn't seem to like this independence one bit. When Henry suggests, "let's all think," Willie responds (maybe sarcastically by this point), "No . . . you let Brewsie do the thinking, that's the way we are in this outfit, we let Brewsie do the thinking" (65). Willie notes that "the guys" won't let Brewsie talk anymore: "they found out from listening to him how to do it and now they all talk and talk and think it sounds just like him" (100–101). But the ideal is not to sound "just like" Brewsie; it is to speak freely and thoughtfully, as Brewsie demonstrates is possible. Willie warns, "look out Brewsie, soon there won't be a thing you can tell them" (67), but Brewsie is probably happy to finally be surrounded by people willing to "get together and think" (11).

Brewsie's kind of talk influences others, but the soldiers agree that he does not speak like a typical leader. Brewsie spends too much time asking questions and deliberating possible answers, sitting among the conferees and asking, "what do you think?" When a young nurse wonders how "the French expect to come back if they have no leaders" (22), Brewsie says that leaders don't lead, or they lead where nobody wants to go, and that the French don't want to go anywhere, they just want homes and fuel, and leaders only manage to get enough of that for themselves (22). Probably because he expects a leader to command people what to think and do, Willie says, "you're no leader, Brewsie, you just talk." Donald Paul asks, "And what do leaders do"; Jo says, "They talk too, but they talk differently" (24).

They talk like Angel Harper, who dictates instead of converses, who is supposed to have been from Mrs. Reynolds's town, and who is discussed in terms of his habits of speech. One woman "did not find him interesting," because "all she noticed about him was that he could not know what to say"; he "just rubbed his fingers and said he could not say what he had to say" (*Mrs. Reynolds*, 46). Elsewhere in *Mrs. Reynolds*, Stein writes:

> Once when [Angel Harper] was twelve he ate twenty macaroons and an apple. He liked it although he never said it. He said that he preferred macaroons to fruit, he said he preferred coffee to potatoes, that is he never said this but he thought that if he said anything about coffee or macaroons or fruit or potatoes he would say that. Just then when he was twelve he knew that what he thought he said and what he said was not what he said. (100)

Angel Harper thinks in set pieces and cannot find the appropriate way to insert his remarks into casual conversation. His awkward silences contrast with the present situation, in which he "talked and talked so everybody had to listen." Angel Harper cannot "participate in the gentle rhythm of being in relation" (Berry, 126). His desire for dictatorship may arise from his inability to speak comfortably in a conversation among equals at school. Angel Harper has created a national power structure that enables him to harp and requires everyone else to listen. Because he is unable to chat, his words have to have consequences.[29]

Throughout *Mrs. Reynolds*, Angel Harper is criticized not only for his style of speech but also for his murderousness and his lack of individuality: "how many people were suffering in summer and suffering in winter because he was fifty. . . . It is difficult to count when so many means more than everybody" (197); "how bitter it was that so many should be dead dead dead, dead because of Angel Harper of the fifty years of Angel Harper, dead dead dead, because of the fifty years of Angel Harper" (193). Over and over, Mrs. Reynolds wishes for Angel Harper's death: "it was really Angel Harper being forty-seven that made her cry and she could only try and hope that he would never be forty-eight" (139; see also 150, 188). When Mrs. Reynolds says, "I know that he will die," Mr. Reynolds says, "that will be a good riddance to bad rubbish" (98). Perhaps Harper can murder because he's not quite alive himself; using her own idiom, Stein sneers that "it is doubtful if he ever was a boy" (86). In other works, Stein questions the purpose of boys who become men: "But you know I know that if a boy is to grow up to be a man what is the use" (*Geographical History*, 127–28). In this way, she asks why the creative individualism and comfortable entity of children so often grow into adult conformity and identity.[30]

A further assertion of Angel Harper's lack of individuality and imagination resides in Stein's claim that he believes what "they say," a voice of false and brutal certainty: "So his life began and he never prayed although he believed in what they said. He always did even when everybody thought he did not. He believed in it a lot, so much so that it would have been much better not so" (*Mrs. Reynolds*, 86). Here, Angel Harper doesn't pray, which may refer to a lack of individual spirituality or creativity—or egosim—but he does put credence in what "they say." The passage may be read as a specific critique of Hitler's Jewish self-hate if we read it as implying that he omits Jewish rituals because he believes what an anti-Semitic "they say." Even if Stein has no idea of Hitler's origins, she depicts Harper as a leader who follows. Having no eye of his own, Angel Harper "never saw when he spoke" (85), and thus he cannot say what he sees.

In *Mrs. Reynolds*, "they" tends to refer to the enemy in the abstract, or to an abstract group that Stein sees as a negative force. Before Mrs. Reynolds dreams of the starving lamb, she has the following conversation with Mr. Reynolds:

And then said Mrs. Reynolds a lamb has died of hunger. What said Mr. Reynolds did I not tell you said Mrs. Reynolds the lamb of the Davilles' has died of hunger. Why said Mr. Reynolds did they not give it something to eat, because said Mrs. Reynolds they had nothing to feed it, and said Mrs. Reynolds they said, and Mrs. Reynolds felt a little queer as she said they say and Mr. Reynolds felt a little queer when she said they say, and they did not go on saying what she was going to say, they went in to dinner and that night just a little earlier than they usually did they went to bed and she did not go before he was ready, they went up to bed together. (184)

Mr. and Mrs. Reynolds may trail off because they do not want to say what "they say," and they cast doubt on the information already conveyed. Certainly they would rather not discuss the possibility of starvation, even the starvation of a lamb (if "the lamb" is even a farm animal at all). They may also be uncomfortably reluctant to believe their neighbors completely (since a lamb could also be killed to protect people from starvation). But they are also suspicious of the idea and the verbal construction of "they say." They do not want to attribute authority to a vaguely defined group, and when they say, "they say," they immediately cast doubt on the information conveyed.

The kind of conversation that Stein prescribes in *Brewsie and Willie* is not much different from the phatic communion I discuss in chapter 3. Pauline says: "wouldn't it just be beautiful if everybody stopped working, and just went out walking, and ate a sundae or an ice-cream soda and went on walking, and then just came home, and had doughnuts and a coke, and then they came in and sing a little and go to bed" (*Brewsie*, 73).[31] Pauline's idea sounds sickly sticky sweet (doughnuts *and* a Coke), but it is followed by Ed's more learned-sounding analysis of what would happen if people stopped going to work: big business would collapse and small businesses could start up. He says, "That sister aint so phony as she sounds, listen" (73). Pauline wants people to walk, eat, and talk—three of Stein's favorite pastimes—which combination may itself be the answer to economic problems. All that loose talk might lead to good answers, and a satisfactory long-term interim solution may be the conversational process itself. Interim solutions are the most satisfying ones anyway, in Stein's universe, and I think in ours. Consider the alternative.

Stein "ain't so phony as she sounds"

It sounds too simple, and too impossible, so we perhaps shake our heads at Stein's naiveté. Louis Bromfield, however, points to her "peculiar variety of naiveté which is the gift of the gods, . . . an innocence which is quite beyond the knowledge and experience of those who are known as sophisticated" (63). He imagines that Stein "was born . . . at a stage of development already beyond sophistication, endowed with that great simplicity which is interested in the value of everything and the price of nothing" (64). If Bromfield cannot make us take Stein seriously, perhaps the congruence between her ideas and those of other less playful thinkers will. For example, Stein's ideas on language and industrialism are surprisingly congruent with those of the highly influential social theorist Herbert Marcuse. In *One-Dimensional Man* (first published in 1964, but growing out of work done in the thirties), Marcuse's analysis of "advanced industrial society" echoes Stein's less systematic discussion of the social costs of industrialism. Voicing a problem and a dream, Stein's G.I. Joe complains that "we got to get on top of industrialism and not have it on top of us" (*Brewsie*, 70). Marcuse also sees a problem with "the technological processes of mechanization and standardization," and he dreams of a future in which these same processes "might release individual energy into a yet uncharted realm of freedom beyond necessity" (Marcuse, 2). Stein and Marcuse describe multiple facets of the problem: limited preprocessed and preapproved choices instead of free-ranging individual and interior thought, no free time to think, and the burden of the production and consumption of indoctrinated "false needs" (4).

Stein and Marcuse are concerned with our acceptance of very limited free choice. Stein's Brewsie worries about the "job men" who "got to articulate yes or no to their bosses, and yes or no to their unions," and yes or no to Gallup polls (*Brewsie*, 103). Marcuse expresses concern that our "advanced industrial civilization" has "reduce[d] the opposition to the discussion and promotion of alternative policies *within* the status quo" (2).[32] He expands on this idea: "Free choice among a wide variety of goods and services does not signify freedom if these goods and services sustain social controls over a life of toil and fear" (7–8). Marcuse also draws parallels between the bosses and the unions: this "integrating trend" of "the laboring class with capitalist society" "enforces a weakening of the negative position of the working class" (31n, 29, 31). In other words, a system that bridges and erases difference disallows opposition.

Stein and Marcuse both understand free time as necessary for open, original thought. Willie, insulting Brock and speaking more truth than he intends, says, "they give you work to shut you up" (Stein, *Brewsie*, 26). Willie again counterpoises talk with work when he says, "talk is good I like talk I like to listen to you Brewsie, but when we get home and dont wear this brown any more we got to have a job, job, job" (54). Brewsie responds, "that's what I want to say, industrialism which produces more than anybody can buy and makes employees out of free men makes 'em stop thinking, stop feeling, makes 'em all feel alike" (55). Marcuse, putting similar content in a contrasting style, writes that "the apparatus imposes its economic and political requirements for defense and expansion on labor time and free time, on the material and intellectual culture" (3). More directly linking free time and bold ideas, Marcuse writes: "Complete automation in the realm of necessity would open the dimension of free time as the one in which man's private *and* societal existence would constitute itself. This would be the historical transcendence toward a new civilization" (37). But industrial jobs keep us from thinking of this possible transcendence.[33]

One important step toward this great "new civilization" is admitting we haven't yet reached it. Both authors challenge the idea that consumerism is purely a liberty. What Marcuse calls "false needs," Stein calls "gadgets." Jo asks, "why we going to go home to jobs just to use up just what we have of iron ore making gadgets to be sold on the installment plan to people worried to death because they have to pay something every month and they'd be lots happier without it" (*Brewsie*, 33). Marcuse also sees constraint in the supposed opportunities of work and consumption: "unfreedom—in the sense of man's subjection to his productive apparatus—is perpetuated and intensified in the form of many liberties and comforts" (32).

These are a few of the reasons Stein and Marcuse believe that economic systems can enable or deny freedom as much as political systems can. It is clear that Stein blamed industrialism for a decline in individualism, and her characterization of the Germans as obedient followers is a fairly transparent reference to Nazism. Marcuse writes that "contemporary industrial society tends to be totalitarian. For 'totalitarian' is not only a terroristic political coordination of society, but also a non-terroristic economic-technical coordination which operates through the manipulation of needs by vested interests" (3). In these several ways, then, Marcuse's understanding of the social costs of advanced industrialism parallels Stein's.

But Stein and Marcuse do not agree only about the sociological effects of industrialism. They also agree that the solution to this problem is linguistic. Marcuse's delineation of the effects of industrialism on society includes a discussion of the way language has been affected, and he mentions ways of counteracting this linguistic disease:

> [The] *functionalization of language helps to repel non-conformist elements from the structure and movement of speech.* Vocabulary and syntax are equally affected. Society expresses its requirements directly in the linguistic material but not without opposition; *the popular language strikes with spiteful and defiant humor at the official and semi-official discourse.* Slang and colloquial speech have rarely been so creative.

It is as if the common man (or his anonymous spokesman) would in his speech assert his humanity against the powers that be, as if the rejection and revolt, subdued in the political sphere, would burst out in the vocabulary that calls things by their names: "head shrinker" and "egghead," "boob tube," "think tank," "beat it" and "dig it," and "gone, man, gone."

However, the defense laboratories and the executive offices, the governments and the machines, the time-keepers and managers, the efficiency experts and the political beauty parlors (which provide leaders with the appropriate make-up) speak a different language and, for the time being, they seem to have the last word. It is the word that orders and organizes, that induces people to do, to buy, and to accept. It is transmitted in a style which is a veritable linguistic creation; *a syntax in which the structure of the sentence is abridged and condensed in such a way that no tension, no "space" is left between the parts of the sen-*tence. This linguistic form militates against a development of meaning. (86; my italics)

If understood as primarily a form of communication, language becomes merely functional, "the concept tends to be absorbed by the word," and further "development of meaning" is prevented (87). Marcuse valorizes the everyday, informal "colloquial speech" of the 1960s as a genre in which people develop and choose words that express what they really mean. And Marcuse has a second, less directly stated, proposal: his condemnation of a lack of space between the parts of a sentence suggests that such space would counteract officialese. Marcuse wants us to use words in ways that allow for a "development of their meaning"—*and thus of our meaning*. He deplores the fact that when one hears a word such as "communist," one "is expected to react in a fixated, specific manner" (91). But when he says that "the functionalization of language expresses an abridgement of meaning which has a political connotation," he means only to change the way we use words that "denote things or occurrences beyond [the] noncontroversial context" of "the objects and implements of daily life, visible nature, vital needs and wants" (87). Marcuse means us to rethink words such as "democracy" and "freedom," "equality" and "peace," but Stein goes even further. Her comment about Hitler's deserving a peace prize makes us rethink "peace," but in *Tender Buttons* she not only makes us resee and rehear (over and over) her favorite concept words, such as "exchange," "change," and "arrange," but she also makes us renegotiate our understandings of words that refer to the objects, food, and rooms of daily living.

In *Tender Buttons*, Stein grants individual words the freedom to mean somewhat independently of the words that surround them in the sentence and paragraph. Stein's placement of words allows them multiple valences, and readers are encouraged (or even forced) to continue calling up connotations of words without ever exactly feeling satisfied enough to stop and declare denotational victory.[34] The close readings in previous chapters demonstrate that the multiple meanings of words enable them to react variously with different words around them, creating many kinds of private relationships. In this way, Stein leaves "space" between her words in which an organic, nonfunctional meaning can grow. Put another way, Stein allows her words self-determination and the freedom to form unique relationships with one another instead of locking them in a kind of totalitarian sentence structure. This careful placement of words in sentences, her refusal to become a totalitarian author who decrees all semantic relationships, corresponds with her desire for humans to escape from formal and informal totalitarian political structures. Developing our own networks of relationships and responsibilities through conversation is, theoretically, an attractive alternative to both tight totalitarianism and, on the other side of the political spectrum, anarchic isolationism in which we deny any interpersonal social or political connections.[35] The failure of syntax is both a symbol of freedom and a means to it.

Readers may become frustrated with what does not seem like an answer, and even frustrated with the way these writers define the problem of modern society: what's wrong, anyway, with technology, the easy satisfaction of real needs, and even the creation and satiation of "false needs"? Of Marcuse's text, a student typically complains: "Besides, he doesn't offer a real solution. Are we just supposed to feel bad about all this?" To accept Marcuse's and Stein's ideas as solutions, we have to get beyond what Marcuse calls "operationalism." Marcuse cites P. W. Bridgeman on the "wide implications of this mode of thought": Bridgeman points out that "we . . . no longer permit ourselves to use as tools in our thinking concepts of which we cannot give an adequate account in terms of operations" (13)[36] Our operationalist tendencies manifest themselves in our dissatisfaction with Stein's and Marcuse's answers. Talking and listening *are* actions or operations (they are things we can at least try to do), but since words and actions are understood as opposites in our society, the suggestion seems empty and necessarily ineffective. "What can we *do?*" is already a question with specific and limiting criteria for the answer it deems acceptable. These criteria do not accept "converse, talk, say playfully and differently" as an answer. As the action-oriented like to complain, "Talk is cheap."

Stein and Marcuse expect people to start listening to themselves, start listening to the clichés of other speakers, and, as a result, speak differently. Clichés are perpetuated by individuals who easily accept political (and other types of) slogans. This neglectful nonthinking in everyday linguistic experience parallels Roland Barthes's idea of "readerly" or "*lisible*" texts, the kind "that merely obey a logic of passive consumption" (Rabaté, 71). Barthes knows an alternative, and he defines another kind of text, the "writerly" or "*scriptible*":

> Why is the writerly our value? Because the goal of literary work (of literature as work) is to make the reader no longer a consumer, but a producer of the text. Our literature is characterized by the pitiless divorce which the literary institution maintains between the producer of the text and its user, between its owner and its customer, between its author and its reader. This reader is thereby plunged into a kind of idleness—he is intransitive; he is, in short, *serious:* instead of functioning himself, instead of gaining access to the magic of the signifier, to the pleasure of writing, he is left with no more than the poor freedom either to accept or reject the text: reading is nothing more than a *referendum.* (Barthes, 4)[37]

So one can only say yes or no to it. But writerly texts "stimulate the reader's active participation" (Rabaté, 71). Stein and Marcuse expect readers and listeners to activate their own attention, concentrating on the readerly texts (written and spoken) that are found everywhere around us in our daily lives. If we begin to approach readerly texts as if they were writerly, then we will notice contradictions and truths, and we will create writerly texts of our own (both in our writing and speaking). Reading these new writerly texts with our new writerly habits could initiate a cycle of inventiveness that might let us see beyond today's horizons of possibility.[38]

Barthes's choice of metaphor also builds on the relationship among language, politics, and economics that I've been exploring in Stein and Marcuse. Barthes uses "producers," "consumers," "owners," and "customers" as metaphors. A writerly text is produced by readers and writers who exist within a different economy from the one to which we are accustomed. The writerly reader does more than idly read, passively buying (or not) that which the author produces. Finally and relatedly, Barthes uses a loose political metaphor to describe a reader's relationship to a text. A reader of a writerly text does more than say yes or no to it, which would be "a poor freedom." Barthes links autocratic writing and passive reading, a capitalist economic system, and a lack of freedom. In a parallel way, Stein and Marcuse link active participation in the creation of texts and spoken conversations, an anti-industrialized economy, and greater individual and political freedom.

Real Ideas

When asked to teach a session of the History of Ideas, a course already in progress at the University of Chicago, Stein asked the regular instructors, Robert Hutchins and Mortimer Adler, "What are the ideas that are important?" Stein noticed that "none of the books read at any time by them was originally written in English" and that these men seemed to think that "there are no ideas which are not sociological or government ideas." Dismayed, she said, "Government is the least interesting thing in human life," and "real ideas are not the relation of human beings as groups but a human being to himself inside him" (Stein, *Everybody's*, 206). Stein was interested in "real ideas," not social systems concocted out of fear, hatred, or other perceived necessity. "Real ideas" involve thoughtful people internally divided enough to question persistently—and both seriously and playfully—the expression of ideas they encounter within and without. I have characterized Stein's valuation of individualism as a political position, but her own focus on individuals suggests that it is an antipolitical position.

The political climate in 1946 may have encouraged Stein to be more explicit about her political—or antipolitical—views. In that year, Albert Camus wrote in the Resistance newspaper *Combat*: "Yes, what we must fight is fear and silence, and with them the spiritual isolation they involve. What we must defend is dialogue and the universal communication of men" (138). And George Orwell, also in 1946, describes the era as a time when "it is broadly true that political writing is bad writing." He goes on to say that if the political writing is any good, then "it will generally be found that the writer is some kind of rebel, expressing private opinions and not a 'party line.'" Developing an image of a human automaton, Orwell goes on:

> Orthodoxy, of whatever color, seems to demand a lifeless, imitative style.
> . . . When one watches some tired hack on the platform *mechanically re-*
> *peating the familiar phrases,* . . . one often has a curious feeling that one
> is not watching a live human being but some kind of dummy: a feeling
> which suddenly becomes stronger at moments when the light catches
> the speaker's spectacles and turns them into blank discs which seem to
> have no eyes behind them. And this is not altogether fanciful. A speaker

who uses that kind of phraseology has gone some distance toward turning himself into a machine. The appropriate noises are coming out of
his larynx, but *his brain is not involved as it would be if he were choosing
his words for himself. . . . And this reduced state of consciousness, if not
indispensable, is at any rate favorable to political conformity.* ("Politics
and the English Language," 362–63; my italics)

Stein's recommendation that we say what we see may have been a necessary
and important reminder in 1946 (as indeed it usually is).

Orwell continues to describe the powerful gravity of conventionality in
"The Prevention of Literature" (also published in 1946): "It is the peculiar-
ity of our age that the rebels against the existing order, at any rate the most
numerous and characteristic of them, are also rebelling against the idea
of individual integrity. 'Daring to stand alone' is ideologically criminal as
well as practically dangerous" (368). Further: "The enemies of intellectual
liberty always try to present their case as a plea for discipline versus individualism" (369). Orwell describes the political groups at both ends of the
political spectrum as demanding loyal adherence in order to be stronger in
opposing one another.[39] If efficiency requires conformity, and revolutionar-
ies want quick, efficient change, then they require conformity even when
it means that they become much more like the political organizations they
are rebelling against. In Orwell's view: "Freedom of the intellect means the
freedom to report what one has seen, heard, and felt, and not to be obliged
to fabricate imaginary facts and feelings" (370). Mr. Reynolds says, "he was
sure that if she felt that way that it was what she ought to say" (Stein, *Mrs.
Reynolds*, 206). "Say what you see," commands Stein. But, in this age of
yes-and-no job men, she wonders, "Oh say can you see" (*Geographical History*, 163).[40] For the United States to survive—as she values it—its anthem
must be a true conversation.

CONCLUSIONS:

Feminine Endings

"The Woman Who Changed the Mind of a Nation"

AFTER THE WAR ended in Europe, in October 1945, Stein started "another opera" with Virgil Thomson; she wrote Van Vechten: "it is to be around Susan B. Anthony and Daniel Webster, that is if it comes off, I think Susan B. Anthony is a nice character for an opera . . . and the title is to be The Mother of us all" (Burns, 2:795). (After Stein's complaint about "too much fathering going on" in the thirties, "the mother of us all" may have seemed like a nice antidote, or at least an alternative.) A nurse in *Brewsie and Willie* reads a book about Anthony, and by mid-November 1945, Stein herself had read Rheta Childe Dorr's biography, *Susan B. Anthony, the Woman Who Changed the Mind of a Nation* (Burns, 2:798n). The subtitle summarizes my own understanding of Stein's potential: if things had somehow been different—if more people had read her innovative work, instead of stopping at the autobiographies and the hearsay—Stein could have changed people's minds such that they could really see, and could even say what they saw. She might have changed the operating systems of the American mind.

Several critics have noted the biographical parallels that Stein drew between Anthony and herself.[1] Of Anthony's lecture tours, Dorr writes: "Although she shocked every community she had a genius for making people think" (249). One newspaper article classed Anthony as "a revolutionist aiming at nothing less than the breaking up of the very foundations of society" (qtd. in Dorr, 246). But the most striking parallel for Stein may have been that Anthony fails to meet her goals and is ridiculed by many prominent people, but stays staunchly herself and gets a hero's welcome when she visits Europe and at her later appearances in the United States. Bridgman says that in *Brewsie and Willie*, Anthony "was offered as a model of self-liberation, who proved that if an individual made sufficient 'noise' he would be heard," but that in the opera, Susan B. recognizes her limited success in convincing others of the power of the individual (342, citing *Brewsie and Willie*, 89). Critics tend to concur that the opera expresses Stein's thoughts on her successes and failures at the end of her career (Brinnin, 399; Bridgman, 341–44). Stein—who began to feel some painful symptoms of her stomach cancer before she had finished the libretto (Bridgman, 341; Brinnin, 341)—may feel she has failed on the grand scale. At the same time, however, she asserts the primacy of individuality, and her own success in becoming and remaining an individual.

It is also important, as Robert K. Martin argues, to remember to read the opera as more than a simple autobiographical piece, for "to read the opera as a work about Stein herself, in which Anthony is simply 'equivalent to Gertrude Stein,' is to rob the text of its rich historical allusiveness and to diminish Stein's attempt at a commentary on American history" (210).[2] For example, Stein's history of America reiterates one sterling fact about the United States: we are a nation built on words—the Declaration of Independence, the Constitution, the law, and the verbal negotiations among individual interpretations of all these words. Anthony consistently challenged the standard readings of laws and constitutional amendments, going so far as to register to vote in 1871 based on a possible reading of the first article of the Fourteenth Amendment, which says all persons born or naturalized in the United States are citizens. The second article says it's a crime to deny *males* over age twenty-one the right to vote but, after her arrest, Anthony went on tour giving a lecture titled, "Is It a Crime for a Citizen of the United States to Vote?" (Dorr, 178, 254–55). Anthony did some writerly reading of her own, and words that are the foundation of the United States often beg for creative reading.

In Stein's opera, Martin points out, Stein highlights the difference between dead words and living words, contrasting "cant phrases repeated without meaning" against "their possible realization in the hands of a real democrat." Martin adds that Stein is calling "for a radical democracy that is true to its past, and that can be awakened by an undermining of the surfaces of an abused language" (214). All this goes to show that Stein is continuing her argument for self-determination, trying to persuade us to the same (but, of course, individualized) behaviors: to see and think and speak for ourselves, from our own perspectives, which involves making sure our language helps instead of hinders in these endeavors.

But *The Mother of Us All* also takes a turn toward disappointment or even resignation. The opera recalls a less sterling fact about the nation:

politicians are expedient, and committed political allies often prove un-reliable. The opera is still playful, still a challenge, still sometimes funny, and consistently, unpredictably Steinian. But what seems to be new in *The Mother of Us All* is the unoriginal distinction Stein draws between the gen-ders. She had never been blind to gender, but now she has come around to clichés. As a young woman, Stein saw herself as male—a husband, a genius. Martin notes a gradual shift throughout the thirties, as Stein's "early male identification gives way" and "she finds her way out of the trap of associating genius with masculinity and hence frees herself from adopting a 'mannish' role" (217; and see Winston, 118).[3] She has asserted that the great literary work of the twentieth century must be done by a woman—though she is so clearly referring to herself that the gender commentary goes largely un-noticed. In *Everybody's Autobiography*, Stein's gender assumptions show, as when she says of Stalin, Mussolini, Roosevelt, Blum, Franco, and Hitler: "There is too much fathering going on just now and there is no doubt about it fathers are depressing. . . . England is the only country now that has not got one and so they are more cheerful there than anywhere. It is a long time now that they have not had any fathering and so their cheerfulness is increasing" (133).

While *The Mother of Us All* continues Stein's "questioning of the entire drive to power over others" (Martin, 217), there's a shift to straightforward, clichéd complaints about men and to valorization of women: the opera's male characters are privileged, selfish, and self-satisfied, and the female characters tend to be insightful, or at least maturing, truly living beings. Simply reading Dorr's biography of Anthony might leave one with this strong impression, as at key moments in the struggle for universal suffrage, the male players are unreliable or even turncoats.[4] Stein's sudden removal from the airy world of writers and painters into one of war and poverty might also have induced her to believe that men—the warmongers of these mas-sive wars—were less than brilliant, and were certainly not enough focused on the individual. And seeing how U.S. soldiers shared what she saw as some of the worst failings of the Germans may have suggested a significant masculine shortcoming.

Susan B. says, "Ladies there is no neutral position for us to assume," and Stein's libretto demonstrates her quick turn toward the nonneutral position (*Mother*, 800). A friendly chat isn't going to work with the foes who confront them. However neutral Stein may have been earlier in her life on the question of the sexes, here males are directly criticized with what start to look like second-wave feminist clichés. Susan B. says to Anne (a character based on Anthony's partner of eighteen years but who plays only a small role in Dorr's biography): "Men . . . are so conservative, so selfish, so boresome and . . . they are so ugly, . . . they are gullible, anybody can convince them" (789). She is disappointed in them for following her (although history shows that they did not when it mattered), but "they are men, and men, well of course they know that they cannot either see or hear unless I tell them so, poor things . . . I do not pity them. Poor things" (790). They cannot see or hear, they cannot notice and think for themselves, in her estimation, but their power probably prevents her from pitying them (though she seems a bit divided on this point, pitying them and not pitying them simultaneously). Another problem with men is that they cannot "be mixed," which I take to mean they cannot hold varying opinions at the same time: "How can anything be really mixed when men are conservative, dull, monotonous, deceived, stupid, unchanging and bullies, how said Susan B. how when men are men can they be mixed" (791).[5] Mixedness makes the French complicated and thoughtful in Stein's play *In Savoy*, and Stein advocates it to Americans in *Brewsie and Willie*. Mixedness also describes the way Americans were divided within themselves and their families during the American Revolutionary and Civil wars, when people fought for their beliefs and (sometimes also) loved the very people they were fighting.[6] With those kinds of complications and individual considerations, as well as the internal and personal search for beliefs, thoughtless crowd behavior is less likely. While championing mixedness, Stein offers a very unmixed summary of male characteristics.

Expressing the need to shut up loud pretentious voices is part of the serious work of Stein's opera (as opposed to most other operas). These voices prevent real conversation. Sometimes Stein includes parts of Daniel Webster's speeches (Winston, 122), and in this context they sound silly, as in: "When this debate sir was to be resumed on Thursday it so happened that it would have been convenient for me to be elsewhere" (*Mother*, 786); and in: "The harvest of neutrality had been great, but we had gathered it all" (787). He makes these grand rhetorical flourishes, regardless of what his interlocuter has said (not that Stein lets the famously straightforward Anthony, as Susan B., say anything that Webster would be able to make much sense of). Later, this famous orator is told he "needs an artichoke" to choke his artfulness (784). Thaddeus S.[tevens] harps on his pet causes: "I believe in public school education, I do not believe in free masons I believe in public school education, I do not believe that every one can do whatever he likes because (a pause) I have not always done what I liked" (791). John Adams thinks he is in love but, always aware of his class and position, he has to keep saying things like "if I had not been an Adams I would have kneeled at your feet" (792). Their love of their own voices and of their stubbornly held opinions, and their own limited (but grandiose) sense of self, keeps them from being able truly to interact.

The crowning example of these great men's self-love is the song that Andrew G., Thaddeus S. and Daniel Webster sing: "We are the chorus of the V.I.P. / Very important persons to every one who can hear and see, we are the chorus of the V.I.P." And: "We are the V.I.P. the very important persons, we have special rights, they ask us first and they wait for us last and wherever we are well there we are everybody knows we are there, we are the V.I.P. Very important persons for everybody to see" (*Mother*, 798, 799). These men get more than their share of attention, and they expect it. Adams says, "If you were silent I would speak" (796); he's used to people respectfully listening to him. One reason they get attention, as Susan B. explains, is that the rich get to talk and not listen; the poor have to listen (799). Stein's stage directions emphasize the problem with conversation: right after "Andrew J. and Thaddeus S. begin to quarrel violently," "Everybody [is] suddenly stricken dumb" (797). A slow chorus begins and ends: "Naughty men, they quarrel so" and "Naughty men naughty men, they are always quarreling" (793). There's no room for discussion and compromise, or even understanding, when the talkers never listen.

Stein also emphasizes that these men who get to do the talking share cookie-cutter thoughts and feelings. They are nothing like George Washington, who, she writes elsewhere, "was fairly famous because he wrote what he saw and he saw what he said" (*Four*, 168). One of the men in *The Mother of Us All* says about another: "they all listen to him, by him I mean me" (*Mother*, 798). These words could suggest a feeling of alienation from the self, but they also might suggest that the speaker agrees with whatever someone else says. Ulysses S. Grant likes only silence, but at least "he was not always quarreling" (804–5, 793). The silenced listeners, however, thoughtlessly agree with the speakers. Christ the Citizen says, "I always repeat everything I hear," and Jo the Loiterer responds (and this is funny), "You sure do" (802). These men talk, or don't, but none of them sees and then talks and listens at the same time. Men compromise with their own sensations, lives, experience: "Men want to be half slave half free. Women want to be all slave or all free, therefore men govern and women know" (803).

And in Stein's lexicon, to know is one of the best things a person can do. Knowledge comes from one's true self. Stein depicts Susan B. as attempting to get people to be themselves, to promote individualism, as well as individual rights—*and* as realizing that she has failed, that the only good that came from her work was incidental, beside the point, or completely personal. (The real Anthony was less self-flagellating, ending her final speech: "Failure is impossible" [qtd. in Dorr, 343]). In emphasizing gender distinctions, Stein seems to relinquish her ideas about individuality, but it is frustration on this very point that seems to lead her to this juncture. Her play's Susan B., too, keeps trying to get the other characters to take a more radical position on individuality. When Jo the Loiterer wants to come inside with a crowd of people, Susan B. says, "A crowd is never allowed but each one of you can come in" (*Mother*, 800). When everyone is on the stage, they say, "Now that we are all here there is nobody down there to hear." "They" seem to think that there are too many heads, too many bosses and talkers, but Susan B. seems to feel fine about talking to people who *aren't* below, who aren't waiting to listen, who are equals, who talk back (802).

For her, people *are* individuals, whether they know it or not. Susan B. reminds them that "even if they love them so, they are alone to live and die, they are alone to sink and swim they are alone to have what they own, to have no ideas but that they are here, to struggle and thirst to do everything first" (802).[7] No matter how loving and how loved, we are alone. Paradoxically however, Susan B. needs other people to validate her endeavors. She needs supporters to pass the laws that would enable women to be self-sufficient, but she is disappointed that people "will not do what they could do and I I will be left alone to die but they will not have done what I need to have done to make it right that I lived my life and fight" (807). Susan B. realizes that "they won't vote my laws, there is always a clause, there is always a pause, they won't vote my laws" (808). Knowing that women would never get the vote through popular referendum, Anthony worked on trying to get state and federal constitutional amendments passed. She came to rely on women activists and words, not male voters.[8]

All this is to say that by the end of her life, Stein was starting to believe that women might have a better chance than men at resisting the progressive death of language, and perhaps even that the female place outside the homogenizing public sphere allowed more, rather than less, of certain freedoms. Stein, after all, did gain freedom of action and thought by having her oldest brother, Michael, handle the money and Alice B. Toklas transact the pragmatic daily duties. It may have been easy for Stein to be patronizing about the way other people earned their livings. She has time to be creative and contemplative, and she can order her life as she pleases. But think of many of the young men Stein would have met: young journalists struggling to be writers, soldiers uncertain of their futures or their future livelihoods, even artists trying to figure out how to make a living at art.

Think of the sensitive young man you took Shakespeare with in college, who went into business: hotel management, a car rental agency, insurance, stocks, or journalism. More likely than not, his language has died, as would the language (and the creativity) of many of the young men Stein met. They speak (or write) in dead phrases: "the bottom line," "maximizing profit," "this isn't about you or me," and "the product sells itself." His words are deader even than those of Daniel Webster, who could revive them into being inspirational and meaningful if he meant to. But Webster is not listening to himself: he even inappropriately refers to Susan B. as a "gentleman," because that's the word he always uses to refer to his adversary in a debate (*Mother*, 788). As Martin says, and I concur: "Language must retain its full playful sense of itself so that it can never made over into [the] rhetoric" of "empty signs," and "language for Adams is power, and it is this kind of linguistic power that Stein's playfulness sets out to contest" (218). In short, "men have failed to fulfil the revolutionary potential of American history" (221). And if the founding fathers have ultimately failed, then it's time to look to the mothers. Stein didn't seem to recognize that mothers were already entering the workforce, too, and becoming conditioned in the same deadening ways.

Sublime Amalgamations

For Stein, mothers offer more, since Stein seems to understand the tendency toward less as masculine. The male characters in *The Mother of Us All* talk like stuck recordings, but even earlier Stein alludes to masculine deficiency. In *The Making of Americans*, she describes the communication between a father and daughter who take long walks together. After their conversation, always the same words on the same path, her father "would be looking at her with that sharp completed look that, always so full of his own understanding, could not leave it open any way to her to reach inside to him to let in any other kind of a meaning" (26). In *Ida*, Andrew also takes walks and talks, and he has a similar limitation: "He listened while he was listening but he did not hear unless he asked to have told what they were telling" (122). *Ida* offers strong evidence of Stein's belief that women are less daunted by "more," in this case the merging of identities. Andrew and Ida's merging in *Ida* makes "Ida more Ida" but "Andrew less Andrew" (90). And Susan B. can hold enough diverse ideas to say, "You are entirely right . . . only I disagree with you" (*Mother*, 789).

Earlier, I speculated that Stein's reading of William James may have convinced her that a change in language could effect change in thought.

I also argued that Stein was interested not only in written words but also in the sounds they produce and the spoken language they can approximately transcribe. I see parallels among those subtle meanings, those often unnoticed sounds, and the implicit relationships formed in the interval between persons in conversation. The synergy of different voices produces a collective subjectivity separate from each speaker's and separate from the meanings of the words themselves.[9] But people's voices cannot converse or converge toward new knowings if they all say the same thing, if they don't have anything to say, or if they are too fearful to speak their ideas. If nothing else, Stein's writing is weird enough to give us something to talk about, and since we cannot contain it with our own words, the conversation continues. Stein's writing, so much of which is inspired by spoken comments, mediates and validates further conversations.

If we resist resisting it, reading Stein's writing can initiate a sublime experience. That which causes the sublime cannot be finally and categorically contained through language. Readers are never assured that they have done the organizing and containing "correctly," which leads us to wonder uncomfortably about whether the unknown phenomena have been properly controlled or not. What has been called the feminine sublime exerts the same overwhelming force on a perceiver, but if the perceiver is "feminine enough," flexible enough about her idea of herself, then the usual reaction, sublime terror, is redirected into a melting together of what is usually (mis)perceived as self and other. The masculine tends to fear the multiple and the other, or, as Stein says in *The Mother of Us All*, men "fear women, fear each other, . . . fear their neighbor . . . fear other countries and then hearten themselves in their fear by crowding together and following each other . . . like animals who stampede" (811). But the feminine subject is said to experience an orgasmic merging, a return to being more, rather than the sublime anxiety or even terror that leads to the shutting down of possibilities.[10] Stein's writing advocates, and perhaps even coaxes and coaches us toward, this feminine subjectivity.

The sublime experience is coded male because of its five male Romantic writers, its Mont Blancs and Xanadus. One of the projects of the French feminists "is to reinvent the sublime as a feminine mode" (Yaeger, 192). Luce Irigaray writes that "we have so many voices to invent in order to express all of us everywhere, even in our gaps, that all the time there is will not be enough. We can never complete the circuit, explore our periphery: we have so many dimensions" (213). But this "horizontal sublime" (Yaeger, 202) can also be seen from a different perspective, or at a different time. Rather than spreading, it can be seen as coming up from interiorities that have become hidden (whether locked up or hiding out) within the confining structures of patriarchy:

> She will not say what she herself wants; moreover, she does not know, or no longer knows, what she wants. . . . One would have to dig down very deep indeed to discover beneath the traces of this civilization, of this history, the vestiges of a more archaic civilization that might give some clue to woman's sexuality. That extremely ancient civilization would undoubtedly have a different alphabet, a different language. . . . Woman's desire would not be expected to speak the same language as man's; woman's desire has doubtless been submerged by the logic that has dominated the West since the time of the Greeks. (Irigaray, 25)

Yaeger calls one type of female sublime (of course there would be many) "the pre-oedipal sublime—[which] offers the most striking revision of the 'oedipal' sublime" (204). Rather than resisting the self's secretly desired union with the (m)other, the subject of the pre-oedipal sublime welcomes the merger:

> We have learned that the subject is "infiltrated with the world" in such a way that "otherness is carried to the very heart of selfhood," and yet have not found a language to bring home the political and aesthetic consequences of this knowledge, to put this knowledge into praxis. I will suggest that the "feminine" sublime becomes an arena for discovering this language; it engenders a zone where self-empowerment and intersubjective bliss entertain one another in an atmosphere free of paranoia. (205)[11]

And I suggest that Stein has already discovered this language. First, Stein's exploration of voice in conversation has gone far toward expressing the essence of speech: motivating but invisible boundaries, subtle codes, patterns of equivocation. In a number of ways, Stein's writing expresses many of the amalgamations possible between the knower and the known or, perhaps more accurately, the knower and the to-be-known or even the potentially unknowable (who or which are often knowers, too). Perhaps Stein has moved past a feminine sublime to an epistemological sublime.

The primacy of conversation and amalgamation for Stein is perhaps why she seems so brutal about the atomic bomb. She says in "Reflection on the Atomic Bomb" that its ability to finalize all things makes it completely uninteresting to her. If the bomb destroys all things, then there is nothing left to be interested by; conversation ends. Her apolitical, even apathetic, stance becomes clearer when she posits that "really nobody else [besides "the people inventing the bomb or the people shooting it off"] can do anything about it so you have to just live along like always," but there is something commendably stubborn in her statement that "it's the living that are interesting not the way of killing them." In other words, you're immortal until you're dead.

On the other hand, if the bomb is "not as destructive as all that" then there will still be "lots left on this earth to be interested or to be interesting." Stein may appear to have lowered her valuation of single individuals (the dead ones, in this case) and raised that of the community (the masses who happen to survive). But she may also be expressing the recognition of how much there is in a single human being's experience. If the universe of one person's experience is infinite, it remains infinite even if it's shortened.

Stein willfully believes in what she feels she can effect, but this atomic bomb doesn't seem to budge when it's the subject of conversation, and so she must overlook it, ignore it, discount it, and insist that people use their "common sense" instead of listening to "so much [intractable?] information." It's such a big scary deal that she cannot turn her human nature's fear into the fertile topic of a masterpiece. The atomic bomb is a weapon she can't seem to defuse with her epistemological stance or her language games, so she wills its irrelevance. But she ends her short piece: "This is a nice story" (reminiscent of Hemingway's "Isn't it pretty to think so" at the end of *The Sun Also Rises*), which suggests she might be aware of the inadequacy of stubbornly willing herself not to believe in the bomb as a harbinger of the likely need for an even newer epistemological shift. Stein values fission rather than fusion, but the atomic bomb's fission models chaos instead of conversation.

Before she comes up against the atomic bomb, Stein uses language as a weapon against singularity and boundedness, and ingeniously rewires it, in work after work, style after style, to express multiplicity and integration. In *The Making of Americans*, Stein emphasizes the influences upon her characters from preestablished familial and national narratives, and in this way investigates the complex interaction between internal and external forces. The methods that reach toward multiplicity in *Tender Buttons* and *Geography and Plays* include developing unique interrelationships between words such that plural meanings are created in the conversation between them; writing from different I-positions in the same sentences or paragraphs; and actually (though not always obviously) writing about multiplicities—more options, more disagreement, more discussion, more growth, more associations. In *Ida,* Ida manifests herself in multiple ways, containing more than one voice or I-position and then dematerializing to the extent that she exists somewhere vaguely between the physical bodies of Ida and others. In *Brewsie and Willie,* Stein characterizes her ideal speaker as someone who can playfully and contrarily converse with oneself and others, change opinions in midsentence, and avoid adamant consistency or selfish "monologuing."

All this intersubjectivity, this sublime multiplicity, may make a reader wonder about one of my premises: that Stein advocates individuality. Perhaps it makes more sense to say that Stein valued individualities. Instead of letting her readers blindly and insincerely build coherent selves by lopping off whole parts of themselves, she induces many things that the "me" has considered "not-me" to come crowding back from the margins to petition for reacceptance (which is not quite the same as reassimilation). And she values our expressing those individualities so that they can communicate and play with one another. Her criticism of American society can be expressed as a critique of the ways people limit themselves and become alike. Stein believed society was becoming uniform; the multiple was merging into the single. The peril of corporate globalization was yet one more twenty-first-century controversy she anticipated. And Stein argues against this centripetal motion. But instead of advocating a reactionary centrifugal force in which each person spins out into space, she imagines an orderly but extremely complicated set of orbits that represent our complex but calculable mutual gravity—and levity.

NOTES

INTRODUCTION

1. By 1996, Marianne DeKoven had come to see Stein's writing as "a powerful utopian project" ("Introduction," 475).

2. Hereafter, Stein's works are cited parenthetically by short title in the text.

3. Clive Bush points out that Stein "was five times alienated from centrist American values. She was a woman, a lesbian, a Jew, an expatriate, and most important of all, an artist." He adds: "From such a vantage point she could offer a profound critique of the psychology produced by the 'normal' world of affairs" (360).

4. Clive Bush and Claudia Franken agree that it's time to risk looking for content in Stein's writing. Too much criticism has already been about whether or not to read her at all, and then whether or not readers should look for meaning.

5. In Hubly's presence, Haas said that Stein enabled the repetitive lyrics of popular contemporary music. Stein's words, as she says in *The Autobiography of Alice B. Toklas* (70), have also gotten "under [our] skin" enough to continually reappear in *Los Angeles Times* headlines: "A Rose Is a Rose, but Not Roseanne" (19 November 1994), "Will the Real Al Gore Please Sit Down: There's No There There within this Media Creature" (5 July 2002), "There's No There There" (19 November 2000), and "A Rose Is a Rose" (27 December 1992, 7 May 1987). "Rose Is a Rose Is a . . . Job?" (25 March 2000) and "For Translation Software, una rosa ist eine rose is a rose" (8 January 1995) are among Stein-inspired headlines that have appeared in the *New York Times*.

6. Putnam cites James, "Remarks," 15.

7. In Perloff, epigraph. This is Marjorie Perloff's own translation of the lines from Wittgenstein, *Culture and Value*, 24.

8. The idea, inspired by pragmatism, that "all intellectual discourse is subject to bias, partialities, and [the] values of its users" has inspired feminist thinkers and has allowed Stein into the feminist camp (Shuler and Tate, 212).

9. Linda Watts writes that "Stein embarks upon an exploration of language as itself an ideological instrument" (*Rapture*, 20). Watts quotes DeKoven's *A Different Language* (150): "If patriarchy is to be transformed at all, it must be transformed not only at its most visible levels (political, social, economic, cultural) but also at the fundamental or radical level of the structures of language which enable meaning." Watts goes on to say: "Language inscribes and serves the social order," and "Stein maintains that a writer's critiques are best targeted at language itself" (*Rapture*, 20).

10. Neil Postman and Charles Weingartner discuss the importance of "crap detecting" in their book *Teaching as a Subversive Activity*: "Those who *are* sensitive to the verbally built-in biases of their 'natural' environment seem 'subversive' to those who are not. There is probably nothing more dangerous to the prejudices of the latter than a man in the process of discovering that the language of his group is limited, misleading, or one-sided. Such a

man is dangerous because he is not easily enlisted on the side of one ideology or another, because he sees beyond the words to the processes which give an ideology its reality" (5).

11. "We" is not a single group with a tendency to say the same kinds of things based on what our identity politics might predict. Instead of political positions, Stein heard noises, sounds, turn taking, insistence, repetition, and copying; she heard what we don't usually hear ourselves, what we don't always know we're saying, what we might not intend anyone else to hear. One of the things we humans are proud of, one that makes us different from other animals, is that we have advanced language skills. "We" are human and "we" speak. If we can speak and hear, we can talk and listen, and most of us do. I don't think identity any more specific than that is relevant here. (I might add that "we" speak English—I am writing and you are reading in English—and different languages and cultures have different "rules" for conversation.) We might not agree on my "we," but we can talk about it, and—for my purposes in this book—that puts us in the same "we" group.

12. Critics have pointed to several other dialogic aspects of Stein's writing. Elizabeth Fifer concludes that "the domain of this discourse is the intimacy of the couple," which is further complicated by Stein's obfuscations in the face of a homophobic readership (131). Harriet Scott Chessman lists several kinds of dialogue in Stein's writing: between characters, between narrator and characters, between readers and words, among words themselves, between writer and words, and between words and "the objects they 'caress' but do not necessarily signify" (3). In spite of this promising list, Chessman expands only on the give-and-take relationship—the dance—into which Stein's writing invites the reader, rightly noting that readers become active in the creative process. Ellen E. Berry suggests another possible conversation when she writes that Stein's texts "wander intertextually" or speak to one another. Stein "grafts" pieces from one text to another, and she reworks themes over and over in different works, such that Berry claims every text is a "rewrite" (9). Berry also notes that A Novel of Thank You is interspersed with "snippets of realistic dialogue," which she assumes come from Stein's real experience, and which "highlight a strategy of saying and unsaying," "tantalizing us with the impulse to interpret the text autobiographically . . . and undercutting this impulse" (82). Stein's writing is also necessarily in dialogue with conventional forms of writing. Alison Rieke, in The Senses of Nonsense, claims that if writers stray too far from normal language their work will not be able to catch the attention of readers, who have to be able to recognize something familiar (9). Stein claimed her medium was the English language (Autobiography, 70, 76), and in keeping herself from straying too far from it, she enabled the conversation between the old and the new to continue.

13. Michael Hoffman, Lisa Ruddick, Steven Meyer, and Bush all discuss Stein in relation to William James, as do many earlier critics. Hoffman, helpfully making it "at least a bit clearer why Gertrude Stein wrote the way she did," points out Stein's emphasis on "verbal communication [as] a set of formalized habits to which no writer is beholden" ("Stein and James," 232–33, 231). Ruddick reminds us that Stein borrowed James's ideas of consciousness but, in leaving pragmatism behind, "used [them] in ways [James] would not have anticipated" ("William James," 63). In "Writing Psychology Over," Meyer discusses habit, but he comes to different conclusions than I do.

14. Quotations in the two previous sentences are from Donne, "The Canonization," line 32, and Jameson, Prison-House of Language.

CHAPTER 1

1. "Literally I count eight" is more difficult to interpret, and my own reading of it is too personal to warrant a place in the main text. Much later, Stein writes: "She had certain habits. . . . Living alone as she did counting was an occupation" (*Ida*, 624). When my daughter was born , I stopped doing intellectual work for a few months, and I found myself counting. I would not be aware of it, but suddenly I would discover myself at some ridiculously high number ("two hundred fifty-eight . . ."). During one confessional phone call, I warned my mother that something weird was happening to me, and she said: "Don't tell me. Let me guess. You're counting. I do too!" I think it's because our minds need work. They don't count for nothing.

2. Studs Terkel's *Working* proves her correct: a welder, a stone mason, an ad man, and others become philosophers when Terkel is listening. They reveal the truths of their own natures, as well as wax eloquent on larger truths.

3. Van Vechten cites Wright, review of *Wars*.

4. For example, although she stopped seeing her brother Leo in 1913, they inevitably stood in some relationship to each other. In 1931 Stein wrote "How she bowed to her brother," a short work that "break[s] up sentences into spoken units moving in pronounced irregular rhythms" that "lurch in uncomfortable, jerking, forward and backward movement 'like the flickers,' full of pauses and hesitations, stuttering in discomfort," and suggest the way a partly deaf person (such as Leo—and even herself later in life) might hear (Dydo, *Stein*, 564). Mimicking a difficult conversation, Stein's opaque work suggests that although she and Leo no longer interact, they still have a complex relationship, one understood differently by each of them. Her curt, almost imperceptible, and ambiguous bow to her brother is similar to the shallow bows Stein makes to her literary relations.

5. Wagner-Martin cites Aldrich, "Confessions," M-114.

6. Sources are Wilder, 187; Stein's letters to Sherwood Anderson (White, *Sherwood Anderson*, 26, 56, 95), Stein's college essays (reprinted in Miller); and *Lectures*, 241, 209. Available at Yale University's Beinecke Rare Book and Manuscript Library, the list of books in her library at her death includes more than two hundred authors from different periods on English literature. Stein owned multiple books by many authors, but her large collections of a few authors are most notable: twenty-three novels by James Fenimore Cooper, eleven novels by Charles Dickens, eight English translations of novels by Alexander Dumas, eight novels by William Dean Howells, six books by Washington Irving, eight titles by Rudyard Kipling, six novels by Frederick Marryat, all three of Samuel Richardson's novels, fifteen Shakespeare plays, ten of Robert Louis Stevenson's adventure novels, eighteen books of fiction (for adults and children) by Frank R. Stockton, five books by Trollope, seven works by Constance Fenimore Woolson, two several-volume sets of Flaubert's works, the twelve-volume *Complete Works* of George Eliot, a sixteen-volume set of *The Arabian Nights*, the *Complete Works* of Lewis Carroll, the eleven-volume *Works* by Samuel Johnson (plus his *Letters*), ten volumes of George Sand's work, the twenty-volume *Complete Works* of W. M. Thackeray, and twelve volumes of Jules Verne's *Works* in addition to twelve novels by Verne.

7. See *www.rootsweb.com~cenfiles/calsanfrancisco/1870/ed39/sanfrancisco/ward01/sanfrancisco-a23.txt*.

8. According to Katz, "First Making," the manuscript of *The Making of Americans* identifies these families as Jewish.

9. *Annales* historians have recently emphasized that everything that happens is historical, although we tend to accept only certain things—those that involve the rich, powerful, or athletic—as "historical events." Many people try to be present when "history is made," but others prefer to make their own.

10. For example, between the turn of the century and World War I, my grandfather and his brothers formed a traveling vaudeville troupe, the Seven Cairns Brothers. Among the memorabilia, we have a picture of the extended family standing by their derailed train car. Thinking the great train robbery was a real event and not a movie, and then mistaking the great train robbery for the great train *wreck*, I long thought that this picture was of the great train wreck—and I thought my family had been involved in an important national disaster. Historical fact, fiction, family and national stories, and a lack of perspective get all mixed up in a child's head—and they may never quite be sorted out.

11. *Making*, 122, 128, 129, 124. This starting over was common in education, perhaps especially with well-off parents who were trying to expand their children's horizons toward Europe. Stein's father enrolled his children in several different schools, took them to several countries with different educational systems and languages of instruction, and hired a variety of tutors. William and Henry James's father did the same thing. After attending multiple schools, William James felt that he'd had a terribly haphazard education and thus felt like something of a fraud.

12. Linking David Hersland's life's progress to *The Arabian Nights*, Stein also points to the structure of her own novel. Her text seems to begin again and again, or it conceives its project over and over—a structure that accurately mimics many American lives. Priscilla Wald in *Reconstituting Americans* treats the first three paragraphs of *The Making of Americans* as three separate beginnings: of "a family narrative, a psychological narrative, and a culminating cultural narrative" (Wald, 254). Stein calls attention to her own recurrent beginnings by repeating phrases such as "now there is here a beginning" throughout her work (see *Making*, 176, 396–97, 692). Often her beginnings signal a new goal; sometimes they are just attempts to regroup, to reach an old goal again. Often she seems to be referring to all 925 pages of her writing as a beginning to some larger project that she will not be able to finish.

13. Reading *The Making of Americans* as a social novel makes it sound like *Main Street*. Stein and Lewis, however, did not recognize their shared interests, and they had no appreciation for each other's work. In *The Making of Americans*, Stein's line of identical fathers is sadly deterministic; sons tend to manifest versions of their fathers' limitations. She leaves little hope for succeeding generations to break free except through thoughtful inaction and death. Lewis places hope in the female line: Carol Kennicott sees her daughter as "a bomb to blow up smugness" and daydreams about "what that baby will see and meddle with before she dies" (432). Later in Stein's life, as I discuss in my conclusions to this book, Stein also seems to place her hope in the female. Although Lewis's novel ends with the birth of Carol's daughter, and Stein's novel ends with the death of the young David Hersland, Stein's unusual style seems to me to offer more hope for the surprising potential of the future.

14. While myth says the true innovators went west, and Mark Twain says the failures did, Stein assumes it was restless people who needed more elbow room—more freedom, more space. If these restless people are successful, if they build up the West to be much like the East and then stay there, they become tamed and conformist themselves. In Stein's view, their youthful conformity is worse than that in areas which have been settled longer (as teenagers tend to exert more peer pressure than adults); real eccentrics must leave the adolescent West for the Old

World: "it takes time to make queer people, and to have others know it, time a certainty of place and means. Custom, passion, and a feel for mother earth are needed to breed vital singularity in any man, and alas, how poor we are in all these three." This "singularity that is neither crazy, sporty, faddish, or a fashion, or low class with distinction" requires them to "flee before the disapproval of our cousins . . . [and] fly to the kindly comfort of an older world accustomed to take all manner of strange forms into its bosom." Stein's "Brother Singulars," born and bred in the newest part of the New World, have to escape to the Old World to find the freedom to develop themselves further, since (Stein asserts) only societies with solid traditions allow for eccentricity (*Making*, 21).

15. James reveals the importance he places on personal discovery and experience when he recommends that one "familiarize one's self with the mammalian brain. Get a sheep's head, a small saw, chisel, scalpel and forceps (all three can best be had from a surgical-instrument maker), and unravel its parts" with the aid of one of a couple of suggested books (*Principles*, 24n).

16. Stein's and Solomons's experiments in the Harvard Psychology Laboratory are described in two articles in the *Psychological Review* for September 1896 and May 1898. In the first article, titled "Normal Motor Automatism," Stein and Solomons discuss the "question of consciousness," and they analyze "attention" and the "habits of attention" at quite some length (Stein and Solomons, *Motor Automatism*, 9, 14, 13). The later article, of which Stein is sole author, was titled "Cultivated Motor Automatism: A Study of Character in Its Relation to Attention" (27).

B. F. Skinner, a notorious reductive mechanist of the human psyche, argued that Stein's early experiments prove that much of her later writing was just "automatic writing." Skinner's argument that Stein performs automatic writing is largely based on the fact that Stein and Solomons themselves were the only subjects of their first set of experiments, and he claims (but does not demonstrate, and I do not see) a similarity between texts such as *Tender Buttons* and the writing produced by distracted writers. According to Skinner, Stein was already developing her unintelligible style a decade before she decided to become an author. In his *Atlantic Monthly* article "Has Gertrude Stein a Secret?" Skinner writes that nobody "can fail to recognize a familiar note [between] these examples of automatic writing" and *Tender Buttons* (52). But not all repetition is alike, and not all nonsense "has very little to say" (56). Skinner concludes his article by saying that he does "not believe in the importance of the part of Miss Stein's writing that does not make sense" and that he kindly advises people "to enjoy the other and very great part [of Stein's work] without puzzlement" (57). He thus takes the mystery out of the mysterious, tries to make an end of the endlessly tantalizing questions that Stein's writing evokes in her readers, and throws away all the yeasty potential of Stein's most exciting writing.

17. Johns Hopkins Medical school opened in 1893 and immediately offered the best medical education in the nation. Admitting women and having the most difficult entrance requirements of any medical school went hand in hand. A group of women approached the trustees of the newly conceived college and promised $100,000 on the condition that women be admitted. The reluctant trustees agreed to admit women *only if* this group of benefactors would donate $500,000. (One cannot help but guess that the trustees thought *that* was the end of *that*.) Managing to raise an additional $100,000, the women's group was stumped—until one woman, Mary Garrett, donated the difference of $300,000. But she had her own conditions: admitted students must have a college degree, have taken premedical studies, and know French and German (Duffy, 277).

18. Ludmerer refers to Thayer's "Self-education under Guidance" (Thayer, *Osler*, 228–46) and quotes from Thayer, "Teaching and Practice," in *Osler*, 191.

19. Ludmerer cites Mall, 85. One student describes Osler's clinical amphitheater: "On these occasions he acted as a fellow student with us, guiding us in our examinations of the patient, causing us to see what we had not previously noted and making us realize that the Hippocratic dictum 'to see, to touch and to hear,' was not all in making a diagnosis, for Laennec introduced the words 'to auscult' and so revealed further facts. But he showed us that all of this went for naught if we did not follow what Louis, the great French clinician, had taught us 'to record.' He made us make careful notes of our findings" (qtd. in Harvey et al., 36; Harvey cites Chesney, 2:127).

20. Stein's grades dropped during her last two years of medical school, and it has been speculated that she was distracted by love, which was almost certainly one factor in her inattention. Wagner-Martin's view is that Stein "boycotted" classes taught by sexist professors (49): "Disguising the anger she felt at the sexism and racism evident during her years at medical school, Gertrude pretended to be apathetic" (50).

21. Early biographers somewhat apologetically acknowledge Stein's apparent acceptance of sexist policies that encouraged female students to do the "mechanic" work of drawing brain tracts (Hobhouse, 24–25; Brinnin, 36). Brinnin even writes that Stein "knew it was absurd to make models of brain tracts" (36; information attributed to Stein's brother Leo). I'm not sure why it would be absurd to diagram processes in which one is interested. (Women used to do most computer programming, too, until someone figured out the great potential in the field.)

22. Barker himself describes the fibers as "concerned in the conduction of sensory impulses toward the somoaesthetic area of the cortex, . . . [but] not at all well understood." Further, "if the fasciculus longitudinalis medialis is to be regarded as one of the paths mediating sensory impulses on their way to the cerebral cortex, this path is almost certainly interrupted in the hypothalamus or thalamus" (*Nervous System*, 726).

CHAPTER 2

1. James asserts that experience can only be what we attend to, and there is plenty we miss. His assertion applies to noticing what's happening around us, but it also applies to our language environment. James gives the example of how we tend to read: because language is written in such habitual phrases, reading becomes almost a "*reflex action*" instead of a "*psychic act*" (*Principles*, 97; his italics). But if we attended more carefully to language—or if we were forced to have the language experience become a psychic act because of the unusual nature of the language confronting us—then the words would inspire our "latent excitement" (89) or "expectant attention" (97), we'd be truly experiencing language, and our minds would continue to be formed.

James also employs an example from language experience when he distinguishes "sensorial blindness" (the physical inability to see) and "psychic blindness" (the mental inability to assign meaning to what one sees): "psychic blindness is inability to recognize the *meaning* of the optical impressions, as when we see a page of Chinese print but it suggests nothing to us" (52; his italics). Psychic blindness is a "*loss of associations* between optical sensations and what they signify," James continues (59). He cannot discuss the ways that attention to experience develops the mind (or fails to develop the mind) without resorting to a discussion of the way signification—necessitating if not exactly equivalent to language—is the medium by which this modification takes place.

James asserted the constant remodification of the brain (227): "We believe the brain to be an organ whose internal equilibrium is always in a state of change"; he compares the brain to a "kaleidoscope" in which "the figures are always rearranging themselves" (239). Different qualities of these "figures" he calls "images," "sensations," "percepts," "concepts," "thoughts," "transitive states," and "feelings of relation"—at least a few of which tend to rise to our consciousness through words, phrases, and sentences.

James also employs examples from language use and experience to demonstrate habitual acts such as repeating the alphabet and saying one's prayers (121), and even the more complex "movements of our tongues and pens" (136), sensitivity to bad grammar, a dog's noticing its name being called, and a young child's recognition of a few words (395).

In short, language is one form of experience, and experience tends to be stored away in our minds as language.

2. James's textbook takes this approach (49–51, 70); so does the 1993 textbook *Contemporary Linguistics* (O'Grady, chap. 9).

3. O'Grady gives an example of a conversation with a Wernicke's patient, a set of utterances that might remind the reader of Stein's short plays.

> How are you today, Mrs. A?
> Yes.
> Have I ever tested you before?
> No. I mean I haven't.
> Can you tell me what your name is?
> No, I don't I . . . right I'm right now here.
> What is your address?
> I [could] if I can help these this like you know . . . to make it. We are seeing for him. That is my father. (351)

Sometimes, severely impaired speakers borrow phonemes and intonation instead of whole words to create something that sounds like English, and this disease is called "jargonaphasia" (O'Grady, 352). Redefined, jargonaphasia could be what Stein is fighting against: prefabricated jargon as our main means of communication, one that doesn't allow us to mean what we want and need to mean.

During Stein's U.S. tour, Morris Fishbein, the editor of the *Journal of the American Medical Association*, compared Stein's writing to the speech of patients with palilalia, palilogia, perseveration, or verbigeration—all speech disorders that involve repetition. A person with palilalia "repeats many times a word, a phrase or a sentence which he has just uttered"; one with palilogia repeats in order to emphasize herself; perseveration occurs because "the original idea persist[s] in the speaker's mind for an undue length of time, keeping fresh ideas from entering"; and verbigeration causes one to repeat "the same sentence over and over" (Meyer, *Irresistible*, 50.). In the interests of full disclosure, I should add that palilalia is said to be brought on by encephalitis—a serious illness I had as a child. Could this be why Stein is so appealing to me? I think, however, that Meyer is right to call Fishbein's idea "absurd" (*Irresistible*, 53).

4. In 1914, Van Vechten records that "some [readers] say that the 'fringe of thought,' so frequently referred to by [William James], may dominate [Stein's] working consciousness" ("How to Read," 155). I haven't found any early reviews to confirm his point.

Bain, to whom James alludes quite often in his *Principles of Pyschology*, similarly describes the effect of a sum of several mild stimuli:

> It might admit of a doubt whether four faint links of contiguous adhesion would be equal to one strong, but it would be against our whole experience of the workings of similarity, to doubt the utility of multiplying faint resemblances, when there was no one sufficiently powerful to effect the revival [of a word or memory]. . . . By raising some single feature almost up to the point of identity, we should do more good than could be done by scattering faint and detached likenesses over the picture. This, however, is not always in our power; and we are glad to find that, when the similarity, in any one particular, is too feeble to suggest the resembling past, the existence of a plurality of weak resemblances will be the equivalent of a single stronger one. (586)

5. Bain in 1855 alludes to the "well-known fact that objects do, on many occasions, bring before the mind their contraries" (599).

6. Steven Meyer reads Stein as disliking habit *and* association, but I see her using her knowledge of mental association to fight against habit ("Writing," 151–52). In other words, habits are pitted against each other. Timothy V. Kaufman-Osborn makes the argument that if we shed all habit, we would shed all means by which to think (190–91). He goes on to say (in his enigmatic way): "Deliberation, elicited from the dialectic between unreflective habit and the habit of reflecting, is one moment within the more comprehensive form of conduct that is 'art'" (194).

7. Linda S. Watts writes: "A reader's uncertainties are no longer regarded as sites of failures but rather as liminal ground, where new possibilities take shape" (*Gertrude Stein*, 10). She also nicely describes "the underlying principles at work in Stein's writing" as creating works that "explore rather than explain" and "complicate rather than enumerate" (25). Living a life in two cultures may also produce this intellectual life; another culture's habits can certainly make one hesitate and doubt one's own, and all, habits.

8. Ruddick then "unravel[s]" this very theory by further analysis of Stein's words, but her choice to argue for Stein's revision of the crucifixion story seems a less convincing—although fascinating—alternative.

9. I hesitate to draw "information" from a novel, but Steward's novels are not the worst place to try to get an idea of Stein's daily life and conversation. Steward seems mainly to write from fact, as most of the description and episodes in his novels correspond to real places and actual happenings. His descriptions of the gardens and terrain around Belignin correspond exactly to those I saw there in 2000, when the current owner was kind enough to invite my family into the gardens and tell us about her childhood luncheons with Stein. Even the far-fetched plot of Steward's *Parisian Lives*, in which a man has a love affair with his own illegitimate son, seems to have been based on the experience of Francis Rose (*Chapters*, 69).

10. My readings are tendentious, some more than others, but readers should not be so overwhelmed by multiplicity as to refuse to see anything at all. Michael J. Hoffman asserts that Stein revitalized the English language, but he is more interested in how Stein upsets generic conventions than in how she chooses words. In *Gertrude Stein*, he argues that it is not necessary or productive to read Stein's words too closely. After describing only two ways to understand the opening lines of Stein's "Kristians Tonny," he suggests that

we leave ourselves open to a polysemous situation in which a sentence can have an infinite number of meanings. . . . It is easy to see into what a linguistic slough of despond we would fall if we troubled ourselves too much with the *sense* of the lines. In treating language so cavalierly, Stein runs the danger of a maddening polysemy; but, in return for taking this chance, she achieves the great pleasure of showing that language can be turned into a plastic instrument stripped of meaning by any writer or speaker who is willing to tamper with its traditional linguistic structures. Stein, more than Joyce or any other writer I can think of, can show us just what ambiguous possibilities are inherent in language. (64–65)

I agree that Stein successfully demonstrates the polysemy of the word, but I do not think that showing there are two meanings has ever proved there are an infinite number of meanings. Instead of finding oneself in a "linguistic slough of despond"—although sloughs and swamps are organic and rich—I would hope that readers would discover themselves in a linguistic realm of opportunity, a glorious web of words full of panoramic prospects and unfolding secrets.

Hoffman cites sections of *Tender Buttons* and ask questions about them, but he argues that his tendency to question is just "further proof of the suggestive power of words and of the inability of even the most self-conscious author to divest them completely of their associative powers" (*Abstractionism*, 183–84). His assumption that Stein was naively attempting to treat words as if they did not have any meaning leads to the conclusion that she has failed. But what if he, and other critics who have made similar arguments, are wrong in their assumption? If we look at the works in Stein's *Geography and Plays* that were written around the same time as *Tender Buttons*, we see not only similarities of structure, but also similarities of word choice. There seem to be certain words—piece, change, single, slice, cousin, whole, disorder, spreading, difference and different, center, more, circle, surface, colors, tending, order, resembling, tender, and silence—that have importance for Stein. These are the words she has come to know.

In the end, Hoffman can conclude only that "*Tender Buttons* is a series of black symbols on a white page" and that all we can do as readers is "admire . . . the wonders of creation" (*Gertrude Stein*, 68). This is not enough of a claim for Stein's art. It is certainly not enough of an accomplishment to support Hoffman's assertion that Stein "is a major writer historically and intrinsically and that she has written some of the finest and most complex books of our time" (9). Hoffman admits that "it is possible to give anything—even a telephone book—a dramatic reading" (73); I would claim that "even a telephone book" can let us notice "black symbols on a white page" and that, if Hoffman is right about Stein's meaninglessness, a thick telephone book might be even more likely to inspire admiration at "the wonders of creation."

Lisa Ruddick, writing since Hoffman's book of essays was published, strikes a healthy balance between vague appreciation of words as sensation and the search for meaning. She reads Stein for the pleasure of the sound and the feel of the words on her tongue, as well as for a hidden meaning. It seems reasonable to think that Stein would disrupt the binarism between these two different kinds of reading as much as she would reject other binarisms. Of *Tender Buttons*, Ruddick writes:

Within poems, moreover, there are invariably words that do not contribute to any continuous idea and whose importance is either in their sheer soundplay or in their ability to dislodge other, more logically embedded words in the vicinity from unitary meanings by stimulating alternative associations. Stein constructs a text that invites the reader to find coherent themes but that also makes him or her choose a point beyond which to stop piecing things together. My readings are not meant to substitute for this experience of uncertainty and mobility.(203)

And neither are mine.

11. Booth is writing about literature that people assume they understand: nursery rhymes, the Gettysburg Address, Ben Jonson poems, a Shakespeare play. He writes: "Great works of art are daredevils . . . always on the point of one or another kind of incoherence" (*Precious*, 35). Stein's *Tender Buttons* teeters the other way, on the edge of coherence.

12. This time, that reminder is accurate etymologically, but it is not always: pronunciation shifts and spelling anomalies often make words remind readers of other words and meanings that are *not* etymological relatives. Allegra Stewart often uses etymology as a key to Stein's writing. In interpreting this paragraph, Stewart traces "quintal" through Egyptian and Arabic to the meaning "pertaining to the fifth," which she in turn links to "the quintessential element, that invisible fire worshiped by the ancient Chaldeans and Egyptians as the principle of creativity," then to a variety of other religious rituals, and finally to Stein's own "religious ritual" of writing (133). Compared to this reading, mine makes the jump from religion to rhetoric much more directly, by listening to the words in their order on the page.

13. It may appear that I'm willfully deciding what all this means, but "to decide" is from the root "caedere," which means "to cut off." I am trying to understand meaning by including rather than cutting off or excluding.

14. Randolph Bourne, writing in 1913, sees a similar role for irony: "Irony was Greek, with all the free, happy play of the Greek spirit about it, letting in fresh air and light into others' minds and our own. It was to the Greek an incomparable method of intercourse, the rub of mind against mind . . . without committing one's self. . . . this pleasant challenging of the world, this insistent judging of experience, this sense of vivid contrasts and incongruities, of comic juxtapositions, of flaring brilliances, and no less heartbreaking impossibilities, of all the little parts of one's world being constantly set off against each other, and made intelligible only by being translated into and defined in each other's terms" (135). He later writes that the ironist's "life is expressed in the social intercourse of ourselves with others. The daily fabric of the life of irony is woven out of our critical communings with ourselves and the personalities of our friends, and the people with whom we come into contact" (137). And finally, like Stein's ideal, Bourne's ironist tries to live and think through true experience, distinguishing it from the secondhand: "We are born into a world that is an inexhaustible store of ready-made ideas, stored up in tradition, in books, and in every medium of communication between our minds and others. All we have to do is accept this predigested nourishment, and ask no questions. We could live a whole life without ever making a really individual response, without providing ourselves out of our own experience with any of the material that our mind works on" (139). Like Stein, "the ironist forces his friends to move their rusty limbs and unhinge the creaking doors of their minds" (145).

15. "The winner loses" is quoted from Stein, "The winner loses: A Picture of Occupied France," *Atlantic*, November 1940, 571–83.

CHAPTER 3

1. Kadlec quotes from James, *Principles*, 238.

2. The definition of conversation in this paragraph is based on the ideas of many thinkers in the fields of conversation and discourse analysis: Sacks, *Lectures*; Schegloff, introduction; Moerman, *Talking*; several of Deborah Tannen's academic and popular books; and Clark and Clark, "Discourse."

3. Picasso's collage is reproduced in Stendhal, 75.

4. I refer the reader to Bowers's careful and perceptive examination of the play *Can You See the Name* (112–17). In the course of this analysis, Bowers points out that "our attention is focused on phonology and orthography, not on meaning," when we notice the way Stein has used homophones (116). I would add, of course, that phonology and orthography themselves point toward meaning.

Betsy Alayne Ryan also asserts that Stein breaks dramatic conventions: "Gertrude Stein's disruption of the alternate reality—or fiction—of the traditional theatre is the unifying principle of all her plays, regardless of period" (67). It shouldn't be surprising to anyone familiar with any of Stein's various styles of writing that she makes us rethink our generic expectations in her drama, too.

5. Probably most full-length plays get around to mentioning food somewhere, but Stein's plays in *Geography and Plays* are short. Half of them are less than five pages long. Six more are between six and twelve pages long. Even these numbers are sometimes misleading: In *Counting Her Dresses* (eleven pages long), the longest act has three lines; the longest speech is two sentences; in short, there is much blank space on those eleven pages (but not many empty stomachs).

6. *Bonne Annee* might remind one of Stein's "The Good Anna," from *Three Lives*, and the words in its one and a half pages often recall that good woman.

7. And my French friend Françoise Tillard, in a discussion of what the 2003 strikers were defending—a way of life, daily pleasures without the impingement of possible future stresses, and not just a couple years more of retirement—tells the truth when she says that when the French eat a leisurely meal together, they talk about the food. Meanwhile, the coffee shop owner was outside bringing a bowl of water and feeding cookies to my dog. Food is love, and an appreciation of the present moment of bodily presence.

8. Cheepen cites Bronislow Malinowski, "Phatic Communion," reprinted in J. Laver and S. Hutcheson, eds., *Communication in Face to Face Interaction* (Middlesex, Eng.: Penguin, 1972), 149.

9. Tannen cites Scollon and Scollon, "Cooking."

10. According to Stein: "They [Gertrude and Leo] certainly are not at all alike. One of them is hearing himself and is having then sound come out of him. One of them is hearing some one and is then having sound come out of her" ("Two," 3). Biographical information concurs that Leo was a bad listener—at least partly caused by his loss of hearing—and that Gertrude was "'a terrific talker, but an elegant listener too'" (Wagner-Martin, 31).

11. Gertrude Stein was called "baby" by her family (Wagner-Martin, 23). This nickname seemed to reemerge on her lecture tour, when she was called "baby" by Toklas and Van Vechten (Burns, 434, 435). She refers to herself as a baby in these letters and as a husband in some of her other writings. For example, she implies it by noting that *The Autobiography of Alice B. Toklas* was almost titled "Wives of Geniuses I Have Sat With" (*Autobiography*, 251).

12. Janet Malcolm might disagree, at least to the extent of arguing that Stein let her position as youngest child influence her behavior quite considerably. She cites Stein's description of being "the baby of the family," which meant that "'nobody can do anything but take care of you'" (Malcolm, 62; the Stein quotes are from *Autobiography*). Malcolm also denies that Stein was staunch or even very vulnerable in Vichy France because Faÿ was watching out for her safety and comfort, but I believe this protection was probably something that evolved, not something Stein was depending on when she decided to stay in France for the war. As the conductor of the couple's transactions, Toklas may have had some dealings with Faÿ on the subject of ration cards and deportation lists, but perhaps Stein did not. And finally, youngest children are often protected, but we (yes, me too) also tend to be careful observers of the social dynamics around us.

13. Bush quotes from a Stein notebook: "Activity is a cheap commodity." He adds: "Like Hannah Arendt [Stein] recognized that the contemplative life was more difficult, and more energy-consuming, than a life of pragmatic action" (346, with a short citation from Stein, Notebook [small grey], 2, note d [Stein papers, Beinecke]).

14. In another lecture, Stein repeated this idea: "Seeing a person in the act of doing something is not interesting, but it is interesting when they are doing nothing for the person is not distracted from being something by doing something. In Paris two American doughboys standing on the corner doing nothing for some time are more interesting than when one of them says let's go home and they move off" (Meyers).

15. Inspired by Stein's *Lectures in America*, a reviewer writes: "Listen, consciously listen the next time a person tells you a story—not to what they are telling you but the way they are telling it. 'And then I sez to him, I sez, sez I, when he asks me what I thinks of it, I sez to him, I sez . . .' Just watch—I mean listen" (Winter, 82).

16. After some staring and pondering and some counting, one might notice that each character speaks the number of paragraphs that corresponds with his name—except in two instances—so we could say that those exceptions are the two exciting scenes, but I think that unlikely. A listener would not know how many paragraphs had been spoken, and just the surprise and excitement generated by the surprising words themselves is going to overshadow any emotion one might feel about discovering this pattern with the number of paragraphs.

17. William James writes: "The stream of our thought is like a river. On the whole easy simple flowing predominates in it, the drift of things is with the pull of gravity, and effortless attention is the rule. But at intervals an obstruction, a set-back, a log-jam occurs, stops the current, creates an eddy, and makes things temporarily move the other way. If a real river could feel, it would feel these eddies and set-backs as places of effort" (*Principles*, 427). There are paragraphs in *Tender Buttons* that have this flowing, pausing, eddying, and then speeding momentum to them, as does, for example, the third paragraph of "Roast Beef" at the beginning of "Food."

18. Stein's distinctions between knowing and understanding may remind readers of those made by Coleridge and Emerson. "Not any nuisance is depressing" looks forward to "A Life" by Howard Nemerov: "Innocence? / In a sense. / In no sense!" (in *The Blue Swallows* [Chicago: U of Chicago P, 1967], 13).

19. But is "use" all words *do* have? Rorty makes the case that language "provides tools for coping with objects rather than representations of objects" (*Philosophy*, 65). One way of using language may be more useful than another, and the more useful, the better, he says, while Stein writes: "do not say that words have a use." But when Rorty tells us "to stop thinking of words as representations and to start thinking of them as nodes in the causal

network which binds the organism together with its environment" (xxiii), his thought seems to parallel Stein's valuation of wordy interaction and mutual causation much more closely. For Rorty, the "goal of inquiry" is the "coordination of behavior" ("to achieve agreement . . . about what to do"). He makes an exception for "simply wordplay" (whatever that means to him), but it is probably something like this wordplay that Stein seems to hold out as the last great hope for creative solutions (xxv).

20. What Marxists claim about economics should remind us of Stein on words: Human beings "become alienated from [products] and . . . increasingly fail to recognize them as products of their labor, thus forgetting their history" (Winders, 488). Stein tries to reacquaint people with their verbal production and rescues words from being alienated from their histories.

Of course, words are never quite clear signals. We just pretend they are. Stein says that people can communicate clearly about "mechanics" but "about every other thing nobody is of the same opinion nobody means the same thing by what they say as the other one means and only the one who is talking thinks he means what he is saying even though he knows very well that that is not what he is saying" (*Everybody's*, 290).

21. Similarly, in "Unharvested"—in which there is a "there there"—Robert Frost seems to be discussing poetic beauty when he appreciates the "scent of ripeness from over a wall" and entreats: "May something go always unharvested! / May much stay out of our stated plan, / Apples or something forgotten and left, / So smelling their sweetness would be no theft" (305, ll. 8, 1, 11–14). Stein's words are so arranged that something must always go unharvested in spite of attempts to do a thorough picking.

To move away from gardening, one might also notice the scent of a hunt in this third paragraph. At a hunt there is "blessing and chasing"; the dogs are "mixed strangely"; the prey is "surrounded" and then sometimes escapes through a "vegetable window"; and if the hunt is "complete" then the kill is "exchange[d] in parts" among the hunters. I imagine a fox hunt, but the "simple melancholy clearly precious and on the surface" might remind some readers of the hunted deer, who was purported to go to the water and weep.

22. This paragraph from *What Happened* most resembles National Book Award nominee Harryette Mullen's poetry in *Trimmings*, published by Tender Buttons Press. Mullen offers vivid social commentary about women's lives, employing punning echoes of common phrases. Musing on Stein, Mullen writes:

> Girt, a good old girl got hipped. They thrive with wives, broad beams. Most worthy girth, providing firm. Foundations in midriff. Across (between) girdled loins, tender girders. Gartered, perhaps, struts. Stretching, a snap crotch. (26)

23. According to Sandra M. Gilbert and Susan Gubar, Stein's giving life to words would be a feminist project. They assert that a representative male author both "generates and imprisons his fictive characters, he silences them by depriving them of autonomy. . . . He silences them and . . . embedding them in the marble of his art—kills them" (14). Gilbert and Gubar describe this tendency as masculine, but both men and women have masculine tendencies—which fact may allow Stein to see her project as epistemologically universal, rather than alternatively feminist. By the end of her life, however, Stein may be coming over to Gilbert and Gubar's feminist conviction (see "Feminine Endings" in the conclusions of this book).

24. Silverman quotes from Sacks, *Lectures*, 2:169.

25. This repetition of "goodbye" means two very different things to me: "I adore you," and

"Would you please just leave already?" There seems to be strife and disagreement in *Do Let Us Go Away*, so it probably means the latter in this case. On the other hand, I think it also is a play on "good buy," since the play just mentioned "100 dollars." (It could *also* mean "I adore you," if the speaker regrets leaving her money with somebody else.) Other parts of the play suggest dissatisfaction with a rental agreement: The landlord hates the dog's barking, the renters hate the loud servants' voices and their impoliteness, the neighbors are annoying, and so forth. *Do Let Us Go Away* is probably a serious conversational proposition, too, addressed either to a partner or to the landlord to release them from the lease.

26. I have assumed that two speakers take turns speaking the lines in these examples. In only a few cases is it at all likely that the same speaker voices subsequent lines, as in the case of "Yes I agree with you. / Yes." Although the lines I have chosen may seem arbitrary, I have selected only what I interpret as entire conversations. One can easily go through the text of this play and draw lines between separate conversations, although there are a few statements that seem to stand alone.

27. That readers do not know how many people are participating in each conversation, or even whether each line is spoken by a different person than spoke the previous line, is another source of ambiguity. To limit this discussion to a manageable size, I again assume that there are two speakers in each conversation, and that subsequent lines are usually spoken by different people.

28. Phillips here misquotes Stein's *Ladies' Voices*, in *Geography and Plays*, 204; the correct words are "made no difference."

29. In her excellent introduction to the 1993 reprint of *Geography and Plays*, Pondrom classifies "Susie Asado" as a "transitional piece" between the style of *Tender Buttons* and that of early plays. As she points out, her classifications are similar to but not identical with those of DeKoven (Pondrom, lvii).

30. Of "Susie Asado" and "Preciosilla," Van Vechten comments that "there is reason to believe these two poems paint a portrait and make an attempt to recapture the rhythm of the same flamenco dancer" (*Selected*, 548). I can hear that possibility, but I am also looking for more. Why *these* words in *this* order? There does not seem to be any question that "Susie Asado" is a portrait of the flamenco dancer La Argentina, but Wagner-Martin goes so far as to say that "Susie" is "a reference to sexual effluvia" (107).

31. Stein's writing is full of these lovely rhymes. Reviewing *Four Saints in Three Acts*, Stark Young writes that the stream of words will not "trouble people who have always known by instinct or cultivation that Mother Goose is better poetry than Longfellow—'Hickory, dickory, dock,' for example, which at least lives in the ear, as compared to 'Be not like dumb, driven cattle,' which is born dead" (72).

32. Cheepen discusses how scapegoating allows conversants to repair interactional trouble (*Predictability*, chapter 5).

33. Janet Flanner reports that Stein's "Shakespeare consisted of leftovers from all sorts of editions of him with omissions of absent volumes which she had lent. She thought that when borrowers did not return a volume it was proof they must be reading it still. Her Shakespeare was mostly limp leather editions or paperbacks held together by elastic bands and she carried them in her pocket and read them when she walked Basket the poodle along the quais" (xv).

34. *Macbeth*, 4.1.10–11, 20–21, 35–36. Numbers in parentheses for Shakespeare's plays cited in the text represent act, scene, and lines.

35. Soap is "an essential ingredient in this private world that Stein's plain language

champions," Koestenbaum imagines. "The little we know we're also happy to rinse off. It's possible to think of Stein's work as one long rinsing or cleaning operation: The sentences that remain are the suds, or the dirt that gathers in the sink basin, traces of a past ablution" (304). Koestenbaum refers to Lady Macbeth, then continues: "The dialectic of progress/stasis that informs all of Stein's compositions (we're getting somewhere, we're getting nowhere) obeys soap's laws: Soap only serves its function in the process of disappearing; you must rub and unmake soap in order to enjoy its cleansing properties; using soap corrects and recapitulates the act of primary autoeroticism" (305).

CHAPTER 4

1. See appendix 1, "Gertrude Stein's American lecture Tour," in Burns and Dydo, 333–51, for the most complete itinerary of her lecture tour: the places she stayed, with whom she ate and where, and to whom she lectured.

2. Blackmer cites Van Vechten, *Peter Whiffle*, 123.

3. Buchalter seems to have caught Stein when she was being as contrary as possible, maybe because the room was too cold, and maybe because she wanted to bait a "zealot" who was present. She said she doesn't "take from" causes, which Buchalter interprets as her not being able to "get excited about formulas for saving the world." She seems just as disgusted with one theory as the next ("the Russians," "the Nazis," humanitarian causes). Disgust with hypocrisy is the primary cause, as she says that the people "who talk and worry about the poor being hungry ought to stay hungry themselves." (Elsewhere, she says that "she had no use for people who lived in comfort and luxury and then advocated Communism" ["A Snub"].) Knowing my own tendency to disagree with certain people, or only on certain days, I think Stein was having one of those days. She was mean about her brother, complained about the cold, threw out other random one-liners on painting and the military, and ("with a sly grin") stated a preference for Baltimore to Buchalter, a reporter for a Washington, D.C., newspaper.

4. W. G. Rogers wrote for the *Springfield Daily Republican*, so he may have written this glowing story; this was the only paper I found that printed a portion of her written lecture "through the courtesy of Miss Stein."

5. Actually, Stein describes several ways of writing, but I've lumped some of them together: "what you intend to write," "what you intended to write," "what has always been intended, by any one, to be written," and "what some one [else?] has intended to write," all seem to be related by intention and planning, as opposed to spontaneity (*Four in America*, 124). Stein seems to do the same lumping when she says, "There are then really there are then two different ways of writing," which have to do with how the "words next to each other make a sound" (124–25).

6. Stein continues to discuss these two kinds of writing in ibid., 125, 129, 131, 135.

7. In a 1924 letter to Sherwood Anderson, Stein praises his *Story Teller's Story* by comparing it to Borrow's *Lavengro*. Fifteen years later, Stein wrote a short essay titled "My Debt to Books" in which she mentions *Lavengro* and Borrow's *Romany Rye* by title in a list with Shakespeare, Trollope, and Edgar Wallace. She continues: "But which have I read the most often, of the novelists, Walter Scott and Anthony Trollope, of the playwriters Shakespeare, of the poets Coleridge, Poe and Wordsworth, at least they stick most to my mind, of miscellaneous George Borrow." Stein would not let anyone borrow her Borrow, "which she had in many kinds of editions because they were too hard to come by" (Flanner, xvi).

Affinities between Stein and Borrow abound. First, they both love and write about Daniel Defoe's *Robinson Crusoe*. Second, their texts often share the hybrid genre of autobiography and novel. Third, Borrow and Stein directly address their readers, as when Borrow commands certain "crotchet[y]" readers to "fling down my book, I do not wish ye to walk any farther in my company" (*Lavengro*, 369). Fourth, they express antiauthoritarian views within the puns and other byways of their prose. For example, in attempting to teach a friend Armenian, Lavengro asks her to decline the Armenian noun "Master"; she "neither likes the word nor the sound," does not want to pluralize masters, and wants to decline them all. Fifth, like Belle, who continually misunderstands Lavengro's Armenian words as English, Stein writes in one of her plays: "Many words spoken to me have seemed English" (*Ladies' Voices*, in *Geography and Plays*, 204). Sixth, Lavengro says that superstition is the soul of poetry (458), and Stein discusses how important superstition is to creativity. Seventh, Lavengro meets an author who credits "a single word in conversation, or some simple accident in a street, or on a road" for "some of the happiest portions" of his writing, and whole works by Stein are indebted to the same kinds of accidents. For example, in *Wars I Have Seen*, she describes what she has overheard in conversation or things that she heard, said, witnessed, or did during her almost daily walk of twelve kilometers to the nearest bakery. Eighth, this same author in Borrow's novel names a painting as his "principal source of inspiration," as Stein credits Cézanne's painting with influencing her creation of *Three Lives* (*Autobiography*, 34). But while this author says, "My neighbors are of opinion that I am a great reader, and so I am, but only of those features—my real library is that picture" (359–60), and while many of Stein's critics have discussed Stein solely in relation to paintings she collected, Stein loved books at least as much. Ninth, Lavengro's extensive discussion of the differences between British English and Scots English parallels Stein's interest in the difference between British English and American English (see *Lectures*, 49–54).

The eighteenth-century English novel is a productive place to look for interesting parallels with Stein's work. William Carlos Williams believed that Stein was anticipated by Laurence Sterne's *Life and Opinions of Tristram Shandy* (Meyer explores some of these connections in *Irresistible Dictation*), and I think there are some interesting parallels between Richardson's *Clarissa* and Stein's *The Making of Americans* (W. Williams, 41–42; and see D. Watson, 220–21). When Toklas published Stein's *How to Write*, the two women were careful to make the book "look like an eighteenth-century copy of a novel by Laurence Sterne [that Alice] had found in London" (Souhami, 176). In *Irresistible Dictation*, Meyer not only explores the connection between Stein and Sterne, but also finds fertile discussion of Stein's possible literary conversation with William Wordsworth, Ralph Waldo Emerson, George Eliot, and Walter Pater—just to list the more literary connections he draws. Meyer writes of his "conviction that texts exist in relation to other texts or they do not exist at all" (xvii).

8. In fact, "divine" and "devil" are *not* etymologically related. "Devil" is derived from a Greek word that means "slanderer," while the oldest relative of "divine" is a Latin word that means "god" or "one inspired by gods." While "divine" maintained the *v* sound, the *v* in "devil" evolved from *f* (*déofol*) *and b* (*diabolus*). Shakespeare might draw on this similarity when Othello speaks of "the divine Desdemona," but probably not (*Othello* 2.1.73).

9. Stein writes in *Autobiography*: "From her eighth year when she absorbed Shakespeare to her fifteenth year when she read Clarissa Harlowe, Fielding, Smollett etcetera and used to worry lest in a few years more she would have read everything and there would be nothing unread to read, she lived continuously with the english language" (74).

Smollett's novel is interesting in its epistolary style, which is quite conversational, and his character types—the overbearing manager of others' lives and the passively good-natured subservient female—are the kind one sees in Stein's early prose, *Three Lives* and *The Making of Americans*. Stein's early writings are full of uneducated, subordinated women who (sometimes) manage to gain some power through language. The "good Anna" needs to work for people who "freely let her do it all" (*Three Lives*, 77) and the "patient, gentle" Lena very much likes being a servant (239) and "was so still and docile, she would never want to do things her own way" (245). In *The Making of Americans*, Stein detours away from the Hersland family's story to tell about the succession of governesses and seamstresses that trooped through their lives.

10. Bramble and Jenkins write in simple and silly malapropisms, which must be the evidence upon which Sandra M. Gilbert and Susan Gubar base their assessment of Smollett. They group him with Sheridan and Fielding, who "construct[ed] cartoon figures" of women and "implied that language itself was almost literally alien to the female tongue" (30–31). But later in their analysis, Gilbert and Gubar recognize the potential of these characters' voices; they describe Jane Austen's characters as "taking on the persona of Mrs. Slipshop or Mrs. Malaprop (that wonderful 'queen of the dictionary') or Tabitha Bramble." In their view: "Austen was indisputably fascinated by double-talk, by conversations that imply the opposite of what they intend, narrative statements that can only confuse, and descriptions that are linguistically sound, but indecipherable or tautological" (127).

11. Other substitutions of near homophones also act as social commentary. To get her housekeeper to behave in her absence, Tabitha reminds her that she "must render accunt, not only to your earthly master, but also to him that is above" (Smollett, 156). It's more likely that her words are meant to remind us more of her attempt to catch a husband than to make any statement about sexuality and submission, but we can note both. The same joke is repeated when she tells her housekeeper and her assistant to "get your accunts ready for inspection" because she and her new husband are on their way home. Smollett does not pass up any opportunity to emphasize Tabitha's sexual obsessions, having her also write: "let Roger search into, and make a general clearance of the slit holes which the maids have in secret" (274); in the same letter, she hopes that when they arrive home, Humphry Clinker's preaching "may have power given to penetrate and instill his goodness, even into your most inward parts" (275).

But when Winifred Jenkins describes the marriage of Tabitha Bramble and Lismahago, who seems to marry her for her money, as "the holy bands of mattermoney," we certainly can't help noticing the comment on this marriage and other marriages of convenience (Smollett, 352). Humphry Clinker successfully converts Winifred to pious (usually spelled "pyehouse" [261]) devotion to Methodism and to "improv[e] in grease and godliness" (262). When Winifred marries Humphry Clinker, Tabitha's long lost illegitimate nephew, Winifred expresses a great truth in the sentiments of her last letter. She hopes that she and Tabitha, her former employer, will be able to adjust to their new social relationship: "I hope she and I will live upon dissent terms of civility—Being, by God's blessing, removed to a higher spear" (353). Her spelling errors—caused again by the near homophones—suggest the likelihood that these two women will not be able to adjust peaceably to their new situation, and even that their disputes will be more rancorous now that their social stations—their "spear[s]" or weapons—are more nearly equal.

The dissidence expressed through mistakes of diction, spelling, grammar, and pronunciation demonstrate the possibilities for the female voice to speak in a male society and with a language taught to educated men but (fortunately) disruptable by uneducated—or even some resistant educated—women. These women can see and understand differently, and make us see differently, because their minds have not been infiltrated by the male point of view. Judith Fetterley in *The Resisting Reader* argues that education makes women masculine, giving them a masculine point of view and masculine values (xx). Tabitha Bramble and Winifred Jenkins have escaped this supposedly masculinizing education and can teach us something, if we refuse to acquiesce to the criticism those characters, especially Tabitha, receive in Smollett's novel.

12. The human mind cannot be right about human nature because human nature is stuck in time and the timeless human mind cannot conceive of that:

> Human nature is not natural it is what anybody does and what anybody does is not natural and therefore it is not interesting.
>
> There is no doubt that human nature is not interesting although the human mind has always tried to be busy about this thing that human nature is interesting and the human mind has made so many efforts always it is doing this thing trying to make it be to itself that human nature is interesting but it is not and so the master-pieces always flatten it out, flatten human nature out so that there is no beginning and middle and ending. (*Geographical History*, 186)

13. Stein's understanding of and appreciation for the history of and relationships between words is important and too often overlooked in Stein criticism. For example, Randa Dubnick observes that Stein "uses words as if they were new and had no history" and that *this* constitutes her "innovative use of language" (xiv). Perhaps this disagreement stems from different definitions of "history." For Dubnick, a word's history may arise from etymology, normal context, and usage—the assumptions that people have come to about the meaning of a word. For me, history is what is carried in the word, which includes etymology (both true and false) but tends to allow us to understand the word anew. Readers must escape history, but words carry their own complex histories (and stories). In addition, individual readers and individual words build their own histories together.

CHAPTER 5

1. Postman is more interested in advertising and big media sources (in news, television shows, and radio) than in privately tendered language. The language Postman discusses, when he's not discussing the images that have replaced it, comes at us like a strong wind to which we bend. It is difficult to reply to, or even to think about (and internalize or reject), much of the fast, loud, often irrational language input we get these days. But I like to imagine that in Stein's day—and I think this is particularly likely in France—give-and-take conversation formed a higher percentage of language experience. Advertising was just starting to take on its current characteristics (Stein was struck by the slogans when she visited the United States in 1934–35). Postman observes that "in the eighteenth and nineteenth centuries those with products to sell . . . assumed that potential buyers were literate, rational, analytical" (*Amusing*, 58). The change to "the nonpropositional use of language" such as "slogans" and "jingles" started in the last decade of the nineteenth century, only a decade before Stein left for France—where, at the beginning of the twenty-first century, advertising is still less smoothly manipulative, still involves less "depth psychology," than in the United States (60).

2. At the outset of *Principles of Psychology*, William James distinguishes two main ways of approaching "the Science of Mental Life." One is "the orthodox 'spiritualistic' theory" and the other is the "'associationist'" school, or *"psychology without a soul."* Stein's theories fall under the second category, about which James writes: "Another and a less obvious way of unifying the chaos is to seek common elements *in* the divers mental facts rather than a common agent behind them, and to explain them constructively by the various forms of arrangement of these elements, as one explains houses by stones and bricks. . . . The very Self or *ego* of the individual comes in this way to be viewed no longer as the pre-existing source of the representations, but rather as their last and most complicated fruit" (15–16). His metaphor of humans and houses emphasizes the common materials we are made up of, rather than any particular qualities of individuality.

3. Hermans and Kempen also cite V. M. Colapietro ("The Vanishing Subject of Contemporary Discourse: A Pragmatic Response," *Journal of Philosophy* 87:11 [November 1990] 644–55) for his analysis of Dewey.

4. Hermans and Kempen credit Michael Holquist, *Dialogism: Bakhtin and His World* (London: Routledge, 1990) for this analysis.

5. The possibility that there is no such thing as "one" may remind the reader of Luce Irigaray's speculations in *The Sex Which Is Not One*. My feeling has long been that Stein is exploring the multiple selves of anyone, not just women, but Stein suggests (and later reaffirms) her belief that multiplicity is a more natural or comfortable state for women than for men.

6. By dyeing her hair to create this beautiful twin, Ida subsumes her plainer self, committing partial suicide by choosing to be "a suicide blond." Ida predicts that she will murder her twin, and Stein critic Ellen Berry (164) asks the thought-provoking question: "If Ida eradicates Winnie, is it an act of suicide or murder or neither or both?"

7. It is also possible to understand the two women in the car as the beauty queen and a companion, and the lost Ida in the road as the original. Later, the walking Ida sees the two women in the car and her dog, Love, is with them. Love is carrying a package that was last in the walking Ida's possession. In a letter to her twin, Ida writes: "the day you won, I saw a funny thing, I saw my dog Love belonging to some one. He did not belong to me he did belong to them. That made me feel very funny, but really it is not true he is here he belongs to me and you and now I will call you Winnie because you are winning everything and I am so happy that you are my twin. Your twin, Ida-Ida" (*Ida*, 621). The letter writer remembers that when a part of her was elected beauty queen she felt distant enough from this twin that it felt like Love belonged to somebody else. While writing, she feels close enough to the twin that they can own the dog together. But her feelings double back, and she gives her famous twin a name different from her own. This passage is further complicated by her mixing singular and plural pronouns ("some one" and "them") and the possibility that the passage could be jointly authored by Ida, Winnie, and the lost Ida. Notice that she signs the letter "Ida-Ida," which was the twin's earlier name. For a different reading of this same episode that emphasizes the dreamlike quality of *Ida*, see Berry, 163–64.

8. In *Ida*, Stein explores the topic of "publicity saints." She told a friend: "I want to write a novel about publicity, a novel where a person is so publicized that there isn't any personality left. I want to write about the effect on people of the Hollywood cinema kind of publicity that takes away all identity" (W. Rogers, 168).

9. Stein also anticipates DeLillo in recognizing the materialist's cure for death: "Another one had it in him to be completely certain in all his acting and his feeling and his living that

to be dead is to be a dead one and so this one must keep on being a live one and must have everything he can be seizing to keep by him" (*Making*, 525). In DeLillo's *White Noise*, Murray says, "Here we don't die, we shop" (38).

10. One way the body influences our ways of knowing results from our standing upright. We tend "to employ an up-down orientation in picking out meaningful structures of our experience," which also influences the metaphors through which we come to know the world—for instance, "more is up" for "no intrinsic reason" except the "structure of [our] bodily interactions" (Hermans and Kempen, 9).

11. Copeland argues that the reason Ida's marriages fail is that she does not know her husbands' true identities when she marries them (154). This hypothesis assumes that the uniforms represent the men's whole, or at least most important, self, which I think has to be incorrect.

12. How people react to our appearance changes with location, culture, and climate. Perhaps this is one reason Ida keeps moving. She may not want to be able to predict how people will react to her any more than she wants to have predictable reactions to their given identities.

13. Stein's obituary in the *Saturday Review* says that "there was an earthy, peasant quality about her and at the same time a spiritual force that was somewhat bewildering to those who expected to find in her the essence of mockery" (Smith).

14. The writer and the cuckoo incident recalls a related moment in Sammy Steward's novel *Parisian Lives*, in which Stein is a character. On a walk, Stein hears a cuckoo and gets "very excited," digs into her pockets for money, and says: "Don't you know the old superstition, if you have money in your pocket when you hear the first cuckoo of the year then you'll have money in your pocket for the next twelve months." She goes on: "Superstitions are my new passion. Take spiders for instance, not in the morning but only in the evening when they are lucky, not at noon when they bring care and worry. . . . But I am a lot more interested in money than in spiders or cuckoos, and now we will have money all year round because the cuckoo said so" (33). In the novel, however, Stein's money is immediately stolen.

15. Posnock quotes Connolly, 371.

16. Posnock cites Pitkin, 301, 300.

17. Stein's own poodle was named Basket (because she tried and failed to teach him to carry one [Wagner-Martin, 190]), and when she got a second dog she named him Basket II. Stein appreciated the fact that when he wasn't trimmed like a poodle, Basket looked like a sheep.

CHAPTER 6

1. "Pith," like "pit," means "the single, central kernel" or "essence," but it also refers to deadly extraction; "doubt" means "to waver" or "to vibrate"—as life does.

2. *Mrs. Reynolds* was written during World War II, although it is not known when Stein completed it. Bridgman reports: "The Yale editors have dated *Mrs. Reynolds* 1940–42, but the eleventh section refers to 23 December 1942, and the twelfth and thirteenth sections were almost certainly written more than a year later" (324). He is correct that the novel contains "references . . . to the springing up of the Resistance, the German debacle in Russia, rumors of the Nazis weakening, and the comforting hum of bombers on their way to Italy" (324), although all these references are so oblique that they could be wishful thinking. Assuming *Mrs. Reynolds* was completed even earlier, Ellen E. Berry describes Stein's "imaginative resistance . . . to the power of fascism, prophetically announcing in 1940 the certainty of Harper's/Hitler's demise" (125). I believe that most of the novel was written

between 1940 and the end of 1942, but that Stein probably added the thirteenth section (pp. 314–330), or even the last few pages, significantly later, after Allied airplanes could be heard overhead.

Wishful thinking and a faith in her book of prophecies encouraged Stein's optimism even before there was any basis for it. Predicting that news of the war's end would be announced in huge typescript, that she and Alice would celebrate the end of the war with cake (which they eventually do), and (incorrectly) that Angel Harper would die before he was fifty-five (Hitler had turned fifty-six ten days before killing himself) are all easy inventions. *Mrs. Reynolds* has a character who "conspires" and is a "deserter," but "the first units of the *maquis* were established in the last two to three months of 1942 . . . and composed of refugees or Jews sought by the authorities, deserters from Vichy youth camps, and workers escaping the *Relève*" (Kedward, *Resistance*, 233). It's less likely she foresaw Mr. and Mrs. Reynolds' joy in response to the sound of planes flying overhead (*Mrs. Reynolds*, 328), but since this is five paragraphs from the end of the novel, it could have been tacked on long after the bulk of the novel was written.

John Whittier-Ferguson convincingly argues that *Mrs. Reynolds* represents the struggle of trying to live as a human mind in time, especially a time of war: "The human mind may seem liberating" when we are reading *The Geographical History of America*, for example, but *Mrs. Reynolds* reveals "a state of mind that is historical in spite of itself" (Whittier-Ferguson, 129). While Whittier-Ferguson offers a convincing and impressive reading of *Mrs. Reynolds*, he ignores the pervasive conversations, only mentioning one in which Mrs. Reynolds is talking to herself (128). In another perceptive reading of *Mrs. Reynolds*, Phoebe Stein Davis emphasizes narrative storytelling over interaction when she alludes to conversation.

3. Stein's letter to Francis Rose in 1946 (qtd. in Bridgman, 335), as well recent criticism (Van Dusen), refers to Stein's life in "occupied" France, but Stein and Toklas spent the war in Bilignin and Culoz, which are in southeastern France and not part of the zone originally officially occupied by the Germans. Considering the nature of the Vichy government, that this part of France was occupied by the Italians in 1942, and that all France was occupied after November 1942, most writers still refer to this area as "occupied France" (Jones, 272; Kedward, *Resistance*, v). Nazi soldiers did crowd Belley after the May 1940 blitzkrieg, but once the armistice was signed in late June, people again began showing lights in the evening and French conscripts came home from their eight months in the trenches at the Maginot Line (Jones, 205, 264; Brinnin, 368–69). In Vichy France, the authorities required that all residents be listed—the mayor of Belley kept Stein and Toklas off that list, ostensibly because they were "obviously too old for life in a concentration camp" (Sevareid, 459) and perhaps because Faÿ told the prefect to keep them safe—curfews were enforced, and at least once, at the very end of the war, German soldiers quartered themselves in Stein and Toklas's home and the women hid upstairs for fear their American accents would be recognized (Stein, *Wars*, 211). A Resistance newspaper describes life in the "free zone" as of January 1942 (and uses the characteristic "they" to describe the enemy): "Here they have not dared to use fire and sword. Here they destroy underhandedly, by means of cold, sickness, and privations." The paper reports that the prisons are crowded with veterans, workers, intellectuals, girls who get caught distributing leaflets, and so on (see Liebling, 192).

4. Whittier-Ferguson explains the false positive connotations of the name as one of Stein's most audacious experiments with the possibility of disconnecting words and things, language and history. To change "Adolf" to "Angel" is not simply to make a semantic

equation but, as we experience a dissonance in the rechristening, to expose our presuppositions about how names should fit the world. That is, Stein presents "Adolf" and "Angel," without commentary, as different, though similar, collections of letters. Our desire for a semantic order that corresponds to an ethical one causes us to read the substitution as a grotesque and deliberate mismatching, an affront to our deepest sense of order.

Whittier-Ferguson perceptively adds, however: "But then, nothing adds up with Angel Harper" (126).

5. The pronoun referring to Mr. Reynolds is not usually capitalized. This capitalization is probably a misprint, and I have not interpreted it as a purposeful choice of Stein's.

6. Or are the two women laughing because they have together just quoted a familiar radio refrain? "well well, as the Englishman who does the propaganda in English from Berlin always says, well well" (Stein, *Wars*, 226). Here I emphasize that silence can communicate and even resist authority, but silence can also be considered "the real crime against humanity," which is what Nadezhda Mandelstam calls it in *Hope against Hope* (43). Writing of her experiences in Stalinist Russia, Mandelstam recalls: "After 1937 people stopped meeting each other altogether, and the secret police were thus well on the way to achieving their ultimate objective. Apart from assuring a constant flow of information, they had isolated people from each other" (34). Several of Stein's readers—Thornton Wilder and Janet Malcolm among them—see Stein's silence in this light. They think that she should have been more up-front about being Jewish, and that she should have confronted Faÿ on his Nazi collaboration and anti-Semitism. But no one reading *Mrs. Reynolds* sensibly can doubt Stein's detestation of the Nazi regime.

7. For a different reading, see Davis, who argues that "Stein undercuts the notion that the battlefields are the only sites of death during war" (583).

8. This statement is in third person, but it imitates Mr. Reynolds's speech patterns. Here Stein emulates Jane Austen's technique of indirect discourse, and she imitates Austen's (related) tendency to write dialogue that is "an exercise in noncommunication" (Brown, 169). Stein suggested to Ernest Hemingway that he read Austen to learn how to represent conversation in writing (Wagner-Martin, 170–71), and he best demonstrates what he learned about subtlety and miscommunication in "Hills Like White Elephants."

9. Stein's regular twelve-kilometer walk "gave her opportunities both to barter for food and to exchange news" (Wagner-Martin, 239). Later in the war, barricades made the walk seventeen kilometers. See Wagner-Martin, 242–43, for more on food shortages.

10. Stein loves questions, but people who see themselves as authorities avoid them. Mandelstam notes similar resistance to polite social forms by the policemen in Stalinist Russia (40, 53).

11. Bridgman (316–18) and Wagner-Martin (246–47) each discuss Stein's interest in Pétain. Bridgman describes Stein's introduction to Pétain's speeches but says it was Toklas who loved Pétain. Wagner-Martin says that the introduction is "vapid," that Stein was commissioned to do it, that Stein saw Pétain as her personal savior, and that Pétain really did help keep the worst from happening in France, multiple claims that seem to work against each other. The best extended argument against Van Dusen is Whittier-Ferguson's, which deals specifically with Stein's interest in Pétain's speeches (118–21), more generally with the difficulty of understanding an author "at odds" with our contemporary scholarly interests and categories (144), and even more generally with the problem of "foreshadowed history"—our tendency to assume that Stein knew what we know now (141). Here, Whittier-Ferguson is alluding to Michael André Bernstein, "Foregone Conclusions: Narrating the Fate of Austro-German-Jewry," *Modernism/Modernity* 1.1 [1994]: 57–79.

12. H. R. Kedward, author of two volumes on the French Resistance, writes that his sources are mainly "memoirs, the Resistance Press, and oral testimony from Resisters themselves." He adds that "there are few, if any, 'official' documents to underpin a study of this kind. In fact, there are very few documents for any kind of history of French Resistance," because "it was clearly in the nature of Resistance activity to avoid all paper records which might fall into the wrong hands" (*Resistance*, vi).

13. For the historical version of maquis techniques and the July 1944 German attack on the maquis in Stein's area of Ain, see Kedward, *In Search of*, 50, 178–79.

14. Stein comments:

> It is funny the different nations begin their broadcasting I wish I knew more languages so that I could know how each one of them does it. The English always begin with here is London, or the B. B. C. home service, or the over seas service, always part of a pleasant home life, of supreme importance to any Englishman or any Englishwoman. The Americans say with poetry and fire, this is the voice of America, and then with modesty and good neighborliness, one of the United Nations, it is the voice of America speaking to you across the Atlantic. Then the Frenchman, say *Frenchmen speaking to Frenchmen*, they always begin like that, and the Belgians are simple and direct, they just announce, radio Belge, and the national anthem, and the Frenchman also say, Honor and Country, and the Swiss so politely say, the studio of Geneva, at the instant of the broadcasting station of Berne will give you the latest news, and Italy says live Mussolini live Italy, and they make a bird noise and then they start, and Germany starts like this, *Germany calling, Germany calling*, in the last war, I said that the camouflage was the distinctive characteristic of each country, each nation stamped itself upon its camouflage, but in this war it is the heading of the broadcast that makes national life so complete and determined. (*Wars*, 155–56; my italics).

Notice that the French radio announcer alludes to speaker and listener, while the German radio announcement leaves out the listener and mentions the speaker (or speaking nation) twice.

15. In his book *Propaganda*, Jacques Ellul writes: "Propaganda must be total" (9). "It furnishes [people] with a complete system for explaining the world"; "it must produce quasi-unanimity, and the opposing faction must become negligible, or in any case cease to be vocal" (11). Competing propaganda on stations that all come from the same radio set precludes its effectiveness.

Mandelstam describes the effects of total propaganda: "Propaganda for historical determinism had deprived us of our will and the power to make our own judgments. We laughed in the faces of the doubters, and ourselves furthered the work of the daily press by repeating its sacramental phrases, by spreading rumors about each new round of arrests ('that's what passive resistance leads to!') and finding excuses for the existing state of affairs" (44).

16. The National Endowment for the Humanities sponsored "A National Conversation on American Pluralism and Identity" from 1994 to 1997. The NEH funded 135 grants totaling $6.26 million to enable forums, conversations, and writing projects, as well as research projects and exhibitions (Hackney, *One America*, 131–62). The goals of the conversations included "transform[ing] into a productive discussion [on American identity] what had already become an ill-tempered argument among scholars" in "drive-by debates" (4), and one participant said: "Too many of our public spaces—think of shopping malls—bring us

together only as consumers, not as citizens" (7). Stein's suggestion is earlier, more open, and much less expensive, and its informality makes it impossible for participants to lose sight of the ultimate goal: "deliberat[ing] with each other," as Amy Gutman puts it (in ibid., 184, 183) "because no single person's point of view contains all the insights on these issues." Clearly, conversation promises no complete solutions, but, as Ellis Close writes, it is important to "keep the conversation going" (qtd. in Hackney, 6, from *Color Blind: Seeing beyond Race in a Race-Obsessed World* [New York: HarperCollins, 1997], 240).

Sheldon Hackney, then chair of the National Endowment for the Humanities and former president of the University of Pennsylvania, writes:

> The challenge of our time is to revitalize our civic life in order to realize a new birth of freedom. All of our people . . . have a responsibility to examine and discuss what unites us as a country, what we share as common American values in a nation composed of so many divergent groups and beliefs. . . .
>
> The conversation that I envision will not be easy. [As Cornel West writes:] ". . . Even the very art of public conversation—the precious activity of communicating with fellow citizens in a spirit of mutual respect and civility—appears to fade amid the backdrop of name-calling and finger-pointing in flat sound bites."
>
> . . . What I envision is a national conversation open to all Americans, a conversation in which all voices need to be heard . . . .
>
> This will be a risky enterprise, because the NEH comes only with questions—not answers. The outcome is therefore unpredictable, contingent as it is on the course of the discussion and on what we learn from each other as we talk. ("National Conversation")

17. Gabriel Tarde argued that "personal relationships" might at least "temp[er] the effects of broader structural modifications" (T. Clark, 57).

18. "Absolute Powerpoint" in the *New Yorker* (28 May 2001) reminds us that this problem is still with us and has grown. "Before there were presentations, there were conversations," and not only did people get to know each other in well-lighted rooms, they also got to ad lib when they had a sudden fresh idea (Parker, 76, 87). As language and experience may limit our perceptions, PowerPoint software seems to limit our ideas and expression. One Stanford professor admitted that he removed a book from his syllabus because he "'couldn't figure out how to PowerPoint it'" (87). Relatedly, a journalist at one of Stein's lectures reports that she "defied our system of note-taking" (Winsten).

19. Jacques Ellul discusses the power of facts in *Propaganda*: "Modern man worships 'facts'—that is, he accepts 'facts' as the ultimate reality. . . . He believes that facts in themselves provide evidence and proof" (xv). Herbert Marcuse also laments our faith in facts: "The range of judgment is confined within a context of facts which excludes judging the context in which the facts are made, man-made, and in which their meaning, function, and development are determined" (115–16).

20. Stein uses the now recognized to be highly objectionable term "niggers." As a result, Donald Paul's statement sounds like an alarmist call for change: If white Americans don't get their act together and prevent what seems the inevitable downfall of all industrial nations, then black Americans will rule. But Stein may have meant it differently. Elsewhere, the GIs agree that it's a relief to be in Europe, where they don't feel called upon to assert their white privilege. They praise the agricultural economy of the South because it would have nicely

balanced the industrialism of the North, if only the slaveholders had peacefully accepted the end of slavery with a buyout instead of fighting the Civil War. And in this book that promotes pioneering, one character says, possibly admiringly, "the only pioneering there is in America these days is done by the Negroes" (*Brewsie*, 65).

21. For a discussion of Stein's understanding of "fathering" in *Mrs. Reynolds*, see Berry, chapter 5.

22. The kind of conformity Stein writes against was certainly evident much earlier than World War II, but she may see her opportunity to do something about it in 1946, now that more people have noticed the way individual rights were given up in order to fight Fascism in that war. Martha Banta's *Taylored Lives* discusses the push for uniformity in all aspects of life between the mid-nineteenth century and the 1930s, tracing the relationship between the efficiency of assembly-line production and human conformity. Julie Abraham makes the point that Stein has long seen herself as one of the "Brother Singulars," the "queer people" who have "vital singularity," and that anyone tracing Stein's idea of an American must take into account her experience as a lesbian (Abraham, 511, quoting phrases from *Making of Americans*, 21).

23. Americans now get weekends off (or did, until overtime became the way to save on worker training and benefits costs), many Americans get substantial vacations, and early retirement is common. What we buy through the "installment plan" and other credit (the products, as well as their accompanying desires and accumulations), however, has also cut into the time we spend thinking. If we have to have a motocross bike, an all-terrain vehicle, and a boat, then we have to spend time caring for those "recreational" vehicles and driving the six hours each way to trails or a desert or a lake just to use them. Ownership, the requisite desire in a "healthy" capitalist industrial society, itself takes time away from our thinking. The very popularity of these activities demonstrates our loss of individualism. That we have to buy things in order to ride them also contrasts with the pastime of making things that can serve as expressions of our individuality—meals, quilts, furniture, clothing, even cars (my dad built his first one).

24. World War I "exposed the political naivete at the heart of pragmatism's tough-minded rhetoric" to radical essayist Randolph Bourne, who "contended that [it was necessary to] . . . reconstruct pragmatism on a new basis—one that accepts 'inexorable' capitalist efficiency rather than free will and choice as the fundamental given of modernity" (qtd. in Posnock, 257, citing Bourne, 322). Bourne makes the case that pragmatist thinkers (liberal realists) are wrong in believing that any war could be "democratic and antiseptic" or controlled to reach only toward ideal outcomes. He concludes: "The pacifists opposed the war because they knew this was an illusion, and because of the myriad hurts they knew war would do the promise of democracy at home. For once the babes and sucklings seem to have been wiser than the children of light" (324). Stein did not see capitalism as the end of pragmatism—possibly because for most of her life she is interested in individualism more for the sake of the individual than for its effects on the larger society—but neither do Marcuse or Rorty or any of the later philosophers who understand human will as an important agent in change. As I suggest at the very end of this book, however, Stein may have seen the atomic bomb as a snag to some of her views.

25. For a very different opinion on Stein's relationship to mass production, see Ann Douglas's *Terrible Honesty*; for example: "Stein loved the effortlessness and abundance created by the new technology of consumer-oriented mass production and saw her own art as its ally and analogue" (127).

26. The Germans were taught to follow orders without thinking: "'We must distrust the intelligence and the conscience,' Hitler counseled, 'and must place our trust in our instincts. We have to regain a new simplicity,'" John Wesley Young reports (68). When defining Hitler's "ideal Nazi," Young writes "that Hitler neglected mentioning mental dexterity as an indispensable trait," and "it is fair to say, and amply borne out by the record, that he preferred followers unaccustomed to doing their own thinking" (67). To get people to react to orders instinctively, the Nazis "form a language of assent and domination [yes and no] whose essential characteristic is its univocacy: for every politically significant word, one meaning" (31). Young cites George Orwell's essay on *Gulliver's Travels*: "One of the aims of totalitarianism is not merely to make sure that people will think the right thoughts, but actually to make them *less conscious*" (30; Orwell, "Politics vs. Literature: An Examination of *Gulliver's Travels*," 291).

Stein is not wrong to see a resemblance to business practices of the time. Banta, citing J. David Houser's 1927 report *What the Employer Thinks: Executives' Attitudes Toward Employees*, writes: "Businessmen shaving the line between workaday brutality and lofty social reforms catch at phrases that are 'clearly substitutes for thought'—phrases 'charged with so much emotion that they resemble shibboleths.'" Houser cites phrases such as "management's responsibility," "the desire to be fair," "employees' ingratitude," "decent treatment," and "it pays in dollars and cents" as examples of how "business uses [words] to fight 'free from any intellectual process'" (Banta, 82–83).

27. Herbert Marcuse says something similar in *One-Dimensional Man*. He criticizes polls for the limited range of acceptable response: Republican, Democrat, and (this poll allowed a third choice) "ambivalent." He writes: "The established parties themselves, their policies, and their machinations are not questioned, nor is the actual difference between them questioned as far as the vital issues are concerned (those of atomic policy and total preparedness), questions which seem essential for the assessment of the democratic processes, unless the analysis operates with a concept of democracy which merely assembles the features of the *established form* of democracy" (118; his italics).

28. Stein criticized Hemingway as being a bit "Rotarian," and Banta reads this as a comment on Hemingway's "tales of male bonding in times of war," which, like "business fiction narratives," emphasized "team-work" and "the 'old spirit' of 'solidarity'" (Banta, 13).

29. Joseph Lane's speech is described very differently from Angel Harper's: "Joseph Lane was leading a regular life"; "he just said how do you do and very well I thank you and led an ordinary life just like that." Angel Harper says, "leave it to me" (*Mrs. Reynolds*, 309).

30. In this sense, "it *is* doubtful whether he was ever a boy." What Stein describes of Angel Harper's childhood does not suggest that he was ever a comfortable entity or creatively imaginative. Stein's descriptions of moments in Angel Harper's life "combine to produce a remarkably complex and vivid impression of a fearful, isolated, and vulnerable child behind the facade of the powerful dictator" (Berry, 130).

31. This suggestion of mass action may also be provoked by the success of women's protests in Vichy France from winter 1941 through spring 1942. Several demonstrations by "housewives" and mothers, particularly one held on *la Fête des mères* (Mother's Day), succeeded in improving food rations—an extra three eggs and three hundred grams of dried vegetables for every ration card (Kedward, *Resistance*, 221–23). With all the fathering going on in centers of power, these demonstrations might have emphasized the differences between mothering and fathering in Stein's mind.

32. Environmentalist Murray Bookchin also asks for a different kind of answer. He argues for an ecological position that does not "tak[e] the present social order for granted"; "it is the prevailing order that sets the terms of any 'compromise' or 'trade-off,' just like the rules of a chess game and the grid of a chess board determine in advance what the players can do—not the dictates of reason and morality." Further: "To 'play by the rules' of the environmental game means that the natural world, including oppressed people, always loses something piece by piece until everything is lost in the end." He argues that capitalism and socialism both "devour the natural world," only one is more "systematic" than the other (15). A woman Stein spoke with during World War II expressed a similar sentiment about adapting to the status quo: "well now as we have all made all our arrangements to live in a state of war I suppose the war will go on" (Stein, *Wars*, 140).

33. Mike LeFevre, a steelworker interviewed by Studs Terkel in the late sixties or early seventies, asks: "What do you think would happen in this country if, for one year, they experimented and gave everybody a twenty-hour week? How do they know that the guy who digs [George] Wallace today doesn't try to resurrect Hitler tomorrow? Or the guy who is mildly disturbed at pollution doesn't decide to go to General Motors and shit on the guy's desk? You can become a fanatic if you had the time. The whole thing is time. . . . Time, that's the important thing" (Terkel, xxxiv).

34. As Roland Barthes writes: "Denotation is not the first meaning, but pretends to be so; under this illusion, it is ultimately no more than the *last* of the connotations (the one which seems both to establish and to close the reading)" (9).

35. This anarchic isolationism that I describe is a straw man, but one that gets propped up quite often in American political arguments. Democrats want the government to imitate and sustain interpersonal relations; Republicans are afraid the government might replace and thereby undermine interpersonal relations. Both want to prevent anarchy, and each sees the other side as promoting or at least enabling it.

36. Marcuse cites Bridgeman, 31. In *Halfway to Revolution: Investigation and Crisis in the Work of Henry Adams, William James, and Gertrude Stein*, Bush denounces this operationalism in literary criticism: "Anglo-American critics tend to market 'continental' philosophers in such a way as to neutralize their efforts by turning their thought into sets of techniques" (5). Stein criticizes a kind of operationalism when she discusses newspaper writing: "The yellow press [has] become stereotyped having become a way of doing a machinery that all the schools of journalism teach and as soon as anybody can teach it it is a way of doing a thing and is not the thing itself and it begins to move backward" ("American Newspapers," 93).

37. DeKoven, who in *Different Language* quotes part of this passage from Barthes, also cites it in reference to Stein's writing, her point being that Stein's insistent writing is a success when, as Stein puts it in *The Making of Americans* (540), the words have "'many meanings many ways of being used to make different meanings to every one'":

> Stein's responsibility is to make this core of meaning capable of evoking and supporting private layers of association. . . . The writing in this style fails precisely when it has no underpinning or core meaning, when it gives itself up completely to repetition of words that have "really existing being" only for Stein. Such writing would deny the reader not only the possibility of active, imaginative participation in the creation of the text, but of reading it at all. (DeKoven, *Different Language*, 57)

I mostly agree with DeKoven. But my understanding of the situation leaves less room for Stein's failure and more room for failure on her readers' side of the interaction. If we learn to be writerly, we will understand greater meaning in our reading of Stein, as well as in the orally and visually transmitted texts of everyday life, no matter how personal or functional their intent.

38. Present-day computerized hypertexts present themselves as "writerly" in that the reader (of the screen) is making choices: "readers choose among pathways within plots that form a mosaic" (Swerdlow, 9). But these choices are limited. A *National Geographic* article reports that "information technologies, for all the attention they receive, lag far behind the power of the human brain. Researchers estimate that the normal brain has a quadrillion connections between its nerve cells, more than all the phone calls made in the U.S. in the past decade," and that "no hypertext novel can achieve what the brain does naturally. . . . Readers react to . . . [a passage from Dostoyevsky] in different ways, creating their own combinations of texture, mood, detail, and emotion" (Swerdlow, 9). In short, our brains can turn any text into a hypertext more effectively than can computer programs—and without the limitations of technology and other people's imaginations. Neural connections, like footnotes, are a hypertext technology that far predates computers.

39. Adamant adherents of a political party may be so offensive that they train their brethren to join the opposing party. In "How Nazis are Made," Ingo Hasselback tells the story of how his childhood in Communist East Berlin prepared him to become a neo-Nazi. His parents' work "to establish the first German 'anti-Fascist' state . . . created . . . a state in which there was nothing to strive for but conformity" (39). His hatred of anti-Fascism led him straight to Fascism; later, seeing himself "rattling on about the Jews," *saying things he didn't know from his own experience,* he realized he "needed to explore some hard questions" and *come up with answers to them on his own* (53). To borrow from "Won't Get Fooled Again," by The Who's Pete Townshend, Hasselback's "new boss" (neo-Nazism) was just like his "old boss" (Communism), and he finally became an entrepreneur, thinking his own thoughts

40. Stein had long been interested in saying and seeing, and even in rephrasing this line from "The Star-Spangled Banner." Melanctha's father "tried to make her say a thing she did not know" (*Three Lives*, 95), and later Melanctha says to Jeff: "I can't say as I see just what you mean," and "I certainly don't just see what you mean by what you say" (120). F. Scott Fitzgerald seems to draw on the distinction between real experience and abstractions in *Tender is the Night*, when he writes of a girl who waves her underwear at some sailors: "Oh, say can you see the tender color of remembered flesh?—while at the stern of the battleship arose in rivalry the Star-Spangled Banner" (297).

CONCLUSIONS

1. See Winston, 117; Van Vechten, "How Many Acts," xii; and Bridgman, 341–45. Toklas, however, insisted to Van Vechten that Stein "didn't at all feel [Susan B.] was she herself," although Stein had respected Anthony for her "heroi[sm]" (Van Vechten, "How Many Acts," xiin5).

2. Martin cites Sutherland, 167n57.

3. Winston understands the character Indiana Elliot as a "less obvious" "alter-ego" for Stein, one "who, in the course of the opera, moves from a young ingenue awed by male authority to assertive (albeit disillusioned) married woman, committed to the suffragist cause" (118). Winston makes a convincing but complicated claim for the relationship between

"Indiana Elliot" and Stein's mentors George Eliot (Marian Evans), Currer Bell (Charlotte Brontë), and George Sand (Aurore Dupin).

4. The passage in 1866 of the Fourteenth Amendment, which extended suffrage to all men, was the biggest blow. The very men who had been allies with women's suffrage—men such as Frederick Douglass, Horace Greeley, Wendell Phillips, George W. Curtis, Henry Ward Beecher, Theodore Tilton, Aaron Powell, and Gerrit Smith (Dorr, 198)—jumped ship, told women to be patient, and got the word "male" put in the Constitution for the first time (185–99). Stein's Susan B. can't get over the way her most powerful efforts went so wrong.

5. Dorr gives a great example of one man who could easily have reacted with mixedness if he hadn't so reactively retreated to a conservative, antisuffrage position. As editor of the *New York Tribune*, Horace Greeley was an early supporter of Anthony, but when he was chair of the committee on suffrage at the New York Constitutional Convention, he was antagonistic to the cause. He is said to have "drawled" in his "acid voice" that "the ballot and the bullet go together. If you vote are you also prepared to fight?" "Certainly, Mr. Greeley," Anthony answered, "Just as you fought in the late war—at the point of a goose-quill." Greeley, an old friend of Anthony, insisted "that the best women he knew did not want to vote"; at that, a suffrage advocate pointed out that he had a petition attesting to the contrary signed by Mrs. Horace Greeley. His pride hurt, Greeley then remained "a life enemy of the women" (189–90). He could have been divided—by personal attachments, by changing circumstances, et cetera—but he retreated to the safe position.

6. Van Vechten, "How Many Acts," xvn9, citing Stein's notes for the program of the Pasadena production of *In Savoy*. There Stein writes of "the divided families, the bitterness, the quarrels and sometimes the denunciations, and yet the natural necessity of their all continuing to live their daily life together, because after all that was all the life they had, besides they were after all the same family or their neighbors, and in the country neighbors are neighbors." She wanted the audience "to realize that French families were divided as our American families were divided in our Civil War and even in our Revolutionary War, and it is complicated and simple, and I hope it will make you feel the French as they really were during the long years of the occupation" (qtd in Van Vechten, xvn9). But this complexity makes Stein look bad in the eyes of her critics. For example, maintaining her friendships with neighbors who were collaborators, and especially with Bernard Faÿ, suggests an unbecoming passivity during World War II. Zofia P. Lesinska asserts that "Stein's dramatization of the complexity of the actual is unparalleled," but that "it is difficult to condone Stein's decision to live comfortably in the South of France under the auspices of Fäy, a Vichyite and a resolute anti-Semite" (40, 25). In short, Lesinska can "defend Stein's war autobiographies as historically and artistically compelling," but like Stein's "early critics and like Van Dusen," she finds "Stein's wartime personal and political choices to be quite objectionable" (24–25). Stein might appreciate the very dividedness of this evaluation, although Lesinka's taking friendship, cordiality, the desire to survive, and the continuation of one's "daily life" (as much as that was possible) as "loyalty to the collaborationist government" is going too far (26). (And trying to survive the winters in the foothills of the Alps is much different from enjoying the war along the Riviera, which is what "the South of France" implies.)

7. Winston (125) points out that Elizabeth Cady Stanton spoke words very similar to these in "The Solitude of Self," her 1892 farewell address to the National Woman Suffrage Association.

8. Of course, constitutional amendments require votes in Congress, and the federal

amendment wasn't passed until 1919, thirteen years after Anthony's death and seventy-two years after the Seneca Falls Convention (Dorr, 339–43, 358).

9. Borrowing from a somewhat different field—R. Keith Sawyer's study of improvisational drama, in which Sawyer uses methods of conversation analysis (which describes "how bottom-up processes lead to emergent macro-structure") augmented by a greater interest in "the 'top-down' processes of social causation" (62)—I note that another investigator has seen conversations grow their own attributes. Sawyer writes that "an analytically distinct entity emerges from collective action and then has causal power over individual action" (57), but he calls this thing that arises from his "theory of collaborative emergence" the "frame" for the conversation rather than a separate causal subjectivity (45). Sawyer also posits that "a properly theorized conceptualization" of "the realm of the emergent intersubjective frame as social fact" might allow us "empirically to investigate—to 'see'—creativity" in process (viii). It might be important to note that in improvisational drama, the participants must quickly negotiate a frame for their interaction (Are we children? Are you a storekeeper and am I a customer? etc.). That's one kind of creativity, but another kind occurs in "real" interactional conversations.

10. See Yaeger, Irigaray, and Kristeva. Elizabeth Gross's chapter "The Body of Signification" also helped me think about the relationship between abjection and the feminine sublime.

11. Yaeger here quotes McCarthy, viii.

BIBLIOGRAPHY

PRIMARY WORKS

Stein, Gertrude. "An American and France." In *What Are Masterpieces*, 59–70. 1940. New York: Pitman, 1970.

———. "American Newspapers." 1935. In *How Writing Is Written*, ed. Robert Bartlett Haas, 89–93. Santa Barbara: Black Sparrow, 1977.

———. "And Now." 1934. In *How Writing Is Written*, ed. Robert Bartlett Haas, 63–66. Santa Barbara: Black Sparrow, 1977.

———. *The Autobiography of Alice B. Toklas*. 1933. New York: Vintage, 1961.

———. *Bee Time Vine and Other Pieces*. Preface and notes by Virgil Thomson. New Haven: Yale UP, 1953.

———. *The Blue Swallows*. Chicago: U of Chicago P; 1967, 13.

———. *Brewsie and Willie*. 1946. London: Brilliance, 1988.

———. "The Capital and Capitals of the United States of America." 1935. In *How Writing Is Written*, ed. Robert Bartlett Haas, 73–76. Santa Barbara: Black Sparrow, 1977.

———. "A Circular Play/A Play in Circles." In *A Stein Reader*, ed. Ulla E. Dydo, 326–42. Evanston, Ill.: Northwestern UP, 1993.

———. "Composition as Explanation." 1926. In *Selected Writings of Gertrude Stein*. Edited by Carl Van Vechten, 511–23. New York: Vintage Books, 1952

———. *Everybody's Autobiography*. 1937. New York: Cooper Square, 1971.

———. *Four in America*. Introduction by Thornton Wilder. New Haven: Yale, 1947.

———. *The Geographical History of America, or The Relation of Human Nature to the Human Mind*. 1936. Introduction by William H. Gass. Baltimore: Johns Hopkins UP, 1995.

———. *Geography and Plays*. 1922. Intro. Cyrena N. Pondrom. Madison: U of Wisconsin P, 1993.

———. "I Came and Here I Am." 1936. In *How Writing Is Written*, ed. Robert Bartlett Haas, 67–72. Los Angeles: Black Sparrow, 1977.

———. *Ida*. 1941. In *Gertrude Stein: Writings, 1932–1946*, 609–704. New York: Library of America, 1998.

———. *In Savoy, or "Yes" Is for Yes for a Very Young Man*. London: Pushkin, 1946.

———. *Last Operas and Plays*. Edited by Carl Van Vechten. New York: Rinehart, 1949.

———. *Lectures in America*. 1935. Boston: Beacon, 1957.

———. "Lifting Belly." In Stein, *Bee Time Vine*, 61–115.

———. "A Long Gay Book." In *Matisse Picasso and Gertrude Stein*. Barton: Something Else, 1972.

———. *The Making of Americans Being a History of a Family's Progress*. 1925. New York: Something Else, 1966.

———. "Matisse." 1912. In *Gertrude Stein: Writings, 1903–1932*, 278–81. New York: Library of America, 1998.

———. *The Mother of Us All.* 1949. In *Gertrude Stein: Writings, 1932–1946*, 779–819. New York: Library of America, 1998.

———. *Mrs. Reynolds.* 1952. Los Angeles: Sun and Moon, 1980.

———. "My Debt to Books." *Books Abroad: An International Quarterly of Comment on Foreign Books* 13.3 (summer 1939): 307–8.

———. *Narration: Four Lectures by Gertrude Stein.* Introduction by Thornton Wilder. Chicago: U of Chicago P, 1935.

———. *A Novel of Thank You.* 1958. Introduction by Steven Meyer. Normal, Ill.: Dalkey, 1994.

———. "Off We All Went to See Germany." In *How Writing Is Written*, ed. Robert Bartlett Haas, 135–41. Santa Barbara: Black Sparrow, 1977. Originally published in *Life*, August 6, 1945.

———. *Paris France.* 1940. New York: Liveright, 1970.

———. *Painted Lace and Other Pieces [1914–1937].* New Haven: Yale UP, 1955.

———. "Picasso." 1938. In *Gertrude Stein: Writings, 1932–1946*, 495–533. New York: Library of America, 1998.

———. "Portraits and Repetition." 1930. In *Gertrude Stein: Writings and Lectures, 1909–1945*, ed. Patricia Meyerowitz, 99–124. Baltimore: Penguin, 1974.

———. "Q.E.D." In *Gertrude Stein: Writings, 1903–1932*, 1–63. New York: Library of America, 1998.

———. "Reflection on the Atomic Bomb." 1947. In *Gertrude Stein: Writings, 1932–1946*, ed. Catharine R. Stimpson and Harriet Chessman, 823. New York: Library of America, 1998.

———. *A Stein Reader.* Edited by Ulla Dydo. Evanston, Ill.: Northwestern UP, 1993.

———. *Tender Buttons.* 1914. Los Angeles: Sun and Moon, n.d.

———. *Three Lives.* 1909. New York: Vintage, 1936.

———. "Two: Gertrude Stein and Her Brother (1910–1912)." In *Two: Gertrude Stein and Her Brother and Other Early Portraits (1908–1912)*, 1–142. Foreword by Janet Flanner. New Haven: Yale UP, 1951.

———. *A Village Are You Ready Not Yet: A Play in Four Acts.* Paris: Galerie Simon, 1928.

———. *Wars I Have Seen.* New York: Random House, 1945.

———. "What Are Master-pieces and Why Are There So Few of Them." 1940. In *Gertrude Stein: Writings and Lectures, 1911–1945*, ed. Patricia Meyerowitz, 148–56. Baltimore: Penguin, 1974.

———. "The Winner Loses: A Picture of Occupied France," *Atlantic*, November 1940, 571–83.

Stein, Gertrude, and Leon M. Solomons. *Motor Automatism.* New York: Phoenix Book Shop, 1969. Originally published as "Normal Motor Automatism" and "Cultivated Motor Automatism: A Study of Character in Its Relation to Attention," *Psychological Review*, September 1896 and May 1898.

SECONDARY WORKS

Books and Journal Articles

Abraham, Julie. "'We are Americans': Gertrude, *Brewsie and Willie.*" *Modern Fiction Studies* 42.3 (fall 1996): 508–27.

Adams, Henry. *The Education of Henry Adams.* 1918. Edited by Ernest Samuels. Boston: Houghton, 1973.

Aiken, Conrad. "We Ask for Bread." Review of *The Making of Americans,* by Gertrude Stein. In Curnutt, 37–40. Originally published in *New Republic,* 4 April 1934.

Aldrich, Mildred. "Confessions of a Breadwinner." Microfilm. Radcliffe College Archive, Schlesinger Library, Radcliffe Institute, Cambridge, Mass.

Alpers, Benjamin L. *Dictators, Democracy, and American Public Culture: Envisioning the Totalitarian Enemy, 1920s-1950s.* Chapel Hill: U of North Carolina P, 2003.

Auden, W. H. "In Memory of W. B. Yeats." In *The Norton Anthology of Modern Poetry,* ed. Richard Ellman and Robert O'Clair, 741–43. New York: Norton, 1973.

Bain, Alexander. *The Senses and the Intellect.* 1855. 4th ed. New York: D. Appleton, 1902.

Banta, Martha. *Taylored Lives: Narrative Productions in the Age of Taylor, Veblen, and Ford.* Chicago: U of Chicago P, 1993.

Barker, Lewellys F. *The Nervous System and Its Constituent Neurones.* New York: Appleton, 1899.

———. *Time and the Physician: The Autobiography of Lewellys F. Barker.* New York: Putnam, 1942.

Barthes, Roland. *S/Z.* Translated by Richard Miller. New York: Noonday, 1988.

Becker, Mary Lamberton. "Books for Young People." Review of *The World Is Round,* by Gertrude Stein. In Curnutt, 114–15. Originally published in *New York Herald-Tribune Books,* 24 September 1939.

Bellah, Robert N., Richard Madsen, William M. Sullivan, Ann Swidler, and Steven M. Tipton. *Habits of the Heart: Individualism and Commitment in American Life.* Berkeley: U of California P, 1996.

Berry, Ellen E. *Curved Thought and Textual Wandering: Gertrude Stein's Postmodernism.* Ann Arbor: U of Michigan P, 1992.

Blackmer, Corrine E. "Selling Taboo Subjects: The Literary Commerce of Gertrude Stein and Carl Van Vechten." In *Marketing Modernisms: Self-Promotion, Canonization, and Rereading,* ed. Kevin J. H. Dettmar and Stephen Watt. Ann Arbor: U of Michigan P, 1996.

Bloom, Harold. *The Anxiety of Influence: A Theory of Poetry.* London: Oxford UP, 1975.

Bookchin, Murray. *Remaking Society: Pathways to a Green Future.* Boston: South End, 1990.

Booth, Stephen. *King Lear, Macbeth, Indefinition, and Tragedy.* New Haven: Yale UP, 1983.

———. *Precious Nonsense: The Gettysburg Address, Ben Jonson's Epitaphs on His Children, and Twelfth Night.* Berkeley: U of California P, 1998.

Borrow, George. *Lavengro: The Scholar, the Gypsy, the Priest.* Oxford: Oxford UP, 1982.

Bourne, Randolph. *The Radical Will: Selected Writings, 1911–1918.* Compiled and edited by Olaf Hansen. New York: Urizen Books, 1977.

Bowers, Jane Palatini. *Gertrude Stein.* New York: St. Martin's, 1993.

Bridgeman, P. W. *The Logic of Modern Physics.* New York: Macmillan, 1928.

Bridgman, Richard. *Gertrude Stein in Pieces.* New York: Oxford UP, 1970.

Brinnin, John Malcolm. *The Third Rose: Gertrude Stein and Her World.* 1959. Reprint, Reading, Mass.: Addison-Wesley, 1987.

Bromfield, Louis. "Gertrude Stein, Experimenter with Words." Review of *The Autobiography of Alice B. Toklas,* by Gertrude Stein. In Curnutt. 63–66. Originally published in *New York Herald-Tribune Books,* 3 September 1933.

Brooks, Van Wyck. *America's Coming-of-Age*. 1915. Reprint, New York: Octagon Books, 1975.

Brown, Lloyd W. *Bits of Ivory: Narrative Techniques in Jane Austen's Fiction*. Baton Rouge: Louisiana State UP, 1973.

Burke, Kenneth. "The Impartial Essence." In *Gertrude Stein Advanced: An Anthology of Criticism*, ed. Richard Kostelanetz, 187–89. Jefferson, N.C.: McFarland, 1990.

———. "Two Brands of Piety." Review of *Four Saints in Three Acts*, by Gertrude Stein. In Curnutt, 70–73. Originally published in *The Nation*, 28 February 1934.

Burns, Edward, ed. *The Letters of Gertrude Stein and Carl Van Vechten, 1913–1946*. 2 vols. New York: Columbia UP, 1986.

Burns, Edward M. and Villa E. Dydo, eds. with William Rice. *The Letters of Gertrude Stein and Thorton Wilder*. New Haven: Yale UP, 1996.

Bush, Clive. *Halfway to Revolution: Investigation and Crisis in the Work of Henry Adams, William James, and Gertrude Stein*. New Haven: Yale UP, 1991.

Camus, Albert. "Toward Dialogue" (30 November 1946). In *Between Hell and Reason: Essays from the Resistance Newspaper Combat, 1944–1947*. Selected and translated by Alexandre de Gramont, 137–40. Hanover: Wesleyan UP, 1991.

Canby, Henry Seidel. "Cheating at Solitaire." Review of *Portraits and Prayers*, by Gertrude Stein. In Curnutt, 79–82. Originally published in *Saturday Review of Literature*, 17 November 1934.

Cheepen, Christine. *The Predictability of Informal Conversation*. London: Pinter, 1988.

Chesney, Alan M. *The Johns Hopkins Hospital and the Johns Hopkins University School of Medicine*. 3 vols. Baltimore: Johns Hopkins UP, 1943.

Chessman, Harriet Scott. *The Public Is Invited to Dance: Representation, the Body, and Dialogue in Gertrude Stein*. Stanford: Stanford UP, 1989.

Clark, Herbert H., and Eve V. Clark. "Discourse Plans." In *Psychology and Language: An Introduction to Psycholinguistics*, 227–37. New York: Harcourt Brace Jovanovich, 1977.

Clark, Terry N. Introduction to *On Communication and Social Influence*, by Gabriel Tarde. Edited by Clark, 1–69. Chicago: U of Chicago P, 1969.

Connolly, William. "Taylor, Foucault, and Otherness." *Political Theory* 13 (August 1985).

Copeland, Carolyn Faunce. *Language and Time and Gertrude Stein*. Iowa City: U of Iowa P, 1975.

Cordasco, Francesco. *Dictionary of American Immigration History*. Metuchen, N.J.: Scarecrow, 1990.

Cowley, Malcolm. "Gertrude Stein, Writer or Word Scientist?" Review of *Selected Writings of Gertrude Stein*, by Gertrude Stein. In Curnutt, 147–50. Originally published in *New York Herald-Tribune Weekly Book Review*, 24 November 1946.

Crawford, John W. "Incitement to Riot." Review of *Geography and Plays*, by Gertrude Stein. In Curnutt, 26–27. Originally published in *New York Call*, 19 August 1923.

"Curious Fiction Study." Review of *Three Lives*, by Gertrude Stein. In Curnutt, 11–12. Originally published in *Chicago Record Herald*, 22 January 1910.

Curnutt, Kirk, ed. *The Critical Response to Gertrude Stein*. Westport, Conn.: Greenwood, 2000.

Davis, Phoebe Stein. "'Even Cake Gets to Have Another Meaning': History, Narrative, and 'Daily Living' in Gertrude Stein's World War II Writings." *Modern Fiction Studies* 44.3 (1998): 568–607.

de Beaugrande, Robert. "Discourse Analysis." In *The Johns Hopkins Guide to Literary Theory and Criticism*, ed. Michael Groden and Martin Kreiswirth, 207–10. Baltimore: Johns Hopkins UP, 1994.

DeKoven, Marianne. *A Different Language: Gertrude Stein's Experimental Writing*. Madison: U of Wisconsin P, 1983.

———. "Introduction: Transformations of Gertrude Stein." *Modern Fiction Studies* 42.3 (fall 1996): 469–83.

———. *Rich and Strange: Gender, History, Modernism*. Princeton: Princeton UP, 1991.

DeLillo, Don. *White Noise*. New York: Penguin, 1986.

Dewey, John. *Democracy and Education: An Introduction to the Philosophy of Education*. New York: Macmillan, 1916.

———. *Experience and Nature*. 1929. Reprint, New York: Dover, 1958.

Dodge, Mabel. "Speculations, or Post-Impressionism in Prose." In Curnutt, 151–54. Originally published in *Art and Decoration*, March 1913.

Dodge Luhan, Mabel, and Gertrude Stein. *A History of Having a Great Many Times Not Continued to Be Friends: Mabel Dodge and Gertrude Stein, 1911–1934*. Edited by Patricia R. Everett. Albuquerque: U of New Mexico P, 1996

Donne, John. "The Canonization." In *The Complete English Poems*, 47–48. London: Penguin, 1971.

Dorr, Rheta Childe. *Susan B. Anthony: The Woman Who Changed the Mind of a Nation*. New York: Frederick A. Stokes, 1928.

Dos Passos, John. *U.S.A.* New York: Modern Library, 1937.

Douglas, Ann. *Terrible Honesty: Mongrel Manhattan in the 1920s*. New York: Farrar, 1995.

Dryden, John. *Selected Poetry and Prose of John Dryden*. Edited by Earl Miner. New York: Modern Library, 1985.

Dubnick, Randa. *The Structure of Obscurity: Gertrude Stein, Language, and Cubism*. Urbana: U of Illinois P, 1984.

Duffy, John. *The Healers: The Rise of the Medical Establishment*. New York: McGraw-Hill, 1976.

Dydo, Ulla E., ed. "*Stanzas in Meditation*: The Other Biography." *Chicago Review* 35. 2 (1985): 4–20.

———. *A Stein Reader*. Evanston, Ill.: Northwestern UP, 1993.

Eagleson, Harvey. "Gertrude Stein: Method in Madness." *Sewanee Review Quarterly* 44.2 (April–June 1936): 164–77.

Eliot, T. S. "Charleston, Hey! Hey!" *Nation and Athenaeum* 29 (January 1927): 595.

———. "Tradition and the Individual Talent." In *Selected Prose of T. S. Eliot*. Edited by Frank Kermode. New York: Harcourt Brace Jovanovich, 1975.

Ellul, Jacques. *Propaganda: The Formation of Men's Attitudes*. Translated by Konrad Kellen and Jean Lerner. New York: Knopf, 1968.

Elson, Ruth Miller. *Guardians of Tradition: American Schoolbooks of the Nineteenth Century*. Lincoln: U of Nebraska P, 1964.

Faÿ, Bernard. "A Rose Is a Rose." Review of *The Autobiography of Alice B. Toklas*, by Gertrude Stein. In Curnutt, 55–63. Originally published in *Saturday Review of Literature*, 2 September 1933.

Fetterley, Judith. *The Resisting Reader: A Feminist Approach to American Fiction*. Bloomington: Indiana UP, 1978.

Fifer, Elizabeth. *Rescued Readings: A Reconstruction of Gertrude Stein's Difficult Texts.* Detroit: Wayne State UP, 1992.

Fitzgerald, F. Scott. *Tender Is the Night.* 1934. New York: Scribner's, 1995.

Flanner, Janet. "Frame for Some Portraits." Foreword to *Two: Gertrude Stein and Her Brother and Other Early Portraits, 1908–1912,* ix-xvii. New Haven: Yale UP, 1951.

Foucault, Michel. *The Order of Things: An Archaeology of the Human Sciences.* New York: Vintage, 1994.

Franken, Claudia. *Gertrude Stein: Writer and Thinker.* Münster: Lit. Verlag, 2000.

Frankenberg, Lloyd. "On First Meeting *Mrs. Reynolds.*" In *Mrs. Reynolds and Five Earlier Novelettes,* by Gertrude Stein, v-xii. New Haven: Yale UP, 1952.

Frieling, Kenneth. "The Becoming of Gertrude Stein's *The Making of Americans.*" In *The Twenties: Fiction, Poetry, Drama,* ed. Warren French, 157–70. DeLand, Fla: Everett/ Edwards, 1975.

Frost, Robert. *The Poetry of Robert Frost.* Edited by Edward Connery Lathem. New York: Holt, Rinehart and Winston, 1969.

"A Futurist Novel." Review of *Three Lives,* by Gertrude Stein. In Curnutt, 12–13. Originally published in *Philadelphia Public Ledger,* 10 April 1915.

"Gertrude Stein in Critical French Eyes." In Curnutt, 32–34. Originally published in *Literary Digest,* 6 February 1926.

Gilbert, Sandra M., and Susan Gubar. *The Madwoman in the Attic: The Woman Writer and the Nineteenth-Century Literary Imagination.* New Haven: Yale UP, 1984.

Goody, Jack. "Alternative Paths to Knowledge in Oral and Literate Cultures." In *Spoken and Written Language: Exploring Orality and Literacy,* ed. Deborah Tannen, 201–15. Norwood, N.J.: Ablex, 1982.

Gopnick, Adam. "Orange and White," Talk of the Town, *New Yorker,* 3 March 2003, 31.

Gordon, Bertram M., ed. *Historical Dictionary of World War II France: The Occupation, Vichy, and the Resistance, 1938–1946.* Westport, Conn.: Greenwood, 1998.

Gross, Elizabeth. "The Body of Signification." In *Abjection, Melancholia, and Love: The Work of Julia Kristeva,* ed. John Fletcher and Andrew Benjamin, 80–103. London: Routledge, 1990.

Hackney, Sheldon. *One America Indivisible: A National Conversation on American Pluralism and Identity.* National Endowment for the Humanities, n.d. (between 1997 and 2000).

———. "Toward a National Conversation." *Responsive Community* 4.3 (summer 1994): 9.

Harvey, A. McGehee, Gert H. Brieger, Susan L. Abrams, and Victor A. McKusick. *A Model of Its Kind: A Centennial History of Medicine at Johns Hopkins.* Baltimore: Johns Hopkins UP, 1989.

Hasselback, Ingo, and Tom Reiss. "How Nazis Are Made." *New Yorker,* 8 January 1996, 36–57.

Hemingway, Ernest. *The Sun Also Rises.* 1926. New York: Scribner's, 1970.

Heritage, John. *Garfinkel and Ethnomethodology.* Cambridge: Polity, 1984.

Hermans, Hubert J. M., and Harry J. G. Kempen. *The Dialogical Self: Meaning as Movement.* San Diego: Academic, 1993.

Hobhouse, Janet. *Everybody Who Was Anybody: A Biography of Gertrude Stein.* New York: Doubleday, 1975.

Hoffman, Michael J. *Critical Essays on Gertrude Stein.* Boston: Hall, 1986.

———. *The Development of Abstractionism in the Writings of Gertrude Stein.* Philadelphia: U of Pennsylvania P, 1965.

————. *Gertrude Stein*. Boston: Twayne, 1976.

————. "Gertrude Stein and William James." *The Personalist: An International Review of Philosophy, Religion, and Literature* 47.2 (spring 1966): 226–33.

Hubly, Erlene. "Gertrude Stein: "When this you see, remember me . . ." *North American Review*, September 1986, 65–74.

Irigaray, Luce. *This Sex Which Is Not One*. Translated by Catherine Porter. Ithaca, N.Y.: Cornell UP, 1985.

James, Henry. *The Portrait of a Lady*. 1881. New York: Signet, 1979.

James, William. "The Hidden Self." In *A William James Reader*, ed. Gay Wilson Allen, 90–108. Boston: Houghton, 1971.

————. *Pragmatism and Other Essays*. 1907, 1909, 1896. Reprint, New York: Washington Square, 1968.

————. *The Principles of Psychology*. 1890. 3 vols. Edited by Frederick H. Burkhardt. Cambridge: Harvard UP, 1981.

————. "Remarks on Spencer's Definition of Mind as Correspondent." In *A William James Reader*, ed. Gay Wilson Allen, 3–15. Boston: Houghton, 1971.

Jameson, Fredric. *Prison-house of Language: A Critical Account of Structuralism and Russian Formalism*. Princeton: Princeton UP, 1972.

Jay, Martin. *The Dialectical Imagination: A History of the Frankfurt School and the Institute of Social Research, 1923–1950*. Boston: Little, Brown, 1973.

Jones, Colin. *The Cambridge Illustrated History of France*. Cambridge: Cambridge UP, 1994.

Jonson, Ben. "Epigrams." In *Poems*, ed. Ian Donaldson, 1–84. London: Oxford UP, 1975.

Kadlec, David. *Mosaic Modernism: Anarchism, Pragmatism, Culture*. Baltimore: Johns Hopkins UP, 2000.

Kahnweiler, Daniel-Henry. Introduction to *Painted Lace and Other Pieces [1914–1937]*, by Gertrude Stein, ix–xviii. New Haven: Yale, 1955.

Kammen, Michael. *Mystic Chords of Memory: The Transformation of Tradition in American Culture*. New York: Vintage Books, 1993.

Katz, Leon. "The First Making of *The Making of Americans*: A Study Based on Her Notebooks and Early Versions of Her Novel (1902–1908)." Ph.D. diss., Columbia U, 1963.

————. "Weininger and *The Making of Americans*." *Twentieth Century Literature* 24.1 (spring 1978): 8–26.

Kaufman-Osborn, Timothy V. *Politics/Sense/Experience: A Pragmatic Inquiry into the Promise of Democracy*. Ithaca, N.Y.: Cornell UP, 1991.

Kedward, H. R. *In Search of the Maquis: Rural Resistance in Southern France, 1942–1944*. Oxford: Clarendon, 1993.

————. *Resistance in Vichy France: A Study of Ideas and Motivations in the Southern Zone, 1940–1942*. Oxford: Oxford UP, 1978.

Kennedy, Alan. *The Psychology of Reading*. London: Methuen, 1984.

Keyser, Antoine. "Introduction to Carl Wernicke." In *Reader in the History of Aphasia: From Gall to Geschwind*, ed. Paul Eling, 63–68. Amsterdam: John Benjamins, 1994.

Koestenbaum, Wayne. "Stein Is Nice." *Parnassus: Poetry in Review* 20.1–2 (1995): 297–319.

Kristeva, Julia. *Powers of Horror: An Essay on Abjection*. Translated by Leon S. Roudiez. New York: Columbia UP, 1982.

Krutch, Joseph Wood. "A Prepare for Saints." Review of *Four Saints in Three Acts*, by Gertrude Stein. In Curnutt, 74–76. Originally published in *The Nation*, 4 April 1934.

Lehman, David. *Signs of the Times: Deconstruction and the Fall of Paul de Man.* New York: Poseidon, 1992.

Leonhirth, William J. "William James and the Uncertain Universe." In *American Pragmatism and Communication Research*, ed. David K. Perry, 89–110. Mahwah, N.J.: Lawrence Erlbaum Associates, 2001.

Lerman, Leo. "A Wonderchild for 72 Years." Review of *Selected Writings of Gertrude Stein*, by Gertrude Stein. In Curnutt, 143–46. Originally published in *Saturday Review*, 2 November 1946.

Lesinska, Zofia P. *Perspectives of Four Women Writers on the Second World War: Gertrude Stein, Janet Flanner, Kay Boyle, and Rebecca West.* New York: Peter Lang, 2002.

Lewis, Sinclair. *Main Street.* New York: Harcourt, 1980.

Liebling, A. J., ed. *The Republic of Silence.* New York: Harcourt, 1947.

Loy, Mina. *The Lost Lunar Baedeker.* Edited by Roger L. Conover. New York: Noonday, 1996.

Ludmerer, Kenneth M. *Learning to Heal: The Development of American Medical Education.* New York: Basic Books, 1985.

Lynd, Robert S., and Helen Merrell Lynd. *Middletown: A Study in Modern American Culture.* 1929. Reprint, San Diego: Harcourt, 1957.

Malcolm, Janet. "Gertrude Stein's War: The Years in Occupied France." *New Yorker*, 2 June 2003, 58–81.

Mall, Franklin Paine. "The Anatomical Course and Laboratory of the Johns Hopkins University." *Bulletin of the Johns Hopkins Hospital* 7 (1896).

Mandelstam, Nadezhda. *Hope against Hope: A Memoir.* Translated by Max Hayward. New York: Atheneum, 1970.

Marcuse, Herbert. *One-Dimensional Man: Studies in the Ideology of Advanced Industrial Society.* 1964. Reprint, with an introduction by Douglas Kellner. Boston: Beacon, 1991.

Martin, Robert K. "The Mother of Us All and American History." In *Gertrude Stein and the Making of Literature*, ed. Shirley Neuman, 210–22. Houndmills, Eng.: Macmillan, 1988.

McCarthy, Thomas. Introduction to *The Theory of Communicative Action*, by Jurgen Habermas, vol. 1, *Reason and the Rationalization of Society.* Boston: Beacon, 1981.

McLuhan, Marshall. *The Gutenberg Galaxy: The Making of Typographic Man.* Toronto: U of Toronto P, 1962.

Mead, George Herbert. "The Social Self." 1913. In *Selected Writings*, ed. Andrew J. Reck, 142–49. Indianapolis: Bobbs-Merrill, 1964.

———. *Mind, Self, and Society from the Standpoint of a Social Behaviorist.* 1934. Edited by Charles W. Morris. Chicago: U of Chicago P, 1962.

Mellow, James R. *Charmed Circle: Gertrude Stein and Company.* New York: Avon, 1975.

Menand, Louis. "The Devil's Disciples." Review of *Dictators, Democracy, and American Public Culture*, by Benjamin Alpers. *New Yorker*, 28 July 2003, 83–87.

———. *The Metaphysical Club.* New York: Farrar, Straus and Giroux, 2001.

Mencken, H. L. "A Cubist Treatise." Review of *Tender Buttons*, by Gertrude Stein. In Curnutt, 14–15. Originally published in *Baltimore Sun*, 6 June 1914.

Meyer, Steven. *Irresistible Dictation: Gertrude Stein and the Correlations of Writing and Science.* Stanford, Calif.: Stanford UP, 2001.

———. "Writing Psychology Over: Gertrude Stein and William James." *Yale Journal of Criticism* 8 (1995): 133–63.

Miller, Rosalind S. *Gertrude Stein: Form and Intelligibility.* New York: Exposition, 1949.

Moerman, Michael. *Talking Culture: Ethnography and Conversation Analysis.* Philadelphia: U of Pennsylvania P, 1988.

Moore, George B. *Gertrude Stein's* The Making of Americans: *Repetition and the Emergence of Modernism.* New York: Peter Lang, 1998.

Moore, Marianne. *The Complete Poems of Marianne Moore.* New York: Macmillan, 1986.

Morrow, Elizabeth. *"All Gaul Is Divided": Letters from Occupied France.* New York: Greystone, 1941.

Morson, Gary Saul, and Caryl Emerson. "M. M. Bakhtin." In *The Johns Hopkins Guide to Literary Theory and Criticism,* ed. Michael Groden and Martin Kreiswirth, 63–68. Baltimore: Johns Hopkins UP, 1994.

Mullen, Harryette. *Trimmings.* New York: Tender Buttons, 1991.

O'Grady, William, Michael Dobrovolsky, and Mark Aronoff. *Contemporary Linguistics: An Introduction.* 2d edition. New York: St. Martin's, 1993.

Ong, Walter J. *Orality and Literacy: The Technologizing of the Word.* London: Methuen, 1982.

Orwell, George. "Politics and the English Language" In *The Orwell Reader: Fiction, Essays, and Reportage by George Orwell,* 355–66. New York: Harcourt, 1956.

———. "Politics vs. Literature: An Examination of *Gulliver's Travels.*" In *The Orwell Reader: Fiction, Essays, and Reportage by George Orwell,* 283–300. New York: Harcourt, 1956.

———. "The Prevention of Literature." In *The Orwell Reader: Fiction, Essays, and Reportage by George Orwell,* 367–79. New York: Harcourt, 1956.

Parker, Ian. "Absolute Powerpoint: Can a Software Package Edit Our Thoughts?" *New Yorker.* 28 May 2001, 76–87.

Pepys, Samuel. Excerpts from *The Diary of Samuel Pepys.* In *Eighteenth-Century English Literature,* ed. Geoffrey Tillotson, Paul Fussell, Jr., and Marshall Waingrow. San Diego: Harcourt Brace Jovanovich, 1969.

Perloff, Marjorie. *Wittgenstein's Ladder: Poetic Language and the Strangeness of the Ordinary.* Chicago: U of Chicago P, 1996.

Phillips, K. J. "Ladies' Voices in Donald Barthelme's *The Dead Father* and Gertrude Stein's *Dialogues.*" *International Fiction Review* 12.1 (winter 1985): 34–37.

Pitkin, Hannah. *Fortune Is a Woman.* Berkeley: U of California P, 1984.

Pondrom, Cyrena N. "An Introduction to the Achievement of Gertrude Stein." In *Geography and Plays,* by Gertrude Stein, vii–lv. Madison: U of Wisconsin P, 1993.

Posnock, Ross. *The Trial of Curiosity: Henry James, William James, and the Challenge of Modernity.* New York: Oxford UP, 1991.

Postman, Neil. *Amusing Ourselves to Death: Public Discourse in the Age of Show Business.* New York: Penguin, 1986.

———. *Conscientious Objections: Stirring Up Trouble about Language, Technology, and Education.* New York: Knopf, 1988.

———. *Technopoly: The Surrender of Culture to Technology.* New York: Vintage, 1993.

Postman, Neil, and Charles Weingartner. *Teaching as a Subversive Activity.* New York: Delacorte, 1969.

Preminger, Alex, ed. *Princeton Encyclopedia of Poetry and Poetics.* Princeton: Princeton UP, 1974.

Preston, John Hyde. "A Conversation with Gertrude Stein." In *Gertrude Stein Remembered,* ed. Linda Simon, 153–65. Lincoln: U of Nebraska P, 1994.

Bibliography   243

Putnam, Hillary. "The Permanence of William James." In *Pragmatism: An Open Question*, 5–26. Oxford: Blackwell, 1995.

———. "Was Wittgenstein a Pragmatist?" In *Pragmatism*, 27–56. Oxford: Blackwell, 1995.

Pychon, Thomas. *The Crying of Lot 49.* 1965. Reprint, New York: Perennial Classics, 1999.

Quintilian. *Quintilian on the Teaching of Speaking and Writing: Translations from Books One, Two, and Ten of the Institutio Oratoria.* Edited by James J. Murphy. Translated by John Selby Watson. Carbondale: Southern Illinois UP, 1987.

Rabaté, Jean-Michel. "Roland Barthes." In *The Johns Hopkins Guide to Literary Theory and Criticism*, ed. Michael Groden and Martin Kreiswirth, 68–73. Baltimore: Johns Hopkins UP, 1994.

Richardson, John. A *Life of Picasso: Volume 1, 1881–1906.* New York: Random House, 1991.

Rieke, Alison. *The Senses of Nonsense.* Iowa City: U of Iowa P, 1992.

Rogers, Robert Emons. "New Outbreaks of Futurism: *Tender Buttons*, Curious Experiment of Gertrude Stein in Literary Anarchy." Review of *Tender Buttons*, by Gertrude Stein. In Curnutt, 18–21. Originally published in *Boston Evening Transcript*, 11 July 1914.

Rogers, W. G. *When This You See Remember Me: Gertrude Stein in Person.* New York: Rinehart, 1948.

Rorty, Richard. *Contingency, Irony, and Solidarity.* Cambridge: Cambridge UP, 1989.

———. *Philosophy and Social Hope.* London: Penguin, 1999.

Rothstein, William G. *American Medical Schools and the Practice of Medicine: A History.* New York: Oxford UP, 1987.

Ruddick, Lisa. *Reading Gertrude Stein: Body, Text, Gnosis.* Ithaca, N.Y.: Cornell UP, 1990.

———. "William James and the Modernism of Gertrude Stein." In *Modernism Reconsidered*, ed. Robert Kiely, 47–63. Cambridge: Harvard UP, 1983.

Ryan, Betsy Alayne. *Gertrude Stein's Theatre of the Absolute.* Ann Arbor, Mich.: UMI Research P, 1984.

Sacks, Harvey. *Lectures on Conversation.* 2 vols. Edited by Gail Jefferson. Oxford: Blackwell, 1992.

Sartre, Jean-Paul. "The Republic of Silence." In *The Republic of Silence*, 498–500. Edited by A. J. Liebling. Translated by Ramon Guthrie. New York: Harcourt, 1947.

Sawyer, R. Keith. *Improvised Dialogues: Emergence and Creativity in Conversation.* Westport, Conn.: Ablex, 2003.

Schegloff, Emanuel A. Introduction to *Lectures on Conversation*, by Harvey Sacks, ed. Gail Jefferson, ix–lxii. Oxford: Blackwell, 1992.

Scollon, Ron, and Suzanne B. K. Scollon. "Cooking It Up and Boiling It Down: Abstracts in Athabaskan Children's Story Retellings." In *Coherence in Spoken and Written Discourse*, ed. Deborah Tannen, 173–97. Norwood, N.J.: Ablex, 1984.

Sevareid, Eric. *Not So Wild a Dream.* New York: Atheneum, 1976.

Shakespeare, William. *Hamlet, Prince of Denmark.* Edited by Philip Edwards. Cambridge: Cambridge UP, 1995.

———. *Macbeth.* Edited by David Bevington. New York: Bantam, 1988.

"The Shape of Things." *Nation*, 10 August 1946, 142–43.

Shepherd, Gregory J. "Pragmatism and Tragedy, Communication and Hope: A Summary Story." In *American Pragmatism and Communication Research*, ed. David K. Perry, 241–54. Mahwah, N.J.: Lawrence Erlbaum Associates, 2001.

Shuler, Sherianne, and Melissa Tate. "Intersections of Feminism and Pragmatism: Possibilities for Communication Theory and Research." In *American Pragmatism and Communication Research*, ed. David K. Perry, 209–24. Mahwah, N.J.: Lawrence Erlbaum Associates, 2001.

Silverman, David. *Harvey Sacks: Social Science and Conversation Analysis*. New York: Oxford UP, 1998.

Simon, Linda. Introduction to *Gertrude Stein Remembered*, ed. Simon, ix–xv. Lincoln: U of Nebraska P, 1994.

Simonson, Peter. "Varieties of Pragmatism and Communication: Visions and Revisions from Peirce to Peters." In *American Pragmatism and Communication Research*, ed. David K. Perry, 1–26. Mahwah, N.J.: Lawrence Erlbaum Associates, 2001.

Sitwell, Edith. "Miss Stein's Stories." Review of *Geography and Plays*, by Gertrude Stein. In Curnutt, 25–26. Originally published in *The Nation and the Anthenœum*, 14 July 1923.

Skinner, B. F. "Has Gertrude Stein a Secret?" *Atlantic*, January 1934, 50–57.

Smith, Harrison. "A Rose for Remembrance." *Saturday Review of Literature*, 10 August 1946, 11.

Smollett, Tobias. *The Expedition of Humphry Clinker*. Oxford: Oxford UP, 1991.

Souhami, Diana. *Gertrude and Alice*. London: Pandora, 1991.

Spenser, Edmund. "The Faerie Queene." In *Edmund Spenser's Poetry*, ed. Hugh Maclean, 1–398. New York: Norton, 1968.

Steiner, Wendy. "Mother." *London Review of Books*. 19 October 1995, 23–24.

"Stein's Way." *Time*. 11 September 1933, 57–60.

Stendhal, Renate. *Gertrude Stein in Words and Pictures: A Photobiography*. Chapel Hill: Algonquin, 1994.

Steward, Samuel M. *Chapters from an Autobiography*. San Francisco: Grey Fox, 1981.

———. *Murder is Murder is Murder*. Boston: Alyson Publications, 1985.

———. *Parisian Lives*. New York: St. Martin's, 1984.

Stewart, Allegra. *Gertrude Stein and the Present*. Cambridge: Harvard UP, 1967.

Sutherland, Donald. *Gertrude Stein: A Biography of Her Work*. New Haven: Yale UP, 1951.

Swerdlow, Joel L. "Information Revolution." *National Geographic*, October 1995, 5–37.

Tannen, Deborah. *The Argument Culture: Stopping America's War of Words*. New York: Ballantine Books, 1999.

———. "The Oral/Literate Continuum in Discourse." In *Spoken and Written Language: Exploring Orality and Literacy*, ed. Deborah Tannen, 1–16. Norwood, N.J.: Ablex, 1982.

Tarde, Gabriel. "Opinion and Conversation." 1898. In *On Communication and Social Influence*, ed. Terry N. Clark, 297–318. Chicago: U of Chicago P, 1969.

———. "The Public and the Crowd." 1901. In *On Communication and Social Influence*, ed. Terry N. Clark, 277–94. Chicago: U of Chicago P, 1969.

Terkel, Studs. *Working: People Talk about What They Do All Day and How They Feel about What They Do*. 1972. Reprint, New York: Pantheon Books, 1974.

Thayer, William Sydney. *Osler and Other Papers*. Baltimore: Johns Hopkins UP, 1931.

Toklas, Alice B. *The Alice B. Toklas Cookbook*. New York: Harper, 1954.

———. *What Is Remembered*. New York: Holt, Rinehart and Winston, 1963.

Tomiche, Anne. "Repetition: Memory and Oblivion. Freud, Duras, and Stein." *Revue de Littérature Comparée* 65.3 (July–September 1991): 261–76.

Townshend, Pete. "Won't Get Fooled Again." on *Who's Next*, 1971.

U.S. Bureau of the Census. *Historical Statistics of the United States: Colonial Times to 1970, Bicentennial Edition, Part 1*. Washington D.C., 1975.

Van Dusen, Wanda. "Portrait of a National Fetish: Gertrude Stein's 'Introduction to the Speeches of Marechal Pétain' (1942)." *Modernism/Modernity* 3.3 (September 1996): 69–92.

Van Vechten, Carl, "How Many Acts Are There in It?" Introduction to *Last Operas and Plays*, by Gertrude Stein, vii–xix. New York: Rinehart, 1949.

———. "How To Read Gertrude Stein." In Curnutt, 154–58. Originally published in *Trend*, August 1914.

———. *Peter Whiffle: His Life and Works*. New York: Knopf, 1922.

———, ed. *Selected Writings of Gertrude Stein*. 1945. Reprint, New York: Vintage, 1962.

Wagner-Martin, Linda. *"Favored Strangers": Gertrude Stein and Her Family*. Totowa, N.J.: Rutgers UP, 1995.

Wald, Priscilla. *Constituting Americans: Cultural Anxiety and Narrative Form*. Durham, N.C.: Duke UP, 1995.

Walker, Jayne L. "History as Repetition: *The Making of Americans*." In *Gertrude Stein*, ed. Harold Bloom, 177–99. New York: Chelsea, 1986.

Watson, Dana Cairns. "'Oh Say What You See': The Conversational Structures and Liberating Senses in Gertrude Stein's Poetry, Plays, and Prose." Ph.D. diss., UCLA, 1996. UMI # 9711582.

Watson, Steven. *Prepare for Saints: Gertrude Stein, Virgil Thomson, and the Mainstreaming of American Modernism*. New York: Random House, 1998.

Watts, Linda S. *Gertrude Stein: A Study of the Short Fiction*. New York: Twayne, 1999.

———. *Rapture Untold: Gender, Mysticism, and the "Moment of Recognition" in Works by Gertrude Stein*. New York: Peter Lang, 1996.

Wernicke, Carl. "The Aphasia Symptom-Complex: A Psychological Study on an Anatomical Basis." 1874. In *Reader in the History of Aphasia: From Gall to Geschwind*, ed. Paul Eling, 69–98. Amsterdam: John Benjamins, 1994.

White, Ray Lewis. *Gertrude Stein and Alice B. Toklas: A Reference Guide*. Boston: G. K. Hall, 1984.

———, ed. *Sherwood Anderson / Gertrude Stein: Correspondence and Personal Essays*. Chapel Hill: U of North Carolina P, 1972.

Whittier-Ferguson, John. "Stein in Time: History, Manuscripts, and Memory." *Modernism/Modernity* 6.1 (1999): 115–51.

Wilder, Thornton. "Gertrude Stein's *The Geographical History of America*." In *American Characteristics and Other Essays*, by Thornton Wilder, 187–92. Edited by Donald Gallup. New York: Harper and Row, 1979.

Williams, William Carlos. "Asphodel, That Greeny Flower: Book 1." In *The William Carlos Williams Reader*, ed. M. L. Rosenthal. New York: New Directions, 1966.

———. "The Work of Gertrude Stein." *Pagany* 1.1 (January–March 1930): 41–45.

Wilson, Edmund. "Gertrude Stein." In Hoffman, *Critical Essays*, 58–62. Excerpt from *Axel's Castle*, by Wilson, originally published New York: Charles Scribner's Sons, 1931.

Winders, James A. "Karl Marx and Friedrich Engels." In *The Johns Hopkins Guide to Literary Theory and Criticism*, ed. Michael Groden and Martin Kreiswirth, 486–91. Baltimore: Johns Hopkins UP, 1994.

Wineapple, Brenda. *Sister Brother: Gertrude and Leo Stein*. New York: Putnam, 1996.

Winston, Elizabeth. "Making History in 'The Mother of Us All.'" *Mosaic* (Winnipeg, Man.) 20.4 (fall 1987): 117–29.

Winter, Ella. "Gertrude Stein Comma." Review of *Lectures in America*, by Gertrude Stein. In Curnutt, 82–85. Originally published in *Pacific Weekly*, 12 April 1935.

Wittgenstein, Ludwig. *Culture and Value*. Edited by G. H. von Wright in collaboration with Heikki Nyman. Translated by Peter Winch. Chicago: U of Chicago P, 1980.

Wittke, Carl F. *We Who Built America: The Saga of the Immigrant*. Ann Arbor, Mich.: P of Western Reserve U, 1939.

Wright, Richard. Review of *Wars I Have Seen*. *PM*, 11 March 1945.

Yaeger, Patricia. "Toward a Feminine Sublime." In *Gender and Theory: Dialogues on Feminist Criticism*, ed. Linda Kauffman, 191–211. New York: Blackwell, 1989.

Young, John Wesley. *Totalitarian Language: Orwell's Newspeak and Its Nazi and Communist Antecedents*. Charlottesville: UP of Virginia, 1991.

Young, Stark. "One Moment Alit." Review of *Four Saints in Three Acts*, by Gertrude Stein. In Hoffman, *Critical Essays*, 71–73. Originally published in *New Republic*, 3 July 1934.

Zurif, Edgar. "Language and the Brain." In *Language: An Invitation to Cognitive Psychology*. Vol. 1, ed. Daniel N. Osherson and Howard Lasnik. Cambridge: MIT P, 1990.

NEWS ARTICLES RELEVANT TO STEIN'S
1934–1935 LECTURE TOUR

"4 Saints in 3 Acts 1 of Many." *New York Sun*, 16 November 1934.

"About Gertrude Stein." Editorial. *Cleveland Press*, 21 December 1934.

Allen, Lester. "Miss Stein Likes Things Cubical." *Boston Post*, 20 November 1934.

Alsop, Joseph W., Jr. "Gertrude Stein Likes to Look at Paintings." *New York Herald Tribune*, 2 November 1934.

———. "Gertrude Stein Says Children Understand Her." *New York Herald Tribune*, 3 November 1934.

Beck, Clyde. "Gertrude Stein Explains Theory of 'Seeing Things.'" *Detroit News*, 13 December 1934.

Boardman, Frances. "Few Lucidities Found Hiding in Stein Lecture." *St. Paul* (Minn.) *Pioneer Press*, 9 December 1934.

Bower, Helen C. "Miss Stein Tells Everything: Detroit Seems to Understand." *Detroit Free Press*, 13 December 1934.

Brickell, Herschel. "Books on Our Table." *New York Post*, 22 November 1934.

Buchalter, Helen. "Gertrude Stein Doesn't 'Take from' Causes, She Tells an Ardent Reformist." *Washington Daily News*, 31 December 1934.

"But a Stein Is a Stein Is a Stein." Review of *Portraits and Prayers*. *New York Times*, 18 November 1934.

Butcher, Fanny. "English Letters to Flower Next in U.S.: Gertrude Stein." *Chicago Daily Tribune*, 26 November 1934.

Chamberlain, John. "Books of the Times." *New York Times*, 7 November 1934, 19.

Davidson, Grace. "Radcliffe Laughs." *Boston Post*, 20 November 1934.

Deene, Dian. Letter to the editor. *New York Sun*, 22 November 1934.

"The Devoted Band." Editorial. *New York Times*, 3 November 1934.

The Dowager. "Gertrude Stein Makes Address at the Arts Club." *Chicago Herald and Examiner*, 26 November 1934.

Dush, Sarah L. "Gertrude Stein Is Here Is Here Here Is." *Ohio State Journal*, 18 December 1934.

"Einstein 'Explains' Theories to Reporters." *Washington, D.C., Sunday Star*, 30 December 1934.

"Elite Fete Fete Elite Miss Stein." *New York Evening Journal*, 17 November 1934.

Evans, A. Judson. "Gertrude Tells All about All but Audience Just Can't Take It." *Richmond Times Dispatch*, 7 February 1935.

"Fancy Writing: Fine If You Like It." Editorial. *New York Evening Journal*, 30 October 1934.

Fessenden, Donald. "Gertrude Stein Too Much for Harvard and Radcliffe; She Wonders If It Is Necessary to Stand Still to Live." *Boston Herald*, 20 November 1934.

Flutterbye, Mme. "Gertrude Stein Attracts Fashionables." *New York Evening Journal*, 17 November 1934.

Frey, Virginia. Letter to the editor, *Chicago Daily Tribune*, 14 March 1935.

"Frying Pan into Palalia." Editorial. *New York Times*, 1 December 1934.

Gannett, Lewis. "Books and Things." *New York Herald Tribune*, 7 November 1934.

Genauer, Emily. "Gertrude Stein, It Seems, Likes to Look at Pictures." *New York World-Telegram*, 2 November 1934.

"Gertrude Stein Arrives and Baffles Reporters by Making Herself Clear." *New York Times*, 25 October 1934.

"Gertrude Stein Baffles Radcliffe; Harvard Understands Informal Talk." *Boston Evening Press*, 20 November 1934.

"Gertrude Stein Discusses Art." *New York Sun*, 2 November 1934.

"Gertrude Stein Explains Work." *Birmingham News*, 17 February 1935.

"Gertrude Stein Home, Upholds Her Simplicity." *New York Herald Tribune*, 25 October 1934.

"Gertrude Stein in Greenwich." *New York Times*, 3 November 1934, sec. 2.

"Gertrude Stein, Noted Writer, Speaks Here Today." *Virginia Gazette*, 8 February 1935.

"Gertrude Stein Speaks on Art to D.C. Guests." *Washington Post*, 30 December 1934.

"Gertrude Stein Talks before College Group." *Virginia Gazette*, 15 February 1935.

"Gertrude Stein Tells Paris She Is 'Wed to America.'" *New York Times*, 13 May 1935.

"Gertrude Stein, Visitor in City, Explores Archives at Foster Hall." *Indianapolis News*, 17 December 1934.

"Gertrude Stein Will Speak on Paintings before Chicago Women's Club." *Chicago Herald and Examiner*, 25 November 1934.

Gilbreth, Frank B. "Gertrude Stein Talks on Nouns." *Charleston News and Courier*, 14 February 1935.

Grey, James C. "Books This Week." *New York Sun*, 2 November 1934.

Guest, Edgar. "Love and a Passing Fancy." *New York Evening Journal*, 30 October 1934.

Hansen, Harry. "The First Reader." *New York World-Telegram*, 5 November 1934.

———. "No Stein Song by First Reader." *New York World-Telegram*, 8 November 1934.

Henry, Thomas R. "Brows of Great Minds Pucker as Einstein Proves His Theory." *Washington, D.C., Evening Star*, 29 December 1934.

Jackson, Joseph Henry. "A Bookman's Notebook." Editorial. *San Francisco Chronicle*, 13 April 1935.

Jewell, Edward Alden. "The Realm of Art: Sounds of Firing on Many Fronts." *New York Times*, 3 March 1935.

Jones, Melissa. "Gertrude Stein Speaks of 'Poetry and Grammar' at Lecture Wednesday." *Columbus Evening Dispatch*, 18 December 1934.

Kennedy, Kenneth R., and Morris H. Rubin. "It Took Two Hardy Men to Do This, Reader; You'd Better Call for Help." *Wisconsin State Journal*, 7 December 1934.

Kennedy, Paul. "Gertrude Stein and Boxing Show in One Evening Leave Reporter Punch Drunk." *Toledo News-Bee*, 20 December 1934.

Kirnon, Hodge. Letter to the editor. *New York Times*, 2 November 1934.

Knoblock, K. T. "'Oils on Flat Surfaces' Are Pleasing to Gertrude Stein." *New Orleans Item*, 20 February 1935.

Laird, Donald A. "Science Explains Gertrude Stein's Word Puzzles." *Washington Herald's American Weekly*, 30 December 1934.

Laurie, Annie. "Sound and Fury—La Stein Speaks." *San Francisco Examiner*, 13 April 1935.

Lawner, Rhoda. Letter to the editor. *New York Sun*, 26 November 1934.

L.B.W. Letter to the Editor. *New York Sun*, 3 December 1934.

Liebling, A. J. "Gertrude Stein Interprets as Poetry is Wed to Music." *New York World-Telegram*, 16 November 1934.

"Literary Enigma in Truth Proves Real Friendly." *Boston Daily Globe*, 20 November 1934.

"Literary Snobbery." Editorial. *New York Times*, 6 February 1935.

"Made Herself Understood." Editorial. *New York Times*, 26 October 1934.

Marer, Helene. Letter to the editor. *New York Sun*, 19 November 1934.

Marlow, James. "Gertrude Stein Doesn't Stammer, Reporter Simply Hears Poorly." *New Orleans Times Picayune*, 19 February 1935.

Marx, Carolyn. "Book Marks for Today." *New York World-Telegram*, 25 October 1934.

———. "Book Marks for Today." *New York World-Telegram*, 26 October 1934.

McClain, John. "On the Sun Deck." *New York Sun*, 25 October 1934.

McDermott, William F. "McDermott on Gertrude." *Cleveland Plain Dealer*, 21 December 1934.

Meyers, Lorene. "Miss Gertrude Stein Sinks Society Writer at Lecture without a Solitary Trace." *Dallas Morning News*, 19 March 1935.

"Miss Stein a Wow." *New York Sun*, 1 November 1934.

"Miss Stein Lets in Some Fresh Air." Editorial. *Chicago Daily Tribune*, 12 March 1935.

"Miss Stein Makes It All Very Clear." *Philadelphia Evening Bulletin*, 16 November 1934.

"Miss Stein Puzzle to Psychiatrists." *New York Times*, 29 November 1934.

"Miss Stein to Talk for Xmas Fund." *New York Evening Journal*, 8 November 1934.

"Miss Stein Speaks to Bewildered 500." *New York Times*, 2 November 1934.

"Miss Stein Uses Saints as Scenery." *New York Times*, 17 November 1934.

"Miss Stein Visits City: No More Words to Conquer." *Cleveland Press*, 22 December 1934.

M.L.K. Letter to the editor. *New York Times*, 8 November 1934.

"Multitude Greets Highbrow Thinking She's Movie Idol." *Dallas Morning News*, 18 March 1935.

Murray, Marian. "Gertrude Stein Lecture Given with Sincerity." *Hartford Daily Times*, 19 January 1935.

O'Connell, Grattan. "Miss Stein Speaks with Meaning Here." *Hartford Courant*, 19 January 1935.

O'Hara, Kenneth. "Greeted Greeted at Airport: Oh Gertrude Oh Stein Here to Here to Talk." *Los Angeles Times*, 30 March 1935.

"A Painting Is a Painting Is a Gertrude Stein Axiom on Art." *Richmond Times Dispatch*, 8 February 1935.

"Paris Aroused over Reply to Gertrude Stein." *Chicago Daily Tribune*, 9 March 1935.

"Passion in Literature." Editorial. *New York Times*, 25 August 1935.

Pereda, Prudencio de. Letter to the editor. *New York Sun*, 23 November 1934.

"Perfecting Language." Editorial. *New York Times*, 19 November 1934.

"Princeton Dazed by Gertrude Stein." *New York Times*, 6 November 1934.

"Radcliffe Giggles It Does Giggle at Her Style." *Boston Daily Globe*, 20 November 1934.

"Recalls Early Endeavors." *Washington, D.C., Evening Star*, 29 December 1934.

[Rogers, W. G.?] "Gertrude Stein Gives Talk before Century Club Here." *Springfield Daily Republican*. 8 January 1935.

———. "Stein Gives Talk at Classical High; About 250 Attend." *Springfield Daily Republican*, 25 January 1935.

"Says Writers Are Confused." *Indianapolis Sunday Star*, 16 December 1934.

Schriftgiesser, Karl. "Gertrude Stein Traces Course of Writing—Chaucer to Stein!" *Washington Post*, 31 December 1934.

"Science Understands." *Evening Star*, 29 December 1934.

"Scientists' Meeting Hears Demand for New Mode of Thinking." *Washington Daily News*, 28 December 1934.

Seeley, Evelyn. "Stein, the Bohemian, Doesn't See Our Life." *New York World-Telegram*, 13 November 1934.

"A Snub, a Snub, a Snub." *San Francisco Examiner*, 8 April 1935.

"Someone Called Stein Sails with Alice B. Toklas." *New York Herald Tribune*, 5 May 1935.

Stafford, Jane. "Science Tells How Gertrude Stein Gets That Way." *Times Picayune Everyweek Magazine*, 17 February 1935.

"Stein Likes Stein Opera." *New York Times*, 9 November 1934.

"Stein Opera Sung by All-Negro Cast." *New York Times*, 9 February 1934.

"Topics of the Times: Made Herself Understood." *New York Times*, 26 October 1934.

"Two Steins." Editorial. *New York Times*, 1 January 1934.

Warren, Lansing. "Gertrude Stein Views Life and Politics." *New York Times Magazine*, 6 May 1934.

Weiss, Helene. Letter to the editor. *New York Sun*, 30 November 1934.

Welshimer, Helen. "I Know I Shall Be Lonely." *New York World-Telegram*, 26 October 1934.

"What Is an Oil Painting?—Gertrude Stein Lets It Out." *Baltimore Sun*, 29 December 1934.

Williams, Edgar. "Policeman in Phone Booth Misses Gertrude Stein Talk." *Baltimore News and Baltimore Post*, 29 December 1934.

Winsten, Archer. "In the Wake of the News." *New York Post*, 6 November 1934.

"Youth Understands, Says Gertrude Stein." *New York Times*, 5 May 1935.

INDEX

Index   255